**HUMAN DEVELOPMENT
REPORT 2021/2022**

Uncertain times, unsettled lives

Shaping our future in a transforming world

Team

Director and lead author
Pedro Conceição

Research and statistics
Cecilia Calderón, Fernanda Pavez Esbry, Moumita Ghorai, Yu-Chieh Hsu, Ghida Ismail, Christina Lengfelder, Brian Lutz, Tasneem Mirza, Rehana Mohammed, Josefin Pasanen, Som Kumar Shrestha, Heriberto Tapia, Carolina Rivera Vázquez, Yuko Yokoi and Yanchun Zhang

Production, digital, communications, operations
Rezarta Godo, Jon Hall, Seockhwan Bryce Hwang, Admir Jahic, Fe Juarez Shanahan, Sarantuya Mend, Ana Porras, Dharshani Seneviratne, Carolina Given Sjolander and Marium Soomro

Foreword

We are living in uncertain times. The Covid-19 pandemic, now in its third year, continues to spin off new variants. The war in Ukraine reverberates throughout the world, causing immense human suffering, including a cost-of-living crisis. Climate and ecological disasters threaten the world daily.

It is seductively easy to discount crises as one-offs, natural to hope for a return to normal. But dousing the latest fire or booting the latest demagogue will be an unwinnable game of whack-a-mole unless we come to grips with the fact that the world is fundamentally changing. There is no going back.

Layers of uncertainty are stacking up and interacting to unsettle our lives in unprecedented ways. People have faced diseases, wars and environmental disruptions before. But the confluence of destabilizing planetary pressures with growing inequalities, sweeping societal transformations to ease those pressures and widespread polarization present new, complex, interacting sources of uncertainty for the world and everyone in it.

That is the new normal. Understanding and responding to it are the goals of the 2021/2022 Human Development Report, *Uncertain Times, Unsettled Lives: Shaping our Future in a Transforming World*. It caps a trilogy of Reports beginning with the 2019 Report on inequalities, followed by the 2020 Report on the risks of the Anthropocene—where humans have become a major force driving dangerous planetary change.

Thirty-two years ago, the very first Human Development Report declared boldly that "people are the real wealth of nations." That powerful refrain has guided UNDP and its Human Development Reports ever since, with its messages and meanings taking on richer hues over time.

People around the world are now telling us that they feel ever more insecure. UNDP's Special Report on Human Security, launched earlier this year, found that six out of seven people worldwide reported feeling insecure about many aspects of their lives, even before the Covid-19 pandemic.

Is it any wonder, then, that many nations are creaking under the strain of polarization, political extremism and demagoguery—all supercharged by social media, artificial intelligence and other powerful technologies?

Or that, in a stunning reversal from just a decade ago, democratic backsliding among countries has become the norm rather than the exception?

Or that, in a stunning first, the global Human Development Index value has declined for two years in a row in the wake of the Covid-19 pandemic?

People are the real wealth of nations, mediated through our relationships with our governments, with our natural environments, with each other. Each new crisis reminds us that when people's capabilities, choices and hopes for the future feel dashed, the wellbeing of their nations and the planet are the accompanying casualties.

Now let us imagine the reverse: what our nations, our planet, would look like if we expanded human development, including people's agency and freedoms. That would be a world where our creativity is unleashed to reimagine our futures, to renew and adapt our institutions, to craft new stories about who we are and what we value. It would be not just a nice-to-have; it would be a must-have when the world is in ongoing, unpredictable flux.

We got a glimpse of what is possible in the Covid-19 pandemic. A battery of new vaccines, including some based on revolutionary technology, saved an estimated 20 million lives in one year. Let that sink in, that extraordinary achievement in the annals of humankind. Equally extraordinary is the number of unnecessary lives lost, especially in low- and middle-income countries, from highly unequal vaccine access. The pandemic has been a painful reminder of how breakdowns in trust and in cooperation, among and within nations, foolishly constrain what we can achieve together.

The hero and the villain in today's uncertainty story are one in the same: human choice. It is far too glib to encourage people to look for silver linings or to state that the glass is half full rather than half empty, for not all choices are the same. Some—arguably the ones most relevant to the fate of our species—are propelled by institutional and cultural inertia, generations in the making.

This year's Report invites us to take a hard look at ossified and oversimplified assumptions about human decision-making. Institutions assume away people's messiness—our emotions, our biases, our sense of belonging—at our peril.

As with its predecessors, the Report also challenges conventional notions of "progress," where self-defeating tradeoffs are being made. Gains in some areas, as in years of schooling or life expectancy, do not compensate for losses in others, as in people's sense of control over their lives. Nor can we enjoy material wealth at the expense of planetary health.

This Report firmly positions human development not just as a goal but as a means to a path forward in uncertain times, reminding us that people—in all our complexity, our diversity, our creativity—are the real wealth of nations.

Achim Steiner
Administrator
United Nations Development Programme

Acknowledgements

We live in a world of worry: the ongoing Covid-19 pandemic, continuing regional and local conflicts, record-breaking temperatures, fires and storms. Many reports document these challenges and initiatives and offer recommendations on how to address them, but this year's Human Development Report is an invitation to take a step back. Many challenges, rather than being separate, may be troubling manifestation of an emerging, new uncertainty complex that is unsettling lives around the world. The 2019 Human Development Report explored inequalities in human development, the 2020 Human Development Report focused on how those inequalities drive and are exacerbated by the dangerous planetary change of the Anthropocene, and the 2022 Special Report on Human Security examined the emergence of new forms of insecurity. The 2021/2022 Human Development Report unites and extends these discussions under the theme of uncertainty—how it is changing, what it means for human development and how we can thrive in the face of it. The lingering effects of the pandemic made preparing the Report challenging, including through delays in key data availability. The Report was made possible because of the encouragement, generosity and contributions of so many, recognized only imperfectly and partially in these acknowledgments.

The members of our Advisory Board, led by Michèle Lamont and Tharman Shanmugaratnam as co-chairs, supported us in multiple and long virtual meetings, providing extensive advice on four versions of lengthy drafts. The other members of the Advisory Board were Olu Ajakaiye, Kaushik Basu, Diane Coyle, Oeindrila Dube, Cai Fang, Marc Fleurbaey, Amadou Hott, Ravi Kanbur, Harini Nagendra, Thomas Piketty, Belinda Reyers, Dan Smith, Qixiang Sun, Ilona Szabó de Carvalho, Krushil Watene and Helga Weisz.

Complementing the advice from our Advisory Board, the Report's Statistical Advisory Panel provided guidance on several methodological and data aspects of the Report—in particular those related to calculating the Report's human development indices. We are grateful to all the panel members: Mario Biggeri, Camilo Ceita, Ludgarde Coppens, Koen Decancq, Marie Haldorson, Jason Hickel, Steve Macfeely, Mohd Uzir Mahidin, Silvia Montoya, Shantanu Mukherjee, Michaela Saisana, Hany Torky and Dany Wazen.

We are thankful for especially close collaborations with our partners: the CUNY Advanced Science Research Center, including Anthony D. Cak, Pamela Green and Charles Vörösmarty; the partnership between the German Institute of Development and Sustainability & V-Dem Institute, University of Gothenburg, including Francesco Burchi, Charlotte Fiedler, Jean Lachapelle, Julia Leininger, Staffan I. Lindberg, Svend-Erik Skanning and Armin Von Schiller; the Global Policy Laboratory at the University of California, Berkeley, including Solomon Hsiang, Jonathan Proctor, Luke Sherman and Jeanette Tseng; the Institute for Economics and Peace, including Andrew Etchell, David Hammond, Steven Killelea and Paulo Pinto; the Peace Research Institute Oslo, including Siri Aas Rustad, Andrew Arasmith and Gudrun Østby; the Stockholm International Peace Research Institute, including Richard Black, Claire McAllister and Jürg Staudenmann; the Stockholm Resilience Centre, including David Collste, Beatrice Crona, Victor Galaz and Louise Hård af Segerstad; and the World Inequality Lab, including Lucas Chancel, Amory Gethin and Clara Martinez-Toledano.

Appreciation is also extended for all the data, written inputs and peer reviews of draft chapters to the Report, including those by Saleem H. Ali, Elisabeth Anderson, Joseph Bak-Coleman, Sajitha Bashir, Marc Bellis, Reinette Biggs, Carl Bruch, Sarah Burch, Andrew Crabtree, Dagomar Degroot, Michael Drinkwater, Kendra Dupuy, Erle C. Ellis, Abeer Elshennawy, Benjamin Enke, Ann Florini, Ricardo Fuentes Nieva, Rachel Gisselquist, Nicole Hassoun, Tatiana Karabchuk, Patrick Keys, Erika Kraemer-Mbula, Gordon LaForge, Yong Sook Lee, Laura Lopes, Crick Lund, Juliana Martinez Franzoni, Jennifer McCoy, John-Andrew McNeish, Frances Mewsigye, Dinsha Mistree, Toby Ord, László Pintér, Tauhidur Rahman, Reagan Redd, Ingrid Robeyns, Michael Roll, Håkon Sælen, Diego Sanchez-Ancochea, Rebecca Sarku, Sunil Sharma, Landry Signé, Raimundo Soto, Casper Sylvest, Julia Thomas, Rens Van Munster and Stacy VanDeveer.

Several consultations with thematic and regional experts and numerous informal consultations with many individuals without a formal advisory role were held in the process of preparing this year's Report. We are grateful for inputs during these consultations from Khalid Abu-Ismail, Adeniran Adedeji, Ravi Agarwal, Faten Aggad, Annette Alstadsaeter, Maria Laura Alzua, Reza Anglingkusumo, Ragnheiour Elin Árnadóttir, Jai Asundi, Joseph Atta-Mensah, Vivienne Badaan, Heidi Bade, Faisal Bari, Amie Bishop, Robert Bissio, Bambang P.S. Brodjonegoro, Vural Çakır, Alvaro Calix, Diego Chaves, Hiker Chiu, Afra Chowdhury, Shomy Chowdhury, Zhang Chuanhong, Tanya Cox, Ann-Sophie Crépin, Alexus D'Marco, Cedric de Coning, Andre de Mello, Rafael del Villar Alrich, Ron Dembo, Patrick Develtere, B Diwan, Ibrahim Elbadawi,

Nisreen Elsaim, Harris Eyre, Ryan Figueiredo, Alexandra Fong, Carlos Garcia, Pablo Garron, Sherine Ghoneim, Juan Carlos Gomez, Vasu Gounden, Carol Graham, Thomas Greminger, Renzo R. Guinto, Jannis Gustke, Oli Henman, Bjørn Høyland, William Hynes, Ipek Ilkaracan, Zubair Iqbal Ghori, Andrey Ivanov, Lysa John, Melanie Judge, Nader Kabbani, Sherif Kamel, John Kay, Nadine Khaouli, Alan Kirman, Atif Kubursi, Geert Laporte, Olivia Lazard, Santiago Levy, Yuefen Li, Kwai-Cheung Lo, Hafsa Mahboub Maalim, Keletso Makofane, Heghine Manasyan, Halvor Mehlum, Claire Melamed, Emel Memis, Juna Miluka, Roman Mogilevskii, Hårvard Mokleiv Nygård, Wevyn Muganda, Felipe Muñoz, Keisuke Nansai, Njuguna Ndung'u, Kathleen Newland, Helga Nowotny, José Antonio Ocampo, Marina Ponti, Tazeen Qureshi, Krishna Ravi Srinivas, Jose Felix Rodriguez, Michael Roll, Heidy Rombouts, Marcela Romero, Sofiane Sahraoui, Djavad Salehi-Esfahani, Sweta Saxena, Ouedraogo Sayouba, Andrew Seele, Joel Simpson, Prathit Singh, Karima Bounemra Ben Soltane, Eduardo Stein, Stephanie Steinmetz, Riad Sultan, Mitzi Jonelle Tan, Daniele Taurino, Julia Thomas, Laura Thompson, Jo Thori Lind, Anna Tsing, Ingunn Tysse Nakkim, Khalid Umar, Bård Vegard Solhjell, Bianca Vidal Bustos, Tanja Winther, Justin Yifu Lin, Jorge Zequeira, Michel Zhou and Andrew Zolli.

We would also like to thank all those who presented in our seminar series: Ingvlid Almås, Simon Anholt, Chris Blattman, Carolina Delgado, Alexander Dill, Pamina Firchow, Aleksandr Gevorkyan, Sharath Guntuku, James Jasper, Shreya Jha, Priyadarshani Joshi, Roudabeh Kishi, Anirudh Krishna, Pushpam Kumar, Jane Muthumbi, Brian O'Callaghan and Sarah White.

Further support was also extended by others too numerous to mention here. Consultations are listed at https://hdr.undp.org/towards-hdr-2022. Contributions, support and assistance from many colleagues across the UN family is gratefully acknowledged. They include Shams Banihani, Naveeda Nazir and Xiaojun Grace Wang of the United Nations Office for South-South Cooperation and Maren Jimenez, Jonathan Perry and Marta Roig of the United Nations Department of Economic and Social Affairs. All UNDP regional and central bureaus and country offices are also acknowledged with much gratitude.

Colleagues in UNDP provided advice and inputs. We are grateful to Aparna Basnyat, Ludo Bok, Camilla Bruckner, Farah Choucair, Mandeep Dhaliwal, Almudena Fernandez, Arvinn Gadgil, Irene Garcia, Boyan Konstantinov, Aarathi Krishnan, Anjali Kwatra, Jeroen Laporte, Sarah Lister, Luis Felipe Lopez Calva, Dylan Lowthian, Guillermina Martin, Ulrika Modeer, Shivani Nayyar, Mansour Ndiaye, Camila Olate, Anna Ortubia, Alejandro Pacheco, Paola Pagliani, Mihail Peleah, Noella Richard, Isabel Saint Malo, Ben Slay, Mirjana Spoljaric Egger, Maria Stage, Anca Stoica, Ludmila Tiganu, Bishwa Tiwari, Alexandra Wide, Kanni Wignajara and Lesley Wright.

We were fortunate to have the support of talented interns and fact checkers—Dayana Benny, Allison Bostrom, Parth Chawla, Maximillian Feichtner, Benjamin Fields, Jeremy Marand, Patricia Nogueira, Themba Nyasulu, Nazifa Rafa, Stephen Sepaniak, Zahraa Shabana, Chin Shian Lee, Anupama Shroff, Yuqing Wang and I Younan An.

The Human Development Report Office also extends its sincere gratitude to the Republic of Korea as well as the Governments of Japan, Portugal and Sweden for their financial contributions. Their ongoing support is much appreciated and remains essential.

We are grateful for the highly professional work of our editors and layout artists at Communications Development Incorporated—led by Bruce Ross-Larson with Joe Caponio, Meta de Coquereaumont, Mike Crumplar, Christopher Trott and Elaine Wilson. Bruce, in particular, has been a constant source of sound advice, inspiration and, not infrequently, motivation.

As always, we are extremely grateful to UNDP Administrator Achim Steiner. Facing the demands of leading an organization during unprecedented times, he always found time to give probing advice and to provide encouragement. He has consistently given the team the freedom to explore and to venture beyond well-trodden paths. At a time when expanding freedoms is essential to navigate uncertainties, we hope to have made good use of that incredible trust and commitment to the editorial independence of every Human Development Report.

Pedro Conceição
Director
Human Development Report Office

Contents

Uncertain times, unsettled lives

Uncertain times, unsettled lives

We live in a world of worry. The ongoing Covid-19 pandemic, which has driven reversals in human development in almost every country and continues to spin off variants unpredictably. War in Ukraine and elsewhere, more human suffering amid a shifting geopolitical order and strained multilateral system. Record-breaking temperatures, fires and storms, each an alarm bell from planetary systems increasingly out of whack. Acute crises are giving way to chronic, layered, interacting uncertainties at a global scale, painting a picture of uncertain times and unsettled lives.

Uncertainty is not new. Humans have long worried about plagues and pestilence, violence and war, floods and droughts. Some societies have been brought to their knees by them. At least as many have embraced emerging, unsettling realities and found clever ways to thrive. There are no inevitabilities, just tough unknowns whose best answer is a doubling down on human development to unleash the creative and cooperative capacities that are so essentially human.

Novel layers of uncertainties are interacting to create new kinds of uncertainty—a new uncertainty complex—never seen in human history (figure 1). In addition to the everyday uncertainty that people have faced since time immemorial, we are now navigating uncharted waters, caught in three volatile crosscurrents:
- The dangerous planetary change of the Anthropocene.[1]
- The pursuit of sweeping societal transformations on par with the Industrial Revolution.
- The vagaries and vacillations of polarized societies.

Navigating this new uncertainty complex is hampered by persistent deprivations and inequalities in human development. The past decade finally placed inequality under a spotlight, but less illuminated were the ways that inequalities and uncertainty contribute to insecurity and vice versa. The variation in opportunity and outcome among and within nations is mirrored by—and interacts with—the volatility that people experience in their lives. Complicating matters is a geopolitical order in flux, hamstringing a multilateral system designed for postwar, not postmillennium, challenges and creaking under the weight of naked national interests.

The Covid-19 pandemic and the war in Ukraine are devastating manifestations of today's uncertainty complex. Each exposes limits of—and cracks in—current global governance. Each has battered

Figure 1 A new uncertainty complex is emerging

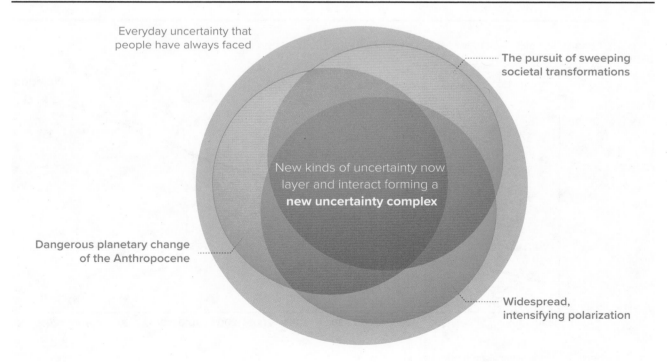

Everyday uncertainty that people have always faced

The pursuit of sweeping societal transformations

New kinds of uncertainty now layer and interact forming a **new uncertainty complex**

Dangerous planetary change of the Anthropocene

Widespread, intensifying polarization

Source: Human Development Report Office.

global supply chains, driving up price volatility in energy, food, fertilizers, commodities and other goods. But it is their interaction that, at the time of this writing, is transforming shocks into an impending global catastrophe. UN Secretary-General António Guterres has repeatedly warned of a prolonged global food crisis due to the confluence of war, pandemic and warming temperatures.[2] Billions of people face the greatest cost-of-living crisis in a generation.[3] Billions already grapple with food insecurity,[4] owing largely to inequalities in wealth and power that determine entitlements to food. A global food crisis will hit them hardest.

Global crises have piled up: the global financial crisis, the ongoing global climate crisis and Covid-19 pandemic, a looming global food crisis. There is a nagging sense that whatever control we have over our lives is slipping away, that the norms and institutions we used to rely on for stability and prosperity are not up to the task of today's uncertainty complex. Feelings of insecurity are on the rise nearly everywhere, a trend that is at least a decade in the making and that well precedes the Covid-19 pandemic and the attendant tailspin in global human development (figure 2).

Even before the Covid-19 pandemic, more than 6 in 7 people at the global level felt insecure.[5] This against a backdrop of incredible global progress (notwithstanding the impacts of the Covid-19 pandemic) over the longer run on conventional measures of well-being, including on many of the human development metrics tracked by the Human Development Report. What is going on? How does the wide-angle lens of human development help us understand and respond to this apparent paradox of progress with insecurity? Such questions animate this year's Report (box 1).

One of the frustrating ironies of the Anthropocene is that while we have more power to influence our future, we do not necessarily have any more control over it. From the climate crisis to far-reaching technological changes, other important forces—many of our own making—are expanding the set of possible outcomes, some unknowable, of any given action. For many, getting from point A to point B in their lives and in their communities feels unclear, unsure, hard —harder still when persistent inequalities, polarization and demagoguery make it difficult to agree on what point B even is and to get moving.

Figure 2 **The global Human Development Index value has declined two years in a row, erasing the gains of the preceding five years**

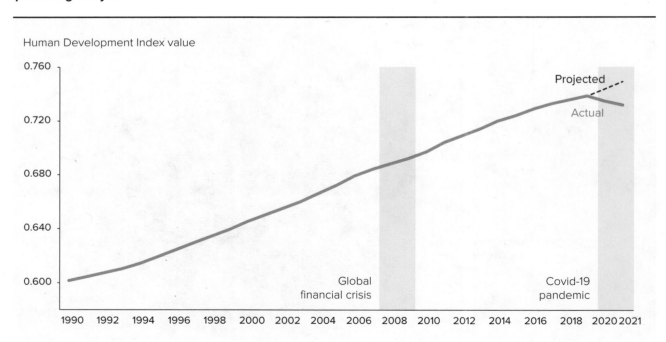

Note: The period of the global financial crisis is indicative.
Source: Human Development Report Office calculations based on data from Barro and Lee (2018), IMF (2021c, 2022), UNDESA (2022a, 2022b), UNESCO Institute for Statistics (2022), UNSD (2022) and World Bank (2022c).

Box 1 The 2021/2022 Human Development Report extends the conversations of earlier Reports

How to understand and navigate today's uncertainty complex—driven by the Anthropocene, by purposeful societal transformation and by intensifying polarization—is the topic of this year's Human Development Report. Much attention over the past decade has been rightly paid to inequalities. Indeed, inequalities and their emerging dimensions were the focus of the 2019 Human Development Report,[1] carried forward into the following year's Report on the socioecological pressures of the Anthropocene.[2] The variations in opportunity and outcome among and within nations also happen within people's lives, giving rise to more and new forms of insecurity, which were explored in the United Nations Development Programme's Special Report on Human Security earlier this year.[3] The 2021/2022 Human Development Report unites and extends these discussions under the theme of uncertainty—how it is changing, what it means for human development and how we can thrive in the face of it.

Notes
1. UNDP 2019. **2.** UNDP 2020a. **3.** UNDP 2022b.

All is not well, but all is not lost, either. Policies that focus on the Three I's—investment, insurance and innovation—will go a long way in helping people navigate the new uncertainty complex and thrive in the face of it (see chapter 6).

- *Investment,* ranging from renewable energy to preparedness for pandemics and extreme natural hazards, will ease planetary pressures and prepare societies to better cope with global shocks. Consider the advances in seismology, tsunami sciences and disaster risk reduction following the 2004 Indian Ocean tsunami.[6] Smart, practical investments pay off.
- *Insurance* does too. It helps protect everyone from the contingencies of an uncertain world. The global surge in social protection in the wake of the Covid-19 pandemic did just that, while underscoring how little social insurance coverage there was before and how much more remains to be done. Investments in universal basic services such as health and education also afford an insurance function.
- *Innovation* in its many forms—technological, economic, cultural—will be vital in responding to unknown and unknowable challenges that humanity will face. While innovation is a whole-of-society affair, government is crucial in this regard: not just in creating the right policy incentives for inclusive innovation but also in being an active partner throughout.

Deeper still are the assumptions underpinning institutions that develop and implement policy at all levels. Assumptions about how people make decisions are often oversimplified. The dominance of these assumptions has occasioned a narrower set of policy options than what is needed to navigate the new uncertainty complex (see chapter 3). Widening the set of policy options starts with recognizing the many cognitive biases and inconsistencies we all have in our decisionmaking. Moreover, what we decide is often rooted in what we value. What we value is in turn rooted in our social context. It is contextual, malleable. Scrutinizing unhelpful social inertias and experimenting with new narratives must be part of the toolbox going forward (see chapter 3).

So must technology. True, technology is more double-edged sword than silver bullet. Fossil-fuel combustion technologies are warming the planet while nuclear fusion promises to bottle the sun, ushering in a new era of limitless, clean energy. With every internet search, retweet and like, our digital footprints generate more data than ever, but we struggle to use it for the common good, and some deliberately misuse it. In a voracious scramble for more of our data, technology giants are concentrating in their hands more and more power over everyone's lives. The trick for us is to bend technology purposefully towards inclusive, creative solutions to challenges old and new rather than allowing it to function like a bull in a china shop, breaking things just because. We need technologies that augment labour rather than displace it, that disrupt selectively rather than indiscriminately (see chapter 4).

As we drift further into this new uncertainty complex, unknown challenges loom—more tough questions without easy answers, more self-defeating opportunities to retreat within borders that are as porous to climate and technology as they have been to Covid-19. If the pandemic is seen as a test run of how we navigate our shared, global future, then we need to learn from it, from the good and the bad, to figure out how to do better. Much better.

The Covid-19 pandemic is a window into a new reality

Now in its third year, the Covid-19 pandemic has exacted a terrible toll in lives and livelihoods around the world. It is more than a long detour from normal; it is a window into a new reality, a painful glimpse into deep, emblematic contradictions, exposing a confluence of fragilities.

On the one hand, an impressive feat of modern science: the development of safe, effective vaccines to a novel virus in less than a year. Having saved tens, perhaps hundreds, of millions of lives over the past century, especially of children, vaccines remain one of humanity's greatest, most cost-effective technological innovations—ever.[7] The battery of Covid-19 vaccines is no exception. In 2021 alone Covid-19 vaccination programmes averted nearly 20 million deaths.[8] It is a lesson of the power of technology to transform lives for the better at a time when we hear so much about the ways technology can do just the opposite.

But access to Covid-19 vaccines remains appallingly low or virtually nonexistent in many low-income countries (figure 3), especially in Africa, which have endured age-specific infection fatality rates twice those of high-income countries.[9] Reaching rural areas with weaker cold chains and fewer healthcare workers remains difficult. Meanwhile, vaccine uptake in many richer countries has stalled, due partly to

Figure 3 Countries' access to Covid-19 vaccines remains highly inequal

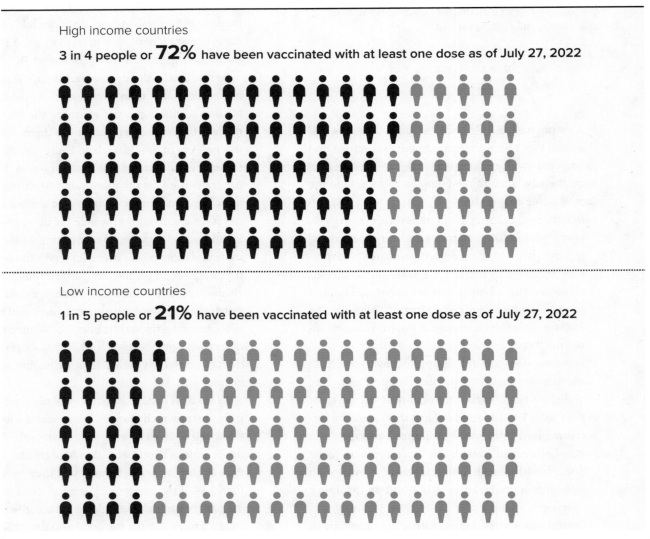

High income countries

3 in 4 people or 72% have been vaccinated with at least one dose as of July 27, 2022

Low income countries

1 in 5 people or 21% have been vaccinated with at least one dose as of July 27, 2022

Source: Global Dashboard for Vaccine Equity (https://data.undp.org/vaccine-equity/), accessed 27 July 2022.

perplexing disputes about vaccines generally.[10] The last mile is long in every country.

Unequal, unjust access to Covid-19 vaccines is one of many inequalities that have weighed heavily throughout the pandemic. Indeed, those inequalities have helped fuel its spread. The groups most likely to be left behind have borne the brunt of its health and economic risks. Women and girls have shouldered even more household and caregiving responsibilities, while violence against them has worsened (see chapter 2).[11] Pre-existing digital divides have widened gaps in children's education access and quality.[12] Some fear a "lost generation" of learners.[13]

For people everywhere the Covid-19 pandemic has generated questions without easy answers, foremost among them: When is this "over"? Answers have proved fleeting, often dashed by upticks in cases or the setting of new restrictions, forcing us back to square one. Global supply chains remain stubbornly knotted, contributing to inflation in all countries —and in some, at rates not seen in decades.[14] The implications of unprecedented monetary and fiscal interventions aiming to rescue ravaged economies, many still scarred by the global financial crisis, remain largely uncertain. They unspool before us in real time and alongside resurgent geopolitical tensions. The pandemic is more than a virus, and it simply is not "over."

With successive waves that have caught countries flat-footed time and time again, ongoing mutability and the seesawing of lockdowns, the Covid-19 pandemic and its seemingly endless twists and turns have—perhaps above all else—entrenched a climate of dogged uncertainty and unsettledness. And this is just one pandemic, having emerged seemingly out of nowhere, like a phantom that cannot be exorcised. We were long warned about the threat of novel respiratory pathogens.[15] As we move deeper into the Anthropocene, we have been warned that there will be more.

A new uncertainty complex is emerging

The impacts of the Covid-19 pandemic on economies pale beside the upheavals expected by powerful new technologies and the hazards and transformations they pose. What do investments in people's education and skills—a key part of human development—look

like in the face of the disorienting pace of technological change, including automation and artificial intelligence? Or in the face of deliberate, necessary energy transitions that would restructure societies? More broadly, amid unprecedented patterns of dangerous planetary change, what capabilities matter and how?

" The impacts of the Covid-19 pandemic on economies pale beside the upheavals expected by powerful new technologies and the hazards and transformations they pose

Recent years have seen more record temperatures, fires and storms around the world, alarming reminders that the climate crisis marches on, alongside other planetary-level changes wrought by the Anthropocene. Biodiversity collapse is one of them. More than 1 million plant and animal species face extinction.[16] As much as the Covid-19 pandemic caught us by surprise, unprepared and fumbling for paths forward, we have even less of an idea of how to live in a world without, say, an abundance of insects. That has not been tried for about 500 million years, when the world's first land plants appeared. This is not a coincidence. Without an abundance of insect pollinators, we face the mindboggling challenge of growing food and other agricultural products at scale.

Human societies and ecological systems have long influenced—and surprised—one another, but not at the scales and speeds of the Anthropocene. Humans are now shaping planetary trajectories,[17] and the dramatically changing baselines—from global temperatures to species diversity—are altering the fundamental frame of reference humans have been operating under for millennia. It is as if the ground beneath our feet is shifting, introducing a new kind of planetary uncertainty for which we have no real guide.

Material cycles, for example, have been upended. For the first time in history, humanmade materials, such as concrete and asphalt, outweigh the Earth's biomass. Microplastics are now everywhere: in country-sized garbage patches in the ocean, in protected forests and distant mountaintops and in people's lungs and blood.[18] Mass coral bleaching is now commonplace rather than extraordinary.[19]

The latest International Panel on Climate Change Report is a "code red for humanity."[20] While we still have the possibility to prevent excessive global warming and avoid the worst scenarios, human-induced changes to our planetary system are expected to continue well into the future. In essence, as science has advanced, the models are, with better precision than before, predicting more volatility.[21]

Any one of the rapid, planetary-level, human-induced changes of the Anthropocene would be enough on its own to inject frightening new uncertainties into the fate of not just individuals, communities or even nations, but of all humankind. Recall just a few decades ago when chlorofluorocarbons entered global consciousness. Or the insecticide known as DDT before that. Or nuclear proliferation before that (and, sadly, still today). The human-induced forces at work in the Anthropocene are not atomized or neatly sequenced. They are not islands of perturbations in a sea of relative stability. Instead, they are stacked on top of each other, interacting and amplifying in unpredictable ways. For the first time in human history, anthropogenic existential threats loom larger than those from natural hazards.[22]

" The layering and interactions of multidimensional risks and the overlapping of threats give rise to new dimensions of uncertainty, if for no other reason than human choices have impacts well beyond our weakened socioecological systems' capacities to absorb them

For this reason, in its portraiture of uncertainty, the Report does not build scenarios. Instead, it explores how three novel sources of uncertainty at the global level stack up to create a new uncertainty complex that is unsettling lives and dragging on human development (see chapter 1):
- The first novel uncertainty is associated with the Anthropocene's dangerous planetary change and its interaction with human inequalities.
- The second is the purposeful if uncertain transition towards new ways of organizing industrial societies —purporting transformations similar to those in the transition from agricultural to industrial societies.[23]
- The third is the intensification of political and social polarization across and within countries—and of misperceptions both about information and across groups of people—facilitated by how new digital technologies are often being used.[24]

The layering and interactions of multidimensional risks and the overlapping of threats give rise to new dimensions of uncertainty, if for no other reason than human choices have impacts well beyond our weakened socioecological systems' capacities to absorb them. In this new uncertainty complex shocks can amplify and interact rather than dissipate; they can be propagated in systems rather than stabilized by them.

Human pulsing of natural systems at unprecedented intensities and scales is one side of the uncertainty coin. On the other are stubborn social deficits, including deficits in human development, which make it more difficult to navigate unpredictable outcomes and to dial down those pulses in the first place. Consider the Covid-19 pandemic, which has as much to do with inequalities, poor leadership and distrust as it does with variants and vaccines. Or competition for environmental resources, competition that does not typically break down into conflict. While stressed ecosystems can parallel grievances, grievances become conflicts due to social imbalances.[25] Political power, inequalities and marginalization contribute more to environmental conflict than does access to natural resources.

Political polarization complicates matters further (figure 4). It has been on the rise, and uncertainty makes it worse and is worsened by it (see chapter 4). Large numbers of people feel frustrated by and alienated from their political systems.[26] In a reversal from just 10 years ago, democratic backsliding is now the prevailing trend across countries.[27] This despite high support globally for democracy. Armed conflicts are also up, including outside so-called fragile contexts.[28] For the first time ever, more than 100 million people are forcibly displaced, most of them within their own countries.[29]

The conjunction of uncertainty and polarization may be paralyzing—delaying action to curb human pressures on the planet. The real paradox of our time may be our inability to act, despite mounting evidence of the distress that human planetary pressures are causing ecological and social systems. Unless we get a handle on the worrying state of human affairs, we face the Anthropocene's vicissitudes with one hand tied behind our backs.

Even when functioning properly, conventional crisis response and risk management mechanisms,

Figure 4 Political polarization is on the rise across the world

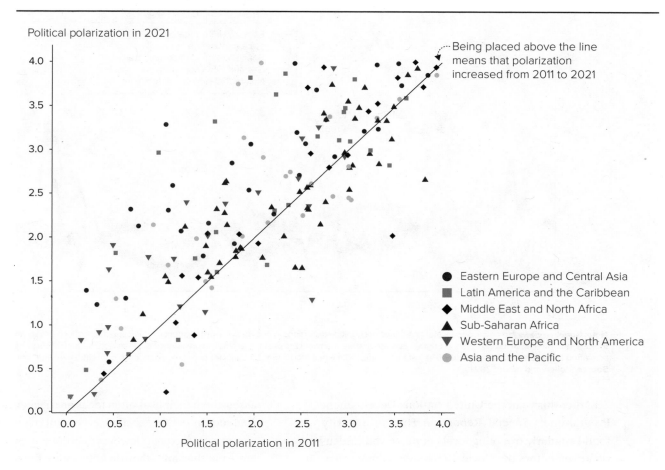

Source: Adapted from Boese and others (2022).

such as various forms of insurance, are not up to the task of global, interconnected disruption. The uncoordinated responses to the Covid-19 pandemic are a case in point. New strategies are needed for tail events synchronized at the global level. Addressing risk through diversification is difficult when volatility affects the entire system rather than only parts of it. Yet, numerous countries around the world have been steadily chipping away at risk sharing in many ways.[30] New forms of work and their uncertainties have become more important in technology-enabled gig economies. Altogether, insecurity has long been on the rise.

And it has been on the rise for some groups more than others. Against a backdrop of novel, interacting uncertainties, people with power, wealth or privilege have the means, to some degree, to protect themselves privately and to shift more of the burden on to others. The groups most likely to be left behind face a world with complex new uncertainties in which most of those uncertainties are directed at them, heaped on persistent discrimination and human rights violations.[31] It is not just that typhoons are getting bigger and deadlier through human impact on the environment; it is also as if, through our social choices, their destructive paths are being directed at the most vulnerable among us.

Feelings of distress are on the rise nearly everywhere

An analysis of more than 14 million books published over the last 125 years in three major languages shows a sharp increase in expressions of anxiety and worry in many parts of the world (figure 5).[32] Other research on smaller time scales reports steady increases in concerns about uncertainty since 2012, well before the Covid-19 outbreak.[33]

Figure 5 Negative views about the world surges to unprecedented highs

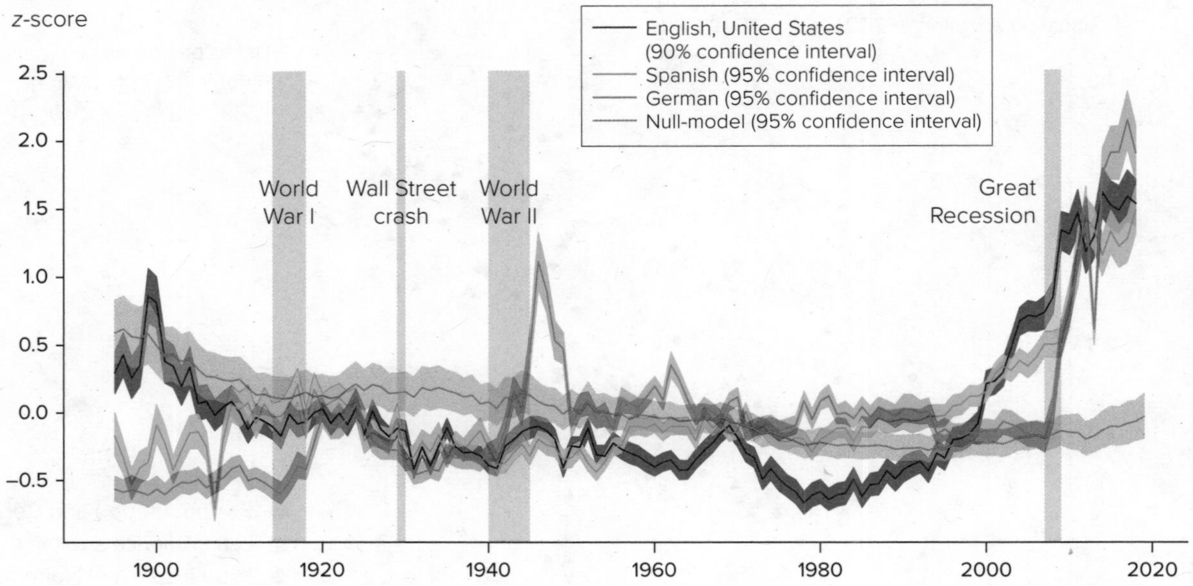

Note: Negative views are defined as textual analogues of cognitive distortions in one- to five-word sequences reflecting depression, anxiety and other distortions, published in 14 million books in English, Spanish and German over the past 125 years. The prevalence of these word sequences in publications are converted to z-scores for comparability. They are compared with a null-model that accounts for over-time changes in publication volumes and standards.
Source: Bollen and others 2021.

Earlier this year, the United Nations Development Programme's Special Report on Human Security found similarly troubling levels of perceived insecurity. Even before the Covid-19 pandemic, more than 6 in 7 people at the global level felt insecure.[34] Perceived human insecurity is high across all Human Development Index (HDI) groups, and it has increased, even in some very high HDI countries (figure 6). Polarization has moved in tandem in recent years. In parallel, there is a breakdown of trust: globally, fewer than 30 percent of people think that most people can be trusted, the lowest value on record (see chapter 4).

These and other data paint a puzzling picture in which people's perceptions about their lives and their societies stand in stark contrast to historically high measures of aggregate wellbeing, including long-standing multidimensional measures of wellbeing, such as the HDI and other indices that accompany this Report. In sum, twin paradoxes: progress with insecurity and progress with polarization.

What is going on?

Too often the answer is reduced to fault-finding inquiries about whether the data or the people are wrong. Most likely, neither. Although people tend to express a holistic view of their lived experience, the questions asked about their lives often focus on specific, measurable subsets of that experience: years of schooling, life expectancy, income. However important these metrics are—and they are—they do not capture the totality of a lived experience. Nor were they ever intended to reflect the full concept of human development, which goes well beyond achievements in wellbeing, such as reducing poverty or hunger, to include equally important notions of freedoms and agency, which together expand the sense of possibility in people's lives. Nor do individual achievements necessarily capture social cohesion and trust, which matter to people in their own right and for working together towards shared goals. In short, the twin paradoxes invite a hard look at narrow conceptions of "progress."

The 2019 Human Development Report emphasized going beyond averages to understand the wide and growing variation in capabilities within many countries. It identified widening gaps in enhanced capabilities, such as access to higher education and life expectancy at age 70, gaps that might also help explain the apparent disconnect between what people say about their lives and what we measure about them. These are not either-or explanations; all are possible, even probable.[35]

Figure 6 Perceived human insecurity is increasing in most countries—even in some very high Human Development Index countries

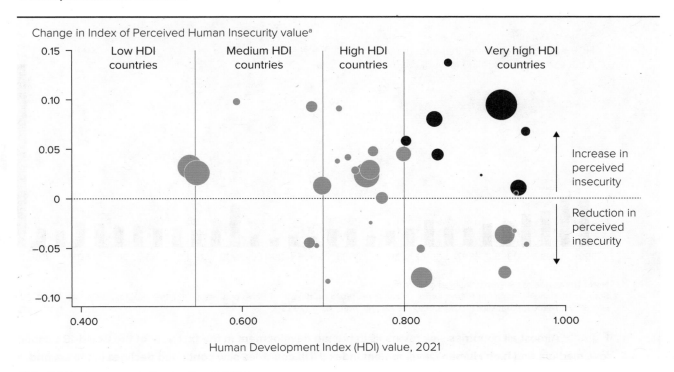

Note: Bubble size represents the country population.
a. Refers to the change in Index of Perceived Human Security value between waves 6 and 7 of the World Values Survey for countries with comparable data.
Source: UNDP 2022b.

Capabilities face more volatile futures while becoming ever more important for helping people navigate the systemic uncertainties of a new epoch. Achieving gains may become harder, securing them harder still. Backsliding may become more sudden or common or both; it has already become evident during the Covid-19 pandemic. For the first time on record, the global HDI value declined, taking the world back to the time just after the adoption of the 2030 Agenda for Sustainable Development and the Paris Agreement. Every year a few different countries experience dips in their respective HDI values. But a whopping 90 percent of countries saw their HDI value drop in either 2020 or 2021 (figure 7), far exceeding the number that experienced reversals in the wake of the global financial crisis. Last year saw some recovery at the global level, but it was partial and uneven: most very high HDI countries notched improvements, while most of the rest experienced ongoing declines (figure 8).

The goal of human development is to help people lead lives they value by expanding their capabilities, which go beyond wellbeing achievements to include agency and freedoms. If uncertainty forms storm clouds over all aspects of human development, then it hurls lightning bolts at the idea of agency. It can disempower. Choices mediate the translation of one's values and commitments into achievements, but the idea of choice becomes ever more abstract, no matter how formally educated or healthy we may be, if we doubt that the choices we make will yield the outcomes we desire. Losing perceived control rather than simply not having it in the first place has its own negative consequences, as do the knock-on effects: a tendency to identify culprits or villains, a distrust of institutions and elites, and greater insularity, nationalism and social discord. Uncertainty can turn up the heat on a toxic brew.

Technology use is a double-edged sword

Powerful new technologies turn it up further. From the news, products and advertisements served up to us to the relationships we build online and in real life, more and more of our lives are being determined

Figure 7 Recent declines on the Human Development Index (HDI) are widespread, with over 90 percent of countries enduring a decline in 2020 or 2021

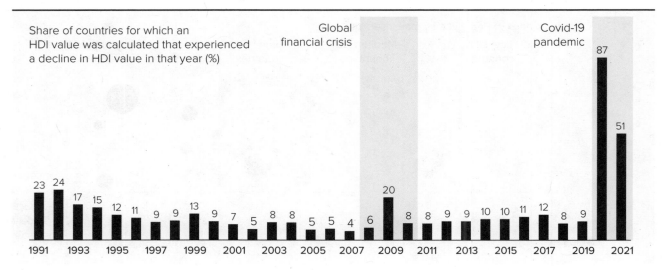

Note: The period of the global financial crisis is indicative.
Source: Human Development Report Office calculations based on data from Barro and Lee (2018), IMF (2021c, 2022), UNDESA (2022a, 2022b), UNESCO Institute for Statistics (2022), UNSD (2022) and World Bank (2022c).

Figure 8 Almost all countries saw reversals in human development in the first year of the Covid-19 pandemic, most low, medium and high Human Development Index (HDI) countries saw continued declines in the second year

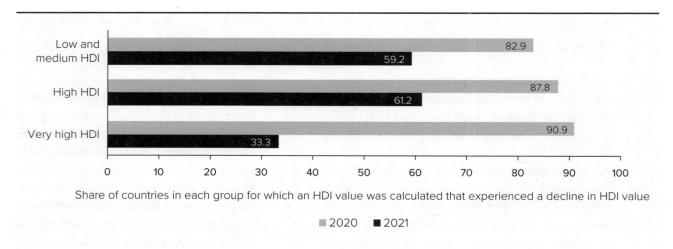

Source: Human Development Report Office calculations based on data from Barro and Lee (2018), IMF (2021c, 2022), UNDESA (2022a, 2022b), UNESCO Institute for Statistics (2022), UNSD (2022) and World Bank (2022c).

by algorithms and, in particular, by artificial intelligence. For people who are online, every aspect of their lives becomes commodifiable data, raising worrying questions about who has access to what information, especially sensitive personal information, and how it is being used.[36]

The political, commercial and personal all get mixed together in social media, which is full of loud echo chambers because they draw eyeballs, which draws advertising and other revenues. At least half the online noise is from bots designed to stir the pot.[37] Misinformation moves faster and farther than information that has been subjected to reasoned scrutiny, sowing distrust and fanning perhaps the gravest kind of uncertainty: not knowing how to distinguish between the two. Making the distinction goes beyond clear-cut objectivism or the reliance on an agreed set of universal facts, scientific or otherwise. Motivated reasoning, in which people select facts, experts and other trusted sources of information that confirm their already-held beliefs, is widespread across political spectra and education levels (see chapter 3). Polarization can take dangerous forms when different groups operate with entirely different sets of facts and, thus, realities, especially when those realities are bound up with group identities. Technologies then turn mere disagreements into pitched battles for survival (see chapter 4).

Given the ways technology use can aggravate at the societal level, its harmful effects at the community and individual levels may come as no surprise. As it is in so many parts of our lives, technology is a double-edged sword. Artificial intelligence will both create and destroy tasks, causing tremendous disruption. Synthetic biology opens new frontiers in health and medicine while raising fundamental questions about what it means to be human. From the invention of writing to Gutenberg's printing press to Marconi's first radio transmissions, technologies have been connecting people ever faster in new ways, now instantaneously and across great distances. Today, telemedicine is especially valuable in digitally connected rural areas and has been vital for mental and physical health during the pandemic.[38]

At the same time, rather paradoxically, technology can isolate. Internet use has been found to reduce offline interaction, political participation and various forms of civic and cultural engagement.[39] The consequences of substituting the digital for the real are complex and will be made more so as virtual worlds —the metaverse—take up more real estate. Cyberbullying is an issue on social media, and angry Twitter mobs, mobilized sometimes by disinformation, can digitally tar and feather someone faster than in real life. Sometimes that spills over into real-life violence or into real-life policy. Digital addiction is a real concern. Random rewards in the form of likes on Instagram or TikTok or the adrenaline rush of clickbait are essentially cognitive hacks that lie at the heart of most real-life casinos (see chapter 2).[40]

Mental wellbeing is under assault

Mental wellbeing is an important, complex issue globally without any single driver, technological or otherwise. Mental distress, whose prevention is a critical aspect of overall mental wellbeing, is aggravated by uncertainties and insecurities of all stripes: by major Anthropocene phenomena, such as climate change; by age-old scourges of discrimination, exclusion, conflict and violence; and by relatively newer entrants, such as social media and other technologies.

The uncertainties of the Anthropocene are expected to undermine people's mental wellbeing through four main pathways: traumatizing events, physical illness, general climate anxiety and food insecurity (see chapter 2). The effects these and other pathways have on children in particular are profound, altering brain and body development, especially in families on lower social rungs, potentially diminishing what children can achieve in life. The 2019 Human Development Report explored how inequalities in human development are perpetuated across generations;[41] it is not difficult to see how the confluence of mental distress, inequality and insecurity foment a similarly injurious intergenerational cycle that drags on human development.

> " The uncertainties of the Anthropocene are expected to undermine people's mental wellbeing through four main pathways: traumatizing events, physical illness, general climate anxiety and food insecurity

Violence—even the threat of violence, its uncertainty—is a major driver of mental distress. Some survivors of and witnesses to violence suffer trauma, which if not addressed properly can develop into post-traumatic stress disorder, among other chronic health conditions, that can weigh heavily on the choices available to them. Violence may be directed at one person or group of people, but it affects everybody in its blast radius. Even perpetrators of violence can suffer trauma due to the violent setting that often surrounds them, as with organized crime or gang violence.[42]

The losses exacted by violence extend well beyond direct physical, mental and emotional injury or trauma. Violence can cause and exacerbate all kinds of insecurities—food, economic and so forth—that are themselves major drivers of mental distress. Many kinds of violence, from interpersonal violence to organized crime to armed conflict, perniciously undermine trust in people we know and in people we do not know. Breakdowns in trust may then beget more instability, more violence.

" Mental disorders weigh on human development in many ways. A health issue themselves, they are often linked to other health challenges. They can impede school attendance and learning, as well as the ability to find a job and be fully productive at it. The stigma that often accompanies mental disorders makes matters worse

Then there is the loss of agency due to violence. The complex interplay of forces, rooted in asymmetries of power, is powerfully at work in intimate partner violence, whose survivors are predominately women and which is correlated with some measures of women's economic dependence (see chapter 2). Channels of dominance at the societal and institutional levels can take concentrated, wicked forms—especially for women, children and older people—behind what are meant to be the safe walls of a home, leaving those subjected to domestic abuse with either the perception or the reality of no escape. The ensuing entrapment of people violates human rights, constrains agency and ultimately undercuts our collective ability to navigate a turbulent new era.

As it has been in so many ways, the Covid-19 pandemic is ominously illustrative. During the first year of the pandemic, the global prevalence of depression and anxiety increased by more than 25 percent.[43] Low-income people, especially those who struggle to afford basic needs such as rent and food, suffered disproportionally in several countries.[44] Women, who assumed most of the additional domestic and care work that emerged during school closures and lockdowns,[45] faced much higher mental distress than before the crisis.[46]

Stressors need not reach the level of globalized trauma to cause mental distress. In fact, one of the most serious economic threats to mental wellbeing seems to stem from repeated financial shocks, such as income loss, especially for poor people and for men.[47] Economic insecurity—or just the perception of such insecurity, even if transitory—is a major factor. Mental distress is one reason why economic dislocations, whether from globalization or automation or phasing out fossil fuels, carry some large, underappreciated risks.

Mental disorders, such as post-traumatic stress disorder and depression, can develop when mental distress is severe and untreated. Almost 1 billion people—roughly one in eight of us—live with a mental disorder,[48] providing a lower-bound estimate of the broader problem of mental distress. Globally, mental health issues are the leading cause of disability. Yet, of those who need mental health attention or treatment, only about 10 percent receive it.[49] On average, countries spend less than 2 percent of their healthcare budgets on mental health.[50]

Mental disorders weigh on human development in many ways. A health issue themselves, they are often linked to other health challenges. They can impede school attendance and learning, as well as the ability to find a job and be fully productive at it. The stigma that often accompanies mental disorders makes matters worse. Mental disorders are uniquely challenging because the primary instrument to navigate life's challenges—the mind—is precisely the thing that people living with a mental disorder may not be able to rely on. The other thing we tend to rely on is relationships. If those also suffer, people are left even more isolated and vulnerable.

Purposeful transformations introduce their own uncertainties

Today's new uncertainty complex is not just about the planetary pressures of the Anthropocene and political and social polarization; it is also about purposeful societal transformations that seek to ease planetary pressures and leverage the positive potential of new technologies (see chapter 1). From energy systems to food production to transportation, easing planetary pressures demands fundamental changes to much of the way the world currently operates. It is a necessary, wildly worthwhile investment—ethically, environmentally, economically—but it comes with its own significant uncertainties, especially for economies, livelihoods and pocketbooks.[51]

The energy transitions required to confront the climate crisis would be challenging even in the best of times. They become more so when stacked on top of inequalities and social fragmentation, the rapid clip of technological disruption and dangerous planetary change. The backlash in some countries to various forms of energy taxation or carbon pricing is a case in point. However welcome new renewable energy technologies may be at competitive market prices, they carry their own environmental costs and risks, including those related to mining to supply the materials for the world's solar panels and wind turbines.[52]

People rightly worry about winners and losers when big change is on the horizon. Yes, the green economy could add more than 24 million jobs worldwide by 2030.[53] This is an exciting opportunity for people and planet. But these jobs will not necessarily be in the same regions that stand to lose jobs as fossil fuel industries shut down. Nor will they require the same skills as a fossil fuel–based economy. No one seems especially interested in a bigger overall pie if his or her piece is feared to be getting much smaller.

Nor do people need forecasts or history books to know that societal transformations—however well planned or not, however "good" or not—can radically reshape the communities they live in, often in unexpected ways where "do-overs" are not possible if things go wrong. Many around the world have lived through transformations, some ongoing, in their lifetimes. They see them with their own eyes. The transformations in energy and materials required now in the Anthropocene portend even more upheavals, which some believe to be as large as the shift from agricultural to industrial societies.[54]

Whether it is the advent of agriculture or the Industrial Revolution, previous tectonic shifts have typically stretched across multiple generations. Now, they can happen within a generation, in a matter of years, introducing a new kind of uncertainty or worry. Whether through foresight or experience, that will influence how people think about and invest in their lives, families and communities and hold their leaders accountable. These are not reasons to give up on a green economy; we cannot afford to throw in the towel. But if we do not understand people's present and future anxieties and address the underlying drivers, if we do not build trust and the promise of a better future, progress towards purposeful, just, sustainable transformations is going to be even harder.

The net result of today's uncertainty complex on development is profound. We might be facing a growing mismatch between what is needed to navigate novel, interacting uncertainties and the current state of affairs, categorized by social arrangements (what to do—in terms of policies, institutions) and the behaviours shaped by social context, culture and narratives (how to do it—in terms of prevalent identities, values and beliefs). The interplay of forces—their scales, speeds, unknown interactions and consequences—have made development pathways simultaneously far less obvious and far more open. What should happen next can no longer be taken for granted. A linear march of progress in which low-income countries chase higher income ones is less relevant. In a sense all countries are developing countries, charting a new planetary course together, regardless of whether they work together to do so.

> " In a sense all countries are developing countries, charting a new planetary course together, regardless of whether they work together to do so

The question is no longer simply how some countries get from point A to point B; instead, it is how all countries start moving from wherever they are to points N, T or W—or letters in some new alphabet—and then course correct along the way. Development is perhaps better seen as a process characterized both by adapting to an unfolding unknown reality and by purposefully transforming economies and societies to ease planetary pressures and advance inclusion.[55]

There is promise and opportunity in uncertainty

If necessity is the mother of invention, then the very forces that give rise to today's uncertainties also offer the means to navigate them. Uncertainty engenders the possibility of change, also for the better. Consider artificial intelligence, a disruptive opportunity at least as much as a disruptive threat. Its potential for enhancing labour is bigger than its potential for automating it. New tasks, new jobs, new industries are all possible (figure 9). Recall that most jobs came into being in part through the task-creating effects of new technologies: around 60 percent of people in the United States are now employed in occupations that did not exist in 1940.[56] We do not, however, have the luxury to wait around for the long run. The negative displacement impacts of artificial intelligence are too big, too likely and too fast, especially if labour-replacing incentives dominate its development. Policies

Figure 9 There is much more scope for artificial intelligence to augment human activity than to automate existing tasks

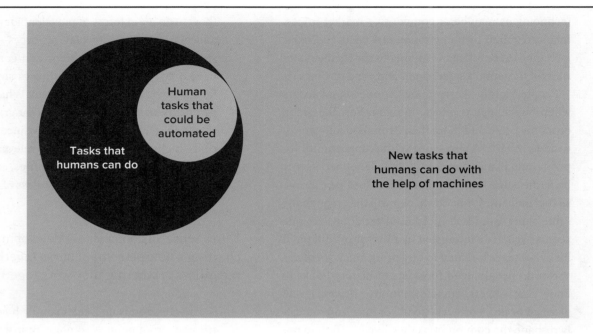

Human tasks that could be automated

Tasks that humans can do

New tasks that humans can do with the help of machines

Note: Figure is illustrative.
Source: Human Development Report Office based on Brynjolfsson (2022).

and institutions must be put into place that nudge artificial intelligence towards people rather than away from them, to unlock and frontload its potential for positive transformation.

We are already witnessing artificial intelligence's upside in many areas (see chapter 5). Among its many climate-related applications, it aids in modelling climate change impacts and in predicting disasters. In education it can facilitate individualized learning and enhance accessibility. In biology it has revolutionized protein folding prediction, a huge boon for medicine.[57]

Among the many things the Covid-19 pandemic broke open was our imaginations. It expanded the reference points for what is possible (see chapter 5). Consider the rapid development and distribution in many (but not all) countries of safe, effective Covid-19 vaccines, some based on new mRNA technologies that hold promise for preventing and treating many other diseases. The pandemic normalized paid sick leave, voluntary social distancing and self-isolation, all important for our response to future pandemics.

The interventions by central banks over the past two years dwarf their interventions in the wake of the global financial crisis about a decade earlier. Fiscal policy saw a sea change, too. Social protection

has surged, protecting many people from even worse impacts of the Covid-19 pandemic while providing large-scale test cases of innovative ideas: linking national registries and databases for eligibility determination; expanding coverage to previously uncovered beneficiaries, such as refugees, migrants and informal workers; and adopting digital verification and delivery systems, among other pathbreaking steps.[58]

Civil society has been breaking new ground, too. In many places the Covid-19 pandemic galvanized civil society organizations to deliver emergency responses, in some cases taking on new functions.[59] In response to expanded emergency government powers, some civil society entities have beefed up watchdog activities, and still others are pushing to address social, economic and political imbalances laid bare by the pandemic.

As the Covid-19 pandemic has shown, the growing mismatch between the world as it is (or is becoming) and conventional ways of understanding and doing things, such that more and more of life lacks an obvious compass or structure, can be seen as an opportunity to do something new. It can be an opportunity to imagine, experiment and create, in ways similar to the work of a scientist or artist. Existing institutions can be transformed, and new ones created, alongside new leaders, social movements and norms. Much like many scientists and artists, who are often responding to practical personal and societal concerns, this process of ongoing, creative reconstruction at all levels is a practical response to today's uncertainty complex. We will have to find ways to renew, adapt and create institutions in the face of their inevitable shortcomings in an unpredictably changing world. We will have to experiment, to cooperate, in order to thrive.

If we do not—if we reinforce the status quo, when the status quo is part of the problem, or limit our aspirations to a "return to normal"—the gap between a changing world and intractable norms and institutions will widen to a chasm. Opportunities for innovation and good leadership then increasingly become dangerous vacuums in power where the allure of simple recipes and the easy gratifications of finger pointing combine to make the problem worse. There is promise and peril in uncertainty and disruption; tipping the scales towards promise—towards hope—is up to us.

An evolving portfolio of perspectives helps in a world of worry

Tipping the scales towards promise requires that we keep testing the fences of conventional thinking, to embrace an evolving portfolio of perspectives from which to draw, mixing and matching as emerging contexts require. For instance, policies and institutions at all levels need to go beyond assuming that people are only, or even predominantly, self-interested (see chapter 3). This assumption remains highly relevant, but it is does not encompass the totality of human behaviour. Its limitations have been highlighted and addressed, at least partially, by complementary and pioneering work in behavioural economics. Still, we must reach for broader perspectives of human decisionmaking, ones that consider the roles of emotions and culture and that explore how people weave together and change value-infused narratives about themselves and the various communities they belong to. For example, our relationship with nature needs renovation, and cultural narratives are the foundation.

" To respond creatively and nimbly to today's uncertainty complex, we need to bring down barriers to people's imaginations, identities and networks, to expand the idea of what is possible in people's lives

Just as we must widen the vista on human behaviour, notions of human development must go beyond a focus on wellbeing achievements, however important they still are, to include the vital roles of agency and freedoms in helping people live lives that they value (see chapter 3). Doing so illuminates the apparent paradoxes of our age: progress with insecurity and progress with polarization. A comprehensive embrace of human development can act as a lodestar through turbulent times when cookie-cutter policy lists simply will not do. To respond creatively and nimbly to today's uncertainty complex, we need to bring down barriers to people's imaginations, identities and networks, to expand the idea of what is possible in people's lives. While crises can present opportunities for pathbreaking action, we will be better off operating deliberately and proactively rather than in a chronic state of emergency response. In an age of layered and interacting uncertainties, freedoms may not translate reliably into desired achievements or outcomes. That is the unfortunate news. But individuals, families and communities can be empowered to experiment, to try new things, for their benefit and for others, without fear of being trapped in poverty, in a single identity or in one cultural narrative.

Rigidities in their many dimensions—in ideas, in networks, in narratives—act as a vise on human creativity; they constrain the generation of new ideas in response to a changing world. Agency and freedoms are antidotes. Policies, institutions and cultural change that promote them tend to be fostered by cultivating four motivating principles: flexibility, solidarity, creativity and inclusion (see also chapter 6). These principles, which can reinforce one another, will go a long way in making policies and institutions more fit for purpose.

The four principles can also have their own internal tensions. Building systems with some stabilizing redundancies, for example, needs to be balanced against nimble response capacities. Still, it is hard to be quick on one's feet if one is constantly getting knocked over by a financial meltdown, novel virus or monster hurricane. Similarly, there is a give and take to creative exploration and concerted, purposeful action anchored in human rights. Striking the right balance among the four motivating principles will be key, and trust is essential to doing so. People will be suspicious of the negotiation table if they fear that the chair will be constantly jerked out from under them. Policy development will be an iterative, trial-and-error process in which we must all learn from each other.

Policies and institutions to invest, insure and innovate

There are no policy panaceas, no one-size-fits-all approaches. Even so, some policies form the building blocks for countries and communities as they navigate today's uncertainty complex towards more hopeful futures. They fall into three overlapping, mutually reinforcing categories: investment, insurance and innovation—the Three I's (figure 10; see also chapter 6).

Investment should connect the dots. Nature-based human development can protect and enhance natural resources while protecting people from shocks, promoting economic and food security and expanding the choices available to them. Such investments are especially relevant at the local level, speaking to the

need for investing in governance that is connected to people on the ground, that builds bridges among policy and institutional silos and that ensures all voices are heard. Investments are needed, too, on the other end—in global public goods. The new uncertainty complex is often driven by global phenomena, so responding to it can require global cooperation. The additional investment to avoid future pandemics is estimated to be only $15 billion a year.[60] This is a tiny fraction of the economic cost of the Covid-19 pandemic, a cost that exceeds $7 trillion in lost production and $16.9 trillion in emergency fiscal responses.[61] Investments in global pandemic preparedness make good sense, given the devastating human costs.

Insurance provides an essential stabilizing force in the face of uncertainty. To start, structures that manage a variety of risk in people's lives, primarily in various forms of social protection, need to be revitalized and modernized, including for people in informal or other precarious employment, such as gig workers. We need to reverse course away from risk segmentation and move towards a broader sharing of risk. More countercyclical social protection measures can be automatically triggered by certain indicators, such as the loss of a job or a drop in income, while ensuring their inclusivity. Such measures played important roles in many countries in protecting people from some of the worst impacts of the global financial

Figure 10 **Making people more secure though investment, insurance and innovation**

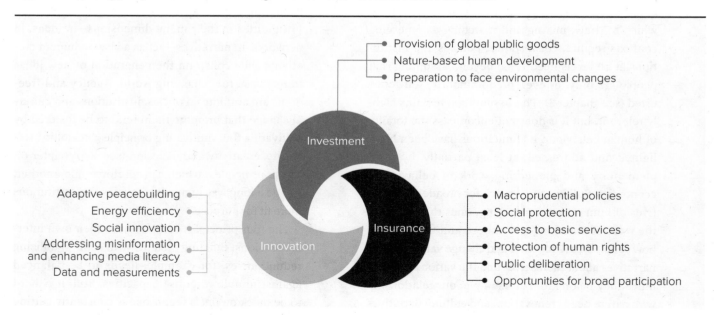

- Provision of global public goods
- Nature-based human development
- Preparation to face environmental changes

Investment

Adaptive peacebuilding
Energy efficiency
Social innovation
Addressing misinformation and enhancing media literacy
Data and measurements

Innovation

Insurance

- Macroprudential policies
- Social protection
- Access to basic services
- Protection of human rights
- Public deliberation
- Opportunities for broad participation

Source: Human Development Report Office.

crisis and the Covid-19 pandemic. One of the benefits of automatic triggers is that they require less political wrangling at already stressful moments, helping target political capital to the unique features of a new challenge rather than continually plugging holes in leaky safety nets.

Universal basic services, such as health and education, are important investments in their own right, as evidenced in the Sustainable Development Goals, and for inclusively expanding human development. They also afford an important insurance function, helping stabilize people in the face of seemingly relentless shocks. This can encourage experimentation. People are loath to try new things if doing so risks their or their family's health and education and threatens to yank them irreversibly down a yawning socioeconomic ladder.

" Innovation will be at the heart of successfully navigating the many unforeseen, unknowable challenges ahead

Investments in preparedness, not just for shocks but also for societal transitions, can be well worth the cost. Equally important are investments in promoting and protecting human rights and in deliberative mechanisms that enable public reasoning in a participatory, inclusive way. Together they help insure against polarization.

Innovation will be at the heart of successfully navigating the many unforeseen, unknowable challenges ahead. Some readymade tools will help, others will be modified and updated for new contexts and still others will be built from scratch. In part, innovation has to do with new technologies and ensuring that they reach everyone. Computational capacities amounting to millions of Apollo missions to the moon are now in the hands of everyone with a smartphone, which is just about everybody.[62] In developing countries mobile phones have reshaped financial transfers and access to information, such as weather forecasts and wholesale market prices. New insurance models are needed that respond to complex new risk paradigms: risks that are increasingly synchronized across geographies and sectors, that span generations and that harm natural resources.

The "right" role for governments in innovation is an important question, and governments have big roles in fostering climates for innovation. There was widespread support when governments threw their full weight behind Covid-19 vaccines, committing to staggering prepurchase orders of then-unproven technologies. Governments were a driving force and active development and distribution partner throughout, ushering in and deploying a lifesaving new technology at astonishing speed. (The contrast with the relatively anaemic action on climate change, no less an emergency than Covid-19, is stark.) Innovation policy frameworks, which are intimately tied to other areas such as competition and patent laws, have enormous implications across sectors, from access to medicines and energy to food and water security.

Innovation does not have to be big to produce big results. Major social media platforms have enacted policies such as notices, warnings and links to resources in a bid to combat misinformation. For example, links to official information by the World Health Organization are suggested under posts mentioning Covid-19 on Instagram, Facebook, YouTube and TikTok. Twitter reminds users when they are sharing an article without opening the link first (see chapter 4). Fact-checking initiatives have been created by users on these same platforms, and media plurality has been strengthened through new and independent outlets that could not exist or have the means to inform in the traditional media landscape, often at the local and grassroot levels. Governments can also take prudent steps to combat misinformation while respecting and promoting people's human rights and freedoms.

Sometimes the answer might not be complex. The simple addition of the retweet button on Twitter has enabled information, including misinformation, to go viral. Modifying its use, as some have argued, could go a long way in curbing some of the more troubling features of social media.[63] Course correcting in this way—practical solutions to practical problems—will be key to navigating the new uncertainty complex.

Innovation is more than technologies as we understand them conventionally in terms of vaccines or smartphones. Equally important is social innovation, which is a whole-of-society endeavour. Adaptive peacebuilding, which focuses on emergent bottom-up, participatory processes rather than adhering to a set recipe, is a case in point.[64] Much can be learned from its application in Rwanda for healing, transitional justice and conflict resolution (see chapter 6).

Cultural change opens opportunities for collective action

Policies and institutions are embedded in social contexts, so aspects such as narratives matter a lot, too. Everyone is immersed in social contexts, with culture understood not as a fixed variable working in the background but as a toolkit that changes over time and that individuals and groups use strategically in society.

When it comes to choices about the future, people appear to be motivated less by accurate scenarios of what the future may hold than by collectively held narratives.[65] Much of the current information about the future, in the form of assessments, such as those issued by the Intergovernmental Panel on Climate Change or Intergovernmental Science-Policy Platform on Biodiversity and Ecosystem Services,[66] are anticipatory. As crucial as they are, it is important to consider also having assessments towards imagining more desirable futures.[67]

The importance of culture is finding its way into many other areas, including economics and law. The work of Robert Shiller explains dynamics in asset prices as well as business cycles in terms of "narrative economics."[68] Karla Hoff and James Walsh suggest that law affects behaviour not only by changing incentives and information (a coordination function) or through its expressive role (as a guidepost for social norms) but also with the potential to change cultural categories.[69]

Shifting culture, for good or ill, is possible and can happen quickly. Education can be a powerful tool to open the potential for new perspectives in younger generations, not just through curricula but also by envisaging schools as spaces of inclusion and diversity. Social recognition by elites of all types, from politicians and celebrities to social media influencers and community leaders, is an important mechanism for cultural change. Media in its many forms plays a big role here. In Bangladesh a popular animated television show reduced the cultural and religious stigma of girls going to school in rural areas and increased their attendance.[70] In Ghana and Kenya the Time to Change campaign made inroads into reducing mental health stigma.[71]

The issue is not just about recipients of programmes or target audiences but also about who is deciding on and delivering the messages. For example, women's representation in political bodies shifts policy priorities and expands aspirations for other women and girls. Social movements have important roles as well in advancing human rights and changing cultural norms and narratives to expand agency and freedoms (see chapter 6).

" Walls between our social connections are perhaps more insidiously damaging and polarizing than walls between nations

Essential to flexible and adaptable narratives, in building trust and social cohesion for more hopeful futures, is the freedom for each person to have and move among different identities in different social contexts (see chapter 4).[72] Walls between our social connections are perhaps more insidiously damaging and polarizing than walls between nations. The bridges that connect different groups are among our most important assets. Good leaders rehabilitate and strengthen them and help us use them—especially in the face of unknowns. Demagogues try to burn them down, replacing fluid connection, exchange and learning with zero-sum, us-versus-them narratives. Instead of trying out cultural scripts precisely when experimentation matters most, people become trapped by them.

Where we go from here is up to us

We must learn to live with today's uncertainty complex, just as we must learn to live with Covid-19. This year's Human Development Report challenges us to aspire to more than mere accommodation, however. By unlocking our human potential, by tapping into our creativity and diversity anchored in trust and solidarity, it challenges us to imagine and create futures in which we thrive. The encouraging words of the late, great poet and civil rights activist Maya Angelou ring as true as ever, reminding us "to bring all our energies to each encounter, to remain flexible enough to notice and admit when what we expected to happen did not happen. We need to remember that we are created creative and can invent new scenarios as frequently as they are needed."[73]

Where we go from here is up to us. One of the great lessons of our species' history is that we can accomplish a lot with very little if we work together towards shared goals. If there is a secret ingredient to human magic, that must be it. The challenges in the Anthropocene and in sweeping societal transformations are huge, even daunting, all the more so for countries and communities struggling with the most dramatic and unjust deprivations. Insecurity and polarization make things worse. Amid so much uncertainty, the truth is that we are not going to get it right, maybe not even most of the time. In this turbulent new era we can set the direction but cannot guarantee the outcome. The good news is that we have more tools than ever to help us navigate and course correct. But no amount of technological wizardry is a substitute for good leadership, collective action or trust. If we can start fixing the human side of the planetary ledger—and this Report tries to highlight how—then the future, however uncertain, will be more promise than peril, just as it should be.

Uncertain times, unsettled lives

Uncertain times, unsettled lives

Uncertainty is not new, but its dimensions today are taking ominous new forms. A new "uncertainty complex" is emerging, never seen before in human history. Part I of this Human Development Report explores what this uncertainty complex is, how it is unsettling lives the world over and what it has to do with human development. Chapter 1 parses the three volatile, interacting strands that constitute the uncertainty complex: the planetary pressures and inequalities of the Anthropocene, the pursuit of societal transformations to ease those pressures and widespread polarization across and within countries. Chapter 2 illuminates how uncertainties of all stripes constrain human development via their negative impacts on mental wellbeing. Chapter 3 argues that narrow assumptions about human behavior, alongside simplistic notions of development progress, limit people's ability to respond creatively to a world in flux. Doubling down on human development in its fullest sense offers a hopeful path forward in uncertain times.

1

A new uncertainty complex

CHAPTER 1

A new uncertainty complex

Feelings of distress have been on the rise for almost everyone everywhere, even before the Covid-19 pandemic. Yet conventional measures of wellbeing suggest that, on average, life has never been better for our species.

What is going on? Why are people so worried, and what worries them?

This chapter argues that a new uncertainty complex is emerging, driven by three novel sources of uncertainty that interact at a global scale:

- The intertwined planetary pressures and inequalities of the Anthropocene.

- The pursuit of just societal transformations to ease those pressures.

- Widespread, intensifying societal polarization, delaying necessary action for change.

Together, they are painting a picture of uncertain times and unsettled lives.

A world of worry in uncertain times

A war between countries in Europe reawakens fear of global nuclear conflagration. A volatile geopolitical context[1] coexists with a pandemic that continues to kill and frighten more than two years since it was declared. Behind the headlines progress in human development has gone into reverse—with worsening trends in poverty, food insecurity, forced displacement and many compounding inequalities.[2] For the first time on record, the global Human Development Index (HDI) has dropped for two years in a row, taking the world back to just after the adoption of the 2030 Agenda for Sustainable Development and the Paris Agreement (figure 1.1). Every year a few countries face declines on the HDI, but over 90 percent of countries saw their HDI value drop in either 2020 or 2021 (figure 1.2). Furthermore, while only a third of very high HDI countries saw a decline in 2021 (compared with over 90 percent in 2020), about 60 percent of low and medium HDI and high HDI countries did (figure 1.3).

There is little doubt that these are uncertain times,[3] as people feel less sure about what the future holds. Even before the Covid-19 pandemic hit, six of seven people in the world reported feeling insecure about many aspects of their lives, with concerns rising the most in very high HDI countries (see chapters 3 and 4 on the links between uncertainty and insecurity).[4]

Life has always been uncertain.[5] The world has faced wars, pandemics and massive natural hazards before. Today's uncertainty is not necessarily any greater than in the past. If anything, given record achievements in average standards of living and incomes, with astonishing technological progress, we could be expected to be more ready than ever to meet uncertain times. Yet, we display high, and often rising, concern about the future. So, what is going on? Why are people so worried, and what worries them? If today's world is not more uncertain than the past's, are today's uncertain times different? If so, how? And how do they relate to human development?

This chapter presents evidence that people are feeling distressed and explores what they may be worrying about. While it cannot be established that there is more uncertainty today than in the past, there is a novel context for uncertainty. The novelty comes from three interacting layers of uncertainty, superimposed on ongoing development challenges. The

Figure 1.1 A drop in global Human Development Index value two years in a row for the first time on record

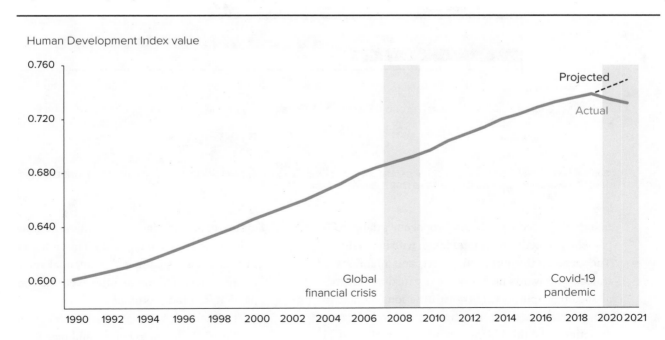

Human Development Index value

Note: The period of the global financial crisis is indicative.
Source: Human Development Report Office calculations based on data from Barro and Lee (2018), IMF (2021c, 2022), UNDESA (2022a, 2022b), UNESCO Institute for Statistics (2022), UNSD (2022) and World Bank (2022c).

Figure 1.2 Drops in Human Development Index values were widespread during the Covid-19 pandemic, with over 90 percent of countries suffering a decline in either 2020 or 2021

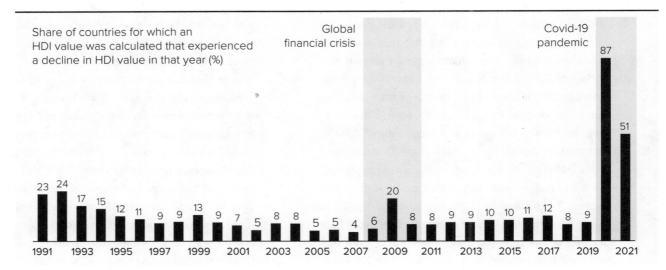

Note: The period of the global financial crisis is indicative.
Source: Human Development Report Office calculations based on data from Barro and Lee (2018), IMF (2021c, 2022), UNDESA (2022a, 2022b), UNESCO Institute for Statistics (2022), UNSD (2022) and World Bank (2022c).

Figure 1.3 While most very high Human Development Index (HDI) countries did not suffer declines on the HDI in 2021, the majority of countries in low and medium HDI and high HDI countries did

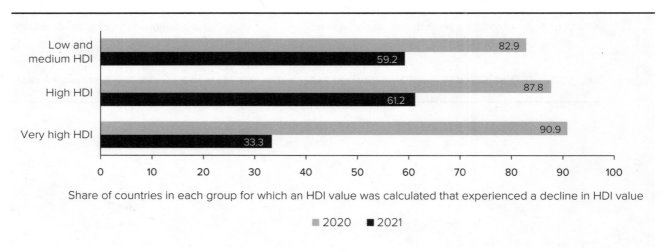

Source: Human Development Report Office calculations based on data from Barro and Lee (2018), IMF (2021c, 2022), UNDESA (2022a, 2022b), UNESCO Institute for Statistics (2022), UNSD (2022) and World Bank (2022c).

first is associated with the Anthropocene's dangerous planetary change and its interaction with inequalities. The second is the purposeful efforts and intentions to transition towards new ways of organizing industrial societies—purporting transformations similar to those in the transition from agricultural to industrial societies.[6] The third is the intensification of political and social polarization across and within countries—and of misperceptions about information and across

groups of people—facilitated by how new digital technologies are often being used.[7] This new and interacting "uncertainty complex" is unequal and universal; it can exacerbate inequalities, yet like the ongoing pandemic, it touches us all.

The interaction of these three layers of uncertainty implies that threats to people and planet compound, with events rippling through our socially and ecologically connected societies in multiple and unpredictable ways. Consider how the war in Ukraine is compounding a global food insecurity crisis.[8] Consider how the Covid-19 pandemic, in addition to the health impacts, also devastated economies and reversed progress in gender equality.[9] Many of the threats, in isolation, are not new. But the confluence of pandemics, the invention of vaccines in record time, the digital proliferation of misinformation, the breakdown of supply chains, the strong market concentrations for essential goods, the loss of biodiversity—have all interacted to present a "complex mixture of the precedented and the unprecedented" at a speed and scale never before seen.[10]

Rising insecurity amid unprecedented material prosperity—for some

Large-scale text analysis identifying language trends in books over the past 125 years reveals a sharp increase in expressions reflecting cognitive distortions associated with depression and other forms of mental distress (see chapter 2).[11] Over the past two decades the language reflecting overly negative perceptions of the world and its future has surged (figure 1.4).[12] Indeed, today's distress levels are unprecedented,[13] exceeding those during the Great Depression and both

world wars. The analysis of more than 14 million books in three languages signals cultural, linguistic and psychological shifts beyond changes in word meaning, writing and publishing standards or the books considered. Indeed, literature has been thought of as mirror of our societies, and studies show that text expressions reflect emotional states[14] and sometimes anticipate broader social and political changes.[15]

Other studies—on, for example, online behaviour[16] and analysis of emotional expressions on social media[17]—echo these findings.[18] The Covid-19 pandemic and uncertainty about the impacts and spread of the disease sparked rapid surges in online searches for acute and health- and economic-related anxiety.[19] While reflecting the concerns of only those with internet access, the measures coincide with survey data[20] across geographic locations.[21] Still other studies show that when events are sudden or unexpected, online behaviour can indicate shared sentiments.[22]

People report feeling more distressed and insecure about their lives and the future. While perceived insecurity is higher in low and medium HDI countries, some of the largest increases in feelings of insecurity are in very high HDI countries (figure 1.5).[23] Insecurity, discontent and pessimism loom large across

Figure 1.4 **Negative views about the world and the future have surged to unprecedented highs**

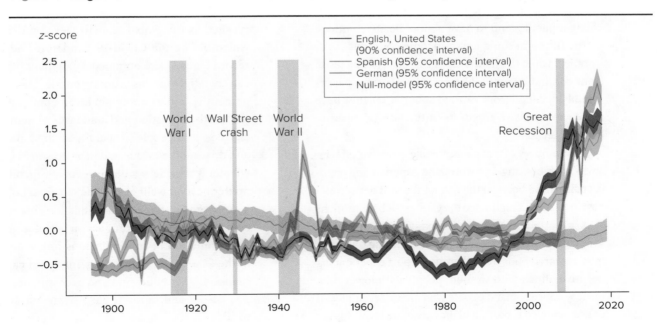

Note: Negative views are defined as textual analogues of cognitive distortions in one- to five-word sequences reflecting depression, anxiety and other distortions, published in 14 million books in English, Spanish and German over the past 125 years. The prevalence of these word sequences are converted to z-scores for comparability. They are compared with a null-model that accounts for over-time changes in publication volumes and standards.
Source: Bollen and others 2021.

Figure 1.5 Perceived insecurity is on the rise in most countries, even in some very high Human Development Index countries

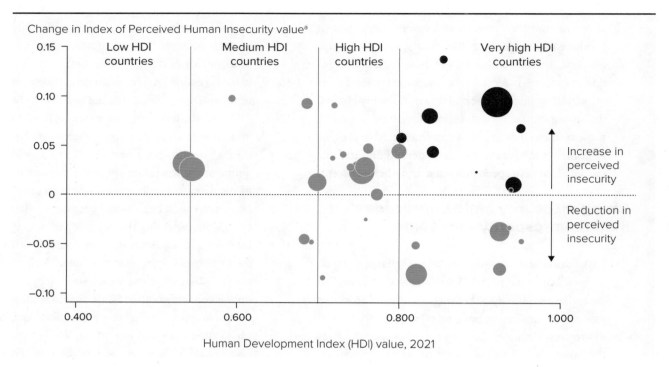

Change in Index of Perceived Human Insecurity value[a]

Note: Bubble size represents the country population.
a. Refers to the change between waves 6 and 7 of the World Values Survey for countries with comparable data.
Source: Human Development Report Office based on World Values Survey data.

all geographic regions, including countries with the highest incomes, with some surveys finding that younger people tend to have a more positive outlook on the future in some lower-income countries.[24] For instance, while the mentions of threats, such as those from conflict or natural hazards, in US newspapers steadily declined from 1900 to about 2010, they have since shot up, with forecasts of further increases in coming decades.[25]

The numbers of people reporting negative affect—stress, sadness, anger or worry and experiencing physical pain—have been on the rise for the past decade and have hit a record high since the Gallup Global Emotions Report started assessing these experiences in 2006.[26] When excluding physical pain and assessing only feelings, research finds that all groups report experiencing negative affect, with women, people with lower than tertiary education and people who are underemployed or unemployed reporting higher absolute levels (figure 1.6). Indeed, a trend of increased stress is discernible across the world and across socioeconomic groups, despite volatility from year to year (figure 1.7).[27]

These patterns of high or increasing worry parallel improvements in some measures of prosperity, such as the global Human Development Index, which before the Covid-19 pandemic had reached record highs.[28] The human development perspective can shed light on this seeming puzzle. Human development is in part about achievements in wellbeing (in health, education and standards of living), a crucial aspect of people's capabilities: their ability to be and do what they value and have reason to value. But chapter 3 considers other aspects of capabilities that matter beyond wellbeing achievements. Looking beyond averages, horizontal inequalities in capabilities across groups—reflected, say, in gender and racial discrimination or in dimensions important for life in the 21st century, including enhanced capabilities such as higher education and access to broadband[29]—persisted and in many cases widened during the pandemic.

And even progress in basic capabilities has stalled or reversed. The Covid-19 pandemic set back the reduction in global extreme poverty, disrupting the

Figure 1.6 Negative affect is increasing for everyone, with persistent by inequalities between groups

Proportion of respondents worldwide experiencing negative affect (%)

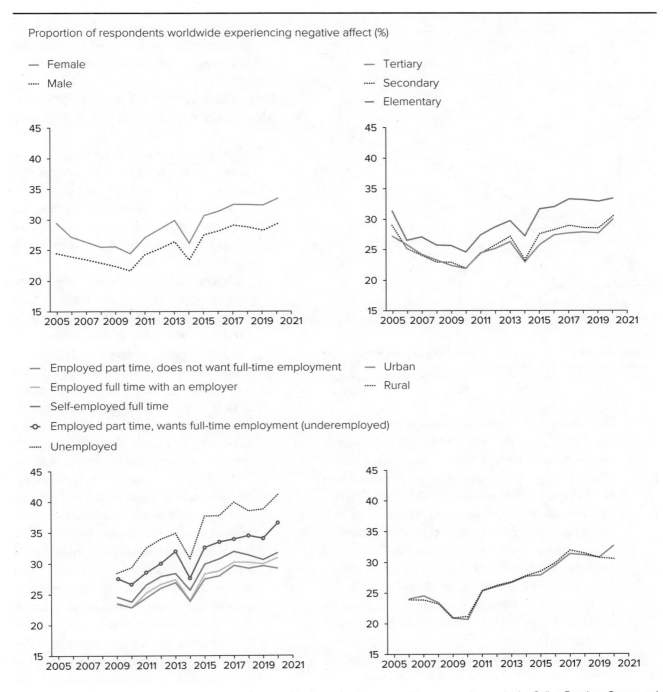

Note: Negative affect is defined as the aggregate of reported feelings of sadness, anguish, worry and anger in the Gallup Emotions Survey and excludes reported feelings of physical pain.
Source: Pinto and others (2022), based on data from Gallup.

steady decline in the number of people living in extreme poverty since 1990. Over the pandemic's first two years an additional 110–150 million people may have been pushed into extreme poverty, adding to the 689 million people worldwide forced to survive on less than $1.90 a day in 2018.[30] Even before the

pandemic, the pace of poverty reduction was slowing —from about 1 percentage point a year in 1990–2015 to half a percentage point a year in 2015–2017.

What is more, at least 1.3 billion people live in multidimensional poverty, facing deprivations in dimensions important for human development—including

Figure 1.7 **Stress is high and rising, independent of education**

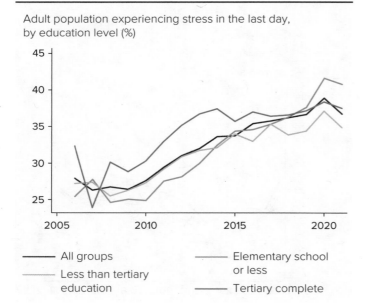

Adult population experiencing stress in the last day, by education level (%)

Legend:
- All groups
- Less than tertiary education
- Elementary school or less
- Tertiary complete

Note: Median values are shown due to inconsistencies in the number of observations across countries and years.
Source: Human Development Report Office based on The Gallup Organization (2022).

health, education and material standards of living. Half of them are children.[31] And while child mortality has declined globally since 1990, children born in the world's poorest countries in the world still have a 1 in 10 risk of not surviving to their fifth birthday, whereas almost all children born in some of the richest countries survive beyond their fifth birthday.[32] The long-term effects of the Covid-19 pandemic and the current inflation in consumer goods prices—especially the increased price of food compounded by the war in the Ukraine—threaten to exacerbate the situation for people living in, or on the brink of, poverty across the world.

These deprivations and inequalities in capabilities pose serious challenges on their own but matter even more when people try to navigate uncertain times—and they matter not only to those excluded and left behind. Indeed, the feedback loops between pre-existing development challenges and a novel context of uncertainty "constitute a systemic challenge to social progress."[33] That provides even more reason to explore why so many people—even if they have met their basic needs—perceive themselves as lacking agency (see chapter 3 for a discussion of agency in the human development

framework) as they look to the future. Doing so requires understanding what is novel about today's uncertain times—the new planetary reality of the Anthropocene, the unprecedented transition from industrial societies and the new forms of political polarization.

Uncertainty driven by dangerous planetary change in the Anthropocene

Never have so many of the planet's systems been knowingly affected by a single species. We humans are driving climate change[34] and harming the integrity of many of the ecosystems that sustain human lives and other species. Our choices are shaping the evolution of life on Earth through legacies that will unfold over millions of years to come.[35]

Climate change, biodiversity loss and many other environmental challenges—from air pollution to plastics use—are receiving individual attention. But the way these and other planetary pressures are interlinked—and the speed, scale and scope of the unprecedented planetary changes unfolding as a result—has motivated a new framing of this current context as the Anthropocene—the age of humans, where humans' impact on the planet is so stark that it is driving dangerous planetary change—which has been formally proposed as a new geological epoch.[36]

The threats to human lives in the Anthropocene are fundamentally unequal, as they will more quickly and intensely affect people and countries that have contributed less in relative and absolute terms to planetary pressures and benefited less from the changes that drive planetary pressures. As the 2020 Human Development Report argued, large and often growing inequalities and power imbalances are a defining feature of the Anthropocene, underpinning the destabilizing dynamics that divert policy attention and may delay action to ease planetary pressures. But given that the threats emanating from dangerous planetary change are driven mainly by humans, the Anthropocene context is creating a responsibility for humanity to act.[37]

If humans have the power to change the planet in harmful and unequalizing ways, they have the obligation to act towards pursuing a safer and more just world.[38] The responsibility to act falls more heavily on those who account for more of the planetary pressures and have more power to change course. People are not inherently destroyers of nature; they have also shaped ecosystems in mutually beneficial ways.[39] So the Anthropocene provides us with not only the responsibility but also the opportunity to pursue human development while easing planetary pressures—the central message of the 2020 Report.

A new planetary reality

Uncertainty in the Anthropocene is about much more than climate change. Even with advances in science and computational power,[40] the multiple feedback loops between social and ecological systems may imply that our "knowledge of the world, its ecosystems and people, their behaviour, values and choices will always be partial."[41] One key unknown is whether people will appreciate, and take the responsibility to act on, the power that we have to stop disrupting planetary processes. Thus, the Anthropocene is characterized by far-reaching and complex interactions between social and planetary systems that engender a layer of novel uncertainty.[42]

Beyond warming temperatures,[43] human-induced planetary pressures result in a natural environment profoundly different from what humans have previously experienced (spotlight 1.1). The frequency and intensity of extreme storms, droughts, wildfires and heatwaves have increased since the 1950s.[44] The intensification of urbanization and agricultural production has disrupted forests, wetlands and grasslands—so much that the amount of human-made materials, such as concrete and asphalt, now outweigh the Earth's biomass.[45] More than 1 million species face extinction, threatening the integrity of whole ecosystems.[46]

> " The Anthropocene is characterized by far-reaching and complex interactions between social and planetary systems that engender a layer of novel uncertainty

These phenomena reinforce each other, magnifying the speed and scale of threats to our natural and social systems. For example, the warming and acidification of oceans provoke migration of fish stocks, affecting food supplies and the livelihoods of coastal communities. Food insecurity and eroded livelihoods can then prompt migration, change land uses and exacerbate

pollution, further weakening ecosystems.[47] As another example, zoonotic diseases are a latent threat: more than 10,000 virus species have the potential to infect humans.[48] These have so far been contained within wild animal populations, but with accelerated climate change and increased human interference with zoonotic reservoirs, animal to human transmission is expected to increase[49] and heighten the risk of new and more frequent pandemics.[50] For example, the intensified human intervention in animal habitats due to agricultural production is associated with more than half of all zoonotic diseases infecting humans since 1940.[51] And climate change may alter the pattern of disease exposure and infections as warmer temperatures change the range of disease-carrying insects.[52]

More volatility is also expected. Climate change is predicted to increase both average temperatures and temperature variability, with temperature fluctuations projected to increase by 100 percent at lower latitudes.[53] More than 40 percent of the world's population depends on water sources affected by high climate variability. By 2080 an estimated 1 billion additional people are expected to be impacted by high climate variability and climate-related water security threats.[54] High weather variability reduces the "ability of economic agents to plan and function effectively"[55] and may impair health[56] and economic productivity.[57] For example, intraday and interday temperature variability is associated with increased mortality risk.[58] Many lower-income countries are disproportionately exposed to increased temperature fluctuations and lack resources to invest in adaptation, leaving them more vulnerable.[59]

Dangerous planetary changes are shifting the baseline of hazards,[60] but because these changes are driven largely by humans, our choices matter. The uncertainty related to the range of possible evolutions in emissions[61] is driven by both the evolution of the climate system and its interaction with the choices we make. Implementing the Paris Agreement in a timely manner increases the world's chances of keeping global average temperature increases below 2°C (figure 1.8).[62] For example, the difference between a 1.5°C and a 2°C increase in global temperature exposes an extra 1.7 billion people to extreme heatwaves.[63]

The uncertainty about dangerous planetary change does not spell unavoidable doom and societal collapse.[64] A balanced reading of the historical record suggests that human societies have, for the most part, been resilient, flexible and able to respond, adapt and thrive when confronting major environmental changes (see spotlight 1.1).[65] Even though the evidence pertains to circumscribed geographic contexts, there is reason to believe that even if not all response options are fully available—for instance, migration when there will be fewer areas with temperatures suitable for human thriving[66]—people retain their ability to adjust and respond, even to a new planetary reality.

Unequal contributions, unequal impacts—planetary pressures and social imbalances reinforcing each other

Countries and groups of people that have contributed less to planetary pressures are projected to bear the largest burdens of dangerous planetary change.[67] For example, mortality and reductions in labour productivity due to warming temperatures will be greater in low- and middle-income countries,[68] leaving them with fewer resources to adapt to planetary pressures and adding layers of vulnerability.

Moreover, climate change is an inequality multiplier. Consider the stark inequalities in contributions to and impacts of carbon dioxide emissions. The top 10 percent of the global income distribution is responsible for almost half of global annual emissions, and the bottom 50 percent, only 12 percent of emissions.[69] The inequalities run even deeper at the top. In 2019 the bottom 50 percent accounted for 1.6 tonnes of carbon dioxide emissions per capita, while the top 10 percent accounted for 31 tonnes per capita, the top 0.1 percent 467 tonnes per capita and

Figure 1.8 The wide range of possible future warming depends on our choices

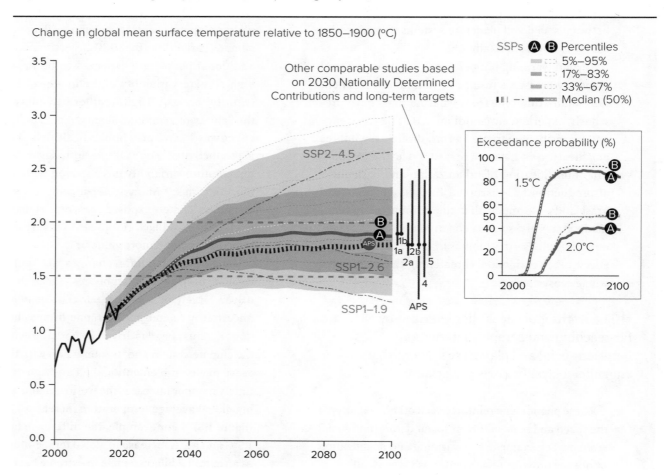

SSP is Shared Socioeconomic Pathway.
Note: The figure shows global warming as a result of officially submitted Nationally Determined Contributions to reduce emissions under the Paris Agreement, as well as the long-term targets at the end of the 2021 United Nations Climate Change Conference (COP 26). It shows a wide range in increased temperature outcomes, depending on whether the base for analysis is Nationally Determined Contributions or only unconditional targets.
Source: Meinshausen and others 2022.

the top 0.01 percent 2,531 tonnes per capita.[70] Since 1990 the top 1 percent have accounted for 21 percent of the increase in emissions.[71] So, within-country inequalities are quickly becoming a defining feature of global carbon dioxide emissions, all while massive between-country inequalities in emissions persist.[72]

" The channel through which planetary pressures are affected by inequality runs through actual choices as well as through aspirations

Those contributing the least to climate change find themselves at the losing end. Unmitigated climate change may drive up to 132 million people into poverty in the coming decade.[73] Planetary pressures may also exacerbate horizontal inequalities or even open new gaps between groups.[74] For instance, future risks of flooding in the United States are expected to affect mainly low-income Black communities.[75] And barriers to women's participation in decisionmaking work against policies and resource allocations that address women's specific vulnerabilities to environmental change.[76]

As seen above, curbing emissions at the top of the income distribution would have a great impact,[77] but when those responsible for planetary pressures are not equally affected by them and believe they have the resources to shield themselves from the adverse effects, incentives to ease planetary pressures are distorted. The choices of high-income earners are associated with consumption and production patterns that account for a disproportionate share of planetary pressures. These choices are driven by many factors, but social norms among high-earners and peer effects influence the lifestyles they expect.[78] Their social context determines not only choices but also aspirations.[79]

The channel through which planetary pressures are affected by inequality runs through actual choices as well as through aspirations. Aspirations can play an important role as an incentive for effort with positive individual and collective outcomes[80] and in enhancing human development.[81] The reference frames of aspirations for adjacent, but lower, income groups are influenced by the behaviour of higher earners. As reference points change, more and more people may be influenced to behave in ways that add to planetary pressures. Such dynamic "expenditure cascades"

show how demand for large housing, large cars and other large goods has increased even where median incomes are stagnant.[82] If access to these positional goods becomes harder and the referent of aspirations is seen to be out of reach, the positive effects of aspiration can instead lead to alienation and frustration.[83] This mismatch between aspiration and realization has implications for people's wellbeing (it can increase depression).[84] But it can also change people's perception of the future from positive to negative and their sense of agency over the future from high to low[85]—leading to more pessimistic views. As a result, there will be less of a concern about how individual behaviour affects future outcomes. And alienation and frustration can, in turn, contribute to polarization, making collective action towards easing planetary pressures more difficult.

No second chances: Existential threats in the Anthropocene

To see how the uncertainties in the Anthropocene are novel, consider existential threats. For the first time in human history, anthropogenic existential threats loom larger than those from natural hazards.[86] This started with the advent of nuclear weapons, with escalating technological power reaching the point where we are able to threaten our own destruction. Nuclear war posed an existential risk:[87] the permanent destruction of humanity's long-term potential. Throughout most of human history, the existential risks to our species emanated exclusively from natural hazards, independent of human action—including large asteroid impacts or massive volcanic events, such as those leading to mass extinction events in the geological timescale.[88] Humans have always had power to inflict much harm on each other and on nature, but only in the Anthropocene have they reached the potential to kill much of the global population and destroy the potential of future societies.[89]

The spectrum of anthropogenic existential threats is large and growing. In addition to the prospect of nuclear war, threats include artificial intelligence (AI), genetic engineering and nanotechnology, as well as the dangers of planetary pressures and their interactions.[90] They may be deliberate, as in the use of nuclear force. Or they may be accidental, such as the spread of a virus from a lab, or they may emerge from ungovernable technological development.[91] Heightened political polarization and conflict may increase the existential threats, including through nuclear war or biological warfare.[92] The drivers of a possible nuclear conflict may be linked, both in exacerbating the risks and in magnifying the impacts for human lives and the planet (spotlight 1.2).[93]

" Easing planetary pressures would entail a fundamental transformation in how societies live, work and interact with nature. This transformation engenders its own novel layer of uncertainty, because, like the Anthropocene reality, it is unprecedented and uncharted

While the existential risks of nuclear war might be easily imagined, the existential risks of slow-onset climate change or biodiversity loss may not be as evident. With continued human pressures on the planet, tipping points—beyond return—can inflict irreversible damage to ecosystems and to the benefits humans derive from them. If tipping points interact, they may have catastrophic and cascading consequences.[94] For example, climate change is provoking Arctic sea-ice loss, which contributes to a slowdown of the Atlantic circulation, which could disrupt the West African monsoon and trigger drought in the Sahel, dry up the Amazon and warm the Southern Ocean, further accelerating the melting of Antarctic ice. Amazon forest dieback would distort the stability of the Earth's biosphere, with large-scale consequences, including massive biodiversity loss and unprecedented rises in carbon dioxide concentrations in the atmosphere.[95] While uncertainty remains about the exact "location" of tipping points and the full consequences of crossing one, they are just "too risky to bet against."[96]

Realizing the power that humans have over our entire planet implies the responsibility to act. Recognizing anthropogenic existential threats also provides an obligation to lower, indeed to eliminate, existential risk. In the same way that the Anthropocene provides a unifying framework to understand how human choices drive planetary pressures that result in disequalizing dangerous planetary change, eliminating existential risk—or promoting existential security— is the ultimate nonrenewable resource and demands

reflecting on the type of institutions needed to reach existential security (spotlight 1.3).

Uncertainty emerges from complex transitions to ease planetary pressures

Adapting to the uncertainty brought about by the Anthropocene reality just described is a tall order. In addition to adaptation, it is crucial to ease the planetary pressures that are driving dangerous planetary changes. Easing planetary pressures will also mitigate some of the uncertainties.[97]

Easing planetary pressures would entail a fundamental transformation in how societies live, work and interact with nature, comparable to the transitions to agricultural societies and from agricultural to industrial societies.[98] That calls for us to work with —not against—nature (spotlight 1.4). This transformation engenders its own novel layer of uncertainty, because, like the Anthropocene reality, it is unprecedented and uncharted. Uncertainty also emanates from the fact that transformations involve multiple social and ecological factors, and their interactions, playing out over the long term of the transitions at stake. Even if many of these transitions have in some ways been charted and modelled (singly or in parts of the world), there is also modelling and analytical uncertainty.

Central in all this is transforming how societies generate energy and use materials.[99] That will involve shifting both production and consumption patterns, underpinned by how human behaviour interacts with institutions. And that interaction shapes, and is shaped by, incentives, social norms and values.

The 2020 Report proposed representing advancing human development while easing planetary pressures as paths taking countries towards the aspirational space of the green triangle in figure 1.9.[100] While the world had moved in that direction over the past 30 years, it has done so far too slowly and in a way that leaves higher human development strongly correlated with greater planetary pressures. The needed scale and speed of this transition should not be oversimplified or minimized, given the ambition of the required shifts[101]—and that, along with complexity of the transition, adds a new layer of uncertainty.[102]

Transitional uncertainty has several dimensions, including those associated with a move towards a

Figure 1.9 **Transforming our world to advance human development while easing planetary pressures**

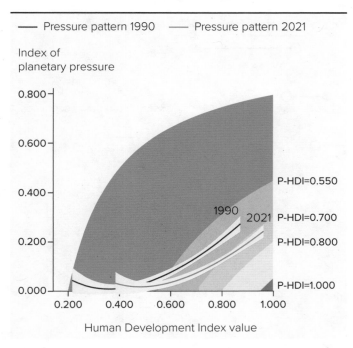

— Pressure pattern 1990   — Pressure pattern 2021

Index of planetary pressure

(y-axis: 0.000, 0.200, 0.400, 0.600, 0.800)

P-HDI=0.550
1990 2021 P-HDI=0.700
P-HDI=0.800
P-HDI=1.000

(x-axis: 0.200, 0.400, 0.600, 0.800, 1.000)

Human Development Index value

Note: Cross-sectional pressure patterns for 1990 and 2021 were calculated using a polynomial regression model. Shaded areas are confidence intervals. The index of planetary pressures is constructed using the per capita levels of carbon dioxide emissions and material footprint in each country (it is 1 minus the adjustment factor for planetary pressures presented in table 7 in the *Statistical Annex*).
Source: Human Development Report Office. See specific sources in tables 2 and 7 in the *Statistical Annex*.

until 2100—but the question remains about how these gains would be distributed across countries and across individuals.[108] If distributional effects are perceived as unfair or if people are left without the support to adapt to a new economic reality, transitions may be met with resistance, dissent and dispute.[109]

The outcomes of past transitions have been largely unplanned and unintentional. But the expansion of knowledge and science and our awareness of the Anthropocene reality imply that the transitions to ease planetary pressures are purposeful and deliberate. The goal of the transitions is clear—to move to the aspirational space of high human development and low planetary pressures—even if much uncertainty remains about the pathways that would take us there.[110]

Uncertainties stem not only from the types of policy choices that are adopted but also from how they are designed and implemented. Success depends on their perception—on their social acceptance by different segments of the public and those that hold positions of power. Transitions depend on technology, and the resulting efficiency gains from it and how they are distributed. Explored here are changes required to ease planetary pressures and the layer of uncertainty associated with energy and resource transitions.

low-carbon economic development path.[103] Beyond the physical uncertainties of climate change are the uncertainties associated with our deliberate policy choices—such as altering carbon taxes, shifting economies away from carbon-intensive industries or adopting new technologies.[104]

Some of the uncertainty is associated with who will win and who will lose as the process unfolds, which will likely differ across regions and groups—recognizing that some are better equipped than others to benefit from new opportunities.[105] One possible manifestation of uncertainty could be economic insecurity (spotlight 1.5). For instance, the green economy could add more than 24 million jobs worldwide by 2030.[106] But these jobs will not necessarily be in the same regions that stand to lose jobs as fossil fuel industries shut down,[107] nor will they require the same set of skills as in a fossil fuel–based economy. The economic gains from phasing out coal could amount to as much as 1.2 percent of global GDP every year

Energy transitions: Making their way, but too slowly and amid great uncertainties

Energy transitions from fossil fuels towards renewables are driven by new technologies and lower costs.[111] While fossil fuels such as coal, natural gas and oil still produce two-thirds of global electricity,[112] renewables are expected to become the dominant source of global energy supply by 2040.[113] But this is only one of many possible future outcomes. The outcomes vary widely under three scenarios of the International Energy Agency: net-zero emissions, stated policy scenarios and announced pledges to reduce greenhouse gas emissions (figure 1.10).

Uncertainty can unfold as consequences emerge. Biofuels, originally thought to be an excellent alternative for fossil fuels, also pose a variety of challenges[114]—with implications for land use,[115] carbon footprint,[116] deforestation impacts,[117] biodiversity loss,[118] water competition[119] and poverty impacts,[120] among others.

Figure 1.10 Energy transitions towards renewables can unfold in different ways for different sectors

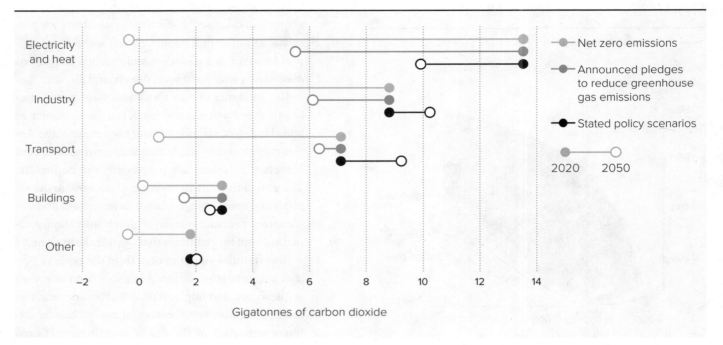

Gigatonnes of carbon dioxide

Legend:
- Net zero emissions
- Announced pledges to reduce greenhouse gas emissions
- Stated policy scenarios
- 2020 — 2050

Source: IRENA 2021.

Uncertainty is also associated with prospects for developing technologies key to the energy transition, which are not yet in place. Consider energy storage, which is critical to addressing the intermittency of supply due to daily and seasonal differences in renewable power. While a handful of technologies are available, much more is needed to enhance technological solutions, lower costs and make transmission more efficient. Even with advances in battery storage, adoption remains limited in most low- and middle-income countries due to policy, financial and regulatory barriers. Options sought beyond short-term energy storage solutions, such as lithium-ion batteries, include sustainable, cost-efficient long-duration energy storage systems, which are a long way off.[121]

Another dimension of uncertainty is how the financial system, which assumes a stable climate, will evolve.[122] A shift away from carbon-intensive assets will expose some investors, who may resist and attempt to slow a move towards a low-carbon path.[123] Governments are now paying more attention to climate-related financial risks. For example, a 2021 executive order by US President Joseph Biden requires clear and accurate disclosure of climate-related financial risks to safeguard physical assets as well as financial markets from climate change–related risks.[124]

The objective is to protect communities and families as the United States transitions to the net-zero emissions target by 2050.

Global and regional mechanisms are also working to facilitate a low-carbon transition in the financial sector. The Task Force for Climate-Related Financial Disclosure seeks to provide investors with information on climate change–related risks in their portfolios. With the same inspiration a consortium of central banks and financial supervisors established the Network for Greening the Financial System.[125] The EU Taxonomy, which classifies environmentally sustainable economic activities, supports transitioning to net-zero emissions by 2050 and implementing the European Green Deal; the EU Delegated Act has been formalized to set the screening criteria for the environmental objectives of new economic activities. And European countries are stepping up various mitigation efforts, such as ending the sale of new diesel- and gas-powered cars in 14 years and imposing tariffs on goods imported from countries with lax environmental laws.[126]

The volatility in oil and gas prices during the Covid-19 pandemic and now as the war in Ukraine unfolds is sending shock waves around the world.[127] Oil-exporting countries experienced large fiscal deficits when oil prices dropped.[128] But a range of factors, including the conflict in Ukraine and economic recovery as Covid-19 concerns have eased, have led to a rapid increase in oil prices, a boon to oil-exporting countries but also a driver of inflation almost everywhere.[129]

The uncertainty associated with energy transitions has unsettled people who perceive it as unjust. French villages and small towns saw protests against rising petrol prices again in 2021, reminiscent of the "yellow vest" movements of 2018, Spain saw demonstrations against energy bills and Greece faced social unrest with the closure of coal mines.[130] This even as a large numbers of jobs are being created in the renewable energy sector.[131] Yet while it is anticipated that more jobs will be created than lost in energy transitions, whether the transitions will be just will depend on how they are managed.[132]

Current global pledges to reduce greenhouse gas emissions cannot safeguard against dangerous climate change.[133] Carbon prices remain far too low to effectively curb emissions. Only 22 percent of global carbon emissions are under a carbon pricing scheme.[134] And implementation remains a challenge even for commitments made to phase out fossil fuel subsidies —no date has been set to achieve the target globally, and 2021 saw the highest increase in fossil fuel subsidies since 2010.[135] Uncertainty associated with the transition can be heightened by the realization that more ambition is needed, along with the resistance to change from powerful lobby groups or public concerns with loss of employment in specific sectors.[136] And the transitions can be drawn out: phasing out coal in Germany, initiated in the 1980s, is still years from completion, with concerns about stranded assets and the insecurity of affected workers and communities.[137]

" Deliberate energy transitions are happening now, backed by policies and supported by social movements

Even so, energy transitions are possible.[138] A move in France to increase nuclear capacity boosted its share of power from 4 percent in 1970 to 40 percent in 1982.[139] The Netherlands went from having coal supply 55 percent of its power and crude oil 43 percent in 1959 to having natural gas supply 50 percent by 1971.[140] Deliberate energy transitions are happening now, backed by policies and supported by social movements.[141]

Uncertainty associated with managing material use to ease planetary pressures

The shift to low-carbon economies will depend in part on extracting minerals and using materials that are key to technologies such as electric cars and solar panels. The same extraction implies land-use change and emissions that not only add to planetary pressures but have also been linked with serious human rights violations.[142] For example, rare earth elements can be located in sensitive ecosystems with high biodiversity, crucial carbon sinks and water resources, which if exploited could irreversibly damage natural resources. Of the 50 million square kilometres of the Earth's land currently being mined, about 8 percent overlaps with protected areas, 7 percent with key biodiversity areas and 16 percent with the remaining areas free of industrial activities and other human pressures.[143] The next wave of renewable energy growth could affect 30 percent of protected areas and key biodiversity areas and compromise 60 percent of the remaining areas free of industrial activities and other human pressures.[144] Ongoing conflict diverts resources and attention from protecting sensitive ecosystems and vulnerable populations. With energy demand projections based on existing policies and policy announcements, mineral demand is expected to double. And under a sustainable development scenario, where energy policies are consistent with the Paris Agreement goals, mineral demand is expected to quadruple (figure 1.11).[145]

Another dimension of uncertainty is related to the future of seabed and space mining. Growing demand for renewables is driving mining companies and start-ups to invest in opportunities under the ocean.[146] Scientists warn that disturbing an otherwise quiet and dark seabed that provides a unique ecosystem for marine life will have ramifications not only locally but also thousands of kilometres away. The first experiment in seabed mining in 1989, DISCOL,[147] demonstrated that species did not recolonize after more than 30 years. With technology ahead of the curve and regulations catching up, the commercial exploitation of seabed mining could be devastating for marine life.

Figure 1.11 The energy transition demands minerals and materials that add to planetary pressures

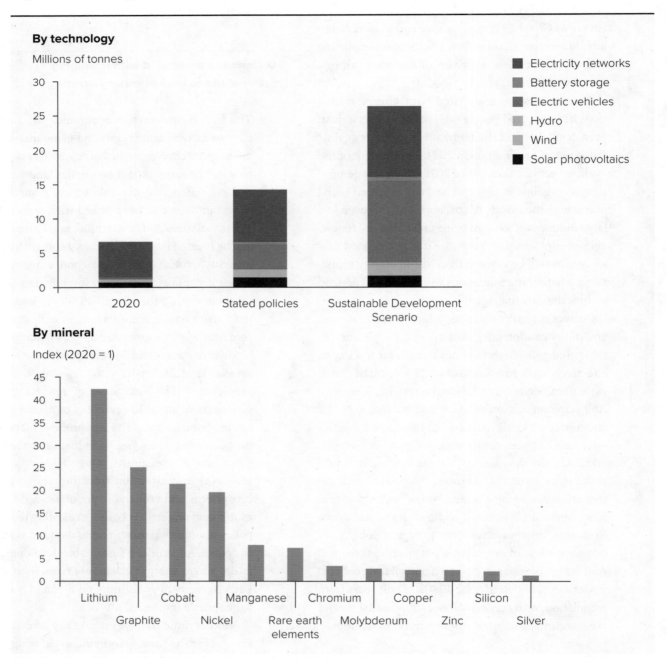

By technology

Millions of tonnes

Legend:
- Electricity networks
- Battery storage
- Electric vehicles
- Hydro
- Wind
- Solar photovoltaics

(x-axis: 2020, Stated policies, Sustainable Development Scenario)

By mineral

Index (2020 = 1)

(x-axis: Lithium, Graphite, Cobalt, Nickel, Manganese, Rare earth elements, Chromium, Molybdenum, Copper, Zinc, Silicon, Silver)

Note: The demand for minerals will depend on the types of renewable energy. For example, copper and silicon are important for solar panels and transmitting power, and lithium, manganese and zinc are important for wind energy (IEA 2021b).
Source: Human Development Report Office compilations based on data from IEA (2021b).

And as technology races ahead to make space mining a near possibility, questions are being raised about regulations.[148] There is no legal agreement among nations to prohibit mining celestial bodies; the two treaties in place allow for free exploration and use of space resources, leaving choices to miners. Moreover, strong pressures to look for answers beyond our own planet may divert attention from ourselves.[149]

The demand for materials goes beyond that for the energy transition. It is adding to planetary pressures with implications that will span deep into the future. A plastic water bottle can remain in nature for approximately 450 years.[150] And since the 1950s we have produced more than 8 billion tonnes of plastic.[151] In 2020 the world's consumption of materials exceeded 100 billion tonnes a year,[152] twice the amount in 1995.[153] By 2060 it is expected to be at least three times that in 1995.[154] Only about 8.6 percent of everything produced is recycled.[155] Human-produced goods are changing the face of the Earth. To give a sense of the scale, for the first time in human history, anthropogenic mass exceeded world's living biomass (figure 1.12).[156]

The challenges with nuclear waste disposal also point to the need to consider material use in a comprehensive way. Nuclear resources that are used to produce clean energy and industrial goods and for military applications also generate radioactive waste, which needs to be stored for more than half a million years—transmitting responsibilities and challenges to distant generations.[157] Much of the waste is temporarily stored underground in tanks, which through wear and tear may leak radioactive material into our soils and water. About 95 percent of the world's nuclear power reactors have produced an estimated 265,000 metric tonnes of spent heavy-metal fuel and 38 million cubic metres of solid nuclear waste.[158]

Anthropogenic activities are also disrupting biogeochemical cycles. Carbon levels are 36 times higher than preindustrial levels, phosphorous levels 13 times higher and nitrogen levels 9 times higher.[159] The nitrogen in fertilizers accumulating in nature pollutes water (excessive nitrates in drinking water), reduces air quality, depletes the ozone layer and accelerates global warming and biodiversity loss.[160] The excessive runoff of nitrogen into rivers and oceans increases algae blooms, which are depleting ocean oxygen and killing aquatic flora and fauna. Satellite images suggest that about 1.15 million square kilometres of the ocean surface may be eutrophic zones,[161] with a large part of them dead zones.[162]

Rapid technological change: A shifting ground beneath our feet

Rapid technological shifts are bringing new ways for humans to interact with technology, and with each

Figure 1.12 **Anthropogenic mass now exceeds the world's total living biomass**

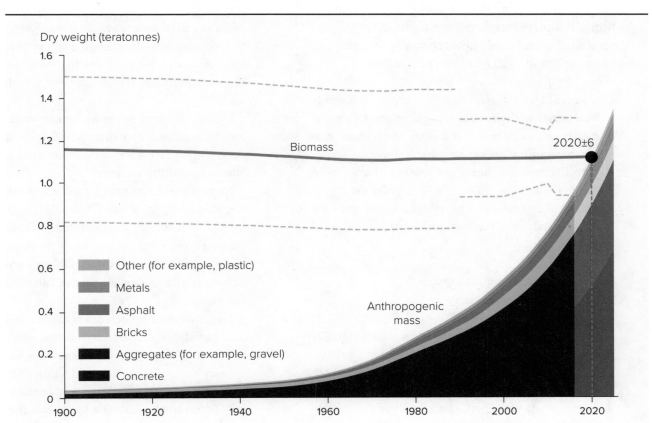

Source: Elhacham and others 2020.

other, creating more novel uncertainties.[163] The potential gains are massive, but what about the distribution of benefits and the differentiated impacts on people? The eventual emergence of general-purpose AI could multiply global GDP per person by a factor of 10—something that historically took the world 190 years to accomplish, from 1820 to 2010.[164] But these massive potential aggregate gains may be concentrated among a few, leaving many behind. One possibility is falling into a Turing trap, where technological and economic power is concentrated and translated into political power, "trapping a powerless majority into an unhappy equilibrium."[165] The backlash against free trade in some high-income countries offers a cautionary tale, given that the aggregate income gains of globalization through comparative advantage and specialization were not distributed to compensate disadvantaged occupations, sectors or regions. The economic winners gained power and lost interest in ensuring the equitable distribution of benefits.[166]

" Recent technological changes outpace our ability to understand their societal implications. Often disruptive, artificial intelligence, social media and other new technologies are changing our lives in fundamental ways

Recent technological changes outpace our ability to understand their societal implications. Often disruptive, AI, social media and other new technologies are changing our lives in fundamental ways.

To illustrate the novel dimensions of uncertainty, the following sections briefly consider the digital age, AI and genetic editing; see chapters 4 and 5 for further analysis of the implications of technological change.

The digital world—transforming human-to-human interaction

Less than 1 percent of the world's technologically stored information was in a digital format in the late 1980s compared with more than 99 percent by 2012.[167] Whether the way we connect to our work, how we communicate with friends and family or what we do in our free time, digital technology has become an indispensable part of many people's lives. In 2010 the number of machines connected to the internet exceeded the number of people connected to it for the first time.[168] Unlike any previous generation, many children born after 2008 have extensive exposure to digital devices early in life.

Tempering the initial optimism about the opportunities of new technologies are downsides or unintended consequences. Mobile phones trace our movements. AI, reducing human effort in sophisticated tasks, can also replicate and amplify stereotypes. Social media, originally meant to connect us, are contributing to divisiveness. These illustrate how new technologies bring along unintended consequences, engendering uncertainty.[169]

Firms are bringing in new technologies at an accelerated pace to automate production and reduce costs. Some jobs are being lost, as in accounting, administration and translation, just as others are created in big data, digital security and robotics engineering. The World Economic Forum projects that by 2025, 97 million new jobs will be created and 85 million jobs will be lost across 15 industries in 26 economies.[170] Industries not keeping pace with the trend towards automation stand to lose competitive edge, as will labourers who do not acquire new skills to keep pace with the changing labour market. This may also have implications for low- and middle-income countries, which may see a reshoring of jobs.[171]

Digitalization is changing human-to-technology and human-to-human interactions, sometimes radically. Online dating is one example of digitalization-altered human interaction.[172]

Human interaction with algorithms has also turned detrimental in many ways.[173] Mobile telephones and social media lift the voices of marginalized and oppressed groups but are also tools for those wishing to do harm.[174] Through these platforms groups with extremist and violent ideologies can expand their followings.[175]

The constant connectedness to social media can have harmful cognitive and emotional effects.[176] Neuroscientists suggest that internet use has altered the way the brain functions, affecting attention and memory and making us less sociable and empathetic.[177] For example, adding a single moral-emotional word to a tweet increases its retweet rate by 19 percent.[178] A post that includes indignant disagreement obtains twice as many likes and three times as many comments.[179] And the high demand for attention, as through the overuse of social media, reduces the time young people have for constructive reflection, shrinking the space for future imagining or reflecting on personal memories.[180]

Artificial intelligence—making choices for us

As our lives become more dependent on AI—from weather forecasts to financial market transactions to analysing DNA—we are delegating human choices. AI is choosing the news and information we are exposed to and suggesting what we should buy.

The use of algorithms in social media results in people's decreased exposure to counterattitudinal news, facilitating the polarization of views.[181] Among millennials in many parts of the world, social media outlets are often the dominant source of news about politics and governments.[182] By recommending automated videos and news, manipulative content now easily reaches viewers, amplifying the spread of disinformation.[183] Social media can also fuel populist, nationalist and xenophobic waves across societies.[184]

AI is getting better at creating counterfeit information and fuelling the spread of disinformation. Consider how generative adversarial networks create counterfeit audios and videos.[185] These technologies can now be easily used through apps to create deepfakes. By 2016 more than 50 percent of internet traffic was generated by bots.[186] Indeed, false information tends to spread more broadly than true information.[187] Social networks can reduce critical assessment and facilitate the diffusion of conspiracy theories.

" As our lives become more dependent on artificial intelligence—from weather forecasts to financial market transactions to analysing DNA—we are delegating human choices

In a similar vein, who is responsible for mistaken AI decisions? Credit applications are rejected, and social media posts are deleted based on AI decisions, while mechanisms to contest these decisions are not fully developed. Many algorithms are opaque, unregulated and difficult to contest.[188] Pattern-recognition algorithms could be applied to target certain people[189] or produce disproportional and biased collateral damages due to imperfections in the code or in training data.[190] The use of AI in the military to deploy autonomous weapons or killer robots raises many questions.[191]

Machine learning is also providing firms with market information that they have never had before, creating new avenues for advertising while potentially encroaching on consumer privacy. When consumers purchase online, they reveal their preferences, and perhaps information about their friends and families, that companies can use to expand market outreach. Such data, often provided inadvertently by consumers, may transfer information to companies without constraints on how it may be used.[192]

Genomic editing—redefining the realm of possibilities

Genomic editing has revolutionized the life sciences and medicine through the possibility of changing the characteristics of living organisms by altering DNA. CRISPR can support the treatment of a range of health conditions with relative ease and efficacy.[193] For the first time it is possible to increase the longevity of children with progeria, a genetic disorder that promotes early aging and to reverse blindness.[194] CRISPR is also being explored for neurodegenerative diseases such as muscular dystrophy, Huntington's disease and Alzheimer's disease.[195]

Genomic editing also raises questions. Somatic cell editing can change the genes of a particular patient, while germline editing of egg and sperm cells can carry the treatment to future generations. Progress in this field has been so rapid that issues around ethics, regulations and societal implications have countries scrambling to catch up. Recently, a researcher alarmed the world by confirming that he had edited the genes of twin babies.[196] There are also many safety concerns. For example, in an embryo a nuclease may not necessarily cut both copies of the target genes or may start dividing before the corrections are complete.[197] Gene editing in rats, cattle, sheep and pigs also shows that it is possible to delete or disable genes in an embryo. Bioethicists argue that it is impossible to obtain consent on germline editing from an embryo or from future generations.[198]

Gene editing in the food industry can enhance productivity and make products resilient to weather and disease.[199] Japan recently authorized a genetically edited tomato variant rich in amino acids (GABA) that can induce relaxation and lower blood pressure.[200] Drought-resistant crops are being developed to keep yields high in times of reduced water supply, and research is under way on whether genetically edited rice could be resistant to flooding.[201]

" The conjunction of uncertainty and polarization may be paralyzing—delaying action to curb human pressures on the planet

How should genetically edited food be regulated and how should consumers be informed? And what about the labelling of genetically edited food? Several biotech companies, agribusinesses and food retailers are behind an antilabelling drive, while others advocate otherwise—but until these questions are answered, uncertainty is likely to persist.[202]

Uncertainty propelled by polarization: Delaying action, adding conflict

Uncertainty opens space for dispersing beliefs[203] and disagreeing on best courses of action.[204] This is not necessarily a problem. Indeed, when facing unpredictability, societies tend to leverage aggregate collective knowledge and narratives to mobilize resilience.[205] But uncertainty can also spur political polarization, especially among those averse to uncertainty.[206] For example, research finds that in the uncertain aftermath of a shock, such as a financial crisis, support for political extremes increases.[207] Political polarization reduces generalized trust and divides society into "us" and "them." It entrenches opinions, undermines public deliberation and may even reach toxic levels, with detrimental effects for democratic freedoms and human rights.[208]

The last decade has seen rapid democratic backsliding and increased political polarization in many societies (see chapter 4).[209] Trust and belief in democracy have been declining in parallel with increasing authoritarianism.[210] Political polarization has been increasing across a diverse set of countries (figure 1.13).

The conjunction of uncertainty and polarization may be paralyzing—delaying action to curb human pressures on the planet. The real paradox of our time may be our inability to act, despite mounting evidence of the distress that human planetary pressures are causing our ecological and social systems. But when perspectives of the future are uncertain, people may draw different conclusions from the same data,[211] and scientific uncertainty can be a basis for political manipulation.[212] Indeed, the spread of disinformation has been found to contribute to deteriorating social attitudes and polarization.[213]

In today's uncertain times cooperation and dialogue have often taken a backseat, as armed conflicts and military spending peak.[214] Wars and violent conflicts pose direct threats to lives and livelihoods and compounding pre-existing vulnerabilities. They add huge layers of uncertainty to people's lives and impede both individual and collective investments in human development.[215] The number of people living in areas affected by violent conflict was reaching record levels even before the war in Ukraine. In 2020 about 1.2 billion people lived within 50 kilometres of a conflict event, almost half of them (560 million) in places outside so-called fragile contexts.[216] Furthermore, a large share of the increase in the number of people living close to conflict events has occurred in settings where conflict is present but results in fewer than 10 fatalities, indicating a shift towards insecurity and uncertainty that go beyond the most violent and deadly conflicts.[217]

Conflict diverts policy attention and resources from sustainable development and can hamper climate change mitigation and adaptation efforts.[218] Studies point to the twin crisis of conflict and planetary disruption (spotlight 1.6). Warming temperatures heighten conflict risks,[219] as documented in history,[220] with temperature surges linked to higher crime and interpersonal violence, even outside armed conflict settings.[221] Nature and natural resources are also becoming a source of contestation.[222] But the links between climate and conflict are not straightforward —they span socioeconomic, political and ecological spheres.[223] Today, some of the places most exposed to climate change coincide with fragile and conflict-ridden contexts, where resources and the capacity for resilience are already low (see spotlight 1.6). Conflict hinders access to much-needed climate financing in fragile and violent conflict contexts.[224] The low-carbon transitions under way can add insecurity by

Figure 1.13 Political polarization is on the rise across the world

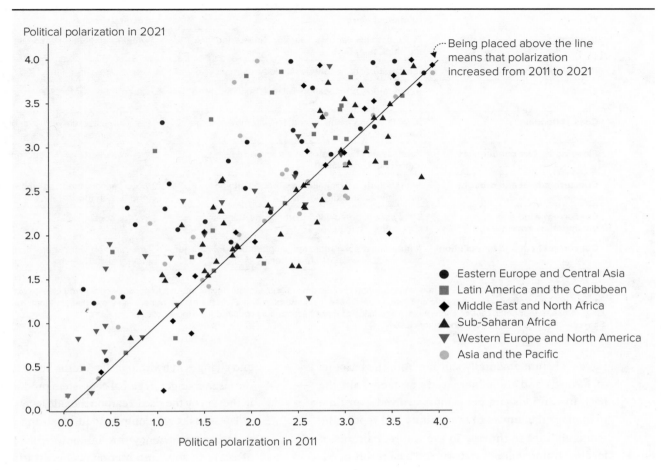

Source: Adapted from Boese and others (2022).

And now for something completely different: Novel and layered drivers of uncertainty

Uncertainties are stacking up and interacting. The novelty of humans' stark impact on the planet, the intentional efforts to transform, the fast pace of technological innovation and human development's embeddedness in nature invite us to take a step back and consider the feedback loops and interlinkages between our social and ecological systems.[225] With close interlinkages threats can easily spill over and multiply—leading to systemic failure.[226] The interaction of different layers of uncertainty makes the current context one of systemwide turbulence.[227] Extreme

opening new areas of contestation—especially when coupled with unequal power dynamics and uncertainties about land ownership (spotlight 1.7).

weather and climate events interact in ever more complex ways, shaped both by physical drivers and by societal contexts.[228] Institutions and behaviours create nonphysical interconnections, with implications for the impact of natural hazards and the severity of future extreme events in a series of complex feedback loops (table 1.1).

These interactions between physical and societal drivers have always been present at the local level. But over the 21st century the world will confront a continuously changing baseline, along with more extreme wet and dry precipitation events that will present adaptation challenges far beyond anything already experienced.[229] In fact, the changing "normal" will be so substantial that, if traditional measures to identify extreme events are based on what has been considered "normal," the entire late 21st century would be a single large extreme event.[230] In other words the interaction of physical drivers and societal

Table 1.1 Climate hazards driven by compounded physical drivers and societal context

Hazard	Climatic drivers	Societal drivers
Drought	Precipitation, evapotranspiration, antecedent soil moisture, temperature	Water management, land-use change
Physiological heat stress	Temperature, atmospheric humidity, diurnal cycle	Urbanization, irrigation
Fire risk	Temperature, precipitation, relative humidity, wind, lightning	Urbanization, deforestation
Coastal flooding	River flow, precipitation, coastal water level, surge, wind speed	Hard infrastructure, removal of natural coastal barriers
Flooding at river confluences	Precipitation, river water levels, large-scale atmospheric circulation	Water management, urbanization
Concurrent heat and drought	Temperature, precipitation, evapotranspiration, atmospheric humidity	Water management, soil management, land-use change
Concurrent wind and precipitation extremes	Wind speed, precipitation, orography, large-scale atmospheric circulation	Few or none
Concurrent heat and air pollution	Temperature, solar radiation, sulphur dioxide, nitrogen oxides, ozone, particulate matter	Urbanization, agricultural and industrial activities

Note: The table provides examples of how compounding climatic drivers and societal drivers interact to produce connected climate extremes. The societal drivers listed are nonexhaustive and include only those that contribute directly to the hazard rather than those that contribute to the impact. Long-term anthropogenic climate change plays into many of these hazards but is omitted here for simplicity.
Source: Adapted from Raymond and others (2020).

forces[231] is fundamentally shifting both the baseline of hazards and their increased variance.[232] In the past, institutions and behaviours evolved over time to manage the impact of uncertainty and reduce the vulnerabilities to threats. In the future, patterns of local adaption will be so disrupted as a result of climate change[233] that we may be ill-equipped to handle nationally and even globally the simultaneous materialization of multiple threats interacting with one another in compounding and novel ways (see box S1.6.1 in spotlight 1.6 for one example of a compounding crisis at the national level).

Droughts have rarely, if ever, affected all the major food producing regions at the same time, providing opportunities for "global insurance" through trade. The decline in food supplies in a drought-affected region could be compensated for by the supply from other regions free of drought. Now, the risk of global crop failure will emerge from more frequent spatially concurrent heatwaves and droughts affecting major breadbaskets for wheat, maize and soybean.[234] Today, there is almost zero probability of the four countries that account for the vast majority of global maize exports suffering simultaneous crop harvest losses greater than 10 percent. But this probability could increase to almost 90 percent under global warming of 4°C.[235] The global impact runs not only through temperature

and changes in hydrological patterns but also through the large changes in global ecosystem productivity set in motion by the rise in carbon dioxide levels.[236]

These risks are compounded by strong pressures to increase efficiency through powerful economies of scale in food production, concentrating global food production in only a few breadbaskets. The homogenization of food consumption habits leaves the world reliant for nourishment on a limited number of crops from a limited number of places.[237] So, behavioural and social choices—diet choices and economic incentives to concentrate production—make us increasingly vulnerable to synchronized crop failures.[238] Furthermore, the loss of crop diversity could destabilize entire ecosystems and have adverse economic and social impacts.[239]

Conflict weaves in additional layers of uncertainty to the increasingly concentrated and homogenous global food production. Consider the war in Ukraine, one of the world's largest wheat producers and exporters. The Russian Federation controls much of the global market share of fertilizer—a key input in agricultural production. The conflict has disrupted grain and fertilizer exports, contributing to a commodity price shock, especially among people living in poverty.[240] Beyond the battle-related deaths and displacements, energy insecurity is looming, a food insecurity crisis is under way and geopolitical instability is on the rise.[241] Indeed, war may be a "trigger of triggers," with global ripple effects.

The Covid-19 pandemic brought together zoonotic disease, inequalities and global socioecological connectivity. Unequal labour market conditions implied that some workers could quickly transition to remote working arrangements, safeguarding health and economic livelihoods, but others had to continue interacting with people or leave their jobs. And while social protection may have determined whether a person had the possibility of forgoing work to follow public health recommendations, political polarization, misinformation and deteriorating trust in science and institutions were also at play, influencing whether people were willing to follow the recommendations of public health authorities.[242]

What the future may hold due to pandemics is a major source of distress,[243] and the Covid-19 pandemic may leave deep scars. Inequality in access to digital technologies may have widened education disparities, setting back children in lower-income countries.[244] While higher-income countries could mobilize massive resources for recovery spending, often by borrowing at record-low interest rates, lower-income countries faced tight fiscal conditions and had to service debt rather than support people in dealing with the pandemic's socioeconomic impacts. Going forward, the differences in recovery spending between developed and developing economies may exacerbate differences in growth trajectories.[245]

Zoonotic diseases and pandemics may be in the limelight, but health threats from anthropogenic impacts on the planet expand beyond that. Accelerated biodiversity loss is a threat to food security, since much of our agricultural production depends on pollinators.[246] Food security is a looming global crisis, with 2.4 billion people facing moderate to severe food insecurity in 2020. The loss of pollinators also affects the diversity and availability of different nutrients.[247] The loss of biodiversity reduces the potential for new medical discoveries and poses a direct threat to local and traditional medicinal practices.[248] Pollution is becoming a major health threat, causing approximately 9 million premature deaths globally in 2015, 92 percent of them in low- and middle-income countries.[249] Exposure to air pollution has also been linked to higher Covid-19 mortality.[250]

A mismatch between interacting uncertainties and resilience strategies

The interaction of uncertainties casts doubt on the effectiveness of some of the resilience strategies that have historically been pursued (see spotlight 1.1). Leveraging trade to cope with local climate extremes affecting food production, building temperature-indifferent energy systems or migrating may be difficult amid layered and interacting uncertainties. Where do we migrate if the entire world is affected by simultaneous natural hazards—or when inequalities and political polarization set up barriers to people's movement? Can we diversify food supplies through imports in a world where increasing temperatures heighten the risk of simultaneous failures of wheat, maize and soybean harvests[251] or where pandemic-induced labour shortages, war and geopolitical tensions weaken global supply chains?[252]

" The interaction of uncertainties casts doubt on the effectiveness of some of the resilience strategies that have historically been pursued. Where do we migrate if the entire world is affected by natural hazards—or when inequalities and political polarization set up barriers to people's movement?

Our common aspirations, as codified in the 2030 Agenda for Sustainable Development and the Universal Declaration of Human Rights, are indivisible. Today, many people are losing faith in our collective ability to meet them.[253] Indeed, democratic practices have been weakening,[254] and the inability of countries to come together quickly enough during the Covid-19 crisis to provide equitable vaccine access, another illustration.[255] UN Secretary-General António Guterres has warned repeatedly of a fraying global world order[256] and has called on nations to rebuild global solidarity and multilateral cooperation in the face of systemic and interconnected threats.[257]

To meet the "confluence of calamities"[258] in the world today, we need more international cooperation, not less, and more solidarity across people, across generations and with the planet. A main challenge to overcome is that action to ease planetary pressures is needed now, but some of the benefits will not materialize until well in the future. Insights from indigenous philosophies bridge these intergenerational gaps and may contribute to foster change. In many of these philosophies, past, present and future generations share "interwoven histories that shape [...] collective lives and the world" and intergenerational responsibilities of "socioenvironmental guardianship" are implied.[259] Restoring our connection with the planet and with ourselves, including across generations, and acting in ways that enhance our shared, intergenerational, collective lives then become central objectives. Yet these perspectives are often marginalized in mainstream policy debates, making the empowerment of indigenous and other marginalized communities not only a matter of justice but also a matter of gaining insights and ideas that could benefit humanity as a whole (spotlight 1.8).[260]

Where we go from here is up to us: will we act in time to avoid the worst consequences, or will polarization drive disagreement and hinder change? Will we address the power imbalances and inequalities that drive planetary pressures and obstruct people's agency? Will the actions taken be enough, and will they benefit everyone, or will they exacerbate inequalities, adding strain to already weakened social contracts and global cooperation? The uncertainty complex we face may seem daunting, but history provides ample evidence of individual and societal resilience. Inaction in the face of deep uncertainty and compounding threats to human development is not an option. Going forward, we need to be courageous enough to challenge the status quo and to look into new places, new people and a diverse set of knowledge traditions for inspiration and solutions.[261] Indeed, human agency can be a major driver of large-scale societal change (see chapter 3).

Beyond crisis and collapse: Climate change in human history

Dagomar Degroot, *Georgetown University*

Today's climate crisis has no precedent in Earth's history, owing to the combination of its speed, eventual magnitude, global scale and human cause. Yet regional and even global climates have changed profoundly and often abruptly over the roughly 300,000-year history of humanity.[1] Anthropologists, archaeologists, economists, geneticists, geographers, historians, linguists and paleo scientists have long attempted to identify how these changes influenced communities and societies. Scholars in this field—recently termed the history of climate and society (HCS)—typically identify relationships between climatic and human histories not only to improve understandings of the past but also to inform forecasts of the hotter future.[2]

For over a century the most influential studies in HCS argued that temperature and precipitation trends and anomalies caused human populations to either collapse or undergo subsistence crises. While HCS scholars have not settled on a common, cross-disciplinary definition of collapse, to them the concept usually involves a disintegration of socioeconomic complexity, leading to depopulation, new political structures and new settlement patterns. HCS scholars have used statistical and qualitative methods to link drought and cooling to the collapse of, for example:

- The Akkadian Empire in the 3rd millennium BCE.
- The societies of the Bronze Age Mediterranean in the 2nd millennium BCE.
- The Western Roman Empire in the 5th and 6th centuries CE.
- The cities of the Classical Maya in the 10th century CE.
- Angkor, capital of the Khmer Empire, in the 15th century CE.
- The Norse settlements of western Greenland in the 15th century CE.[3]

When examining well-documented and often comparatively recent periods and places, HCS scholars usually concentrate on subsistence crises that culminated in political transformation but not collapse. In such studies crises typically afflicted only one state—for example, during dynastic transitions in ancient Egypt or Imperial China—but occasionally also entire continents, in western Eurasia during the 14th or 17th century, for instance. In this scholarship the worst-affected civilizations were those with subsistence strategies, hydraulic infrastructure, military and demographic pressures, or inefficient and unpopular governments that left them vulnerable to environmental disruption.[4]

HCS studies of collapse and crisis inform common fears that present-day civilizations cannot survive continued global warming.[5] Today's climate change will indeed reduce agricultural productivity; limit the availability of freshwater; increase the severity of droughts, heat waves and tropical cyclones; and reshape coastal environments on a speed and scale that could provoke destabilizing societal responses.[6] Yet the disproportionate emphasis on collapse and crisis in HCS scholarship partly reflects systematic biases in how studies in the field are designed, rather than the most common historical responses to climate change.[7]

HCS scholars are increasingly exploring the resilience of past populations to climatic changes and anomalies. Definitions of resilience in climate-related fields long privileged "bouncing back" in the wake of disaster and were eventually criticized for assuming that social change is inherently undesirable. Critics argued moreover that the concept distracted from the more urgent priority of mitigating human greenhouse gas emissions. They claimed that focusing on resilience encouraged the assumption that disasters are inevitable—naturalizing sources of vulnerability in marginalized populations—and that it displaced responsibility for avoiding disaster from governments to individuals.[8]

Yet people of the past plainly found ways to cope with climate changes, and there is no term as accessible as resilience to describe their achievements. Nor is there any doubt that governments must foster resilience to the human-caused warming that is already baked into the current climate crisis. Today, the Intergovernmental Panel on Climate Change (IPCC) uses the term resilience to mean the ability of coupled human and natural systems "to cope with a hazardous event or trend or disturbance, responding or reorganizing in ways that maintain their essential function, identity and structure."[9] It therefore encompasses adaptation, which the IPCC defines as the "process of adjustment to actual or expected climate and its effects, in order to moderate harm or exploit beneficial opportunities."[10] Neither adaptation nor resilience is automatically a positive quality. Both may preserve unjust systems and come at the expense of vulnerable populations. In particular, the resilience of a society, government, institution or culture across decades or centuries may belie the vulnerability of ordinary people to extreme weather.[11]

Scholars in different disciplines have attempted to identify historical examples of resilience in diverse ways. Archaeologists, for example, have perhaps overstressed "adaptionist" understandings of past responses to climate change. Many have defined resilience using resilience theory, a method based on the adaptive cycle model, in which social-ecological systems gradually lose resilience as they grow in size and complexity, then regain it after they collapse. Yet today there is widespread disagreement over how—and whether—to use resilience theory. Interdisciplinary collaborations therefore typically use broad conceptualizations of resilience, most of which roughly align with the IPCC's definition.[12]

One recent approach is to identify common pathways followed by populations that were broadly resilient in the face of past climate changes—meaning that they avoided serious or sustained demographic loss. This approach can emphasize both the diversity of resilient responses to past climate changes and the existence of shared strategies that may inform present-day climate policy.[13] There are at least five of these pathways (figure S1.1.1):

- Identifying new opportunities in local and regional environments.
- Maintaining or developing resilient energy systems.
- Exploiting diverse resources through trade.
- Adapting institutions to new climatic risks.
- Migrating to new environments.

Populations that followed the first pathway exploited regional or local environments that responded to global or hemispheric climate changes in ways that benefitted how these populations had organized their societies. The most striking examples date back to the Pleistocene, the geological epoch in which cycles in Earth's orbit and rotation repeatedly altered greenhouse gas concentrations enough to trigger alternating glacial and interglacial periods. In glacial periods advancing ice sheets trapped water previously in the oceans, lowering sea levels and creating land bridges that humans exploited to migrate across the Earth. The same forces responsible for glacial and interglacial periods also strengthened monsoon systems, periodically "greening" the Sahara and helping pastoralists migrate through and thrive in what is now the world's largest desert. Pastoralists, in turn, may have delayed the redesertification of parts of the Sahara by sustaining healthy grassland ecosystems.[14]

Well into the Holocene, the recent geological epoch characterized by a relatively stable interglacial climate, similar dynamics played out across smaller scales in time and space. In the Eastern Mediterranean precipitation increased during winter, the region's wet season, during the 6th century CE. Pastoral and agricultural communities benefitted from higher rainfall because the taxation system of the Eastern Mediterranean allowed them to easily transport agricultural commodities to population centres. Rising productivity encouraged elites to invest in market-oriented agriculture; new dams, channels, pools and other infrastructure then allowed farmers to manage water more effectively.[15]

The second pathway involved developing or exploiting energy systems for transportation, industry and human subsistence that did not respond directly to shifts in temperature or precipitation. As European temperatures declined in the 6th century, communities in Frisia (in today's northern Netherlands) thrived by consuming dairy and meat from livestock, supplemented by fish, shellfish and waterfowl. This subsistence strategy was less sensitive to cooling than others in Europe, many of which depended on cultivating grains that were sensitive to variations in temperature.[16] In the same century subsistence strategies across much of Finland and in northern Sweden and Norway did not depend on crop cultivation and in

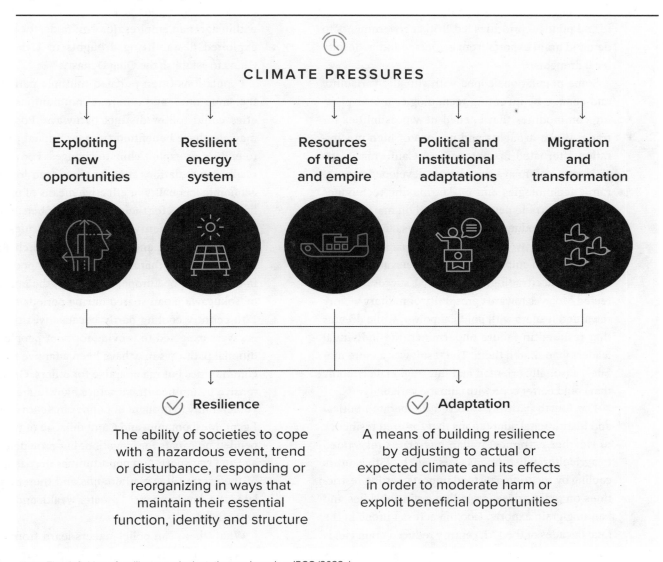

CLIMATE PRESSURES

| Exploiting new opportunities | Resilient energy system | Resources of trade and empire | Political and institutional adaptations | Migration and transformation |

Resilience

The ability of societies to cope with a hazardous event, trend or disturbance, responding or reorganizing in ways that maintain their essential function, identity and structure

Adaptation

A means of building resilience by adjusting to actual or expected climate and its effects in order to moderate harm or exploit beneficial opportunities

Note: The definition of resilience and adaptation are based on IPCC (2022a).
Source: Created by Hans Sell, Michelle O'Reilly and Dagomar Degroot.

fact primarily exploited wild food resources such as birds, freshwater fish, seals and terrestrial mammals. Changes in temperature affected the availability and accessibility of these resources in diverse ways.[17]

In Kraków, Poland, firewood prices rose as winter temperatures declined in the 17th, 18th and 19th centuries. Because the city occupied an increasingly peripheral position within larger polities, state authorities did not act to relieve high fuel prices. The city's inhabitants therefore shifted decisively from wood to coal for heating. Coal was more reliable and less expensive than firewood—and therefore beneficial for household budgets.[18]

To follow the third pathway, populations exploited the benefits of trade—including trade within imperial borders—to cope with climate change. Weather rarely affected far-flung regions simultaneously or equally. Trade therefore allowed populations to thrive despite climatic anomalies by importing commodities that were less available locally, owing in part to extreme weather. The integration of European and then global grain markets in the 2nd millennium CE eventually buffered populations at the centre of trading networks from increases in food prices that were influenced by precipitation or temperature anomalies.[19] At the same time these networks could render populations on their periphery more vulnerable to extreme weather. In the late 19th century millions died when economic and political priorities led British governments to demand grain exports from colonized India, despite local droughts.[20]

Some populations coped with climatic variability and change by inventing technologies and exploiting commodities that opened new possibilities for trade. When droughts and periods of high precipitation alternated in southeastern California in the 15th century, Mojava settlements developed new ceramic technologies and basket-making techniques to establish trade networks centred on maize, beans and squash produced by nearby Kwatsáan communities.[21] These networks fostered the expansion of a dynamic "dream culture" that further elevated Mojave long-distance trading. Dreams that successfully directed Mojaves towards prosperity or military victory rewarded leaders with political power, while dreams that resulted in failure undermined the individual leaders who shared them. The result was a more mobile, seasonally oriented and interregional economy that could better cope with climatic variability.[22]

The fourth pathway involved deliberate political and institutional adaptations that fostered resilience to weather extremes. Italian city-states responded to agricultural disruptions worsened by 13th century cooling by securing new food imports, setting restrictions on grain prices, providing grain subsidies and banning grain exports. Cooling across Europe in the final decades of the 17th century reduced grain yields and tax revenues across France just as grain supplies were already strained by military provisions. French administrators struggled to respond effectively, and harvest failures in 1693 and 1694 led to catastrophic famines.[23] When similar conditions returned in 1709, however, administrators negotiated emergency grain imports from Algeria that effectively eased food shortages.[24]

Finally, populations took the fifth pathway by migrating to either escape or exploit the impacts of climate change in local environments. Climate refugees migrating to escape the desertification of the eastern Sahara likely helped establish Pharaonic Egypt.[25] Across Eurasia, pastoral societies later threatened agrarian empires when precipitation changes either allowed them to rear more horses or threatened grasslands that otherwise sustained them. Some migrations by pastoralists responded to subsistence crises—and thus political and military vulnerability—within agrarian empires. Jurchen raids, for instance, exploited destabilizing droughts in 17th century China to establish the Qing Dynasty.[26]

Populations often pursued multiple pathways at the same time, and different communities in societies could follow distinct pathways. Populations may also have benefitted from additional pathways to endure or exploit climate changes. For example, resilient populations may have enjoyed low socioeconomic inequality or effective means of providing life's necessities for their poorest members. A robust culture of civic charity in Dutch coastal cities helped insulate the 16th and 17th century Dutch Republic from famines that affected primarily poor people in other parts of Europe.[27] Similarly, the population of Tokugawa Japan soared during periods of severe 17th century cooling partly because wealthy farmers were expected to provide for poor people.[28] Additional pathways may have been adaptive for some communities but maladaptive for others. Capital-intensive hydraulic infrastructure likely increased the vulnerability to drought of polities in South America, Egypt, Mesopotamia and Cambodia, all of which depended on canals for irrigation, but provided drainage and transportation opportunities in coastal areas of the present-day Netherlands and thereby stimulated the development of greater wealth and military potential.[29]

What, then, can policymakers learn from the diverse experiences of climate change in the past to build resilience to today's human-caused warming? One lesson may be that the impacts of climate change on populations were and are determined as much by human socioeconomic, cultural and political arrangements as the magnitude of environmental transformations. Communities, therefore, are rarely doomed to a particular fate; under all but the most extreme emissions scenarios, substantial scope remains for human adaptation and prosperity.

More specifically, the past reveals that adaptations to build resilience may involve identifying and exploiting what rare opportunities warming may provide, developing energy systems that both mitigate emissions and are resilient to extreme weather, diversifying sources of energy and commodities, restoring or maintaining flexible political and legal systems that prioritize redundancies over efficiencies and normalizing climate migration. The past may also reveal that tackling inequality and poverty—in particular, through policies that further environmental justice for historically marginalized populations—will foster resilience to global warming. And it may indicate that capital-intensive interventions to adapt to climate change have the potential to become sources of vulnerability. More HCS scholarship will further clarify the lessons of the past, lessons that may offer compelling reasons for hope and suggest strategies for sustainable human development in the decades to come.

NOTES

1   Osman and others 2021; Tierney and others 2020.

2   Degroot and others 2021.

3   See, for example, Brooke (2015) and Weiss (2017).

4   See, for instance, Campbell (2016) and Parker (2013).

5   See, for example, Begley (2021).

6   IPCC 2021.

7   Degroot and others 2021.

8   Soens 2020.

9   IPCC 2022a.

10 IPCC 2022a.

11 Izdebski, Mordechai and White 2018; Soens 2018; Van Bavel and others 2020.

12 Bradtmöller, Grimm and Riel-Salvatore 2017; Riede 2008.

13 Degroot and others 2021.

14 Brierley, Manning and Maslin 2018; Claussen, Dallmeyer and Bader 2017; Timmermann and Friedrich 2016.

15 Decker 2009; Izdebski and others 2016.

16 Devroey 2003; Knol and Ijssennagger 2017; Vos 2015.

17 Oinonen and others 2020; Tvauri 2014.

18 Miodunka 2020.

19 Epstein 2006.

20 Davis 2002.

21 Anderson 2005.

22 Zappia 2014.

23 Berger 1976; Lachvier 1991; Campbell and others 2017; Guillet and others 2017; Lavigne and others 2013.

24 Goubert 1982.

25 Lieberman and Gordon 2018.

26 Brook 2010; Cui and others 2019.

27 Curtis and Dijkman 2019.

28 Parker 2013.

29 Buckley and others 2010; Degroot 2018; de Souza and others 2019; Gill 2000; Manning and others 2017.

The nuclear–environment nexus and human development in the Anthropocene

Rens van Munster, *Danish Institute for International Studies,* and **Casper Sylvest,** *University of Southern Denmark, Department of History*

When Paul Crutzen and Eugene Stoermer coined the term Anthropocene in 2000 to denote an epoch characterized by the geological impact of the human species on planet Earth, these effects were already evident.[1] Since then, geologists and other scientists have debated the starting point of the Anthropocene. Among the contenders is the dispersion of radioactive isotopes from widespread nuclear testing during the 1950s—an indicator also singled out by the Anthropocene Working Group under the International Commission on Stratigraphy.[2] Meanwhile, the Anthropocene has become both a ubiquitous scientific concept and a potent political symbol that extends to the Earth's climate and ecosystems. As a result, questions of extinction and survival loom large in political debates about human development in this new epoch. Such debates echo those around the Cold War nuclear arms race, and there are good reasons for scrutinizing the intellectual and political links between the nuclear age and the current predicament. Indeed, a closer examination of the nuclear–environment nexus offers a prescient perspective on the persistent links between militarization and anthropogenic reconfigurations of the planet.

Historically, the connections between nuclear weapons and the environment are both multiple and deep. That nature could be controlled and manipulated was an integral part of the notion of security during the Cold War. The postwar development of such scientific disciplines as meteorology, glaciology and oceanography took place in a close relationship with the preparations for nuclear war, since adequate understanding of the effects of these weapons—vital for strategy and defence—depended on ecological knowledge. Over time these branches of science produced a new understanding of the Earth and its interacting systems, which in turn fostered conceptions of security as common and tied to the natural environment.

Nuclear testing and uncertainties about the effects of radioactive fallout gave rise to scientific measurements and environmental concerns, entanglements that persist to this day in climate modelling.[3] Antinuclear activists and movements unrelentingly criticized the arms race and the attendant risks of nuclear deterrence while exploiting scientific uncertainty and disagreement to expand political responsibility in time and space. Temporally, the effects of nuclear weapons revolved around future generations. And spatially, the effects transgressed any ground zero and came to include concern for both humanity and the planet, later symbolized in iconic photos of a living yet fragile Earth taken from space. The nuclear arms race paradoxically sparked a more ecocentric conception of the environment.[4]

The 1980s, when détente had given way to the second Cold War, witnessed an intensification and emerging synthesis of such links, especially striking in the work of Jonathan Schell, author of the best-selling *The Fate of the Earth* (1982).[5] The book, which compels people to imagine the extinction of the human species as a way of cultivating a global ecological awareness that included the fate of future generations, played a central role in the "nuclear freeze" movement and primed the public for debates about nuclear winter. Drawing on the latest insights from Earth system science, Schell concluded that the environmental effects of nuclear war would most likely leave Earth uninhabitable for humans. The political lesson taught by science was clear: the survival of the human species depended on functioning Earth systems and had to be seen in a broader ecological framework. To Schell, nuclear weapons symbolized not only modernity's inability to recognize its own self-destructiveness but also a hubris in humans' belief that the threat to complex, fragile and highly interdependent ecosystems could be rationally managed and contained.[6]

After the turn of the millennium, Schell's understanding of the entanglements between nuclear weapons and climate issues led him to recognize the value of the Anthropocene as an idea that explicitly foregrounds the connections between Western modernity and human technological prowess on the one hand and climate change, species extinction and biodiversity loss on the other. To Schell the Anthropocene called for reflecting more deeply on human–Earth relations and expanding the conventional horizons of space, time, community and agency. Yet, valuing ourselves as humans in relation to nature and other forms of life involves a heavy ethical and political responsibility, and Schell clearly feared that humans were not up to the task at a time when their technological power forcefully set the species apart from the rest of creation. Ultimately, however, Schell insisted on the role of human beings as "chief valuer" and maintained that a true embrace of this responsibility would decentre the human, whether by installing sober lessons about humility, prudence and the limits of a narrow technological rationality or by promoting more ecocentric valuations of the world, as expressed in ideas about interspecies entanglements, companionship and "nature-based" solutions to climate change.[7]

Schell's work is a reminder of the deep relationship between nuclear weapons and the environment in the Anthropocene. Nuclear weapons are detrimental to human development and risk jeopardizing the ecological systems on which it depends. The vast economic resources required for the production, maintenance and stockpiling of nuclear weapons divert funds away from human development and achieving the Sustainable Development Goals. Nuclear war would also have grave humanitarian consequences, including large-scale displacements, long-term harm to human health, restricted access to food and catastrophic damage to the environment. Some scientists predict that even a limited nuclear war could set off a global nuclear winter.[8] In a nuclear-armed world survivability and sustainability are tightly entwined.

Source: This spotlight also builds on Bilgrami (2020), Steffen and others (2011) and UNODA (2018).

NOTES

1   Crutzen and Stoermer 2000.

2   See Working Group on the Anthropocene 2019.

3   For example, Doel (2003), Edwards (2012) and Masco (2010).

4   Worster 1985.

5   Schell 1982.

6   van Munster and Sylvest 2021.

7   See Schell's late essays on "Nature and Value" and "The Human Shadow," posthumously published in Bilgrami (2020).

8   Witze 2020.

What kind of institution is needed for existential security?

Toby Ord, *Senior Research Fellow, The Future of Humanity Institute, University of Oxford, United Kingdom*

Humanity has faced many natural existential risks over the 3,000 centuries we have survived so far—such as risks from asteroid impacts or supervolcanic eruptions. But the anthropogenic risks we now face appear much greater in probability and continue to rise as our power over the world grows ever greater.[1] It is unclear whether we can survive another three centuries, let alone three thousand.

To survive, we need to achieve two things. We must first bring the current level of existential risk down—putting out the fires we already face from the threat of nuclear war and climate change. But we cannot always be fighting fires. A defining feature of existential risk is that there are no second chances—a single existential catastrophe would be our permanent undoing. So we must also create the equivalent of fire brigades and fire-safety codes—making institutional changes to ensure that existential risk (including that from new technologies and developments) stays low forever.

If we can achieve both these things, we will have reached existential security: a return to comparative safety, where we have ended the era of heightened risk to humanity.[2] This would be no utopia. Existential security would not guarantee universal human development or freedom—or health and prosperity. But it would be necessary to achieve any of those things—a foundation on which they rest.

One way to look at our current position is that humanity faces a high and unsustainable level of risk. Indeed, we can see this as one of the most fundamental kinds of sustainability. Think of the probability that humanity will continue to survive and flourish over a time span comparable with the 3,000 centuries we have lived so far. Each year that our time of heightened risk goes on, this probability of a successful future drops. And nothing we ever do could restore that chance. The probability of humanity surviving to live out its potential is the ultimate nonrenewable resource: something we depend on completely—with no possible substitutes—but are frittering away. Existential security means stabilizing humanity's survival curve—greatly reducing the risk and ensuring that it stays low. Only by doing so can we keep the probability of long-term survival high (figure S1.3.1).

What would be required to stem this loss—to reach existential security?

A large part of the answer has to come from international institutions. Existential security is inherently international: the risks that could destroy us transcend national boundaries, and finding ways forward that never once succumb to an existential catastrophe will require international coordination. Meeting this challenge would be an extremely difficult but necessary task. Here are some broad outlines of what it would require.

As Carl Sagan wrote: "The world-altering powers that technology has delivered into our hands now require a degree of consideration and foresight that has never before been asked of us."[3] We need the foresight to see the risks while they are still on the horizon, providing time to steer around them or, if that is impossible, to prepare to meet them. This involves knowing how to ask the right questions about future dangers. And while being able to accurately answer such questions is impossible, great progress is being made in systematically assigning well-calibrated and accurate probabilities to them.[4] An institution aimed at existential security would need to harness this progress and be at the forefront of forecasting expertise.

It would also require extremely high trust: from both the public and the elites across many different nation states. Perhaps it could learn from the Intergovernmental Panel on Climate Change, with its attempts to neutrally establish the current state of scientific consensus on climate change in a transparent manner, with input from all nations.

An institution for existential security would need extremely strong coordinating ability. Because existential risk threatens a common foundation on which

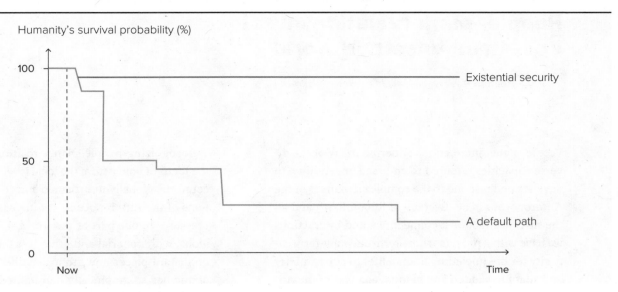

Source: Author's creation.

all of our varied hopes and futures are built, it is in every nation's interest to avoid it. But because different strategies and tactics for avoiding risk will have burdens that fall unevenly upon the nations, there are still great challenges for coordinating a path forward that everyone can accept.

Finally, such an institution would require a great deal of buy-in. This would have to be both strong and lasting.

Strong buy-in would be required before the idea of an institution to govern existential risks could even get off the ground, as nations will not lightly make the sacrifices in sovereignty that would be required. While there is not sufficient buy-in at the moment, this may change over years or decades as people slowly face up to the gravity of the threats facing humanity. And just as the United Nations was formed in the wake of the crisis and catastrophe of the Second World War, in the wake of new global crises and threats, the idea of new institutions with the power to achieve existential security may move quickly from unthinkable to inevitable.

Our resolve would have to be lasting. National constitutions provide proof that building institutional constraints that last hundreds of years is possible. Designing a constitution means setting in place the parameters for our descendants to operate across generations—as well as the means to adjust those parameters if circumstances change in unforeseen ways. Building institutions to reach existential security would have much in common with formulating a constitution—not just for a nation, but for humanity, and with a focus on ensuring that each generation cooperates to give succeeding generations the chance the exist and flourish in their turn.

Source: This spotlight also builds on Bostrom (2013), Leslie (1996), Ord (2020), Parfit (1984), Sagan (1983) and Schell (1982).

NOTES

1   Snyder-Beattie, Ord and Bonsall 2019.

2   Ord 2020.

3   Sagan 1994, p. 316–317.

4   Tetlock and Gardner 2015.

People–planet relationships in an uncertain, unsettled world

Belinda Reyers, *University of Pretoria and Beijer Institute of Ecological Economics of the Royal Swedish Academy of Sciences*

People–planet interactions underpin many of the diverse capacities required to embrace uncertainty, to navigate and respond to the complex dynamics of the Anthropocene. The diversity of life on Earth and all the myriad functions, connections and interactions we have with it provides short-term and long-term capacity for life (including human life) to persist under and adapt to sudden and gradual changes of the Anthropocene. As dominant models of development—with their emphasis on industrialization, resource exploitation and urbanization—continue to erode biodiversity and human interactions with it, we lose options and opportunities, reducing flexibility and adaptive capacity. Worryingly, these declines further push other planetary pressures such as climate change and pollution ever closer to dangerous thresholds.[1]

A focus on human–nature relationships and transformative capacities moves away from the risk reduction approaches that have become dominant as ways to manage uncertainty but that often fail to address the complex causes of planetary pressures and inequality.[2] Instead, by foregrounding on relationships, policy can overcome problematic divisions between nature and development to focus on the quality of relationships connecting people and planet and on reconfiguring relationships to enhance capacities to navigate uncertain futures.[3] For example, new indicators emerging from indigenous community monitoring systems feature relationships connecting people and nature, such as indicators of the condition of the human–biodiversity relationship[4] and indicators that monitor relationships and feedbacks between the social and ecological components of a place.[5] Such monitoring systems do not treat the social and ecological parts as separable. They focus instead on what connects them and could prove a valuable way forward for more integrated approaches to assessing human development progress.

Recognizing people–planet relationships widens the focus of policy from the local level to take into account the globally intertwined social-ecological systems of the Anthropocene. An increase in planetary pressures in one part of the world ripples across regions, with material and other less tangible impacts on distant places and groups, as the Covid-19 pandemic has so graphically highlighted. The Anthropocene is a heightened state of interconnectedness where social-ecological teleconnections and power asymmetries in global systems require new forms of solidarity for the interdependencies and realities of the Anthropocene.[6] Transitions in one country from nonrenewable energy sources (fossil fuels) towards renewable energy (solar)—done in solidarity with groups and places where the mineral resources (cobalt or lithium) for these technologies reside—will likely have very different outcomes for human development from local transitions that do not account for such distant impacts and dynamics.[7]

Inclusion and participation, so central to the human development journey, can also have blind spots. Focusing on people–planet relationships highlights additional barriers and potentially new dimensions of inclusiveness. It opens avenues to explore moral or ethical questions around including nonhuman entities and the risks and impacts imposed on those entities through various policy choices. This expansion of care and concern in human development is a lively topic receiving increasing attention as the interconnection and impact of our relationship with the natural world becomes more apparent.[8] It is strengthened as development policy engages more deeply with multiple knowledge and value systems that reject the separation of human and nonhuman or of nature and people.

Biocultural approaches, for example, portray human livelihoods, landscapes and ecosystems as having coevolved over long periods of time.

Biocultural diversity is the "diversity of life in all its manifestations—biological, cultural, and linguistic—which are interrelated within a complex socio-ecological adaptive system."[9]

Taking into account the dynamics of the Anthropocene, where complex social-ecological interactions result in lag effects and where today's choices are committing the planet to global-scale changes that will span thousands of years,[10] it becomes apparent that inclusion and participation have an important temporal dimension and that policy must innovate to include young people and consider future generations whose realities are being shaped for the long term by actions and choices taken today.

Innovation and human development have long gone hand in hand. In the context of the Anthropocene, there is, however, a risk that many of the innovative policies, practices and interventions that exist and are emerging will all stay small, localized and short term—tinkering at the edges without fundamentally rewiring development models and approaches to truly contend with the Anthropocene, the scale of its planetary pressures and the economic and political systems and asymmetries on which it is based.[11] Innovations that do not consider what needs to be built up and broken down, what needs protection and how to manage power asymmetries and participation can end up increasing vulnerability and eroding sustainability and resilience.[12]

Substituting one innovation (such as fossil fuel) with another (such as renewable energy) without addressing justice and sustainability of the transition will reduce emissions but will also likely defer many other impacts and risks to another place, group and time, without necessarily improving energy access and democracy.[13] As the 2020 Human Development Report made clear: "We must reorient our approach from solving discrete siloed problems to navigating multidimensional, interconnected and increasingly universal predicaments."[14] By anchoring innovation in deliberate considerations of people–planet relationships, the interconnections and interdependencies become clear and offer novel opportunities for human development in an uncertain future.[15] These interdependencies are not only material flows of energy, resources and waste; they are also intangible but essential in how they shape identities, cultures, relationships, minds, mental and physical wellbeing, and ultimately freedoms and choices in ways we often realize only when lost.[16]

Without acknowledging these relationships in the human development journey, dangerous feedbacks and negative people–planet relationships will undermine human development gains.[17] Previous innovations that have ignored these relationships to the detriment of the environment, vulnerable groups, local adaptive capacities and cultural practices are legion.[18] On the other hand, research exploring persistent poverty traps that considers social-ecological interactions highlights not only important causes of these traps but also novel pathways out of poverty.[19] As Michele-Lee Moore and colleagues point out, it is "the capacity to see, interrogate, and reimagine" these people–planet relationships that will create the disruptive and radical changes needed for transformations to sustainability.[20]

NOTES

1	Mace and others 2014; Steffen and others 2015.
2	Reyers and others 2022.
3	Haider and others 2021.
4	Lyver and others 2017.
5	Thompson and others 2020.
6	Rocha, Peterson and Biggs 2015.
7	Lèbre and others 2020.
8	Díaz and others 2019; Lee 2020.
9	Maffi 2005, p. 602.
10	Keys and others 2019.
11	Eriksen and others 2021; Hooli 2016.
12	Olsson and others 2017.
13	Lèbre and others 2020.
14	UNDP 2020b, p 5.
15	Moore and others 2014.
16	Njwambe, Cocks and Vetter 2019.
17	Olsson and others 2017
18	Haider and others 2021.
19	Lade and others 2017.
20	Moore and others 2018, p. 38.

On economic insecurity

Jonathan Perry, Marta Roig and **Maren Jiménez,** *United Nations Department of Economic and Social Affairs*

Economic security is a cornerstone of wellbeing. Economic stability and some degree of predictability enable people to plan and invest in their future and that of their children. They encourage innovation, reinforce social connections and build trust in others and in institutions.[1] Worry and anxiety about the future have negative health outcomes, ranging from mental health problems to heart disease and increased risk of obesity, including among children.[2] Pervasive economic insecurity generates popular discontent and imperils political stability.

Even before the Covid-19 pandemic, many people found themselves and their families on shaky economic ground. Growing employment instability and work that is increasingly precarious and poorly paid, together with persistent joblessness, are root causes of rising economic insecurity in high-income countries. In low- and middle-income countries high informal employment continues to affect income stability. People can no longer rely on stable, decent work to provide economic stability throughout their lives—a trend compounded by the Covid-19 pandemic and an emerging climate crisis.

Increased awareness of climate change and its many implications has injected growing uncertainty about the future and raised people's concerns about their wellbeing in the long run. Even though the effects are shaping anxieties worldwide, the impacts will be uneven. People in the poorest countries, particularly children and young people, stand to lose the most.

Indeed, people in poverty are more exposed to adverse events, from ill health to the growing impacts of systemic shocks such as climate change and pandemics, and have fewer resources to cope with and recover from their consequences. However, many people who are not poor by national or international standards are or feel economically insecure as well. In fact, while economic security and confidence in the future have traditionally been defining features of the middle class, this group is feeling increasingly insecure.[3] Workers in the informal economy and the growing number of people under nonstandard contractual arrangements are highly insecure, as are people with lower education levels, women, younger adults, members of racial and ethnic minorities and heads of single-parent households.[4]

Despite its significance, growing economic insecurity has stayed under the policy radar in many countries. Experts find fault in the fact that it is not adequately reflected in standard national statistics.[5] Indeed, many measurement issues related to insecurity are still unresolved, and empirical research on developing countries is scarce.

Whatever the method used to assess economic risks, the implications of these risks depend crucially on the buffers available. Catastrophic expenses and large debts drive falls into poverty when social protection systems do not help guard against risks or cover their effects. Even in developed countries with comprehensive social protection systems, comparative cross-country data suggest that public transfers protect only about 40 percent of adults against large drops in disposable income (drops of 25 percent of disposable income or above).[6]

Not only are risks growing, but policies are also not keeping up with current trends. Public institutions, policies and governance systems are struggling to adapt to rapidly changing needs across countries. Social protection coverage is often contingent on a traditional formal employer–employee relationship, and many schemes are not portable across jobs. Labour market institutions and regulations are also challenged by the growing diversification of working arrangements.

There are, however, policy innovations in both developed and developing countries that demonstrate the capacity of social protection systems, labour market institutions and public services to adapt to changing circumstances. These include new forms of social protection that adequately cover informal workers, migrant workers or those with nonstandard contracts.[7] There are also agile programmes that automatically scale up in response to systemic shocks, such as pandemics or climate-related emergencies. Some groups of informal workers have pursued new models of collective representation to protect their interests, namely through cooperatives, self-help groups and associations. Some of these new organizations have helped workers connect and undertake collective action, but many lack the legal capacity to negotiate working conditions. A key challenge for these organizations is that many informal workers are not considered workers under the law and therefore do not have bargaining rights. In some countries—Canada, Germany and Sweden, for instance—collective bargaining rights have been extended to some categories of self-employed workers.[8]

Providing economic security remains a key role of the state and its institutions and is a foundation of the social contract between government and citizens. Many governments spend a substantial share of GDP to safeguard against hardship-causing losses, through social protection systems, healthcare and other public services. This is a crucial moment to reflect on how to adapt past policies and institutions to a new socioeconomic reality.

Large-scale crises heighten risk and insecurity and have, at times, opened a path to renew the social contract. The unprecedented income support and health measures put in place by many governments as a response to the Covid-19 pandemic attest to the primary role that the state continues to play in confronting economic risk and insecurity. Policy responses to the crisis have ranged from direct payroll support to employers to covering income losses in informal employment to rent payments and eviction moratoriums, not to mention expanding healthcare coverage in traditionally underserved areas.[9]

However, many of these measures are temporary. Most of them leave beneficiaries just as vulnerable to future shocks once they are removed. Comprehensive, universal social protection systems, when in place, play a much more durable role in protecting workers and in reducing the prevalence of poverty than short-term, ad hoc measures, since they act as automatic stabilizers. They provide basic income security at all times and therefore enhance people's capacity to manage and overcome shocks.

Countries with social protection systems already in place were able to scale them up quickly during the Covid-19 pandemic. Investments in building and expanding social protection systems in some Latin American countries over the past decades have cushioned the fallout from the crisis, at least in the short term.[10] Many other low- and middle-income countries entered the crisis on weak financial footing, however. Their ability to expand social protection has been constrained by lack of fiscal space as well as by a lack of existing mechanisms on which to build. Overall, the financial support to individuals and families has varied dramatically across countries, as has access to vaccines and thus the speed of economic recovery. Without urgent corrective action from the international community, the current crisis is likely to widen disparities both within and between countries.[11]

Focusing on the challenges people face today—from increasingly precarious employment to inadequate healthcare and difficulty accessing social protection, housing and other public services—can narrow social, economic and political divides and guard against the next global crisis.

NOTES

1   For a broad assessment of economic insecurity and its measurement, see Stiglitz, Fitoussi and Durand (2018).

2   See Rohde and others (2017) and Watson and Osberg (2017).

3   Hacker 2018b.

4   Hacker 2018a.

5   Durand, Fitoussi and Stiglitz 2018; Stiglitz, Fitoussi and Durand 2018.

6   On average, although the percentage varies widely across countries. See Hacker (2018a).

7   See, for instance, ADB 2016.

8   For details of specific programmes in these countries, see OECD (2019b).

9   ILO 2020a.

10   Blofield, Giambruno and Pribble 2021; Lustig and others 2019.

11   Ferreira 2021.

Building an environment of peace in a new era of risk

Environment of Peace Initiative, *Stockholm International Peace Research Institute*

Humanity has entered a new era of risk created by the confluence of twin crises—one rooted in the darkening global security horizon, the other stemming from ongoing environmental destruction. The risks are complex and often unpredictable. While failing to address either crisis adequately, governments are not paying enough attention to the crossover points where the most dangerous situations are emerging.

There are more hungry and displaced people than a decade ago,[1] twice as many state-based conflicts and twice as many deaths in those conflicts.[2] Governments are spending more on their military forces.[3] Even before the war in Ukraine, nuclear states were increasing the number of warheads being held in readiness for use.[4] Meanwhile, the impacts of climate change are worsening,[5] plastic pollution and resource depletion continue almost unabated and the health of ecosystems declines.

Half a century ago, at the United Nations Conference on the Human Environment in Stockholm, governments formally recognized that ecological integrity is essential to human development.[6] Now, the consequences of declining ecological integrity are clear. The countries facing the greatest ecological threat are statistically likely to be among the least peaceful. They also tend to be marked by fragility and low capacity for resilience.[7] Half of ongoing UN peace operations are in the countries with the highest exposure to climate change impacts.[8]

A climate change impact or the disappearance of an important food resource does not axiomatically cause insecurity and conflict, but it does increase the risk.[9] The risk will be heightened if the society in question is already tense, fragile or insecure and will be lower if it is well-governed and well-resourced (box S1.6.1). Additionally, insecurity can lead to people taking decisions that damage environmental integrity.

To succeed, transitions must be just and peaceful

Turning back the tide of environmental decline is necessary in order to reduce the risks and secure an environment of peace. It will entail major transitions in such sectors as energy, industry and land use.[10] Transitions need to occur quickly and successfully. However, interventions aiming to tackle an environmental problem can exacerbate insecurity or cause a different form of environmental damage.

In the 2000s the rush to biofuels led to landgrabs in the Global South as producers looked to meet demand stimulated by policy choices in the Global North. This contributed to soaring food prices and resultant unrest in countries such as Burkina Faso, Egypt and Haiti.[11]

Building hydropower dams has altogether displaced an estimated 80 million people on every inhabited continent.[12] In Myanmar dam building has forced displaced people into areas populated by other ethnic groups, leading to clashes.[13] Once in place, dams restrict water availability for downstream use, disrupt biodiversity and fish stocks important for food, flood farmland and divide communities.

Meeting the Paris Agreement 1.5°C target could entail a 10-fold expansion of hydropower in Africa.[14] Governments and companies such as airlines propose increased biofuel production.[15] Unless a different approach is taken, conflict and displacement could result again.

With the sixth mass extinction of species in Earth's history possibly under way, attempts to protect nature and biodiversity are at a crunch point. More than 90 governments now support the goal of protecting 30 percent of the Earth's surface through conservation by 2030, the so-called 30×30 initiative,[16] which is up for negotiation at the 2022 UN Convention on Biological Diversity summit.[17] However, with 300 million people living in key biodiversity areas, 30×30 has

Environment of Peace Initiative, Stockholm International Peace Research Institute

Haiti, the lowest income country in the Americas, has been beset by decades of political instability, natural hazards (including a massive earthquake in the Southern Peninsula of the country in 2010) and removal of tree cover, in turn leaving communities exposed to storms and landslides.[1] In January 2020 the Haitian Parliament dissolved after elections were postponed, with President Jovenel Moïse attempting to rule by decree against a backdrop of continuing public unrest.[2] Two months later Haiti reported its first cases of Covid-19. The government declared a health emergency, with a familiar mix of school and business closures, limitations on transport and gatherings, and a night-time curfew.[3]

With three-fifths of the population already below the poverty line and antigovernment sentiment running high,[4] people refused to abide by the regulations, boosting the infection rate.[5] Agricultural production fell, and food prices rose by more than 25 percent.[6] In August tropical storm Laura came to Haiti, ruining 50–80 percent of certain crops in the southeast.[7] Unusually dry months followed, depressing harvests by up to 80 percent. Entering 2021, food prices were running 40 percent above normal.[8]

In May 2021, with Covid-19 cases soaring, the government redeclared a state of emergency.[9] In July tropical storm Elsa hit the same southeast regions devastated by Laura the previous year.[10] Four days later, for reasons that remain unclear, gunmen assassinated President Moïse, unleashing a further period of political turmoil.[11] Soon afterward, the United Nations Food and Agriculture Organization declared that nearly half the Haitian population was in acute food insecurity.[12]

Perhaps a country with stable politics could have coped with the two storms in quick succession. Perhaps without the restrictions around Covid-19, political order could have been restored. But the combination of the previous decades of environmental destruction and political turmoil, unrest in the streets, Covid-19 and two major storms dealt Haiti a systemic blow. Millions have been left without sufficient food or prospects, the only certainty being that more insecurity lies ahead.

Notes
1. USAID 2020. **2.** Freedom House 2021. **3.** Díaz-Bonilla and others 2021. **4.** Freedom House 2021; USAID 2020. **5.** Fujita and Sabogal 2021. **6.** Díaz-Bonilla and others 2021. **7.** UN OCHA 2020. **8.** FEWS NET 2021a. **9.** FEWS NET 2021b. **10.** FAO 2021. **11.** BBC News 2021. **12.** FAO 2021.

provoked concern over land rights, indigenous peoples' rights and food security.[18] Two UN Special Rapporteurs have warned of "fortress conservation."[19]

Wind and solar power, set to become the main energy sources in a rapidly decarbonizing world, have historically generated very little conflict. However, there are potential issues at both ends of the product lifecycle, as there are with batteries for energy storage and electric vehicles. At the source end, concerns focus on the human rights abuses connected with some mining operations for minerals such as lithium, cobalt and rare earth elements.[20] At the disposal end, wind turbines, solar panels and batteries need to be made fully recyclable, to avoid the creation of potentially huge waste streams.[21]

The urgency of the crisis in nature and climate change is so acute that rapid and profound transitions are needed to halt and reverse it. Failure to do so will inevitably lead to further security risks associated with continuously rising impacts. However, failure to enact transitions in a fair and peaceful manner will be a sure-fire recipe for both creating further insecurity and conflict risks and compromising the prospects of success.

Beginnings of a new security

Despite the gravity of the global situation, there are hopeful signs from community projects up to the supranational institution level.

Recognition within the United Nations of the relationship between environmental degradation and security dates back to at least January 1992, when the Security Council declared that "non-military sources of instability in the economic, social, humanitarian and ecological fields have become threats to peace and security."[22] The link has since been acknowledged in many other declarations and initiatives, including the Sustainable Development Goals and the

Sustaining Peace initiative.[23] Nevertheless, security and environmental agendas have largely progressed along separate tracks. The creation of the Climate Security Mechanism in 2018 has built a bridge, but the serial vetoing of resolutions on climate change and security within the Security Council is one bar to fuller coordination.

Several regional blocs also acknowledge the links between environmental degradation and security, including the African Union, the European Union, the Organisation for Security and Co-operation in Europe and the Association of Southeast Asian Nations. The African Union recognizes that addressing human impacts on the planet, such as climate change, will reduce the risk of conflict and commits to tackling them as a route to securing development.[24]

At the operational level, the UN Assistance Mission in Somalia represents an important step forward. It is the first mission to include a dedicated environmental and climate security adviser.[25] The United Nations is deploying similar advisers elsewhere.

Civil society organizations and international agencies have launched many initiatives that build peace and address environmental degradation simultaneously in historically conflict-prone areas. In the Sahel, where climate change impacts and overuse of water have exacerbated tension between pastoralists and farmers, multiple projects are improving resource management and animal health, facilitating access to markets, helping pastoralists diversify sources of income and managing conflict.[26] Across the borders of Israel, Jordan and the State of Palestine, the nongovernmental organization EcoPeace builds mutual understanding among communities whose security is impacted by shortfalls in water and energy access relating to environmental decline.[27] In Uganda the Strengthening Resilience and Inclusive Governance project aims to defuse tensions between refugees and host communities who would otherwise be competing for the same charcoal resources and in the process would use it unsustainably.[28] All these examples can be learned from and scaled up.

Towards an environment of peace

There are, broadly, two areas in which governments and other decisionmaking institutions need to take action to mitigate the growing threat to peace posed by the twin crises.

One is to link up responses to insecurity and environmental degradation, at every level from policymaking down to projects, so that manifestations of the crises are tackled holistically. This cannot be only about responses to emerging situations—it must also be anticipatory, involving horizon scanning, forecasting, knowledge sharing and resilience building.

The second is to get on with solving the underlying environmental threats. Security risks will keep growing until society rebuilds the natural resource base, restores biodiversity, aggressively limits pollution and reduces greenhouse gas emissions to net-zero. Moves to do this must be undertaken in a just and peaceful way—but they must be undertaken.

The Stockholm International Peace Research Institute report *Environment of Peace*,[29] launched in May 2022, concludes with six recommendations for action and five principles to guide them. The principles include approaching the crises cooperatively, because a nationalistic approach to threats faced in common is clearly illogical and inefficient. Governments need to combine far-sighted vision and strategy with urgent action and to adapt strategies as they go along because the manifestations of the twin crises will evolve. All the transitions needed to halt and reverse environmental degradation, including climate change, must be enacted justly and peacefully—which also implies enacting them inclusively, ensuring that affected people are involved in decisionmaking and share in the benefits.

The recommendations themselves include some that will build resilience. For example:

- All governments should carry out a risk assessment on the security risks posed by environmental decline.
- All transboundary resources such as river basins should be covered by resource-sharing agreements, and those agreements should be made fit for purpose in an era of climate change.
- Early warning systems for conflict should include indicators of environmental change.

Others address root causes. For example:

- Governments should, as far and fast as possible, stop funding conflict risk through building up weaponry and subsidising fossil fuels and instead fund environmental restoration and peace.

- The public and private sectors should proactively identify and reduce conflict risks in the clean technology supply chain.
- Indigenous peoples and other marginalized groups should routinely be involved in making decisions that concern them.

All the recommendations can be implemented within the next few years. And all should be. Governments agreed, in approving the Working Group 2 report from the Intergovernmental Panel on Climate Change in February 2022, that there is "a brief and rapidly closing window to secure a liveable and sustainable future for all."[30] The context of its words was climate change; but they are equally applicable across the entire risk landscape of the twin security and environmental crises. With the escalating risks having been identified, it is clearly in every government's self-interest to act.

NOTES

1   UNHCR 2021; von Grebmer and others 2021.

2   Pettersson and others 2021.

3   Lopes da Silva, Tian and Marksteiner 2021.

4   Kristensen and Korda 2021.

5   IPCC 2022b.

6   UN 1972.

7   IEP 2021, p. 4.

8   Krampe 2021.

9   Mobjörk, Krampe and Tarif 2021.

10 IPCC 2019, p. 15; Lebling and others 2020, p. 8.

11 Headey and Fan 2010; Zoellick 2008.

12 Walicki, Ioannides and Tilt 2017.

13 International Rivers Network 2011.

14 IEA 2021a.

15 European Commission 2021; ICAO 2019.

16 High Ambition Coalition for Nature and People 2022.

17 The Open-ended Working Group on the Post-2020 Global Biodiversity Framework 2022.

18 Rights and Resources Initiative 2020.

19 Boyd and Keene 2021; Tauli-Corpuz, Alcorn and Molnar 2018.

20 Searcey, Lipton and Gilbertson 2021.

21 Harper and others 2019; Månberger and Stenqvist 2018; Morse 2021; Pavel and others 2017.

22 United Nations Security Council 1992.

23 UN 2020b.

24 African Union 2015.

25 Hodder 2021.

26 World Bank 2017a, 2022a, 2022b.

27 EcoPeace Middle East n.d.

28 CARE 2019.

29 Black and others 2022.

30 See note 6 in IPCC (2022b).

Low-carbon transformations: A green resource curse?

New low-carbon technologies such as electric vehicles and renewable energy generation will require much larger inputs of nonrenewable minerals than are needed for high-carbon energy sources, such as petroleum-powered cars.[1] In many instances these minerals are found in a very limited number of locations, often low- and middle-income countries.[2]

Africa hosts some of the largest reserves of many of the minerals used to produce low-carbon technologies at scale.[3] And by 2040 renewable energy is projected to account for 75 percent of Africa's new power generation and 40 percent of its total power generation.[4] These two trends could boost economic growth and improve living standards. But many resource-rich countries have suffered from a "resource curse," with resource wealth fuelling violent conflict, heightened poverty and social inequality.[5] The shift to low-carbon technologies and renewable energy raises concerns about potential "green resource curses."

There are multiple channels for low-carbon transitions to lead to conflict and dispossession. A recent mapping of renewable energy projects and conflict sites across five African countries revealed a substantial correlation. Proximity to a renewable energy site was strongly associated with higher conflict risk across green activities, ranging from establishing renewable energy projects to green mineral mining to producing renewable energy.[6]

Establishing and operating renewable energy projects are frequently fraught with tension over land acquisition, employment opportunities and benefit sharing—often compounded by a lack of consultation with existing landowners and users, especially where customary land users may lack written documentation of their claims. Grievances were compounded by concerns about local employment opportunities and the lack of a mechanism for reinvesting project revenues in the local community.[7] Moreover, many residents in the communities closest to the project sites were not afforded access to the national electric grid, despite ceding their historical lands for project development.

Tensions often persist after projects become operational. Key reasons include limited employment opportunities and a perceived lack of benefit sharing among the communities most impacted by such projects. When the benefits and value produced from such projects are seen as benefitting far-away elites or a rival status group, the potential for conflict is high. This risk can be reduced by including local communities and indigenous and marginalized groups in project planning.

Green mineral mining is also a classic example of a potential resource curse. From cobalt and coltan in the Democratic Republic of the Congo to lithium in Zambia and Zimbabwe to copper across much of southern Africa, the region holds enough mineral wealth to support the mass production of low-carbon technologies.[8] Yet, resource curse dynamics are a threat where economic diversification is limited, institutions are weak and potential for resource capture is high.

Even where conflict is less prevalent, many such projects are plagued by unsafe conditions, environmental degradation and benefits that fail to accrue to the local communities.[9] Voluntary governance initiatives, such as limiting the sale of conflict diamonds, can help prevent green resource curse dynamics but require coordination across the supply chain of mineral producers, processers and consumers.

The adverse impacts associated with renewable energy production have yet to reach the conflicts sparked by fossil fuel production. But given the projected growth of renewable energy, active policy interventions will be needed to reduce conflict risks associated with low-carbon transitions.[10]

Source: This spotlight builds on Aas Rustad and others (2022).

NOTES

1   Leonard and others 2022; Aas Rustad and others 2022.

2   See, for example, IEA (2021b).

3   Aas Rustad and others 2022; IEA 2021b.

4   IEA 2014, 2019.

5   Aas Rustad and others 2022; Leonard and others 2022.

6   Aas Rustad and others 2022.

7   Aas Rustad and others 2022; Schilling, Locham and Scheffran 2018.

8   Aas Rustad and others 2022; IEA 2021b; Leonard and others 2022.

9   Aas Rustad and others 2022; Frankel, Mucha and Sadof 2018; Ochab 2020.

10   Leonard and others 2022; Schilling, Locham and Scheffran 2018.

The new uncertainty complex and intergenerational justice

Krushil Watene (Ngāti Manu, Te Hikutu, Ngāti Whātua o Orākei, Tonga), *Massey University, New Zealand*

Pursuing socioenvironmental justice now and leaving a thriving planet for the generations that follow require both knowledge and imagination. Not only do we need to know how to pursue and realize such things as social justice and ecosystem health, but we also need to be able to imagine relationships and responsibilities far beyond our own temporally and spatially bound lives. For instance, to "[meet] the needs of the present without compromising the ability of future generations to meet their own needs,"[1] we must both know what meeting needs requires now and be able to imagine what the lives of future generations might be like in a range of different and distant futures.

Philosophers have developed several theories of intergenerational justice that animate the normative underpinnings of our responsibilities to future generations.[2] Some theories take the view that justice requires that we imagine ourselves choosing principles to govern intergenerational responsibilities. To enforce fairness, the choice procedure removes knowledge of exactly which generation we (the decisionmakers) will belong to.[3] Other theories contend that justice requires that we imagine having to justify any courses of action we take now directly to our descendants who will inherit the consequences of those actions.[4] For other theories justice requires that we imagine ourselves situated such that we must justify our actions now directly to our ancestors given their values, aspirations and expectations.[5] Similarly, other theories start out from the contention that justice requires we imagine ourselves as part of connected and overlapping intergenerational communities extending backwards and forwards in time.[6] In line with this view Indigenous philosophies situate each generation as part of a "series of never-ending beginnings"[7] —each born in the imaginations of generations past, with the responsibility to set the course for the journeys that follow.[8]

Our cultural values, narratives and practices have a vital role in protecting and enabling intergenerational links—connecting past, present and future generations.[9] Polynesian ocean-voyaging narratives, for example, trace descent lines across the expanses of the Pacific Ocean, the largest body of water on Earth, in some cases all the way to the Southern Ocean and Antarctica.[10] Land-based narratives story ancestral migrations that weave networks of communities into the land and waterways—embedding connections and responsibilities through and across multiple generations.[11] Socioenvironmental practices enact values that preserve relationships and knowledge transmission.[12] Together, these theories, cultural values and practices provide critical conceptual and cognitive tools that bridge distant people and places in ways that situate the current generation as having responsibilities as part of a far-reaching intergenerational community.[13]

Our theories, values and practices are grounded in the aspiration to leave behind a thriving planet. This aspiration is reflected in the way we live our individual and collective lives hopeful that what we value, create and pursue will endure. It is similarly reflected in the way we make policies based in part on the legacies that those policies will chart and enable in the long run. There tends to be, in other words, "a conceptual connection between valuing something and wanting it to be sustained."[14] Indeed, what we leave behind for future generations shapes not just how meaningful their lives will be but how meaningful our lives can be said to have been as well.

The uncertainty complex outlined in this year's Report, while reinforcing this aspiration, highlights a more fundamental aspiration and challenge as well: namely, that there will be a future of some sort at all. While previous generations have largely been able to take a stable planetary system for granted, our generation faces the challenge of ensuring the planet's long-term survival. Such a predicament reinforces the urgent need for pathways through which different ideas, fresh perspectives and appropriate socioenvironmental practices can be enabled and enacted now. More specifically, our collective challenge provides an opportunity to adopt the kind of long-term intergenerational thinking that grounds Indigenous (and many other) philosophies—which Tim Mulgan refers to as "multigenerationalism."[15] According to this view, the best way to find meaning in the world today is to embark on projects spanning several generations that come to fruition only long after the present generation is gone.

To do multigenerationalism well, or even at all, however, we must remember what we truly need to flourish,[16] and we must be courageous enough to remake our local and global systems in ways that will truly enable and sustain that flourishing.[17] What is more, we have to find the courage to radically change our values and narratives so that our descendants might still be here to pursue planetary wellbeing and justice long after we are gone.[18] Perhaps most important, we must have "radical hope"[19]—we must hope for a world that we know may never materialize in the future and yet still find the courage to hold the course towards that future anyway.

NOTES

1 WCED 1987, p. 37.

2 See, for instance, Gardiner (forthcoming) and Mulgan and others (2021).

3 Rawls 1971.

4 Darwall 2009; Mulgan 2018.

5 Watene 2022.

6 De-Shalit 1995.

7 Jackson 2020, p. 99.

8 Kelbessa 2022; Watene 2022, forthcoming; Whyte 2013.

9 Epeli Hao'ofa 2008; IPBES 2019b; Kimmerer 2013; Mutu and McCully 2003.

10 Wehi and others 2021a, 2021b.

11 See, for instance, Watene (forthcoming).

12 Grix and Watene 2022.

13 Watene 2022.

14 Scheffler 2013, p. 60.

15 Mulgan forthcoming.

16 Grix and McKibbin 2015, p. 292–306.

17 Táíwò 2022; Watene 2022.

18 Bendik-Keymer 2016; Táíwò 2022.

19 Lear 2006. See also van der Lugt (2022) and Whyte (2017).

Unsettled minds in uncertain times

Mental distress—an obstacle to human development

CHAPTER 2

Unsettled minds in uncertain times:
Mental distress—an obstacle to human development

Unsettled lives mean unsettled minds.

What does that have to do with human development?

This chapter makes the case that mental distress weighs on human development in many ways, ultimately limiting people's freedom to live the lives they have reason to value. The effects are especially damaging to children and can perpetuate inequality in intergenerational cycles of mental distress and socioeconomic hardship. Breaking these cycles requires action from people and policymakers on three fronts: preventing distress, mitigating crises and building psychological resilience.

The preceding chapter documented the novel and unprecedented uncertainties affecting people's lives. This chapter dives into how uncertainty can cause mental distress,[1] with implications for the way people feel, think, act and interact with each other throughout their lives, restraining their freedom to achieve and to live lives they have reason to value.[2] It shows how mental distress can constrain human development and reinforce and perpetuate inequalities. It also emphasizes early childhood—as crucial for developing the brain and body but subject to the devastating consequences of toxic stress.

Mental wellbeing shapes the way people think, act and interact.[3] Individual emotion,[4] perception, cognition and motivation[5] are set in a social context of circumstances, relationships and culture.[6] Emotions, such as anger, can drive people to interpersonal violence or to violent conflict, but they can also trigger actions against injustices (see chapter 3).[7] And emotions can help in dealing with an unpredictable world (with some arguing that emotions reflect evolutionary adaptations).[8] Healthy regulation of emotions and overall mental wellbeing are crucial for peaceful and cohesive societies—and thus for human development.

" Healthy regulation of emotions and overall mental wellbeing are crucial for peaceful and cohesive societies— and thus for human development

Mental distress can hinder people from developing their full potential.[9] For instance, even when free high-quality education is universally available, a student suffering from anxiety and insomnia has the choice to go to school but may not be able to concentrate because of mental distress and will thus not be able to learn as easily as her peers. These individual limitations in one aspect of human development can be carried over to other dimensions and different stages of the lifecycle, as when the same student later seeks employment, and can even act intergenerationally through distress during pregnancy and beyond.

A crucial task for people and policymakers is thus to prevent and mitigate mental distress. Since not all adversity can be prevented or mitigated, this chapter and the policy options presented in chapter 6 emphasize the importance of psychological resilience that enables people to thrive despite adversity and that is intrinsically linked to agency, a critical component of human development (see chapter 3).[10]

How mental distress constrains human development

In the absence of psychological resilience, mental distress can result in mental disorders. These are associated with poor education achievements,[11] low productivity at work,[12] poverty,[13] premature and excess mortality[14] and poor overall health. Many people suffer from mental health–related problems, commonly measured by the number of diagnosed mental disorders (spotlight 2.1).

To understand the links among mental distress, mental wellbeing and human development, the capabilities approach—focusing on the capabilities that enable people to expand their freedoms to do and be what they value and have reason to value—can be helpful. Capabilities are a combination of things a person is able to do or be—the various functionings he or she can achieve.[15] Each person has his or her conversion function, with individual conversion factors that determine the ability to turn resources into capabilities (figure 2.1).

While mental wellbeing can influence choices and behaviour at multiple stages and can be a functioning itself, mental distress shapes individual conversion factors, affecting each person's ability to convert goods and services into capabilities. The complete set of achieved functionings also affects the amount and intensity of mental distress a person is exposed to. For example, a person with high income can afford to live in a safe neighbourhood, but a person with low income may not. So, the low-income person will be exposed to more mental distress caused by neighbourhood insecurity, which in turn will affect her conversion factors.

In childhood

The impact of mental distress on conversion factors, and thus capability sets, shapes not only children's individual lives but also human development prospects in adult life, with implications for society. Exposure to frequent or long-term toxic stress or adversity,

Figure 2.1 Mental distress constrains freedom to achieve, choices and achievements

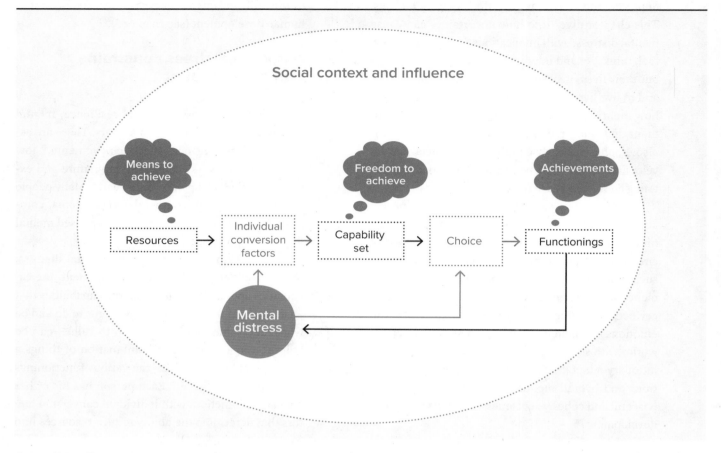

Source: Human Development Report Office based on Lengfelder (2021) and Robeyns (2017).

combined with weak support systems, impairs the development of neural circuits responsible for emotional self-regulation, cognition and behaviour.[16] In some cases this creates long-term physical and mental health problems, including damage to the developing brain.[17] A child's developing brain sets the foundation for future learning, behaviour and health.[18] Damages are difficult, though not impossible, to remedy later in life.

When stressors such as domestic violence, child maltreatment or extreme poverty activate the stress response system frequently or over an extended period, physiological responses that usually deal with short-term stress remain activated or become permanently calibrated to activate more easily and do not turn off as readily as they should. They then can overwhelm the biological system (called allostatic overload) and impair the development of neural connections (figure 2.2).[19] Abundant empirical evidence shows that this process, apart from causing

(chronic) mental disorders, can increase the possibility of obesity, cancer, diabetes, cardiovascular disease, substance abuse, autoimmune disease, impaired cognition and interpersonal and self-directed violence.[20] And even without mental disorders, emotions and cognition can be impaired with a similar effect on some parts of the body, since processes in the brain are linked with those in the microbiome and the gut.[21]

These interactions shape the possibilities for learning, earning good income and leading a long and healthy life. They can thus constrain the conversion function and the ability to turn resources into capabilities and may shape choices with potentially long-lasting effects throughout the lifecycle. Basic trust established during infancy[22] and supportive relationships with caregivers and other adults in the community can buffer some of these effects[23] and build resilience. Role models are especially important, as is perceived self-efficacy—both shape children's aspirations and beliefs in how much they can achieve.[24] But when caregivers and other adults in the social network themselves face adversity or permanent stressors, these support structures may be weak or even counterproductive. Severe maternal distress also seems to alter DNA.[25] Mothers' exposure to adversity can increase defensive behaviour among offspring, which might be biologically useful in malign environments but can also lead to pathologies, even among children raised in safe environments after the adversity subsides.[26]

Such children are not necessarily doomed for life. Multiple biological, psychological, social and ecological systems interact to build resilience, which helps them absorb some distress throughout the lifecycle.

The interplay of individual, social and community factors can produce secure attachments, cognitive reappraisals, family cohesion, social structures and support networks.[27] Exposure to nature can also make a difference. People, particularly children,[28] who are frequently exposed to nature or spend much time outdoors tend to be more resilient to adversity and mental distress than those who do not.[29]

In adulthood

For adults severe mental distress can impair capabilities in a similar way—but at a time when the development of the brain and other organs is already

Figure 2.2 Connecting mental and physical health

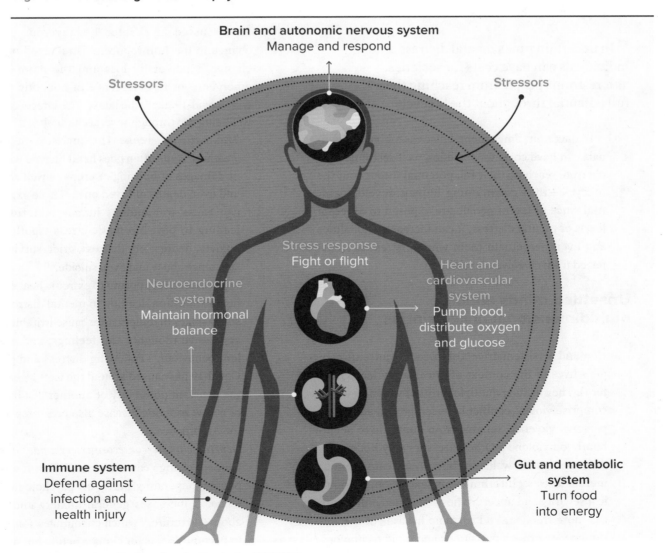

Source: National Scientific Council on the Developing Child 2020.

advanced or concluded. Still, adults who suffer from mental distress over an extended period have impaired conversion factors, resulting in constrained capability sets (or freedoms to achieve). That includes the ability to continue learning, to work and earn income, to lead a long and healthy life, to have attachments to things and people, to form perceptions of good and bad, to plan one's own life, to affiliate with others, to care about other species and to enjoy recreational activities[30]—even if external conditions are favourable. Some external conditions, such as access to information or health services, can also help build psychological resilience among adults, which can absorb some of the stress and provide room to deal with future adversity.[31] Mental health at older ages partly reflects individual adversities and resilience, but some other mental disorders common among older people have other causes.[32]

" In uncertain times mental distress among individuals can have costs for societies, as it restrains people from reaching their full potential throughout the lifecycle

In uncertain times mental distress among individuals can have costs for societies, as it restrains people from reaching their full potential throughout the lifecycle—thus constraining human development. And since different people are exposed to different levels of mental distress, it can increase inequalities and even perpetuate them when distress is transferred from caregivers to children.

Unsettled minds amid multidimensional uncertainties

New and persistent drivers of insecurity unsettle people's lives in the context of uncertainty (see chapter 1). They include multiple forms of violence, which comprise violent conflict between groups and interpersonal violence, ranging from domestic to neighbourhood violence. Other stressors may not always threaten physical wellbeing but can still cause serious mental distress: discrimination, exclusion, economic insecurity and uncertainties associated either with the more frequent and extreme hazards of the Anthropocene or with transitions and rapid technological change, as with digitalization.

The Anthropocene context is a driver of uncertainty without precedent in human history. It is manifest not only in climate change but also in biodiversity loss and the depletion and contamination of natural resources.[33] Efforts to ease planetary pressures are also a source of uncertainty, driving real or perceived threats associated with the transitions in economic and social systems in a context of rapid digital transformation. Precarious jobs, digital inequality, cyberattacks, data fraud and concentrated digital power can all cause serious mental distress. This section discusses evidence showing how these manifestations of uncertainty affect mental wellbeing and can also drive inequalities in human development.

Minds pressured in the Anthropocene

As discussed in chapter 1, dangerous planetary change in the Anthropocene is reflected in climate change, biodiversity loss and the more frequent emergence or re-emergence of zoonotic diseases, with Covid-19 likely the latest. The effects on mental wellbeing run through several channels:

- *Traumatizing events.* The increase in extreme weather events often goes hand in hand with losses or damages of housing or crops as well as injuries and even deaths of loved ones. These experiences can cause tremendous human suffering, often leading to post-traumatic stress (spotlight 2.2), anxiety, depression, distress, grief, survivor guilt, substance abuse and even suicide.[34]
- *Physical illness.* Exposure to extreme heat can cause heat exhaustion, leading to mental distress.[35] And sharp spikes in temperature cause irritability, more aggressive thoughts and feelings, and even violent behaviour.[36] Following distress and grief that Covid-19 has caused around the world (see below), the constant possibility of another deadly variant or a new zoonotic disease also pressures minds in the Anthropocene.
- *General climate- or eco-anxiety and solastalgia.* Climate change can have two different effects on people, depending partly on psychological resilience. It increases general anxiety and worries about the future,[37] which encourages some people to become agents for climate action but may leave others feeling anxious and incapable of changing

anything.[38] Young people claim that governments around the world have dismissed or neglected their requests for urgent action.[39] Indigenous peoples from around the world, among the most affected by climate change, have suffered mental distress over seasonal changes and acute weather events.[40]

- *Food insecurity.* With increasing extreme weather events disrupting food production and access, food insecurity is on the rise again after decades of decline.[41] In addition to being a threat to physical health, it is also a serious mental stressor.[42] It has been associated with psychological distress in both low and high human development countries.[43] In several African countries women and older people are especially affected. The most effective interventions target livelihoods as opposed to income only.[44]

- *Biodiversity loss.* Biodiversity loss can drive mental distress, especially among indigenous and marginalized communities, leading to longer-term adverse psychological and behavioural impacts, such as increased family stress, amplification of previous trauma, greater likelihood of substance abuse and higher prevalence of suicide ideation.[45] While causal mechanisms are yet to be fully understood, some reasons can include that biodiversity loss causes disruptions to physical health through altered food systems or leads to a different sense of place that can undermine cultural practices and knowledge systems. Moreover, it can impair self-determination by reducing the sufficiency of locally available resources, and it can result in a loss of social capital as community members rely increasingly on outside sources of aid and income rather than on one another.[46]

The adverse consequences of climate change are already affecting people who more directly depend on agriculture and natural resources for their livelihoods, including those in communities in rural, coastal, mountainous or forest areas, many of them indigenous.[47] Since many of these people live in low-income countries and are already disadvantaged, mental distress and its effects on the conversion factors can further increase inequalities in freedoms to achieve.

The depletion of natural resources and land-use changes through deforestation and for agricultural use are putting pressures on biodiversity and threatening the integrity of ecosystem functions, with several unknown threats potentially to come, including more frequent zoonotic diseases.[48] As discussed in chapter 1, the Covid-19 pandemic may be the latest but surely will not be the last, with implications that include multiple lockdowns all over the world that may cause mental distress in the future as they did during Covid-19.[49]

" Biodiversity loss can drive mental distress, especially among indigenous and marginalized communities, leading to longer-term adverse psychological and behavioural impacts

During the first year of the Covid-19 pandemic, the global prevalence of depression and anxiety increased by more than 25 percent.[50] The increase was greater among women than men, most likely because women were more affected by the socioeconomic consequences of lockdowns.[51] In a global survey 77 percent of respondents reported moderate to severe stress and poor sleep, and 59 percent suffered from anxiety and 35 percent from depression (only 18 percent had previously been diagnosed with a mental disorder).[52] Young people suffered—most likely because of missed opportunities during multiple lockdowns.[53] People with low incomes, struggling to afford basic needs such as rent and food, suffered disproportionally in several countries.[54]

Women, who took on most of the additional domestic and care work that emerged during school closures and lockdowns,[55] faced more mental distress than before the Covid-19 pandemic.[56] A cross-country survey found that 27 percent of women struggled with mental distress, compared with 10 percent of men. Women cited their escalating unpaid care burden as a critical stressor, alongside concerns about food, healthcare and livelihoods. Given the links among employment, income, food security and mental health, it is noteworthy that 55 percent of women reported income loss as the top impact of the pandemic (compared with 34 percent of men) and that 41 percent of women (versus 30 percent of men) reported not having enough food.[57] Ethnic minorities of both sexes were severely affected in the United Kingdom, with the largest increase in mental distress among men with a background from Bangladesh, India or Pakistan (figure 2.3).[58]

Figure 2.3 In the United Kingdom mental distress is most prevalent among female minority groups, but mental distress among male minority groups increased most during the Covid-19 pandemic

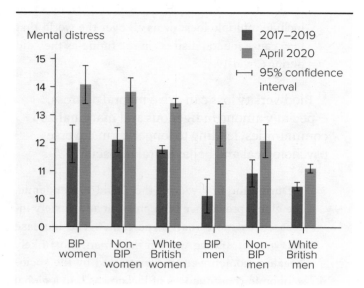

BIP refers to people with a background from Bangladesh, India or Pakistan.
Note: Changes in mental distress were measured by the 12-item General Health Questionnaire. Higher scores (on a scale of 0 to 36) mean more mental distress.
Source: Proto and Quintana-Domeque 2021.

More than two years into the Covid-19 pandemic, worries about the virus have somewhat dissipated in parts of the world. But anxiety about new variants—and the possibility of mandatory quarantines, lockdowns and cancellations—remains around the globe. The abrupt halt and related uncertainty that the pandemic inflicted on many people's lives will likely linger for some time.

Economic insecurity drives mental distress

Economic insecurity—expressed in periods of low income, unemployment, poor working conditions, poverty, housing instability and financial shocks—can cause mental distress. Even the perception that such outcomes could materialize may give people reason to worry, particularly in contexts of economic precariousness or dislocations. And even when these dislocations are transitory or small relative to the scale of an economy, they can loom as scary threats in particular regions or sectors.[59]

The causal relation also works in reverse: people with impaired mental (and physical) health have fewer employment opportunities and can face income penalties for their conditions.[60] Especially in economic contexts where brain-based skills such as emotional intelligence, creativity, cognitive flexibility, self-control or system thinking matter more than manual skills,[61] mental wellbeing is increasingly important to thrive in the professional world, while the lack of it can further exacerbate disadvantages. In other contexts where people work in agriculture, they are being increasingly exposed to the stresses of extreme weather events that jeopardize their source of income and food security—and with it both physical and mental wellbeing.

The association of economic insecurity with mental distress starts very early in life, indeed in the mother's womb. Some foetuses are exposed to more stress and worry related to poverty, malnutrition, violence or environmental irritants associated with poverty (such as pollution or extreme temperatures) than others.[62] The intergenerational effect continues during childhood when parents' mental distress impairs children's wellbeing, with effects into adulthood.[63] If the situation continues throughout childhood, this can lead to long-term adaptive behaviour and pathologies that are hard to break later in life.[64] For instance, children who grow up with food insecurity often continue binge eating even after hardship is overcome.[65] These effects can be buffered by social institutions or informal aid in the community, such as cash transfers to mothers, which have been shown to improve infant brain activity and subsequent cognitive skills and mental wellbeing.[66]

Even less severe conditions of low socioeconomic status and related social structures can affect children's brain and body development, cognitive functioning and mental and physical health. For example, children in families who live in crowded, chaotic or noisy conditions or unsafe neighbourhoods and who lack organization and daily routines are usually exposed to higher mental distress.[67] And the belief in how much one is capable of achieving—which is usually lower in low socioeconomic status families—can diminish children's aspirations and achievements.[68] These factors can accumulate,[69] which is in line with models of cumulative advantage and disadvantage that look at socioeconomic disparities in general and health disparities in particular.[70] The 2019 Human Development Report analysed in detail how this mechanism acts in intergenerational ways, perpetuating multidimensional inequalities in human development.[71]

During adulthood perceived and actual economic insecurity as well as anticipated future downside risks are detrimental for mental wellbeing at all incomes, especially for men.[72] Income shocks have been shown to increase suicides in some contexts, an effect that can be mitigated by cash transfers.[73] One of the most serious economic threats to mental wellbeing stems from repeated financial shocks, such as income loss, especially for poor people and for men.[74] Shocks already experienced, such as unemployment, worsen expectations for the future and reduce life satisfaction.[75] Continued employment is not only important to avoid financial stress; it also has positive psychosocial effects, such as stimulating the feeling of belonging to a community and contributing productively to society.[76]

Persistent low incomes are also associated with poorer mental health and wellbeing, especially when generating a sense of scarcity or insufficiency compared with peers in the community.[77] People at the lower end of the income spectrum suffer from mental distress 1.5–3 times as often as people at the higher end[78] and are more likely to experience violent crime and traumatic events,[79] which can make some people want to leave their place of origin (box 2.1). However, even people with higher incomes can experience resentment and frustrations due to financial concerns, especially when aspirations are very high and the social environment is such that people perceive high inequality compared with their peers.[80]

Status incongruence is an important concept here. For example, having a high level of education in a manual occupation or low-skilled nonmanual occupation has been shown to cause emotional discomfort, such as feelings of shame and anxiety,[81] pessimistic outlooks and overall poor mental wellbeing. With rising education levels and labour markets that are unable to absorb all qualified labour, cases of status incongruence have increased and are expected to become even more prevalent.[82] Positive expectations and belief in the ability to achieve one's goals can partially compensate for negative effects on mental wellbeing.[83] Finally, at older ages a higher debt burden

Box 2.1 Multidimensional uncertainties may make some people subject to human trafficking—another source of severe mental distress

Multidimensional uncertainties make some people want to look for a better future elsewhere. But bureaucratic obstacles often stand in the way of free migration, so that some people fall victim to human trafficking. Networks of organized crime consisting of traffickers typically make false promises of education or job opportunities using fraudulent employment agencies to trick victims before applying violence and coercion.[1] The experience of being trafficked is often traumatic, with restriction of movement and violence, and fear of being discovered, detained and deported.[2] An Ethiopia-based study found that among human trafficked returnees the prevalence of depression was about 58 percent, that of anxiety 52 percent and that of post-traumatic stress disorder (PTSD) 35 percent. Restricted movement was associated with anxiety, depression and PTSD, whereas experiencing violence during trafficking was linked to anxiety and PTSD. Detention contributed to all three disorders.[3]

A study of trafficked women and girls from Monterrey and Reynosa (Mexico) found that all of the study's participants were experiencing feelings of tension, stress, anxiety, worry and anger and that most of them were crying more than usual (86 percent), lacking appetite (86 percent) and having suicidal thoughts (80 percent).[4] Among human trafficking survivors in the Greater Mekong subregion, men, women and children who had experienced violence during trafficking faced a higher prevalence of anxiety, depression and PTSD than those who did not.[5] In addition to experiencing mental distress, many victims of human trafficking do not find what they had expected at their destination but face new challenges, such as adaptation to a new environment and sometimes even dependence and human rights violations from their traffickers.

From a human development perspective human trafficking takes away people's agency and freedoms as well as the possibility for them to make their own choices and determine their futures. Managing safe migration is crucial to tackling human trafficking and should be taken up through cooperation and partnership among countries.

Notes
1. UNODC 2021. 2. Acharya and Sanchez 2018; Gezie and others 2018; Iglesias-Rios and others 2018; Mumey and others 2020; Ottisova and others 2018. 3. Gezie and others 2018. 4. Acharya and Sanchez 2018. 5. Iglesias-Rios and others 2018.

can cause social and emotional loneliness, independent of social participation, social network size, and previous states of anxiety or depression.[84] Moreover, there is a growing understanding of the long-term impacts of income downturns.[85] When an economic downturn coincides with a health shock, as with Covid-19, the implications can be magnified and perpetuated across generations.[86] The channel for much of the lasting scarring to take hold relates primarily to behavioural and psychological impacts that have implications throughout life, even after the economy bounces back.[87]

Causality also runs the other way. Mental distress lowers people's ability to work productively and distorts the way people think, with consequences for the way they search for work, interact with people and carry out their work.[88] Alleviating financial worries improves workers' productivity, making them more attentive, faster and less prone to mistakes,[89] as poverty appears to burden cognitive capacity (but see the discussion in chapter 3 suggesting that the burden may be contingent on social context).[90] It can also modify the content of cognition, adding a monetary perspective to many dimensions of life, which is difficult to suppress and may shape decisionmaking and social relationships.[91] Conversely, poverty alleviation can improve socialization and other noncognitive skills, such as agreeableness and conscientiousness, while diminishing hostility and aggression.[92]

Severe mental distress can undermine physical health, which can lead to an inability to carry out certain work—and increase health spending where there are gaps in health insurance or public provision of health services.[93] Furthermore, mental distress can result in job loss or income decline, not least because it affects preferences, beliefs, cognitive functioning and ultimately economic decisionmaking.[94] People with depression earn about 34 percent less than the average person, people with bipolar disorder about 38 percent less and people with schizophrenia about 74 percent less. People with these conditions also face a much higher risk of no income and disability.[95] And the lack of income can cause even more mental distress. The circular relation has been found to nearly double the negative impact of financial shocks, explaining low financial resilience in a long-term mental distress–poverty trap.[96]

The circular and intergenerational relation between economic insecurity and mental distress can perpetuate economic inequality across generations (figure 2.4).

Figure 2.4 **The circular and intergenerational relation between economic insecurity and mental distress can perpetuate economic inequality across generations**

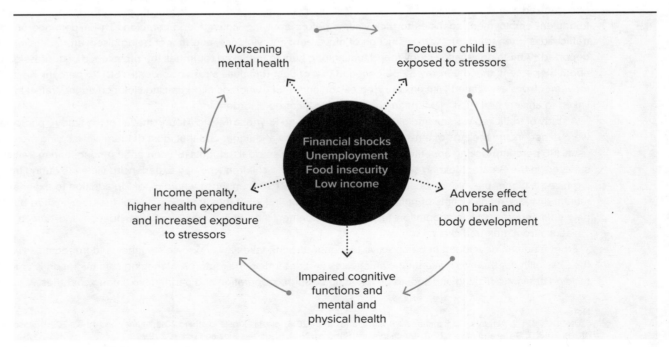

Source: Human Development Report Office.

Digital technologies can generally improve life, as they facilitate many processes, increase efficiency and connect people from different parts of the world. They can even accelerate the achievement of the Sustainable Development Goals (SDGs).[97] A recent study covering more than 200 countries found that mobile phone access was associated with higher gender equality through multiple channels (lower maternal mortality, better information about sexual and reproductive health services, higher empowerment to make independent decisions, with larger gains among the least developed countries and among the most disadvantaged groups).[98] In this sense digitalization can contribute to empowerment, essential for mental wellbeing.

But the benefits of these new technologies also come with challenges. Digitalization poses several social and economic threats, including, but not limited to, lower labour demand for some tasks,[99] digital inequality and exclusion,[100] cybercrime and the related theft of financial resources and personal information,[101] transfer of decisionmaking powers to machines, digital power concentration,[102] digital addictions[103] and violence,[104] and reduced personal life security.[105] One of the most serious challenges of digitalization is digital inequality.[106] Poor people and those with existing mental disorders have a higher probability of being digitally excluded, which potentially increases inequalities in other areas.[107]

Some of these challenges can cause mental distress, despite the fact that some of the benefits of digital technologies foster mental wellbeing (figure 2.5). For instance, cyberharassment and cyberstalking have been associated with anxiety, panic attacks, suicidal ideation[108] and depression.[109] Mobile devices, social networks and cloud computing services can be used to stalk people and conduct surveillance.[110] Digital platforms such as Facebook, Instagram and Twitter can be used in a similar way as well as for social comparison, negative interactions, cyberbullying, and sharing violent content and violent or discriminative language.[111] This has been associated with mental distress and suicidal behaviour, with the highest prevalence among girls.[112] Older people may feel excluded from socialization when the younger

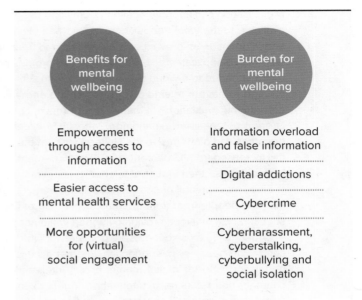

Figure 2.5 Digitalization is a double-edged sword for mental wellbeing

Source: Human Development Report Office.

generation spends time on social media or with other technologies.

Digital exclusion can be found among healthcare services. While digital healthcare services can provide substantial benefits for people with fast internet connections and digital skills—and thus have potential to widen access to health services among some remote populations (box 2.2)—people without these advantages are less likely to benefit from services.[113]

While access to information can be empowering, abundant and sometimes false information (which is easy to distribute through social media) can also be a source of anxiety. Not only can people feel anxious because of too much and sometimes contradictory information, but they may also stress about information that is not even true. During the early stages of the Covid-19 pandemic, and often continuing beyond, false information about the virus, its cures and vaccines went viral on communication platforms such as Facebook and Twitter, causing anxiety in many people.[114] The abundance of information seems to constitute a stressor (information overload), making it more likely that people share false information.[115]

Another way digitalization can cause mental distress is obsessive use of digital technologies, digital platforms and digital devices.[116] Obsessive smartphone use can result in chronic sleep

Box 2.2 Potential of telehealth for increasing access to mental healthcare

Digitalization can improve health systems and the provision of healthcare services[1] if digital technologies are readily available to the whole population. Mobile and electronic interventions allow easy access to mental health services and information on prevention, counselling and treatment.[2] Telehealth, which involves telephone or video via various web-based applications,[3] has gained global prominence over the years. By 2016 more than 50 percent of countries that responded to a World Health Organization survey reported having a national telehealth policy, about 70 percent claimed to have a teleradiology programme and approximately 25 percent said they had conducted a telehealth programme evaluation.[4] In many parts of Africa, particularly in rural areas populated mostly by young people, there is great potential for expanding telehealth services.[5] The Covid-19 pandemic massively increased telehealth programmes and platforms. In the United Kingdom the proportion of doctor's appointments over the phone or by video call increased from 13 percent in 2019 to 48 percent by mid-2020.[6] In some East Asia and Pacific countries[7] and in the United States,[8] the number of telehealth users more than doubled in the first month of the pandemic.

Since most mental health services do not require physical examinations, digital services are especially promising, allowing people from remote areas to get help online without traveling long distances. Such services can be more time and cost efficient, providing support while people wait for face-to-face interventions.[9]

Undermining these benefits are poor network infrastructure, inadequate funding to support telehealth programmes, competing health system priorities, internet access inequalities and a lack of digital skills among all or parts of the population.[10] So for digital mental health interventions to improve health outcomes without increasing inequality, countries need to increase telehealth budgets, expand internet access in deprived communities and empower people from these communities through education and training on how to use digital devices and platforms.

Notes
1. Ricciardi and others 2019. 2. Apolinário-Hagen 2017. 3. Aref-Adib and Hassiotis 2021. 4. WHO 2016. 5. Holst and others 2020. 6. ITU 2021. 7. Data are for Australia, China, Indonesia and Singapore. Kapur and Boulton 2021. 8. Koonin and others 2020. 9. Mental Health Foundation 2021. 10. Kearns and Whitley 2019; Skinner, Biscope and Poland 2003; WHO 2016.

deprivation and undermines cognitive control and socioemotional functioning.[117] Digital technology can also promote gambling—an activity associated with mental disorders.[118] Young people in particular appear to engage in digital gambling on social platforms, smartphones and specialized websites.[119] The World Health Organization has recognized gaming disorder as a mental health issue, given its adverse health impacts and increasing prevalence.[120]

Cybercrime, such as fraud, theft, scams and other forms of online financial exploitation, can cause excessive worrying and anxiety and has been linked to depression among older adults.[121] Moreover, internet use reduces offline interaction, political participation and civic cultural engagement,[122] increasing the likelihood of social isolation.[123] By contrast, digital technology can also create social engagement opportunities that help eliminate loneliness and social isolation[124] and improve wellbeing[125]—for example, by connecting to people with similar interests or problems over long distances (self-help forums). By doing so, digital technology can also alleviate mental distress.[126]

Violence scares, unsettles and scars lives

Given the direct threat to physical integrity, most forms of violence cause mental distress, often leading to mental disorders such as post-traumatic stress disorder (PTSD), anxiety and depression, and each form of violence comes with additional challenges depending on context and setting. Interpersonal violence includes domestic and community violence, such as intimate partner violence, child or elder abuse and assaults by strangers. Collective violence occurs between larger groups, such as organized crime and armed conflicts.[127]

Interpersonal violence can increase inequalities in opportunity

Psychologically, domestic violence is extremely toxic, as the home is a place that should provide protection and safety, constituting a location to rest and relax away from other environmental stressors. When several forms of domestic violence happen simultaneously, they can create a vicious cycle of dependence and abuse. For instance, the perpetrator controls the household's financial resources, making the victim financially dependent,[128] while invoking fear and undermining self-worth and self-esteem through verbal abuse, constant criticism and social isolation, which can lead to a withdrawal from the labour force, housing stress and ultimately a loss of self-identity.[129] The key here is dominance over the partner through emotional, economic or psychological abuse,[130] which then substantially limits the possibilities to escape physical violence as well. This mechanism is reflected in data showing that in countries with lower female labour force participation, more women experience intimate partner violence (figure 2.6). While men can certainly also be affected, the majority of intimate partner violence survivors are women.[131]

Bisexual and gay men report worse psychological consequences following intimate partner violence than straight men.[132] This is possibly due to the combined burden of mental stressors, including discrimination, and social pressures of internalized masculinity norms suggesting that men should be more resistant to oppression and violence.[133] Due to gender stereotypes in some criminal justice systems, there also appears to be hesitance to report assaults out of fear of being misjudged as the perpetrator. In various country contexts men who had filed police reports recounted that authorities had responded to their plea for help with suspicion, ridicule or even arrest.[134]

When older people live in a household with family members, which is common in some cultural contexts, domestic violence can also be directed towards them, affecting their physical and mental health.[135] This happens more frequently among older people with physical disabilities (49 percent) and with psychological disabilities (7 percent). Many, but not all, affected older people are female (63 percent).[136]

Figure 2.6 Intimate partner violence increases with economic dependence

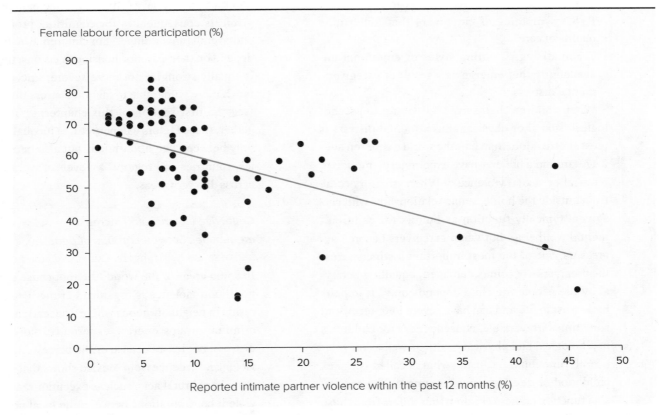

Note: Reported intimate partner violence within the past 12 months includes women and girls over age 15 who have experienced physical and/or sexual partner violence. Female labour force participation refers to the percentage of women ages 15–64 participating in the labour force for the most recent data year available. Only countries with data on female labour force participation for 2019 or later are included to allow for direct comparisons with the most recent United Nations Population Fund dataset on intimate partner violence. Similarly, only countries with data on female labour force participation for women ages 15–64 are included to control for potential effects of age. The statistically significant correlation coefficient is −0.53019.
Source: Human Development Report Office calculations using data from ILO (2021a) and UNFPA (2021).

The consequences of domestic violence for mental wellbeing range from milder symptoms such as elevated psychological stress to full-fledged clinical presentations of mental disorders such as PTSD, phobias, substance abuse, depression and anxiety.[137] Survivors of physical domestic violence are also prone to traumatic brain injury, with devastating consequences for their ability to function in society, including to work and socialize.[138] All of this can eventually result in a loss of agency, when individuals no longer feel able to shape and change their circumstances, lose hope altogether and become vulnerable to revictimization.[139]

" More than half the world's children ages 2–17—around a billion—have experienced emotional, physical or sexual violence, with devastating consequences for their mental wellbeing

Even when physical attacks are not targeted towards them, children are affected through three channels:

- Witnessing attacks on one of their caregivers.
- PTSD symptoms of caregivers that undermine quality of care.
- Traumatizing parenting styles or emotional unavailability that emerge as a result of caregivers' mental distress.[140]

When children themselves fall victim to psychological, sexual or physical abuse, mental distress is most severe. More than half the world's children ages 2–17—around a billion—have experienced emotional, physical or sexual violence.[141] When stressors come from outside the home, stable relationships with caregivers typically function as buffers for children's mental wellbeing. But when caregivers become aggressors, one of the most important instincts—trust in caregivers—becomes damaged, equalling betrayal by the people the child depends on.[142] It impairs basic trust in life and can have severe long-term, and sometimes irreversible, consequences for children's psychological and physical health as well as for their overall functioning, causing what is called complex childhood or developmental trauma.[143] The conversion function of these children thus differs from those of children who grew up in a nonviolent household, unless a very favourable combination of resilient building factors comes together and absorbs part of the toxic stress the child has suffered.[144] Culturally

aligned interventions are crucial here, as discussions of domestic violence are still taboo in many societies, hindering social workers from intervening and making mental health treatments available for children.

Community violence ranges from isolated acts of assault by strangers or acquaintances, such as bullying, armed robbery and sexual abuse, to workplace and institutional violence.[145] Neighbourhoods are not simply the physical locations in which we reside; they are also places with intricate socioeconomic-spatial connections (box 2.3).[146] While neighbourhood characteristics—including education and healthcare facilities, transport connectivity and crime levels as well as perceived safety and social cohesion—may affect outcomes such as health, education and income,[147] these same outcomes in turn determine which neighbourhoods are accessible to people.[148] This effect constitutes an obstacle to intra- and intergenerational mobility, as it can trap people in cycles of low income, poor health and education, and surroundings prone to amplifying these disadvantages.[149] Mental distress is an additional risk factor in this trap, given its consequences for cognition, productivity and overall functioning.[150] For children, who typically depend on their parents' housing decisions, the effect is equally strong, if not more severe, since they are much more vulnerable to mental distress than adults (see the first section of this chapter).[151] Taken together, these factors can perpetuate inequalities, not only between neighbourhoods but also between cities, countries and regions, as levels of violence vary across different areas.

Collective violence can increase inequalities between groups of people

In some areas of the world, the root cause of neighbourhood violence is organized crime. People who reside in neighbourhoods where drug cartels or other criminal groups operate experience more mental distress, not least because of the perceived threat of violence. Evidence from Mexico shows that information about brutal acts, such as executions, and about violent confrontations between the local police and criminal groups has caused substantial mental distress for community members. On some occasions this information may be diffused purposely to instil fear in the community.[152] Mental distress caused

Box 2.3 Neighbourhood violence is bad, but uncertainty around it can make it even worse

Direct exposure to violence and the possibility of experiencing violence as a resident of a neighbourhood that is perceived as unsafe are significant risk factors for mental distress. Across Buenos Aires, Lima, Medellín, Mexico City and São Paulo exposure to interpersonal violence—for example, being beaten up, witnessing death or someone getting injured, being mugged or threatened with a weapon, and sexual violence—and the experience of living in neighbourhoods with a higher prevalence of violent crime (after individual violence exposure is accounted for) are associated with higher odds of anxiety and mood disorders.[1]

In Baltimore, Maryland, survey respondents living in violent crime hotspots report higher rates of depression (61 percent higher) and post-traumatic stress disorder (85 percent higher) than residents in coldspots.[2] Depression can be caused by indirect exposure or other factors related to living in violent neighbourhoods. In some cases the perceived level of violence in the neighbourhood and the uncertainty around being exposed to it can be at least as troubling.

Adolescents in California who perceive their neighbourhood as unsafe are twice as likely to experience serious mental distress as their peers who perceive their neighbourhood as safe. They are also more likely to suffer from distress than adolescents who live in neighbourhoods that are considered violent based on objective measures (box figure 1).[3]

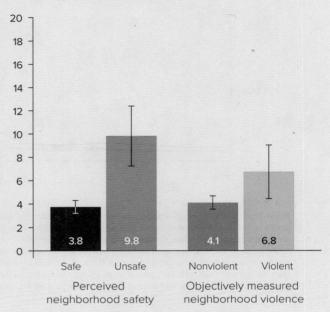

Box figure 1 Perceived risk can induce more stress than actual risk

Share of adolescents in California with serious psychological distress (%)

Note: Whiskers indicate the 95 percent confidence interval.
Source: Goldman-Mellor and others 2016.

Mental distress can also be exacerbated by an interplay of other factors. Several of these factors in a population-based survey of adults living in a group of *favelas* (slums) in Rio de Janeiro—specifically being younger, female or unemployed; having a lower income; and having experienced and fearing neighbourhood violence—were separately and significantly associated with poorer mental health outcomes. These factors, together with past experiences of violence and the fear of violence, were also significantly associated with higher levels of mental distress.[4]

Notes
1. Benjet and others 2019. 2. Weisburd and others 2018. 3. Goldman-Mellor and others 2016. 4. Cruz and others 2021.

---

by organized crime is not limited to victims and the community. Members of criminal groups also suffer from mental distress because of chronic exposure to violence, potentially increasing cycles of violence, as some types of mental distress can result in aggressive behaviour.[153]

Violence during protests, riots and clashes with the police can cause emotional imbalances, fears, worries and even psychological trauma. Over the past decade protests, sometimes accompanied by related political violence, increased substantially, until the

Covid-19 pandemic hit (figure 2.7).[154] When political climates change and authorities do not fully respect the right to freedom of expression, people may sense repression and start feeling impotent or powerless.

Sometimes, frustration throughout the population can also turn into clashes between protesters and police, causing mental distress. A protester from India claims, "[I] freeze up, feel[ing] numb and uncertain anytime [I] see a policeman, or someone wielding a lathi, or when streetlights go off. ... I see people break down in gatherings... friends

Figure 2.7 Increases in political violence have meant more uncertainty for many people

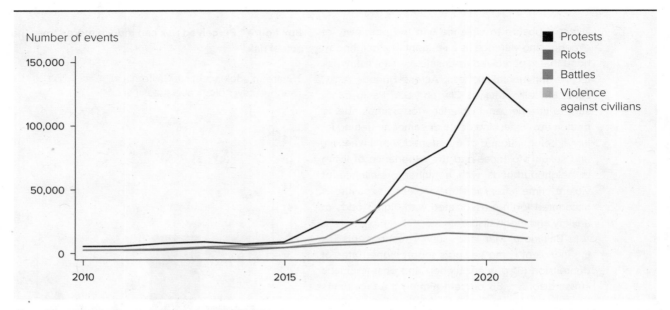

Note: *Protest* is defined as a public demonstration in which the participants do not engage in violence, though violence may be used against them. *Battle* is defined as a violent interaction between two politically organized armed groups at a particular time and location. Battles can occur between armed and organized state, nonstate and external groups and in any combination therein. *Riot* is defined as a violent event where demonstrators or mobs engage in disruptive acts, including but not limited to rock throwing, property destruction and the like. *Violence against civilians* is defined as violent events where an organized armed group deliberately inflicts violence upon unarmed noncombatants. The perpetrators of such acts include state forces and their affiliates, rebels, militias, and external or other forces (ACLED 2019).
Source: Human Development Report Office calculations using data from ACLED (2021).

getting full-blown panic attacks."[155] The effect can be as severe as the ones caused by armed conflict, in which WHO estimates the PTSD rate to be a little over 21 percent.[156] A study from Hong Kong Special Administrative Region, China, found a combined prevalence of depression and PTSD of 21.8 percent among the adult population during the 2019–2020 social unrest. There was also a strong association between heavy politics-related social media use and mental distress, attributable to emotion contagion.[157] Following violence in Syrian Arab Republic, civilians expressed panic attacks, especially towards the possibility of "disappearing" while being transferred in detainment.[158] The Syrian conflict also shows how collective violence, such as riots, battles or violence against civilians can escalate into armed conflicts and civil wars.[159]

When that happens, severe and long-lasting mental distress can be the consequence for large parts of the population, given the nature of traumatic experiences related to war settings. From the early 2000s until the outbreak of the war in Ukraine, there have been few interstate conflicts, but the past decade has witnessed a surge in battle-related deaths due to civil conflicts, some subject to foreign state interventions.[160] In postwar settings about one in five people suffer from mental health conditions.[161] PTSD is very common among war survivors, affecting about 354 million adult war survivors,[162] not least because of the direct threat to experiencing violence and the constant possibility of loss or injury of loved ones.[163] Grief and sadness have been related to addictive behaviour, particularly to increased substance abuse.[164] This may put an additional burden on public health systems, considering the long-term consequences of substance abuse for mental and physical health.

Globally comparative data on the prevalence of PTSD remains a challenge, but more specific examples from war torn countries can provide deeper insights into the number of affected people and into the mechanisms and causalities behind them. Due to recurrent wars and armed conflicts in Iraq, for example, the prevalence of PTSD among young people ages 17–19 is 25 percent,[165] and more than two-thirds of adult men suffer from anxiety and emotional instability.[166] In Nigeria the Boko Haram insurgency has contributed to major mental distress, including severe emotional disorders, psychological distress, psychotic disorders, PTSD and depression.[167] The militia sexually assaults women and girls,[168] leading to social isolation, depression and suicidal ideation.[169] Military personnel stationed in Nigerian armed conflict zones also have a high probability of suffering from PTSD and avoidance symptoms.[170] But survivors are often not diagnosed with PTSD and do not identify their condition as such. There are other, culturally aligned explanations for what people feel and go through, and following those, people may seek alternative approaches to integrative health and mental wellbeing.[171]

About 450 million children—or one in six—currently live in conflict zones, with devastating consequences for their mental health,[172] including PTSD.[173] The PTSD prevalence rate was 44 percent among child survivors of the Rwandan genocide and 87 percent among children exposed to the bombings in Gaza.[174] In Nigeria Boko Haram has recruited young children to join its militia, causing severe mental distress associated with warfare.[175] Some of these effects can be long-lasting if not adequately treated: children who survived the Viet Nam war show increased symptoms of depression in adulthood.[176]

Apart from the threat to physical integrity, armed conflicts can expose people to displacement, destroy critical infrastructure, disrupt supply chains, hinder investment and thus undermine economic growth and development, possibly resulting in massive unemployment—all adding to mental distress of large parts of the population.[177] When armed conflict forces people to leave their homes, this complicates the overall situation even further. As of mid-2022 at least 100 million people are estimated to have been forcibly displaced from their homes worldwide due to conflict, with major displacements in Afghanistan, Burkina Faso, Democratic Republic of the Congo, Ethiopia, Myanmar, Nigeria and Ukraine.[178]

The war in Ukraine has caused a major increase in displaced people, with more than 7 million internally displaced persons and more than 5.6 million refugees.[179] Children, who account for about half of the displaced, become exposed to all sorts of mental distress.[180] Globally, there are now nearly 37 million displaced children—the highest number ever recorded.[181] When displaced, people may lose their material possessions, community affiliations and social support networks. And if they flee to another country, possibly even their civic duties, access to social services, professions, occupational identity and much else—all risk factors for mental distress that affect people's capabilities sets.[182] In such an environment where people suffer from impaired health, limited education opportunities and unemployment, mental distress is more likely to set in but less likely to be treated because resources are desperately needed on all ends. Indeed, countries experiencing conflict present the widest gap between people who need mental healthcare services and people who have access to them.[183] Community-level approaches are promising for facilitating access to mental healthcare services in these settings (box 2.4).

" Some groups of people have been excluded, disrespected and discriminated against for centuries, with devastating effects on their mental wellbeing and human development at large

Because some groups of people are affected more by violence than others, and thus suffer more from mental distress than others, the alteration of their conversion factors limits their freedom to achieve and thus increases inequality of opportunity across neighbourhoods, districts and even countries, depending on the level of violence people are experiencing (and on access to mental healthcare services and other resources that can mitigate distress). Moreover, the exposure to violence can itself create vicious cycles of even more violence if left unattended.

Discrimination unsettles minds by attacking human dignity

Some groups of people—including women; certain ethnic groups; people of colour; people who identify as lesbian, gay, bisexual, transgender, queer, intersex or other sexual minority (LGBTQI+); and people with disabilities—have been excluded, disrespected and discriminated against for centuries, with devastating effects on their mental wellbeing and human development at large. At the institutional level discriminatory norms and laws of some countries still bias the criminal justice system and block access to high-quality education and health services, economic

Box 2.4 Tackling mental distress at the community level

The rationale behind community-based mental health services is that they tend to have greater acceptability among the population—and better accessibility and affordability than most other healthcare options. They typically enable family involvement, are less prone to stigma and discrimination, promote mental health awareness and have enhanced clinical effectiveness given the involvement of trusted local providers.[1] One example is the Mental Health Innovation Network's Basic Needs Mental Health and Development Model, which has reached more than 650,000 people and their family members in different low- and middle-income countries. It has increased access to treatment among service users by 84 percent, and users have reported a 75 percent reduction in symptoms—all while costing only $9.67 a month per person.[2] In some countries, including Rwanda, South Sudan and Mexico, tackling mental distress at the community level has become an important part of the public health strategy.

Rwanda

The 1994 genocide in Rwanda has had numerous long-lasting adverse effects on mental health among citizens, including high rates of depression and post-traumatic stress disorder (PTSD).[3] Like other countries, Rwanda has made efforts to address the population's mental distress. In seeking to ensure the availability of mental health services at the community level by 2024,[4] the government has used several strategies, such as establishing mental health facilities in all community units and health centres, enhancing the quality of mental healthcare by constructing a National Mental Health Care Center, and improving reporting and surveillance systems to manage and conduct patient follow-ups.[5] Over time the government has decentralized mental healthcare and maintained at least one psychologist and psychiatric nurse per hospital.[6] Such interventions help the people who suffer from mental disorders to heal, to establish strong social networks at the community level and to become emotionally more resilient.[7]

South Sudan

South Sudan's people also struggle with mental distress, such as depression, anxiety and PTSD caused by conflict, violence, economic hardship and poor access to healthcare, among others.[8] To help people suffering from mental distress, including those who have experienced armed conflict and violence, the International Committee of the Red Cross's mental health teams provide counselling services in South Sudanese health facilities such as primary healthcare centres, physical rehabilitation centres and surgical wards.[9] This approach is similar to the Rwandan one in that it tries to leverage local public health infrastructure and trusted networks to spread access to mental healthcare.

Mexico

Mexico's mental health policy involves increasing public mental health awareness, community care and outpatient services as well as keeping the need for hospitalization to a minimum, among others.[10] Specifically, to address mental disorders, Mexico uses the community mental healthcare model, which involves developing outpatient clinics, rehabilitation centres and sheltered homes,[11] to ensure access to mental health services even in remote areas.[12]

Notes
1. Kohrt and others 2018. **2.** MHIN 2022. **3.** Rwanda Ministry of Health 2018. **4.** Rwanda Ministry of Heatlh 2018. **5.** Rwanda Ministry of Health 2018. **6.** Smith and others 2017. **7.** Hynie and others 2015. **8.** ICRC 2020. **9.** ICRC 2020. **10.** Block and others 2020. **11.** Alvarado and others 2012. **12.** Block and others 2020.

opportunities and wealth accumulation, attacking human dignity and increasing inequalities.[184]

Since many measures of development capture outcomes at the aggregate level, horizontal inequalities often remain unrevealed, resulting in policies that fail to address structural discrimination. But people also suffer from discrimination in their daily lives, when attacked or excluded by peers, colleagues or neighbours or on the streets. Both types of discrimination can cause mental distress and interact with inequalities,

mutually reinforcing each other and creating intergenerational cycles of inequality and discrimination.

Structural discrimination reinforces inequalities

Structural discrimination and racism have been found to increase overall health disparities through several channels,[185] including mental distress, environmental adversities and unequal healthcare.[186] Discrimination can be seen as a latent form of violence, constituting a psychological stressor that has been empirically related to depression; anxiety; delinquent behaviour; alcohol, tobacco and drug use as coping mechanisms; metabolic disease; cardiovascular disease; low birth weight; and prematurity.[187] Structural or systemic discrimination can sometimes turn into actual violence, going hand in hand with human rights violations. The most extreme case is genocide, but other forms of human rights violations and disrespect of human dignity have left entire minority groups, such as the Rohingya or Yazidi populations, with serious mental health problems as well.[188] Exclusion and discrimination can impair certain groups' mental wellbeing, as with migrants who struggle in adapting to the host country, specifically with cultural congruity, identity and even bereavement.[189] Culturally aligned healing approaches are especially important here, because different people believe in different things, which may alter the effectiveness of some mental health interventions.

In the case of racism, the effect on mental wellbeing can be intergenerational: vicarious racism —that is racism experienced by parents and then transmitted to children—can affect children's mental, physical and socioemotional health (some examples include increased body mass index, depression, anxiety, substance use, delays in cognitive development and increased healthcare use for sick visits).[190] This effect runs mainly through children's increased threat perception, harsher parenting practices, more complicated parent–child relationships and racial socialization—that is the information children receive about race and racism.[191] Younger children are at higher risk of developing long-term defensive patterns when indirectly exposed to racism (see above about the effects of threat on long-term behavioural consequences). Children who are affected by discrimination and have insufficient psychological resilience or resources to build it may become even more disadvantaged with respect to their peers.

Interpersonal discrimination harms societies

Structural discrimination involving institutions, rules, and norms is not the only attack on people's dignity. Discrimination and exclusion among peers, colleagues or neighbours or on the streets may also leave psychological scars that last a lifetime if untreated.

Apart from race and ethnicity people are sometimes discriminated against due to their sexual orientation or gender identity. In some countries LGBTQI+ people have 4.5 percent stronger symptoms of depression and a 40 percent higher social interaction anxiety rate than their non-LGBTQI+ counterparts.[192] When minority statuses overlap—for example, when an LGBTQI+ person identifies as ethnic minority—the effects of discrimination may multiply, making the person more vulnerable than individuals with a single minority status.[193] LGBTQI+ young people appear to be especially vulnerable to discrimination—important, given their delicate stage of development and identity formation. Some national surveys on this minority group have found that:

- More than 75 percent of LGBTQI+ young people report having experienced discrimination based on their sexual orientation or gender identity.
- More than half of transgender and nonbinary young people have seriously considered suicide within the past year, 71 percent experienced symptoms of anxiety disorder and roughly 62 percent have had major depressive disorder.[194]
- Almost all survey participants (95 percent) report difficulty sleeping at night, and 70 percent had felt worthless or hopeless during the past week.
- Only 26 percent of participants feel safe at school.[195]

The two major mental disorders are also more common among LGBTQI+ young people, though there is no significant variance between different ethnic identities (figure 2.8).[196]

" Mental distress caused by exclusion, disrespect and discrimination is one more factor that can increase multidimensional inequalities within societies

Mental distress caused by exclusion, disrespect and discrimination is one more factor that can increase multidimensional inequalities within societies. Where discrimination does not directly increase health disparities, the mechanism runs through mental distress, which ultimately impairs physical health, hindering people from developing their full potential and living lives they have reason to value. These disadvantaged people then have different conversion factors from their peers—and thus different capability sets (freedom to achieve)—which further increases

Figure 2.8 High levels of mental distress among young people who identify as lesbian, gay, bisexual, transgender, queer, intersex or other sexual minority (LGBTQI+)

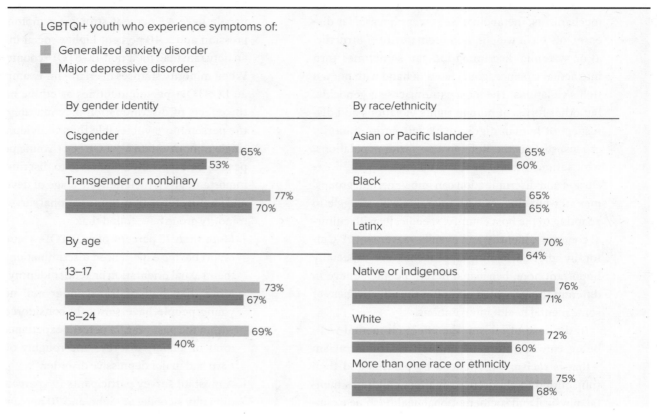

LGBTQI+ youth who experience symptoms of:
- Generalized anxiety disorder
- Major depressive disorder

By gender identity

Cisgender
- 65%
- 53%

Transgender or nonbinary
- 77%
- 70%

By age

13–17
- 73%
- 67%

18–24
- 69%
- 40%

By race/ethnicity

Asian or Pacific Islander
- 65%
- 60%

Black
- 65%
- 65%

Latinx
- 70%
- 64%

Native or indigenous
- 76%
- 71%

White
- 72%
- 60%

More than one race or ethnicity
- 75%
- 68%

Source: The Trevor Project 2021.

multidimensional inequalities. In some cases this will further exacerbate discrimination, exclusion and disrespect because victims are often blamed for their disadvantaged condition in meritocratic societies.[197] It is up to us to stand up against discrimination, protect each other mutually in socially cohesive societies and exercise agency when it comes to resilience building.

Human development in uncertain times

This chapter shows how mental stressors do not act in a vacuum; they are interconnected and may reinforce each other,[198] particularly in the context of uncertainty described in chapter 1. At the same time multiple systemic factors can help build resilience,[199] as explored in part II of the Report. Different sources of toxic stress affect not only people's mental wellbeing but also their physical health, especially at an early stage of the lifecycle, given that body and brain are still developing. Child, youth and even foetal development are functions of socioeconomic, political and

social structures, among many others, all of which determine the level of adversities and distress people are exposed to. So, individual conversion factors—meaning each individual's ability to convert resources into capabilities (freedom to achieve) and later into functionings (achievements)—will vary between people and throughout the lifecycle. The intergenerational effect of this mechanism is remarkable due to the strong impact of toxic stress and adversities during pregnancy and early childhood. Mental distress can also affect the capability set of adults, as several examples throughout the chapter show. In both cases the expansion of capabilities will be hindered, restraining people's choices to live lives they have reason to value. Mental distress can thus shape individuals' levels of human development as well as the aggregate level of human development of countries and regions, with consequences for inequality within and between countries and regions (figure 2.9).

This chapter shows the implications of uncertain times—from economic insecurity to anthropogenic

Figure 2.9 Human development amid multidimensional uncertainties

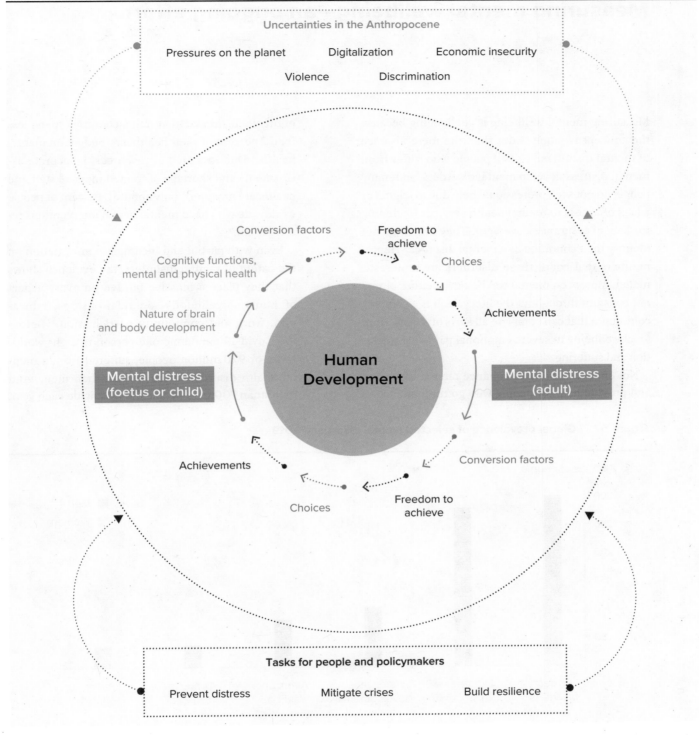

Source: Human Development Report Office.

pressures, digitalization, violence, discrimination and exclusion—for mental distress and how mental distress can in turn constrain human development for some people in some places, potentially increasing inequalities. Tasks for people and policymakers to prevent mental distress, mitigate crises and build psychological resilience are noted in figure 2.9 and are elaborated in part II of the Report.

Measuring mental wellbeing—an ongoing effort

Measuring mental wellbeing is challenging because the concept is much wider than the mere absence of mental disorders.[1] Not all people who suffer from mental distress develop mental disorders, and many people do not seek professional help due to stigma or a lack of access to mental health services (including for lack of insurance coverage). They may thus not identify their condition as a mental disorder.[2] Hence, numbers that count these disorders are underestimated. Moreover, mental wellbeing is neither binary nor constant throughout the lifecycle. It is a complex continuum that can comprise all sorts of stages, from ideal wellbeing to severe emotional pain, disorientation and suffering.[3]

Not enough is done to enhance mental wellbeing and provide help for people who go through phases of mental distress. On average, countries spend less than 2 percent of their healthcare budget on mental health.[4] Due to a lack of resources, inaccurate assessments and shortage of trained medical staff and healthcare providers, only about 10 percent of people worldwide who need mental health interventions receive them.[5]

Even with partial and incomplete information on the extent of mental disorders, the evidence shows that they place a massive burden on every aspect of human livelihoods—on relationships, education, work and community participation.[6] Before the Covid-19 pandemic one person in eight worldwide, or 970 million people, suffered from a mental health disorder, more women than men.[7] And more than 700,000 people die by suicide each year,

Figure S2.1.1 Global prevalence of selected mental disorders, 2019

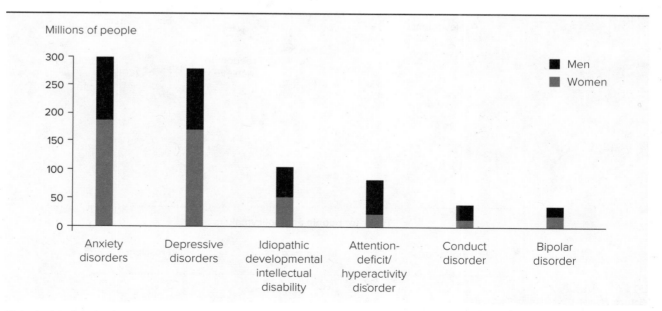

Note: Anxiety disorders incorporate disability caused by experiences of intense fear and distress in combination with other physiological symptoms. Depressive disorders include disability from major depressive disorder and dysthymia; major depressive disorder involves the experience of depressed mood or loss of interest or pleasure almost all day, every day, for two weeks, and dysthymia symptoms are less severe but chronic. Idiopathic developmental intellectual disability captures the health loss resulting from intellectual disability that arises from any unknown source. Attention-deficit/hyperactivity disorder is an externalizing disorder, incorporating disability from persistent inattention and/or hyperactivity/impulsivity. Conduct disorder occurs in those under age 18 and incorporates disability from antisocial behaviour that violates basic rights of others or major age-appropriate societal norms. Bipolar disorder is a mood disorder incorporating disability from manic, hypomanic or major depressive episodes (IHME 2021).
Source: Human Development Report Office calculations using data from IHME (2021).

predominantly in low- and middle-income countries, accounting for 1 in 100 deaths globally (the second leading cause of death among those ages 15–29). But for every death by suicide there are at least 20 more attempts, an expression of severe human suffering.[8] Although more men than women die by suicide, more women attempt suicide.[9]

Mental health problems are also the single leading cause of disability worldwide.[10] Children, adolescents and older people are most affected. WHO estimates that, globally, approximately 20 percent of children and adolescents[11] and about 15 percent of people age 60 and older suffer from mental disorders.[12] The most common mental disorders are anxiety (affecting 300 million people worldwide) and depression (affecting 280 million people; figure S2.1.1).[13] Most of these people live with their condition without ever receiving treatment.[14] Much more work is needed to statistically embrace the concept of mental wellbeing, develop adequate measurements for it and offer universal services to enhance it.

The cause of diagnosed mental disorders varies with context and evolves over time, interacting with several factors, from genes to the environment. Only about 26 percent of the variation in anxiety[15] and 37 percent of the variation in depression is due to variation in genes (heritability).[16] For other mental disorders the proportion can be higher.[17] This chapter focuses on the effects of distress on mental wellbeing for which nonheritable factors are most relevant.

NOTES

1   While the literature still lacks of a clear definition of mental wellbeing, the World Health Organization (WHO) defines mental health as "a state of well-being in which every individual realizes his or her own potential, can cope with the normal stresses of life, can work productively and fruitfully, and is able to make a contribution to her or his community" (WHO 2022b).

2   WHO 2022c.

3   UNICEF 2021c; WHO 2022c.

4   WHO 2022c.

5   PAHO 2019; WHO 2021c.

6   WHO 2021e, 2022b.

7   WHO 2022c.

8   WHO 2021d, 2021f.

9   WHO 2022c.

10   PAHO 2019.

11   WHO 2021f.

12   WHO 2017.

13   IHME 2021.

14   WHO 2022c.

15   Purves and others 2020.

16   Lee and others 2013.

17   Lee and others 2013.

Post-traumatic stress disorder—not just from combat

Post-traumatic stress disorder (PTSD) has become known mostly as a psychological condition common among war veterans who have returned from combat and been severely traumatized by their experiences on the battlefield. Less known is that PTSD is common among the general population, caused by child abuse, domestic violence, life-threatening accidents, political violence, human rights violations and disasters associated with natural hazards.

Trauma is "a direct personal experience of an event that involves actual or threatened death or serious injury, or other threat to one's physical integrity; or witnessing an event that involves death, injury, or a threat to the physical integrity of another person; or learning about unexpected or violent death, serious harm, or threat of death or injury experienced by a family member or other close associate."[1]

A wide range of symptoms can develop (table S2.2.1). As every human being and each traumatic event differs, strength, duration and types of symptoms vary among survivors. Initially, traumatic experiences trigger the "fight or flight" response in

Table S2.2.1 Symptoms of post-traumatic stress disorder among adults and children

Symptoms among adults	Symptoms among children

→ Avoidance of thoughts, feelings or conversations associated with the event as well as of people, places or activities that may trigger recollections of the event
→ Trauma-related thoughts or feelings (such as fear, horror, anger, guilt or shame)
→ Intrusion: Recurrent, involuntary and intrusive recollections
→ Dissociative reactions
→ Inability to remember an important aspect of the event (not due to head injury, alcohol or drugs)—usually caused by dissociative amnesia
→ Persistent and exaggerated negative beliefs
→ Persistent inability to experience positive emotions
→ Diminished interest or participation in activities
→ All summarized as depression
→ Persistent, distorted cognitions about the cause or consequences of the event and possible blame on self or others
→ Feelings of detachment or estrangement from others
→ Irritable or aggressive behaviour and angry outbursts
→ Reckless or self-destructive behaviour
→ Hypervigilance
→ Exaggerated startle response
→ Concentration problems
→ Sleep disturbance (traumatic nightmares)
	→ Affect dysregulation
	→ Aggression against self and others
	→ Unmodulated aggression and impulse control
	→ Dissociative symptoms (numbing, splitting, fragmentation)
	→ Depression
	→ Separation anxiety disorder
	→ Oppositional defiant disorder
	→ Phobic disorders
	→ Disturbed attachment patterns
	→ Rapid behavioural regressions and shifts in emotional states
	→ Loss of autonomous strivings
	→ Failure to achieve developmental competencies
	→ Altered schemas of the world
	→ Anticipatory behaviour and traumatic expectations
	→ Chronic feelings of ineffectiveness
	→ Impaired memory
	→ Diminished concentration
	→ Visceral dysregulation and muscular contraction
	→ Anxiety
	→ Somatization (for example, gastrointestinal distress, migraines, chronic back conditions)
	→ Attentional and dissociative problems
	→ Difficulty negotiating relationships with caregivers, peers and, subsequently, intimate partners
	→ Chronic inflammation
	→ Type 2 diabetes
	→ Obesity
	→ Especially with sexual assault:
	  • Substance abuse
	  • Borderline and antisocial personality
	  • Eating, dissociative, affective, somatoform, cardiovascular, metabolic, immunological and sexual disorders
	  • The loss of bodily regulation in the areas of sleep, food and self-care
	  • The apparent lack of awareness of danger and resulting self-endangering behaviours
	  • Self-hatred and self-blame

Source: Lengfelder (2021) based on American Psychiatric Association (2013), Center on the Developing Child (2013), Danese and Lewis (2017), Danese and others (2014), Hackett and Steptoe (2017), Heller and LaPierre (2012) and Van der Kolk and others (2005).

the body. When this biological response is not processed, as through rapid eye movement sleep or therapy, it remains activated in later life, when it is no longer necessary or useful. Trauma survivors then remain hypervigilant, with startling responses long after the traumatic event.[2] They may also develop depression—persistent and exaggerated negative beliefs about themselves, others and the world, combined with an inability to experience positive feelings and a loss of interest in activities important before the trauma. Depressed individuals may feel detached or estranged from others with an increasing feeling of isolation, exacerbating the negative worldview.[3]

Some individuals tend to avoid thoughts or emotions related to the traumatic event, whereas others experience especially strong emotions or thoughts related to the trauma. The disproportional significance of the trauma can impede focus on other aspects of life. Some thoughts can be intrusive, leading to involuntary recollections of memory that had been lost due to fragmentation or (partial) amnesia.[4] Other consequences may include concentration problems, sleep disturbances,[5] or aggressive, reckless or self-destructive behaviour.[6]

Early childhood trauma is a special case in which the impact on daily life goes beyond the symptoms of regular PTSD.[7] Even after children are removed from the traumatizing setting, problems with self-regulation, emotional adaptability, relating to others and self-understanding may continue throughout life.[8] And post-traumatic stress in early childhood is associated with obesity, chronic inflammation and type 2 diabetes.[9] Chronic dissociation and partial amnesia are two common symptoms of early childhood trauma that can affect brain functioning and development with long-lasting consequences.[10] Chronic dissociation detaches real-life situations from emotions, suppressing natural responses (such as crying when something sad happens), which are important for mental wellbeing. Difficulty with recalling memories from one's childhood may lead to distorted identity formation when it is unclear what happened where, when or why during certain stages of one's life, and it may cause self-doubt when feeling unable to rely on one's own mind and memory.

NOTES

1 American Psychiatric Association 2013.

2 Herman 1992; Levine 2008, 2010; Levine and Frederick 1997; Van der Kolk 2015; Van der Kolk and others 2005.

3 American Psychiatric Association 2013.

4 Van der Kolk and Fisler 1995.

5 Herman 1992.

6 American Psychiatric Association 2013.

7 Some of the symptoms of adult and childhood trauma overlap, but they are usually stronger in early childhood trauma (Heller and LaPierre 2012).

8 Center on the Developing Child 2013; McEwen and McEwen 2017.

9 Danese and Lewis 2017; Danese and others 2014; Hackett and Steptoe 2017.

10 Heller and LaPierre 2012.

Harnessing human development to navigate uncertain times

CHAPTER 3

Harnessing human development to navigate uncertain times

There is promise and peril in uncertainty. Tipping the scales towards promise is up to us.

But how do we do this?

This chapter doubles down on human development writ large. Wellbeing achievements matter, but more is needed to expand people's agency and freedoms to help us navigate and flourish in uncertain times.

This chapter also argues for widening the vista on human behaviour, going beyond models of rational self-interest to include emotions, cognitive biases and the critical roles of culture.

Enhancing human development in uncertain times: The end, but also the means, to navigate uncertainty

Being sensitive to what is happening in the world today implies taking notice of a novel uncertainty complex that is unsettling people's lives, as chapters 1 and 2 documented. But uncertainty, engendering the possibility of change, can also mobilize action and be a source of hope. It is not that more unpredictability is better—but that the glaring, and often increasing, injustices prevailing today call for change. So does the imperative to ease planetary pressures. They both call for transformation, as does the 2030 Agenda for Sustainable Development, subtitled "Transforming Our World."

Transformation is an opportunity to shape a world that is more just for people living today and in the future—by addressing behavioural inadequacies and institutional and policy gaps.[1] So how are the deficiencies to be addressed?[2] Behavioural change and institutional and policy reform are mutually interdependent: institutional choices and their effectiveness in shaping better outcomes are contingent on behaviours and on varying social, economic, political and cultural circumstances.[3] The interaction of behaviours and institutions is shaped by public reasoning and procedures of social choice (figure 3.1).[4] Given that outcomes are contingent on behaviour and circumstances, how can social choice be shaped so that it advances a transformation to a more just world while easing planetary pressures?

This is where doubling down on human development comes in. Advancing human development, the aspiration behind every Human Development Report, is not only the end but also the means for people to strive for change that leads to better outcomes by harnessing diverse and plural views in productive ways. Human development is about expanding capabilities, so equitably expanding capabilities is central in assessing development progress and evaluating policies.[5]

Capabilities are not exhausted with wellbeing achievements. One key distinction relates to the difference between advancing a person's wellbeing and promoting a person's agency (spotlight 3.1; see also spotlight 3.2).

Doubling down on human development (wellbeing and agency) opens the space to explore options to shape our future. Many institutions are designed and policies implemented based on specific behavioural assumptions (that people are rational only if they pursue the maximization of their individual wellbeing while assuming that everyone else is doing the same). But it is possible to draw on a richer understanding of human behaviour and motivation.[6] Central to the human development approach is the emphasis on people's ability to participate individually and collectively in public reasoning—subjecting prevalent beliefs and purported reasons to critical examination and retaining those to be sustained after doing so.

The pursuit of human development recognizes that people have plural identities and affiliations and value a plurality of dimensions, often simultaneously. Broadening the vista of how people behave, briefly reviewed below, suggests how an approach centred on the pursuit of human development may be the means to navigate uncertainty. Human development leverages a richer understanding of how people behave as well as the potential for social choice, through individual and public scrutiny of beliefs and reasons, to marshal institutions and public policies that advance justice while easing planetary pressures. How to do so in practice is the subject of part II of the Report.

Widening the vista of human behaviour

Many institutional designs and policy recommendations assume that people behave as "rational"[7] agents (see spotlight 3.3). Much can be accomplished by using this assumption to descriptively understand many social and economic processes and to

Figure 3.1 Behavioural change and institutional reform are mutually dependent

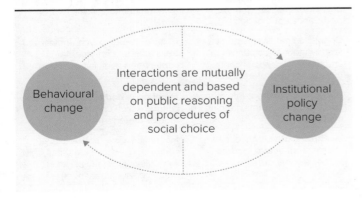

Source: Human Development Report Office.

normatively clarify the implications of different social choices (column 1 in table 3.1). But descriptively, this assumption corresponds to a very limited way of representing how people make choices. For instance, it poses very high demands on people's cognitive processing power, which has long motivated alternative framings of bounded rationality.[8] It also corresponds to a very narrow understanding of the role of the social context,[9] which has motivated arguments specifying how social embeddedness matters.[10] The explosion of behavioural economics and behavioural science has documented many deviations in actual human behaviour from what this assumption would predict.[11] The role of emotions, and how people come to reach and stick to beliefs, has also been increasingly explored. This has provided a broader framework for understanding human behaviour and why it sometimes seems hard for people to act individually and collectively in the face of uncertainty. This broader understanding widens the set of justifications and inspiration for policies and institutions (column 2 in table 3.1).

The human development approach's consideration of agency alongside wellbeing highlights the relevance of expanding beyond the assumption that choices are driven exclusively by the pursuit of the welfare of individuals, interest groups or countries—recognizing that this pursuit does matter and often dominates.[12] But it need not be the exclusive driver of choice. Amartya Sen described people who are assumed to always exclusively pursue egoistically individual payoffs while assuming that everyone else is doing the same as "rational fools,"[13] because mutual choices based on this assumption often lead to suboptimal outcomes for all involved.[14] He argued further that elements such as the choice process (including the menu of available options to choose from) and the fact that choices may have to be made even if a judgment has not been fully completed also point to a richer set of determinants of choice than maximizing individual material interests. That opens space for "the sociological exploration of the complex values that influence people's conduct."[15]

Recent evidence from cognitive neuroscience nuances the commonly held view that what people value is simply what gives them happiness, rewards or pleasantness. People can value something because of the goals they are pursuing, and these goals (and therefore, what they value) can change with circumstances (for example, a compass is more important than a diamond for someone lost in the desert). This goal-dependent usefulness is critical in guiding behaviour and constructing value—and is particularly important when circumstances change.[16] But what people value is not only associated with need; it can also be the result of notions of responsibility.[17] The notion of responsibility could be influenced by social norms of conduct or individual ethical reflection but takes us to the realm of agency. In particular, Sen argued that responsibility could be crucial in what he called the "operation of 'environmental values,' which is one of the reasons why the market analogy

Table 3.1 Behavioural assumptions: Determinants and scope of interventions to shape choices

	"Rational" agent	Behavioural agent	Encultured agent
Individual determinants of choice	Preferences (stable, autonomous); beliefs (isolated from preferences, based on collecting and processing information)	Preferences (can be fickle), beliefs (can be motivated), plus emotions (can change preferences and beliefs)	Preferences, beliefs, emotions shaped by social constructs (cultural mental models)
Cognition	Maximizes utility and assumes everyone else is doing the same	Cognitive limitations and biases (endowment effect) universal and hardwired, social context (norms, social preferences)	Culture shapes psychological traits; culture contingent on context and evolving over time
Social determinants of choice	Prices, rules of the game (emerge from a unique equilibrium)	Prices, rules of the game, plus social context (norms, framing of choices)	Experience and exposure to culture, which creates mental models (categories)
Scope of actions to shape choices	Incentives to correct market failures (externalities), governance (improve the rules of the game)	Incentives, governance, plus choice architecture (nudge, prime), social norms	Incentives, governance, social context, plus social identities, worldviews, narratives (which prime certain behaviours)

Source: Human Development Report Office based on Hoff and Stiglitz (2016).

is often quite deceptive in assessing 'existence values' of what people try actively to preserve in nature."[18]

" People tend to make choices under what is called narrow framing. That is, they do not evaluate all possible outcomes and weigh them against one another but focus on one or a few that are more salient for different reasons

The insights briefly reviewed here are not new, but today's uncertain times make them more relevant—and may, in fact, call for completely new analytical tools (spotlight 3.4; see also spotlight 3.5). Going beyond the "rational" agent and the behavioural agent and recognizing the role of the broader social context in shaping people's choices gets us to the encultured agent (column 3 in table 3.1).[19] This provides an even wider scope of interventions, one that includes a more prominent account of the role of the social context and the potential of widening ways of intervening to confront today's uncertain times. In building this argument, the chapter explains the relevance of the human development approach to seize that potential.

A psychologically richer description of behaviour under uncertainty

One example where the deviations of the rational choice model matters for the analysis in this Report relates to how people make choices under uncertainty. In many cases choices appear to be based on the evaluation of changes in wellbeing from a certain reference point,[20] as opposed to being based on the evaluation of levels of wellbeing.[21] There might be a deep biological and cognitive foundation for this,[22] given that human perceptual systems are broadly adaptive: what we find cold or hot or bright or dark is driven in part by a contrast with a frame of reference, typically our recent experience with temperature or light.[23]

People often seem to give greater weight to losses than gains when making choices. That is, they are often more reluctant to choose an outcome where there is a chance of losing $100 than one where there is the same chance of gaining the same amount—loss aversion.[24] This can account for the status quo bias,[25] or the endowment effect, where people ask for more

compensation to sell something they already own than what they would be willing to pay if they did not own it yet—a rational agent would have no reason to value the same thing differently.[26] A related behaviour is probability weighting, where people attribute a higher probability to events that have actually very low probability of occurring (say, winning the lottery), while assuming that events with very high probability of occurring are less likely than they are in reality.[27]

Something that sociologists have emphasized for a long time is that people often look at money as something other than a fungible and homogeneous flow of income. In many cases they construct mental accounts attributing different meanings and values to different flows of income depending on factors ranging from how the money was earned to what it was meant for.[28] Money also serves different functions, from offering for a sense of autonomy to being valued for the security that it provides for the future, which can vary across cultural contexts and across the income distribution.[29] Finally—and the list could go on even for this narrow set of behaviours linked to choice under uncertainty—people tend to make choices under what is called narrow framing.[30] That is, they do not evaluate all possible outcomes and weigh them against one another but focus on one or a few that are more salient for different reasons (because they are surprising, say).[31]

To illustrate how this set of deviations from the rational choice model can matter in the context of changes to address the challenges discussed in this Report, imagine the following scenario. A policymaker shows how existing fossil fuel subsidies are inefficient and regressive, are polluting the air and could be phased out and replaced by income transfers or public spending on health and education, at the same time giving incentives for less energy-intensive investments and innovations that help to fight climate change.[32]

How would a behavioural agent look at the proposal? Possible deviations from rational choice (interlinked, not necessarily sequential and separate) include the following. First, the subsidy becomes salient (the agent might not even have known before that something like this was in place) and a primary focus of valuation (narrow framing). Second, the endowment effect would suggest that the behavioural agent is not inclined to simply accept losing something she already has. Third, as appealing as the potential gains from the policy are to the climate change–aware behavioural agent, loss aversion can dominate, and the prospective gains might not compensate for the prospective losses.[33] Fourth, mental accounts mean that all the money may already be destined for purposes and goals from which the agent will not want to deviate. Fifth, even though the policymaker is of unimpeachable integrity and very likely to follow through with the compensation scheme, probability weighting could come to the fore, leading the behavioural agent to believe that it is not that likely.

" Now widely recognized and accepted, cognitive biases have opened a much richer understanding of human behaviour and a wider scope for the range of policies and institutions that may be considered beyond those that emanate from the rational choice model

At a minimum the behavioural agent could be expected to be less supportive, if not outright oppose, phasing out the fossil fuel subsidy, independent of political economy and framing effects. In reality, powerful economic interests seek to sway public opinion against removing fossil fuel subsidies to keep their economic and political power,[34] possibly crafting narratives that build on some of these behavioural insights. The scenario does not imply that the behavioural agent is beyond the reach of reason: each of the steps could be critically scrutinized, even if this could be complex and cognitively demanding. Nor is it inevitable that everyone will oppose the removal of fossil fuel subsidies—quite the contrary, as the discussion below suggests. This scenario is meant simply to illustrate how a psychologically richer description of behaviour under uncertainty opens space to consider a wider scope beyond material incentives to shape people's choices.[35]

Now widely recognized and accepted, cognitive biases (with reference to what would be expected behaviour as a "rational" agent) and cognitive limitations (people are unable to process as much information as would need to happen under a rational choice model) have opened a much richer understanding of human behaviour. This understanding can widen the range of policies and institutions that

may be considered beyond those that emanate from the rational choice model. The implications continue to be explored in fields ranging from optimal taxation[36] to issues that draw on progress in behavioural economics as an example of the "golden age of social science."[37] Prospect theory (which accounts for several of the biases associated with behaviour under uncertainty)[38] has been used for insights from politics[39] to international relations.[40] This has inspired policy interest in "nudging" or "priming" interventions that preserve the freedom of choice but change the choice architecture in ways that seek to "correct" for cognitive biases.[41] These nonfiscal and nonregulatory actions steer people to behave in a certain way but fully preserve freedom of choice. One example is the Save More Tomorrow initiative, behavioural interventions nudging people to save more, whose principles have been incorporated in the United States' 2006 Pension Protection Act.[42]

No single unified model accounts for all the documented cognitive biases.[43] So an intervention seeking to address one type of bias may affect behaviour in a negative way elsewhere.[44] Some behavioural interventions can even become too salient and backfire, such as displaying death counts in street signs to encourage safer driving, which has been shown to increase car crashes.[45] Nudges aim at intervening in situations where people think fast and automatically, implying that they make decisions in a different way from when they are able to think slowly and reflectively.[46] But this dichotomy may imply that opportunities are missed by recognizing that it is possible to incorporate elements of reflection even in nudges[47] or to boost people's ability to make decisions, enhancing their agency in making choices.[48] The effectiveness of nudges and boosts may also vary depending on the cultural context.[49]

More than reviewing all relevant biases and their implications, the purpose here is to suggest that cognitive biases and limitations often shape how people behave, particularly in contexts of uncertainty. But that behaviour, even if it deviates from what the rational choice model predicts, does not imply that people are lacking in reason—much of the behaviour may actually be preferable, particularly to deal with uncertainty.[50] Thus, awareness of these considerations has heightened relevance when confronting uncertainties. A promising development with potentially far-reaching policy implications is identifying fundamental cognitive processes that can account for many of the observed behavioural choices under uncertainty (spotlight 3.6).

When emotions make preferences fickle

The emotion of fear—triggered by the belief of a threat—tends to make people more risk averse, while anger tends to make them more risk seeking.[51] This is just an example of how beliefs can change preferences through emotions.[52] Rational choice theory assumes not only that beliefs and preferences both matter but also that they are delinked. Emotions result from gathering information, learning and experience.[53] Thinking and feeling are simultaneous processes that cognitively shape an individual's perception, attention, learning, memory, reasoning and problem solving—affecting even the direction of cognitive biases. For instance, sadness—growing globally over the last decade, with more intensity among the less educated—often reverses the endowment effect: when people are sad, choice prices exceed selling prices (figure 3.2).[54] Sadness can also heighten addictive substance use.[55] In addition, anger can account for major changes in political history that

rational choice alone cannot explain,[56] and emotions more broadly can be decisive in accounts of historical action and thought.[57] Hope can lead to choices that enhance health[58] and mediate the relation between income and subjective measures of wellbeing.[59]

The relevance of emotions seems to have deep neuro-anatomical foundations, as seen in the way people with different types of brain injuries make decisions.[60] Recent neuroscience findings suggest that rational decisionmaking may depend on prior accurate emotional processing.[61] Even though some of the specific findings may not be conclusive,[62] a growing body of evidence documents multiple ways that emotions matter when making choices,[63] generating "the rise of affectivism."[64] A full emotion-imbued model of choice has been proposed.[65]

An instinctive sentiment of anger that can trigger a risky course of action—which, in insight and after critical reasoning is seen as harmful to oneself or others—can be dangerous. By contrast, emotions are often triggered by reasoned understanding of connections—for instance, the cause of manifest injustice that makes one angry about discrimination or torture. Angry rhetoric in the writings of Mary Wollstonecraft in the 19th century against the inequalities suffered by women was followed by a strong appeal to reason for the equality of rights of all human beings.[66]

Figure 3.2 **People are experiencing more sadness**

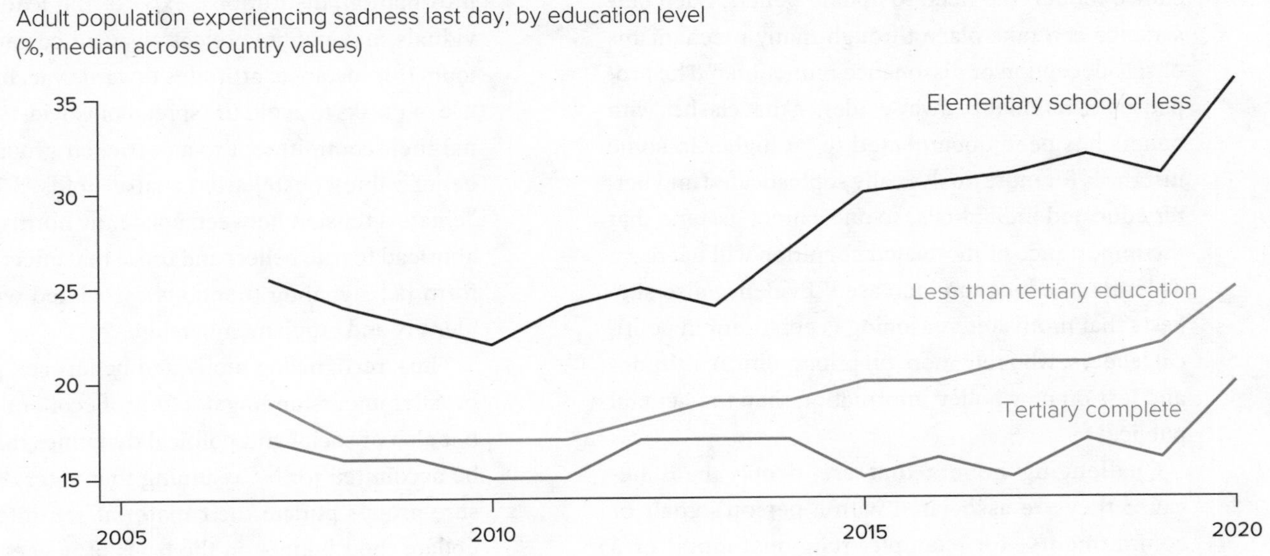

Adult population experiencing sadness last day, by education level
(%, median across country values)

Source: Human Development Report Office based on data from Gallup.

That emotions matter for behaviour is not, however, a negation of rationality or reason or a justification for not subjecting emotions to reasoned appraisal in the same way that motivations and beliefs need to be.

Motivated beliefs and motivated reasoning: When more and better information may not be enough

Preferences, goals and motivations can directly affect beliefs, as a rapidly growing literature on motivated beliefs and motivated reasoning documents—people distort how they process new information in the direction of beliefs they favour.[67] In rational choice, beliefs are based on rationally processing information, and people cannot be systematically fooled. But beliefs also fulfil psychological and other needs, with implications for behaviour and choice.

One example of motivated reasoning is wishful thinking, which seems to have a positive valence value, making people feel better and more optimistic about the world, thus also having an emotional component. But it also has a functional value, allowing people to persist in a task under adversity.[68] However, it may also support dangerous behaviours, such as persisting in smoking, believing that one's health will not be affected, despite all the scientific evidence to the contrary.[69]

Beliefs about oneself or the world can persist despite information that would suggest (in a rational choice model) the need to update beliefs. Such persistence can take place through many mechanisms of self-deception or dissonance reduction.[70] The propensity to rationalize away evidence that clashes with beliefs has been documented to be higher in some instances for more analytically sophisticated and better educated individuals, so one cannot assume that the importance of motivated cognition will decrease as levels of education increase.[71] Evidence also suggests that motivated reasoning is persistent in political leaders, who rely more on prior political attitudes and less on new policy information than the general public.[72]

Challenging beliefs that are deeply held because they are associated with a person's goals or commitments—for example, religious, moral or a salient aspect of a person's identity or politics—can trigger strong emotional responses of anger or even hate and disgust.[73] Motivated reasoning can lead to beliefs becoming more polarized around issues such as immigration, income mobility and how to handle crime.[74] That is, some of the cleavages in beliefs are tied not necessarily to material interests but to different worldviews or social identity. And when these acquire more salience, polarization can become more correlated across issues, leading to "belief-value constellations,"[75] where people associate more with a group based on shared ideas rather than economic interests.[76]

> " Recognizing motivated beliefs can provide a broader understanding not only of economic choices but also of social and political dynamics that cannot be accounted for by assuming that voters and pressure groups pursue their material self-interest and update their beliefs on the basis of new evidence

One illustration of the potential implications of motivated reasoning is associated with (epistemic) norms that shape what people consider to be true, in addition to individual reasoning.[77] Children at very young age (age 4, with some rudimentary aspects emerging during infancy) can determine beliefs that are the norm in their context and identify false beliefs —according to the prevailing social norm.[78] Different groups may assume different epistemic norms that place different levels of trust on different sources of information, institutions, experts and leaders. Individuals may publicly reject or avoid certain behaviours (for instance, attitudes towards vaccines or the use of masks to avoid the spread of Covid-19)[79] to signal their commitment to a particular group and the belief-value constellation that it holds.[80] This may "create a tension between epistemic norms that reliably lead to true beliefs and those that effectively perform [...] signaling functions associated with social identity and group membership."[81]

Thus, recognizing motivated beliefs can provide a broader understanding not only of economic choices but also of social and political dynamics that cannot be accounted for by assuming that voters and pressure groups pursue their material self-interest and update their beliefs on the basis of new evidence.[82] Another very compelling application of motivated beliefs could be how people may convince themselves that climate change is not going to be too bad purely because it helps them justify not taking action.[83] Understanding motivated reasoning provides a lens to understand some dynamics of polarization noted in chapter 1 and explored further in part II of the Report. How goals and values can motivate beliefs may be relevant when we confront novel uncertainties and particularly when there is a reversal in the importance given in public debate to sentiments rather than reasons. Since the 1980s there has been a reversal in a trend dating from the mid-19th century of rational language dominating sentiment-laden language in fact-based argument (figure 3.3).[84]

This evidence does not suggest that beliefs are never or even infrequently updated based on new information. But it shows how motivated cognition can provide a richer understanding of human behaviour.[85] It also shows that polarization should not be seen as inevitable and preordained—and that the affirmation of a more salient social identity, above all others, should not be seen to uniquely define a person and thus be accepted without scrutiny.[86] Even more important from a human development perspective, individual reasoning and public deliberation are powerful drivers of social change—people are not helpless prisoners of one single social identity, of their emotions

Figure 3.3 The Great Reversal from rationality to sentiment in fact-based argument

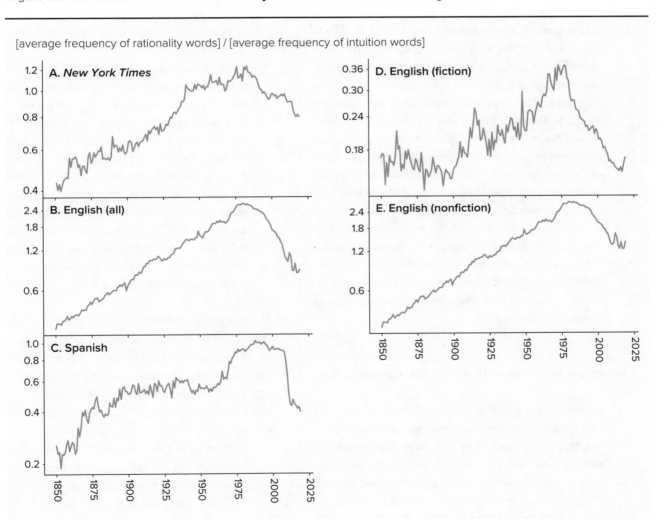

[average frequency of rationality words] / [average frequency of intuition words]

Note: Sun (2022) suggests a different interpretation of the changes in language, associating them with a shift from more formal to more informal terms, but Scheffer and others (2022) argue that their interpretation holds. Ratio of intuition- to rationality-related words in the *New York Times* (A) and various book corpora represented in the Google n-gram database (B–E), with the lines portraying the ratio of the mean relative frequencies of sets of rationality-related and intuition-related flag words used in the analysis.
Source: Scheffer and others 2021.

or of motivated beliefs. Indeed, harnessing diversity of goals, motivations, values, beliefs and emotions depends on how behaviours interact with institutions and the procedures of social choice that can harness plurality in productive ways, as explored next.

Behavioural and institutional change: Mobilizing human development towards a hopeful future

As argued earlier, behavioural changes and institutional reforms are interdependent. And the richer understanding of human behaviour just reviewed suggests much more scope for change in both than may be commonly assumed. This is central to explore how to draw from a context of uncertainty to mobilize action towards a more hopeful future. That scope expands even further with the understanding that cognitive biases and limitations are not hardwired and universal to all humans in the same way[87]—and are not necessarily an inherent part of our psychology.[88] Similarly, the role of emotions in changing preferences and driving behaviour is also context contingent. Emotions play a role in people's conforming with social norms, but the salience of doing so to avoid either shame or guilt depends on the cultural context.[89] It has been argued that socialization and cultural context determine which emotions matter for behaviour and how.[90] And preferences and the motivations that may drive certain beliefs—across domains, from attitudes towards risk to preferences for equity and income distribution—vary widely across individuals and across countries.[91]

Bringing culture back in: How the social context matters

Recognizing culture (discussed below) is only part of a broader and more fundamental point: the need to give greater salience to how social contexts shape preferences, perceptions and cognition—not only what people do but also who people believe they are. That takes us from the rational agent and beyond the behavioural agent to the encultured agent (see table 3.1).[92] Recent insights from sociology have reconceptualized culture from something that stays in the background of political and economic life towards a much more dynamic, fluid and adaptable toolkit.

This implies a two-way causal effect between culture and institutions.[93] It also means that people select strategically from the toolkit to provide meaning, interpretation and justification for their behaviour.[94] Studies of poverty that focus on how scarcity taxes people's cognitive capacities and functions[95] would benefit from considering how people perceive and identify needs based on what they take from the cultural toolkit available to them.[96] When uncertainty becomes salient, different groups of young people buffer themselves against a murky future in different ways, drawing on the cultural toolkits available to them.[97] This perspective on culture is inspiring fresh takes on economic development, exploring how highly adaptable and fluid cultural configurations interact with political power and economic incentives to generate different social, economic and political outcomes.[98]

An emerging account of how cultural variation takes hold comes from the field of cultural evolution,[99] even if it remains a hotly debated perspective.[100] In this account psychological traits coevolve with the broader cultural context in combinations that make societies better adapted to different circumstances over time.[101] These perspectives also suggest that what is assumed to be universal human behaviour is often based on what is observed from a sliver of humanity.[102] Thus, there is a much broader diversity of behaviours, psychology and institutions across the world and over time. And there is even more variation within than across cultures.[103]

" Recognizing culture is only part of a broader and more fundamental point: the need to give greater salience to how social contexts shape preferences, perceptions and cognition—not only what people do but also who people believe they are

Culture, in these accounts, "represents information stored in people's heads that got there through cultural learning or direct experience induced by various cultural products, like norms, technologies, languages or institutions."[104] Cultures can vary in systematic ways on dimensions ranging from how tight cultural norms are enforced[105] to how individualistic they are.[106] But cultures cannot be firmly categorized in different boxes—and even less so in dichotomous ways, such as associating individualistic cultures with "the West" and interdependent cultures with "the East."[107]

In cultural evolution accounts, cultural change is driven largely by the emergence of culture and psychological traits that are better adapted to cope with the new environment.[108] Over time this has resulted in culture-psychology combinations that have enabled people to cooperate at larger scales—millions of strangers in today's societies—devising specific social arrangements (institutions, policies) resulting in ever more complex and sophisticated technologies, leading to higher income and material wellbeing.[109] Cultural evolution is one way of accounting for changes in moral values, with variations around the world associated in part with how different societies have responded to the problem of cooperation.[110]

A mismatch of behavioural patterns and institutional settings in today's uncertain times?

Culture is both persistent, which helps people navigate and make decisions in their social world, and changeable, particularly when that social world or the environment around it is altered.[111] When uncertainty is heightened or changes, the potential for a cultural mismatch increases between those relying on prevailing culture and those attempting to innovate to adapt to the new circumstances.[112] Cultural change can play a role in how the social context influences the emergence of behaviour and institutional configurations. But as Amartya Sen argued: "Paying reflective ethical attention to behaviour neither nullifies, nor is nullified by, the importance of evolutionary forces."[113] Ethical reasoning has been described as a powerful way of "escaping from tribalism," manifest in patterns of moral progress that are less and less exclusionary of groups of people.[114] It also offers opportunities for norm-based governance to address global collective action challenges, such as climate change.[115]

Evolutionary processes and ethical reasoning may have interacted in reaching the current prevailing configurations of behaviours and institutions. But today's uncertain times have novel elements that present fundamentally new challenges, and those configurations may not be a good match. Some of the challenges of the Anthropocene are existential;

others require cooperation not only with people alive today but also with people who do not yet exist—that is, with the future.[116] The Anthropocene reality of shared challenges at the planetary scale requires cooperation—or, at a minimum, coordination—across countries.

> " There is tension between conforming to the prevailing institutions (including norms) and behaviours that have moved the world towards record achievements in material wellbeing—and the lack of response from those norms, institutions and behaviours to a novel and unprecedented context

Individual solutions for shared challenges can create tensions between self-reliance and collective efficiency. One country or group of people may be able to afford to stay protected from a pandemic through private means. That can make cooperation and even coordination more difficult, in a modern tragedy of the commons.[117] Certainty about biophysical thresholds of climate change and other dangerous patterns of planetary change that would spell catastrophe would make coordination by self-interested agents more likely. But great uncertainty about those thresholds makes collective action less likely and harder.[118]

So, today's uncertain times may be characterized in part as a mismatch between the cultural configurations that have enabled certain development paths thus far[119] and the layered novel uncertainties of the Anthropocene, transitions and polarization. Disagreements and even conflict in societies may reflect that mismatch. There is tension between conforming to the prevailing institutions (including norms) and behaviours that have moved the world towards record achievements in material wellbeing—and the lack of response from those norms, institutions and behaviours to a novel and unprecedented context.

This mismatch could be playing out in many dimensions. One has to do with generational inequalities in exposure to climate extremes. For the cohort born in 1960, exposure to lifetime heat waves is essentially the same across climate change scenarios. But even if temperatures stay below 1.5°C above preindustrial levels, the cohort born in 2020 will suffer four times more exposure—and seven times more under current pledges (figure 3.4). No surprise,

Figure 3.4 Younger generations will be four to seven times more exposed to heat waves in their lifetimes than older generations

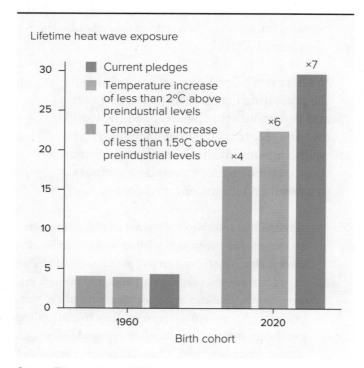

Source: Thiery and others 2021.

then, that young people ages 16–25 around the world report associating climate change with a range of emotions with negative affect, from anger to anxiety: two-thirds report feeling sad, and two-thirds report feeling afraid.[120] Another facet of disagreement is the differences across groups of people in either doubting or denying climate change. Groups in Europe more concerned about their economic security and less certain about the future are much more likely to reject climate change—and to be "less prosperous, more rural and more economically dependent on fossil fuels."[121] And individualistic attitudes are associated with less concern for environmental action[122] and less wearing of masks during the Covid-19 pandemic.[123]

The potential of this mismatch, and the broader range of determinants of human behaviour beyond rational and behavioural agents, also opens opportunities to mobilize uncertain times for better individual and social outcomes. The insights from rational choice and the emphasis on incentives remain relevant. Understanding how the context in the moment

of decision influences choices, one of the insights of behavioural science, and the role of emotions and motivated reasoning widens the scope beyond incentives shaping the choices of self-interested agents. But recognizing the role of culture further widens the scope. It takes us beyond considering how interests and institutions drive people's behaviour, to recognize the power of ideas.[124]

Ideas with the power to shape individual and collective choice range from social identities and worldviews[125] to narratives and frames.[126] Joel Mokyr has emphasized "cultural entrepreneurs" as agents able to change the beliefs of others during momentous transformations in history, such as during the Enlightenment and the Industrial Revolution.[127] Caroline Schill and colleagues argue that this more "dynamic understanding of human behaviour" is essential in the Anthropocene.[128]

This Report extends the argument to today's uncertain times.[129] It looks at current disagreements and differences in perspective across groups of people less as a motive for despair and more as the kind of diversity and pluralism that may be needed in an open-ended pursuit of the innovations—social, technological, institutional—required to respond to novel and unprecedented challenges. In the "paradox of diversity," this pursuit may require longer lead times to agree on collective actions and implement collective decisions.[130] As David Byrne sings: "The future is certain; give us time to work it out." This paradox gives even more reason to address inequalities perceived as unfair or divisive, while preserving the plurality of views and an open, reasoned, public debate.[131]

Advancing human development to learn, and to expand the scope for learning, in uncertain times

Chapter 1 documented how novel layers of interacting uncertainties are heightening feelings of insecurity,[132] pointing to a disconnect between wellbeing achievements and security. What do we hold on to, then, when even our sense of direction seems submerged in uncertainty? Wellbeing achievements with insecurity and progress with polarization[133] cast doubt on seeing development as a smooth process of progress in wellbeing achievements. Ideas, institutions and policies seeking to advance development are not delivering as expected, but they are also opening new and dangerous problems by undermining the ecological integrity of our biosphere and leaving many people behind.[134]

Where we go from here is up to us. Our planet and societies have gone through periods of change and volatility before. But one key feature making this era unique is humans' role in driving threats—and our potential ability to shape the changes to build a more hopeful future (spotlight 3.7).[135] A real paradox of our time is our tentativeness to act despite mounting evidence of the distress that our pursuit of development is inflicting on our societies and planet. One contribution of this Report is to explore how understanding uncertainty and its relation to individual and collective choices can explain why action may be delayed, even in the face of looming threats, and to suggest ways forward that move us beyond paralysis.[136]

Why might societies not adequately respond to uncertainty? Consider the interaction between the different multilayered uncertainties and both behaviour and institutions (figure 3.5). Societies respond to shocks through multiple institutional and policy mechanisms. These institutions are often designed to absorb the shocks and moderate the threats that people confront. Under the rational choice model this process depends on state capacity, resource distribution and social preferences, as with the way societies

manage the potential tensions between social insurance and individual responsibility.[137]

Now consider how social arrangements (institutions and policies) are influenced by a wider set of individual and social factors interacting with an evolving reality. In the presence of new threats, people's behaviour is strongly mediated by their perceived uncertainty.[138] This perception comes through different channels. First is the increase in residual uncertainty, the one not absorbed by the collective response. Second is the perceived adequacy of the social response and the extent to which previous beliefs about how things work hold, which determines confidence in institutions and trust within and across groups. Third is the social and cultural context that defines the interpretation of the new threats in the light of prevailing narratives. Is it a sign of personal failure? Will this affect my position and future prospects in society?[139] Fourth are the emotions surrounding the increased uncertainty, ranging from fear to indifference to hope. The same shock can thus cause different levels of perceived individual uncertainty, depending on the prevailing narratives about underlying processes and the perceived effectiveness of policies.

Uncertainty for individuals shapes both individual behaviour and attitudes, with an impact on social interactions. Collective responses to uncertainty that

Figure 3.5 Individual and collective responses to uncertainty can drive uncertainty loops

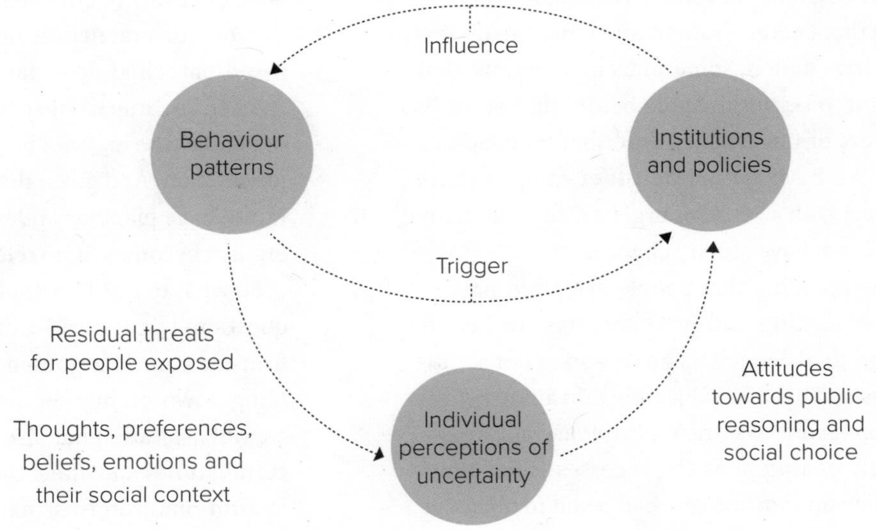

Source: Human Development Report Office.

are perceived as ineffective or unfair can trigger animosity and polarization—especially in the presence of political narratives that manipulate the situation to deepen societal divides.[140] Such polarization has been documented in several countries in the response to the Covid-19 pandemic,[141] where the public health measures put in place were resisted less because of a personal assessment of risks of, for instance, being vaccinated, and more because they represented a set of behaviours that defined expected group behaviours. Disbelief in climate change is associated more with political allegiance than with misinformation.[142] This animosity and polarization then drive not only the specific collective response but also how the collective response interacts with the threat, eventually heightening uncertainty. Thus, the high and in many cases rising perceptions of insecurity may be accounted for in this type of uncertainty loop.

Expanding human development to foster learning and public reasoning

The broader understanding of human behaviour highlighted in this chapter helps account for some of the choices that so many people are making around the world, resulting in patterns ranging from political polarization to the rejection or dilution of the science of climate change and pandemics. But understanding does not mean resignation. Recognizing the role of emotions does not mean that we should wait until catastrophic outcomes become emotionally salient to act. Events that become salient and emotionally resonant can drive action, sometimes in directions that were thought to be unthinkable before that event.[143] But the layers of uncertainty described in chapter 1 imply that we have no option other than to think ahead and act with a sense of urgency, since in many cases we will not have second chances.[144]

And understanding that people are often prey to motivated reasoning and hold steadfast to beliefs that are hard to dislodge[145] is no reason to not scrutinize reasons and beliefs. Subjecting prevailing beliefs and alleged reasons to critical examination, through appropriately comprehensive processes (see below) and with relevant information, can result in objective beliefs. Indeed, research has shown that uncertainty about other people's political beliefs and attitudes

can drive people to tighten their own beliefs.[146] Because people often misconceive others' attitudes and values, polarization may be cemented in spaces and on issues where differences in attitudes or opinions are, in fact, fairly small.[147] This so-called "false polarization" has been found to drive actual political polarization.[148] Understanding the processes that create misconceptions opens space for interventions that may correct them and mitigate political polarization.[149]

" Subjecting prevailing beliefs and alleged reasons to critical examination, through appropriately comprehensive processes and with relevant information, can result in objective beliefs

This scrutiny of reasons and beliefs should happen at the individual level, but here we have to be mindful also of the cognitive limitations and biases discussed earlier in the chapter (see also spotlight 3.6). That is why public reasoning—always important under any circumstances—acquires heightened relevance in today's world. Our individual brains are limited, but our collective brain[150] is far more powerful. A plurality of sources of voice and power is not a weakness in today's uncertain times but can be a source of strength, provided processes sustained by democratic practices ensure that public reasoning takes place in a context and through processes where what carries the day is not always a powerful economic or political group or a highly motivated believer who refuses to subject beliefs to critical examination.[151] Processes of democratic practice, at multiple scales, need to also avoid parochial dominance and welcome perspectives from "impartial spectators"—that is, the views of people who may not be part of a particular political jurisdiction. And given that the novel layers of uncertainty have planetary relevance, the role of multilateralism becomes more relevant than ever.[152]

So what to do? Part II of the Report addresses this question, but as part I closes, it is important to reaffirm the central argument of this chapter, that doubling down on human development is not only the central aspiration but also the means to navigate uncertain times and effect the behavioural changes and institutional reforms that would allow us to shape a more hopeful future. Advancing human development means pursuing all aspects of capabilities, not just the drive to enhance wellbeing achievements. Agency matters, as do freedoms in both wellbeing and agency—options that need to remain wide as the search for the appropriate set of institutions and behaviours is still open-ended. In a sense expanding human development in uncertain times can also be a learning process, where capabilities—wellbeing and agency, achievements and freedoms—allow for changes in behaviour and institutions to take shape in addition to expanding the scope for learning. Confronting the layers of uncertainty that we face today is about enhancing cooperation at multiple scales and about the "agility of the mind" to use new and appropriate frames to understand our world and the responses needed to address the challenges that we confront.[153]

Part II of the Report proposes motivating principles whose cultivation can enable public reasoning, as well as priority policy areas, so that human development is advanced in a way that enables people to harness uncertainty towards a more hopeful world—more just for people living now and in the future.

How agency differs from wellbeing

Agency is the ability to hold values and make commitments that may—or may not—advance the person's wellbeing.[1] The person may be committed to fighting climate change to an extent that she skips school or forgoes a well-paying job, choices that may not advance wellbeing but would express agency. Another important distinction is between actual achievements and the options or freedoms available to people, regardless of their choices. Independent of what people end up securing, the options or freedoms available to people are inherently valuable.[2]

These distinctions result in four aspects of capabilities of interest:

- Achievements in wellbeing.
- Achievements in agency.
- Freedoms in wellbeing.
- Freedoms in agency.[3]

In assessing development progress, the spotlight tends to shine more on wellbeing achievements, such as standards of living, and much less on the freedoms available to people and their agency.[4]

But these four aspects of capabilities are relevant in the context of drawing on the human development approach to support behavioural change and institutional reform to navigate today's uncertain times. Chapters 1 and 2 suggest the need to go beyond—not replace—considering wellbeing achievements alone—for two reasons. First, the spotlight on wellbeing achievements may leave other aspects of life that matter to people in the shadows—such as feeling very or increasingly insecure, despite high wellbeing achievements. Second, there is no guarantee that focusing on wellbeing achievements alone would equip people with the capabilities to navigate today's uncertain times—and particularly to lead fundamental transformational change to adapt and transition away from the layers of novel uncertainty that characterize today's world.

Freedoms and agency have always been intrinsically important. They are also instrumentally important, as in facilitating collective action to provide public goods.[5] And they may be indispensable where societies have to explore largely uncharted transitions to an aspirational space of expanding human development while easing planetary pressures.[6]

Human development, understood as expanding the four aspects of capabilities, thus becomes both the end and the means. Agency acquires relevance because it is difficult, if not impossible, to conceive of people leading the required transformations if they are seen only as potential receivers of assistance, as simply "vehicles of wellbeing,"[7] as mere patients—rather than as agents able to judge, to commit and to give priority to goals and values that may go beyond advancing their wellbeing. Recognizing agency affirms people not only as the subject of wellbeing- or welfare- enhancing policies (though these are important) but also as active promoters and catalysts of social and economic change[8]—beyond their own narrow self-interest.

NOTES

1   Sen (1985) suggested that the neglect of agency is shadowed by the consideration that people are geared exclusively to purse their material self-interest.

2   Sen (1985) argued that the neglect of options results from assuming that only actual achievements, or what people end up choosing, counts. See Sen (1999) for an elaboration on the perspective of seeing development as freedom. This refers primarily to what Sen called opportunity freedoms, recognizing that process freedoms, some of which may not be associated with capabilities, also matter.

3   The original framing around these four categories of capabilities was proposed in Sen (1985). The discussion here, including the examples, draws mainly from the simplified treatment in Sen (2009b).

4   These four aspects of capability often reinforce one another but need not. For instance, being well nourished is certainly something important for human life and part of the wellbeing aspect of capabilities. But sometimes a commitment to fasting (for religious or political reasons), which is in the realm of the agency aspect of capabilities, may override the overwhelming importance that being well-nourished has for most people, most of the time. And while the state should have an obligation to ensure that everyone has the freedom to be well-nourished, just because the wellbeing achievement of being well-nourished matters does not imply that the state should ban fasting. That would be a limitation not only in people's freedoms in wellbeing achievements, by precluding the possibility of choosing not to eat, but also in their agency, by excluding the possibility of making a commitment to fasting (Sen 1985).

5   Shi and others 2020.

6   In standard rational choice theory models, discussed later in the chapter, temporal-dependent and context-dependent preferences are often seen as suboptimal deviations from normative choice. But recent evidence shows how adaptation of preferences is crucial for efficiently representing information in volatile and uncertain contexts: "Value adaptation confers distinct benefits to a decision maker in a dynamic world" (Khaw, Glimcher and Louie 2017, p. 2700).

7   Sen 2009b, p. 288.

8   Indeed, civil society organizations, community initiatives, social movements and activists around the world work tirelessly using their agency to bring about social change.

Agency, ideas and the origins of the regulatory welfare state

Elisabeth Anderson, *New York University Abu Dhabi*

Can an individual change the course of policy history? Might such individuals be motivated by shared ideas from which they do not stand to directly benefit? The answer to both questions, I argue in my recent book, *Agents of Reform: Child Labor and the Origins of the Welfare State,* is a qualified yes. Under certain conditions, and only with cooperation from others, individual middle-class reformers exercised decisive influence over early legislation to protect workers. Acting on culturally embedded ideas about why industrial labour conditions were problematic, they exercised creative agency to build political coalitions and surmount institutional barriers to change. At a time when labour still lacked the power to demand protective legislation on its own, these reformers deserve much of the credit for bringing the regulatory welfare state into being.

Regulatory welfare refers to the web of policies that protect workers by limiting employers' arbitrary power over them. Child labour laws enacted in the 1830s and 1840s were the first of these efforts to intervene in the relationship between the new industrial bourgeoisie and the "free" labour it employed. These laws formed the bedrock on which vital protections for adult workers—including occupational health and safety regulations as well as the normal working day—were eventually built. Still, scholars tend to pay little attention to this regulatory side of the welfare state. *Agents of Reform* aims to correct this through seven case studies of the political origins of child labour and factory inspection legislation in 19th century Belgium, France, Germany and the United States.

Throughout much of the 19th century, working-class people were politically marginalized. In many countries they could not even vote. Moreover, many workers did not regard child labour as a problem requiring legislative attention; some depended on their children's earnings to survive, and others were more focused on issues of direct concern to adult men. Under these conditions it was middle-class reformers who spearheaded efforts to enact child labour laws and later to create the factory inspection systems needed to enforce them.

One puzzle is why these reformers bothered to put time and energy into advocating for policies from which they themselves did not stand to directly benefit. Understanding this requires excavating the ideas that motivated them—and these, it turns out, were surprisingly diverse. Ideologically, child labour and factory inspection reformers ran the gamut from classical liberalism to religious conservatism to democratic socialism. What united them, however, was the belief that excessive and premature labour inflicted lasting damage on children's minds, bodies and souls. Allowing such abuses to continue posed a dire threat, not only to working-class children's wellbeing but also to the nation as a whole. How they interpreted this threat varied. For instance, some saw child workers as potential criminals or revolutionaries who required the disciplining influence of school, whereas other regarded them as national resources whose human capital was being squandered. Ideas such as these informed reformers' understandings of the child labour problem and drove them to pursue legislation. They were not, at least not in a direct sense, motivated by simple self-interest.

Of course, not all would-be reformers were equally influential. They needed allies. Scrutinizing how some succeeded while others did not reveals that effective reformers distinguished themselves in two ways: alliance-building and problem solving.

Alliance-building

Reformers used a variety of alliance-building strategies—including framing, citation, piggybacking, compromise and expertise-signalling—in ways that accorded with the priorities and expectations of the audiences they needed to convince. Take the first of these strategies: frames are ideas that political actors deploy to convert audiences into allies. To be effective, frames must resonate with audience members' existing ideas or interests; otherwise, they will fall flat and can even backfire.[1]

To illustrate this, compare how two reformers—one successful, one not—framed the child labour problem at key coalition-building moments. When Charles Dupin, a French legislator, argued before the Chamber of Peers that child labour rendered "the country weak in military powers, and poor in all the occupations of peace,"[2] he was cleverly framing the issue as vital to France's economic and national security interests. He went on to argue that working children were likely to grow up to be criminals and deviants who would destabilize the social order. Such frames appealed directly to the concerns of political elites and helped Dupin build a solid coalition around his proposed child labour bill.

In contrast, when Édouard Ducpétiaux, a Belgian public administrator, framed child labour as a grave violation of children's rights, his argument was soon used against him by chambers of commerce that were institutionally empowered to weigh in on economic legislation—and whose support Ducpétiaux needed to move forward. The notion that children had rights that sometimes trumped those of fathers had not yet been established by law or custom, so the employers accused Ducpétiaux of trying to upend the sacred privileges of the *pater familias* in a misguided pursuit of "foreign" policy goals. Missteps such as these contributed to Ducpétiaux's failure as a child labour reformer and, by extension, to Belgium's inability to enact child labour regulation until much later in the 19th century.

Problem solving

The second way successful reformers distinguished themselves was through their willingness to try creative, and at times risky, problem-solving strategies. When political opponents repeatedly impeded their reform ambitions, they reacted by subverting normal policymaking channels in unconventional ways. For example, when Theodor Lohmann, a Prussian commerce ministry official, found his quest for a Reich-wide system of factory inspection thwarted at every turn by his formidable boss, Otto von Bismarck, he refused to give up. Instead, he went behind the chancellor's back, penning anonymous op-ed articles to drum up support, enlisting friends to lobby their political contacts and, most decisively, secretly sharing his own factory inspection bill with leaders of Germany's second most powerful political party. By forging an unauthorized and highly risky alliance with the legislative branch, Lohmann was eventually able to harness the Reichstag's power and circumvent Bismarck's executive authority. Without Lohmann's bold interventions, Germany would not have been able to mandate factory inspections across the empire, at least not until after the end of Bismarck's reign.

*   *   *

Research on agency and policy change often highlights policy or institutional entrepreneurs and stresses that these actors are first and foremost coalition-builders.[3] My analysis builds on this literature by specifying various micro-level relational strategies through which reformers forge alliances and overcome institutional barriers. In doing so, it lends precision to the general claim that their agency matters. It shows, furthermore, that 19th century labour protections were not simply the outcome of dedicated reformers' compassion or morality. Rather, protections were enacted when reformers persuaded lawmakers that working children posed hidden threats, or harboured latent resources, that were relevant to the interests of elites and the state. At a time when labour's political power has eroded and policy progress still requires substantial buy-in from political elites, these insights remain relevant for social welfare reformers today.

Source: Anderson 2018, 2021; Béland and Cox 2016; Fligstein and McAdam 2012; Kingdon 1984; Mintrom 1997; Sheingate 2003.

NOTES

1   See, for example, Snow and Benford 1988.

2   Parlement Français 1840, p. 82.

3   See, for example, Béland and Cox 2016; Fligstein and McAdam 2012; Kingdon 1984; Mintrom 1997; Sheingate 2003.

The "rational" agent and rational choice theory

An agent (someone who acts) makes a rational choice when acting to do as well as she believes she can to achieve her preferences.[1] There are three independent ingredients in rational choice: stable preferences, rational information processing and beliefs, and maximization.[2] What someone desires (preferences) is autonomous and does not change. It is what moves people to pursue their individual self-interest, their own wellbeing (their utility). They form their belief based on information collected to help the agent make a specific decision. For instance, if someone prefers not to get wet after leaving the house, how does she choose whether to grab an umbrella? Rational choice assumes that she makes the decision based on the combination of the preference (to not get wet) and the belief about whether it is going to rain—for instance, by looking out the window or consulting weather forecasts, depending on how important it is for her to not get wet.[3]

This concept of agent is very general and is widely used to describe and explain human behaviour with economic models,[4] framing rational choice as maximizing individual welfare (typically represented by a utility function that translates consumption choices into welfare).[5] Preferences are thus represented by a utility function that each person seeks to maximize. Powerful extensions account for more general contexts. When two or more agents are in a situation where their choices depend on what others do, they need to form rational expectations (that is, assume that everyone else behaves according to rational choice) about what the others will do. This type of interdependent decisionmaking is studied in game theory, which can be applied to many economic, political and social settings. More relevant for this Report, where there is uncertainty—that is, where different outcomes are possible, each with a different level of utility associated with it—the model is reframed as expected utility theory. The utility (which represents the agent's preferences) associated with each possible outcome is weighed by its probability of occurring and averaged out in the form of expected utility, which then represents what the agent seeks to maximize.

Under well-specified conditions (for instance, everyone has access to the same information), economic agents make choices for what to consume and produce, exchanging what they are endowed with in markets, leading to an economic equilibrium that is reached after all the agents make their best possible choice in fulfilling their individual motivations.[6] The economic equilibrium is such that no agents can improve their utility without harming someone else's—designated as Pareto optimality. These results are often the justification for many policies and institutions. Their scope is justified as correcting violations of the conditions under which this equilibrium emerges (that is, correcting market failures, ranging from externalities, when choices have side effects that are not included in the moment of choice, to situations in which some agents have more information than others). Policies and institutions often focus on structuring incentives—changing prices through taxes, for instance, to bring the actual conditions under which people make choices closer to the specified conditions under which the model yields the desired Pareto optimum equilibrium.

NOTES

1   The description of rational choice in this spotlight draws heavily from Elster (2021b). A more extensive treatment is presented in Elster (2015).

2   A canonical statement comes from Becker (1976, p. 143): "all human behaviour can be viewed as involving participants who maximize their utility, form a stable set of preferences and accumulate an optimal amount of information and other inputs in a variety of markets."

3   The example also comes from Elster (2021b).

4   Much of the inspiration for the discussion in this spotlight comes from Hoff and Stiglitz (2016).

5   A set of axioms that are behaviourally plausible and impose a logical structure to the acts of choice that are allowed to take place is also included (for example, if someone prefers apples to oranges and oranges to pears, she also has to prefer apples to pears). For a formal treatment, including some of the extensions discussed in this paragraph, see Mas-Colell, Whinston and Green (1995). Key axioms are meant to ensure behaviour where there is consistency of choice, but Sen (1993) argued that seemingly inconsistent behaviours do not imply lack of rationality, since they may reflect the consistent use of decision strategies based on rules. Sen (2002) argued that there is no way to establish internal consistency of choice without referring to something external to the act of choice (such as values or norms). Arkes, Gigerenzer and Hertwig (2016) argue that coherence in choice cannot be a universal benchmark of rationality.

6   The model formalizes Adam Smith's intuition that the pursuit of self-interest in the context of potentially mutually beneficial economic exchange would make everyone better off, without the need for moral commitments to doing something good or under the direction of a supra-individual authority. It is ironic that Adam Smith is remembered primarily for this insight, when much of his work was to explore the importance of different motivations for human behaviour, including the role of moral commitments or social expectations about what is acceptable behaviour. These observations draw from Sen (2009b).

How can societies make progress in uncertain times? A question taking on new forms, calling for new analytical tools

Diane Coyle, *Cambridge University.*

In unsettled times the perpetual question of how human societies can progress takes on new forms. This Report diagnoses the multiple sources of insecurity and distress affecting so many people around the world at present and in doing so explores some possible actions policymakers might take. Even setting aside immediate pressures such as conflict-related food shortages and price increases, two long-term challenges face all of us. One is dealing with the consequences of climate change. The other is responding to the structural economic and social changes being brought about by disruptive digital technologies. A long time in the making, both need action now, or they will increase inequalities and insecurities beyond the intolerable levels they have already reached.

Tackling these challenges will require new analytical tools. This is because the phenomena of environmental damage on the one hand and digital transformation on the other do not conform to the assumptions underlying much conventional economic analysis and policy recommendations. Both areas are rife with what economists refer to as externalities or spillovers, whereby decisions have byproducts in the form of substantial consequences for others as well as the decisionmaker. Examples are businesses that emit pollutants or carbon dioxide, causing environmental and societal damage they do not have to pay for, or in the digital domain the provision of personal data that reveal information about other individuals —or conversely that enable platforms to provide a better service to all their users. Environmental externalities are usually negative, as natural resources are so often unpriced. Digital externalities can be either negative or positive.

In textbook economics the rule of thumb is that market prices capture the relevant information for the best use and allocation of resources; but it is also textbook economics that this presumption does not hold when there are pervasive externalities. On the contrary such situations of market failure pose collective action problems. Individual incentives lead to worse outcomes than are possible if there is coordination, led by either governments and public bodies or community-organized institutions, as in the inspiring work of Elinor Ostrom.

Yet although this is well known, standard economic policy tools continue to assume a simpler world where it can be reasonably believed that individual business or personal decisions generally lead to good economic outcomes, while individual market failures can be tackled one by one with specific solutions. This default way of thinking about economic policy, deeply embedded in the education and traditions of policymakers for decades, needs to change. The world has changed beyond recognition from those mental models of individual choice.

To give one example, digital business models using data and algorithms to deliver services are becoming increasingly widespread in many countries. They hold great promise for individual consumers—for example, enhancing access to low-cost financial services or providing access to markets for small and medium enterprises. But they need an appropriate policy framework to govern their use of data and ensure markets remain open for new entrants.

Data are a key resource in the digital economy, but data's features are not like a standard economic good. Data are "nonrival" in that they can be used by many people simultaneously and are not depleted, and data can cause harm (a negative externality) by unintentionally revealing too much information about people at the expense of their privacy and offer benefits (positive externalities) when different pieces of data are joined to provide useful information. Businesses that acquire a lot of data about users can also turn those data into a barrier to entry to limit their competition, as they are in a much better position to both improve service and earn revenues.

Since 2019 the debate about competition policy has increasingly recognized the challenge posed by the dominance of a few companies in digital markets, which are sometimes described as "winner takes all" or "superstar" markets. However, progress in changing policies to tackle market dominance has been slow, even in the United Kingdom and the United States, where the academic and policy debate started a few years ago. The everyday, practical policy tools for analysis and remedies do not yet exist.

What is more, debates about appropriate governance policies for data more generally are in their early stages. Should data be "owned" as if a piece of property when the information that data provide is always relational or contextual? If so, given that using data creates so much value, who should be assigned property rights: the collector or the original subject or source? If not, what framework of access rights and responsibilities would generate value for society? How should data users be required to take account of data bias due to the inequality of society—and indeed of people who have no data "voice," whose activities and needs are not measured?

Another example of an area with many open questions, due to the absence so far of an appropriate benchmark policy framework, is biodiversity policies. Partha Dasgupta's 2020 landmark review of the economics of biodiversity for Her Majesty's Treasury in the United Kingdom synthesized the relevant theoretical framework, but again the spadework needs to be done to turn conceptual insights into practical interventions. How can early warning of irreversible tipping points in ecosystems be recognized? What is the appropriate geographic scope for measuring and acting on biodiversity loss? How does it integrate with agricultural productivity or affect human health?

In both arenas, environmental and digital, there has been considerable excellent academic research at the frontier of knowledge. But to turn this into actionable insights, the default presumption needs to be that this is a world of tipping points, multiple possible outcomes depending on current choices, externalities and collective action problems. The economic analysis needs to be integrated with scientific or technical knowledge to deliver practical policy tools. Different datasets are required, going beyond standard economic metrics and dashboards.

There are active debates among researchers and policymakers alike about these kinds of challenges and much recent progress—such as the development of statistical standards for measuring natural capital and ecosystem services. But shaping an appropriate mindset for this uncertain, unstable and interconnected world remains a challenge.

Source: Based on Coyle (2021).

Norms and cooperation in a multipolar world: Beyond economics

Kaushik Basu, *Cornell University*

As the world battles multiple onslaughts—from the fracturing of society, caused by the shifting rules of economic and social interaction, in turn caused by the rapid advance in digital technology, to the rise in climate-related disasters, the Covid-19 pandemic that waxes and wanes but refuses to go, and to the war in Ukraine—it is time to rethink not just our policies but also the foundations of the social sciences. Since much of today's policy challenge relates to economics, economists have written extensively on these themes, much of it captured in this Report. There is, however, a growing contribution from neighbouring disciplines—philosophy, politics and sociology—that provide insights for economists and urge them to question some of the assumptions hidden deep in the woodwork of their own discipline. It is important to realize that the world that we analyse is partly a construction of our discipline.[1] As we try to understand society, which is on the one hand steadily globalizing and on the other becoming politically polarized with rising conflict across and within nations, it is critical to trespass boundaries and draw on these alternate disciplinary paradigms.

Since the Age of Enlightenment, and even before that, philosophers have been aware of the need for society to nurture cooperation. Some of this happens naturally from the nudges of the invisible hand, but we also need agreements and conventions that coordinate the behaviours of individuals. Such agreements seem like an impossible task for our vast, multipolar world. Hope lies in the fact that we now have a better understanding of how cooperation happens and why it often breaks down. This is because of one instrument that the Enlightenment philosophers did not have but their progenies do, to wit, game theory. As a result, there has been a spate of recent writing that formalizes ideas from the 17th and 18th centuries and helps us think of new ways to manage society, avert conflict and foster development.[2]

This new literature is helping us grapple with real-world problems, from conflict and social inequality to the role of political leaders. We understand these better than ever before. How do leaders acquire power? Why do they have such influence over individuals, at times hurting the very people who follow them? Surprisingly, much of the leader's ability to stir action among people arises from nothing but the beliefs of ordinary individuals. The statements and orders of the leader create focal points. You believe that, given a leader's order or suggestion of order, others will follow it, and that in turn makes it in your interest to follow it as well. When such a confluence of beliefs occurs, a speech or even an utterance by a leader can unleash torrents of behaviour among individuals, propped up by nothing more than beliefs of what other individuals will do.

This kind of analysis can be brought to bear on practical matters, such as the responsibility people bear towards their community[3] and a leader's responsibility for the behaviour of his or her followers. The convention is to hold a leader responsible for certain group behaviour if it can be shown that unleashing such behaviour was the leader's intention. Following the above analysis, it can be argued that a leader should also be held responsible for unwarranted group behaviour if the leader could reasonably be shown to have been aware that his or her speech or behaviour would result in the group behaviour, even if that was not the leader's intention.[4] This altered view can have large implications for how we interpret the law, regulate and punish.

Because of the large influence of economists, much of the formal analysis remains confined to individually rational behaviour. We try to explain all forms of cooperation by reference to self-interest. This often leads to exciting mathematical models, but one consequence of this obsession is we forget that universal self-interested behaviour is one of those assumptions in the woodwork, which we take for granted but is not true.

Virtually all human beings carry some form of moral compasses in their heads. They desist from numerous behaviours not out of self-interest but because their ethics, often deontological principles, do not permit them. I believe we do not pick other people's pockets not because, after doing a cost-benefit analysis, we conclude that the cost of picking pockets outweighs the benefit, but because this is an inbuilt moral code in us.

This, in turn, raises questions about the very meaning of cooperation. Was the cooperation of Adam Smith the same as that of philosophers and scholars of politics?[5] Basing our evaluation on a wider disciplinary foundation also raises vital questions about value, worth and equality. We can stigmatize individuals, banish individuals to the margins and exacerbate inequities in a variety of ways.[6] These inequities can give rise to fractures and polarizations that have little to do with economic inequality.

Because these are subjects on the fringes of the social sciences, we know little about the connection between the nature of norms and moral codes we adhere to and the level of our economic growth and wellbeing. There is need for more research on this. It is arguable that to sustain economic development, we need concurrent moral progress. Michele Moody-Adams argues that what is moral "progress" can be contested, but we can nevertheless take a stance on it, and she expressed optimism that moral progress can be advanced.[7] Allen Buchanan and Russell Powell take the agenda forward, showing that this can be carried over to codes of inclusivity, which are critically important in today's polarized world.[8]

As we understand these motivations that go beyond individual rationality, we can try to cultivate moral instincts that lead to greater harmony and cooperation in society. The crux of the challenge is to think of codes of behaviour that individuals as well as collectivities such as nations adhere to. The aim is to have agreements, such as minimal constitutions, that are scientifically constructed. This will not rule out conflict since the roots of some conflicts go beyond self-interest.[9] Nevertheless, by nurturing certain codes of behaviour, which are often innately in us anyway, we can hope to stimulate empathy and further the collective good for the world.

NOTES

1   Mitchell 2005.

2   Basu 2022; Moehler 2019; Thrasher and Vallier 2015; Vanderschraaf 2019.

3   Deb 2020.

4   Basu 2022.

5   Brennan and Sayre-McCord 2018.

6   Goffman 1963; Lamont 2018; Lindbeck, Nyberg and Weibull 1999.

7   Moody-Adams 1999.

8   Buchanan and Powell 2018.

9   Muldoon and others 2014.

Cognitive uncertainty

Benjamin Enke, *Harvard University*

Many of the most important challenges facing humankind require tradeoffs involving uncertainty and time. For instance, climate change mitigation measures are risky in the sense that we do not know precisely how well they will work. Moreover, climate action involves intertemporal tradeoffs because it delivers benefits primarily in the future but accrues costs today. In contexts like these, adequate decisionmaking by policymakers and individuals requires sophisticated reasoning about risk and time. Yet, a key insight from recent research in behavioural economics is that many economically relevant decisions that involve risk or intertemporal tradeoffs are cognitively very difficult. Consider the following two illustrative examples:

- Suppose you are offered an investment that pays $1,000 with a probability of 35 percent and nothing with a probability of 65 percent. How much would you be willing to pay for such an asset? Maybe $220? Are you sure? How about $185? Or $342?
- Now suppose you actually won $1,000 and your banker offers you a safe annual interest rate of 4 percent. How much of your new wealth would you like to save at this interest rate rather than spend this year? $600? Are you sure? Not $775 or $452?

These examples illustrate a principle that is very general: in a large range of decisions, people exhibit cognitive uncertainty, meaning that they do not know which decision is actually best for them, given their preferences. Cognitive uncertainty refers to a purely internal —cognitive—form of uncertainty, rather than objective uncertainty about the physical world. Cognitive uncertainty is the result of people's imperfect ability to determine the optimal course of action in complex situations. The empirical reality that people often exhibit cognitive uncertainty contrasts with the approach traditionally taken by behavioural economists, which is to assume that people may make mistakes but are not aware of their own cognitive imperfections.[1]

Why is cognitive uncertainty important? A main reason is that a growing number of experiments and surveys document that when people are cognitively uncertain, they anchor on a so-called cognitive default decision.[2] A cognitive default decision is the naïve decision people would make in the absence of any deliberation: what they would do if they did not really think about it. In contexts with which people have experience, this could be a decision they previously made. In contexts with which people do not have experience, the cognitive default is often to pick something intermediate or a compromise. Regardless of what the decision is, much evidence shows that when people are cognitively uncertain, they anchor on, or regress to, a cognitive default.[3] As a result, people's decisions are often poorly calibrated to the prevailing set of circumstances, in particular under new environmental conditions.

The following sections explore these abstract ideas in more concrete contexts, by studying how people think about probabilities (uncertainty) and intertemporal tradeoffs and then by discussing more speculatively how cognitive uncertainty and cognitive default decisions may matter for understanding and addressing current societal challenges.

Decisionmaking under uncertainty

Almost all economically relevant decisions involve some risk. As a result, much research in economics and psychology studies how people learn from information, how they make predictions about future events (such as the probability that they will lose their job) and how they choose among different investment strategies (such as whether and how to invest in the stock market). All these domains require people to process probabilities. Yet, substantial research has documented that people have a pronounced tendency to make decisions that look as if they implicitly treat all probabilities to some degree alike, which produces a compression-to-the-centre effect (figure S3.6.1).[4]

Figure S3.6.1 People have a pronounced tendency to make decisions that look as if they implicitly treat all probabilities to some degree alike

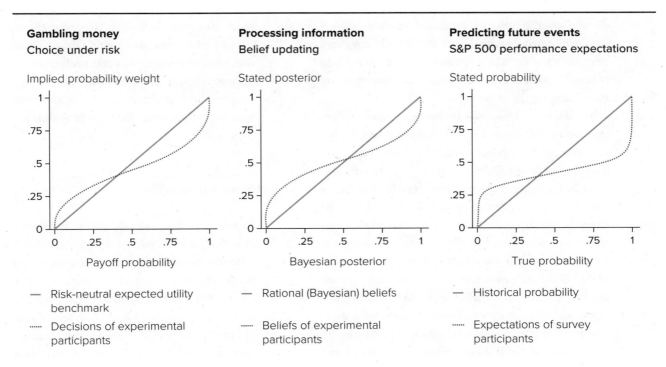

Gambling money
Choice under risk

Implied probability weight

Payoff probability

— Risk-neutral expected utility benchmark

····· Decisions of experimental participants

Processing information
Belief updating

Stated posterior

Bayesian posterior

— Rational (Bayesian) beliefs

····· Beliefs of experimental participants

Predicting future events
S&P 500 performance expectations

Stated probability

True probability

— Historical probability

····· Expectations of survey participants

Source: Enke and Graeber 2019.

The left panel of figure S3.6.1 shows the canonical probability weighting function that depicts how people typically weight probabilities when they choose among different monetary gambles. For example, people overweight a 5 percent chance of winning $100 but underweight a 95 percent chance of winning that amount. Thus, in essence, people treat both high and low probabilities as more intermediate than they really are. This is a regularity that economists have devoted much attention to, as it helps explain phenomena such as casino gambling, the overpricing of positively skewed financial assets, the equity premium and why people prefer insurance policies with low deductibles.[5]

The middle panel illustrates a common way in which people's inferences from new information tend to be systematically wrong. When people receive information suggesting that a specified event is objectively very unlikely to occur, they often overestimate such small probabilities. On the other hand, when people receive information suggesting that an event is very likely to occur, they underestimate such high probabilities, which again leads to a compression effect towards the centre.

Finally, the right panel shows a typical pattern regarding people's expectations of how much the stock market will go up, as a function of objective probabilities. Again, people's probability estimates are typically heavily compressed towards the centre, which means that people are overly optimistic as far as very unlikely scenarios are unconcerned but overly pessimistic when it comes to very likely scenarios.

The similarity of compression effects in these three probability domains is striking. Yet, until recently, economists and psychologists often viewed them as separate phenomena, rather than as being driven by a common cognitive mechanism.[6]

One way of jointly accounting for these patterns across different domains is the simple insight that people find it cognitively difficult to think about probabilities and, therefore, anchor on an intermediate cognitive default decision.[7] The main idea is that people mentally start out from an intermediate decision, something that is far from the extremes and feels moderate. Upon deliberation, they then insufficiently adjust in the direction of the rational decision (the decision that would be expected under a standard rational choice model). Crucially, the idea is that the magnitude of the adjustment towards the rational decision decreases in cognitive uncertainty. Thus, people who are extremely cognitively uncertain will decide based purely on the cognitive default decision, while people who do not exhibit any cognitive uncertainty will make a rational decision. According to this hypothesis, cognitively uncertain decisions are more compressed towards the centre.

Testing of this hypothesis through a series of experiments and surveys that measured people's cognitive uncertainty revealed that in all three decision domains in figure S3.6.1, the gist of the results was the same: higher cognitive uncertainty is strongly associated with greater compression of decisions towards the centre (figure S3.6.2).[8] Intuitively, this makes sense: when people do not know how to value a risky asset, or if they do not know how to form probabilistic estimates about variables such as stock market returns, they anchor on an intermediate decision and then only partially adjust away from it. As a result, cognitively uncertain people overestimate the probability of unlikely events and overweight low probabilities when they translate them into risky decisions. Likewise, cognitively uncertain people underestimate the probability of likely events and underweight low probabilities when they translate them into risky decisions. However, these patterns do not arise because people have acquired domain-specific errors or even preferences—instead, they reflect a general heuristic according to which people find it difficult to think about probabilities and, therefore, treat different probabilities to some degree alike.

Intertemporal decisions

Consider now an entirely different set of decisions, in which people trade off money (or other goods) at different points in time. For example, an experiment participant may be asked whether she would prefer to receive $90 today or $100 in a year from now. A large body of empirical work has documented that people's intertemporal decisions are often characterized by a type of compression effect that is very similar to the one seen in the case of probabilities.[9]

Figure S3.6.2 Higher cognitive uncertainty is strongly associated with greater compression of decisions towards the centre

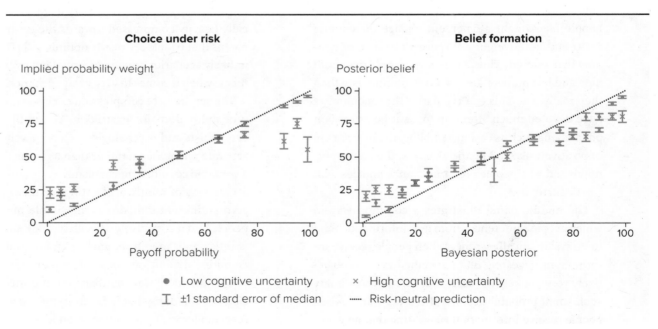

Note: The left panel illustrates the probability weighting function in choices between monetary lotteries, and the right panel shows reported beliefs in laboratory belief formation experiments.
Source: Enke and Graeber 2019.

S3.6.3 illustrates this by showing how much people typically value a payment of $100 to be received at different points in time. For example, the left panel shows that, on average, people value $100 in nine months roughly as much as $60 today and that they value $100 in four years as much as $40 today. The main takeaway is that people's decisions seem to treat different time delays to some degree alike. For example, people seem to behave as if it makes almost no difference to them whether they receive $100 in two years or in three. Overall, this leads to a compression effect, according to which people's valuation of a delayed payment of $100 is again compressed towards an intermediate value of roughly $50.

Popular models such as the standard discounted expected utility model, or models of present bias,[10] cannot explain these puzzling patterns. For example, the extreme compression effect towards the centre also occurs when people make decisions that involve tradeoffs between two future dates (right panel of figure S3.6.3), such that present bias cannot play a role.

One hypothesis is that these patterns do not (only) reflect present bias or other nonstandard preferences but that they are again driven by complexity and resulting cognitive uncertainty.[11] The intuition is that when people are cognitively uncertain about exactly how much a payment of $100 in three years is worth to them today, they again anchor on an intermediate cognitive default decision and then adjust from there —but insufficiently so. According to this hypothesis, relative to the benchmark of a rational decisionmaker, people with cognitive uncertainty will look less patient over short horizons (because the intermediate cognitive default "drags down" their patience), yet they will appear more patient over long horizons.

Experiments measuring people's cognitive uncertainty when making these types of intertemporal decisions show that cognitive uncertainty is strongly predictive of the degree to which people's intertemporal decisions seem to treat all time delays alike (figure S3.6.4).[12] As a result, cognitively uncertain people exhibit excessively high impatience over short horizons, such as in tradeoffs between today and in three months. However, in contrast to conventional preferences-based accounts of intertemporal choice, such impatience does not largely reflect genuinely

Figure S3.6.3 People's decisions about value seem to treat different time delays to some degree alike

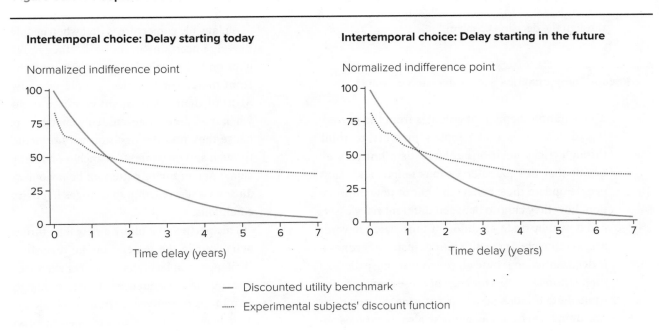

— Discounted utility benchmark

···· Experimental subjects' discount function

Note: The left panel shows people's typical behaviour in tradeoffs between the present and the future, and the right panel shows people's typical behaviour in tradeoffs between two different future points in time.
Source: Enke and Graeber 2021.

Figure S3.6.4 Cognitive uncertainty is strongly predictive of the degree to which people's intertemporal decisions seem to treat all time delays alike

Experimental results: Intertemporal choice

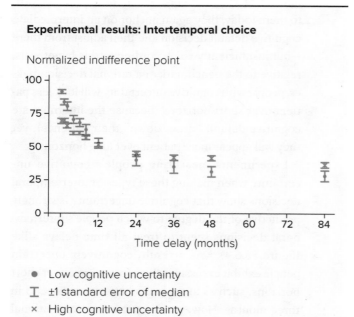

Normalized indifference point

- ● Low cognitive uncertainty
- I ±1 standard error of median
- × High cognitive uncertainty

Note: The dots show how much participants value a cash payment or food voucher of $100 at different points in time.
Source: Enke and Graeber 2021.

low patience but instead people's inability to think through the decision problem.

Recap: Commonalities across decision domains

The common theme that emerges from the preceding discussion is that people's inability to think through tricky decision problems is a unifying element that ties together various behaviours. How people update their beliefs in light of new information, how they choose between different risky assets and how they trade off different time-dated rewards are, in principle, three different domains of economic decisionmaking. Indeed, economists have devised sophisticated models for each of these domains. Yet, while there is much benefit in focusing on each decision domain in isolation, doing so also sometimes obscures important commonalities across domains. In particular, we have seen that people are often unsure what the best decision is, that cognitive uncertainty is strongly linked to taking "intermediate" decisions

that make it seem as if people treat different probabilities and time delays alike and that this mechanism generates many of the famous empirical regularities that behavioural economists and psychologists have accumulated over the years. According to the logic of cognitive uncertainty, these regularities are all intimately linked.

Potential implications for societal challenges

The main takeaway from the studies summarized above is that when people are cognitively uncertain —that is, when they find a decision problem difficult to think through—they anchor on a cognitive default and then insufficiently adjust in the direction of the rational decision. As a result, decisions look as if people underreact to changes in the prevailing circumstances such as the probabilities of different events.

In experiments the default decision is consistently intermediate in nature, which could reflect a naïve diversification or compromise logic. Yet, these choice experiments all involve contexts with which most people have limited or no experience. This raises the question what constitutes people's cognitive default decision in situations with which they do have experience, as is usually the case in reality.

A plausible conjecture is that when people are cognitively uncertain "in the wild," they intuitively anchor on their typical past decision and then adjust from there. For instance, people who always save $100 of their salary might continue to do so even when the interest rate suddenly changes—purely because they find the decision very difficult to think through and they therefore anchor on their past decision.[13] Again, such a pattern of behaviour would produce an underreaction to changes in environmental conditions.

This perspective offers a new lens through which behaviour in the general public regarding societal challenges can be understood. For example, thinking through the consequences of climate change for one's own life is cognitively extremely challenging. Even if we knew for certain that temperatures will rise by 3°C over the next 30 years, it is very hard (even for experts) to think through how this would affect the structure of our economies and lifestyles. In other words it is most likely true that people exhibit very high cognitive uncertainty when thinking through which personal decisions they should take in light of climate change. Which skills will be valued 30 years from now? How should I optimally behave in light of these changes? How and where should I optimally choose to live given these developments?

Even in the absence of any objective uncertainty about the physical word, these questions are cognitively extremely difficult to think through. This cognitive difficulty may induce people to anchor on the cognitive default of making the same decisions as in the past, which then mechanically produces an underreaction to changes in economic and climatic conditions. For example, the relatively low investment into climate change adaptation in the past may serve as a cognitive anchor for determining today's investments. If true, this would suggest that the apparent underreaction in the population to new economic or climatic conditions partly reflects the cognitive difficulty of thinking through complex topics, rather than necessarily selfish or short-sighted preferences. This account is potentially valuable because it adds a new perspective and policy prescription. Rather than lament about people's preferences or even try to change them, policymakers may be more successful at inducing people to adjust their behaviours by helping them imagine and think through a future with climate change: what people's lives will look like, which types of jobs they will be competing for, how they will commute to work and what their children will learn. Only when people understand the implications of abstract policy discussions for which decisions they need to make to prepare themselves for the future—once people have reduced their cognitive uncertainty—may they be able to make the decisions that policymakers and international organizations are hoping for.

NOTES

1   Benjamin 2019.

2   Enke and Graeber 2019, 2021; Xiang and others 2021.

3   Enke and Graeber 2019, 2021; Xiang and others 2021.

4   Benjamin 2019; Fischhoff and Bruine De Bruin 1999; Kahneman and Tversky 1979.

5   See Barberis (2013) for a review.

6   For example, Kahneman and Tversky's (1979) prospect theory applies only to how people translate probabilistic beliefs into decisions; it remains silent on how people form probabilistic beliefs in the first place. Similarly, formal economic and psychological models of belief formation sometimes predict that reported beliefs are overly compressed towards 50:50, but they do not predict that people's risky decisions are compressed functions of beliefs (see Benjamin 2019 for a review).

7   Enke and Graeber 2019. The idea that people exhibit noise in processing probabilities is present in various theoretical models, including Erev, Wallsten and Budescu (1994), Khaw, Li and Woodford (2021) and Viscusi 1985, 1989.

8   Enke and Graeber 2019.

9   See, for example, Cohen and others (2020) for a review.

10   Laibson 1997.

11   Enke and Graeber 2021.

12   Enke and Graeber 2021.

13   For example, D'Acunto and others (2021) document that people with lower cognitive skills react less to changes in interest rates than their higher-ability counterparts. This may reflect that people entertain a cognitive default decision of repeating what they did in the past.

Human agency can help restore biodiversity: The case of forest transitions

Erle C. Ellis, *University of Maryland, Baltimore County*

Biodiversity losses are increasingly recognized as a global crisis demanding transformative changes in human societies to halt further losses and to better conserve and restore biodiversity.[1] Forest habitats generally sustain more species than other terrestrial biomes, and moist tropical forests are among the most biodiverse ecosystems on Earth.[2] As a result, the conversion, degradation and fragmentation of forests and other biodiverse wild habitats by agriculture and other intensive land uses are currently the leading cause of biodiversity losses across the terrestrial biosphere.[3]

For more than a century, human demands for food, fibre and other land use products have soared to sustain the growth of increasingly well-off populations and their choice of richer diets, including animal products and other land-demanding commodities.[4] To meet these demands, land use for crops and pastures have replaced forests and other habitats across more than 35 percent of Earth's ice-free land area.[5] Yet despite this alarming long-term trend, the global area of agricultural land has not increased significantly since the 1990s, even while the amount of food produced per capita has risen faster than population for more than half a century.[6]

Biodiversity losses remain a serious concern as the global area used for intensive crops continues to grow, both within existing agricultural areas and through deforestation, especially in less developed tropical regions, where biodiversity losses from land conversion are greatest.[7] Nevertheless, tropical deforestation appears to be slowing, and forests and other wild habitats are regenerating in the more developed temperate regions of the world where less suitable agricultural land is being abandoned.[8] Though it remains unlikely that global forest area in 2030 could increase by 3 percent relative to 2015 to meet target 1.1 of the United Nations Strategic Plan for Forests, annual net loss of forests has been nearly halved since the 1990s, to about 0.1 percent a year, as a result of declining deforestation rates and increasing forest regeneration

rates.[9] Clearly, some forest trends are going in the right direction, especially in the more developed regions of the world.

The large-scale regeneration of forests following the abandonment of agricultural land was first identified as a general pattern of forest recovery in developed regions of Europe starting in the late 1800s.[10] In recent decades these so-called forest transitions, defined as sustained regional shifts from net deforestation to net reforestation, are increasingly being observed in contemporary temperate and tropical regions around the world.[11] The early forest transitions of Europe, the United States and elsewhere were first explained by an economic development pathway in which urbanization and industrialization drove labour scarcity in agriculture, leading to agricultural intensification to increase total production using the most suitable lands, enabling profits to be maximized and leading to the abandonment of less productive agricultural lands, where forests then regenerated spontaneously.[12]

More recently, "economic" forest transitions have also been explained, to some degree, through "land use displacement pathways," in which forests recover in one region while potentially being lost in another, when agricultural demands are outsourced through globalized supply chains, often to developing regions of the tropics.[13] In land use displacement pathways the biodiversity benefits of forest regeneration may be reversed many times over, unless the receiving agricultural region has very high yields (and therefore lower net land area requirements), owing to the higher biodiversity of most tropical regions and the potential for land use conversions through deforestation.[14] Additional pathways towards forest transitions have emerged in recent decades, including state and nongovernmental organization–supported tree planting programmes and through land use policies and regulatory pathways supporting forest conservation and restoration to meet international targets for carbon and biodiversity.[15]

Global supply chain transparency initiatives and voluntary certification of sustainable production are helping reduce losses of tropical forests produced through land use displacement.[16] But there is still a long way to go.[17] Even though forest transitions are increasingly evident around the world, including in many developing tropical regions,[18] at the global scale, biodiversity losses remain inevitable whenever land use is simply exported to other regions,[19] unless their productivity is substantially higher or their biodiversity is substantially lower.

The ultimate prospects for a global forest transition to halt losses of biodiversity will depend on the degree to which commodity demands can be met by increasingly intensive land use practices that shrink land demand overall—the classic "economic" pathway of urban and industrial development—combined with efforts to prioritize the conservation and restoration of the most biodiverse regions on Earth.[20] The pace of this development, including urbanization and agricultural intensification, and the governance of global commodity supply chains[21] will ultimately determine not only the fate of Earth's remaining biodiversity but also the future of human opportunities with respect to food, housing, employment, recreation and other essential conditions.

NOTES

1   Díaz and others 2019; IPBES 2019b; Pereira, Navarro and Martins 2012; WWF 2020.

2   Barlow and others 2018; FAO and UNEP 2020.

3   Díaz and others 2019; IPBES 2019b; WWF 2020.

4   Alexander and others 2015; Ellis 2019; Sanderson, Walston and Robinson 2018.

5   Ramankutty and others 2018.

6   Ellis 2019; FAO 2017.

7   Barlow and others 2018; Curtis and others 2018; Ramankutty and others 2018.

8   FAO and UNEP 2020; Keenan and others 2015.

9   FAO and UNEP 2020.

10 Mather 1992; Rudel and others 2020.

11 Ellis 2021; Meyfroidt and others 2018; Rudel and others 2020.

12 Meyfroidt and others 2018; Rudel and others 2020.

13 Meyfroidt and Lambin 2011; Meyfroidt and others 2018; Rudel and others 2020.

14 Schwarzmueller and Kastner 2022.

15 Meyfroidt and others 2018; Rudel and others 2020; Wolff and others 2018.

16 Lambin and others 2018.

17 Curtis and others 2018.

18 Hosonuma and others 2012.

19 Meyfroidt and Lambin 2011.

20 Curtis and others 2018; Ferreira and others 2018; Meyfroidt and Lambin 2011; Strassburg and others 2020.

21 Chung and Liu 2022; Lambin and others 2018; Pimm 2022.

Shaping our future in a transforming world

Shaping our future in a transforming world

Beyond causing frustration and unsettling minds (chapter 2), the uncertainties described in chapter 1 can also undermine the ability to act collectively. Uncertainty has different manifestations. At the individual level it can be seen in the form of human insecurity. This chapter shows that perceptions of insecurity are associated with mistrust and with political polarization—people who feel insecure trust others less and are more prone to politically extreme positions. Meanwhile, changes to our information systems are reshaping how people form beliefs and how they interact with one another. The social changes brought on by rapidly evolving digital communications technology place additional pressures on human interaction. Together, these two shifts are jeopardizing public deliberation and social choice (chapter 4). But uncertainty can also open new possibilities for action, since it can reframe what is perceived as possible and needed: this is explored in chapter 5, on the way to chapter 6, which provides suggestions on the way forward.

What's standing in the way of our acting together?

CHAPTER 4

What's standing in the way of our acting together?

The paradox of our time is paralysis: we know what the problems are, we have more tools than ever to address them, but we are failing to act.

Why? What is getting in the way?

This chapter points to polarization and how uncertainty and insecurity can exacerbate it. Trust is down; political extremism is up. Hyperinformation is sowing division. Spaces for public deliberation are shrinking right when they are needed most.

The unprecedented multilayered uncertainties —coming from the Anthropocene context, social and technological transformations and political polarization—test our social, economic and political institutions, as well as the patterns of behaviour that shape and are shaped by those institutions. The link between the two, as chapter 3 discusses, is the result of procedures of social choice, reflected in how societies craft collective responses.

Why has it proven so difficult to craft these collective responses, which demand changes in both behaviour and institutions, despite clear evidence of harm to come for people, societies and the planet? Chapter 3 argues that current configurations of behaviour and institutions are not responding effectively to a novel context of uncertainty. This mismatch increases the importance of processes of public deliberation and social choice in shaping the behavioural and institutional changes needed in an uncertain world. Processes of social choice that harness people's diverse goals, motivations, beliefs and emotions can be a powerful driver of social change.

However, in many countries today, processes of public deliberation and social choice are coming under strain amid intensifying political polarization and divisiveness.[1] Political polarization can be understood as "the extent to which citizens become ideologically entrenched in their own values and political beliefs, thereby increasing the divide with citizens who hold different values and political beliefs."[2] Polarization tends to make people close in on their in-groups and be reluctant to interact, exchange and communicate with out-groups. Affective polarization —the tendency to view out-group members negatively and in-group members positively[3]—antagonizes people across partisan lines.[4] This animosity is added to the other forms of issue-based and ideological polarization between groups that have long been studied in sociology and political science.[5]

This chapter explores how polarization can intensify because of two intertwined developments. First, the unsettling of people's lives and experiences of human insecurity. Second, the massive economic, social and political shift driven by a rapidly changing (digital) information context. It discusses how political polarization might diminish the space for imaginative, effective and just actions needed today, before suggesting how we might break the hold of

uncertainty on collective responses, taking us from a confused reacting mode to a purposeful harnessing of uncertainty towards a hopeful future.

Uncertain times, divided societies

The layers of uncertainty discussed in chapter 1 are interacting to produce new shocks and dislocations. But uncertainty is not only about shocks and dislocations; it is also about growing gaps in our collective ability to "make sense" of the world when deciding our actions. Progress in recent decades has been remarkable in many aspects of human development, particularly in wellbeing achievements, despite marked (and in some cases increasing) inequalities (see chapter 1).[6] But despite widespread progress in wellbeing achievements, around half the population does not see progress in their living standards relative to those of their parents. About 40 percent of those who have more education than their parents do not perceive intergenerational progress, vividly showing how expectations of higher future living standards are being dashed.[7]

Uncertainty and human insecurity parallel increases in polarization

When uncertainty translates into unsettled lives and human insecurity, it can increase polarization, impacting processes of social choice. Building on the analysis in chapter 3, the following discussion highlights the importance of considering beliefs, motivations and emotions as factors accounting for why it seems hard for people to act individually and collectively in the face of uncertainty. Together, these factors shape the issues people find important, people's attitudes and behaviours towards others, and the actions people support or undertake themselves.[8]

" When uncertainty translates into unsettled lives and human insecurity, it can increase polarization, impacting the processes of social choice

What is the connection between uncertain times and a range of beliefs that matter for public deliberation? Here we use the World Values Survey, whose representative sample covers around 80 percent of the global population, to check how people's perceptions of insecurity appear connected with beliefs that worsen polarization. Perceived human insecurity is a partial measure of individual uncertainty that mirrors how people's fundamental freedoms (from want, fear and indignity) are being affected today (box 4.1). We first show how perceived human insecurity is connected with people's feelings of agency and control over their lives and with their trust in others. The evidence here suggests that greater human insecurity is linked to lower individual agency and trust. We then explore associations between perceived human insecurity and people's political preferences, showing that greater human insecurity is linked to people holding extreme political preferences. The combination of high insecurity, lower interpersonal trust and high polarization is more prevalent in low Human Development Index (HDI) countries and among lower-income people.

Greater human insecurity is linked with lower individual agency and trust

Human insecurity can directly restrict human agency. High human insecurity reduces people's ability to make autonomous decisions because of lack of resources, because of fear or because of social discrimination. These effects often extend to the overall perception of agency to make choices over their own lives: people with greater human insecurity tend to perceive lower agency (figure 4.1).[9]

Trust in one another influences prospects for cooperation in a group. People tend to trust people closer to them (such as family) more than people whom they do not know or who have a different social background (as with different nationalities or religions). Lower trust in socially "distant" people influences social discrimination,[10] among other socioeconomic outcomes.[11] This pattern tends to be stronger across individuals with low incomes and with greater human insecurity (figure 4.2).[12] In other words people with high incomes and high human security have greater trust in people from more socially distant groups.

Addressing the common challenges that we confront today requires cooperation in contexts beyond those where intragroup cooperation tends to be high—in particular, addressing planetary challenges

Box 4.1 The Index of Perceived Human Insecurity

To track human insecurity, we use the Index of Perceived Human Insecurity. It is based on wave 6 (2010–2014) and wave 7 (2015–2022) of the World Values Survey[1] and reflects mainly a pre-Covid-19 context. The index is computed for 77 countries and territories, covering around 80 percent of the global population. It combines 17 variables covering violent conflict and socioeconomic, personal and community-level insecurity. These insecurities reflect challenges to freedom from want, freedom from fear and freedom from indignity.

- For insecurity from violent conflict, the index uses variables reflecting worries about a war involving the country of residence, a civil war or a terrorist attack.
- For socioeconomic insecurity the index uses variables representing explicit worries (losing a job, not being able to give children education) and actual deprivations in health, food and economic security.
- For insecurity at the personal and community levels, the index uses variables of exposure to crime, change in habits because of security concerns, overall safety perception of the neighbourhood and assessment of specific risks (including robbery, alcohol and drugs on the streets, abuse by law enforcement and racism).

Note
1. See Haerpfer and others (2022).
Source: Human Development Report Office based on UNDP (2022b).

implies collaboration not only between governments but also across other institutions (chapter 6). Interpersonal trust (the most general trust, in essentially any human being) has been declining over time. Globally, fewer than 30 percent of people think that "most people can be trusted," the lowest recorded value. There is a close association between interpersonal trust and human security.[13]

Greater human insecurity is linked to political extremism

Greater human insecurity is also linked to political extremism, understood as attitudes and behaviours representing polar views or the single-minded pursuit of one goal over others.[14] We capture the first aspect using preferences along the left-right political spectrum. People experiencing greater human insecurity tend to have a stronger preference for the polar extremes of the political spectrum: the proportion of

Figure 4.1 Greater insecurity is associated with lower personal agency

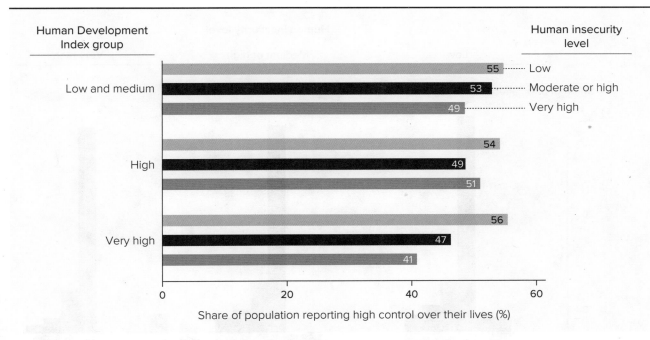

Share of population reporting high control over their lives (%)

Source: Human Development Report Office based on World Values Survey, waves 6 and 7. See Haerpfer and others (2022).

Figure 4.2 Trust declines with social distance more steeply at lower incomes and higher insecurity

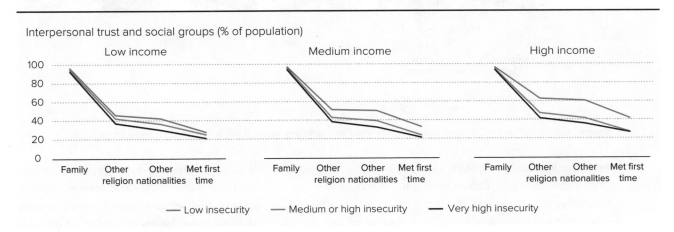

Source: Human Development Report Office based on World Values Survey, waves 6 and 7. See Haerpfer and others (2022).

people with extreme political preferences is twice as large among those feeling very insecure as among those feeling relatively secure (figure 4.3).[15]

Moreover, people experiencing greater human insecurity tend to have preferences for extreme views about the government's role in the economy (full government responsibility at one extreme and full individual responsibility at the other; figure 4.4).[16]

This is a barrier for public deliberation in uncertain times: where insecurity is higher, increased polarization of views about the role of the government in the economy can lead to a vicious cycle that makes more difficult the search for social insurance mechanisms in the very societies that need them the most.[17]

How does uncertainty affect polarization?

Research on polarization points to several factors that might cause people to harden their beliefs about their

Figure 4.3 Greater insecurity is linked to political extremism

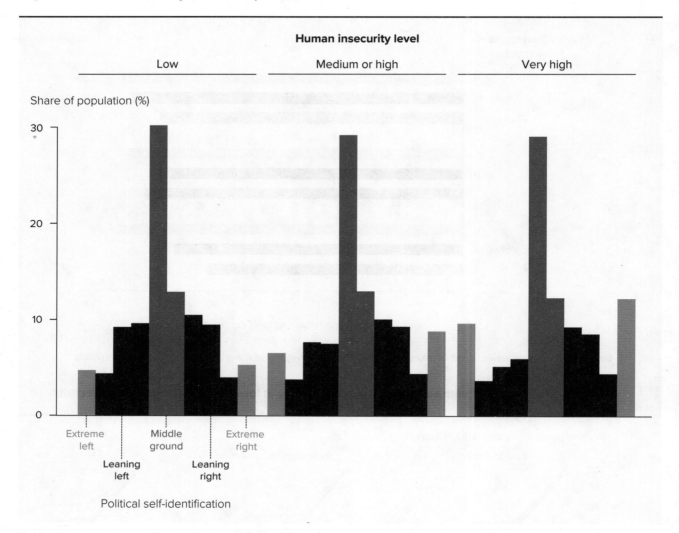

Source: Human Development Report Office based on World Values Survey, waves 6 and 7. See Haerpfer and others (2022).

own in-groups and out-groups. Here, we consider evidence on some of the factors known to contribute to polarization:

- Behavioural drivers affected by a context of uncertainty can intensify people's identification with their own social groups. Adding to this is that people in one group are also generally prone to forming incorrect beliefs about people in other groups, with implications for prospects of cooperation across groups.
- Institutional drivers, particularly those associated with inequalities and disruptive changes in our information systems.

The empirical evidence presented above suggests that individual uncertainty (proxied by perceived human insecurity) is associated with a particular set

of beliefs: diminished agency, lack of trust in others and more extreme political beliefs. The next section expands this discussion to additional behavioural factors that can contribute to polarization, as well as institutional conditions that drive polarization.

Behavioural factors

There is some evidence of a causal link between multiple manifestations of uncertainty and political polarization.[18] It comes from different disciplines, with several noting the need for humans to reduce or "resolve" uncertainty.[19] For instance, the "need for closure" or the "desire for a definite answer on some topic, any answer as opposed to confusion and ambiguity..."[20] appears as a key motivation for human behaviour.

Figure 4.4 Insecurity is associated with polarization on preferences over government versus individual responsibility

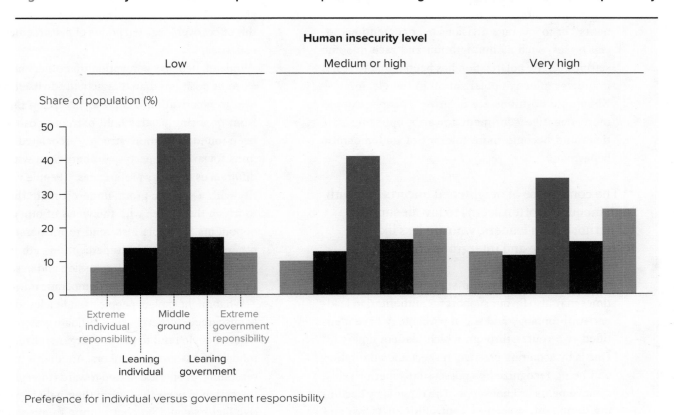

Preference for individual versus government responsibility

Source: Human Development Report Office based on World Values Survey, waves 6 and 7. See Haerpfer and others (2022).

According to the significance quest theory, people need social worth and significance.[21] This need is activated by deprivation (rooted in failure, humiliation or rejection) or incentivization (the opportunity to boost one's significance), which are linked to manifestations of human insecurity and uncertainty in general. When activated, the quest for significance enhances ideological narratives that support the values of people's group or culture that give meaning to their lives. As a result, people can be attracted to affiliating with social identities that become an "antidote" to uncertainty, social identities that are in part affirmed as being different—at the limit, completely opposite—from others, which can lead to polarization.[22]

Another form of adjustment could be through group identification, as in the uncertainty identity theory: feelings of uncertainty (particularly related to self) motivate people to identify with, switch to or reform social groups in order to cope with those feelings.[23] Self-uncertainty strengthens group identification, favouring groups with greater distinctiveness

and clear leadership. Through this process self-uncertainty facilitates radicalization (self-identification with more extreme groups and well-delimited identities), potentially culminating in the support of more authoritarian leaders.[24] More generally, experimental analysis of brain activity through magnetic resonance imaging indicates that people with greater intolerance of uncertainty are more likely to show more neural synchrony with politically like-minded peers and less with opponents, fuelling the formation of polarized beliefs.[25]

These mechanisms can be exploited by political entities and leaders, targeting individuals struggling with high personal uncertainty through compelling narratives that are embraced even if they include the justification of extreme behaviours, such as political violence.[26] Attractive extreme political ideologies often connect to people's distress, cognitive simplicity (such as a black-and-white perception of the social world), overconfidence in judgment and intolerance towards alternative views because of perceived moral superiority.[27] Elites are often politically incentivized to fuel polarization, with direct negative campaigns, uncivil discourse and vitriol against political opponents[28] or to leverage divisions over contentious social issues, such as immigration and race in some settings.[29] Elite polarization has been found to result in greater affective polarization in the electorate—when elite positions are polarized, people express more negative sentiment towards opposing parties[30] and become more tolerant of undemocratic behaviour.[31]

> " The confluence of heightened uncertainty with high inequality often seems to favour support for authoritarian leaders, who are less likely to foster intragroup and intergroup cooperation

The style of leadership supported in uncertain times may also favour support for authoritarian leaders. Anthropology and social psychology have identified two routes through which leaders emerge.[32] One is by acquiring prestige, respect and admiration and being recognized as possessing superior skills, achievements or knowledge. The other is by becoming dominant, assertive, controlling, decisive and confident, often coercing or inducing fear. In contexts of economic uncertainty dominant leaders often appear to have greater appeal than prestige leaders.[33] And higher economic inequality also attracts and often favours support for dominance-oriented leaders, with inequality also providing incentives for leaders to pursue their own self-interest over the interests of the groups they lead.[34] The confluence of heightened uncertainty with high inequality thus often seems to favour support for authoritarian leaders, who are less likely to foster intragroup and intergroup cooperation.

Polarization has to do with a group forming negative beliefs about other out-groups, and people are generally prone to forming such beliefs in an incorrect way. A substantial body of evidence shows that people's perceptions about others are generally biased.[35] People can misjudge what other individuals in society think, feel and do.[36] Not only is misperception of others widespread, it also tends to be asymmetric: far more people hold beliefs about others that fall on one side of the truth over the other.[37] In particular, people harbour greater misperceptions when considering those outside their own social groups than those closer to them. Inaccurate perceptions about out-groups are widespread, with evidence to this effect over localized points of disagreement in 26 countries.[38]

Indeed, people's perception that others hold more extreme positions than they actually do itself contributes to polarization. People's perception that those from opposing parties hold extreme positions has been found to be more strongly associated with animus towards out-party members than with actual differences in policy preferences.[39] People who identify with a specific group underestimate the extent to which they agree with the views of other groups' opponents.[40] People also tend to misperceive how others view them. These perceptions are uniquely associated with hostility, aggression and in some settings a willingness to violate democratic norms.[41]

What might explain people's tendencies to routinely misperceive others? One candidate is stereotyping, where people tend to adopt overgeneralized mental models of out-group members. Another is motivated reasoning: people are biased towards interpreting information in ways that affirm their beliefs. So, affective factors could be contributing to misperception (rather than the other way around—misperceptions causing people to have negative attitudes towards others).[42]

Institutional factors
The rise in polarization today comes alongside progress in other dimensions of human wellbeing—greater economic prosperity, uptake of new technologies, and improvements in health, education and gender equality—and despite the formal strengthening of socioeconomic institutions (box 4.2). Increasing polarization amid greater progress signals that what is often called "development" may not always deliver for people as expected.

In-group–out-group polarization can be framed in the context of the potential mismatch discussed in chapter 3. A rapid transformation with new layers of uncertainty can shake norms and values that are ill matched to current realities. This triggers advocates of new responses, risking polarization between advocates for change and those rejecting or alienated by change.[43] Intragroup cohesiveness can increase when people are confronted with threats but often at the expense of intergroup cooperation.

Box 4.2 Progress with polarization in the global Positive Peace Index

The Positive Peace Index measures the positive peace of 163 countries, covering 99.6 percent of the world population. Positive peace is defined as the attitudes, institutions and structures that create and sustain peaceful societies. It is based on more than 45,700 data series, indices and attitudinal survey variables in conjunction with current thinking about the drivers of violent conflict, resilience and peacefulness. The index covers eight pillars, using three indicators for each. The pillars are:

- Well-functioning government.
- Equitable distribution of resources.
- Free flow of information.
- Good relations with neighbours.
- High human capital.
- Acceptance of the rights of others.
- Low corruption.
- Sound business environment.

The 24 indicators fall into three domains:

- Attitudes, which measure social views, tensions or perceptions.
- Institutions, which are associated with the functioning of the formal and informal organizations that manage and influence the socioeconomic system.
- Structures, which are embedded in the framework of society, such as poverty and equality, or are the result of aggregate activity, such as GDP.

The six indicators in the attitudes domain are factionalized elites, group grievance, quality of information, exclusion by socioeconomic condition, hostility to foreigners and freedom of the press. These indicators were used as proxies for social attitudes—that is, the way individuals and groups perceive and interact within their society.

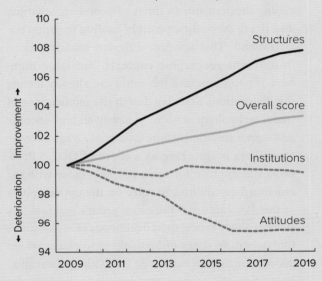

Box figure 1 Improvements on the Positive Peace Index over the past decade have been driven by progress in the structures domain rather than in the attitudes domain

Positive Peace Index score (2009 = 100)

Source: Pinto and others 2022.

- Deteriorations in attitudes are changes in social perceptions and patterns of interactions among individuals and groups that lead to more social disharmony, more violence or fear thereof, deeper political instability or more disruptive economic inefficiencies.
- Improvements in attitudes are changes in social perceptions and patterns of interaction among individuals and groups that lead to enhanced social cohesion, less violence, more political cooperation, greater institutional transparency and economic efficiencies.

Using this classification framework, the data suggest a steep divergence in development patterns over the past 10 years (box figure 1). The global average of the structures domain suggests uninterrupted progress, as gauges of aggregate economic performance, scientific and technological development, and business indicators have continually improved since 2009. By contrast, the global averages of the attitudes domain have deteriorated markedly—a proxy for polarization. The institutions domain has also deteriorated, though modestly.

This is the paradox of economic and business progress with increasing social polarization. Despite improvements in aggregate economic performance, technological advancement and business opportunities, societies appear to have become less harmonious, and political preferences appear to have become more factionalized and intolerant.

Source: Pinto and others 2022.

For instance, after violent conflict, trust and cooperation increase within groups but not between them.[44] War also seems to increase religiosity, another form of affiliating with a social group based on shared beliefs.[45] People seek to reduce ambivalence in their perception of others by creating clear "us" and "them" boundaries.[46] The tightening[47] of social norms and their heightened enforcement or sanctioning are also a collective response to cope with threats and uncertainty[48]—perhaps an evolved cultural adaption to deal collectively with uncertainty.[49] But mismatches can occur when some societies overtighten norms in the face of perceived tangible threats and loosen them in the face of real threats.[50]

Economic hardship and income inequality might parallel trends in polarization.[51] Beliefs and behaviours prioritizing in-group affiliation can emerge as coping mechanisms in times of economic volatility and rising inequality, possibly leading to group polarization.[52] This acquires different manifestations in different geographic contexts, but large numbers of people around the world are already feeling the dislocations associated with the implications of trade, technology or both. In nearly all high-income and upper middle-income countries, wage income to workers is shrinking as a share of GDP.[53] Prospects will improve for some people— those with the enhanced capabilities to seize on the opportunities of the 21st century.[54] But other groups will feel less secure—those seeing their livelihoods or social status threatened. In times of hardship or in places where dislocations cause economic hardship, polarization intensifies, and support can increase for leaders who reject pluralism, including those hostile to foreigners and migrants.[55]

Inequalities, and perceptions of inequality,[56] may undermine the basic promise of fundamental political equality.[57] It is argued that we are witnessing the secession from political life[58] of those at the very top, isolated and disconnected through their privilege, and those at the very bottom, disaffected and disenfranchised in their agency and voice. These inequalities—especially income and wealth inequality—have an impact on political engagement,[59] which often translates into low political participation among the most disadvantaged.[60] Institutions have sometimes struggled to safeguard the integrity of the rituals of choice whereby societies can collectively and iteratively design their fate and determine the winning and losing political positions without undermining formal systems and without disagreement turning into disrespect of others and of institutions.[61] In recent decades inequalities have been accompanied by rising nationalism and identity-based politics in many countries. There is substantial variation across countries in how class-based inequalities interact with other social divides, leading to diverse patterns in political cleavages; how political institutions manage these cleavages also influences dynamics between groups (spotlight 4.1).

" Inequalities, and perceptions of inequality, may undermine the basic promise of fundamental political equality

Widening inequalities and worsening prospects for many workers around the world are connected to the global rise of market power of some firms: as the winner-takes-all structure of new technologies paired with challenged antitrust policies allows some companies to thrive with high profits, while lower shares of income accrue to workers.[62] The rise in market power can lead to monopolistic competition, raising company profits while keeping worker wages low.[63] Firms that were able to innovate in new information platforms are now giants of technology. These "superstar" firms, with a high capacity to innovate and very high profits, have seen rising market power. Their markups (the difference between sales prices and production costs) are high, contributing to the decline in the labour's share of income.[64]

Hyper-information is powering social division and polarization

As chapter 3 argues, we may be confronting a mismatch between behaviour and the institutions that exist now and those required to navigate through a new context of multilayered uncertainties.[65] In addition, the world faces another mismatch between the availability of information (about people's actions, interactions and perceptions, captured through multiple platforms and social media) and our ability to effectively harness it in processes of social choice.[66] Changes to how we produce and share information are part of a broader social and cultural change. The ubiquity of information and communications technology today signifies a substantially different world from just a few decades ago. Technological advances are dramatically altering how people form their beliefs and values and how these are transmitted through social connections and networks. People interacting with one another on digital networks are engaging in new cultural practices.[67] New social groups and networks can emerge online that are widely distributed and decentralized, involving only loosely connected individuals. As this section discusses, the social changes generated by the rapidly evolving (digital) information ecosystem are introducing new vulnerabilities to processes of public deliberation, even as they support collective action in other ways.

Advances in digital technology are disrupting social networks

In many respects digital social media can support processes of public deliberation. The free flow of information is fundamental to democratic processes. Accurate information allows people to develop well-informed policy preferences, hold those in power accountable and participate meaningfully in democratic debate. Information is an important part of any strategy to address the complex challenges before us. For instance, information about the extent and scale of climate change is important for spurring actions to minimize human-induced pressures on the planet. And technologies for sharing information, such as social media, play an important role in supporting collective action. Digital social media provide new ways for groups to interact, find common ground and even organize into movements. There are several such examples of digital media supporting collective action, from protesting racial or ethnic violence to advocating for workers' rights and the rights of gender-diverse groups and indigenous peoples. Communications technology promises a means for marginalized, minoritized or threatened groups to organize and effect change.

However, recent advances in digital communications technology have also been disruptive to our social networks, more so than communications advances in the past (box 4.3). There are at least four key changes in our social systems as a result of rapid advances in information and communications technology.[68] They have dramatically altered the stability and functionality of social networks.

- *Changes in scale.* Social networks have expanded massively in scale, to nearly 7.8 billion people.[69] The sheer number of people involved complicates

decisionmaking, cooperation and coordination.[70] Mechanisms for cooperation or coordination may be scale-dependent, and new institutions may be required to meet these functions as social networks grow so large.[71] Changes in scale can undermine cooperation and impede consensus.[72]

" Digital social media provide new ways for groups to interact, find common ground and even organize into movements, but recent advances in digital communications technology have also been disruptive to our social networks, more so than communications advances in the past

- *Changes in structure.* The structure of human social networks has changed. A large population combined with technology that connects otherwise disparate groups allows for network structures that were not previously possible. Where humans had social connections with at most a few hundred others in the past, online media platforms now connect much larger networks of people to one another, as do traditional media sources. Positive aspects of these networks include the greater possibility of collaboration across borders, the diffusion of scientific ideas and expansion of the networks of those who may otherwise be isolated. However, some features of these networks, such as long ties and inequality of influence, can facilitate harm.[73] For instance, these networks can foster echo chambers and spread misleading or inaccurate information.
- *Information fidelity.* New communications technology allows for information to be transmitted without decay or noise across several degrees of separation.[74] This makes it easy for false and misleading information to spread fast and widely. Rapid information flows may overwhelm cognitive processes and lead to less accurate decisions.[75] Because information is cheaper to produce and distribute, low quality information can spread more easily.
- *Algorithmic decisionmaking.* Algorithms are widely used to filter, curate and display information online. When designed to share information based on user preferences and usage patterns, they work as feedback loops and drive new content exposures

Box 4.3 Advances in digital communications risk destabilizing societies

Our species has enjoyed a comparatively stable existence for more than 100,000 years. Humans lived and spread in loosely connected hunter-gatherer groups numbering in the tens or low hundreds. Our biology at that time was not fundamentally different from what it is today, exhibiting rich cultural features such as tool use, social bonds, language, intergroup conflict, art and knowledge sharing.

The stability of our species, by almost any measure, changed dramatically with the first agricultural revolution 12,000 years ago. Growing crops and raising animals led many hunter-gather groups to abandon a mobile lifestyle to form settlements. Organized labour distribution allowed larger groups to coexist in a given geographic area. Converting land for agricultural use provided nutrition to support rapid population growth. Further technological advances fundamentally altered how most humans interact. Writing, for instance, opened the potential for ledgers, economies, codified laws and sequestering of wealth. The printing press enabled large-scale distribution of information by those able to afford the upfront production costs.

The Industrial Revolution enabled us to extract and convert natural resources at a dramatically faster pace. Photography, radio, telephony, powered transit and television fostered communication across vast spaces at high speed. These advances caused subsequent generations to bear less and less similarity to previous ones. Although technology has brought us many things, stability is not among them.

Discussions of digital communications technology, from social media and search engines to artificial intelligence and cryptocurrency, often occur against this backdrop. Scholars, technologists, politicians and lay people often argue that the internet is simply our generation's printing press. Harms are seen as mere growing pains and a far cry from existential. Our continuing existence is held up as evidence of a collective behavioural invisible hand that will guide us forward much as it brought us here.

However, there are reasons to believe that digital communication technologies today are both quantitatively and qualitatively distinct from past advances. Engineering decisions that reshape our society can now be deployed instantaneously and without oversight to billions of users, dramatically outpacing historical adoption timelines and creating novel challenges for evidence-based regulation. Further differentiating current advances from past ones, modern communication technology leverages vast datasets and complex algorithms to couple social systems to technological ones.

Most important, past technological advances have not produced stable social dynamics, particularly in our interactions with the natural world. Digital communications technology, while nascent, has more potential than any past advance to alter social dynamics. Given the precarious state of our natural world and global inequalities, disruptions that bring about further instability are existential threats for many.

Source: Bak-Coleman 2022.

---

that become more extreme over time.[76] Given people's tendency to seek friendly social environments, algorithmic feedback may narrow the information and networks that users are exposed to: so they can induce biases in perceived reality and contribute to polarization.[77] The algorithms that online media platforms use are typically proprietary, and there is limited transparency in how algorithmic decisions for information flows might be altering human collective behaviour.[78]

Disruptive changes in information systems can compromise public deliberation

The changes described above are altering processes of public deliberation. More information and larger networks are not unequivocally empowering. Alongside benign or socially beneficial information flows, unreliable and unverified information can also be transmitted with ease through today's social networks. One area of concern is the proliferation of misinformation.[79] Online spaces have become hotbeds of politically motivated misinformation, with negative effects on social dynamics and processes, such as elections[80] and treatment of minorities.[81] While misinformation itself is not a new phenomenon, online media have increased the reach, influence and impact of inaccurate information.[82] Misinformation can emerge from a range of actors, including governments, groups and bots designed to convince people that they are authentic users.[83] The spread of false information can be especially harmful in times of crisis, as clearly demonstrated during the Covid-19 pandemic. In many parts of the world, waves of unreliable information preceded increases in Covid-19 infections.[84]

" Social media might lead people to perceive political divisions to be more extreme, to become more affectively polarized and enclosed in their own views and to have hostile or negative discourse about others be rewarded or reinforced through increased engagement in social media

Human cognition can facilitate the spread and influence of misinformation. In contrast to models of rational choice, people routinely rely on mental shortcuts to bypass some of the information they encounter when making decisions (see chapter 3).[85] Heuristics allow people to reduce the complexity of these judgments to a more manageable scale. It is in conjunction with people's cognitive and behavioural tendencies that today's advanced communications technologies can strain how societies process information and form beliefs. For instance, that fake posts spread wider and faster than truthful news online has been attributed to humans being more likely to spread fake information rather than to those outcomes being an artefact of algorithmic choices.[86] People tend to turn towards information that reinforces their existing beliefs—a manifestation of confirmation bias. "Repulsion" away from opposing viewpoints is also a powerful motivator.[87]

Algorithmic decisionmaking and feedback in online spaces can influence the flow of information in unpredictable, and often opaque, ways. Some design characteristics of online media platforms can facilitate polarization. Recommendation algorithms can shape how information spreads on social networks, encouraging people to vote against their interests.[88] Research from Twitter's Machine Learning, Ethics, Transparency and Accountability Team indicated that their content recommendation algorithms appear to amplify right-leaning politicians across the majority of countries surveyed.[89] Although they could not identify why the algorithm exhibited this behaviour, it is conceivable that such unexpected algorithmic behaviour could affect democratic outcomes in ways that external observers cannot evaluate.

Interactions on social media can increase perceptions of difference.[90] Selective exposure to like-minded attitudinal content increases polarization by reinforcing existing attitudes.[91] There is evidence of political sorting on social networks: people adjust their online social ties to avoid encountering news from nonpreferred sources, leading to homogenized online networks.[92] Moreover, negative discourse about the out-group can get positive reinforcements through increased engagement on social media in comparison to language about the in-group.[93]

Put plainly, social media might lead people to perceive political divisions to be more extreme, to become more affectively polarized and enclosed in their own views and to have hostile or negative discourse about others be rewarded or reinforced through increased engagement in social media. Although social media are certainly not responsible for all polarization, they have provided a space for new tactics and paths towards misinformation and polarization.[94]

Polarization harms public deliberation in uncertain times

As the analysis here shows, uncertainty creates fertile ground for political polarization, with worrying consequences for public deliberation, precisely when societies must come together to tackle emerging threats. Polarization is much more than simple differences in preferences or beliefs. After all, differences between groups of people need not impede our ability to work together and generate sound policy. Some differences between people are often beneficial.[95] And holding many different interests, identities and social connections can constrain social fragmentation. Even where people disagree on ideological grounds or policy issues, they are less likely to experience political isolation by virtue of their rich social interactions and overlapping identities.[96] When people share beliefs across groups, the space for healthy interaction and deliberation increases.

Rather than a matter of differing preferences or beliefs, the polarization documented in many societies today is more pernicious: "the normal multiplicity of differences in the society increasingly align along a single dimension, cross-cutting differences become reinforcing, and people increasingly perceive and describe politics and society in terms of 'us' versus 'them.'"[97] In other words polarization has to do with deepening social divisions between groups, where intergroup relationships become hostile and disharmonious, distrust between groups intensifies, opposing groups tend towards more extreme positions and the scope for cooperation diminishes.

In many settings polarization is spilling over into spaces that would otherwise have been ones of coexistence, such as families and neighbourhoods.[98] When social networks become segregated, groups have limited information about others' preferences, diminishing impulses towards cooperation and coordination. Rather than any differences over values, it is the breakdown in communication between groups that impedes public deliberation.[99] Coming to consensus on issues takes longer when opposing groups are homogenized, and deliberation within homogeneous groups tends to lead people to adopt more extreme positions that they otherwise would on their own.[100] Polarization contributes to discontent with democratic systems. In a polarized society one group ("us") may see the actions of other opposing groups ("them") as impeding its efforts to shape policy within democratic systems.

" Severe polarization can make people blind to the fact that there are strategies where all sides can gain

Frustration with democratic processes can be the result, especially where impulses for collaboration have already been weakened by processes of group homogenization.[101] Democratic institutions themselves can struggle to accommodate the priorities of deeply polarized groups, resulting in deadlocks and public disaffection.[102] In-group–out-group polarization can become a driving factor in supporting authoritarian leaders,[103] thus putting democratic processes under strain.[104] Accounting for the rise of radical and populist parties, scholars have shown that declining trust in institutions is associated with diminishing support for traditional insider parties.[105] People's tolerance for undemocratic actions increases, creating conditions for democratic decline or even reversal. There is evidence of the erosion of attitudes towards democracy and peaceful deliberation in high HDI countries associated with human insecurity (spotlight 4.2).[106] In national politics polarization advantages leaders that shun negotiation and compromise

and does lasting damage to the norms that underpin democracy, such as tolerance for differing views.[107]

The rise in political polarization is occurring in the context of a long-term, global disaffection with democratic practices.[108] The Varieties of Democracy approach makes an effort to capture this process and argues that there has been a deterioration of critical ingredients of democracy (figure 4.5). Freedom of expression is declining in around 35 countries, more than three times the number where it is increasing. Similarly, deliberation is in decline in more than four times the number of countries where it is improving. Clean elections, rule of law and freedom of association are also in decline in more countries than where they are improving.

Severe polarization can make people blind to the fact that there are strategies where all sides can gain. Instead, they may end up behaving as though life is a zero-sum game. This dynamic can be self-reinforcing: "the less they [*people*] undertake joint collective actions, the more their perceptions of difference, and the more likely it is that they will perceive their interests to be zero-sum."[109] Dynamics of polarization affect not just how people feel about others who think differently but also how people act. For example, in the United States social distancing behaviours, using masks, getting vaccinated and beliefs about risk during the Covid-19 pandemic correlate with partisan divisions.[110] Polarization also makes international cooperation harder. For example, party polarization has negative consequences for national commitments to international environmental agreements.[111] We risk losing some of the benefits of living in plural societies—a diversity of knowledge and ideas as well as decisionmaking that is responsive to as many people and groups as possible.[112]

Worryingly, polarization is difficult to reverse when it involves a positive feedback mechanism. When positive feedback increases (such as political parties adopting more extreme positions), polarization can ascend to a tipping point, after which it becomes a self-reinforcing, runaway process.[113] And once it has set in, polarization is hard to reverse, even in the face of external shocks.[114]

The discussion in this chapter explains how polarization may emerge and persist in a context of uncertainty and how the appeal of authoritarian leaders may increase. But these are not mechanistic and predetermined outcomes. Greater uncertainty does not

Figure 4.5 Ten years ago there were more countries where critical elements for democratic governance were improving than declining—today, the situation is reversed

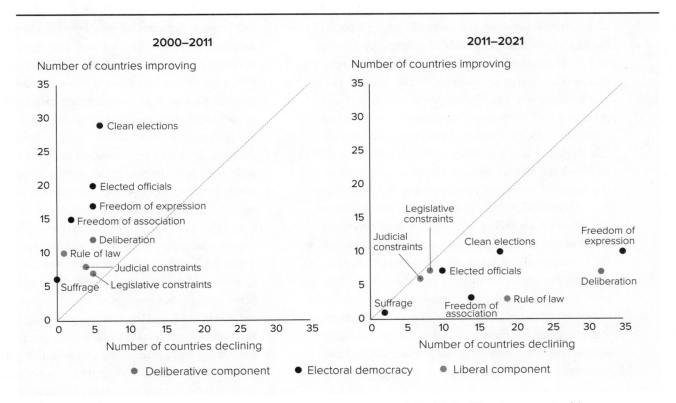

Note: Figure shows the number of countries improving and declining significantly and substantially for different components of democracy.
Source: Boese and others 2022.

have to lead to polarization. There are multiple examples in history where uncertainty was faced through broad collaboration. With uncertainty people can turn to values that go beyond strategic thinking about seeking the pursuit of self-interest alone. If there is trust, that value can be solidarity.

Experimental evidence indicates that uncertainty can affect the morality of individuals. Participants in experiments appeared less likely to lie and more likely to share resources under uncertainty, reducing the scope for purely strategic self-interested behaviour.[115] More important, the power of reasoning and public deliberation is not diminished in uncertain times, particularly when the broad notion of capabilities, emphasizing agency and freedoms, is considered.

Breaking the hold of uncertainty on collective action

Political polarization associated with human insecurity, and the inadequacy of our institutions in times of

change is standing in the way of more decisive joint action to face common challenges. Despite clear progress on many fronts, human insecurity is putting people under stress and pulling people apart. Human insecurity is associated with lower interpersonal trust and tendencies towards political extremism.

Meanwhile, rapid changes in information systems are a source of added instability in our social systems. Many of the challenges of sustaining information systems that support democratic deliberation are not new. After all, the spread of misleading information, censorship and other impediments to democratic debate existed long before the advent of digital communications technologies. The difference today is that our information systems now operate at such a broad scale that they pose a systemic challenge to public deliberation, just when our ability to act together to deal with large-scale societal challenges is so critical.

Development progress—with achievements in different dimensions of human development—has gone along with institutions that have structured human interactions[116] and made that very progress possible. But as chapter 3 argues, we may be reaching a point of mismatch between the institutions and social configurations that have enabled progress up to now and those required to face new challenges exemplified by the uncertainty complex.[117] The two processes contributing to polarization today may reflect this mismatch—of institutions inadequately responding to people's unsettledness and insecurity and to a rapidly changing (digital) information context. How do we break the vicious cycle of increased polarization, the reduced space for collaboration, the multilayered uncertainties? Advancing human development (in terms of wellbeing and agency, achievements and freedoms) remains the foundation for shaping the behavioural and institutional changes needed to navigate our uncertain times. Expanding capabilities provides a way to enhance the diversity of voices involved in public deliberation to this end, to the extent that processes of deliberation allow for the full range people's beliefs and motivations to be scrutinized and reasoned.

" Polarization impedes public deliberation, thereby working against the cooperation needed to address novel, multilayered uncertainties

Polarization impedes public deliberation, thereby working against the cooperation needed to address novel, multilayered uncertainties. Two critical elements are deeply interconnected in breaking the hold of uncertainty on collective action.

First, tackling people's unsettledness and human insecurity. Thriving under uncertainty requires human security, overcoming the mismatch between aspiration and achievements.[118] Our ability to implement the many transformations needed today—local, national and global—depends on our ability to agree on what needs to be done, to generate broad social support and then to implement creative policy change amid uncertainty. Addressing the basic drivers of unsettledness and insecurity in people's lives is essential.

Existing strategies for human security need to be upgraded. An expanded concept of human security for the Anthropocene combines strategies of protection, empowerment and solidarity (where solidarity recognizes the interdependence among people and between people and the planet).[119] This agenda depends on several actions, and there are some practical examples, such as strengthening social protection systems with built-in adaptive capabilities. Robust social protection not only allows people to better weather shocks but also helps sustain people's wellbeing and broad participation in decisionmaking. In other words effective social protection systems can support agency. To directly address the spread of polarization, policies that seek to counter the feedback cycle between inequality and polarization are also crucial.[120]

Second, steering the expansion of social networks to advance human development. It is imperative to acknowledge that the digital world occupies a central role in our social interactions and to set principles and norms to guide its expansion, so it favours human flourishing and an equitable and effective collective deliberation. A hands-off approach is not enough—there is little to suggest that an information ecosystem organized for narrow private interests (including boosting engagement, ad sales or short-term profit) might organically evolve into a space for free, open and informed collective deliberation.[121] Principles of stewardship, comparable to managing complex ecosystems, have relevance for strengthening our information systems.[122] Within this framework three steps can be considered:

• Increasing transparency over how companies opt to sort, filter and display information to users.
• Improving access and equity in leveraging information and communications technology.
• Enhancing our understanding more broadly of how new technologies are shaping public discourse and deliberation.[123]

As detailed in the following chapter, new opportunities for transformation are emerging against a backdrop of rapid technological change and the recent Covid-19 crisis. Chapter 6 suggests a way forward, with a framework for action in uncertain times.

Inequality and the structure of political conflict in democracies: A global and historical perspective

Amory Gethin *(Paris School of Economics—École des hautes études en sciences sociales and World Inequality Lab),* **Clara Martínez-Toledano** *(Imperial College London and World Inequality Lab),* **Thomas Piketty** *(Paris School of Economics—École des hautes études en sciences sociales and World Inequality Lab)*

In our new book, *Political Cleavages and Social Inequalities,*[1] we investigate where and how class divides emerge and how they interact with other social conflicts (ethnic, regional, generational, gender and the like). In what contexts do we see inequality become politically salient and why? What determines the strength of identity-based divides, and how do these conflicts interact with the structure of social inequalities? Drawing on a unique set of surveys conducted between 1948 and 2020 in 50 countries on five continents, our volume sheds new light on these questions and provides a new data source to investigate voting behaviours in a global and historical perspective: the World Political Cleavages and Inequality Database (http://wpid.world).

Among the many findings of the book, three interesting facts emerge from the analysis of this new dataset.

The intensity of class divisions varies widely in contemporary democracies

We document a gradual decoupling of two complementary measures of social class in many European and North American democracies: income and education. In the early post–World War II decades the party systems of these democracies were class-based: social democratic and affiliated parties represented both the low-education and the low-income electorates, whereas conservative and affiliated parties represented both high-education and high-income voters (figure S4.1.1). These party systems have gradually evolved towards what we can call multi-elite party systems: social democratic and affiliated parties have become the parties of higher-educated elites, while conservative and affiliated parties remain the parties of high-income elites.

In contrast to the gradual decoupling between income and education that we find in many European and North American democracies, in other regions there are large variations in the configuration and intensity of class divides. These variations can often be explained by the relative importance of other dimensions of political conflict. The interaction among class, regional, ethnic, religious, generational, gender and other forms of divides thus plays a key role in determining the ways through which inequalities are politically represented in democracies around the world today.

Ethnic diversity is not synonymous with ethnic conflict

Another major finding of our global perspective on political divides is that ethnic and religious conflicts vary widely across countries and over time. In particular, more diverse countries are not necessarily those where ethnic or religious conflicts are more intense. Instead, varieties of political cleavage structures can be accounted for in part by history, such as the ability of national liberation movements to bring together voters from different origins. They also have an important socioeconomic component: in democracies where ethnoreligious groups tend to cluster across regions and differ markedly in their standards of living, political parties also tend to reflect ethnic affiliations to a greater extent.

Identity politics take different forms

The large variations in class and sociocultural divides in contemporary democracies point to a more general pattern. Political cleavages can take multiple forms, depending on the nature of underlying social conflicts and on the ability of political parties to embody these conflicts in the democratic arena.

Figure S4.1.1 The emergence of multi-elite party systems in Australia, Europe and North America

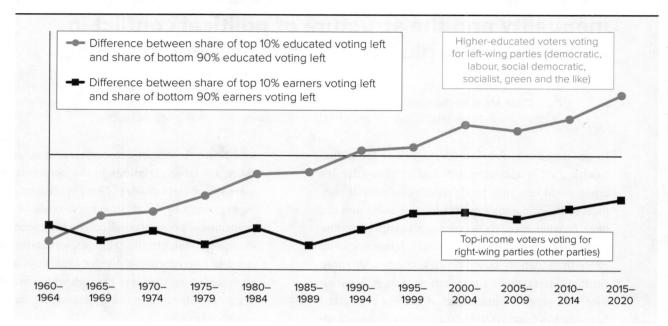

Note: In the 1960s both higher-educated and high-income voters were less likely to vote for left-wing (democratic, labour, social democratic, socialist, green) parties than lower-educated and low-income voters by more than 10 percentage points. The left vote has gradually become associated with higher-education voters, giving rise to a multi-elite party system. Data are five-year averages for Australia, Canada, Denmark, France, Germany, Italy, the Netherlands, Norway, Sweden, Switzerland, the United Kingdom and the United States. Estimates control for income, education, age, gender, religion, church attendance, rural or urban location, region, race, ethnicity, employment status and marital status (in country-years for which data are available).
Source: Authors' calculations based on data from the World Political Cleavages and Inequality Database (http://wpid.world).

In European and North American democracies, for instance, the rise of conflicts over immigration and the environment have come together with the decline of class divides and of traditional left-wing parties, perhaps because they are perceived as unable to propose convincing redistributive platforms. It has also coincided with a decline in turnout among low-income and lower-educated voters, pointing to a more general dissatisfaction among these voters with the functioning of democracy. Nonetheless, the shift to identity politics observed in many democracies today is neither inevitable nor generalized. In several countries outside Europe and North America the class-based dimension of political conflicts has intensified in recent decades.

NOTE

1   Gethin, Martínez-Toledano and Piketty 2021.

Support for democracy under strain: Evidence from very high Human Development Index countries

Democratic institutions are means to deliver on collective choices. Uncertainty can affect this role, through polarization, which in turn can affect beliefs about democratic institutions. Overall, support for democracy is high globally. But the share of people considering democracy very important is sensitive to the perceptions of human insecurity, particularly in very high Human Development Index (HDI) countries and among high-income groups (figure S4.2.1, left panel). Moreover, people's justification of violence as a political tool also appears highly connected with human insecurity, in particular among high-income

segments (figure S4.2.1, right panel).[1] Among high-income groups, an insecure person is more than twice as likely to justify violence or not consider democracy very important than a secure person. These results indicate a potentially destabilizing dynamic of negative attitudes towards cooperation at the top. This trend should be of concern, considering that people affected by high insecurity account for more than 40 percent of the population in very high HDI countries (even before the Covid-19 pandemic).

Why are people in higher HDI countries more sensitive to human insecurity (measured by attitudes and

Figure S4.2.1 **Support for democracy drops with insecurity in wealthier groups**

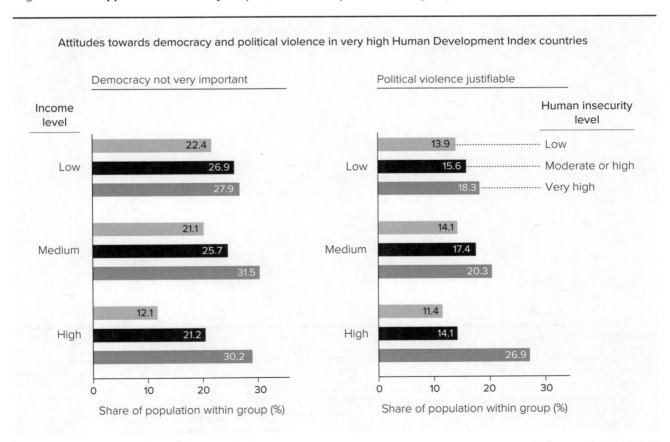

Attitudes towards democracy and political violence in very high Human Development Index countries

Note: Values are pooled individual-based data with equal weights across countries. Left panel refers to responses of 1–7 on a scale of 1–10; right panel refers to responses of 4–10 on a scale of 1–10.
Source: Human Development Report Office based on World Values Survey, waves 6 and 7. See Haerpfer and others (2022).

perceptions)?[2] People near the top of the HDI generally enjoy greater human security than those living in lower HDI settings. And because people near the top of the HDI have known greater human security, they are likely to feel "entitled" to it and therefore perceive insecurity as a loss. This may be a reason why people in higher HDI countries derive more distress from human insecurity.[3]

The feeling of uncertainty across HDI categories can also be affected by the mismatch between expectations and reality: people suffering insecurity in very high HDI countries and high-income countries are more likely to experience the cognitive dissonance of development-with-insecurity: income, a measure of worth and success that often guides people's behaviour and incentives, cannot in these extreme cases protect against threats, as could be typically expected. As market-based mechanisms of security and regular state-based policies struggle to deliver, authoritarian approaches might become attractive, consistent with the earlier discussion on the appeal of dominant-type leaders.

Source: Human Development Report Office.

NOTES

1   All differences between people perceiving very high human insecurity and people perceiving low human insecurity are statistically significant at the 1 percent level.

2   The index of perceived insecurity is built using a linear aggregation of insecurity threats and cannot account for their subjective impact on people. See UNDP (2022b).

3   The higher sensitivity of wealthier groups to human insecurity is consistent with the existence of endowment effects (Thaler 1980)—people living in a context of high human security (both on an objective and subjective basis) will tend to value more the benefits of a high human security environment —and with loss aversion (Tversky and Kahneman 1991, p. 1047)—"losses (outcomes below the reference status) loom larger than corresponding gains (outcomes above the reference state)." In line with the idea that the loss aversion theory can be context specific (Gal and Rucker 2018), the text elaborates further about the meaning of loss in a context of a very high HDI country.

5

Advancing human development in uncertain times

CHAPTER 5

Advancing human development in uncertain times

Uncertainty need not be paralyzing. In fact, it presents opportunities to test the fences of conventional thinking and to pursue reimagined futures.

What do those opportunities look like today? How big are they?

As this chapter argues: huge.

Among the many things the Covid-19 pandemic broke open was our imaginations, from revolutionary vaccines to unprecedented fiscal and monetary interventions. Rapidly evolving technologies, such as artificial intelligence and synthetic biology, and frontier ones, such as nuclear fusion, could usher in a new era of prosperity for people and planet. Opportunities abound. It is up to us to steer them towards human development.

Uncertainty need not lead to negative outcomes. A context of uncertainty and change can also alter the reference for what is possible or desirable, opening new opportunities to expand human development along the four aspects of capabilities highlighted in chapter 3: wellbeing achievements (typically the dominant focus of assessments of progress and policies), wellbeing freedoms, agency freedoms and agency achievements.

Transformational change happens against the backdrop of the uncertainties discussed in part I. Some of the implications associated with climate change are daunting, as the most recent Intergovernmental Panel on Climate Change assessments have highlighted.[1] But the ability of societies to respond is not predetermined. A recent model of human behaviour that looked at the interactions among social, political, economic, technical and climate systems found that interactions at the individual, community, national and global scales could lead to substantial mitigation action.[2] In fact, the reality of the Anthropocene is that human agency signals hope to consciously manage planetary ecosystems in a way that eases planetary pressures.[3]

This chapter calls attention to the potential for expanding human development in uncertain times. It argues that such an expansion can be leveraged in part precisely because uncertain times provide a context where individuals and society see more fundamental changes as possible or required. Uncertainty itself can be a source of knowledge to be mobilized to act differently,[4] something that empowers individuals and societies to adopt fundamental changes in choices,[5] that leads people to act according to new moral codes[6] and that can enhance cooperation when it gives more salience to thinking about the future.[7] It has even been suggested that the greatest source of political legitimacy may need to evolve beyond process legitimacy (complying with procedures that link people's aspirations and preferences to political decisions) and substantive legitimacy (delivering outcomes that matter to people). It can also come from promissory legitimacy (justifying decisions and persuading others to act based on claims about what the future will hold).[8] With democracy, uncertainty announces the freedom to choose. By institutionalizing an iterative and evolving configuration of winners and losers, uncertainty over political outcomes keeps many different possibilities open, thereby supporting pluralism and participation.[9] Uncertainty can thus help tap into people's energy and appetite for change.

Uncertainty forces us to make choices—between sticking to known paths and exploring new ones, between yielding to paralysis and polarization or tackling them head on.[10] Both bleaker and more optimistic scenarios may seem plausible, but the paths are open and will be shaped by choices. Multiple narratives are being discussed and debated about what the future holds,[11] and this diversity can be mobilized to enable people to cooperate.[12] When old ways of doing things seem to no longer work and development pathways seem less obvious than in the past, the opportunities for rethinking ideas and practices open up.[13] Uncertainty can provide fertile ground for experimentation, innovation and purposeful transformation.[14] In other words, it is possible to embrace uncertainty and not be paralyzed by it.[15] We can do much today to ensure human thriving and flourishing, even in times of crisis and turbulence.

" It is possible to embrace uncertainty and not be paralyzed by it. We can do much today to ensure human thriving and flourishing, even in times of crisis and turbulence

This chapter considers some of those possibilities. It explores the example offered by technological advances, arguing that the context of uncertainty provides a space for steering technological progress in ways that advance human development. It also shows that times of crisis can alter the horizon of what is possible. Even amid significant failures, the Covid-19 pandemic has changed our reference points for what we can achieve in many aspects of life. These are examples of the new possibilities in today's uncertain world.

Technological innovation opens new possibilities

Technological advances have been behind vast improvements in human life and flourishing. They have been the engine of economic growth—powering the Industrial Revolution, building cities and allowing movement of people and goods. The printing press and photography have expanded human knowledge.

Communication technologies have linked people across vast distances, allowed for rapid dissemination of information and expanded our social connections in large-scale networks. Numerous innovations in health, from anaesthetics to vaccines, have allowed us to live longer and healthier lives.

However, technological innovation does not happen in a vacuum, nor does it have a life of its own: technology is us. Our social, economic and political choices—about where innovation can be directed, to what priorities and to serve which people—determine how technology changes and how innovations advance human development. Consider the sobering case of vaccine deployment during the Covid-19 pandemic. Advances in science and manufacturing allowed for multiple, highly effective vaccines against Covid-19 to be developed in record time, in a remarkable feat of modern science. But amid a global failure to share vaccines equitably, wide disparities have emerged: by June 2022 less than 15 percent of people in low-income countries had received a full protocol of Covid-19 vaccines, compared with nearly 75 percent of people in high-income countries.[16] Unequal access to lifesaving vaccines has had a tragic toll on human lives and wellbeing.

“ Our social, economic and political choices —about where innovation can be directed, to what priorities and to serve which people— determine how technology changes and how innovations advance human development

This startling disparity in vaccine access reflects in part patterns in the diffusion of technological innovations. The share of the population that benefits is small when a new technology is introduced; then typically the share grows slowly at first, then increases very quickly after a threshold is reached and then slows down as the share of the population with access approaches 100 percent—in what is well known in technology diffusion studies as an S curve. Depending on the innovation at stake, often those with higher income, power and social status benefit from technological advancements first. This pattern is well documented, in particular, for health innovations,[17] in part because initial adopters have better access to information.[18] Disparities in health outcomes have been found to increase for diseases with better tools

for prevention and treatment, because people with more resources are better able to use new knowledge.[19] As such, an acceleration in new health-related technology can worsen health gradients within and between countries for a time, even as it eventually drives improvements at large.[20] In terms of Covid-19 vaccines, while the gap between richer and poorer countries has decreased over time, there is still a long way to go.[21]

The initial stage of the technological diffusion process—of remarkable improvements alongside widening gaps—is eventually closed, not only as technological innovations become more affordable, but also as complementary changes in economic and social arrangements foster both greater benefits and lower prices due to further diffusion.[22] At the same time, those excluded as the technology diffuses to a larger and larger share of the population are doubly disadvantaged, in that not only do they lack the benefits of the innovation, but they are also left outside what is increasingly the norm. The ongoing digital revolution is an example, promising to vastly improve the world's production possibilities but risking leaving a substantial proportion of people excluded and ultimately worse off if insufficient attention is paid to those exclusions.[23]

Past technological advances have generated great disruptions alongside opportunities and deep anxieties about the future, as well as the promise of progress to come. Rapid technological change is part of the uncertainty complex gripping the world today. New technologies are upending our economies and societies, and many aspects of our social systems will need to adjust before the vast potential of technological innovation can advance human development. As argued in the 2019 Human Development Report, these adjustments must unequivocally pay attention to inequalities if another great divergence is to be avoided.[24] The shift from concentrated access and wide inequality to convergence over time depends on social and political choices. Amid technological change as rapid and destabilizing as we are seeing today, the need for institutional and behavioural transformation becomes not only more salient but also necessary and actionable. Periods of turbulence have prompted radical new policies in the past: in Britain the Industrial Revolution saw far-reaching interventions to improve labour and working conditions (including regulating work hours and taxing incomes), which helped convert the structural change in the economy into improved opportunity and wellbeing.[25]

The initial stages of diffusion are characterized by growing inequality in access and typically also social dislocation. But this context is an opportunity for action: the choices made at this stage determine the trajectory to come. Expanding human development becomes even more important at this stage, with the concern for inequalities at the centre, implying that uncertain times need not be seen as an impediment to action; rather, they provide a context in which new possibilities for action emerge.

Many of today's hopes for positive transformational change rely on technological innovations. New technologies have helped deliver rapid advances in human development. For instance, in health, antibiotics and vaccines vastly improved life expectancy in just a few decades in Africa, Asia, and Latin America; in Europe the same improvement took well over a century, from the early 1800s, when such technology did not exist.[26] More recent technological advances have been crucial for curbing human-induced pressures on the planet —enabling more efficient land use, more sustainable food systems and a transition away from fossil fuels. Technological changes affect human capabilities in multiple ways: they not only expand people's ability to do more things (as an enabler), but they also affect our social context and people's agency.[27] Innovation is more than new inventions or machines; it is about new ideas for doing things and taking advantage of existing resources to make those ideas come to fruition. In this respect innovation is linked to agency—people's ability to act on their values, ideas and priorities. It is a broad process of transformation, where human initiative and creativity interact with social, economic and political choices.

Technological advances are offering transformative potential

Today, several developments in science and technology signal the potential for far-reaching transformation. There have been major developments in computing, biology and energy, as discussed in chapter 1. These advances are occurring in what has been described as the exponential age, fostered by remarkable improvements in computing power and connections across people and machines.[28] Exponential development in new technologies is not simply about individual inventions—it is the result of several new technologies developing in parallel and nourishing one another.[29] In digital technologies our capacity to generate innovations on the back of old or existing technologies has greatly expanded. Many important technologies today are standardized and interoperable[30]—that is, made compatible with other technologies by design. The internet is based on standard web protocols, and much modern software development relies on modular, standard code blocks. These conditions help make breakthrough innovations possible.

" Disruptive change in major technological sectors has the potential to dramatically alter societies and economies

Economic and political conditions are an important part of this picture. The availability of markets for new goods and services, facilitated by trade and globalization, has helped new technologies diffuse widely. This has enabled us to engage in learning by doing: more production allows us to learn how to further improve the production process. This learning effect is an essential driver behind the exponential development of solar power technology.[31] Our networks for sharing information are also larger and more complex than ever, facilitating flows of data, ideas and know-how. Consider some factors that made Covid-19 vaccines possible, such as global scientific collaboration, open data sharing and the release of the latest research on preprint servers—all capabilities based on information networks.[32] Spurred by the Covid-19 crisis, advances in mRNA vaccine technology are now opening new possibilities for controlling disease.[33]

Disruptive change in major technological sectors has the potential to dramatically alter societies and economies. Many new technologies are general purpose, with applications beyond a single sector. General purpose technologies are transformative because they create new products and processes and new ways of organizing economic activity. The general-purpose technologies of today include new forms of computing (such as artificial intelligence), among many others, with a dizzying array of applications for advancing human development. The following sections consider some of the possibilities offered by technological advances in energy, computing and biology.

That even the most beneficial advances often generate negative consequences only heightens the importance of purposefully managing technological disruption. Technological change is far from deterministic—the related risks and impacts and the prospects for positive transformation are all ultimately shaped by social and political choices. Even as rapid technological change fosters uncertainty, it also opens space for action. There is enormous potential to be realized, and with the right policies and actions in place (as discussed in depth in chapter 6), the future should be one of remarkable gains for human development.

Renewable energy technologies are getting better and cheaper

Making progress on clean energy is essential for breaking the patterns of human wellbeing improvements generating planetary pressures. Because energy is so crucial to overall human development, energy consumption is unlikely to ease in the near future, particularly in developing countries. So, in the absence of technological advancements towards plentiful clean energy, there are few viable paths to mitigating planetary pressures.

On the technological front there are remarkable positive signals both as outcomes and as processes. New capacity additions were dominated by renewable energy, accounting for 72 percent of additions worldwide in 2019.[34] The costs of renewable energy technology and energy storage have declined dramatically in recent years. The price of utility-scale solar photovoltaics dropped by 89 percent from 2009 to 2019 (figure 5.1).[35] The price of lithium-ion batteries has fallen by 97 percent since their commercial introduction in 1991.[36] Maturing technology contributes to cost and price reductions. For solar power technology, installed capacity has increased exponentially, accompanied by exponential declines in the cost of solar modules.[37] Since the 1970s the unit costs of solar photovoltaics have fallen by 24 percent each time the cumulative installed capacity has doubled.

The equivalent learning rate for lithium-ion batteries has been around 20 percent.[38] Other energy storage technologies have followed similarly steep learning curves.[39] Batteries are also becoming smaller and lighter. Between 1991 and 2018 the energy density of lithium-ion batteries rose 3.4-fold.[40] The dramatic cost reductions in renewable energy technologies have consistently exceeded expectations: contrary to the projected average annual cost reduction of 2.6 percent between 2010 and 2020 (based on 2,905 global energy-economy models), solar photovoltaics costs declined by 15 percent a year over the same period (figure 5.2).[41]

There have been major breakthroughs in nuclear fusion. Leveraging nuclear fusion's enormous potential will require substantial innovations before it can be deployed at scale. This transition will take time, but recent developments provide some grounds for optimism. There have been important advances in some nuclear fusion experiments, and at least three may soon generate energy gain factors (the ratio of fusion power to externally applied heating power) greater than 1—the National Ignition Facility and SPARC are expected to do so in the 2020s, and ITER by 2040.[42] In February 2022 scientists at the Joint European Torus generated more than double the previous record for energy generated in a fusion reaction, a major step towards nuclear fusion becoming a viable clean energy source.[43] There are also signs of new technologies interacting in ways that can accelerate progress. Machine learning techniques are being used in the tokamak configuration (a form of magnetic confinement used in nuclear fusion research).[44]

" Making progress on clean energy is essential for breaking the patterns of human wellbeing improvements generating planetary pressures

But the path forward is likely to be volatile in the context of uncertainty that we confront today. During the Covid-19 pandemic progress in clean energy innovation may have been affected by pressures on public and private budgets, creating a riskier environment for clean energy venture capital and disrupting global supply chains. Global carbon dioxide emissions declined by 5.8 percent in 2020, as the pandemic affected demand for oil and coal, but rebounded by

Figure 5.1 The cost of renewable energy has declined dramatically

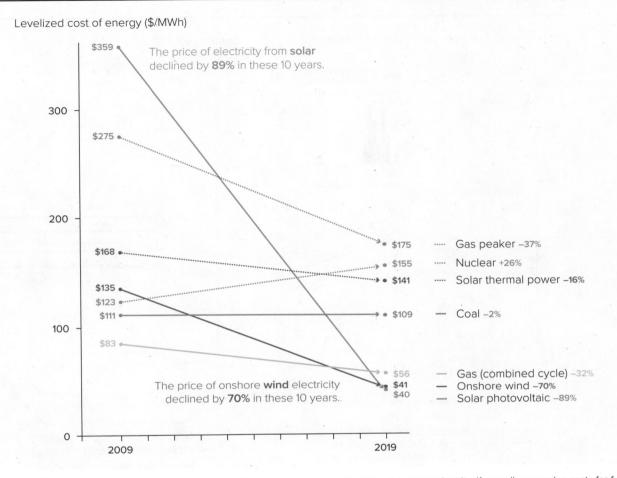

Levelized cost of energy ($/MWh)

The price of electricity from **solar** declined by **89%** in these 10 years.

$359
$275
$175 ····· Gas peaker –37%
$168
$155 ····· Nuclear +26%
$141 ····· Solar thermal power –16%
$135
$123
$111
$109 —— Coal –2%
$83

$56 —— Gas (combined cycle) –32%
$41 —— Onshore wind –70%
$40 —— Solar photovoltaic –89%

The price of onshore **wind** electricity declined by **70%** in these 10 years.

300

200

100

0

2009   2019

Note: Prices are expressed in levelized cost of energy, which captures the cost of building the power plant itself as well as ongoing costs for fuel and operating the plant over its lifetime.
Source: Roser 2020.

nearly 5 percent in 2021, approaching the 2018–2019 peak.[45] Still, the pandemic could present a unique opportunity to leverage clean energy innovation, given the global demand for a greener recovery.[46] New players with new ideas aiming to displace high-carbon producers and to scale up quickly may find a supportive environment if they are able to enter the market at the right moment. Economic stimulus plans could be an opportunity to boost clean energy technology innovation. This potential is being underused: a review of 75 International Monetary Fund (IMF) programmes in 65 countries shows that the indicator for the green recovery is very low, at 0.59 (on a scale of 0 to 3).[47]

Today, there is potential for expansion in this area. The International Energy Agency's Energy Technology Perspectives Clean Energy Technology Guide includes information on the maturity level of more than 400 technology designs and components, as well as a compilation of cost and performance improvement targets and leading players in the field.[48] Some 5 percent of technology designs and components analysed are at a mature stage. Around 60 percent are not commercially available today, and 35 percent are at the early adoption phase.[49]

Leveraging artificial intelligence for augmentation of the demand for labour

Rapid advances in computing over the past decade have drawn attention to the possibilities of powerful artificial intelligence (AI). Some of the biggest

Figure 5.2 Contrary to the projected average annual cost reduction of 2.6 percent between 2010 and 2020, solar photovoltaics costs declined by 15 percent a year over the same period

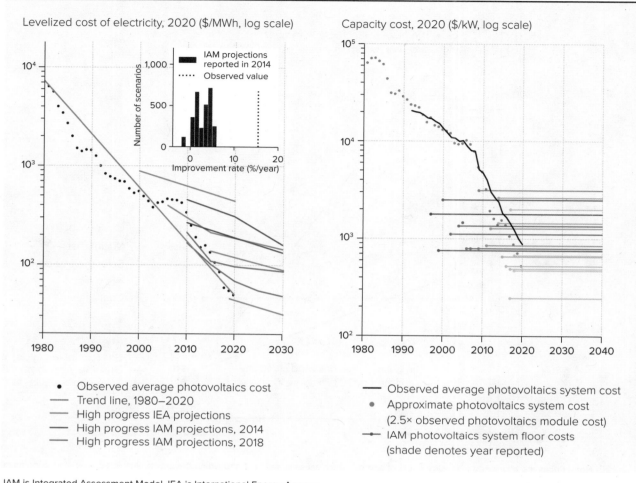

IAM is Integrated Assessment Model. IEA is International Energy Agency.
Source: Way and others 2021.

opportunities for applying AI are in automation that augments—rather than replaces—demand for human tasks across various sectors of the economy. AI-based systems are driving major technological developments in several applications, such as autonomous vehicles, medical diagnosis and inventory management, to name a few.[50] This means that some tasks can be performed by machines, but there is little evidence that machines can replace whole occupations.[51] Instead, applications for machine learning (a subset of AI) that have exploded in numerous fields are opening an array of new possibilities for advancing human wellbeing. For climate change, machine learning is aiding in predicting disasters and modelling climate change impacts, among many other applications. In healthcare, machine learning is offering

new ways to detect and diagnose disease.[52] Machine learning applications have the potential to improve education outcomes through individualized learning techniques and accessibility applications.[53]

Augmenting what humans can achieve by using AI in a complementary way rather than substituting what humans can do offers enormous promise—what people can achieve with these machines can be greater than what people might achieve without them (figure 5.3). AI applications can supplement human cognitive tasks. For instance, there is evidence of AI's potential for supporting human decisionmaking through teaching people cognitive strategies.[54] By augmenting the process of technological invention, AI applications could vastly increase the rate at which human capacities further expand.[55]

Figure 5.3 Opportunities for augmenting human activity are far greater than opportunities to automate existing tasks

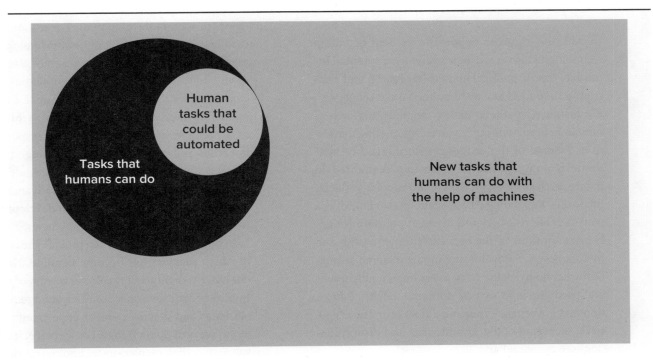

Note: Figure is illustrative.
Source: Human Development Report Office based on Brynjolfsson (2022).

One of the most widely discussed impacts of AI relates to its effects on the world of work. The possibility of labour displacement is a source of anxiety, as it has been in previous waves of automation.[56] AI-induced labour displacement could exacerbate inequality, both within and between countries.[57] But AI also offers labour-enhancing potential.[58] When machines replace labour, workers' bargaining power and influence diminish; in contrast, when AI augments human activity, people remain important for value creation and continue to wield power and influence. There is some evidence that the augmentation effects of introducing AI can outweigh the effects of automation, but this requires appropriate incentives.[59] Moreover, introducing technology can generate new tasks and activities that demand human labour.[60] Most jobs performed today came into being in part through the task-creating effects of new technologies: in the United States around 60 percent of people are now employed in occupations that did not exist in 1940.[61] Expanding AI into the world of work could similarly generate new tasks, new occupations and new industries altogether.

Harnessing synthetic biology

Advances on several fronts are now propelling what has been described the Synthetic Age, where biological systems can be redesigned and re-engineered for a variety of useful purposes.[62] Synthetic biology builds on advances in multiple fields over the past decade, including dramatic declines in the cost of DNA sequencing and synthesis, the development of sophisticated gene editing tools such as CRISPR and high-powered computational tools.[63]

Redesigning organisms to have new abilities could have numerous applications in health, agriculture, manufacturing and ecosystem management. Synthetic biology is supporting new advances in medicine—for treating cancer,[64] improving cell-based and gene therapies[65] and developing new drugs.[66] In agriculture there are now possibilities for engineering nitrogen fixation in crops and increasing crop resistance to pests and pathogens.[67] Potential applications of synthetic biology in managing the environment include breaking down pollutants[68] and supporting biodiversity and habitat restoration.[69] There is also potential for developing synthetic alternatives to fossil fuels.[70]

In addition to great opportunities, fast-changing technologies also create new challenges: potential for misuse, thorny political and ethical issues, and risks from unintended and even unknown consequences. For instance, synthetic biology applications such as human genome editing involve urgent ethical questions.[71] Some of the challenges introduced by synthetic biology applications are unprecedented in nature, such as the novel risks of introducing artificial life forms. Expanding AI applications also introduces considerable risks. AI and digitization more broadly can contribute to the concentration of wealth and market power.[72] Beyond the impact in some sectors of the economy, using AI to assist human judgement and predictions in several domains (health, education and governance to name a few) introduces new risks, including of algorithmic bias and discrimination (see chapters 1 and 2).[73]

" Given the speed at which technological advances are unfolding, there is the risk that, without appropriate incentives and regulation, new problems might accumulate just as rapidly while long-standing ones are further exacerbated

The potential of these technologies, coupled with the new challenges they pose, increases the importance of purposefully steering technological progress in ways that expand human capabilities. Indeed, given the speed at which technological advances are unfolding, there is the risk that, without appropriate incentives and regulation, new problems might accumulate just as rapidly while long-standing ones (such as inequalities) are further exacerbated. Many new technological advances reflect what has been considered an era where societal implications are exceedingly complex and require sophisticated governance and policymaking.[74] New social and ethical questions might unfold faster than appropriate responses can be formed.[75] Moreover, the Covid-19 pandemic has generated an enormous setback for human development progress. It is in this context that the double-edged sword of technological change must be wielded carefully.

These conditions highlight the importance of purposefully advancing the full potential of new technologies for human development. For instance, rather than leaving the evolution of new technologies up to markets or to the narrow incentives of a few actors alone, actively steering new technologies towards expanding human capacities is essential. Policy and regulatory interventions are important in this respect, as is a broader evolution of norms for responsible innovation and avoiding harm. Opening spaces for broad deliberation and overcoming the gulf between technical and social debates on new advances will be essential for advancing the human development potential of the disruptive new technologies.[76]

A context of uncertainty can provide the conditions in which such actions become possible. Navigating our current reality will require new ways of thinking. In these conditions opportunities emerge to rethink old ideas and practices and to experiment with different ways of doing things. For instance, it has been suggested that managing technological disruption today demands rethinking competition policy and antitrust regulation.[77] Things that once appeared impossible or infeasible are becoming possible in governance, science, technology and innovation. Indeed, as the next section discusses, times of crisis can alter our reference points for what we can achieve—and open new avenues for action in uncertain times.

The Covid-19 pandemic: A window into a new reality

The Covid-19 pandemic has exerted a vast human toll, not only through loss of life but also through long-term damage to economies and communities. It is the greatest global crisis in human development since World War II. Harmonized information since 1950 for income per capita and life expectancy shows the magnitude of the crisis and its global character in historical perspective (figure 5.4): in 2020, 85 percent of countries experienced a decline in income per capita, and 70 percent of countries and territories faced a reduction in life expectancy at birth. The comparison of income and life expectancy also reminds us of the importance of looking beyond income: despite significant economic recovery in 2021, the health crisis intensified, with two-thirds of countries recording even further reductions in life expectancy at birth.

Figure 5.4 The Covid-19 pandemic led to an unprecedented synchronized and multidimensional crisis

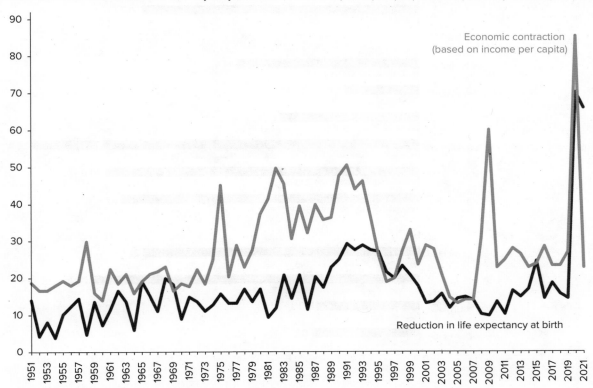

Share of countries and territories with a yearly reduction in income per capita (red) or life expectancy at birth (blue) (%)

Note: Based on countries with available data in each year. Data for 2020 and 2021 are preliminary estimates.
Source: Human Development Report Office calculations based on data from Bolt and van Zanden (2020), IMF (2022), UNDESA (2022a), UNSD (2022) and World Bank (2022c).

The Covid-19-Adjusted Human Development Index quantifies the depth of the crisis from a multidimensional perspective. The index retains the standard Human Development Index (HDI) dimensions but modifies the expected years of schooling indicator to reflect the effects of school closures and the availability of online learning on effective attendance rates.[78] The Covid-19 pandemic touched nearly every person in the world, with all regions facing declines (figure 5.5). In 2020 the world experienced a loss in Covid-19-adjusted HDI value equivalent to more than one-fifth of the progress from 1990 to 2019. Latin America and the Caribbean was the most affected region, losing in one year the equivalent of 30 percent of its pre-Covid-19 progress since 1990.

In 2021 there was a recovery, but it was partial and uneven. For very high HDI countries the 2020

Covid-19-adjusted HDI shock was not as large as across other country groups, but it was more sustained, with a slow recovery in 2021.

Crises on such a large scale hold up a mirror to societies. Covid-19 has laid bare the vast prepandemic disparities in people's ability to cope with shocks to access healthcare and to rebuild from loss. The pandemic has exposed the fragilities in global coordination mechanisms in pandemic preparedness and response. The Independent Panel for Pandemic Preparedness and Response found "gaps and failings at every critical juncture of preparedness": containment measures that were too slow, a lack of coordinated global leadership, emergency funding that took too long to materialize, and large holes in social protection systems.[79] The unequal access to lifesaving Covid-19 vaccines demonstrated a tragic failure of global solidarity.[80] These failures played a role in

Figure 5.5 **Widespread but unequal declines in Covid-19-adjusted Human Development Index (HDI) value: Regional and group aggregates**

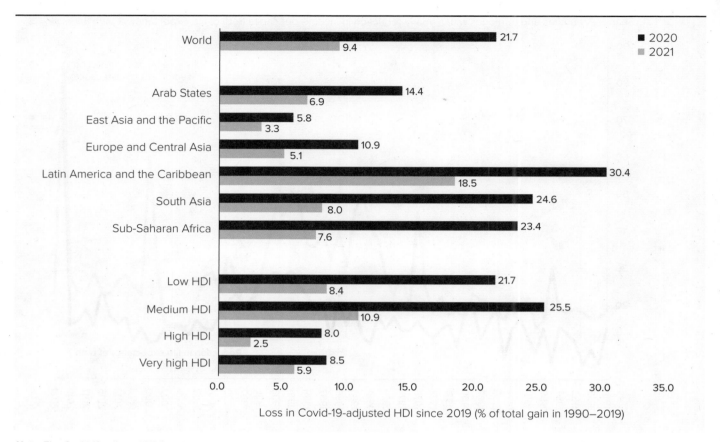

Loss in Covid-19-adjusted HDI since 2019 (% of total gain in 1990–2019)

Note: The Covid-19-adjusted HDI retains the standard HDI dimensions but modifies the expected years of schooling indicator to reflect the effects of school closures and the availability of online learning on effective attendance rates.
Source: Human Development Report Office.

the pandemic's disproportionate impacts on people around the world.

Yet, even as crises mirror weaknesses and injustice, the current crisis also shows us that there are opportunities. Wars, pandemics and disasters can trigger far-reaching change. The 1918 flu pandemic helped spur investments in medicine in some countries, and the bubonic plague triggered efforts to improve sanitation and working conditions.[81] At other times shocks have fostered repressive or harmful policies or not resulted in change.[82] Opportunities for positive transformations are context-specific and far from inevitable (box 5.1). The next section suggests that amid significant collective failures the world's response to the pandemic offers new possibilities for transformation. In our response to Covid-19 are new reference points for what we can achieve in times of crisis—triggering breakthrough

technological innovation, delivering inclusive social protection and changing social norms.

New reference points for technological breakthroughs

Less than two years after the novel coronavirus strain was identified, multiple highly effective vaccines against Covid-19 were deployed around the world.[83] The availability of vaccines for Covid-19 was a crucial turning point. The speed of developing these vaccines—just 11 months after the SARS-CoV-2 sequence was published—is a remarkable achievement. This outcome was made possible in part by years of scientific work, including three decades of prior research into RNA-based vaccines, now deployed for the first time to tackle Covid-19. The history of mRNA vaccine development starts in the 1960s.[84] But only

Box 5.1 The Covid-19 pandemic as an opportunity? A call for a contextual approach

Do shocks create opportunities for policy change? How can the Covid-19 pandemic help ensure that in the future most of the population has access to clean water, sanitation, healthcare, school services and other social benefits as a matter of right? These questions have surfaced in the aftermath of a pandemic that upended all dimensions of everyday life. Progressive policymakers, social activists and international organizations have identified the current crisis as an opportunity to promote radical policy change.

An important body of research identifies shocks as triggers for policy change. Pandemics have also generated opportunities for change as early as the 14th century, contributing to the growth of public institutions and the modern state.[1] The extent to which pandemics have triggered opportunities for inclusionary change has depended at least in part on the role of ideas—including scientific ideas—and how they have shaped the narratives regarding policy responses. Each narrative is a story about a problem and its sometimes-obvious solution.[2]

Analytic frameworks that move beyond grand proclamations about how shocks enhance opportunities for inclusive social policies can be useful. To determine whether such policies have created longer term opportunities, we propose focusing on three key variables. First are the incentives that the policy tools themselves create.[3] Second are the responses to shocks that can also modify the distribution of power among state actors. Third are the narratives that are particularly important as a mechanism for change—one that deserves special attention here. In this way ideas are a power resource to define what the problem subject to state intervention is, frame possible and desirable outcomes and lead policy implementation.[4]

Opportunities are context-specific and revolve around the combination of narratives, policy tools and pro-equity state actors. Take the emergency cash transfers under the Bono Proteger programme, which buffered the sudden loss of income in Costa Rica. The pandemic, along with high uncertainty and fear of social unrest, lifted constraints and made space to implement new policy measures. The programme empowered state entities focused on advancing social goals and created openings for new narratives and policy tools.[5] A second lesson is that the pandemic may leave as many challenges as opportunities when narratives of austerity, including the claim that more taxes are not politically possible or even desirable, take hold.

This reminds us of the power of the idea that states should live within their means, which often also implies that they should avoid increasing taxes as much as possible. Austerity is as much a scientific idea as it is a moral imperative linked to moderation and sacrifice.[6] It alters the relationship between the state and citizens and has become a powerful tool against serious attempts towards redistribution.[7] In recent decades, austerity has become appealing for conservative political actors critical of the welfare state, because it is "politically more expedient to argue that the government lives above its means than to directly attack the poor."[8]

To further advance and fight this dominant narrative, much needs to change. The combination of state weaknesses and pro-status quo actors (such as the economic elites) that ended up inhibiting rapid use of the opportunities created to expand inclusive social policy should be analysed further.

Notes
1. McMillen 2006. **2.** Stone 2011. **3.** Martínez Franzoni and Sánchez-Ancochea 2016; Pierson 1994; Pribble 2013. **4.** Swinkels 2020. **5.** Costa Rica responded to the Covid-19 pandemic and lockdowns by adopting an emergency cash transfer programme, Bono Proteger, which provided 676,340 people (13 percent of the population) two to three payments of up to $214 each (Contraloría General de la República de Costa Rica 2020). Martínez Franzoni and Sánchez-Ancochea (2022a) compared the Costa Rican experience with that in Guatemala and El Salvador and reached similar conclusions. **6.** Schui 2014. **7.** Blyth 2013. **8.** Jabko 2013, p. 706.
Source: Martínez Franzoni and Sánchez-Ancochea 2022b.

in 1993 was the first vaccine tested for influenza in mice. Commercial research and development started only in the late 1990s, with the US Defense Advanced Research Projects Agency financing a large part of the research. This long history of development made possible vaccine development from when the pandemic started.

Even as these advances in vaccine technology built off a pre-existing foundation, the Covid-19 emergency injected an unparalleled sense of urgency into scientific work, producing a systemic shift in supply and demand. Addressing the pandemic through vaccination became a mission, and vaccine supply chains emerged.[85] Moreover, thanks to the steady reduction of DNA sequencing time, many countries could receive current information on prevailing strains of the virus and to act accordingly. Publication pipelines worked overtime to keep up with the rapidly emerging research.[86] The rate of Covid-19-related therapies in research pipelines and the academic publication rate of Covid-19 articles exceeded that of recent Ebola, Zika and H1N1 crises by at least an order of magnitude.[87]

The success of vaccine development shows that governments, industry and academia can work together to great effect in a crisis. Regulatory processes were deployed to support the acceleration of clinical development, trials and emergency use authorization. Governments provided large investments in manufacturing capacity and in supporting private research and development. Manufacturing pipelines were developed alongside clinical trials to allow for rapid scale-up. Government investments helped support development of several potential vaccine candidates, increasing the odds that at least a few might be successful. The United States and Germany were the largest investors in vaccine research and development, providing about $2 billion and $1.5 billion respectively to pharmaceutical companies.[88] Covid-19 also propelled major technological advances in our ability to develop vaccines for future diseases: novel RNA technology appears set to permanently transform how vaccines can be developed and manufactured in the future.[89]

New reference points for social protection and economic policy

In the more than two years since the SARS-CoV-2 virus was first identified, governments have adopted new and unprecedented policy measures to protect vulnerable populations and national economies from lasting damage.[90]

Instruments of economic policy have been deployed at an extraordinary scale. In August 2021 the IMF issued $650 billion equivalent in new Special Drawing Rights, the largest in the fund's history —even if the process took much longer than what would have been feasible. The new Special Drawing Rights provided vital support for national economies as governments battled the health and economic damage the pandemic wrought. A G20-sponsored Debt Service Suspension Initiative granted 73 countries temporary relief on debt-service payments until December 2021. Government fiscal responses were among the largest in recent history, totalling $16 trillion in support between April 2020 and April 2021.[91] These resources were poured into helping households and businesses survive the crisis through a variety of instruments, including direct transfers, expanded benefits, payment deferrals and liquidity injections. To deliver these massive financial support measures, governments moved to rapidly upgrade existing social protection systems and develop new facilities, such as for digital payments.

" The response to the Covid-19 pandemic has reminded us how people-centric policies can substantially enhance human wellbeing

The response to the Covid-19 pandemic has also reminded us how people-centric policies can substantially enhance human wellbeing. As the pandemic's economic, social and health impacts mounted, governments around the world deployed a flurry of expansive social protection measures to support people through the crisis. More than 1,600 social protection measures were reported across virtually all countries and territories in February 2020 and January 2021.[92] The scope and scale of these measures were unprecedented in many settings. In several countries governments expanded protections for losses of livelihoods and income (see monetary support measures in figure 5.6). Many began to extend direct transfers, in the form of cash payments and guaranteed income. Where transfer programmes already existed, governments increased benefits and expanded coverage to include more recipients.[93] By the end of 2020, cash transfers had reached nearly 1.1 billion people worldwide, with coverage growing by 240 percent on average relative to prepandemic levels.[94] By some estimates almost 17 percent of the world's people saw at least one Covid-19-related cash transfer payment between 2020 and 2021.[95] Several countries delivered one-off payments to their populations on a universal or near-universal basis.[96] In addition to cushioning the blow of lost livelihoods, income support programmes helped stem the spread of Covid-19. In low-income countries income support measures were found effective in reducing the growth rate of Covid-19 cases, and in middle-income countries they helped reduce both case growth rates and deaths linked to Covid-19.[97]

Figure 5.6 Most countries implemented monetary support and health measures during the Covid-19 pandemic

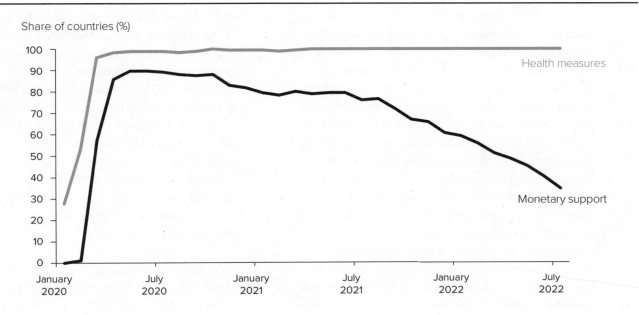

Note: Figure tracks the "flow" of active policies across around the world, displaying the percentage of countries that had any active monetary and health measures in any given month during the Covid-19 pandemic. Data are for 177 countries. Monetary support refers to measures considered income support and debt or contract relief. Health measures refers to testing policy, contact tracing, emergency investment in healthcare, investment in vaccines and vaccination policy.
Source: Human Development Report Office based on Hale and others (2021) and Oxford COVID-19 Government Response Tracker (https://www.bsg.ox.ac.uk/research/research-projects/covid-19-government-response-tracker, accessed 29 July 2022).

Many social protection schemes saw unprecedented expansions in scope, reaching groups that have been excluded from support in the past, such as informal sector workers and the self-employed.[98] Governments of several countries provided food aid, delivering baskets of staples and essential foods to households for free.[99] Some suspended routine payments and contributions, including for utility bills, loans and pension schemes. Mobile payment systems were deployed to deliver financial support—in Bangladesh, Jordan and Mali for instance—to minimize the need to visit banks and service providers in person. Countries turned to online application systems to reach as many of their citizens as they could. Brazil expanded coverage for households already registered as potential beneficiaries and then registered about 27 million households within a few weeks through an online system.[100]

Since Covid-19 triggered a public health crisis, measures to expand health coverage were deployed around the world (see health measures in figure 5.6). Several countries sought to ensure that facilities to identify, diagnose and treat Covid-19 were readily available at low or no cost. Many countries sought to close gaps in health coverage by expanding existing schemes to cover additional segments of their populations, such as temporary and migrant workers. Paid sick leave and other forms of support were expanded, such as compensation for earnings lost due to self-isolation and quarantine.[101]

These efforts reflected the urgency of the crisis, and emergency measures are unlikely to remain in place indefinitely, as figure 5.6 seems to confirm. But they have demonstrated that inequalities and gaps in social protection are not insurmountable. They have shown that governments can do more to make social protection a reality. And they have shown that interventions in income security and healthcare in particular can make an enormous difference to people's lives. The Covid-19 pandemic may have helped broaden public appreciation for social protection and improve government experience with delivering it. And it has added to a growing evidence base on the effectiveness of relatively untested social protection measures, such as guaranteed basic incomes.

The Covid-19 pandemic has also brought previously neglected concerns to the forefront of the reform agenda. Bridging digital disparities has become more urgent than ever, as the pandemic made affordable internet access essential for education as schools closed (recognizing, though, that it should not be seen as a replacement for in-person education). Governments around the world ramped up e-government facilities to continue delivering essential government services, manage new demands (including administering expanded social protection programmes) and provide dedicated Covid-19 information portals.[102] Living with Covid-19 is providing new impetus to digitalization efforts, bolstered by a renewed awareness that going online can create new possibilities for public administration and that strengthening internet access and infrastructure could be essential for resilience against future disasters.[103]

Tools such as nowcasting (providing real-time information about economic and social processes as they unfold, as opposed to waiting for official statistical information) are already gaining traction in efforts to understand and respond to the fast-moving crisis presented by Covid-19. Alternative data sources such as mobility data, congestion data, mobile payment patterns and internet search activity are being incorporated into models for understanding outbreak patterns and economic activity.[104]

This spate of policy activism, through ramped up social protection and new delivery mechanisms, may have reset public expectations of what governments are able to do, at least for some people. If sustained, a new mindset about what governments can do for people opens new possibilities to transform economic policy thinking and approaches as we confront the challenges ahead.

New reference points for altering norms and behaviour

Covid-19 showed us that people all over the world are willing to dramatically alter their everyday conduct in service of a common purpose. Although responses to the Covid-19 pandemic became the focus of divisions in society sometimes associated with political polarization, as discussed in chapter 3, there was remarkable and unprecedented behavioural and institutional change. Combating the spread of Covid-19 required a range of social and behavioural changes such as social distancing, contact tracing, masking and restrictions on gatherings. These changes could not have

been sustained without voluntary cooperation from the vast majority of the world's population. A survey of people in 58 countries during the early stages of the pandemic showed high voluntary compliance with several behavioural measures: 91 percent of respondents reported that they did not attend any social gatherings, 78 percent said that they stayed home in the week before the survey and 93 percent said that they would have informed people around them if they experienced Covid-19 symptoms.[105] A different study of pandemic-related behaviour in 28 countries in August 2020 found that 58 percent of respondents reported always or frequently avoiding having guests in their homes and that 78 percent reported always or frequently avoiding crowds.[106]

" Covid-19 showed us that people all over the world are willing to dramatically alter their everyday conduct in service of a common purpose

Behaviours that were exceedingly rare in many societies becoming commonplace, such as wearing masks, suggests the emergence of new social norms. This means that people are motivated not only by the need to protect themselves but also by a sense of shared responsibility, a perception that others are doing the same or the possibility of social disapproval for noncompliance. People in several countries reported feeling proud of their contribution to stopping the spread of Covid-19 and believing that they were setting a good example by wearing a mask.[107] A variety of interventions based on new social norms engendered by Covid-19 can be considered for future disease control, including normalizing paid sick leave, voluntary social distancing and self-isolation in the event of exposure to infection.[108]

*   *   *

The foreseeable future remains one of uncertainty. Social upheaval, climate and environmental crises and rapidly changing technology may be here to stay for some time. The Covid-19 pandemic has given us a glimpse of the kinds of reality we may need to confront. It has also shown us who we are in times of crises, how we can mobilize with a sense of common purpose and how we may yet shape our common destiny. The extent to which we succeed in this era of uncertainty is up to us.

Our ability to manage this new reality will be strengthened only with a new resolve for far-reaching change. The pandemic has disrupted the world, and it is unlikely, even undesirable, that things will return to how they once were. And there is much more left to do. Our response to the crisis has shown us some of the possibilities for ensuring that the world will be more just and resilient. We have seen that it is possible to substantially reorient people's relationships with governments and that this reorientation can deliver enormous improvements to people's lives. The pandemic showed that social protection can work better where it corresponds to how people actually live, work and navigate times of crisis. We saw how people possess an immeasurable capacity to care for one another—and how our ties to one another provide an invisible infrastructure for human flourishing. We saw also that our ability to spur technological innovation can dramatically expand our possibilities for surviving and thriving. More than any single technology or invention, it is our capacity for innovation at large that matters the most. Technological advances will be vital for the structural changes needed in our economies and society. The direction of technological change remains up to us, and much can be achieved by turning its potential to tackle the challenges we face.

Charting paths to transformation

Navigating uncertainty to expand human development

Charting paths to transformation:
Navigating uncertainty to expand human development

The hero and the villain in today's uncertainty story is one and the same: human choices.

So, what practical choices can be made for the better?

This chapter emphasizes policies that focus on the Three I's: investment, insurance and innovation. Together, these will promote, protect and stimulate human development for people and planet to flourish in the face of new uncertainties.

Culture plays a big role, too. The chapter identifies three enablers of cultural change: education to cultivate evolving values, social recognition to legitimize them and representation to protect their inclusiveness and translate them into policies.

Enhancing human development—by expanding freedoms and achievements in wellbeing and agency—is an open-ended process filled with new possibilities. Uncertainty is part of that journey, and as human ingenuity pushes forward the frontier of the possible, new unintended consequences are bound to arise, good and bad. And new challenges can mean room for new opportunities. To thrive under uncertainty, as important as averting the negative consequences of well-intended actions, is to grab the opportunities that emerge.

Today we seem to be living through several unintended consequences of progress, as reflected in part in the three layers of uncertainty—the dangerous planetary changes in the Anthropocene, the unpredictability in uncharted transitions, and the social division and polarization of societies. Our choices and the values that underpin them have at times promoted socially, economically and environmentally unsustainable policies and development paths. Inequalities have allowed a few to benefit while many get left behind.

" Our choices and the values that underpin them have at times promoted socially, economically and environmentally unsustainable policies and development paths

The image of the "empty box" in chapter 1, with no country so far achieving a very high Human Development Index (HDI) value with low pressures on the planet, suggests that our societies need to devise new ways of pursuing development. Chasing higher GDP per capita or even higher HDI values alone is not enough.

The call is thus for transformational change, which requires enhancing social arrangements to address people's insecurity and unsettledness. But this provides only a partial response. We are not confronting a small adjustment or transitory imbalance. We are navigating uncharted territory, where social and planetary systems are adjusting simultaneously. The assumption in much economic analysis that all other conditions remain unchanged does not hold.

Transformational change may be needed beyond policies and institutional arrangements. Societies also might need to shift social norms, beliefs and values (introduced in chapter 3 as culture). The

Dasgupta Review on the economics of biodiversity argues for ensuring that societies' demands on nature do not exceed nature's sustainable supply, for adopting different metrics of economic success and for transforming our institutions and systems—particularly those in finance and education—to enable these changes and sustain them for future generations.[1] But the review goes further, coming to a startling conclusion: "No social mechanism can meet this problem in its entirety, meaning that no institution can be devised to enforce socially responsible conduct."[2]

The problem is that humans are embedded in nature, so current and future wellbeing depends on maintaining the integrity of the biosphere, yet people's conduct is undermining that very integrity. As if this were not challenging enough, the Dasgupta Review argues that "unlike the economics of climate change, [...] the economics of biodiversity [...] requires not only national and intergovernmental engagement, but engagement by communities and civil societies throughout the world."[3] How, then, can such a problem be solved? If these conclusions are startling, the recommendation on what to do may seem even more so: "It would seem then that, ultimately, we each have to serve as judge and jury for our own actions. And that cannot happen unless we develop an affection for Nature and its processes."[4]

Social mechanisms to address collective problems usually rely on appealing to people's interests (such as price incentives to tax pollution) or creating institutions (property rights over land or a specific resource, such as a forest). Interests and institutions clearly matter, but the headline recommendation of the Dasgupta Review can be interpreted to take us to the world of ideas—or of culture (chapter 3).

And why invoke the relevance of ideas, of culture, now? Many communities in history have had a deep affection for nature. Chief Elesi of Odogbolu living in Nigeria stated in 1917: "I conceive that land belongs to a vast family of which many are dead, few are living and countless others unborn."[5] The 2020 Human Development Report documented how indigenous peoples over time have held—and today in many communities around the world continue to hold—beliefs and values that reflect "an affection for Nature and its processes."[6] Many are persecuted and killed when their actions based on such beliefs come into conflict with interests shaped by existing institutions, from mining to expanding agriculture.[7] But now the challenges that we confront go beyond climate change and preserving the integrity of biodiversity functions: these are but two of the manifestations of our Anthropocene context.

In addition to dangerous planetary change, the other layers of uncertainty documented in this Report are unsettling people's lives. The conflicts that play out at the local level between indigenous peoples and firms or authorities are a microcosm of a broader set of tensions that may not be resolved by arbitrating between competing interests. It seems reasonable to suggest, in addition to re-examining policies and institutions (which is typically the remit of work such as the Human Development Report), that the cultural context—the ideas, broadly defined to include practices, beliefs, norms, values and technologies—also bears re-examining to explore a way forward as we navigate today's uncertain world.

Examining culture opens new vistas for the range of possible actions by those in positions of power and the potential for new social mechanisms to address the unprecedented challenges we are confronting today. But that requires two things. First is broadening our perspective on the determinants of people's choices. And second is reflecting on more recent perspectives about what culture is, how it changes across contexts and over time and how it is used by people in strategic ways, rather than as a fixed latent variable working silently in the background. Key for both is recognizing the importance of agency and freedom, the tenets of the human development approach (chapter 3).

A framework to embrace uncertainty

Navigating the uncertainty complex demands doubling down on human development to ensure that people have the capabilities to harness the potential embedded in uncertain times. "The cunning of uncertainty opens new spaces and facilitates the emergence of alternative options. Ambiguities permit boundary crossings where closure between knowledge domains or areas of strictly defined expertise have reigned. Ambiguities do not mean that everything becomes fuzzy and porous or that anything goes. They mean acknowledging that social life is full of contradictions and that social beings have the ability to navigate between them. Once they have

the necessary resources, they also negotiate with each other viable options for living together."[8]

" Navigating the uncertainty complex demands doubling down on human development to ensure that people have the capabilities to harness the potential embedded in uncertain times

We propose a two-tier framework to respond to a dual gap in our uncertain times. On the one hand, a mismatch between current social arrangements struggling to promote human security and to tackle people's unsettledness. On the other hand, a mismatch between prevalent beliefs and values and what might be needed to navigate through the uncertainty complex (figure 6.1).

The first tier is about what to do, with a focus on concrete transformations on three fronts: investment, insurance and innovation.

- Investment, in the capabilities people will need to enable socioeconomic and planetary conditions for human flourishing.
- Insurance, to protect people from the unavoidable contingencies of uncertain times, safeguarding their capabilities, including their fundamental freedoms (enhancing human security).
- Innovation, to foster capabilities that might not exist today.

The second tier is about how to generate the broader social and contextual conditions for change to take hold, acknowledging the role of culture as described in chapter 3.

- Education, to strengthen agency and encourage people to shape their own future.
- Recognition, to acknowledge human rights and respect for people's identities and values to change scripts and narratives that build hope in society.
- Representation, to amplify the power and voice that strengthen representation and agency.

Insights from cultural change suggest cultivating motivating principles that can both enhance social arrangements and shape cultural evolution in uncertain times.[9] The motivating principles highlighted in this Report are flexibility, creativity, solidarity and inclusion (spotlight 6.1).

No single set of policy recommendations can suit every context and every country, but using these principles as a compass can help navigate through the layers

Figure 6.1 A two-tier framework for transformation

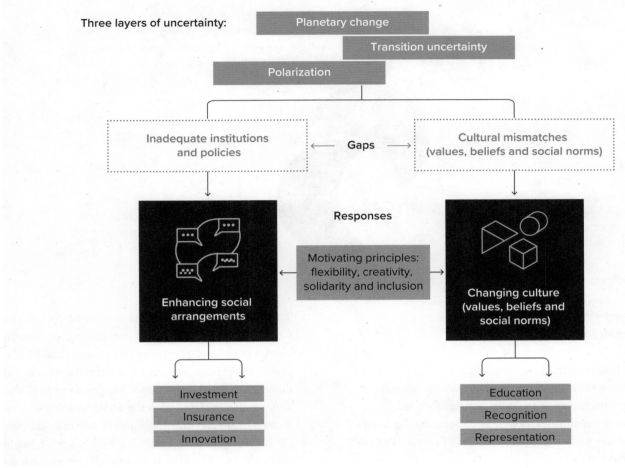

Source: Human Development Report Office.

of uncertainty and inspire people to embrace uncertainty. Flexibility, creativity, solidarity and inclusion build pathways to transformation by strengthening resilience[10] and agency,[11] as they increase communities' capacity to thrive in environments characterized by change. For instance, in the context of societal responses to Covid-19 in the G7 countries, differences in solidarity and agency were much more marked than in the economic and environmental policies pursued, pointing to the importance of supplementing economic policies with solidarity- and agency-enhancing actions.[12]

Investment, insurance and innovation towards continually expanding human development

Thriving under uncertainty is possible. Three policy building blocks that would shape transformations to expand human development could provide support in facing the layers of uncertainty from dangerous planetary change, uncharted transitions and polarization. The first is investment, encompassing people and financial and natural resources. The second is insurance mechanisms that guarantee protection or compensation in the case of shocks or threats emanating from planetary imbalances or insecurities and that can bring a greater sense of control. The third is innovation, to embrace change, looking for new solutions through creativity, iterative learning and diverse perspectives. Investment, insurance and innovation all safeguard and promote agency, thus advancing human development. Implementing these mechanisms aims to grow opportunities for the future while advancing human potential in the present.[13] Figure 6.2 identifies some of the policy examples explored below.

Figure 6.2 Making people more secure though investment, insurance and innovation

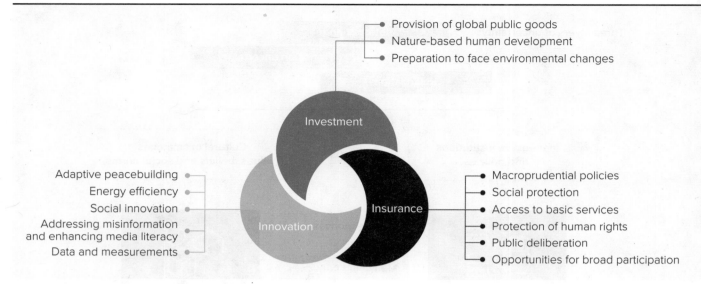

- Provision of global public goods
- Nature-based human development
- Preparation to face environmental changes

Investment

Innovation

Insurance

- Adaptive peacebuilding
- Energy efficiency
- Social innovation
- Addressing misinformation and enhancing media literacy
- Data and measurements

- Macroprudential policies
- Social protection
- Access to basic services
- Protection of human rights
- Public deliberation
- Opportunities for broad participation

Source: Human Development Report Office.

Investment—in capabilities to thrive under uncertainty

The first building block encompasses investment in the capabilities required to successfully navigate an uncertain future. It includes policies focused on enhancing capabilities as well as on forming the assets to do so—meaning different forms of capital, including natural capital.

The context of multilayered uncertainties sets up new challenges but also new possibilities for the long-standing aspiration to provide global public goods.[14] On the challenges the three layers of uncertainty render investments in global public goods more difficult: the planetary scale of the Anthropocene's challenges generates a mismatch with the geographic scope of national governments,[15] while political polarization and transition uncertainty complicate how domestic priorities are weighed against international challenges. This was made starkly clear during the Covid-19 pandemic, as the world struggled and failed to ensure universal access to personal protective equipment and then vaccines, despite having the scientific, technological and financial capacities to make the investments needed to do so.[16]

But the uncertainty complex also makes the case for investing in providing global public goods more compelling. The additional investment to avoid future pandemics is estimated to be $15 billion a year.[17]

This is a tiny fraction of the economic cost of the Covid-19 pandemic (without considering any human cost in lives lost or learning lost): more than $7 trillion in lost production and more than $16.9 trillion in emergency fiscal responses.[18] The investment is also very small compared with the $650 billion dollar issuance of special drawing rights.[19] The rational case for investing in global public goods has been made many times, as has the need to craft appropriate arrangements that sustain international coordination or cooperation.[20]

But with the recognition of the uncertainty complex lies the opportunity to look across the interactions of the layers of uncertainty and not only work through formal existing structures and rules but also encourage experimentation and innovation.[21] This can be advanced by recognizing that providing global public goods in a context of novel uncertainty can be enhanced with institutions of multilevel governance offering compelling narratives that foster cooperation and coordination through the legitimacy of envisioning better futures.[22] These institutions would embrace uncertainty, which means adopting policies and strategies robust to many alternative futures. Normative goals—if formulated with participation, flexibility to iterate and informed rigorous research—could help produce assessments that offer more robust policy options beyond just alerting the world of the extreme possibilities to come.[23] They could be even more robust if these assessments took a holistic view, focusing on the behaviour of the individual components and agents in socioecological systems as well as their interactions and relationships.[24]

Investment is also essential in complex governance systems (governmental and beyond) that can experiment, respond quickly, draw on all relevant knowledge and account for heterogeneity of societies, while overcoming the power imbalances that entrench vested interests. This would promote inclusion and build trust for sustained collective action and solidarity (box 6.1). Investing in governance also means crafting systems that can redress inequality and provide individual and group recognition to enable dignity by, among other things, strengthening social policies and fostering civic (re)engagement and participation.[25]

Investment is also needed in nature-based human development, including bottom-up efforts that rely

---

Box 6.1 Governance for systemic and transformational change

The Anthropocene represents a complex set of crises of a kind humanity has not previously confronted. Human impact on the planet and unsustainable economic and social systems virtually guarantee environmental and societal upheaval for the foreseeable future. Every polity will experience the effects for generations to come.

Complexity theory helps us understand what it takes to manage such systemic problems: holistic analysis, constant experimentation and the inclusion of many disciplines and perspectives. But our existing governance processes are designed largely to sort people and issues into siloed boxes onto which "optimal" procedures can be applied, sandpapering away the diversity and volatility that characterize reality.

It is entirely possible to govern for the complex systemic problems we confront.[1] Such governance must focus not just on the behaviour of individual components and actors in interrelated systems but also on their interactions and relationships.[2] It must adopt policies and strategies that are robust to alternative futures and adaptable in the face of rapid change. Specifically, it must aim to (re)build social capital at scale, build meaningful networks across decision silos and create effective, inclusive layers of governance that keep decisionmaking as close to local knowledge as possible. To those ends governance should be based on four principles: systemic thinking, transparency, social inclusion and subsidiarity.

The most important change that Anthropocene governance requires is the shift to systemic thinking and decisionmaking. Some of the actions decisionmakers can take are mapping the system using social or organizational network analysis;[3] employing tools such as scenario-based planning for a variety of alternative outcomes and conditions;[4] and continuously monitoring, evaluating and assessing the impact of policies.

Transparency in governance refers to the degree to which information is available to all stakeholders and enables them to have an informed voice in decisions and assess the choices made by insiders.[5] It is essential both for accountability and for making governance effective and responsive, as meaningful transparency permits feedback on how well policies and experiments are working and what adaptations may be needed.

Inclusion in governance refers to expanding meaningful participation to a wide array of stakeholders and ensuring they have both deliberative and decisionmaking powers. Governance must prioritize inclusivity for three reasons: it is necessary for reducing power imbalances, networks with a diverse and distributed structure are more resilient to shocks and disruptions, and greater inclusion fosters legitimacy.

Subsidiarity made possible by adequate transparency and inclusion then becomes a key principle for creating resilience in a multilayered governance structure. It refers to how "social and political issues should be dealt with at the most immediate level consistent with their adequate resolution."[6] If practised well, governance based on subsidiarity can bolster the efficacy and legitimacy of policy responses because local authorities tend to be physically closer, more connected and more visible to the people they serve.

Governance based on these principles gives humanity its best shot at effectively and justly transforming the existing systems for creating, using and disposing of the material substrate of human society. Such governance has the potential to shift us towards greater adaptability, to strengthen the societal trust that is key to effective governance in challenging times and to improve prospects for sustainable development in the Anthropocene.

Notes
1. Florini, LaForge and Sharma 2022. 2. Colander and Roland 2014; Florini, LaForge and Sharma 2022. 3. Yang, Keller and Zheng 2016. 4. Kupers and Wilkinson 2014. 5. Florini 2013. 6. Arato, Cohen and von Busekist 2018, p. 43.

on the inclusion, participation and knowledge of local communities and indigenous peoples,[26] leveraging their potential to both learn and scale up transformative change.[27] Examples include investing in green areas to manage the risk of extreme temperatures, reducing ecosystem-based disaster risk, improving water quality, ensuring water availability and improving agricultural practices to ensure food security. The value of these efforts often goes beyond the contributions to communities. So, instead of treating them as isolated initiatives, countries should integrate them into national development priorities across domains, including water security, food security, disaster risk reduction and economic performance. Nature-based human development both relies on and can enhance the agency of local communities and indigenous peoples; it also provides for diverse visions of what is a good life, incorporates justice and inclusion in conservation and promotes education and knowledge sharing.[28]

" Investing in mechanisms that prepare local communities to face rapid environmental changes such as food insecurity can increase agency and freedoms by fostering inclusion and solidarity

Investing in mechanisms that prepare local communities to face rapid environmental changes[29] such as food insecurity can increase agency and freedoms by fostering inclusion and solidarity (spotlight 6.2).

Insurance—against the interacting layers of uncertainty

Insurance guarantees protection or compensation against shocks emanating from the interacting layers of uncertainty. A key goal is to enhance human security. As chapter 4 describes, human insecurity not only constrains agency and fundamental freedoms but also hinders collective action. People have always confronted adverse outcomes—illness, death or injuries that preclude someone from providing for the household—and extended families, friends and local communities have often been a source of support.

Charities or religious institutions have sometimes helped. Groups engaged in dangerous occupations such as mining established mutual societies

for an injured or incapacitated member of the group to receive support from the others, and some market insurance eventually developed out of these arrangements.

It is critical to expand market insurance, under properly regulated frameworks that protect users and address several of the well-known market failures in insurance markets (including moral hazard and adverse selection). Equally important, market insurance providers will face the challenge of innovating to offer services that address the novel context of uncertainty, for which existing actuarial practices may not be fully adequate.

It is also crucial to expand, and innovate in, social insurance. Over the 20th century government-funded social insurance programmes expanded around the world. Public social welfare spending in Organisation for Economic Co-operation and Development (OECD) countries grew from a median of 0.4 percent of GDP in 1900 to 18.6 percent in 2017. Private (mandatory and voluntary) social welfare spending has also increased in recent decades, from a median of 1.1 percent of GDP in OECD countries in 1980 to 2.1 percent in 2017—reaching more than 10 percent in the Netherlands, Switzerland and the United States.[30]

There is great diversity across countries in the level and categories of spending, in the mix of taxation to fund government programmes and in the reliance on private provision. But the bulk of the increase in OECD countries is related to contributory social insurance programmes to support older people and to pay for healthcare expenses, with both workers and employees contributing to fund government programmes. Denmark and New Zealand rely, instead, on general tax revenues only. Most striking, however, is how much less spending there is in non-OECD countries: total social protection spending increased from a median of 4.5 percent of GDP in 2000 to only 6.3 percent in 2015 in 46 countries that account for most of the world's population. In several African countries less than 3 percent of the population living in the bottom 40 percent of the income distribution is expected to rely on support from governments or nongovernmental organizations—and the rest were most likely to rely on family and friends (box 6.2).[31]

Macroprudential measures can be implemented to promote financial stability, in part learning from the lessons of the global financial crisis. Most central

Box 6.2 The heightened importance of expanding and innovating in social protection

Expanding and improving social insurance, recognized as important for a while, acquire heightened relevance in today's uncertain times. Social insurance enhances human security and can stimulate risk taking and investment, supporting other elements of institutional change and policies. The reverse also holds: some investments can provide insurance. For instance, investments in nature-based human development can be an effective tool for achieving resilience to shocks.[1]

Key policies in this area relate to social protection[2] that can shield people against shocks, achieving a dual purpose: protection and promotion.[3] The need to balance both raises questions about the appropriate mix of targeted and universal policies. The interaction of inequalities, hierarchical power imbalances, polarization and conflicts can complicate reaching consensus for social policies.[4] Social protection income and providing public goods can reduce inequality while preventing political polarization, potentially reversing entrenched polarized attitudes.[5] So it is important to deliver mechanisms that reach everyone, independent of economic status. For instance, a social protection model that was born to tackle social protection simultaneously with climate adaptation and disaster risks is adaptative social protection.[6] Adaptative social protection builds safety nets (savings, insurance, information) to prepare households to act on unforeseen situations, so they can smooth consumption, retain assets and reduce exposure to shocks.[7]

Notes
1. Dasgupta 2021; DeFries 2020; UNDP 2020a. 2. Social protection is concerned with protecting and helping those who are poor, marginalized or dealing with increased risks. Social protection includes a set of measures provided by the state, such as social assistance (noncontributory transfers in cash, vouchers, in-kind, free waivers and subsidies), social insurance, social care services and labour market programmes (Carter and others 2019). 3. Drèze and Sen 1989. 4. Ravallion 2017. 5. Stewart, Plotkin and McCarty 2021. 6. Arnall and others 2010; Bahadur and others 2015; Davies and others 2013. 7. Bowen and others 2020.

banks have stability objectives, and they apply different tools that work as insurance instruments to build resilience.[32] The most common mechanisms are countercyclical capital buffers and capital requirements, which serve as a shock absorber, sector-specific capital requirements for the banking sector, and loan-to-income or loan-to-value ratios that increase bank capital above the minimum.[33] Although in most countries these instruments are under the Central Bank's control, in some (such as Brazil and South Africa) decisionmaking responsibility is shared. Not all countries have the same mechanisms available—for example, Argentina, Brazil, Chile, China, Colombia, Peru and Türkiye use other prudential instruments such as reserve or cash requirements on domestic deposits. Reducing the costs of future systemic shocks and containing vulnerabilities require building macroeconomic prudency and coordinating with monetary policy.[34]

Approaches such as state-contingent debt instruments can help economies respond to shocks quickly and predictably. These instruments enable countries to manage their sovereign debt payments depending on changes in their capacity to pay as a direct result of shocks.[35] Mexico, Nigeria and Venezuela have linked these instruments to commodity prices (such as oil prices); Argentina, Greece and Ukraine have linked them to GDP variations; and Barbados and Grenada have linked them to the effects of natural hazards. State-contingent debt instruments act as insurance that gives countries the space to apply countercyclical and stabilization policies that are immediately triggered after well-specified adverse events take place. After the event, and by contract, either the maturity or the volume of payments to creditors (or both) is adjusted to give more fiscal space to the sovereign debtor. Creditors can count on a predictable response as specified in the contract, as opposed to being subject to ad hoc and unpredictable processes of potential debt restructuring.[36]

Access to financial services can greatly contribute to people's abilities to navigate changing and uncertain economic conditions. Financial inclusion can reduce poverty and inequality through access to credit and insurance.[37] Moreover, digital banking and payment, loan and credit services enable wider financial inclusion, especially among underserved groups and in low- and middle-income countries.[38] Financial literacy is an important accompaniment to greater financial inclusion because it develops tools, knowledge, confidence and awareness related to personal and business finances. Important state-led and private initiatives exist to strengthen these capabilities—for example, by incorporating financial literacy content in education curricula.[39]

One of the main challenges policymakers face is inadequate coverage of the people most likely to be left behind. Targeted social policies that are based on income can easily exclude informal workers. Such policies might have requirements that leave individuals at higher risk of slipping through the cracks.[40] With these challenges combining with other recent threats, such as the Covid-19 pandemic, the focus of the debate has shifted more to universalism. An example to take advantage of the structures that have already been built is the implementation of systems that benefit all, such as universal access to health, education, care or income.[41]

A minimum guaranteed income has been tested through pilot projects in India, Kenya and Namibia.[42] One of the main operational challenges for these programmes is that they are financed by taxation, and countries with lower incomes have limited formal tax systems and income data.[43] Another concern is that a minimum guaranteed income does not provide an integrated solution across other human development dimensions, so it could divert resources from other government-subsidized or universal services, such as education, and distort economic incentives. However, a universal basic income needs to be seen not only in the context of the world today—in which limited government resources and acute needs may tilt the argument towards targeted transfers—but also as preparing for the world of tomorrow, when the nature of future work may change.[44]

Many have advocated shifting the debate towards universal basic services, to guarantee that everyone meets their basic needs and has expanded opportunities and participation independent from contingencies.[45] Universal access to services can still lead to inequalities in human development. And as the recent Special Report on Human Security points out, universalism must consider equity and quality and not just cover essential needs.[46] In some countries health and education are already built on universal basic service principles, but this can be expanded to housing, care, transportation, information, security and nutrition.[47] Universal access to mental health services[48] enables people to deal with mental distress and thrive, and these services could be offered within existing social structures, such as schools and community centres.

> " Good practices in promoting human rights point towards identifying what binds us together and engaging people in dialogue about human rights in their daily lives

Universal basic services are also based on solidarity, as it recognizes that needs and the responsibility to fulfil them are shared in the collective. A study of 19 countries in Latin America and the Caribbean determined that policies across the region explicitly mention that no child or adolescent should be left out of the education system and designed methodologies based on the Universal Design for Learning.[49] In El Salvador's Modelo Escuela Inclusiva de Tiempo Pleno, flexible pedagogic programmes were adapted for different students based on inclusion principles.[50] The study also highlights that the challenge for inclusive education is achieving not just a technical change but also a social change. When approaching universal policies in practice, it is important to consider all actors (teachers, administrators, parents), create local support networks and transform the institutional culture with a shift in attitudes and norms.[51]

Protecting human rights can work as insurance by shielding people in times of uncertainty (box 6.3). Mechanisms that rebuild trust and promote understanding,[52] respect, inclusion and equality can help in navigating conflicts and impacts of displacement. In some cases policy design and programme selection that consider human and environmental rights can be helpful in a context of contested and uncertain futures.[53] Examples include strategic impact assessments, regulatory impact assessments and cost-benefit analyses that consider both international and local regulations, such as access to water and full citizenship and recognition of people who identify as lesbian, gay, bisexual, transgender, intersex or another sexual minority (LGBTQI+).[54]

Good practices in promoting human rights point towards identifying what binds us together and engaging people in dialogue about human rights in their daily lives.[55] Practices such as volunteerism and policy mechanisms that favor inclusion and that enhance deliberative processes can also be interpreted

In a context of uncertainty, it is extremely difficult (maybe impossible) to think of ideal scenarios or optimal policies. Even more so in a context of a plurality of views, where decisions are heavily affected by cultural context and emotions (chapter 3).[1] Amartya Sen advocated that it is possible to make progress in assessing policy objectives without necessarily searching for the conditions of an ideal world. The key is to identify "clearly remediable injustices."[2] Not an easy task, either. But humanity has made remarkable progress in defining some normative principles that should remain valid in the new context. Probably the most important consensus is encoded in the internationally agreed 1948 Universal Declaration of Human Rights.

Human rights and human development are linked.[3] Their concepts have a common motivation, and several human rights can be seen as rights to capabilities. However, capabilities tend to refer to the opportunity to choose among different alternatives for what one would like to do (opportunity freedoms), while human rights also encompass the chance to choose freely (process freedoms).[4]

In times of change and deep uncertainty, human rights become even more salient to guide our collective actions for three main reasons.

First, in a context of deep social and planetary transformations, is that they retain the focus on people.

Second is their emphasis on fundamental freedoms, which depend not only on achievements but also on the agency of people (a dimension that has often been missing in public discussions; see chapter 3). In this space human security is a subset of these fundamental freedoms (freedom from fear, from want and from indignity), explicitly mentioned in the preamble of the Universal Declaration of Human Rights.

Third is their universality. This defines a space of equality across all people on the planet. The 2019 Human Development Report highlights that this condition (inherited by the description of several Sustainable Development Goals) allows the analysis of inequalities to be refocused beyond income, including on the gaps in agency and freedoms.[5] The 2020 Human Development Report underscores that the lack of recognition of human rights amid dangerous planetary change can perpetuate discrimination and injustice and makes navigation harder in the Anthropocene context.[6]

The universality of human rights also ensures their validity in the expanding digital world. This is critical for protecting the right to participate in the cultural life of communities, the right to freedom of expression while addressing online hate speech and disinformation, and the right to privacy.[7]

Notes
1. As indicated in the introduction of this chapter, in these times humans will have to serve as judge and jury for their own actions (Dasgupta 2021). **2.** See discussion in Sen (2009b). **3.** Sen 2005. **4.** Sen 2005. **5.** UNDP 2019. **6.** Leach and others 2018; UNDP 2020a. **7.** Bachelet 2022.

as advancing insurance (spotlight 6.3) in addition to promoting human rights.

Innovation—expanding societies' chances to thrive in uncertainty

Innovation refers to mechanisms that look for new approaches through creativity and iterative learning drawing from diverse perspectives. As chapter 5 mentions, technological innovation can expand societies' chances for thriving in uncertainty. It is important to prioritize investments in research and science to push the frontiers of knowledge and mobilize technological change to complement, and not replace, people. As chapter 1 highlights, it is also fundamental to innovate responsibly, addressing

justice and sustainability seeking to avoid power concentration.

Peacebuilding is one space where innovative approaches are being applied to manage complexity. Born out of new understanding of complexity and resilience, adaptive peacebuilding prioritizes iterative learning to sustain peace, where peace is seen as a continuous process rather than an end.[56] Drawing on insights from complexity theory, the approach recognizes that peacebuilding must respond to continuously changing circumstances. The objectives for peacebuilders then become working with communities and people affected by conflict, facilitating the creation of self-organized and resilient social institutions that can embrace uncertainties and channelling nonviolent responses to stressors and shocks.[57] This is achieved through participatory decisionmaking, constant iteration and variety of solutions.[58] Lessons from church-based groups, local nongovernmental organizations and government initiatives for adaptive peacebuilding in Rwanda point to focusing on local needs for transitional justice. Religious institutions facilitated spaces for Hutu, Tutsi and Twa to come together and process their grief and honour their loved ones after the genocide. Civil society leaders encouraged Rwandans to take advantage of their cultural repertoires for healing. Through *kwihangana*,[59] communities achieved conflict resolution through patience and gift giving. Local nongovernmental organizations focused on tackling socioeconomic conditions and the mental health of women who had faced sexual violence. The government implemented efforts to resonate with local adaptive peacebuilding strategies,[60] teaching reconciliation in schools and providing a space for commemoration and public memory.

Because shocks, crises and conflicts can have serious effects on mental wellbeing, they should ideally be prevented. This is not always possible, but measures can be implemented to mitigate crises, and innovations can help improve mental wellbeing—for example, mechanisms that connect mental wellbeing to peacebuilding or psychological resilience building techniques.[61] (See spotlight 6.4 for an elaboration of the framework "Preventing distress, mitigating crises and building resilience" introduced in figure 2.9 in chapter 2).

" Even well-intended policies can overlook conditions that affect the groups most likely to be left behind. In these cases social movements and community initiatives innovate and experiment with alternative views, codes, values and practices using symbols, teach-ins, educational workshops and awareness raising

Urban communities are likely to have stronger networks due to the high density and proximity of services, actors and resources,[62] which set the conditions for innovative initiatives. In India it is very common that in the name of solidarity, communities mobilize to establish small-scale decentralized composting plants. The Residents' Initiative for a Safe Environment started in Bengaluru with 1,200 households coordinating waste separation and collection at composting sites. The initiative depended on engaging many households without external support and on their willingness to contribute financially.[63]

Innovation requires creative energy to address complex problems through community interactions.[64] Dangerous planetary change and new threats are pushing some countries to transition to clean energy systems. In India one of the challenges of distributing energy is rural areas, so the country has introduced the National Solar Mission, with mechanisms to encourage community-based off-grid projects.[65] Two initiatives based in the provinces of Rajasthan and Uttar Pradesh have attempted different solutions to bring electricity to their communities.

Innovative organized actions can strengthen the individual and community repertoires and power, influence decisionmakers and transform traditional social norms and cultural behaviours.

Community involvement can also ensure that policies reflect people's priorities. Even well-intended policies can overlook conditions that affect the groups most likely to be left behind. In these cases social movements and community initiatives innovate and experiment with alternative views, codes, values and practices[66] using symbols, teach-ins, educational workshops and awareness raising.[67] In Israel a welfare-to-work programme was implemented to benefit the long-term unemployed, requiring all adults from beneficiary households to participate full time. But the programme did not account for the needs of those dependent on unpaid care work. A local group of men and women in one of the areas that lack day-care facilities started advocating for their right to participate in the labour market and to have access to care. The group organized a participatory needs assessment to express the needs of the community.[68] This example aligns with inclusive localism, focused on empowering and investing in the capabilities and agency of local communities.[69]

Innovation can also result from recombination or iteration.[70] Initiatives such as Thinking and Working Politically and Problem-Driven Iterative Adaptation have an advantage when the problem is complex, the context is novel or the solutions are contentious.[71] For instance, the organization Funda Wande was created based on the fact that 58 percent of children in South Africa were unable to read for meaning in any language at the end of grade 4.[72] The organization aimed to improve children's reading skills. Using the iterative adaptation approach[73] to deconstruct the problem, it identified four main causes: weak institutional functionality, undue union influence, weak teacher content and pedagogical skills, and wasted learning time.

" Another area that requires innovation is tackling misinformation. Major social media platforms have enacted policies such as notices, warnings and links to resources on misinformation

Local actors, native language speakers, teachers and other relevant stakeholders were brought in for another diagnosis, which identified teacher training and reading materials as action entry points. In Eastern Cape and Limpopo, two of the worst performing provinces, iterating and revising practices led to teaching materials being produced in local languages, thereby adapting them to each setting. Only a cheaper set of materials in native languages would accomplish widespread readership. The organization currently runs its programme in 30 schools in Eastern Cape, 80 schools in Limpopo and 50 schools in Western Cape.[74]

Another area that requires innovation is tackling misinformation. Social media have transformed the methods, speed and scale of spreading misinformation, especially where it is organized and intentional (spotlight 6.5). Major social media platforms have enacted policies such as notices, warnings and links to resources on misinformation. For example, links to official information by the World Health Organization are suggested under posts mentioning Covid-19 on Facebook, Instagram, TikTok and YouTube. And Twitter alerts users who share an article without opening the link first. At the same time fact-checking initiatives have been created by users of these platforms, and media plurality has been strengthened through new and independent outlets that could not exist or have the means to inform in the traditional media landscape, often at the local and grassroot levels.

Innovation is also important when it comes to new ways of measuring human development (box 6.4). Motivated scientists can fulfil a social role[75]—for example, in contributing to green transitions through advocating for taxes on pollution.[76] Committed researchers and scientists who let their values guide their work are a powerful force, as they can draw society's attention to the perils of climate change[77] or other development challenges. In this sense there is also a need to expand the research and measurement of social norms (perceptions and values),[78] as understanding them is also key to socially coordinating people.[79] Beyond data collection, research is developing models to predict social norm change and methodological tools to test the causal effect of social norms.[80]

Drawing from cultural change

For investment, insurance and innovation strategies to promote agency and advance human development, opportunities for common deliberation to accompany cultural change are important (figure 6.3). Building a solid institutional capacity open to diversity and deliberation can be seen as insurance in uncertain times. Under uncertainty, mismatches between current and needed institutions can emerge.[81] Strengthening intergroup contact[82] can reduce hostilities against other parties and provide opportunities for common deliberation that fosters cultural change.[83]

Education, social recognition and representation[84] are some of the ways stakeholders can encourage cultural change supportive of investment, insurance and innovation.[85]

Education to cultivate evolving values

Education—a powerful tool to instil reasoning and critical thinking, opening possibilities for new values and attitudes in younger generations—is key for agency. It can encourage people to act regarding climate change and other Anthropocene pressures, providing them with ownership and agency to shape their own future and hold decisionmakers to account.[86] Governments and other organizations have explored myriad education curricula to shape the next generations' wellbeing. One is comprehensive sexuality education,[87] an approach that schools around the world are implementing to improve sexual reproductive health, prevent dating violence and increase understanding

Box 6.4 Augmenting the resolution of the Human Development Index values using satellite imagery and artificial intelligence

Data collection to measure human development is challenging. It is difficult to get accurate and high-quality information for some regions across the globe. In this context remote technology and satellite imagery can help researchers and decisionmakers observe, explore and evaluate the status of human development[1] in a timely, consistent and affordable way[2] and can fill gaps in official statistics.[3]

The availability of geolocalized and satellite imagery data can inform decisionmakers of where to implement policies, who to target and how to allocate resources efficiently.[4] For example, targeted policies or programmes that require monitoring Human Development Index (HDI) values at the local level. The United Nations Development Programme (UNDP) estimates HDI values at the national level based on country-level data, but some countries produce subnational estimates. There have been prior efforts to measure HDI values locally, producing a snapshot at the state or province level using survey and administrative data,[5] but these remain spatially coarse and expensive to produce.

A recent collaboration between UNDP and academic researchers uses daytime and night-time satellite imagery to estimate HDI values at highly disaggregated geographic resolution (box figure 1).[6] Using a machine-learning technique, it is possible to train an artificial intelligence algorithm that associates image elements with HDI values, employing these image elements to estimate HDI values at the local scale.

Box figure 1 Estimates of Human Development Index values at the state or province and county levels in selected countries of Africa, the Middle East and Latin America

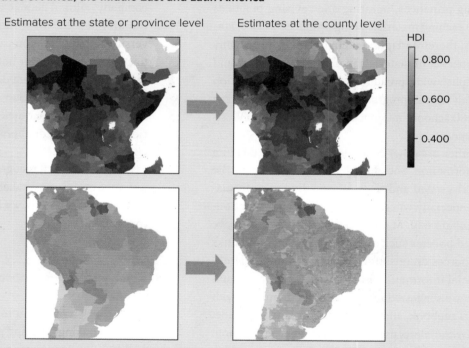

Estimates at the state or province level

Estimates at the county level

HDI
0.800
0.600
0.400

Source: Based on Sherman and others (2022) and Smits and Permanyer (2019). Maps from https://globaldatalab.org/shdi/maps/.

These results are experimental since there are no official local HDI values to fully validate these estimates. Nevertheless, new measurement tools are promising and have great potential to be scaled up, with appropriate benchmarking and data calibration.[7] Combining satellite imagery and machine learning is an exciting direction for future research to expand how the HDI is used for decisionmaking.

Notes
1. Doll, Muller and Elvidge 2000. 2. Qi, Wang and Sutton 2021. 3. Andreano and others 2021. 4. Bedi, Coudouel and Simler 2007. 5. Smits and Permanyer 2019. 6. Sherman and others 2022. 7. Head and others 2017.
Source: Human Development Report Office based on Sherman and others (2022).

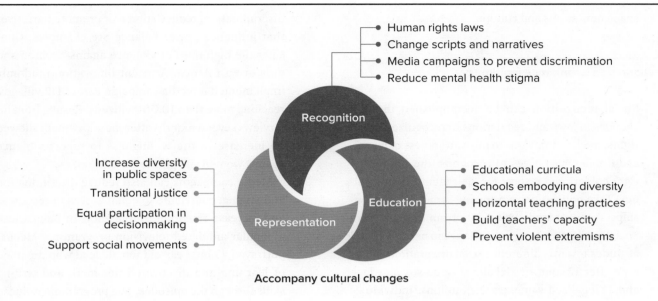

Human rights laws
Change scripts and narratives
Media campaigns to prevent discrimination
Reduce mental health stigma

Recognition

Increase diversity in public spaces
Transitional justice
Equal participation in decisionmaking
Support social movements

Representation

Education

Educational curricula
Schools embodying diversity
Horizontal teaching practices
Build teachers' capacity
Prevent violent extremisms

Accompany cultural changes

Source: Human Development Report Office based on Lamont (forthcoming).

of diverse sexual orientation and gender identities. The curriculum has contributed to the normalization of same-sex romantic relationships and the reduction of homophobia and homophobic bullying and harassment in schools. It has also led to shifting norms around intimate partner violence, leading to the reduction of such cases as a result.[88]

Discussions of the role of education for change in social norms envisage schools as a space that embodies inclusion and diversity. Teaching practices also affect students' beliefs and trust in institutions. Education not only dictates the content of students' learning—the what—but also the how and with whom. The how relates to teaching practices that have an impact on student beliefs and world views. In some cases educational attainment shapes one's beliefs. Across countries women with higher educational attainment are less likely to believe that husbands are justified in beating their wives if they argue.[89] In addition, research sheds light on how different teaching styles have divergent impacts on students' values. Students who are taught with horizontal teaching practices that entail working in groups on projects are more likely to participate in civic life, believe in cooperation with others and tolerate different ideas.[90]

The question of with whom students receive education is equally critical. Education that provides space

for students of various backgrounds contributes to norm changes, especially tolerance for differences and diversity.[91] For example, students can understand by their lived experiences that gender does not determine one's ability to learn or perform. Teachers' attitudes towards female students also affect how students view equality among the sexes. In India, when the government of Delhi made a policy to provide at least 20 percent of the seating in elite schools to students from low-income households, students with high economic status were more understanding and had less discriminatory views against the poor students.[92] Hence, regular personal interactions enabled by the inclusion and diversity policy in education destigmatized economically marginalized individuals.

By the same token, efforts to prevent violent extremism through education aim to use education to create a space for inclusion and a sense of belonging for young people at risk of joining violent extremist groups. Here, education serves as an alternative for such young people, as one underlying driver to join violent extremist groups appears to be feeling excluded and marginalized in the community and seeking a sense of belonging in militia groups.[93] Education also provides new knowledge and fosters critical thinking to strengthen students' resilience and prevent them from subscribing to extremist ideologies when exposed to them. It can thus be a catalyst for norm change and an instrument that empowers students to shape new norms and culture.

Recognition to enhance legitimacy

Social recognition can be accomplished through changes in laws and regulations to recognize human rights, media campaigns to raise awareness or changes in policy narratives to recognize the interest of right holders and respect for their identities and values. Take policies on recognizing same-sex relationships. A recent study using data from the European Social Surveys evaluated the change in narratives and attitudes towards different sexual orientations in Europe after 17 countries legalized same-sex marriage and 11 legalized same-sex civil unions. Individuals living in countries with legal recognition of same-sex relationships showed more positive attitudes towards LGBT people. These results are consistent with legitimacy models, where legal recognition legitimates a group in society and attitudes towards the group adjust as a result.[94]

" Social recognition can help change scripts and narratives to portray groups in different ways and build hope in society

Social recognition can help change scripts and narratives to portray groups in different ways and build hope in society. Climate change activism among indigenous young people in New Zealand has faced multiple challenges to transforming narratives, such as anthropocentrism, racism, adultism or generic recommendations to fight planetary change. Nevertheless, through activism and changes in education Māori youth narratives based on stories of colonization and indigenous systems of values and beliefs have had a ripple effect, enabling children and young people to feel a sense of hope and empowerment.[95] "Governance of climate and natural resources emerges best when rooted in stories about human purpose, identity, duty and responsibility."[96]

Nondiscrimination mechanisms can enhance an individual's ability to choose. These include preventing those most likely to be left behind from being discriminated against in access to resources such as health, education, land, natural resources, and labour and financial markets. Media campaigns to prevent discrimination, reduce stigma or promote narratives that influence power balance are examples. Consider the high rates of violence against women and girls in East Africa. A recent innovation randomly implemented a media campaign across 112 villages, reaching more than 10,000 citizens. Results from interviews several months after the experiment showed an increase in the willingness to report violence against women and girls to the authorities.[97]

Media campaigns can also reduce discrimination and stigma, contribute to equal access to resources and increase freedoms and agency. In Bangladesh a popular animated television programme, Meena, portrayed a nine-year-old female lead who dreamed of learning and discovered her math and writing skills through the episodes. The programme reduced the cultural and religious stigma of girls going to school in rural areas and increased their attendance.[98] It focused on describing how religious and cultural practices can generate discrimination and affect girls' lives and health. By influencing beliefs around girls accessing education, the narratives could balance power and change social norms.

More attention is needed as well to dismantle stigmatization of mental health, which can be achieved by changing social norms and narratives.[99] In Ghana and Kenya the Time to Change Global campaign tackled stigma and discrimination against mental health, disseminating on social media videos of real experiences with stigma and myths about mental health. According to an evaluation, there was a significant positive impact: in Ghana the desire to socially distance from people with mental health challenges was reduced, and in Kenya knowledge of mental health increased.[100] Narratives can thus work as lenses that allow people to look at mental health from a different perspective.

Representation to advance inclusiveness

Finally, representation, power and voice can foster people's ability to influence and participate while encouraging others. Increasing the representation, power and voice of diverse experiences in public spaces, institutions, governance processes, leadership positions, art, film, photography, music and writing can shape the definitions of who matters, foster their agency and encourage other people to participate. Recent research to explore the impact of women's representation in Cameroon's parliament found that their presence increases their participation in decisionmaking structures and influences the topics the parliament debates.[101]

Considering intergenerational relationships can also point out mechanisms related to reparations, reconciliation and transitional justice.[102] Australia's parliament issued an official acknowledgment and apology to the Stolen Generations[103] and their families and a report outlining recommendations to support reconciliation.[104] The Community Arts Network started a program to amplify the voices of indigenous elders to tell their stories of oppression, suffering and survival. The common elements in their narratives were cycles of dispossession, consequences of dispossession in their lives, and cultural continuity and survival. Through spaces of representation the indigenous elders gave voice to their history as part of healing, and the wider community was asked to acknowledge the stories and legacy to understand the land they inhabit.[105]

Participating in decisionmaking and building social networks are key to strengthen representation and agency. Inclusion is essential for devolving decisionmaking power to local contexts, through which equal participation and cooperation at the community level can be achieved.[106] In Kutna Hora, Czechia, the government conducted participatory budgeting with young people and children in 2019. Both primary and high school students participated in the local government's budget allocation. Each class appointed representatives to present a project on behalf of their schools for the budget from the school level up to the municipal level. Young people filled the role of coordinators in the local rounds of budget allocations. In the final phase the budget allocation was opened for all the students to vote. The initial idea from the local government was for young people to experience democracy on their own as executers and decisionmakers. In contrast with similar exercises, this case was motivated by the objective of incorporating young people.[107]

Collective action and social movements shaping culture and coping with uncertainty

Collective action, through social movements and community-level initiatives, can be a source of inspiration for researchers, policymakers and advocates (spotlights 6.6 and 6.7).

To redress inequalities and provide equal opportunities for people to expand their agency and foster human development, transformation is imperative at the level of social norms and culture. Social movements are key to achieving that.

Where we go from here is our choice

We must learn to live with uncertain times and unsettled lives. This year's Human Development Report challenges us to aspire to more than mere accommodation. Unlocking our human potential will require us to let flexibility, creativity, solidarity and inclusion guide us to imagine and create futures in which we thrive.

Where we go from here is our choice. One of the great lessons of our species' history is that we can accomplish a lot with very little if we work in solidarity towards shared goals. Dangerous planetary change, uncharted transitions and polarization are making uncertainty more challenging. Even so, we have more tools than ever to help navigate and course correct, and no amount of technological wizardry is a substitute for good leadership, social cohesion or trust. If we can start fixing the human side of the planetary ledger—and this Report tries to highlight how—then the future, however uncertain, will be more promise than peril, just as it should be.

Principles to be cultivated to navigate uncertainty

Flexibility should be understood as rejecting one-size-fits-all policy solutions and deliberately practicing iteration, variation and recombination in policymaking. For instance, chapter 4 builds on the need to upgrade strategies for human security such as strengthening social protection systems with built-in adaptive capabilities. Practices such as feedback loops, iterative learning and iterative design can be valuable tools to navigate uncertain contexts and find solutions that adapt best to different contexts and moments.

A key factor for creating knowledge and transmitting ideas is cumulative cultural evolution.[1] Because evolution does not necessarily mean efficiency and equality of outcomes, it requires strategies to favour flexibility, allowing adaptation to constantly changing conditions. But efficiency and flexibility need not be interchangeable in policy outcomes if flexibility is based on dynamic mechanisms to enable change.[2] In fact, a balance of both can be superior in uncertain contexts.[3]

Creativity would have a hard time thriving in homogeneous and rigid contexts, and adequate context-aware solutions are hard to find through safe repetition of a narrow set of policies. In chapter 3 successful policy reformers were characterized by their willingness to try creative problem-solving strategies. Uncertainty means we are always facing new and multifaceted challenges. Solutions to these challenges can emerge only in environments with matching dynamism. Chapter 5 points out how our ability to thrive under uncertainty and achieve transformations will depend on creative policy change. In practice, creativity requires exploring tools and approaches such as iterative learning, diverse perspectives and risk management. Creativity depends on societies' interconnectedness, the fidelity of the information and learning transmitted, and cultural trait diversity.[4]

Solidarity should be understood as recognizing our interconnectedness. "Solidarity does not assume that our struggles are the same struggles, or that our pain is the same pain, or that our hope is for the same future. Solidarity involves commitment, and work, as well as the recognition that even if we do not have the same feelings, or the same lives, or the same bodies, we do live in common ground."[5] For example, redistributive policies such as robust social protection recognize how inequities in agency, freedoms and capabilities have direct and indirect consequences for all individuals, groups and societies.

Incorporating solidarity means acknowledging that our lives are interconnected by the multidimensional impacts of our choices and our shared physical, economic and social spaces. In the face of uncertainty, people can turn to default values that go beyond strategic thinking, and in an environment of trust, the default can be solidarity (chapter 4). And transitions to renewable energy can be done in solidarity with the groups and places where the resources reside (chapter 1), while unsustainable arrangements could prevent the consolidation of human development gains for everyone.

Inclusion can enable transformations, as seen in examples throughout the Report. Chapter 4 highlights ensuring access and equity in communications technology. Chapters 2 and 5 discuss regulating artificial intelligence to address algorithmic bias and discrimination. Inclusiveness goes beyond increasing participation and diversity; it requires shifts in institutions' norms and attitudes and the cooperation of relevant stakeholders, society and policymakers to address the roots of unequal treatment.[6]

These four motivating principles are nonexhaustive, but balancing them could help chart paths to transformation. Driving transformation requires acknowledging the links and tensions between them. These principles are not mutually exclusive. They often coexist and enable each other. For instance, inclusion can unlock innovation.[7] Exposure to diversity (of people, practices and institutions)[8] motivates people to learn,[9] and iterative learning is part of innovation.[10]

Solidarity and inclusion[11] are interdependent. Solidarity requires recognizing and incorporating the diversity of individuals, groups, perspectives and lived experiences that coexist. At the same time greater inclusion contributes to solidarity by fighting divisiveness and inequalities. Social movements can teach us a lot about solidarity in the search for inclusion, leading the way to leave no one behind. Institutions can support the transformations pushed by social movements and community initiatives by listening to the diverse voices of those whose rights are being abridged, allocating resources and informing their research agendas to complement collective actions.[12]

Beyond the multiple intersections there also might be some tensions between these motivating principles. The paradox of diversity represents an example, as chapter 3 discusses.[13] Cultural trait diversity has perhaps the largest potential to empower creativity because it increases the recombinatorial possibilities. But it also increases coordination costs due to the multitude of perspectives. To address this, the cultural evolution approach analyses how high cultural trait diversity allows for an evolution of approaches favouring the traits that best adapt to the current circumstances,[14] understanding that these traits might fall out of favour if the circumstances change. This requires a high tolerance for diversity, but it also means that there will be inequality of outcomes because some approaches borne out of the recombination might fail and be discarded. However, the successful ones will spread and benefit all.[15] So, although it is generally possible to align flexibility, creativity, solidarity and inclusion, there is not a straightforward path for them to work together, and tensions might mean compromises along the way.

NOTES

1   Muthukrishna and Henrich 2016.

2   Adler, Goldoftas and Levine 1999.

3   Phillips, Chang and Su 2019.

4   Schimmelpfennig and others 2022. Cultural trait diversity refers to the differences in beliefs, behaviours, assumptions, values, technologies and other transmissible traits.

5   Ahmed 2013, p. 189.

6   UNESCO 2021.

7   Hewlett, Marshall and Sherbin 2013.

8   Swidler 2013.

9   Garrett 2016; Gutiérrez and Rogoff 2003.

10 For instance, a recent study presented evidence at the country level on how social tolerance towards homosexuality is positively correlated with positive attitudes towards greater technological innovation (Vu 2022).

11 Going forward, this transformation should be guided by stressing equal dignity and voice and solidarity among members of the community (Bowles and Carlin 2021).

12 Levine 2019.

13 The tension between traits adapted to a specific context and the need for diversity to enable adaptation to new contexts is present even in the collective behaviour of bacteria (Mattingly and Emonet 2022).

14 Schimmelpfennig and others 2022.

15 Schimmelpfennig and others 2022.

How local communities confront rapid environmental change

Consider South Africa, where impoverished rural communities have become proactive in improving their quality of life. Women have organized initiatives that range from local saving clubs and cooperatives to traditional craft and barter systems.[1] For the Zamukphila Women's Community Project, women in Upsher villages formed a vegetable-growing community, growing 70 percent to sell on the roadsides and the rest for self-consumption. The project received support from a corporation that allocated a piece of irrigated land adjacent to the village, while the women provided fertilizer and seeds.[2]

Another project in South Africa—the Mansomani initiative, led by Black women—mobilized community support to convert a piece of land into an irrigated sugar cane field and liaise with a local sugar mill. This helped secure a source of income for community producers. Key success factors were leadership, which persisted for more than 20 years, and external support. In this line, external agents, such as nongovernmental organizations, or governments can support initiatives sensitive to local needs and aspirations, preserving the community's agency.[3] Through this

project women used what was already in place—land and irrigation—and invested in crop resources to have more economic independence and be better prepared to face shocks.

In 2012 a group of practitioners in Democratic Republic of the Congo started the African Institute for Integrated Responses to Violence Against Women and HIVAIDS at the Panzi Hospital to research mental health in African contexts. The hospital partnered with a local feminist organization to provide counselling and training in Kiswahili. Capacity building of medical staff along with individual and group counselling sessions using music and dance to facilitate healing and livelihood therapy provided for land and tools for women to restart farming or rebuild assets.[4] Building women's emotional and economic agency translated into more inclusion in political spaces, empowering the women to express solidarity by organizing themselves to raise funds by selling local products.[5] Having the perspective of local women affected by the same structural inequalities facilitated coordination and communication and opened a different array of possible solutions.

NOTES

1 Nel and Binns 2000.

2 Nel and Binns 2000.

3 Nel and Binns 2000.

4 Allowing women who are experiencing distress, stigmatization and isolation to embody positive states of spiritual and social connection can help them heal as they find feelings of connection and belonging in collective voice, movement and creative self-expression (Horn 2020).

5 Horn 2020.

How volunteerism, inclusion and deliberation can work as insurance

Volunteerism can be seen as collective insurance rooted in solidarity that can prepare communities for environmental shocks. In Sudan during seasons of either high demand or drought, communities work together through *nafeer* (calls to mobilize), where people help each other plant and harvest crops. The military engages as well, protecting the harvests from theft and reconstructing mosques and other buildings damaged during conflict. Without trust, collaboration and communication to build a sense of solidarity, this activity could not be accomplished by just one farmer. But when people come together, crops can be harvested faster and more productively.[1]

Policy mechanisms that favour inclusion typically remove barriers or discriminatory attitudes and behaviours to ensure people's participation in social, economic, political and civic spheres.[2] Equal participation fosters agency and increases diversity through opportunities and choice. Inclusion can work as insurance. For example, including smallholder farmers in the design, business models and decisionmaking of digital platform providers would go a long way towards enabling the full potential and benefits of information and communications technology innovations in Africa.[3] There is rising demand for inclusion policies as women, indigenous peoples and migrants continue to be excluded.[4] Since 2017 the Colombian government has provided a special permit to grant Venezuelan immigrants permission to work. In general, the programme has expanded access to the labour market, but barriers such as recognition of credentials or access to financial markets persist, limiting the opportunities for immigrant workers.[5] As part of a set of flexible and inclusive assessment methods, the Netherlands has been working with local migrant and refugee organizations to offer proof of Dutch-equivalent credentials and facilitate the assessment and recognition of Syrian nationals' qualifications.[6]

Deliberation can serve as insurance for polarization[7] and is one of the keys to achieving recognition.[8] Although a natural human capacity, deliberation requires intentional and concerted efforts: rules, to prompt inclusive and civil deliberation; stories that make sense, provide meaning and instil a collective sense of commitment; leadership that engages citizens in a deliberative rhetoric; outcomes that matter to people; and the possibility to pass on and learn the skills to instil a culture of deliberation.[9] Deliberation is especially important for enabling public reasoning in a participatory and inclusive way, where ideas are represented and put forth by all groups irrespective of their political, economic or other status (see chapter 4). Even in the absence of organized deliberation, contact among groups has been shown to decrease dehumanization across groups[10] and reduce hostility.[11] However, negative contact can exacerbate hostilities,[12] pointing to the importance of setting up deliberation and intergroup contact for success through the conditions and settings in which they are encouraged. Beyond deliberation, voting is effective as well because it allows citizens to restrain defectors and reassures cooperative citizens that their efforts are not futile. Accompanying cultural change could consist of a shift in the mindset from exclusively seeking self-interest to believing that people can make decisions for the greater good.[13]

NOTES

1   Lough and others 2018.
2   Yang and others 2016.
3   Sarku 2022.
4   Yang and others 2016.
5   Selee and Bolter 2022.
6   Desiderio 2016.
7   Fishkin and others 2021.
8   Fuentes-Nieva 2022.
9   Ryfe 2005.
10   Bruneau and others 2021.
11   Wojcieszak and Warner 2020.
12   Wojcieszak and Warner 2020.
13   Hauser and others 2014.

Addressing mental distress: Capabilities for people and policymakers

Mental distress can become an obstacle to human development under certain circumstances (see chapter 2). To avoid this, policymakers as well as people themselves can take action and prevent situations that cause mental distress, mitigate crises and build psychological resilience without leaving anyone behind.

Preventing distress

The first layer of policies to tackle the cycle of distress and constrained human development consists of preventing distress. Building safe environments through strong national institutions and international cooperation is the ideal setting. Socioeconomic policymaking can contribute to this goal. Income support, for instance, has been shown to significantly decrease mental distress of children and young people living in a household.[1] Education is key to empowerment, enabling people to filter good-quality information out of abundant information during the digital age. It can also encourage people to take action regarding climate change and other anthropogenic pressures, proving them with ownership and agency to shape their own future.[2] And it can prevent discrimination.[3]

Diplomacy and negotiation can prevent some violent conflicts. But other conflicts can be stopped from turning violent at a much earlier stage through socially cohesive communities as well as tightly knit support networks.[4] Moreover, social embeddedness —social connections and interpersonal relationships within social networks and group identities—has been found to reduce stress and anxiety.[5] In the face of threat and uncertainty, cultural norms are crucial to keep societies cohesive and organized.[6]

Mitigating crises

As demonstrated by the Covid-19 pandemic, as well as by multiple extreme weather events around the globe, crisis prevention may not always be possible in the light of unprecedented threats. In that case socioeconomic policies can provide transitionary continuity and stability. During multiple lockdowns caused by the pandemic, economies with strong social contracts and robust social protection schemes caused fewer worries to the people and were less affected by economic consequences.[7] Examples include universal emergency payments comparable to a temporary universal basic income[8] and some traditional social protection policies such as extended sickness benefits, unemployment protection and benefits for families and older people.[9] The pandemic has shown that strong social institutions can help mitigate crises by contributing to stability. But some of these measures can also help during extreme weather events, when droughts or floods impair harvests, or when livelihoods are damaged during armed conflicts. Relying on tightly knit social protection schemes assures people's livelihoods and can thus alleviate mental distress until crises are overcome.

Building resilience

Not all uncertainties and crises can be prevented or mitigated, but this does not mean that people have to develop mental disorders. With universal access to mental health services as well as other culturally aligned resilience building and healing approaches,[10] people are often able to absorb mental distress and thrive in the context of uncertainties. Many of these services could be offered within existing social structures, such as schools and community centres.

There is a wide variety of mental health and well-being interventions, but some have proven especially effective for distress. For example, eye movement desensitization and reprocessing has shown significant improvement of post-traumatic stress disorder symptoms,[11] including in veterans and children,[12] exceeding the success of pharmacotherapy.[13] Yoga can alleviate anxiety, depression and somatization[14] and release stress-related muscle tensions that can cause migraines.[15] Mindfulness exercises and meditation have been used in psychotherapy for a long time,[16] and empirical evidence shows that they can improve depression[17] and aggressive behaviour.[18] Accessible at large scale, this can break cycles of violence and mental distress—one step towards building peaceful societies. More attention needs to be paid to providing universal access to these and other techniques as well as to dismantling stigmatization around mental health. Narratives within the policy discourse can help achieve this and foster hope collectively.[19]

Source: Human Development Report Office.

NOTES

1   Angeles and others 2019; Costello and others 2003.

2   UNDP 2020a.

3   Gronholm and others 2017; Jaramillo 2022; UN 2013; Winthrop 2020.

4   Aall and Crocker 2019.

5   Jetten and others 2009.

6   Jackson, Gelfand and Ember 2020.

7   Abdoul-Azize and El Gamil 2021; Razavi and others 2020.

8   See Serbia, Singapore and the United States.

9   Razavi and others 2020. Other examples include supporting companies in retaining workers through employment retention benefits in order to prevent unemployment, as was the case in Denmark, Dominican Republic, Germany, Italy, Japan, Malaysia, Netherlands and Thailand; active labour market policies to facilitate job skill-matching, online counselling and job mediation, such as in Belgium, China, Estonia, Republic of Korea and Malaysia; and expanded family leave and childcare benefits during school closures.

10 Dein 2020; Igreja, Kleijn and Richters 2006; Kpobi and Swartz 2019.

11 American Psychiatric Association 2013; Shapiro 1996.

12 van den Berg and others 2015. For a study on veterans, see Silver, Rogers and Russell (2008). For the effect on children see Rodenburg and others (2009). Results may vary according to levels of dissociation in patients, which have been found to reduce the effectiveness of eye movement desensitization and reprocessing therapy (Bae, Kim and Park 2016). However, in that case, the therapy can be combined with mindfulness exercises that can reduce dissociation.

13 van der Kolk and others 2007.

14 Brown and Gerbarg 2005; Saeed, Antonacci and Bloch 2010. For anxiety, see also Gabriel and others (2018).

15 Gabriel and others 2018.

16 Smith 1975.

17 Butler and others 2008.

18 Singh and others 2007.

19 Lamont 2019. On the controversy around the concept of hope, see Schlosser (2013).

Social media misinformation and freedom of expression

Social media has transformed the landscape of consumption and diffusion of misinformation. People can now immediately find and share content with billions of other users online through platforms such as Facebook, Instagram, LinkedIn, Reddit, Snapchat, TikTok, Twitter, WhatsApp and YouTube, among many others. Publicity, the arts, entertainment, commerce, advocacy, education, journalism and even public entities have adapted strategies to reach users in online socialization spaces. The same applies to the distribution of news. By 2021 close to 60 percent of users in some world regions were using platforms such as Facebook and WhatsApp to get their news (figure S6.5.1).[1]

Along with the potential benefits of rapidly expanding virtual social spaces, social media provide fertile ground for spreading misinformation[2] and fake news,[3] and the targeted and intentional use of platforms to enhance polarization and radicalization.[4] Prominent social media platforms have been called to action on this front by users, policymakers, authorities and their own conviction.

The policy discussion on misinformation often finds tension in the intersection between freedom of expression and both the importance of accurate, verified and trustworthy diffusion of information and the determination of boundaries of respect and civility in online behaviour. "We want to help people stay informed without stifling productive public discourse.

There is also a fine line between false news and satire or opinion."[5] "It's not just what we take down, but how we treat all the content we leave up that gives us the best path forward. (...) An overly aggressive approach towards removals would also have a chilling effect on free speech."[6] Big social media platforms now have policies and guidelines on misinformation and have developed varying strategies to combat it, ranging from user-initiated reporting features to removal of misinformation and restriction of accounts.

Governing bodies, national and international, have shown more interest in the effects of media misinformation. The UN Secretary-General's Roadmap for Digital Cooperation and the upcoming Global Digital Compact in the context of the Common Agenda incorporate prioritizing digital trust and security for the present and future of digital development.[7] Policy recommendations on misinformation at the international level highlight the importance of protecting human rights and freedom of expression; emphasizing methods that build trust, media literacy and cooperation; and emphasizing the dangers of overusing and misusing censorship.[8]

The European Union has increased its regulation on disinformation and the use of social media. The European Commission developed an action plan that includes a Code of Practice on Disinformation, the European Digital Media Observatory and the European Democracy Action Plan, with guidelines for

Figure S6.5.1 A considerable portion of users across the world get their news from social media platforms

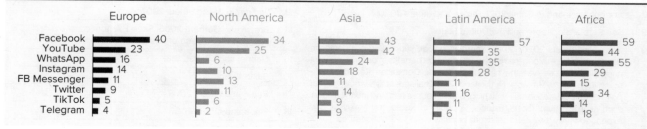

Source: Newman and others 2022.

obligations and accountability of online platforms.[9] The Digital Services Act, a "comprehensive set of new rules regulating the responsibilities of digital services that act as intermediaries within the EU to connect consumers with goods, services and content,"[10] was agreed in April 2022 and will reshape the obligations and relationships between digital services and governance structures in Europe. This will set new rules and enforcement mechanisms on digital activities, including managing misinformation.

NOTES

1   Newman and others 2022.

2   Waszak, Kasprzycka-Waszak and Kubanek 2018.

3   Di Domenico and others 2021.

4   Thompson 2011; Tucker and others 2018.

5   Meta 2022.

6   Mohan 2021.

7   UN 2020c.

8   UN 2022b.

9   European Parliament, European Council and European Economic and Social Committee and European Committee of the Regions 2018.

10   European Commission 2022.

Collective action and social movements shaping culture and coping with uncertainty

Whether it pushes to change cultural configurations or attempts to adapt to hardship, collective action has a transformative power that transmits ideas and shapes narratives and perceptions that can be vital for adaptation.[1]

In the face of uncertainty and institutional shortcomings,[2] feelings of shared discontent and dissatisfaction can motivate a push for solidarity within communities or social groups. This can translate into collective organization and action in search of community resilience and better development outcomes. Social movements are a clear example of how people's choices have supported transformations. Throughout history the world has witnessed the power of social movements, where people connected by a shared purpose or common identity have triggered transformational change for entire societies.[3]

A wide range of social movements develop because of unmet expectations and moral beliefs of fairness and social justice.[4] Some do so through collective identity.[5] In all cases the process is linked to emotions and cultural ideas with the power to transform a personal goal or interest, to adopt the goals and interests of a group.[6] Individuals involving themselves in a social movement develop a shared normative perspective or shared concerns for change that give them a sense of common purpose.[7]

Individuals join social movements and sustain their mobilization because of rational, emotional, behavioural, leadership, organizational and social-normative factors.[8] Even though emotions are present in every phase of the lifecycle of a social movement[9] and they positively motivate individuals, they have often been dismissed or unjustly judged by outsiders.[10] For instance, protestors are often portrayed as irrational or immature,[11] hostile or violent, or as needing to be disciplined.[12] The study of emotions in politics and social movements emerged to recognize that emotions permeate any political action,[13] shape movements' goals and determine their success. This analysis can provide insights to necessary changes for transformation by encouraging new ways of thinking and approaching policy mechanisms.

For a social movement to succeed, one of the most important factors is for it to lead towards social change and transformation as well as strategic choices.[14] Social movements can emerge when a large group of people become distressed by a particular situation or driven by leaders who mobilize people and facilitate broader awareness of concerns, then coalesce when they become more organized to raise awareness and mobilize resources. After formal and informal institutions take notice of a movement and bureaucratize it, a social movement can follow several paths before starting to decline (figure S6.6.1).[15]

Successful social movements have demonstrated a commitment to changing norms and attitudes, not just policy reforms. For instance, LGBTQI+ advocates used polling research to reframe public campaign messages on rights to include wording on love and commitment as well; this eventually turned into the "Love is love" slogan and contributed to change in marriage laws.[16]

The frequency of social protests increased by an average of 11.5 percent a year between 2009 and 2019 across all regions of the world, with the largest concentration of activity in the Middle East and North Africa and the fastest growth in Sub-Saharan Africa.[17] The Covid-19 pandemic halted mass protests from March to May 2020, but rather than disappearing, social movements adapted to the pandemic measures and bounced back as restrictions eased.[18]

Identity social movements arise to challenge traditional understandings of power distribution and reframe how certain groups are perceived. These movements aim to reclaim and transform narratives around identity for a group that has been historically discriminated against and oppressed. Confronting traditional beliefs and behaviours constitutes a reclaim of power and provides a sense of agency,

Figure S6.6.1 Social movements connect collective action with institutions

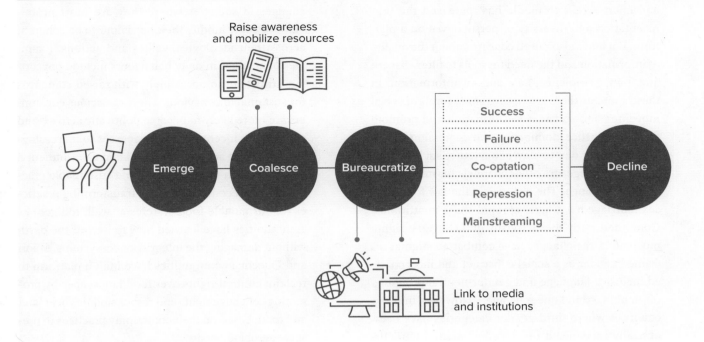

Source: Human Development Report Office elaboration adapted from Blumer (1995), Mauss (1975) and Tilly (1977).

pride, self-confidence and equality.[19] This type of movement is both reformative and transformative, as it looks to expand opportunities but also freedoms. Take the example of the feminist movement (spotlight 6.7).

Although powerful in their transformative capacity and as examples of in-group solidarity, identity-based struggles may also reify adversarial narratives between groups and reaffirm structural and social divisions based on certain identity dimensions. This can bring about challenges in broader global cooperation and can lead to violence and conflict. It can also overshadow the freedom that exists within self-identification and the overlapping multidimensional identities across the world. This is especially concerning for movements that seek to encroach on the freedoms of others. As argued in chapter 3, key to addressing these challenges is recognizing that each person comprises multiple, overlapping identities that can acquire different salience depending on context and can change over time.

Social movements' enduring impacts permeate cultural repertoires and transform societies. They can change the way we live, make us question traditional beliefs, reposition identities and eliminate stereotypes and prejudices. The policy changes that have emerged from protests and movements have depended on broad changes in public attitudes.[20] Mobilizations change culture through different channels: public opinion, memories, language and lifestyle, the media, and political and nonpolitical institutions.[21] They are a way to give momentum and directionality to the feedback cycle between social attitudes and norms and institutional and policy responses.

The nature and tone of media coverage can shift public opinion perceptions, even if indirectly. A study documenting public opinion change as an outcome of the feminist movement in the United States argues that the media coverage had a significant effect on gender attitudes, such that the public started reconsidering traditional roles and adopting alternative views.[22] Although traditional news outlets still dominate news gathering in Europe and the United States[23] and have a strong influence over politics, social media has impacted these dynamics significantly in recent years as the circulation of news stories is increasingly featured on platforms such as Facebook, Instagram, TikTok, Twitter and YouTube. Through media and social media, activists have defied traditional portrayals of groups, combated stigma and increased the representation of groups among writers, producers and performers.[24] More decentralized and open access to media has increased the representation and diversity of perspectives on a platform. But it has also raised concerns about the quality of information and the need for tools to filter, discern and manage violence, hate and misinformation. In these contexts there is a risk for some forms of social movements to spread misinformation and promote forms of injustice, domination and oppression.

Changes in day-to-day behaviours, such as lifestyle or language, are other channels for movements to trigger change. The changes in the law for same-sex marriage has triggered rapid shifts in attitudes. Combined with the activism of LGBTQI+ rights movement, the changes have combatted stigma, reframed gender as a social construct and incorporated inclusive language and gender-neutral pronouns for nonbinary and queer people.[25] However, in some countries where third-gender categories have been officially recognized for decades, many LGBTQI+ activists are campaigning against the forceful imposition of third-gender pronouns, highlighting the importance of people having the agency to determine their own identity rather than having it imposed on them by outside actors.[26] Thanks to the feminist movement the terms machismo or male chauvinist, feminist and sexist have become more widely used and understood.[27]

Other movements such as those linked to environmentalism and social justice have produced lifestyle changes in societies where they are most prominent.[28] People modify their behaviour to be coherent across their ideologies, values and actions. Examples of changes in daily behaviours include boycotting firms that do not comply with raised standards for sustainable behaviour. These conscious consumers are more likely to become politically active[29] and can present incentives for businesses to increasingly declare and act on their social and environmental principles with more inclusive and sustainable practices.[30] Local communities are transforming practices for sustainable food systems as well. Indigenous communities have learned how to live off the earth without damaging the integrity of ecosystems. Māori and Quechua communities have built a platform to reclaim cultural rights over food landscapes by promoting collective rights and responsibilities over land and food, based on their community practices to preserve agrobiodiversity.[31]

When individuals belonging to a community perceive that government institutions or authorities are unreliable and unsupportive, policies and regulation might seem insufficient. This creates a need for action, and collaboration is used as a coping mechanism.[32] In these contexts social movements are rooted in solidarity, key for overcoming injustice, domination and oppression.[33]

NOTES

1. Around the 1980s efforts from social movements to transform dominant cultural behaviours and identities began to be recognized (Goodwin and Jasper 2006; Johnston, Larana and Gusfield 1994).

2. Fransen and others 2021.

3. Zald, Morrill and Rao 2005.

4. Jenkins, Wallace and Fullerton 2008.

5. Polletta and Jasper 2001.

6. Social movements have questioned the status quo—policies, institutions and structures—and have shed light on human rights violations, discrimination and violence (Blumer 1951; Christiansen 2009).

7. DeFronzo and Gill 2020; James and Van Seters 2014.

8. Bate, Bevan and Robert 2004.

9. Jasper 2011.

10. Ferree 1992; Flam 1990.

11. Goodwin, Jasper and Polletta 2000.

12. Jasper 2021.

13. Goodwin and Jasper 2006.

14. Crutchfield 2018. Being leaderfull implies having an effective leader and people willing to share power and lead from behind, empowering multiple local grassroots leaders and people with a "lived experience" to speak and act on behalf of the issue they are defending.

15. Blumer 1951; Christiansen 2009.

16. Crutchfield 2018.

17. Brannen, Haig and Schmidt 2020, p. 1.

18. Pleyers 2020.

19. DeFronzo and Gill 2020; Gill and DeFronzo 2009.

20. Amenta and Polletta 2019. The cultural impacts from mobilization have been documented in the political and economic arenas (Bosi, Giugni and Uba 2016; Snow and others 2018).

21. Amenta and Polletta 2019.

22. Banaszak and Ondercin 2016.

23. Mitchell and others 2016; Taylor and Keeter 2010. As highlighted in spotlight 6.3, in Africa and South Asia, in particular, a far higher share of the population consumes news through social media apps.

24. Cockrill and Biggs 2018; Perlman 2016.

25 One of the key elements of the media discourse has been the stigmatized condition, which is seen first as involuntary and even linked to fate (Garretson and Suhay 2016).

26 Human Rights Watch 2020b, 2021; Khadgi 2021.

27 Mansbridge and Flaster 2007.

28 Haenfler, Johnson and Jones 2012.

29 Willis and Schor 2012.

30 Crutchfield 2018.

31 Huambachano 2020.

32 Fransen and others 2021.

33 Gould 2018.

Feminist mobilizations defying gender social norms

Women's and feminist movements have advanced women's rights across a variety of issues, both nationally and globally. Feminist mobilizations are associated with better legal rights to participate in economic life, greater representation in politics, better support for paid and unpaid domestic care work, better protection from sexual harassment, better access to land tenure, financial inclusion,[1] overcoming stigma and raising awareness around violence against women and girls.[2] Feminist mobilizations have grown across every Human Development Index (HDI) group. Low and medium HDI countries have seen the greatest increases in autonomy and strength of feminist movements (figure S6.7.1). Low HDI countries that have seen a greater increase in feminist movements

include Burkina Faso, Haiti, Liberia, Rwanda, Senegal and Uganda. Among medium HDI countries, Bangladesh, Cameroon, India and Morocco, among others, have. South Asia and Latin America have had the highest Feminist Mobilization Index scores on average since 1995, while the Arab States have had the lowest.

Feminist mobilizations defy stereotypes, redefine boundaries and expand agency for women and girls. They can open pathways to enhanced wellbeing and agency for women occupying spaces in all spheres of life, using their voices to bring new perspectives, participate equally in society and hold governments and others in positions of power accountable. Countries with powerful feminist movements or higher women's representation in parliaments adopted an average of five more gender-sensitive measures in response to the Covid-19 pandemic than countries without these features.[3] Activists in these countries developed feminist plans and gender budget assessments in addition to demanding action to address violence against women and girls and to improve access to public services. Two examples are the Gender and Covid-19 Roundtable with 79 civil society organizations in Chile[4] and the Women's Caucus in Brazil's legislature[5] (Bancada Feminina) advocating for facilities that aid women and girls who are subject to violence to be declared essential public services.

Women's participation in social movements has promoted changes in traditional gender norms through two main pathways: policy reforms and reframing gender roles and power relations.[6] Countries with a lower presence of women's movements or protests (as measured by the Feminist Mobilization Index) have the highest biases against gender equality and women's empowerment (as measured by the Gender Social Norms Index; figure S6.7.2; see also box S6.7.1). The elevated risks and costs of women mobilizing in these contexts are probably

Figure S6.7.1 Feminist mobilizations have grown in autonomy and strength across every Human Development Index group

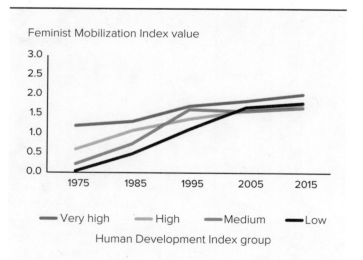

Feminist Mobilization Index value

Human Development Index group

— Very high — High — Medium — Low

Note: The Feminist Mobilization Index combines autonomy and strength of movements using a dichotomous coding: FMI = Existence + (Strength*Autonomy). A country without a feminist movement at all is scored a 0 (FMI = 0 + [0*0] = 0). The index awards 1 point for the existence of a movement, so a country with a feminist movement of some variety that is either not strong or not autonomous is scored a 1 (1 + [1*0] or 1 + [0*1]). A country with a strong and autonomous feminist movement is scored a 2 (1 + [1*1]). The countries with the strongest autonomous movements are scored a 3 (1 + [2*1] = 3).
Source: Forester and others 2022.

Figure S6.7.2 Countries with less feminist movements have higher biases against gender equality and women's empowerment

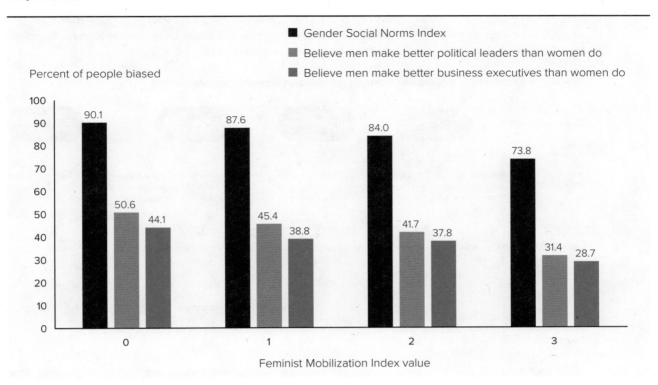

Source: UNDP 2020b; Forester and others 2022.

much higher, feeding into a vicious cycle. The association between the presence of biases and lower feminist mobilization appears in political and economic dimensions: in countries with lower feminist mobilizations, almost 50 percent of people think men make better political leaders and more than 40 percent think they make better business executives than women.

How are biases against gender equality and women's empowerment changing? The 2022 Gender Social Norms Index

Gender inequalities persist, and recent shocks, including planetary imbalances, the Covid-19 pandemic and economic crises, are aggravating the current scenario for women all over the world. The Gender Inequality Index (GII) reveals a lack of global improvement in its dimensions, with the world value stagnating at 0.465 for the past three years. Alarmingly, all regions experienced a decline in GII value from 2019 to 2020 except South Asia, which

experienced an increase; from 2020 to 2021 all regions except the Arab States and East Asia and the Pacific registered a decline.[7] While women have seen some progress in basic capabilities, there are still challenges in areas that involve greater agency and power. In 59 countries adult women are more educated than adult men. In those same countries the income gender gap is 39 percent.[8] Behind these calculations social norms help us understand these dynamics of power imbalances.

According to the Gender Social Norms Index, 91 percent of men and 88 percent of women show at least one clear bias against gender equality in areas such as politics, economics, education, intimate partner violence and women's reproductive rights (figure S6.7.3; see also box S6.7.1). Men have high biases in thinking that men make better political leaders than women do (52.8 percent) and that men should have more right to a job than women (50.2 percent). Women present fewer biases across all dimensions.

This year's Gender Social Norms Index results provide hope, showing an improvement from the first

Box S6.7.1 The Gender Social Norms Index—measuring biases, prejudices and beliefs

The Gender Social Norms Index, introduced in the 2019 Human Development Report, comprises four dimensions—political, educational, economic and physical integrity. It is constructed based on responses to seven questions from the World Values Survey, which are used to create seven indicators (box figure 1).

Box figure 1 How social beliefs can obstruct gender and women's empowerment

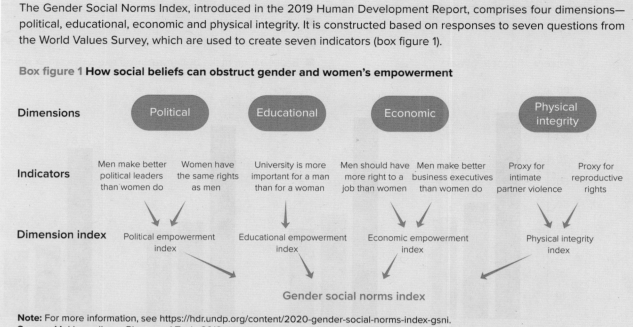

Note: For more information, see https://hdr.undp.org/content/2020-gender-social-norms-index-gsni.
Source: Mukhopadhyay, Rivera and Tapia 2019.

For each indicator a variable takes the value of 1 when an individual has a bias and 0 when the individual does not. The core index value is an aggregation based on the "union approach," which measures the percentage of people with biases, independent of the number of biases. In many instances it might take only one bias from one person to block a woman's progress in society.

This year's index covers two sets of countries and territories. The first set consists of countries and territories with data for wave 5 (2005–2009), wave 6 (2010–2014) or wave 7 (2017–2022) of the World Values Survey (accessed April 2022) and uses the latest data available. This set includes 76 countries and territories, accounting for more than 84 percent of the global population. The second set consists of only countries and territories with data for wave 6 and wave 7. This set includes 37 countries and territories, accounting for 48 percent of the global population.

Source: Mukhopadhyay, Rivera-Vazquez and Tapia 2019; UNDP 2020b.

time it was calculated. On average, biases against gender equality and women's empowerment declined from 2010–2014 to 2017–2022 (table S6.7.1).

Most countries and territories with time-series data showed progress: women in 23 countries and territories and men in 26 countries and territories showed reduced biases against gender equality and women's empowerment (figure S6.7.4). Progress in the share of people with no bias was greater in Germany, New Zealand, Singapore and Japan. But there were reversals in several countries, among women in 14 countries and men in 11 countries. The greatest reversals took place in the Republic of Korea, Mexico, Chile and Iraq.

Expanding human development and drawing cultural change in a patriarchal society

In line with the two-tier framework presented in chapter 6, the different policy blocks can support the task of defying gender social norms. Investing in gender-sensitive responses to shocks, especially initiatives that build partnerships between governments and civil society,[9] can help women better cope with uncertainty. Strengthening and expanding social protection systems to cover women can work as insurance, increasing their bargaining power at the household level, promoting financial inclusion, supporting long-term income generation and building

Figure S6.7.3 Only 10.3 percent of people worldwide have no gender social norms biases, including 11.5 percent of women and 8.9 percent of men

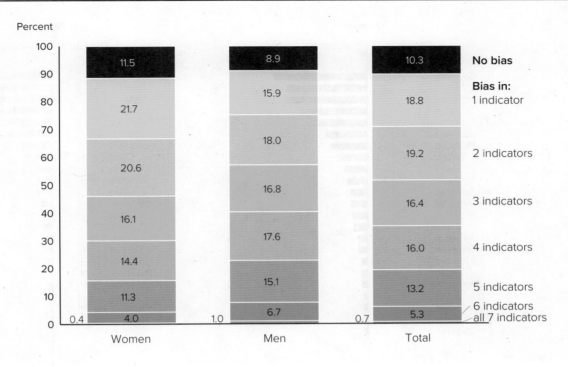

Note: Based on 76 countries and territories with data from wave 6 (2010–2014) or wave 7 (2017–2022) of the World Values Survey, accounting for 84 percent of the global population. Averages are weighted based on the population age 15 and older from United Nations Department of Economic and Social Affairs population data.
Source: Human Development Report Office based on data from the World Values Survey, accessed April 2022.

Table S6.7.1 Percentage of people with at least one bias against gender equality, 2010–2014 and 2017–2022

Group	Percent of people		Change (percentage points)
	2010–2014	2017–2022	
Women	86.5	84.3	−2.2
Men	90.5	87.5	−3.1
Total	88.5	85.7	−2.7

Note: Based on 37 countries and territories with data from wave 6 (2010–2014) and wave 7 (2017–2022) of the World Values Survey, accounting for 48 percent of the global population. Averages are weighted based on the population age 15 and older from United Nations Department of Economic and Social Affairs population data.
Source: Human Development Report Office based on data from the World Values Survey, accessed April 2022.

agency.[10] Encouraging innovative interventions can be a tipping point for traditional norms—for instance, taking advantage of social media to amplify the messages of feminist movements or incorporating new narratives in daily practices or cultural or artistic activities.

The second tier that targets cultural mismatches can go a long way in shifting gender traditional norms—for example, through gender transformative education.[11] This approach uses the whole education system (policies, pedagogies and community engagement) to transform stereotypes, attitudes and practices regarding power relations and gender binaries by raising critical consciousness about the root cause of inequalities. Increasing women's representation in public spaces, institutions, governance processes and leadership positions can change stereotypes and support changes in laws and policies defending women's rights. Recognizing the relevance of shifting social norms for gender equality or of women's right to body and physical integrity can help change scripts and narratives to portray women in a certain way and to build hope.

Feminist movements and women's different forms of resistance and action have come a long way, so amid uncertainty, we can imagine and build a feminist future. In the face of uncertainty and shocks,

Figure S6.7.4 Most countries saw progress on bias against gender equality and women's empowerment between 2010–2014 and 2017–2022—but several countries saw reversals

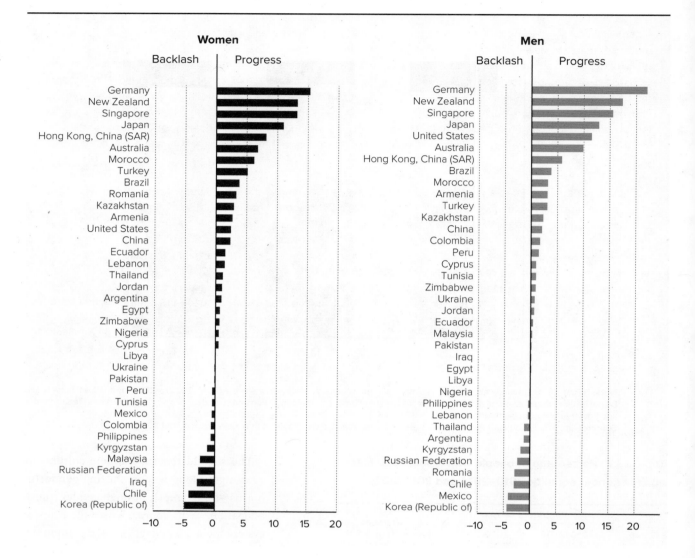

Note: Based on 37 countries and territories with data from wave 6 (2010–2014) and wave 7 (2017–2022) of the World Values Survey, accounting for 48 percent of the global population.
Source: Human Development Report Office based on data from the World Values Survey, accessed April 2022.

advocates and social movements can demand governments and institutions act to prevent disproportionate increases in and intensity of inequalities. Grassroots and community-level organizations and feminist collectives, as relevant actors within broader

movements, can be vital sources of knowledge, experience and perspectives to enable transformation. There is great potential in community-based interventions—apart from institutional reforms—that could be leveraged to move the needle on social norms.

NOTES

1 Weldon and others 2018.

2 Sahay 2021; UN Women and UNDP 2022.

3 UN Women and UNDP 2022, p. 10.

4 Senate of the Republic of Chile 2020.

5 Prange de Oliveira 2021.

6 Jimenez, Harper and George 2021.

7   The GII is a composite metric of gender inequality using three dimensions: reproductive health, empowerment and the labour market. A low GII value indicates low inequality between women and men, and a high GII value indicates high inequality between women and men.

8   Calculations based on data from table 4 in the *Statistical Annex.*

9   UN Women and UNDP 2022.

10   Plank, Marcus and Jones 2018.

11   UNICEF 2021b. Argentina, India, Nepal, Sierra Leone, Uganda and Zimbabwe are already implementing models based on this approach.

Gender Social Norms Index values for most recent available period (76 countries and territories with data from wave 6 or wave 7 and 12 countries or territories with data from wave 5)

Country or territory	Period	Gender Social Norms Index (percent of people with at least one bias)				Percent of people biased, by dimension			
		Total	Women	Men	People with no bias	Political	Educational	Economic	Physical integrity
Countries with data from wave 6 (2010–2014) or wave 7 (2017–2022)									
Algeria	2010–2014	98.67	97.47	99.84	1.33	80.08	37.17	74.08	91.83
Andorra	2017–2022	43.13	41.62	44.60	56.87	23.61	2.59	15.84	21.22
Argentina	2017–2022	74.28	72.01	76.70	25.72	33.90	13.56	24.63	59.82
Armenia	2017–2022	92.07	90.46	95.57	7.93	56.09	18.23	67.29	66.64
Australia	2017–2022	37.01	32.05	43.89	62.99	22.89	2.59	13.29	18.92
Azerbaijan	2010–2014	98.70	97.60	99.80	1.30	83.73	30.24	90.72	70.06
Bangladesh	2017–2022	99.42	99.18	99.66	0.58	66.83	42.83	86.58	87.83
Belarus	2010–2014	90.42	86.81	94.90	9.58	77.85	21.24	58.24	55.50
Bolivia (Plurinational State of)	2017–2022	91.29	90.41	92.19	8.71	37.88	21.67	38.03	82.20
Brazil	2017–2022	86.32	85.97	86.75	13.68	37.80	9.59	30.76	76.73
Canada	2017–2022	41.14	34.00	47.94	58.86	27.87	7.02	16.25	24.24
Chile	2017–2022	79.90	77.19	82.91	20.10	56.00	23.40	35.70	56.90
China	2017–2022	91.77	89.92	94.01	8.23	57.44	21.05	56.46	74.57
Colombia	2017–2022	91.18	92.76	89.61	8.82	54.14	18.16	28.16	81.58
Cyprus	2017–2022	81.80	78.19	85.68	18.20	47.40	15.50	51.60	60.20
Ecuador	2017–2022	92.33	91.55	93.19	7.67	51.17	22.08	38.42	81.00
Egypt	2017–2022	99.58	99.31	99.84	0.42	86.58	30.00	93.58	90.42
Estonia	2010–2014	78.28	73.73	83.92	21.72	57.53	16.18	45.79	41.55
Ethiopia	2017–2022	98.86	98.85	98.87	1.14	44.23	16.02	61.54	95.12
Georgia	2010–2014	94.68	93.37	96.20	5.32	65.89	18.14	66.97	76.87
Germany	2017–2022	40.18	36.18	44.41	59.82	13.15	4.19	15.25	25.46
Ghana	2010–2014	98.97	98.83	99.10	1.03	84.47	27.58	76.55	90.34
Greece	2017–2022	64.92	56.99	73.89	35.08	28.67	7.75	45.75	31.75
Guatemala	2017–2022	89.59	88.94	90.31	10.41	58.75	15.38	28.89	76.32
Haiti	2010–2014	98.95	98.04	99.90	1.05	74.95	59.67	71.84	88.48
Hong Kong, China (SAR)	2017–2022	80.82	78.63	83.40	19.18	50.12	18.46	42.27	59.33
India	2010–2014	99.09	98.71	99.39	0.91	64.10	35.24	69.91	92.82
Indonesia	2017–2022	99.66	99.71	99.59	0.34	77.66	43.91	84.28	94.06
Iran (Islamic Republic of)	2017–2022	95.53	93.72	97.26	4.47	66.84	46.90	77.45	67.31
Iraq	2017–2022	98.92	98.14	99.67	1.08	83.83	31.50	87.08	87.42
Japan	2017–2022	63.41	61.86	65.42	36.59	34.44	12.49	34.29	30.75
Jordan	2017–2022	98.50	98.15	98.85	1.50	83.04	24.44	87.45	81.46
Kazakhstan	2017–2022	93.42	91.70	95.49	6.58	65.60	27.82	65.75	74.92
Kenya	2017–2022	95.66	94.69	96.55	4.34	71.41	17.85	50.39	85.47
Korea (Republic of)	2017–2022	89.88	86.83	93.08	10.12	72.85	33.73	65.54	59.20
Kuwait	2010–2014	98.31	96.72	99.25	1.69	88.10	36.45	77.13	85.80

(continued)

Country or territory	Period	Gender Social Norms Index (percent of people with at least one bias)				Percent of people biased, by dimension			
		Total	Women	Men	People with no bias	Political	Educational	Economic	Physical integrity
Kyrgyzstan	2017–2022	98.08	97.58	98.91	1.92	77.17	51.83	83.08	90.08
Lebanon	2017–2022	95.58	93.17	98.00	4.42	66.83	15.08	67.83	83.83
Libya	2017–2022	99.67	99.48	99.84	0.33	82.86	30.60	81.61	93.39
Malaysia	2017–2022	99.54	99.70	99.39	0.46	91.77	36.10	59.79	84.62
Mexico	2017–2022	90.18	88.81	91.53	9.82	56.98	18.67	32.85	73.18
Mongolia	2017–2022	97.44	97.40	97.47	2.56	74.18	31.62	66.73	80.16
Morocco	2017–2022	93.67	90.83	96.50	6.33	61.92	20.42	63.42	79.67
Myanmar	2017–2022	99.42	99.67	99.17	0.58	74.50	52.50	89.17	94.42
Netherlands	2010–2014	44.16	37.82	51.47	55.84	21.29	4.63	13.56	27.92
New Zealand	2017–2022	34.44	31.14	38.41	65.56	14.47	2.65	8.99	20.34
Nicaragua	2017–2022	93.17	92.80	93.55	6.83	44.08	20.92	34.33	86.00
Nigeria	2017–2022	99.51	99.01	100.00	0.49	85.53	41.47	79.30	89.98
Pakistan	2017–2022	99.80	99.79	99.81	0.20	84.56	59.50	91.63	92.23
Palestine, State of	2010–2014	98.20	97.46	98.98	1.80	89.30	26.70	79.50	84.00
Peru	2017–2022	89.07	88.68	89.46	10.93	40.07	14.14	32.21	76.79
Philippines	2017–2022	99.50	99.67	99.33	0.50	75.33	43.50	77.83	92.83
Poland	2010–2014	81.37	80.19	82.77	18.63	44.31	11.80	42.44	57.04
Qatar	2010–2014	99.81	99.83	99.80	0.19	91.51	27.45	81.70	87.55
Romania	2017–2022	86.63	83.03	92.15	13.37	49.40	19.09	52.51	63.96
Russian Federation	2017–2022	91.44	88.06	96.25	8.56	68.18	26.69	66.52	58.62
Rwanda	2010–2014	99.15	99.22	99.08	0.85	67.78	36.15	65.68	97.64
Serbia	2017–2022	77.63	70.33	85.60	22.37	42.35	10.42	29.64	57.17
Singapore	2017–2022	77.63	77.02	78.35	22.37	49.35	17.40	37.82	56.56
Slovenia	2010–2014	61.09	55.36	68.89	38.91	33.58	8.04	25.91	33.68
South Africa	2010–2014	97.14	96.32	97.96	2.86	75.73	37.69	55.28	89.69
Spain	2010–2014	53.49	51.89	55.17	46.51	29.52	11.52	20.27	32.04
Sweden	2010–2014	31.76	30.14	33.57	68.24	15.92	2.57	8.87	17.83
Tajikistan	2017–2022	99.92	99.83	100.00	0.08	78.33	51.67	78.08	97.50
Thailand	2017–2022	95.47	95.08	95.85	4.53	65.87	31.40	53.80	81.20
Trinidad and Tobago	2010–2014	87.39	85.77	89.36	12.61	39.14	5.61	37.74	74.77
Tunisia	2017–2022	96.77	95.22	98.57	3.23	82.95	24.75	71.03	77.24
Türkiye	2017–2022	91.64	89.40	93.87	8.36	68.86	32.01	63.98	76.02
Ukraine	2017–2022	86.11	82.35	91.60	13.89	51.12	23.04	52.60	66.18
United States	2017–2022	50.65	51.49	49.93	49.35	34.82	8.59	13.79	31.55
Uruguay	2010–2014	78.60	79.36	77.75	21.40	28.60	9.20	34.30	57.30
Uzbekistan	2010–2014	97.93	97.50	98.62	2.07	78.67	48.60	80.33	84.27
Venezuela (Bolivarian Republic of)	2017–2022	92.35	91.28	93.52	7.65	55.80	17.90	31.01	80.84

(continued)

Country or territory	Period	Gender Social Norms Index (percent of people with at least one bias)				Percent of people biased, by dimension			
		Total	Women	Men	People with no bias	Political	Educational	Economic	Physical integrity
Viet Nam	2017–2022	93.75	92.98	94.68	6.25	65.08	27.67	64.33	77.75
Yemen	2010–2014	98.70	97.81	99.60	1.30	87.40	45.30	87.20	85.40
Zimbabwe	2017–2022	98.68	98.86	98.50	1.32	61.56	14.24	55.14	95.47
Overall average[a]	Most recent year available	89.70	88.48	91.07	10.30	59.85	27.39	58.74	76.09
Countries with data from wave 5 (2005–2009)									
Bulgaria	2005–2009	78.22	69.98	87.99	21.78	53.15	10.79	36.16	44.86
Burkina Faso	2005–2009	98.57	98.25	98.84	1.43	65.65	33.05	77.12	90.48
Finland	2005–2009	52.47	45.71	59.71	47.53	25.15	6.80	23.87	31.16
France	2005–2009	57.24	57.01	57.50	42.76	36.16	6.89	26.07	23.18
Hungary	2005–2009	67.33	63.13	72.13	32.67	42.90	18.67	38.23	33.37
Italy	2005–2009	64.43	60.36	68.51	35.57	17.98	7.81	29.35	47.83
Mali	2005–2009	99.48	99.21	99.74	0.52	81.36	47.39	88.53	91.92
Moldova (Republic of)	2005–2009	90.73	89.47	92.12	9.27	60.33	16.73	58.80	67.21
Norway	2005–2009	42.15	39.92	44.36	57.85	19.51	3.71	21.85	18.15
Switzerland	2005–2009	56.89	56.14	57.81	43.11	21.11	8.70	29.01	32.39
United Kingdom	2005–2009	57.73	52.17	63.48	42.27	26.42	6.82	25.17	35.16
Zambia	2005–2009	97.07	95.54	98.55	2.93	65.87	23.53	55.33	89.93

a. Averages are weighted based on the population age 15 and older from United Nations Department of Economic and Social Affairs population data for the 76 countries and territories with data from wave 6 (2010–2014) or wave 7 (2017–2022) of the World Values Survey, accounting for 84 percent of the global population.
Source: Human Development Report Office based on data from the World Values Survey, accessed April 2022.

Notes
and
references

Notes

OVERVIEW

1   Cognizant of ongoing discussions about whether the Anthropocene can be defined as a new geological epoch, the Report adopts the perspective of the Anthropocene as an ongoing geological event (Bauer and others 2021.) as well as a historical event. As Wagner-Pacifici (2017, p. 1) argues: "Historical events provoke an enormous sense of uncertainty. The world seems out of whack, and everyday routines are, at the least, disrupted. People often experience a vertiginous sensation that a new reality or era may be in the making, but it is one that does not yet have a clear shape and trajectory, or determined consequences. [Events imply a] complex dynamic of 'unknowing' and then reknowing a world transformed by events." With relevance to the layer of uncertainty associated with the Anthropocene emphasized in the Report, the author continues: "[P]lanetary environmental crisis is an event in which the ground *becomes* the event." (Wagner-Pacifici 2017, p. 165).

2   UN 2022c, 2022d.

3   UN Global Crisis Response Group on Food 2022.

4   FAO and others 2021.

5   UNDP 2022b.

6   Satake 2014.

7   Toor and others (2021) estimate that the vaccines covered in their study averted 50 million deaths from 2000 to 2019. See also van Panhuis and others (2013) for US estimates since the early 20th century.

8   Watson and others 2022.

9   Levin and others 2022.

10   Mathieu and others (2021) based on data from Our World in Data (https://ourworldindata.org/covid-vaccinations, accessed 7 June 2022).

11   UN Women 2021a.

12   Haelermans 2022; Saavedra 2021.

13   Gill and Saavedra 2022; UNICEF 2020a.

14   Reinhart and Graf von Luckner 2022.

15   Payne and Bellamy 2014.

16   IPBES 2019b; Pörtner and others 2021.

17   See UNDP (2020a).

18   Jenner 2022.

19   Hughes and others 2018.

20   UN 2021d.

21   IPCC 2021.

22   Ord 2020. We are grateful to Toby Ord for contributing text to this paragraph.

23   These two layers of uncertainty echo the framing emanating from assessments of the implications of climate change for financial stability (see, for instance, BIS 2021), which distinguishes between two sources of risk when it comes to valuing assets: physical risks and transition risks. Physical risks are associated with how hazards exacerbated by climate change can lower asset values—for instance, how floods can lower the value of houses located near the sea or in flood-prone areas. Transition risks are associated with changes in regulation or consumer tastes that can result in stranded assets—for instance, if coal-fired power plants are forbidden or rejected by consumers, the value of coal mining and coal-fired power plants can collapse. Chapter 1 extends this framework by looking beyond physical risks of climate change to consider the broader set of challenges associated with the Anthropocene context and by looking beyond the climate transition to consider the broader set of elements associated with a transition to ease planetary pressures.

24   Pinto and others 2022.

25   See the discussion in chapter 2 of Black and others (2022).

26   Diamond 2015; Hyde 2020.

27   Boese and others 2022.

28   Østby, Aas Rustad and Arasmith 2021; UNDP 2022b

29   UNHCR 2022c.

30   Hinrichs 2021; ILO 2018a.

31   See UNDP (2019).

32   Bollen and others 2021.

33   For example, Ahir, Bloom and Furceri (2022) constructed a World Uncertainty Index based on text analysis of Economist Intelligence Unit reports. They found that concerns about uncertainty have been steadily increasing since 2012, with the onset of the Covid-19 pandemic prompting a historical peak on the index.

34   UNDP 2022b.

35   UNDP 2019.

36   See Zuboff (2019).

37   Zeifman 2017.

38   Demeke and others 2021; Palozzi, Schettini and Chirico 2020.

39   Geraci and others 2018.

40   See Polak and Trottier (2020).

41   UNDP 2019.

42   Connolly and Jackson 2019; Maguen and others 2009; Nydegger and others 2019; Osman and Wood 2018.

43   WHO 2022a.

44   Newson and others 2021.

45   Even before the pandemic, women already assumed the lion's share of unpaid care work, and given containment measures, they shouldered even more responsibilities tending to their children while working remotely in some cases (Andrew and others 2020; Power 2020; Seedat and Rondon 2021; UN Women 2021b).

46   Etheridge and Spantig 2020; Hammarberg and others 2020; UN Women 2021b; Wade and others 2021; WHO 2022a; Xue and McMunn 2021.

47   Watson and Osberg 2017.

48   *The Lancet Global Health* 2020.

49   PAHO 2019.

50   WHO 2022b.

51   See Black and others (2022) for an exploration of the environment—security nexus, including an elaboration of different kinds of risks that must be managed in just transitions, with guiding principles and recommendations for how to do so.

52   Sonter and others 2020.

53   Kimbrough 2021.

54   Folke and others 2021; Zaremba 2022.

55   "Transformations, like adaptations, are also coming to be seen not as discrete events but rather as dynamical cascades entailing multidimensional regime shifts and associated qualitative changes in development pathways" (Clark and Harley 2020, p. 355).

56   Autor, Salomons and Seegmiller 2021.

57   Baek and others 2021; Tunyasuvunakool and others 2021.

58   Hammad, Bacil and Soares 2021.

59   Youngs 2020.

60   Okonjo-Iweala, Shanmugaratnam and Summers 2021.

61   IMF 2021b.

62   According to Statista (2022), there were nearly 6.6 billion smartphone subscriptions in 2022, about 84 percent of the global population. Another 1 billion subscriptions are expected to be added over the next five years.

63 Weiss 2022.

64 See de Coning (2018).

65 Clark and Harley 2020, p. 367.

66 IPBES 2019a.

67 Mach and Field 2017; Pereira and others 2020.

68 Shiller 2019.

69 Hoff and Walsh 2019.

70 Anis and White 2017.

71 Potts and Henderson 2021.

72 Baldassarri and Page 2021.

73 Angelou 1993, p. 65–66.

PART I

CHAPTER 1

1   At the start of 2022, UN Secretary-General António Guterres warned world leaders of increasing divergence between countries, prompting a "recipe for instability" (UN 2022a), echoing the need to strengthen multilateralism to meet humanity's greatest challenges, which was set out in the Secretary-General's report *Our Common Agenda* (UN 2021c).

2   For example, the Covid-19 pandemic forced an unprecedented human development reversal, with decreases in life expectancy at birth for two consecutive years (UNDP 2022b). Some 1.3 billion people live in multidimensional poverty, as of 2021 (UNDP and OPHI 2020). And inequalities across groups and in important aspects of human development are on the rise (UNDP 2019).

3   Uncertainty has been defined as the topic of the decade by International Monetary Fund Managing Director Kristalina Georgieva 2020): "If I had to identify a theme at the outset of the new decade, it would be increasing uncertainty." A time of shifting geopolitics, increasing instability and global tensions has also been identified by United Nations Security Council (2021).

4   UNDP 2022b. For further evidence on discontent, anxieties and feelings of insecurity, including in some of the richest countries in the world, see Pinto and others (2022), Pew Research Center (2021) and UNDP (2022b).

5   "Uncertainty" is used in this chapter and in the Report to refer to a broad set of possible future outcomes that are not known in advance with certitude. In economics there is a long tradition of thinking about uncertainty, as in the contributions by Keynes (1909) and Knight (1921). Today, the economics literature on choice under uncertainty distinguishes between choice under risk (when there is a probability distribution associated with a set of possible events) and choice under ambiguity (when the set of possible events is known but the probability distribution is unknown). Choices on climate change mitigation are typically analysed as choices under risk, given that a set of possible outcomes is known and there are different ways of estimating

the probability distributions associated with them (even though there are disagreements over what the probability distribution is). In this context climate change is a source, or driver, of uncertainty, not because we do not know that something bad might happen and not even because we cannot estimate how likely it is for that to happen, but because future outcomes are not certain but rather are defined today in probabilistic terms. Crucially, our own actions can (still) shape the direction of our climate, which makes future outcomes contingent on our choices, among other things. Probabilities associated with uncertain events can be estimated in different ways. For recurrent events frequency of past events is a common approach, including in the insurance industry. For rare or unprecedented future events models or expert elicitation can suggest distributions associated with future events. When no probability distribution can be derived for future events that can be specified, we confront choice under ambiguity. And, of course, there is also the possibility of confronting an event that has never been imagined. All these possibilities fall under the broad umbrella of uncertainty in this Report.

6   These two layers of uncertainty echo the framing emanating from assessments of the implications of climate change for financial stability (see, for instance, BIS 2021), which distinguish between two sources of risk when it comes to valuation of assets: physical risks and transition risks. Physical risks are associated with how hazards exacerbated by climate change can lower asset values—for instance, how floods can lower the value of houses located near the sea or in flood-prone areas. Transition risks are associated with changes in regulation or consumer tastes that can result in stranded assets—for instance, if coal-fired power plants are either forbidden or rejected by consumers, the value of coal mining and coal-fired power plants can collapse. This chapter extends this framework by looking beyond physical risks of climate change to consider the broader set of challenges associated with the Anthropocene context, as well as looking beyond the climate transition to consider the broader set of elements associated with a transition to ease planetary pressures.

7   Pinto and others 2022.

8   Delgado 2022.

9   See figure 2.10 in UNDP (2020a).

10 Ellis 2022, p. 15.

11 Bollen and others 2021.

12 Bollen and others 2021; Ahir, Bloom and Furceri 2018.

13 The analysis predates the Covid-19 pandemic and as such would not reflect any effects of the pandemic.

14 Dodds and others 2015.

15 Martins and Baumard 2020.

16 Fan and others 2019; Helliwell and others 2022; Maurer and Holbach 2016.

17 Helliwell and others 2022; Jaidka and others 2020.

18 For example, Ahir, Bloom and Furceri (2022) constructed a World Uncertainty Index based on text analysis of Economist Intelligence Unit reports. They found that concerns about uncertainty have been steadily increasing since 2012, with the onset of the Covid-19 pandemic prompting a historical peak of the index.

19 Ayers and others 2020; Fetzer and others 2021. See also the Computational Story Lab (n.d.).

20 Helliwell and others 2022.

21 Jaidka and others 2020.

22 Maurer and Holbach 2016. See also Computational Story Lab (n.d.) on the influence of events on expressions of happiness on Twitter.

23 The findings are akin to other studies that show growing public discontent and serious deteriorations in social attitudes towards democracy, science and governments (EIU 2021; Foa and others 2020; Institute for Economics & Peace 2020).

24 Pinto and others 2022. For example, a recent study found that a majority of people in 17 advanced economies believe that the children growing up today will be financially worse off than their parents (Pew Research Center 2021). Yet other studies point towards young people holding more optimistic views of their future and the future of the world, at least prior to the Covid-19 pandemic (Ipsos and Bill & Melinda Gates Foundation 2018), particularly those in developing countries (UNICEF 2021a).

25 Choi and others 2022.

26 The Gallup Organization 2022.

27 Psychology research shows that while uncertainty in controlled situations—such as gambling—may be exciting, uncertainty is also a major cause of stress, especially among those with low tolerance of uncertainty or when linked to situations in which we cannot rely on previous experience to inform decisionmaking (Grupe and Nitschke 2013; Harvard Medical School 2020; Tanovic, Gee and Joormann 2018).

28 Pinto and others 2022; UNDP 2022b.

29 UNDP 2019.

30 World Bank 2020a.

31 UNDP and OPHI 2020.

32 Roser 2021.

33 Fleurbaey 2018, p. 42.

34 IPCC 2021, 2022b.

35 Malhi 2017.

36 The final adoption of a new epoch by the stratigraphic community remains under consideration (Voosen 2022a). The proposal was formally put forward by a working group set up to consider the evidence in favour of a new geological epoch (Zalasiewicz and others 2017). Recently, a suggestion was made to characterize the Anthropocene as an unfolding geological event, rather than a geological epoch with clear markers (Bauer and others 2021). See the 2020 Human Development

Report (UNDP 2020a) for a review of the evidence, as well as the debate from multiple perspectives from the natural sciences, social sciences and humanities that the Anthropocene frame has motivated.

37 UNDP 2020a.

38 The argument that having power over something creates an obligation to act (either towards improving an outcome or stop something that is harmful) has a long tradition in ethical reasoning. For instance, it was invoked by Buddha as the argument for why humans should not harm nonhuman life. This example and argument draw from Sen (2009b).

39 Ellis 2021; Ellis and others 2021.

40 Marra and others 2021.

41 Reyers 2017.

42 Polasky and others 2020. See also Lenton (2019) and Lovejoy (2019).

43 The latest IPCC report shows that it is virtually impossible that the acceleration of global warming since 1970 has a geological cause. Without stark action, human-induced emissions are expected to increase average temperatures by 1.5°C within the next 20 years, with potential catastrophic consequences for humans (IPCC 2021).

44 IPCC 2021.

45 Elhacham and others 2020.

46 IPBES 2019b; Pörtner and others 2021.

47 IPCC 2022b.

48 Carlson and others 2022.

49 Carlson and others 2022.

50 Marani and others 2021.

51 Rohr and others 2019.

52 WHO 2021g.

53 Kotz, Wenz and Levermann 2021.

54 CUNY Advanced Science Research Center 2021; see also Vörösmärty and others 2020.

55 Kotz and others 2021, p. 319.

56 Guo and others 2016.

57 Kotz, Wenz and Levermann 2021.

58 Guo and others 2016.

59 Kotz and others 2021.

60 Keys and others 2019.

61 Climate simulations are susceptible to an inherent model uncertainty—across and within models (Barnett, Brock and Hansen 2020). Some major sources of uncertainty are derived from the evolution of greenhouse gas emissions—which will be influenced by human choices and policies—and the feedback loops between different ecosystem processes (Hausfather and others 2022). For example, implementing a carbon tax will impact the cost of carbon, influence consumption and production choices and ultimately affect emissions. But the optimal rate of such a tax is difficult to identify, due to uncertainty about the true social cost of carbon (Barnett, Brock and Hansen 2020) and whether

people will accept such a tax (see, for example, the "yellow vest" fuel tax protests in France). Thus, the assumptions made when projecting future temperatures may lead to vastly different conclusions (Hausfather and others 2022), and researchers have been raising a warning flag for a new generation of "hot models" that overestimate temperature increases (Voosen 2022b). Averaging projections from different models is one way to deal with model uncertainty, but too-hot models may exaggerate the impact of emissions on warming. The latest IPCC report instead modelled results based on different degrees of warming, again illustrating the wide range of possible outcomes. Inherent uncertainty in climate models does not mean that warming is not happening; indeed, the latest IPCC report shows that average temperatures on Earth are now 1°C higher than before the Industrial Revolution, which without reasonable doubt is due to human-induced emissions (IPCC 2021). How emissions will evolve going forward, and what their impact will be on temperatures and the planet, is largely up to us.

62 See for example, the latest IPCC report, which integrates cross-disciplinary insights into the assessments of climate change risks. Based on an understanding of the interdependent adaptation of human societies and ecosystems, the report shows that—in the context of climate change—human responses to climate change add new layers of opportunity and risk (IPCC 2022b).

63 Dosio and others 2018.

64 History can provide important insights. Sometimes history is invoked to provide cautionary tales for today's world based on narratives of ecocides in the past, in which "civilizational collapse" was the outcome of overusing natural resources. A popular reading of this narrative was based on Diamond (2005). Recognizing that "[t]he chief practical use of history is to deliver us from plausible historical analogies" (James Bryce, cited in Müller 2002, p. 5), a more recent account of the historical record, made possible in part by advances in technologies ranging from Earth observation to the analysis of DNA deep into the past, suggests that this account has been oversimplified.

65 Degroot 2019; Degroot and others 2021.

66 Xu and others 2020.

67 UNDP 2020a.

68 UNDP 2022b.

69 Chancel and others 2022.

70 See table 6.6 in Chancel and others (2022).

71 Chancel and others 2022.

72 Chancel and others 2022.

73 Jafino and others 2020.

74 For example, pollution is a major health threat, causing one in six deaths every year. Over time, there has been a decrease in poverty-related pollution-related deaths, such as death due to polluted drinking water, but deaths due pollution from industrialization, such as toxic chemicals, have increased by

more than 60 percent since the start of the 21st century, indicating that new gaps in pollution inequality are opening (Fuller and others 2022).

75 Wing and others 2022.

76 Osman-Elasha n.d.

77 Some have even argued that the unequal dynamics of climate change are reason for "limitarianism" in income and wealth (Robeyns 2019).

78 Frank 2020.

79 Appadurai 2004.

80 La Ferrara 2019; Fruttero, Muller and Calvo-González 2021.

81 Conradie and Robeyns 2013.

82 Frank 2020.

83 Genicot and Ray 2017, 2020.

84 Greenaway, Frye and Cruwys 2015.

85 Lybbert and Wydick 2018.

86 Ord 2020. We are grateful to Toby Ord for contributing text to this paragraph.

87 The idea has developed through Bostrom (2013), Leslie (1996), Ord (2020), Parfit (1984), Sagan (1983) and Schell (1982).

88 Sears 2020.

89 Bostrom 2002.

90 Bostrom 2002, 2013; Sears 2020.

91 Bostrom 2002.

92 Sears 2020, 2021.

93 The Bulletin Science and Security Board 2021.

94 Lenton and others 2019.

95 Boulton, Lenton and Boers 2022; Huntingford and others 2008.

96 Lenton and others 2019, p. 512.

97 A scenario where the world at large meets targets set by the Paris Agreement by undertaking national reforms in a steady, steadfast manner will pose different transitional risks compared with a scenario where changes take place abruptly. In an adverse scenario, where changes are too late and too sudden, transitional uncertainties will be amplified, transcending through different parts of our economy and society (Gros and others 2016).

98 UNDP 2020a.

99 One way of taking an integrated perspective on the multiple transitions to ease planetary pressures and incorporating the role of technological change is to draw on the approach of the 2020 Human Development Report (UNDP 2020a). Every form of life uses energy and materials and sends them back to nature, but the footprint of humans far exceeds that of any other species. For most of human history, the use of energy and materials was not too far from the limits of their biological metabolism; it was not until the Industrial Revolution that humans began to capture and use energy and materials at a scale comparable to the biosphere. Sociometabolic research provides

deeper insights into how society interacts with nature and studies biophysical flows across them and how such a relationship evolves over time (Haberl and others 2011). Bringing the disciplines of economics and sociology together with earth and natural sciences, it explores how matter and energy change forms as they are extracted and used by societies. In human history major advances in technology followed transitions to higher energy inputs and altered material cycles, leading to new social and environmental orders. In many cases the step increases in energy resulted in more waste products disrupting the environment, initially on a local scale and now at the planetary scale (Lenton, Pichler and Weisz 2016).

100 UNDP 2020a.

101 Smil 2022.

102 Smil 2022.

103 Bai and others 2016.

104 Cai 2020.

105 Balta-Ozkan, Watson and Mocca 2015; Gambhir, Green and Pearson 2018.

106 ILO 2018b.

107 Bergant, Mano and Shibata 2022.

108 Bolton, Adrian and Kleinnijenhuis 2022.

109 Lieu and others 2020.

110 Haberl and others 2011; Krausmann and others 2008; UNDP 2020a.

111 The global weighted-average levelized cost of utility-scale solar photovoltaics fell by 85 percent between 2010 and 2020; during the same period the global weighted-average cost of electricity from onshore wind projects fell by 56 percent (IRENA 2021).

112 IEA 2021c.

113 BP 2020.

114 Graham-Rowe 2011.

115 Rulli and others 2016.

116 Jeswani, Chilvers and Azapagic 2020.

117 Verdade, Piña and Rosalino 2015.

118 Webb and Coates 2012.

119 Oehlschlaeger, Wang and Sexton 2013.

120 Hertel 2009.

121 Sepulveda and others 2021.

122 Bolton and others 2020; NGFS 2019.

123 Campiglio and others 2018.

124 The White House 2022.

125 NGFS 2021.

126 Erlanger and Sengupta 2021.

127 Peszko and others 2020.

128 Engebretsen and Anderson 2020.

129 Smith and Brower 2022.

130 Alderman 2021.

131 The renewable energy sector currently employs 12 million people worldwide, with the sector expected to grow to provide 114 million jobs, assuming current policies and pledges are successfully executed. (IRENA and ILO 2021).

132 Lazer 2021.

133 Hausfather and Forster 2021; IEA 2020a; UNEP 2021.

134 World Bank 2020b.

135 IEA 2022.

136 Timperley 2021.

137 Vinichenko, Cherp and Jewell 2021.

138 Sovacool 2016.

139 Sovacool 2016.

140 Sovacool 2016.

141 Fouquet 2016.

142 Lazard and Youngs 2021. Both agriculture and mining, human activities that exert pressures on the planet, have been linked to serious human rights issues in low- and middle-income countries. For example, almost 70 percent of all child labour and almost 30 percent of people in modern slavery are found in agriculture. Hazardous work conditions, child labour and other violations are linked to artisanal mining of various metals (Sellare and others 2022).

143 Sonter and others 2020.

144 Rehbein and others 2020.

145 These estimates vary considerably across studies depending on model assumptions of anticipated policies, types of technologies and timeframe, among others; however, even under an ambitious assumption of reuse and recycle, the rate of mining will have to increase multifold (Hund and others 2020; IEA 2021b; Sovacool and others 2020).

146 Heffernan 2019.

147 Helmholtz Centre for Ocean Research Kiel 2021.

148 Race 2019.

149 UNDP 2020a.

150 WWF Australia 2021.

151 Hataway 2017.

152 Circle Economy 2020.

153 MaterialFlows 2022.

154 Bringezu and others 2017; OECD 2019a.

155 Circle Economy 2020; Veidis and others 2022.

156 Elhacham and others 2020.

157 OECD 2020a.

158 IAEA 2018.

159 Schlesinger and Bernhardt 2013.

160 Kinzig and Socolow 1994.

161 Eutrophication happens when the mineral and nutrient levels in a body of water increase excessively. When nutrient levels are too high, dead zones—low oxygen zones in bodies of water—appear (National Geographic 2022).

162 de Raús Maúre and others 2021.

163 The title of this section was inspired by Basu (2021).

164 Russell 2022.

165 Brynjolfsson 2022, p. 282.

166 Autor, Dorn and Hanson (2016) contrast the narratives around the benefits of free trade with the asymmetric impacts across sectors and regions in the United States.

167 Hilbert 2022.

168 Evans 2011.

169 Some authors propose distinguishing among risk, resolvable uncertainty and radical uncertainty (Kay and King 2020). In this approach risk is seen as a failure to fulfil the central elements of the reference narrative. Resolvable uncertainty is uncertainty that can be resolved by looking something up or that can be represented by a known probability distribution of outcomes. With radical uncertainty, however, there is no similar means of resolving the uncertainty—we simply do not know.

170 WEF 2020a.

171 Studley 2021.

172 Business of Apps 2022.

173 Hilbert 2022.

174 Jacob and Akpan 2015.

175 Mirchandani 2018; Mutahi and Kimari 2017.

176 Midgley and others 2021.

177 Neophytou, Manwell and Eikelboom 2021.

178 Brady and others 2017.

179 Messing and Weisel 2017.

180 Immordino-Yang, Christodoulou and Singh 2012.

181 Levy 2021.

182 Mitchell, Gottfried and Matsa 2015.

183 Kreps 2020.

184 Nowotny 2021.

185 OpenAI and Pilipiszyn 2022.

186 Imperva 2016.

187 Vosoughi, Roy and Aral 2018.

188 O'Neil 2016.

189 Ciancaglini and others 2020.

190 Hill 2020.

191 de Ágreda 2020.

192 Acemoglu 2021.

193 Meenakshi 2022.

194 Meenakshi 2022.

195 Prabhune 2022.

196 Cyranoski and Ledford 2018.

197 Mehravar and others 2019.

198 Lanphier and others 2015.

199 Waltz 2022.

200 Waltz and Nature Biotechnology 2021.

201 Aslam and others 2022.

202 Selfa, Lindberg and Bain 2021.

203 Stiglitz and Guzman 2021.

204 Polasky and others 2020.

205 Kay and King 2020.

206 Klein and Kruglanski 2013; van Baar, Halpern and FeldmanHall 2021.

207 Funke, Schularick and Trebesch 2016.

208 Boese and others 2022.

209 Boese and others 2022.

210 Boese and others 2022; International IDEA 2021; Repucci and Slipowitz 2022.

211 Stiglitz and Guzman 2021.

212 Druckman 2017.

213 Pinto and others 2022.

214 Lopes da Silva, Tian and Marksteiner 2021; Pettersson and others 2021.

215 UNDP 2022b.

216 Aas Rustad 2021; UNDP 2022b.

217 Arasmith, Østby and Aas Rustad 2022.

218 Collins, Florin and Sachs 2021; Darbyshire 2021.

219 Burke, Hsiang and Miguel 2015; Hsiang, Burke and Miguel 2013; Mach and Kraan 2021.

220 McCool and others 2022.

221 UNDP 2022b.

222 Consider the 20-fold increase in water-related conflicts since 1970 (SIPRI 2021) or the contestations around mineral resources (Aas Rustad and others 2022).

223 Lazard 2021.

224 UNDP 2021a.

225 Keys and others 2019; Polasky and others 2020; Wassénius and Crona 2022. See also UNDP (2020a).

226 Helbing 2013.

227 Crona, Folke and Galaz 2021.

228 Raymond and others 2020.

229 Stevenson and others 2022.

230 Stevenson and others 2022.

231 Raymond and others 2020.

232 Zscheischler and others 2020.

233 Aguirre-Liguori and others 2019.

234 Anderson and others 2019; Gaupp and others 2020; Raymond and others 2022; Sarhadi and others 2018; Zscheischler and others 2020.

235 Tigchelaar and others 2018.

236 Quéré and Mayot 2022.

237 Indeed, wheat, rice and corn make up 51 percent of the global diet (UNDP 2020a).

238 Anderson and others 2019.

239 Hynes and others 2020.

240 Kirby 2022; Krugman 2022; Menker 2022.

241 Pomeroy 2022.

242 Dryhurst and others 2020; Hromatko, Tonković and Vranic 2021; Kreps and Kriner 2020.

243 Research shows that spillovers of pathogens from animals to humans are likely to have caused many viral pandemics since the start of the 20th century (Bernstein and others 2022); zoonotic disease outbreaks triggering pandemics are likely to become even more frequent in the coming decades because of increasing human interference with our natural environment (Marani and others 2021).

244 Gill and Saavedra 2022.

245 O'Callaghan and Murdock 2021.

246 Marshman, Blay-Palmer and Landman 2019.

247 UNDP 2022b.

248 Alves and Rosa 2007.

249 Landrigan and others 2018.

250 Cole, Ozgen and Strobl 2020.

251 Gaupp and others 2020.

252 Georgieva, Gopinath and Pazarbasioglu 2022.

253 Studies show an overall decline in trust in institutions, governments and democracy—see, for example (Foa and others 2020; UNDP 2022b).

254 Boese and others 2022; International IDEA 2021.

255 Okonjo-Iweala, Shanmugaratnam and Summers 2021.

256 For example, in 2018 UN Secretary-General António Guterres warned world leaders of an "increasingly chaotic" world order (Nichols 2018). The words were echoed in his opening of the 2020 World Economic Forum Annual Meeting, where he used two words to describe the state of the world: "uncertainty and instability" (WEF 2020b). In 2022 Guterres sounded the alarm for increasing divergence between countries, prompting a recipe for instability UN (2022a).

257 UN 2021c.

258 Georgieva, Gopinath and Pazarbasioglu 2022.

259 See page 6 and onwards in Watene (2022).

260 Watene 2022.

261 We are grateful to Krushil Watene for these suggestions.

CHAPTER 2

1 Distress is defined as "the negative stress response, often involving negative affect and physiological reactivity: a type of stress that results from being overwhelmed by demands, losses, or perceived threats." It implies "a negative emotional state in which the specific quality of the emotion is unspecified or unidentifiable" (American Psychological Association 2022).

2 These concepts are based on Sen (1999).

3 Mani and others 2013; Ridley and others 2020; WHO 2022b.

4 Martha Nussbaum and others have repeatedly argued that emotions are crucial in the debate of human development. Nussbaum considers emotions one of her 10 fundamental capabilities, pointing out the importance of love, grief, longing, gratitude and justified anger without having these emotions distorted by fear and anxiety (Nussbaum 2003a). Other important works include Comim (2011), Hirai, Comim and Ikemoto (2016) and Nussbaum (1995, 2003b).

5 Pessoa 2019.

6 The influence of culture has been well established in the literature for decades. Not only do different cultures have different "tool kits" with habits, skills and styles that people use to develop action strategies, but most important, patterns of human thought develop in cultural settings, shaping the functioning of our minds. In unsettled times culture also shapes people's behaviour through persisting ideologies that people apply to determine their actions (Lamont and others 2017; Nisbett and Norenzayan 2002; Swidler 1986; Tomasello 2016).

7 The literature finds, for instance, that fearful people have a stronger risk aversion than angry people, who tend to make risk-seeking choices (Lerner and Keltner 2001).

8 Gordon and Mendes 2021.

9 Human development is the process of enlarging people's choices so that each and every individual can develop his or her full potential (UNDP 1990).

10 The concept of resilience is used in many different ways in the psychology literature but is used here in the sense of mental immunity, in which people do not develop mental disorders despite facing toxic stress (Davydov and others 2010).

11 Brännlund, Strandh and Nilsson 2017.

12 Bubonya, Cobb-Clark and Wooden 2017.

13 Callander and Schofield 2018.

14 Saxena 2018.

15 Sen 1979, 1989, 1997a, 1999, 2008.

16 McEwen and McEwen 2017.

17 Center on the Developing Child 2013, 2021; National Scientific Council on the Developing Child 2020.

18 Center on the Developing Child 2021.

19 McEwen and McEwen 2017; National Scientific Council on the Developing Child 2020.

20 Dallman 2010; Danese and Lewis 2017; Danese and others 2014; Evans and Wachs 2010; Hackett and Steptoe 2017; Hughes and others 2017; Morris and others 2019.

21 Ignatow 2021.

22 Basic trust refers to the trust that is developed during infancy when needs are met by caregivers. The baby develops trust in itself, the world and those who surround it. This trust develops further during childhood, when children can consistently rely on caregivers (Erikson 1993).

23 Center on the Developing Child 2013, 2021; McEwen and McEwen 2017.

24   On perceived self-efficacy, see Wuepper and Lybbert (2017). On the importance of role models, see Frye (2019).

25   Youssef and others 2018.

26   Diorio and Meaney 2007.

27   Robeyns 2017; Ungar and Theron 2020.

28   Nature-based learning approaches have shown particularly effective (Yiğit-Gençten 2022).

29   Crabtree 2022a; Bratman and others 2019; Soga and others 2021; Tillmann and others 2018. Since this is a new area of research, some of these studies point out that more research is needed to fully confirm this effect and explain the channels through which it works.

30   Lengfelder 2021. These are what Martha Nussbaum considers essential capabilities (Nussbaum 2003a, 2015).

31   Ungar and Theron 2020.

32   For example, more than 55 million people around the world live with dementia, with almost 10 million new cases every year. Dementia results from a variety of diseases and injuries with impact on the brain. Alzheimer's disease is the most common form of dementia and contributes to about 60–70 percent of cases (WHO 2021b).

33   UNDP 2020a.

34   Berry, Bowen and Kjellstrom 2010; Berry and others 2018; Cianconi, Betrò and Janiri 2020; Crabtree 2012; Hayes and others 2018; Padhy and others 2015; Palinkas and Wong 2020.

35   Berry, Bowen and Kjellstrom 2010.

36   Cianconi, Betrò and Janiri 2020; Miles-Novelo and Anderson 2019; Padhy and others 2015.

37   For a detailed analysis about this—including two case studies, one on Finland and one on Tuvalu—see Crabtree (2022b).

38   Clayton 2020; Taylor 2020.

39   A recent survey involving 10,000 young people (ages 16-25) from 10 countries from around the world found that over 60 percent of young people are sad, afraid or anxious about climate change. Many of them feel that governments are failing young people (65 percent) or are even lying about the impact of their actions in response to climate change (64 percent). Only a few think that governments act in line with recommendations from scientific research (36 percent; Thompson 2021).

40   Middleton and others 2020.

41   UNDP 2020a.

42   National Scientific Council on the Developing Child 2020.

43   Carter and others 2011; Hjelm and others 2017; McLaughlin and others 2012. In New Zealand distress was higher among women and girls than among men and boys, while in the United States adolescents' mental health was impaired by food insecurity, with the effect remaining significant even after extreme poverty was controlled for.

44   Trudell and others 2021.

45   Cunsolo and Ellis. 2018; Maguire 2020; Middleton and others 2020; Willox and others 2013.

46   Middleton and others 2020. Interactions between biodiversity and mental wellbeing remain poorly understood, with studies conducted among wealthier populations yielding mixed and inconclusive results (Hedin and others 2022; IPBES 2019a; Marselle and others 2019). This suggests there may be differential impacts of biodiversity loss on different groups of people, with certain species more central to the identity of some social groups than others (IPBES 2019a, p. 323–324; Marselle and others 2019; see also Wheeler and others 2015).

47   Altman and Jordan 2018; Ebi and others 2007; Gentle and Maraseni 2012; Tankari 2018.

48   Carlson and others 2022.

49   Czeisler and others 2020; Gao and others 2020; WHO 2022a.

50   WHO 2022a.

51   WHO 2022c.

52   Varma and others 2021. The survey included 1,653 participants across 63 countries.

53   ILO 2020b; Tamarit and others 2020; Tang and others 2021; UNICEF 2020b; Wathelet and others 2020; WHO 2022a. See also Newson and others (2021), which tracks mental wellbeing levels in Australia, Canada, New Zealand, the United Kingdom, the United States and the substantial English-speaking populations of India, Singapore and South Africa among people ages 19–24.

54   Newson and others 2021.

55   Even prior to the Covid-19 pandemic, women had already assumed the lion's share of unpaid care work, and given containment measures, they shouldered even more responsibilities trying to tend to their children while working remotely, in some cases (Andrew and others 2020; Power 2020; Seedat and Rondon 2021; UN Women 2021b).

56   Etheridge and Spantig 2020; Hammarberg and others 2020; UN Women 2021b; Wade and others 2021; WHO 2022a; Xue and McMunn 2021.

57   The survey involved 6,200 women and 4,000 men in close to 40 countries (CARE 2020). Its findings were echoed by another multicountry study in which female caregivers of children ages 5–18 across Australia, Canada, the United Kingdom and the United States experienced higher levels of distress, anxiety and post-traumatic stress than male caregivers (Wade and others 2021).

58   Proto and Quintana-Domeque 2021.

59   Bender and Theodossiou 2018; Christian, Hensel and Roth 2019; Hjelm and others 2017; Johnston, Shields and Suziedelyte 2020; Kopasker, Montagna and Bender 2018; Martin-Carrasco and others 2016; Ridley and others 2020.

60   Biasi, Dahl and Moser 2021; Ridley and others 2020.

61   Smith and others 2021.

62   Persson and Rossin-Slater 2018; Ridley and others 2020.

63   McEwen and McEwen 2017. A study from Ghana shows that in cacao-producing regions decreases in cacao prices by the time a child is born have adverse effects on the child's mental health that last until adulthood and can result in fewer economic opportunities (Adhvaryu, Fenske and Nyshadham 2019).

64   Diorio and Meaney 2007.

65   National Scientific Council on the Developing Child 2020.

66   Troller-Renfree and others 2022. Similarly, another study from Malawi shows how unconditional cash transfers improve mental health among young people, especially among young women (Angeles and others 2019). In a different setting unconditional cash transfers in Zambia did not reduce stress levels, even though stress levels were highly correlated with perceived food insecurity, which was improved by the extra income (Hjelm and others 2017). The positive effect of cash transfers on mental wellbeing is also valid for adults in low- and middle-income countries (McGuire, Kaiser and Bach-Mortensen 2022).

67   Evans and Kim 2012; Evans and Wachs 2010; McEwen and McEwen 2017.

68   Wuepper and Lybbert 2017.

69   Evans, Li and Whipple 2013.

70   Evans, Li and Whipple 2013; O'Rand and Hamil-Luker 2005. For a more general perspective, including on the intergenerational effects of adversities, see Deaton (2003, 2013b), Heckman (2019) and Heckman and Rubinstein (2001).

71   UNDP 2019.

72   Kopasker, Montagna and Bender 2018.

73   Christian, Hensel and Roth 2019. The mitigation of mental health issues through cash transfers and other government programmes has been observed in other settings as well. See endnote 66 on African case studies and Cooney and Shaefer (2021) for an example from the United States.

74   Watson and Osberg 2017.

75   Knabe and Rätzel 2011.

76   Hussam and others 2021. See also UNDP (2015).

77   Even if some of the evidence remains contested, as argued in O'Donnell and others (2021).

78   Lund and others 2010. When comparing socioeconomic status within countries, people with low socioeconomic status in developed countries suffer higher psychological burden than people with low socioeconomic in developing countries. Religion may play a role in this association, as religious norms alleviate the burden of poverty (Berkessel and others 2021). In countries with a strong longstanding presence of Christian churches, one of the cultural differences that was identified with respect to other countries was less conformity and more individualism among people

(Gelfand 2019). Alternative or complementary explanations, apart from church influence, are the effect of perceived inequality, social comparison and peer pressure that cause psychological burden for the low-income population in some developed countries (Wilkinson and Pickett 2009).

79   Marmot 2005; Ridley and others 2020.

80   Genicot and Ray 2020; McKenzie, Mohpal and Yang 2021. See also UNDP (2019).

81   The ability to appear in public without shame, first suggested by Adam Smith, is crucial to the human development approach, not least because it impacts agency—the ability to act and bring about change (Sen 2005).

82   Lundberg, Kristenson and Starrin 2009. For some people, growing prosperity is reflected in the "American Dream" of faring better than one's parents, which may be more difficult to achieve now than it was a few decades ago—not least because of a mismatch between expectations based on past conditions and available opportunities in the present (hysteresis; Lamont 2019). See also commentary by Frye (2019). On the argument about hysteresis, see Ayala-Hurtado (2021). In light of massive uncertainties, cultural braiding—the process of "creatively redefining, melding and combining elements from pre-existing cultural repertoires that form the cultural supply on which people draw to form their worldviews"—may help younger generations overcome the mismatch between expectations and reality and adapt to and navigate an unpredictable future (Zilberstein, Lamont and Sanchez 2021, p. 3).

83   Pleeging, Burger and van Exel 2021. Education and political systems seem to play a role in the relation among believe, hope and well-being. Case and Deaton (2015, 2020) find that "deaths of despair" (deaths due to substance abuse or suicide) have risen substantially among the middle-aged White working population without college degree in the United States since the 1990s. The authors make psychological distress partly caused by the capitalist system responsible for this development. However, parts of their argument have been contested. Ruhm (2018)'s study of different counties in the United States argues that the effect of economic decline on mortality is minimal.

84   Loibl and others 2021.

85   Evidence for the United States has consistently shown that college graduates who begin their working lives in a recession earn less for up to 15 years than those that start work when an economy is expanding (Kahn 2010; Oreopoulos, von Wachter and Heisz 2012; Oyer 2006; Wozniak 2010). This effect is magnified for high school graduates, and the negative effects extend beyond income, also affecting health, leading to higher mortality than those who enter the labour force during prosperous times (Schwandt and Von Wachter 2019, 2020).

86   For instance, a study found that the bad luck of young men who suffered a health shock (the study considered only the effect of paternal ancestry) negatively influenced the health of descendants up to grandchildren, with a magnitude as important as in utero conditions or children's socioeconomic status (Costa 2021).

87   Bianchi, Bianchi and Song 2021. It is also linked to higher risk aversion (evidence from Japan in Shigeoka 2019), reflecting a long-term scarring of beliefs, in a persistent expectation of a higher likelihood of an extreme negative shock in the future, with long-term costs that are many times higher than the short-term costs typically accounted for when there are losses in economic output (Kozlowski, Veldkamp and Venkateswaran 2020).

88   Mani and others 2013; Ridley and others 2020.

89   Kaur and others 2021.

90   de Bruijn and Antonides 2021; Mani and others 2013.

91   Shah and others 2018. For impacts on economic decisionmaking based on scarcity theory, see de Bruijn and Antonides (2021).

92   Mehra, Stopnitzky and Alloush 2018.

93   For adults with chronic physical illnesses and obesity, see Shen, Sambamoorthi and Rust (2008). For adults with diabetes, see Vamos and others (2009). For a randomized controlled trial on whether mental health interventions can reduce overall health costs, see Weobong and others (2017).

94   Ridley and others 2020.

95   Biasi, Dahl and Moser 2021. Psychological treatments have been shown to be effective and are often able to mitigate this effect, eliminating up to a third of the income penalty. The benefits of treatments are strongest among people with lower income, which indicates potential for decreasing income inequality.

96   Alloush 2021.

97   UN 2021a. Some examples include artificial intelligence–enabled frontier technologies improving health outcomes by diagnosing various diseases, saving lives and boosting life expectancy; digital learning technologies enhancing education outcomes by providing virtual learning platforms and access to education to everyone with an internet connection, regardless of their geographic location, through artificial intelligence technologies and blockchain-powered systems; public service delivery being made more accountable, accessible and less bureaucratically burdensome; and programmes and policies becoming more accurate and responsive due to big data.

98   Rotondi and others 2020.

99   ILO 2021b.

100   Robinson, Wiborg and Schulz 2018; Robinson and others 2020a; Robinson and others 2020b.

101   Agrafiotis and others 2018; Gandhi and others 2011; Kovacevic and Nikolic 2015; Purplesec 2021; Wang, D'Cruze and Wood 2019.

102   Khan 2017.

103   Dávideková 2016; Singh and Singh 2019.

104   Freed and others 2017; Kazan 2020.

105   Khandii 2019.

106   UNDP 2019.

107   Greer and others 2019.

108   Although there is no consensus on a definition, suicidal ideations can be broadly understood as "a range of contemplations, wishes, and preoccupations with death and suicide" (Harmer and others 2022, p. 1).

109   Stevens, Nurse and Arief 2020.

110   Freed and others 2017.

111   Kazan 2020.

112   Abi-Jaoude, Naylor and Pignatiello 2020.

113   This type of analysis should not be limited to dichotomous measures such as access or no access but should consider different dimensions of digital inequality, including inequality in equipment, autonomy of use, skill, social support and the purposes for which the technology is used. Since these inequalities change quickly, institutional aspects should be considered to understand patterns and interactions involving the private sector, consumer choices and government policies (DiMaggio and Hargittai 2001).

114   In Wuhan, China, frequent social media use was associated with symptoms of anxiety during the first outbreak (January–February 2020; Gao and others 2020). Other studies from around the world confirm that too much or incorrect information can cause anxiety among social media users (Tasnim, Hossain and Mazumder 2020).

115   Bermes 2021.

116   Dávideková 2016; Lee and others 2014; Singh and Singh 2019.

117   Abi-Jaoude, Naylor and Pignatiello 2020.

118   Awaworyi Churchill and Farrell 2018.

119   King and others 2014.

120   See WHO (2018).

121   Lichtenberg, Stickney and Paulson 2013; Lichtenberg and others 2016.

122   Geraci and others 2018.

123   Geraci and others 2018.

124   Barbosa Neves and others 2019.

125   Amundsen 2021.

126   Amundsen 2021.

127   WHO 2021a.

128   Postmus and others 2020.

129   Benavides, Berry and Mangus 2019; Moulding and others 2021; Shen and Kusunoki 2019; WHO 2012.

130   UN 2021b.

131   Bates 2020b; Walker and others 2020; WHO 2012; Wörmann and others 2021.

132   Dickerson-Amaya and Coston 2019.

133   Bates 2020a; Dickerson-Amaya and Coston 2019; Walker and others 2020.

134 Bates 2020a; Dickerson-Amaya and Coston 2019; Walker and others 2020.

135 Yekefallah and others 2018.

136 Frazão and others 2014.

137 Jones, Hughes and Unterstaller 2001; Kumar and others 2005; Roberts and others 1998. In the United States, for instance, 69 percent of women and 34 percent of men who had experienced sexual or physical violence with an intimate partner during their lifetime report suffering from symptoms of PTSD, being fearful, being concerned for safety, needing medical care or needing help from law enforcement and missed at least one day of work or school (Smith and others 2018). Similarly, a retrospective cohort study in the United Kingdom found that women who had been exposed to intimate partner violence were nearly three times as likely to be diagnosed with mental disorders, almost twice as likely to suffer from anxiety and three times as likely to be depressed as unexposed women (Chandan and others 2020). Likewise, a national survey from El Salvador observed that women who had experienced intimate partner violence showed a significantly higher prevalence of mental disorders and suicidal tendencies than those who had not (Navarro-Mantas, de Lemus and Megías 2021).

138 Cimino and others 2019; Daugherty and others 2020; Ivany and others 2018; Smirl and others 2019.

139 Brenisen 2020.

140 Greene and others 2018. See also Hornor (2005) and Silva and others (2019).

141 Data refer to the year prior to the survey (Hillis and others 2016).

142 Freyd 1994. The theory of betrayal has been contested with regards to its claims about the development of partial amnesia following a betrayal trauma by McNally (2007). For a response, see Freyd, DePrince and Gleaves (2007).

143 Heller and LaPierre 2012; Van der Kolk 2015.

144 Ungar and Theron 2020.

145 WHO 2021a.

146 Petrović, Manley and van Ham 2020.

147 Abass and Tucker 2018; Lee and Waite 2018; Papachristou and others 2019; Petrović, Manley and van Ham 2020; Ruiz and others 2019; Zhang, Zhou and Kwan 2019.

148 Boyle and others 2019; Izuan and others 2018; Jonsson, Vartanova and Södergren 2018; Salvatore and Grundy 2021; Satariano 2019.

149 For a detailed analysis on this effect, see UNDP (2019).

150 Alloush and Bloem 2020. The study used national panel data from South Africa and found a strong link between exposure to heightened levels of neighbourhood violence and depressive symptoms, especially among poor people living in urban neighbourhoods. It argues that a psychological poverty trap arises when individuals with lower incomes live in neighbourhoods with lower rent and

housing prices, which are often disproportionately affected by violence, with detrimental consequences on mental health and thus abilities to work and generate income.

151 See also Fowler and others (2009) and McCoy, Roy and Raver (2016). In Bogotá a singular violent crime event near children's homes is associated with an increase in children's mental health conditions (Cuartas and Leventhal 2020). Supporting the literature cited in the first section of the chapter, the strength of this effect was also related to parents' mental health.

152 Martínez and Atuesta 2018.

153 Connolly and Jackson 2019; Dierkhising, Sánchez and Gutierrez 2019; Nydegger and others 2019; Osman and Wood 2018; Whaling and Sharkey 2020.

154 ACLED 2021.

155 First Post 2020.

156 Ni and others 2020.

157 Ni and others 2020.

158 Human Rights Watch 2020a.

159 The incidence of armed conflict, especially in African countries (for example, Ethiopia, Democratic Republic of Congo, Mozambique Nigeria and Rwanda), has risen following the defeat of the Islamic State in both Iraq and Syrian Arab Republic, which compelled these groups to move their efforts to Africa (together with other cross-border jihadi groups; Pettersson and Öberg 2020).

160 Davies, Pettersson and Öberg 2021. The data include only conflicts with an average of 25 or more battle-related deaths and in which at least one side of the conflict parties is the government of a state.

161 WHO 2021f.

162 Hoppen and Morina 2019.

163 Boelen, de Keijser and Smid 2015.

164 Dorison and others 2020.

165 Lafta, Aziz and AlObaidi 2014.

166 Al-Nuaimi, Hamad and Lafta 2015.

167 Adesina, Adesanya and Olufadewa 2020.

168 Adesina, Kanmodi and Merrick 2019.

169 Humanitarian Pratice Network 2017.

170 Dami and others 2018.

171 Dein 2020; Igreja, Kleijn and Richters 2006; Kpobi and Swartz 2019.

172 Save the Children 2021; Strømme and others 2020.

173 Pritchard and Choonara 2017.

174 Bosqui, Marshoud and Shannon 2017.

175 Adesina, Adesanya and Olufadewa 2020.

176 Singhal 2019.

177 Awaworyi Churchill and others 2021; Gates and others 2012; Kadir and others 2018.

178 UNHCR 2022a.

179 UNHCR 2022b. Data are as of 5 July 2022.

180 Kadir and others 2018.

181 UNICEF 2022.

182 Lengfelder 2021; Shultz and others 2019.

183 Occhipinti and others 2021.

184 National Academies of Sciences 2017.

185 Schwandt and others 2021.

186 UNDP 2019; Williams and Sternthal 2010.

187 Clark and others 1999; Pachter and Coll 2009; Straiton, Aambø and Johansen 2019; Szaflarski and Bauldry 2019.

188 For examples on Rohingya refugees, see Riley and others (2017) and Tay and others (2019). Not all mental distress among this minority group is due to past traumas of persecution; continued stressors and assaults on human dignity in some refugee camps are important factors influencing refugees' mental wellbeing and health as well (Riley and others 2017). For examples on the Yazidi population, who suffered from war crimes conducted by the Islamic State, see Rovera (2014).

189 Bhugra and Becker 2005.

190 Heard-Garris and others 2018.

191 Heard-Garris and others 2018.

192 Stojanovski and others 2018.

193 Golembe and others 2020; Hsieh and Ruther 2016; Khan, Ilcisin and Saxton 2017; National Academies of Sciences 2017.

194 The Trevor Project 2021.

195 Human Rights Campaign 2018.

196 The Trevor Project 2021.

197 Lamont 2019; UNDP 2019.

198 Occhipinti and others 2021.

199 Ungar and Theron 2020.

CHAPTER 3

1 Institutions in the broadest sense, as proposed by Douglass North to represent formal rules as well as social norms and expectations (North 1990), and including social arrangements that take the form of regulations and other public policies.

2 One approach would be to assume how people behave and then define an ideal set of institutions that would deliver intended outcomes based on those behavioural assumptions. "There is a long tradition in economic and social analysis of identifying the realization of justice with what is taken to be the right institutional structure. There are a great many examples of such a concentration on institutions, with powerful advocacy for alternative institutional visions of a just society, varying from the panacea of wonderfully performing free markets and free trade to the Shangri-La of socially owned means of production and magically efficient central planning. There are, however, good evidential reasons to think that none of these grand institutional formulae typically deliver what their visionary advocates hope, and that their actual success in generating good social

realizations is thoroughly contingent on varying social, economic, political and cultural circumstances" (Sen 2009b, p. 83). Thus, this approach, always fraught, may be particularly unsuited to novel uncertain times in which a fundamental transformation is being pursued.

3   Sen 2009b.

4   This argument is based on Sen (2009b), contrasting contractual approaches to justice, exemplified by several theories of the social contract, with an approach based on social choice, in which the world is constantly assessed, and injustices are addressed through public reasoning that determines institutions and behaviour.

5   Recognizing that capabilities are not the only thing that matters. International cooperation for development and social and economic policies often focus on one aspect of capabilities: the deprivations and inequalities in opportunities leading to achievements in wellbeing, such as having income to meet basic standards of living and being healthy and educated enough to participate in economic, social and political life. There is good reason for this focus when the claims for assistance from others or from the state are associated with deprivations in these capabilities. This focus assumes even greater force when someone is living in extreme poverty or suffering from hunger. Human Development Reports over the years have emphasized wellbeing achievements associated with basic capabilities in standards of living, health or education—also the inspiration for the Human Development Index (HDI). The HDI provides a natural way to compare countries and assess development progress over time, in a more informationally plural way than relying narrowly on national income. The reversal in HDI values documented in chapter 1 shows how important it is to continue pursuing this emphasis.

6   "The possibilities of affecting human behaviour through means other than economic incentives may be a great deal more substantial than is typically assumed in the economic literature. The rigid correspondence between choice, preferences, and welfare assumed in traditional economic theory makes the analysis simpler but also rules out important avenues of social and economic change" (Sen 1973, p. 254).

7   Rational in quotation marks to signify the narrow perspective that assumes that people behave rationally only if they behave according to these assumptions. Behaviour deviating from these assumptions does not imply that it is irrational, only that it does not conform to the assumptions.

8   As early as 1955, Herbert Simon (1955, p. 99) wrote: "Broadly stated, the task is to replace the global rationality of economic man with the kind of rational behaviour that is compatible with the access to information and the computational capacities that are actually possessed by organisms, including man, in the kinds of environments in which such organisms exist." Daniel Kahneman (2003), a leading contributor to behavioural science, titled his review of his contributions to the field that were recognized with a Nobel Prize "Maps of Bounded Rationality."

9   While the standard economic model includes social determinants (that is, elements that are shared and not attached exclusively to agents), they are typically limited to either prices or the "rules of the game" that may be in place to constrain choice. The rules of the game are often equated with institutions, in the broad sense proposed by North (1990) to represent formal rules as well as social norms and expectations. They are part of individual beliefs that enter rational choice. For a broader discussion of the (underappreciated) relevance of beliefs, see Basu (2018). As Hoff and Stiglitz (2016) argue, these social determinants influence only the choice sets available to agents, not any social determinants of the actual choice.

10 Granovetter 1985, 2005. More recently, Greif and Mokyr (2017, p. 25) argued that beliefs (which Douglass North assumed to be individually held) are actually socially constructed on the basis of cognitive rules that "summarize society's beliefs and experience."

11 For many years some of these findings were popularized among economists in a feature of the *Journal of Economic Perspectives* titled "Anomalies." In one of the contributions, it was explained that "economics can be distinguished from other social sciences by the belief that most (all?) behaviour can be explained by assuming that rational agents with stable, well-defined preferences interact in markets that (eventually) clear. An empirical result qualifies as an anomaly if it is difficult to 'rationalize' or if implausible assumptions are necessary to explain it within the paradigm" (Rabin and Thaler 2001, p. 219). An early review of the impact of a more complex understanding of human psychology in economics is Rabin (1998). A more recent review of the field is Thaler (2018). Implications for development economics have been reviewed in World Bank (2015), Demeritt and Hoff (2018) and Kremer, Rao and Schilbach (2019).

12 [Economic analysis] "underestimates that [a human] is a social animal and that his choices are not rigidly bound to his own preferences only. I do not find it difficult to believe that birds and bees and dogs and cats do reveal their preferences by their choice; it is with human beings that the proposition is not particularly persuasive. An act of choice for this social animal is, in a fundamental sense, always a social act" (Sen 1973, pp. 252–253).

13 Sen 1977.

14 Paraphrasing from Dawes and Thaler (1988, p. 196).

15 Sen 1997b, p. 749.

16 A change in goals triggers a reorganization of the neural representation of value, which explains flexible behaviour Castegnetti, Zurita and Martino (2021).

17 Which may or may not be mediated through personal wellbeing.

18 Sen 1997b, p. 751. For the interplay among narratives and imperatives and more reasoning, see Bénabou, Falk and Tirole (2018).

19 Hoff and Stiglitz 2016.

20 Some interesting evidence about the relevance of reference points comes from the times that marathon runners take to complete the course, which are significantly bunched around round numbers (that is, at 3 hours, 3.5 hours and so on; Allen and others 2017).

21 Unlike what is assumed in expected utility theory, as described in spotlight 3.3 (Tversky and Kahneman 1974).

22 The neural basis for loss aversion is documented in Tom and others (2007). On the role of the amygdala in the brain, see Martino, Camerer and Adolphs (2010), but for caution interpreting some of this evidence, see Eklund, Nichols and Knutsson (2016).

23 Frank 2020.

24 Tversky and Kahneman 1974. The reference point that people use to make these valuations can be based on either something people actually have or some expectation about what they believe may or should happen (Kőszegi and Rabin 2006, 2007).

25 Samuelson and Zeckhauser 1988.

26 Rabin and Thaler 2001.

27 Tversky and Kahneman 1992. Although evidence suggests that the way in which people acquire information about probabilities matters: this behaviour is observed when probabilities are described but not necessarily when they are learned from experience (Hotaling and others, 2019).

28 Zelizer 1989, 2017.

29 Cohen, Shin and Liu 2019; Collins and others 2009.

30 Narrow framing was proposed to account for the evaluation of a specific risk separately from other risks, along with insights from prospect theory by Benartzi and Thaler (1995) to explain the equity premium puzzle (the fact that average returns on risky assets such as real estate and stocks historically exceed those of safe assets such as short-term bonds) by much more than expected utility theory would predict. For the regularity of this differential in returns across countries and over time, see Jordà and others (2019).

31 Bordalo, Gennaioli and Shleifer 2012, 2021.

32 The case has been made many times and in a very compelling way, as reviewed in chapter 5 of the 2020 Human Development Report (UNDP 2020a), for instance.

33 Present bias, giving greater weight to prospective gains that are coming sooner rather than later (O'Donoghue and Rabin 1999) might also contribute to the behavioural agent giving pause.

34 Erickson and others 2020; Oreskes 2019; Oreskes and Conway 2011; Supran and Oreskes 2021.

35 More generally, Atkinson and Jacquet (2022) show how many of the cognitive biases, or psychological traits more broadly, that are invoked as reasons why people will oppose action on climate change have a counterargument that suggests they could also drive

behaviour that would support action against climate change. See also Berman 2022.

36   Farhi and Gabaix 2020.

37   Buyalskaya, Gallo and Camerer 2021.

38   For a review of prospect theory, see Kahneman and Tversky (2013) and Barberis (2013).

39   Alesina and Passarelli 2019.

40   Levy 1997.

41   Thaler and Sunstein 2003.

42   http://www.shlomobenartzi.com/save-more-tomorrow.

43   Dean and Ortoleva 2019.

44   And conversely, behaviour learned as a result of an intervention in one domain may extend to others, obviating the need to design nudges for every single bias (Jarvstad 2021).

45   Hall and Madsen 2022.

46   Kahneman 2011.

47   Banerjee and John 2021.

48   Hertwig 2017.

49   Yan and others 2020.

50   Gigerenzer and Gaissmaier 2011; Mousavi and Gigerenzer 2017.

51   Druckman and McDermott 2008; Lerner and Keltner 2001; Meier forthcoming.

52   As noted by Sen (2009b, p. 50), Adam Smith discussed extensively the central role of emotions in *Theory of Moral Sentiments*, arguing that reasoning and feeling were deeply intertwined activities. Sometimes emotions are presented as "irrational," something that Sen (2009b) rejects, in line with Smith's view. For explorations of the role of emotions in behaviour, see Elster (1998) and Loewenstein (2000).

53   LeDoux and Brown 2017.

54   Lerner, Small and Loewenstein 2004.

55   Dorison and others 2020.

56   Elster 2021a.

57   Lynch, Broomhall and Davidson 2019.

58   Long and others 2020.

59   Pleeging, Burger and van Exel 2020.

60   See Bechara, Damasio and Damasio (2000), who suggest that bioregulatory processes—some conscious, others unconscious—take expression in the form of emotions that make it impossible to separate the emotional from the other elements involved in decisionmaking.

61   Bechara and Damasio 2005.

62   Dunn, Dalgleish and Lawrence 2006.

63   Blanchette and Richards 2010; FeldmanHall and Chang 2018.

64   Dukes and others 2021.

65   Lerner and others 2015.

66   This example, and the discussion in this paragraph, borrows from Sen (2009b).

67   For the review that inspired the discussion in this section, see Bénabou and Tirole (2016).

68   For the valence and instrumental value of optimism, the extent to which people hold generalized favourable expectancies about the future, see Carver, Scheier and Segerstrom (2010).

69   As argued in Elster (2015).

70   Bénabou and Tirole 2016. identify three mechanisms: strategic ignorance (for instance, refusing to be tested for Huntington's disease, despite knowing that one is at risk), denial of reality (rationalizing, distorting or dampening warning signs of, for instance, a housing market crash before the incontrovertible crash does happen) and self-signalling (pushing through work even though one feels sick, to validate the belief that all is fine).

71   Kahan 2013; Kahan and others 2017a, 2017b. Even though the robustness of some of these findings is under scrutiny (Tappin, Pennycook and Rand 2020), perhaps the more relevant and robust point is that higher cognitive achievements do not impede motivated reasoning.

72   Christensen and Moynihan 2020.

73   Martinez 2022.

74   Thaler 2020; Van Bavel and others 2022.

75   Barron, Becker and Huck 2022.

76   Bonomi, Gennaioli and Tabellini 2021. In his empirical account of income and voter patterns, Piketty (2020) demonstrates a shift in many countries in political preferences across income groups, where class-based or income-based voting seem to have given way to voting patterns along other fault lines, such as education (see also spotlight 4.1 in chapter 4).

77   For an argument as to how epistemic norms are social norms, see Henderson (2020). Levy (2022, p. xiii) puts it succinctly: "[T]hose who come to hold bad beliefs do so for roughly the same sorts of reasons as those who come to hold good beliefs. It isn't because they're irrational and we're not. It is largely because we defer to reliable sources of evidence and they defer to unreliable. This deference, which may be explicit or implicit, is itself rational on both sides. Given that we're epistemically social animals, it's largely through deference that we come to know about the world and generate further knowledge."

78   O'Madagain and Tomasello 2022; Tomasello 2018, 2020.

79   Levy 2021; Schmelz and Bowles 2022; Scoville and others 2022.

80   Kahan and others 2017a; Schaffner and Luks 2018.

81   Henrich and others 2022, p. 13.

82   For an example of models contrasting political choice based on interests versus ideas (based on identity or world views), see Ash, Mukand and Rodrik (2021).

83   We are grateful to Benjamin Enke of Harvard University for this suggestion through direct communication.

84   "If we want to effectively reduce political polarization, we need to recognize the biases that our brains impose in processing and the ways that broader institutions (e.g., media and political systems) may shape our thoughts and feelings. [...] Only once we realize that we are all subject to many layers of influence that our brains seamlessly convince constitute 'reality' will we then be able to successfully reduce political polarization" (Moore-Berg and others 2020, p. 28553).

85   See, for instance, Sharot and Sunstein (2020). Box-Steffensmeier and others (2022) provide a review of emerging findings and directions for future research on the understanding of human behaviour.

86   As Sen (2009a, p. 288) wrote: "Once the priority of a social affiliation (chosen or unchosen) is accepted as an integral part of one's 'overall identity,' something substantial is lost. This includes the ability to recognize easily that one has to decide on one's social affiliations, which does not compromise one's personal identity."

87   Henrich and others (2022) review evidence of how many cognitive biases vary across societies, with some disappearing or reversing, including overconfidence, risk aversion, the gambler's fallacy, the hot hand fallacy, the representative heuristic, neglecting regression to the mean, functional fixity and the endowment effect. A more nuanced view is that some features are universal, but their manifestations vary across cultures. For instance, hyperbolic discounting (discounting the immediate future more than the far future) was shown to be present in 53 countries but with great heterogeneity for shorter time horizons across countries (Wang, Rieger and Hens 2016). They also appear to vary across people depending on measures of analytical sophistication and education level (Frederick 2005).

88   Even if there are differing views on what is and is not universal, see Cosmides and Tooby (2013), Cosmides, Barrett and Tooby (2010) and Pinker (2010). For an evolutionary account of the origins of hyperbolic discounting (not limited to humans), see Dasgupta and Maskin (2005). Often psychological evolutionary arguments are based on time-shifted rationality theories, which explain what is now described as a cognitive bias that deviates from rational choice as resulting from the persistence of cognition traits that evolved to adapt to environments in the evolutionary past. For instance, Jaeger and others (2020) present evidence that links the magnitude of the endowment effect to evolutionary salience of different items.

89   Henrich 2020. The type of norm in question, whether it is injunctive (prescribing behaviour) or descriptive (where people follow how others behaviour), also matters on the type of emotion that has greater salience (Elster 2015).

90   Frank 1988.

91   Almås and others 2022; Falk and others 2018; Huppert and others 2019.

92   To use the expression of Hoff and Stiglitz (2016). See also Hoff and Stiglitz (2016), LeDoux and Brown (2017) and Tyng and others (2017).

93   Alesina and Giuliano 2015.

94   This description draws from Acemoglu and Robinson (2021). Key contributions to this understanding of culture include DiMaggio 1997, Patterson 2014 and Swidler 1986. An early account of culture consistent with this perspective comes from Geertz (1973). See also Amenta and Polletta (2019) and Bonn (2015). That a person's sense of self has behavioural implications is recognized in economic models of identity such as those by Akerlof and Kranton (2000), but those models do not specify where identity comes from, as recognized and explored in Huettel and Kranton (2012) and Kranton and others (2020). This perspective from sociology offers an answer to the question of where a sense of self comes about and how.

95   Schilbach, Schofield and Mullainathan 2016; Schofield and Venkataramani 2021.

96   See Lamont and others (2017) for an exploration of the implications of this perspective on these studies. Indeed, Lambe and others (2020) show that development interventions that build their understanding of behaviour change as contextual, taking place in relation to complex socioecological systems that also evolve over time, are more successful in creating robust and long-lasting change.

97   Sanchez, Lamont and Zilberstein 2022.

98   This includes Acemoglu (2022), Acemoglu and Robinson (2021, 2022), Acemoglu, Egorov and Sonin (2020) and Lowes and others (2017).

99   Richerson, Gavrilets and de Waal (2021) provide a recent statement of the achievements and potential contributions of this perspective.

100 For an illustration of critiques and responses, see, for instance, Henrich and others (2016) and Richerson and others (2016). See also Mesoudi (2016, 2021) and Sterelny (2017).

101 Apicella, Norenzayan and Henrich 2020; Henrich 2020.

102 The sliver of humanity has been associated with the acronym WEIRD—Western, educated, individualistic, rich and democratic, referring to the overwhelming overrepresentation of people with these characteristics in experimental findings in behavioural economics. Sometimes observed behaviour by WEIRD people deviates from the rational choice model—thus, described as some of the biases discussed above—in other cases behaviour consistent with rational choice is observed in non-WEIRD populations (Apicella, Norenzayan and Henrich 2020; Henrich 2020; Henrich, Heine and Norenzayan 2010a, 2010b; Muthukrishna and others 2020).

103 Falk and others 2018.

104 Henrich and others 2022, p. 3. Culture develops and is transmitted through social learning and affects not only how people solve specific problems but also how they conceptualize the world and think of their selves. Culture shapes "core aspects of our attention, perception, thought, memory, reasoning, motivations, mentalizing abilities, decision heuristics/biases or moral intuitions, [...and] what constitutes a good argument or solid evidence" (Henrich and others 2022, p. 1). Boyd, Richerson and Henrich 2011.

105 Gelfand and others 2011; Jackson, Gelfand and Ember 2020.

106 Gelfand and Jackson 2016.

107 Morris, Chiu and Liu 2015; Vignoles and others 2016. The huge variation in beliefs and values occurs even within a shared cultural setting. In fact, a set of cultural attributes and the psychological traits associated with it do not have a one-to-one counterpart at the individual level (Na and others 2010). That is, just because one society can be associated with a cultural and psychological package characterized by, say, more individualistic traits and another society can be characterized by more interdependent psychological traits does not mean that everyone in the first society is individualistic and everyone in the second is not. For instance, Markus (2016) and Markus and Kitayama (1991) have shown that the United States is a more individualistic culture valuing independence than Japan but that within the United States. However, Grusky, Hall and Markus (2019) found that some disadvantaged groups in the United States behave in a way and have an understanding of the self that values interdependence more than independence. Lamont (2000) shows how different racial and socioeconomic groups in different countries construct different frames of how they live dignified lives, in cultural contexts that are dominated by individualistic and materialistic pursuits are culturally dominant signifiers of value.

108 Henrich and others 2016; Kwon, Wormley and Varnum 2021; Varnum and Grossmann 2021.

109 Henrich and Muthukrishna 2021; Muthukrishna, Henrich and Slingerland 2021.

110 Enke 2019.

111 Nunn (2022), which provides the basis for the discussion in this paragraph.

112 Buggle and Durante 2021; Giuliano and Nunn 2020.

113 Sen 1997b, p. 749.

114 Buchanan 2020.

115 Raymond, Kelly and Hennes 2021; Raymond and others 2014.

116 Hauser and others 2014.

117 Gross and Böhm 2020; Gross and Dreu 2019; Gross and others 2020.

118 Barrett and Dannenberg 2012; Dannenberg and Barrett 2018.

119 Particularly the WEIRD package, perhaps a reason for why it is emulated in many different contexts, as argued in Henrich (2020). For instance, Santos, Varnum and Grossmann (2017) document increases in individualist practices and values across 78 countries over the past 50 years or so.

120 Thompson 2021.

121 Lübke 2021, p. 153.

122 Eom and others 2016.

123 Lu, Jin and English 2021.

124 We are thankful for Ravi Kanbur's suggestion of using the "3 I's" framework. Institutions can be formal—government structures, laws and regulations—or informal—social norms, habits and customs—and they are generally understood as "rules" or constraints that guide behaviour and give meaning to social life (Breukers and Wolsink, 2007; Hall 1997; North 1990; Scott 2008). Interests can be understood as the agendas of different groups or the preferences and power embedded in policy actors. Ideas refer to the knowledge and values held by actors regarding what or how things are and ought to be (Pomey and others 2010; Shearer and others 2016).

125 Ash, Mukand and Rodrik 2021.

126 Akerlof 2020; Akerlof and Snower 2016; Meckling and Allan 2020; Shiller 2017.

127 Mokyr 2013, 2016. For instance, creating a culture of innovation drew from cultural entrepreneurs such as Francis Bacon and Isaac Newton, who created focal points around which people could coordinate new beliefs—focal points in game theory enable people to coordinate their actions without the need for cooperation. For a related, also culture-based, but slightly different argument, see also Mokyr (2013).

128 Schill and others 2019, p 1075.

129 For models of development that can follow different paths—more or less "green"—depending on "ideas," broadly defined, see Besley and Persson (2020, 2021) and Persson and Tabellini (2020).

130 Schimmelpfennig and others 2022.

131 Hauser and Norton 2017.

132 UNDP 2022b.

133 Pinto and others 2022; UNDP 2022b.

134 UNDP 2019.

135 UNDP 2020a.

136 Polasky and others 2020.

137 Hacker 2018c.

138 Hogg 2021.

139 Sandel 2020.

140 Funke, Schularick and Trebesch 2016.

141 See, for example, Makridis and Rothwell (2020) on how polarization and partisanship influenced the effectiveness of public health policies and Bruine de Bruin, Saw and Goldman (2020) on how political preferences determined risk perceptions and willingness to follow public health mandates in the United States during the pandemic.

142 Levy 2022.

143 Bordalo, Gennaioli and Shleifer 2012, 2021.

144 Similarly, recognizing that evolutionary processes may play a role in the changes of behaviour and institutions is important to understand cultural variation and change but does not mean that purposeful reasoning is abandoned as we wait for selection to do its work. We may not have enough time to wait

for relevant evolutionary processes to play out. Here, again, we have to think ahead.

145 To use the expression of Sen (2009b) when discussing how beliefs created under specific "positional features" form and are hard to change. The example given by Sen is that of someone in a position who does not have knowledge of distance-dependent projections and no other information about the sun and the moon as seen from Earth and concludes that they are of the same size (as they appear to be when observed from Earth).

146 Lees 2022.

147 Mernyk and others 2022.

148 Fernbach and Van Boven 2022.

149 Fernbach and Van Boven 2022. See also, for example, experimental evidence by Bursztyn, González and Yanagizawa-Drott (2018), who show that men in Saudi Arabia tend to underestimate the support for female labour force participation among their neighbours and that revealing information about the actual level of support tends to shift attitudes in favour of women working outside the home.

150 Muthukrishna and Henrich 2016.

151 Indeed, part of the deteriorating support for democratic processes noted in chapter 1 may be found in perceptions of a system that is unfair and rigged, stacked against the average person, where those process fail to effectively channel different voices and deliver on concerns. Pinto and others (2022) note declining attitudes towards democracy alongside increased perceptions of corruption and government inefficiency. UNDP (2021b) shows how the stark concentration of power in Latin America seems to translate into a high share of people believing that their countries are run in the interest of the few, rather than in the interest of the citizens.

152 We are grateful to Belinda Reyers for suggesting that it is useful to understand what shapes people's behaviour and the multiple processes through with behavioural change and institutional reform interact and appreciate the inherent uncertainty associated with it. But that is no reason to be resigned but rather to think ahead, even acknowledging that uncertainty will not be resolved. As argued in chapter 1, what is required to ease planetary pressures and to navigate uncertain futures are transformative changes: we must go beyond adapting to existing conditions, towards strengthening capacities for transformations. Specific capacities, such as learning and reflexivity, engaging with complex dynamics and diversity, navigating across scales and responding to emergent processes, have been found to be crucial (Moore and others 2018). Existing development practice has highlighted capacities such as coordinated decisionmaking, collective action and the capacities to innovate and experiment and is exploring the potential of transformative capacities such as shift in attitudes towards innovation and changes in cultural gender norms, agency and leadership (Reyers and others 2022). From a planetary perspective the global biosphere and the diversity of life on Earth form a critical aspect of capacities

for transformative change. Biodiversity not only mitigates, buffers and provides adaptive capacities to respond to the turbulence and uncertainty of the Anthropocene; it also represents an undervalued and underexplored source of options, innovation, capacities and opportunities for human development in an uncertain future. Moreover, transformative change will ultimately depend on collective capacities to see and analyse the whole system, its social and ecological components, their dynamics and especially capacities to make visible and reimagine the interdependencies that connect them (Moore and others 2018).

153 As argued in Cukier, Mayer-Schönberger and de Véricourt (2022).

PART II

CHAPTER 4

1 McCoy, Rahman and Somer 2018.

2 van Prooijen 2021, p. 2.

3 Iyengar, Sood and Lelkes 2012.

4 Hobolt, Leeper and Tilley 2021.

5 Wilson, Parker and Feinberg 2020.

6 See, for instance, UNDP (2019).

7 Human Development Report Office calculations based on data from the World Values Survey, Wave 7 (Haerpfer and others 2022). Data are weighted averages within countries, with every country equally weighted.

8 Indeed, the Positive Peace Index developed by the Institute for Economics and Peace documents a decline in cooperative social attitudes. This decline is linked to people's diminished tolerance for differing views, declining trust in governments and reduced faith in democratic institutions (Pinto and others 2022).

9 Perceived agency is lower for people facing greater human insecurity than for people experiencing low human insecurity. Results are statistically significant at the 1 percent level for low and medium HDI and very high HDI countries and territories. Results are statistically significant at the 5 percent level for high HDI countries and territories.

10 For instance, people who express low trust in people with other religions are 10 percentage points more likely to mention them as undesirable neighbours. Human Development Report Office calculations based on data from the World Values Survey, wave 7 (Haerpfer and others 2022).

11 Enke 2019; Enke, Rodriguez-Padilla and Zimmermann 2021.

12 The level of trust towards people met for the first time is greater for people perceiving low human insecurity than for people perceiving very high human insecurity. Results are statistically significant at the 1 percent level for all income groups.

13 UNDP 2022b.

14 von Hippel and Fox 2021.

15 The preference for extreme political positions (left and right) is greater for people perceiving very high human insecurity than for people perceiving low human insecurity. Results are statistically significant at the 1 percent level.

16 The preferences for extreme views on government responsibility and individual responsibility are significantly greater for people perceiving very high insecurity than for people perceiving low human insecurity. Results are statistically significant at the 1 percent level.

17 As part of this debate, the design of social insurance policies has been greatly affected by the characterization of moral hazard in the economics literature: in the presence of asymmetric information, protecting people against risks might increase risk-taking behaviour. At least in the United States, this has been a contributing factor to a shift in the distribution of risks, increasing people's exposure to different types of shocks. See Hacker (2018c).

18 For some of the mechanisms, see Jonas and others (2014).

19 FeldmanHall and Shenhav 2019.

20 Kruglanski 1989, p. 13.

21 Kruglanski and others 2022.

22 Kruglanski and others 2014; Webber and others 2018.

23 Hogg 2007, 2021.

24 Hogg 2021.

25 van Baar, Halpern and FeldmanHall 2021.

26 Webber and others 2020.

27 van Prooijen and Krouwel 2019.

28 Boxell, Gentzkow and Shapiro 2020; Wilson, Parker and Feinberg 2020.

29 Gidron, Adams and Horne 2020; Wilson, Parker and Feinberg 2020. For instance, the priming of national identity in political discourse has been shown to fuel polarization among people opposed to immigration. See Wojcieszak and Garrett (2018).

30 Banda and Cluverius 2018.

31 Graham and Svolik 2020.

32 Cheng and others 2013; Garfield, von Rueden and Hagen 2019; Henrich and Gil-White 2001; Maner and Case 2016; McClanahan, Maner and Cheng 2021. The two types of leadership are characterized by distinct nonverbal displays (Witkower and others 2020). On the variations and commonalities in characteristics of leaders across cultures, see Garfield, Syme and Hagen (2020).

33 Kakkar and Sivanathan 2017.

34 Ronay, Maddux and von Hippel 2020.

35 Bursztyn and Yang 2021; Stone 2020.

36 Bursztyn and Yang 2021.

37 Bursztyn and Yang 2021.

38 Ruggeri and others 2021.

39 Enders and Armaly 2018.

40 Dorison, Minson and Rogers 2019.

41 Kteily, Hodson and Bruneau 2016; Lees and Cikara 2021.

42 There is evidence that "negative affective orientations toward out-groups cause individuals to perceive greater ideological and issue-based differences between parties and candidates, irrespective of the truth" (Armaly and Enders 2021, p. 10).

43 Gelfand 2021; Norris and Inglehart 2016.

44 Bauer and others 2016.

45 Henrich and others 2019.

46 Durante and others 2017.

47 The framework of cultural tightness-looseness, as developed by Gelfand, Nishii and Raver (2006), presents cultural tightness as the presence of stronger social norms and sanctioning of them within societies. For empirical evidence that tighter social norms are associated with greater exposure to threats, see Gelfand and others (2011).

48 Gelfand 2021.

49 Roos and others 2015.

50 Gelfand 2021.

51 Gidron, Adams and Horne 2020; Stewart, McCarty and Bryson 2020.

52 Stewart, McCarty and Bryson 2020.

53 Basu 2021.

54 UNDP 2019.

55 Funke, Schularick and Trebesch 2016.

56 Silagadze and others 2022.

57 Müller 2021, p. 69.

58 Müller 2021.

59 Lindh and McCall 2020.

60 Schäfer and Schwander 2019.

61 Müller 2021.

62 Eeckhout 2021.

63 Azar, Marinescu and Steinbaum 2019; Barkai 2020; Benmelech, Bergman and Kim 2022.

64 Autor and others 2020.

65 Nunn 2022.

66 Azhar 2021.

67 Deuze 2006.

68 Bak-Coleman and others 2021.

69 Bak-Coleman and others 2021.

70 Galesic, Barkoczi and Katsikopoulos 2018; Kao and Couzin 2014.

71 Barfuss and others 2020; Dunbar 1992; Henrich 2018.

72 Galam 2004; Kao and Couzin 2014.

73 Brady and others 2017; Guriev, Melnikov and Zhuravskaya 2019; Narayanan and others 2018.

74 Vosoughi, Roy and Aral 2018.

75 Bago, Rand and Pennycook 2020; Chittka, Skorupski and Raine 2009.

76 Evans 2008; Nguyen and others 2014.

77 Bakshy, Messing and Adamic 2015; Bozdag 2013; Nguyen and others 2014; Toff and Nielsen 2018.

78 Stoyanovich, Bavel and West 2020.

79 Calo and others 2021; Tucker and others 2018.

80 Bennett and Livingston 2018.

81 Whitten-Woodring and others 2020.

82 Farrell and Schneier 2019.

83 Keller and others 2021.

84 Gallotti and others 2020.

85 Steenbergen and Colombo 2018.

86 Vosoughi, Roy and Aral 2018.

87 Sabin-Miller and Abrams 2020.

88 Stewart and others 2019.

89 Huszár and others 2021.

90 Barnidge 2018.

91 Knobloch-Westerwick and others 2015.

92 Tokita, Guess and Tarnita 2021.

93 Rathje, Van Bavel and van der Linden 2021.

94 Tucker and others 2018.

95 Kawakatsu and others 2021; Vasconcelos and others 2021.

96 Baldassarri and Page 2021.

97 Somer and McCoy (2018), p. 2, as quoted in McCoy, Rahman and Somer (2018).

98 McCoy, Rahman and Somer 2018.

99 Somer and McCoy 2018.

100 Golub and Jackson 2012; Sunstein 1999.

101 Somer and McCoy 2018.

102 McCoy, Rahman and Somer 2018.

103 Orhan 2022.

104 Levitsky and Ziblatt 2018.

105 Petrarca, Giebler and Weßels 2022.

106 McCoy, Rahman and Somer 2018.

107 Carothers and O'Donohue 2019; McCoy, Rahman and Somer 2018.

108 Diamond 2015; Hyde 2020.

109 Somer 2005, p.120.

110 Allcott and others 2020.

111 Perrings, Hechter and Mamada 2021.

112 Vasconcelos and others 2021.

113 Axelrod, Daymude and Forrest 2021; Somer and McCoy 2018.

114 Macy and others 2021.

115 Chen and Zhong 2021.

116 Taking the definition by North (1991).

117 Nunn 2022.

118 Carver, Scheier and Segerstrom 2010.

119 UNDP 2022b.

120 Stewart, Plotkin and McCarty 2021.

121 Bak-Coleman and others 2021.

122 Bak-Coleman and others 2021.

123 For a more detailed consideration of opportunities for improving information systems, see Bak-Coleman (2022).

CHAPTER 5

1 IPCC 2022b.

2 Moore and others 2022.

3 Lehman and others 2021.

4 Lewandowsky, Ballard and Pancost 2015.

5 Nowotny 2015.

6 Chen and Zhong 2021. With moral codes themselves potentially evolving, including to encompass what has been described as "earth altruism" by Österblom and Paasche (2021).

7 Barfuss and others 2020; Santos and Pacheco 2011.

8 Beckert 2020.

9 See Müller (2021) and Przeworski (1991).

10 Schipper and others 2021.

11 Hulme 2020; Lövbrand and others 2015; Pancost 2017.

12 Barfuss and Mann 2022; Domingos and others 2020; Santos and Pacheco 2011; Santos, Santos and Pacheco 2008.

13 Nightingale and others 2020.

14 Hoey and Schröder 2022.

15 Nowotny 2015.

16 Our World in Data 2022.

17 See Clouston and others (2016), Cutler, Deaton and Lleras-Muney (2006) and Deaton (2013a).

18 Glied and Lleras-Muney 2008.

19 Phelan and Link 2005.

20 Cutler, Deaton and Lleras-Muney 2006.

21 Suárez-Álvarez and López-Menéndez 2022.

22 Vickers and Ziebarth 2019.

23 Basu, Caspi and Hockett 2021.

24 UNDP 2019.

25 Basu, Caspi and Hockett 2021.

26 UNDP 2001.

27 See, for example, Coeckelbergh (2011), Haenssgen and Ariana (2018), Oosterlaken (2009), Oosterlaken and Hoven (2012) and Robeyns (2005).

28 See Azhar (2021).

29 Azhar 2021; Brynjolfsson and McAfee 2015.

30 Azhar 2021.

31 Roser 2020.

32 See Bak-Coleman and Bergstrom (2022).

33 Jain and others 2021; Pardi and others 2018.

34 IRENA 2020.

35 Roser 2020.

36 Ziegler and Trancik 2021.

37 Roser 2020.

38 IEA 2020b.

39 Schmidt and others 2017.

40 Ziegler and Trancik 2021.

41 Way and others 2021.

42 Wurzel and Hsu 2022.

43 Gibney 2022.

44 Degrave and others 2022.

45 IEA 2021d.

46 IEA 2020b.

47 Gallagher and Franco Maldonado 2020.

48 IEA 2020a.

49 The guide includes 11 technology readiness levels, which could be summarized in broader readiness categories: mature, early adoption, demonstration and prototype. Mature technology has reached sizeable deployment, and only incremental innovations are expected. Early adoption technology means that some designs have reached markets and policy support is required for scale-up. But there are competing designs being validated at the demonstration and prototype phases. Offshore power, wind power, electric batteries and heat pumps are examples. Examples of demonstration designs are carbon capture in cement kilns, electrolytic hydrogen-based ammonia and methanol, and large long-distance battery-electric ships. Prototype designs are at prototype stage of a certain scale. Ammonia-powered vessels, electrolytic hydrogen-based steel production and direct air capture are examples of large prototypes. Battery-electric aircraft and direct electrification of primary steelmaking are examples of small prototypes. Technologies at the concept stage have just been formulated but need to be validated. Lithium-air batteries and electrifying a steam cracker for olefins production are examples.

50 Brynjolfsson 2022.

51 As discussed in the 2019 Human Development Report (UNDP 2019).

52 Dean 2022.

53 Dean 2022.

54 Callaway and others 2022.

55 Brynjolfsson 2022.

56 Furman and Seamans 2018.

57 Alonso and others 2020; Furman and Seamans 2018.

58 See Frank and others (2019) and Genz (2022).

59 Brynjolfsson 2022; Malone, Rus and Laubacher 2020.

60 Acemoglu and Restrepo 2019; Autor, Salomons and Seegmiller 2021.

61 Autor, Salomons and Seegmiller 2021.

62 Preston 2018.

63 Meng and Ellis 2020; National Academy of Engineering and Council 2013.

64 June and others 2018.

65 Collins and Curiel 2021; Katz and others 2018.

66 Trosset and Carbonell 2015.

67 Rogers and Oldroyd 2014; Wurtzel and others 2019.

68 Lorenzo and others 2018.

69 Redford and others 2014.

70 The Royal Society 2019; Schmidt 2010.

71 Evans 2021.

72 Acemoglu and Restrepo 2020; Eeckhout 2021; Korinek and Stiglitz 2021.

73 The threats associated with the proliferation of digital technologies are also covered in depth in UNDP (2022b).

74 Funtowicz and Ravetz 1993.

75 Khushf 2006.

76 Jasanoff and Hurlbut 2018; Scheufele and others 2021; Yu, Xue and Barrangou 2021.

77 Basu, Caspi and Hockett 2021.

78 See box 1.1 in UNDP (2022b). See also Abdalla and others (2020).

79 See The Independent Panel for Pandemic Preparedness and Response (2021).

80 See UNDP (2022b).

81 See Martínez-Franzoni and Sánchez-Ancochea (2022b).

82 Martínez Franzoni and Sánchez-Ancochea 2022b.

83 Baker 2021.

84 Dolgin 2021b.

85 Bown 2021.

86 Kupferschmidt 2020.

87 Bryan, Lemus and Marshall 2020.

88 Knowledge Portal on Innovation and Access to Medicines (https://www.knowledgeportalia.org/covid19-r-d-funding). See also McCarthy (2021).

89 Ball 2020; Dolgin 2021a.

90 Gentilini and others 2021.

91 IMF 2021a.

92 ILO 2021c.

93 Fang, Kennedy and Resnick 2020.

94 Gentilini 2021.

95 Gentilini and others 2021.

96 Gentilini and others 2021.

97 Fajardo-Gonzalez and Sandoval 2021.

98 International Social Security Association 2021.

99 Fang, Kennedy and Resnick 2020.

100 Gentilini and others 2021.

101 Heymann and others 2020; OECD 2020b.

102 UN 2020a.

103 Barrero, Bloom and Davis 2021.

104 Buell and others 2021; Sampi and Jooste 2020.

105 Fetzer and others 2020.

106 Imperial College London 2020b.

107 Imperial College London 2020a.

108 Levy and Savulescu 2021.

CHAPTER 6

1 Drawn from HM Treasury (2021).

2 Dasgupta 2021, p. 6.

3 Dasgupta 2021, p. 33.

4 Dasgupta 2021, p. 6.

5 Cited in Nunn (2022), p. 31.

6 UNDP 2020a.

7 UNDP 2020a.

8 Nowotny 2015, p. 16–17.

9 Nunn (2021) defined a function where cultural transmission of knowledge depends on inclusion, creativity and solidarity to produce adaptative (Payne and Wagner 2019; Pigliucci 2008) responses to new scenarios and circumstances (Schimmelpfennig and others 2022).

10 Community resilience plays a major role in coping with shocks. In this context community resilience can be understood as the existence, development and engagement of community resources by community members to thrive in an environment characterized by change, uncertainty, unpredictability and surprise.

11 Results from a cross-sectional and longitudinal research case study reveal that community organizing elevates psychological empowerment and civic engagement over time (Speer, Christens and Peterson 2021).

12 Miranda and Snower 2022.

13 UNDP 2015.

14 UNDP 2022b.

15 Florini, LaForge and Sharma 2022.

16 Okonjo-Iweala, Shanmugaratnam and Summers 2021.

17 Okonjo-Iweala, Shanmugaratnam and Summers 2021.

18 IMF 2021b.

19 IMF 2021b.

20 Such arrangements depend in practice on the efficacy of processes for making and implementing major decisions throughout society—in a word, governance (Florini, LaForge and Sharma 2022). Governance is the process through which state and nonstate actors interact to design and implement policies within a given set of formal and informal rules that shape and are shaped by power (World Bank 2017b). There are many impediments to governance, from the distortion of information by powerful economic interests that diluted support to policies ranging from tobacco consumption control to climate change mitigation (as reviewed in chapter 3) to corruption. Empirical evidence shows that corruption and poor governance correlate

with lower economic growth, investment and tax revenue (Cerra and others 2021). And governments that are captured by vested interests are liable to hinder societally needed changes rather than bring them about (Steinberger 2018).

21 Florini, LaForge and Sharma 2022.

22 Snower 2020.

23 Mach and Field 2017.

24 Florini, LaForge and Sharma 2022.

25 Fuentes-Nieva 2022.

26 Supporting the practices of indigenous peoples that sustain biodiversity is key, especially since lands managed by indigenous peoples—around 25 percent of global land area—host an estimated 80 percent of global biodiversity (UNDP 2020a).

27 UNDP 2020a.

28 McGregor 2009; Whyte 2013.

29 McCrea, Walton and Leonard 2014.

30 Fishback 2022.

31 This paragraph is based on Fishback (2022).

32 Upper 2017.

33 Zurbrügg 2022.

34 Edwards 2021; Upper 2017; Zurbrügg 2022.

35 IMF 2017.

36 IMF 2017.

37 Cicchiello and others 2021; Huambachano 2018.

38 Demirguc-Kunt and others 2022.

39 Kasman, Heuberger and Hammond 2018.

40 Hanna and Olken 2018; Ravallion 2017.

41 Molina and Ortiz-Juarez 2020; Yang and others 2016.

42 Ruckert, Huynh and Labonté 2018.

43 Hanna and Olken 2018.

44 Korinek and Stiglitz 2021.

45 Coote and Percy 2020; Gough 2021.

46 UNDP 2022b.

47 Gough 2019.

48 Dein 2020; Igreja, Kleijn and Richters 2006; Kpobi and Swartz 2019. Income support has shown to significantly decrease mental distress of children and young people living in the household (Angeles and others 2019; Costello and others 2003)

49 UNESCO 2021.

50 Pinto Benítez and others 2014.

51 UNESCO 2021.

52 Building trust is an essential component of the UN Secretary-General's *Our Common Agenda* (UN 2021c). According to that report, "now is the time to renew the social contract between governments and their people and within societies" (p. 4). Mechanisms to rebuild trust and embrace a comprehensive vision of human rights also include updated governance arrangements to deliver better public goods, health coverage, education, skills, decent work and housing, as well as universal access to the internet by 2030 as a basic human right.

53 Mach and Field 2017; OHCHR and the Heinrich Böll Foundation 2018.

54 OHCHR 2019.

55 The Centre for Human Rights Education in Lahore, Pakistan, has created spaces for debate on the relevance of religious tolerance and respect. Rwadari Tehreek (Movement for Pluralism) is using social media in innovative ways and giving training sessions for sharing individual stories and highlighting commonalities among different religions. OHCHR and Equitas–International Centre for Human Rights Education 2022.

56 De Coning 2020b.

57 De Coning 2020b.

58 De Coning 2020a.

59 Zraly and Nyirazinyoye 2010.

60 Burnet 2021.

61 A practical guide to integrating mental health programming into peacebuilding processes can be found in UNDP (2022a).

62 Fransen and others 2021.

63 Zurbrügg and others 2004.

64 De Moor 2013; Denning and Yaholkovsky 2008.

65 Joshi and Yenneti 2020.

66 Juris 2004.

67 Almeida 2019.

68 Badarne 2008.

69 Rajan 2021.

70 Recombination has far more potential to drive innovation than incremental improvement or luck (Schimmelpfennig and others 2022).

71 Roll 2021.

72 Samji and Kapoor 2022.

73 The Problem Driven Iterative Adaptation Approach, introduced in Andrews, Pritchett and Woolcock (2013), focuses on solving local performance problems by creating an environment that encourages positive deviance and experimentation through experiential learning by including constant feedback loops in the design and implementation of a project, not just ex post with evaluation.

74 Funda Wande 2021; Samji and Kapoor 2022.

75 Besley and Persson 2021, 2022.

76 Besley and Persson 2021.

77 Besley and Persson 2021.

78 UNDP 2022b.

79 Andrighetto and Vriens 2022.

80 Andrighetto and Vriens 2022; Szekely and others 2021.

81 See Nunn (2022).

82 Bruneau and others 2021.

83 Amsalem, Merkley and Loewen 2022.

84 Lamont forthcoming.

85 Culture is directly linked to the three forms of equity: recognitional, distributional and procedural (UNDP 2020a).

86 UNDP 2020a.

87 "A curriculum-based process of teaching and learning about the cognitive, emotional, physical and social aspects of sexuality. It aims to equip children and young people with knowledge, skills, attitudes and values that will empower them to realize their health, wellbeing and dignity; develop respectful social and sexual relationships; consider how their choices affect their own wellbeing and that of others; and understand and ensure the protection of their rights throughout their lives" (UNESCO 2018, p. 16).

88 Goldfarb and Lieberman 2021.

89 Klugman and others 2014.

90 Algan, Cahuc and Shleifer 2013.

91 Marcus 2018.

92 Rao 2019.

93 UNESCO 2017.

94 Aksoy and others 2020.

95 Ritchie 2021.

96 Hulme 2020, p. 311.

97 Green, Wilke and Cooper 2020.

98 Anis and White 2017.

99 Lamont 2019. On the controversy around the concept of hope, see Schlosser (2013).

100 Potts and Henderson 2021.

101 Fokum, Fonjong and Adams 2020.

102 Okeja and Watene 2020; Watene 2022; Watene and Palmer 2020.

103 "The Stolen Generations refers to those children of Aboriginal and Torres Strait Islander descent systematically removed from their families under various government policies rooted in assimilationist ideology" (Quayle and Sonn 2019, p. 47).

104 Aboriginal and Torres Strait Islander Healing Foundation Development Team 2009.

105 Quayle and Sonn 2019.

106 Collier and others 2021.

107 Bal 2021.

References

Aall, P., and Crocker, C. A. 2019. "Building Resilience and Social Cohesion in Conflict." *Global Policy* 10: 68–75.

Aas Rustad, S. 2021. "Conflict Trends." Background box contribution for 2022 Special Report on Human Security, UNDP-HDRO, New York.

Aas Rustad, S., Reagan, R., Bruch, C., Dupuy, K., Mwesigye, F., McNeish, J.-A., and VanDeveer, S. 2022. "Green Curses Renewable Energy and Conflict in Africa." Background paper for Human Development Report 2021/2022, UNDP–HDRO, New York.

Abass, Z. I., and Tucker, R. 2018. "Residential Satisfaction in Low-Density Australian Suburbs: The Impact of Social and Physical Context on Neighbourhood Contentment." *Journal of Environmental Psychology* 56: 36–45.

Abdalla, S. M., Maani, N., Ettman, C. K., and Galea, S. 2020. "Claiming Health as a Public Good in the Post-Covid-19 Era." *Development* 63(2): 200–204.

Abdoul-Azize, H. T., and El Gamil, R. 2021. "Social Protection as a Key Tool in Crisis Management: Learnt Lessons from the Covid-19 Pandemic." *Global Social Welfare* 8(1): 107–116.

Abi Rafeh, L. 2020. "For Arab Women and Girls, the Crisis Is Just Beginning." *Al Jazeera*, 4 May.

Abi-Jaoude, E., Naylor, K. T., and Pignatiello, A. 2020. "Smartphones, Social Media Use and Youth Mental Health." *Canadian Medical Association Journal* 192(6): 136–141.

Aboriginal and Torres Strait Islander Healing Foundation Development Team. 2009. *Voices from the Campfires: Establishing the Aboriginal and Torres Strait Islander Healing Foundation: Report.* Canberra: Department of Families, Housing, Community Services and Indigenous Affairs.

Acemoglu, D. 2021. "Harms of AI." NBER Working Paper 29247, National Bureau of Economic Research, Cambridge, MA.

Acemoglu, D. 2022. "Obedience in the Labour Market and Social Mobility: A Socioeconomic Approach." *Economica* 89(S1) S2–37.

Acemoglu, D., and Restrepo, P. 2019. "Automation and New Tasks: How Technology Displaces and Reinstates Labor." *Journal of Economic Perspectives* 33(2): 3–30.

Acemoglu, D., and Restrepo, P. 2020. "The Wrong Kind of A.I.? Artificial Intelligence and the Future of Labour Demand." *Cambridge Journal of Regions, Economy and Society, Cambridge Political Economy Society* 13(1): 25–35.

Acemoglu, D., and Robinson, J. A. 2021. "Culture, Institutions and Social Equilibria: A Framework." NBER Working Paper 28832, National Bureau of Economic Research Cambridge, MA.

Acemoglu, D., and Robinson, J. 2022. "Non-Modernization: Power–Culture Trajectories and the Dynamics of Political Institutions." *Annual Review of Political Science* 25(1): 323–339.

Acemoglu, D., Egorov, G., and Sonin, K. 2020. "Institutional Change and Institutional Persistence." NBER Working Paper 27852, National Bureau of Economic Research, Cambridge, MA.

Acharya, A. K., and Sanchez, M. L. M. 2018. "Trafficking of Women in US-Mexican Border Cities: An Analysis on the Physical and Mental Health Condition of Victims." *Journal of Trafficking and Human Exploitation* 2(1): 1–17.

ACLED (Armed Conflict Location and Event Data Project). 2019. "Armed Conflict Location & Event Data Project (ACLED) Codebook." https://acleddata.com/acleddatanew/wp-content/uploads/dlm_uploads/2019/01/ACLED_Codebook_2019FINAL.docx.pdf.

ACLED (Armed Conflict Location and Event Data Project). 2021. "Data Export Tool." https://acleddata.com/data-export-tool/. Accessed 5 October 2021.

ADB (Asian Development Bank). 2016. *Social Protection for Informal Workers in Asia.* Manila.

Adesina, M., Adesanya, T., and Olufadewa, I. 2020. "Mental Health and Conflict in Nigeria: An Overview." *European Journal of Environment and Public Health* 4(1): 1–4.

Adesina, M. A., Kanmodi, K. K., and Merrick, J. 2019. *The Boko Haram Terror: Adversary to the Wellbeing of Nigerian Kids.* New York: Nova Science.

Adhvaryu, A., Fenske, J., and Nyshadham, A. 2019. "Early Life Circumstance and Adult Mental Health." *Journal of Political Economy* 127(4): 1516–1549.

Adler, P. S., Goldoftas, B., and Levine, D. I. 1999. "Flexibility Versus Efficiency? A Case Study of Model Changeovers in the Toyota Production System." *Organization Science* 10(1): 43–68.

African Union. 2015. *Agenda 2063: The Africa We Want.* Addis Ababa. https://au.int/sites/default/files/documents/36204-doc-agenda2063_popular_version_en.pdf.

Agrafiotis, I., Nurse, J. R., Goldsmith, M., Creese, S., and Upton, D. 2018. "A Taxonomy of Cyber-Harms: Defining the Impacts of Cyber-Attacks and Understanding How They Propagate." *Journal of Cybersecurity* 4(1): 1–15.

Aguirre-Liguori, J. A., Ramírez-Barahona, S., Tiffin, P., and Eguiarte, L. E. 2019. "Climate Change Is Predicted to Disrupt Patterns of Local Adaptation in Wild and Cultivated Maize." *Proceedings of the Royal Society B: Biological Sciences* 286(1906): 20190486.

Ahir, H., Bloom, N., and Furceri, D. 2018. "The World Uncertainty Index." https://ssrn.com/abstract=3275033.

Ahir, H., Bloom, N., and Furceri, D. 2022. "The World Uncertainty Index." NBER Working Paper 29763, National Bureau of Economic Research, Cambridge, MA.

Ahmed, S. 2013. *The Cultural Politics of Emotion.* London: Routledge.

Akerlof, G. A. 2020. "Sins of Omission and the Practice of Economics." *Journal of Economic Literature* 58(2): 405–418.

Akerlof, G. A., and Kranton, R. E. 2000. "Economics and Identity." *The Quarterly Journal of Economics* 115(3): 715–753.

Akerlof, G. A., and Snower, D. J. 2016. "Bread and Bullets." *Journal of Economic Behavior & Organization (Part B)* 126: 58–71.

Aksoy, C. G., Carpenter, C. S., De Haas, R., and Tran, K. D. 2020. "Do Laws Shape Attitudes? Evidence from Same-Sex Relationship Recognition Policies in Europe." *European Economic Review* 124: 103399.

Al-Ali, N. 2020. "Covid-19 and Feminism in the Global South: Challenges, Initiatives and Dilemmas." *European Journal of Women's Studies* 27(4): 333–347.

Alderman, L. 2021. "Europe Fears That Rising Cost of Climate Action Is Stirring Anger." *New York Times*, 1 November.

Alesina, A., and Giuliano, P. 2015. "Culture and Institutions." *Journal of Economic Literature* 53(4): 898–944.

Alesina, A., and Passarelli, F. 2019. "Loss Aversion in Politics." *American Journal of Political Science* 63(4): 936–947.

Alexander, P., Rounsevell, M. D. A., Dislich, C., Dodson, J. R., Engström, K., and Moran, D. 2015. "Drivers for Global Agricultural Land Use Change: The Nexus of Diet, Population, Yield and Bioenergy." *Global Environmental Change* 35: 138–147.

Algan, Y., Cahuc, P., and Shleifer, A. 2013. "Teaching Practices and Social Capital." *American Economic Journal: Applied Economics* 5(3): 189–210.

Allcott, H., Boxell, L., Conway, J., Gentzkow, M., Thaler, M., and Yang, D. 2020. "Polarization and Public Health: Partisan Differences in Social Distancing During the Coronavirus Pandemic." *Journal of Public Economics* 191: 104254.

Allen, E. J., Dechow, P. M., Pope, D. G., and Wu, G. 2017. "Reference-Dependent Preferences: Evidence from Marathon Runners." *Management Science* 63(6): 1657–1672.

Alloush, M. 2021. "Income, Psychological Well-Being, and the Dynamics of Poverty." http://barrett.dyson. cornell.edu/NEUDC/paper_73.pdf. Accessed 27 August 2021.

Alloush, M., and Bloem, J. R. 2020. "Neighborhood Violence, Poverty, and Psychological Well-Being." Paper presented at the 2020 Annual Meeting of the Agricultural and Applied Economics Association, 26–28 July, Kansas City, MO. https://ideas.repec.org/p/ags/aaea20/304341.html. Accessed 22 September 2021.

Almås, I., Cappelen, A. W., Sørensen, E. Ø., and Tungodden, B. 2022. "Global Evidence on the Selfish Rich Inequality Hypothesis." *Proceedings of the National Academy of Sciences* 119(3): e2109690119.

Almeida, P. 2019. *Social Movements: The Structure of Collective Mobilization.* Oakland, CA: University of California Press.

Al-Nuaimi, M. A., Hamad, R. A., and Lafta, R. K. 2015. "Effects of Witnessing or Exposure to Community Violence on Mental Health of Iraqi Men." *Qatar Medical Journal* 2015(1): 10.

Alonso, C., Berg, A., Kothari, S., Papageorgiou, C., and Rehma, S. 2020. "Will the AI Revolution Cause a Great Divergence?" IMF Working Paper 2020/184, International Monetary Fund, Washington, DC.

Altman, J., and Jordan, K. 2018. "Impact of Climate Change on Indigenous Australians: Submission to the Garnaut Climate Change Review." https://caepr. cass.anu.edu.au/research/publications/impact-climate -change-indigenous-australians-submission-garnaut -climate-change. Accessed 10 August 2022.

Alvarado, R., Minoletti, A., González, F. T., Küstner, B. M., Madariaga, C., and Sepúlveda, R. 2012. "Development of Community Care for People with Schizophrenia in Chile." *International Journal of Mental Health* 41(1): 48–61.

Alves, R., and Rosa, I. M. 2007. "Biodiversity, Traditional Medicine and Public Health: Where Do They Meet?" *Journal of Ethnobiology and Ethnomedicine* 3(1): 1–9.

Amenta, E., and Polletta, F. 2019. "The Cultural Impacts of Social Movements." *Annual Review of Sociology* 45: 279–299.

American Psychiatric Association. 2013. *Diagnostic and Statistical Manual of Mental Disorders.* Fifth Edition. Washington, DC: American Psychiatric Publisher.

American Psychological Association. 2022. "Distress." In *APA Dictionary of Psychology.* https:// dictionary.apa.org/distress. Accessed 1 June 2022.

Amsalem, E., Merkley, E., and Loewen, P. J. 2022. "Does Talking to the Other Side Reduce Inter-Party Hostility? Evidence from Three Studies." *Political Communication* 39(1): 61–78.

Amundsen, D. 2021. "Digital Technologies as a Panacea for Social Isolation and Loneliness among Older Adults: An Intervention Model for Flourishing and Well-being: Visual Technologies as a Panacea for Social Isolation." *Video Journal of Education and Pedagogy* 5(1): 1–14.

Anderson, E. 2018. "Policy Entrepreneurs and the Origins of the Regulatory Welfare State: Child Labor Reform in Nineteenth-Century Europe." *American Sociological Review* 83(1): 173–211.

Anderson, E. 2021. *Agents of Reform: Child Labor and the Origins of the Welfare State.* Princeton, NJ: Princeton University Press.

Anderson, M. K. 2005. *Tending the Wild: Native American Knowledge and the Management of California's Natural Resources.* Oakland, CA: University of California Press.

Anderson, W., Seager, R., Baethgen, W., Cane, M., and You, L. 2019. "Synchronous Crop Failures and Climate-Forced Production Variability." *Science Advances* 5(7): eaaw1976.

Andreano, M. S., Benedetti, R., Piersimoni, F., and Savio, G. 2021. "Mapping Poverty of Latin American and Caribbean Countries from Heaven through Night-Light Satellite Images." *Social Indicators Research* 156(2): 533–562.

Andrew, A., Cattan, S., Costa Dias, M., Farquharson, C., Kraftman, L., Krutikova, S., Phimister, A., and Sevilla, A. 2020. "The Gendered Division of Paid and Domestic Work under Lockdown." IZA Discussion Paper 13500, Institute of Labor Economics, Bonn, Germany. https://ftp.iza.org/dp13500.pdf.

Andrews, M., Pritchett, L., and Woolcock, M. 2013. "Escaping Capability Traps through Problem Driven Iterative Adaptation (PDIA)." *World Development* 51: 234–244.

Andrighetto, G., and Vriens, E. 2022. "A Research Agenda for the Study of Social Norm Change." *Philosophical Transactions of the Royal Society A* 380(2227): 20200411.

Angeles, G., de Hoop, J., Handa, S., Kilburn, K., Milazzo, A., Peterman, A., and Malawi Social Cash Transfer Evaluation Team. 2019. "Government of Malawi's Unconditional Cash Transfer Improves Youth Mental Health." *Social Science & Medicine* 225: 108–119.

Angelou, M. 1993. *Wouldn't Take Nothing for My Journey Now.* New York: Random House.

Anis, F., and White, J. 2017. "The Meena Communicative Initiative in Bangladesh." In Plows, V., and Whitburn, B., (eds.), *Inclusive Education: Making Sense of Everyday Practice.* Rotterdam, The Netherlands: Sense Publishers.

Apicella, C., Norenzayan, A., and Henrich, J. 2020. "Beyond WEIRD: A Review of the Last Decade and a Look Ahead to the Global Laboratory of the Future." *Evolution and Human Behavior* 41(5): 319–329.

Apolinário-Hagen, J. 2017. "Current Perspectives on E-Mental-Health Self-Help Treatments: Exploring the 'Black Box' of Public Views, Perceptions, and Attitudes toward the Digitalization of Mental Health Care." In Menvielle, L., Audrain-Pontevia, A.-F., and Menvielle, W., (eds.), *The Digitization of Healthcare: New Challenges and Opportunities.* New York: Palgrave Macmillan.

Appadurai, A. 2004. "The Capacity to Aspire: Culture and the Terms of Recognition." In Rao, V., and Walton, M., (eds.), *Culture and Public Action.* Stanford, CA: Stanford University Press.

Arasmith, A., Østby, G., and Aas Rustad, S. 2022. "Patterns and Trends of Conflict-Affected Populations, 1990–2020: Advancing a New Measurement Framework." Background paper for Human Development Report 2021/2022, UNDP–HDRO, New York.

Arato, A., Cohen, J. L., and von Busekist, A. 2018. *Forms of Pluralism and Democratic Constitutionalism.* New York: Columbia University Press.

Aref-Adib, G., and Hassiotis, A. 2021. "Frontline 2020: The New Age for Telemental Health." *The Lancet Psychiatry* 8(1): 3–4.

Arkes, H. R., Gigerenzer, G., and Hertwig, R. 2016. "How Bad Is Incoherence?" *Decision* 3(1): 20–39.

Armaly, M., and Enders, A. 2021. "The Role of Affective Orientations in Promoting Perceived Polarization." *Political Science Research and Methods* 9(3): 615–626.

Arnall, A., Oswald, K., Davies, M., Mitchell, T., and Coirolo, C. 2010. "Adaptive Social Protection: Mapping the Evidence and Policy Context in the Agriculture Sector in South Asia." *IDS Working Papers* 2010(345): 1–92.

Ash, E., Mukand, S., and Rodrik, D. 2021. "Economic Interests, Worldviews, and Identities: Theory and Evidence on Ideational Politics." NBER Working Paper 29474, National Bureau of Economic Research, Cambridge, MA.

Aslam, S., Gul, N., Aslam, S., and Eslamian, S. 2022. "Biotechnology and Flood-Resistant Rice." In Eslamian, S., and Eslamian, F., (eds.), *Flood Handbook.* Boca Raton, FL: CRC Press.

Atkinson, Q. D., and Jacquet, J. 2022. "Challenging the Idea That Humans Are Not Designed to Solve Climate Change." *Perspectives on Psychological Science* 17(3): 619–630.

Autor, D. H., Dorn, D., and Hanson, G. H. 2016. "The China Shock: Learning from Labor-Market Adjustment to Large Changes in Trade." *Annual Review of Economics* 8(1): 205–240.

Autor, D., Dorn, D., Katz, L., Patterson, C., and Reenen, J. V. 2020. "The Fall of the Labor Share and the Rise of Superstar Firms." *The Quarterly Journal of Economics* 135(2): 645–709.

Autor, D., Salomons, A., and Seegmiller, B. 2021. "New Frontiers: The Origins and Content of New Work, 1940–2018." Working Paper, Massachusetts Institute of Technology, Cambridge, MA.

Awaworyi Churchill, S., and Farrell, L. 2018. "The Impact of Gambling on Depression: New Evidence from England and Scotland." *Economic Modelling* 68: 475–483.

Awaworyi Churchill, S., Munyanyi, M. E., Smyth, R., and Trinh, T.-A. 2021. "Early Life Shocks and Entrepreneurship: Evidence from the Vietnam War." *Journal of Business Research* 124: 506–518.

Axelrod, R., Daymude, J. J., and Forrest, S. 2021. "Preventing Extreme Polarization of Political Attitudes."

Proceedings of the National Academy of Sciences 118(50): e2102139118.

Ayala-Hurtado, E. 2021. "Narrative Continuity/Rupture: Projected Professional Futures Amid Pervasive Employment Precarity." *Work and Occupations* 49(1): 45–78.

Ayers, J. W., Leas, E. C., Johnson, D. C., Poliak, A., Althouse, B. M., Dredze, M., and Nobles, A. L. 2020. "Internet Searches for Acute Anxiety During the Early Stages of the Covid-19 Pandemic." *JAMA Internal Medicine* 180(12): 1706–1707.

Azar, J., Marinescu, I., and Steinbaum, M. 2019. "Measuring Labor Market Power Two Ways." *AEA Papers and Proceedings* 109: 317–321.

Azhar, A. 2021. *The Exponential Age: How Accelerating Technology Is Transforming Business, Politics and Society.* New York, NY: Diversion Books.

Bachelet, M. 2022. "Human Rights and Democracy in the Digital Age." Office of the United Nations High Commissioner for Human Rights, Geneva. https://www.ohchr.org/en/statements/2022/04/human-rights-and-democracy-digital-age. Accessed 25 August 2022.

Badarne, M.-O. 2008. "'Flower by Flower, We Make a Garden': Palestinian Women Organising for Economic Justice." *Gender & Development* 16(3): 509–521.

Bae, H., Kim, D., and Park, Y. C. 2016. "Dissociation Predicts Treatment Response in Eye-Movement Desensitization and Reprocessing for Posttraumatic Stress Disorder." *Journal of Trauma & Dissociation* 17(1): 112–130.

Baek, M., DiMaio, F., Anishchenko, I., Dauparas, J., Ovchinnikov, S., Lee, G. R., Wang, J., and others. 2021. "Accurate Prediction of Protein Structures and Interactions Using a Three-Track Neural Network." *Science* 373(6557): 871–876.

Bago, B., Rand, D., and Pennycook, G. 2020. "Fake News, Fast and Slow: Deliberation Reduces Belief in False (but Not True) News Headlines." *Journal of Experimental Psychology: General* 149(8): 1608–1613.

Bahadur, A. V., Peters, K., Wilkinson, E., Pichon, F., Gray, K., and Tanner, T. 2015. "The 3As: Tracking Resilience across BRACED." Working paper, Building Resistance and Adaptation to Climate Extremes and Disasters, London.

Bai, X., Van Der Leeuw, S., O'Brien, K., Berkhout, F., Biermann, F., Brondizio, E. S., Cudennec, C., and others. 2016. "Plausible and Desirable Futures in the Anthropocene: A New Research Agenda." *Global Environmental Change* 39(2016): 351–362.

Bak-Coleman, J. 2022. "Promoting Sustainability and Equity in Global Social Systems." Background paper for Human Development Report 2021/2022, UNDP–HDRO, New York.

Bak-Coleman, J., and Bergstrom, C. 2022. "A High-Speed Scientific Hive Mind Emerged from the Covid Pandemic." *Scientific American* 326(3): 34–36.

Bak-Coleman, J. B, Alfano, M., Barfuss, W., Bergstrom, C. T., Centeno, M. A., Couzin, I. D., Donges, J. F., and others. 2021. "Stewardship of Global Collective Behavior." *Proceedings of the National Academy of Sciences* 118(27): e2025764118.

Baker, S. 2021. "The Coronavirus Vaccines Have Shattered Expectations." *Axios*, 8 February.

Bakshy, E., Messing, S., and Adamic, L. A. 2015. "Exposure to Ideologically Diverse News and Opinion on Facebook." *Science* 348: 1130–1132.

Bal, M. 2021. "Youth Engagement in Participatory Budgeting. Case Study of Kutná Hora (2019–2020)." *Slovak Journal of Public Policy and Public Administration* 8(2).

Baldassarri, D., and Page, S. E. 2021. "The Emergence and Perils of Polarization." *Proceedings of the National Academy of Sciences* 118(50): e2116863118.

Ball, P. 2020. "The Lightning-Fast Quest for Covid Vaccines — and What It Means for Other Diseases." *Nature* 589: 16–18.

Balta-Ozkan, N., Watson, T., and Mocca, E. 2015. "Spatially Uneven Development and Low Carbon Transitions: Insights from Urban and Regional Planning." *Energy Policy* 85: 500–510.

Banaszak, L. A., and Ondercin, H. L. 2016. "Public Opinion as a Movement Outcome: The Case of the US Women's Movement." *Mobilization: An International Quarterly* 21(3): 361–378.

Banda, K. K., and Cluverius, J. 2018. "Elite Polarization, Party Extremity, and Affective Polarization." *Electoral Studies* 56: 90–101.

Banerjee, S., and John, P. 2021. "Nudge Plus: Incorporating Reflection into Behavioral Public Policy." *Behavioural Public Policy*: 1–16.

Barberis, N. C. 2013. "Thirty Years of Prospect Theory in Economics: A Review and Assessment." *Journal of Economic Perspectives* 27(1): 173–196.

Barbosa Neves, B., Franz, R., Judges, R., Beermann, C., and Baecker, R. 2019. "Can Digital Technology Enhance Social Connectedness among Older Adults? A Feasibility Study." *Journal of Applied Gerontology* 38(1): 49–72.

Barfuss, W., and Mann, R. P. 2022. "Modeling the Effects of Environmental and Perceptual Uncertainty Using Deterministic Reinforcement Learning Dynamics with Partial Observability." *Physical Review E* 105(3): 034409.

Barfuss, W., Donges, J. F., Vasconcelos, V. V., Kurths, J., and Levin, S. A. 2020. "Caring for the Future Can Turn Tragedy into Comedy for Long-Term Collective Action under Risk of Collapse." *Proceedings of the National Academy of Sciences* 117(23): 12915–12922.

Barkai, S. 2020. "Declining Labor and Capital Shares." *The Journal of Finance* 75(2): 2421–2463.

Barlow, J., França, F., Gardner, T. A., Hicks, C. C., Lennox, G. D., Berenguer, E., Castello, L., and others. 2018. "The Future of Hyperdiverse Tropical Ecosystems." *Nature* 559(7715): 517–526.

Barnett, M., Brock, W., and Hansen, L. P. 2020. "Pricing Uncertainty Induced by Climate Change." *The Review of Financial Studies* 33(3): 1024–1066.

Barnidge, M. 2018. "Social Affect and Political Disagreement on Social Media." *Social Media+ Society* 4(3): 2056305118797721.

Barrero, J. M., Bloom, N., and Davis, S. J. 2021. "Internet Access and Its Implications for Productivity, Inequality, and Resilience." NBER Working Paper 29102, National Bureau of Economic Research, Cambridge, MA.

Barrett, S., and Dannenberg, A. 2012. "Climate Negotiations under Scientific Uncertainty." *Proceedings of the National Academy of Sciences* 109(43): 17372–17376.

Barro, R. J., and Lee, J. W. 2018. Dataset of Educational Attainment, June 2018 Revision. http://www.barrolee.com. Accessed 7 April 2022.

Barron, K., Becker, A., and Huck, S. 2022. "Motivated Political Reasoning: The Emergence of Belief-Value Constellations." Unpublished paper.

Basu, K. 2018. *The Republic of Beliefs: A New Approach to Law and Economics.* Princeton, NJ: Princeton University Press.

Basu, K. 2021. "The Ground Beneath Our Feet." *Oxford Review of Economic Policy* 37(4): 783–793.

Basu, K. 2022. "Why Have Leaders at All? Hume and Hobbes, with a Dash of Nash." *Homo Oeconomicus*.

Basu, K., Caspi, A., and Hockett, R. 2021. "Markets and Regulation in the Age of Big Tech." *Capitalism and Society* 15(1).

Bate, S., Bevan, H., and Robert, G. 2004. "Towards a Million Change Agents. A Review of the Social Movements Literature: Implications for Large Scale Change in the NHS." NHS Modernisation Agency.

Bates, E. A. 2020a. "No One Would Ever Believe Me: An Exploration of the Impact of Intimate Partner Violence Victimization on Men." *Psychology of Men & Masculinities* 21(4): 497–507.

Bates, E. A. 2020b. "Walking on Egg Shells: A Qualitative Examination of Men's Experiences of Intimate Partner Violence." *Psychology of Men & Masculinities* 21(1): 13–24.

Bauer, A. M., Edgeworth, M., Edwards, L. E., Ellis, E. C., Gibbard, P., and Merritts, D. J. 2021. "Anthropocene: Event or Epoch?" *Nature* 597(7876): 332.

Bauer, M., Blattman, C., Chytilová, J., Henrich, J., Miguel, E., and Mitts, T. 2016. "Can War Foster Cooperation?" *Journal of Economic Perspectives* 30(3): 249–274.

BBC News. 2021. "Haiti President's Assassination: What We Know So Far." *BBC News*, 12 July.

Bechara, A., and Damasio, A. R. 2005. "The Somatic Marker Hypothesis: A Neural Theory of Economic Decision." *Games and Economic Behavior* 52(2): 336–372.

Bechara, A., Damasio, H., and Damasio, A. R. 2000. "Emotion, Decision Making and the Orbitofrontal Cortex." *Cerebral Cortex* 10(3): 295–307.

Becker, G. S. 1976. *The Economic Approach to Human Behavior.* Chicago, IL: Chicago University Press.

Beckert, J. 2020. "The Exhausted Futures of Neoliberalism: From Promissory Legitimacy to Social Anomy." *Journal of Cultural Economy* 13(3): 318–330.

Bedi, T., Coudouel, A., and Simler, K. 2007. *More Than a Pretty Picture: Using Poverty Maps to Design Better Policies and Interventions.* Washington, DC: World Bank.

Begley, C. 2021. *The Next Apocalypse: The Art and Science of Survival.* New York: Basic Books.

Béland, D., and Cox, R. H. 2016. "Ideas as Coalition Magnets: Coalition Building, Policy Entrepreneurs, and Power Relations." *Journal of European Public Policy* 23(3): 428–445.

Bénabou, R., and Tirole, J. 2016. "Mindful Economics: The Production, Consumption, and Value of Beliefs." *Journal of Economic Perspectives* 30(3): 141–164.

Bénabou, R., Falk, A., and Tirole, J. 2018. "Narratives, Imperatives, and Moral Reasoning." NBER Working Paper 24798, National Bureau of Economic Research, Cambridge, MA.

Benartzi, S., and Thaler, R. H. 1995. "Myopic Loss Aversion and the Equity Premium Puzzle." *The Quarterly Journal of Economics* 110(1): 73–92.

Benavides, M. O., Berry, O. O., and Mangus, M. 2019. "Intimate Partner Violence: A Guide for Psychiatrists Treating IPV Survivors." American Psychiatric Association. https://www.psychiatry.org/psychiatrists/cultural-competency/education/intimate-partner-violence. Accessed 28 Aug 2021.

Bender, K. A., and Theodossiou, I. 2018. "The Unintended Consequences of Flexicurity: The Health Consequences of Flexible Employment." *Review of Income and Wealth* 64(4): 777–799.

Bendik-Keymer, J. D. 2016. "'Goodness Itself Must Change' – Anthroponomy in an Age of Socially-Caused, Planetary Environmental Change." *Ethics & Bioethics* 6(3–4): 187–202.

Benjamin, D. J. 2019. "Errors in Probabilistic Reasoning and Judgment Biases." In Bernheim, B. D., Dellavigna, S., and Laibson, D., (eds.), *Handbook of Behavioral Economics: Applications and Foundations 1.* Amsterdam: North-Holland Publishing Company.

Benjet, C., Sampson, L., Yu, S., Kessler, R., Zaslavsky, A., Evans-Lacko, S., Martins, S., and others. 2019. "Associations between Neighborhood-Level Violence and Individual Mental Disorders: Results from the World Mental Health Surveys in Five Latin American Cities." *Psychiatry Research* 282: 2–22.

Benmelech, E., Bergman, N., and Kim, H. 2022. "Strong Employers and Weak Employees: How Does Employer Concentration Affect Wages?" *Journal of Human Resources* 57(S): S200–S250.

Bennett, W. L., and Livingston, S. 2018. "The Disinformation Order: Disruptive Communication and the Decline of Democratic Institutions." *European Journal of Communication* 33(2): 122–139.

Bergant, K., Mano, R., and Shibata, I. 2022. "From Polluting to Green Jobs: A Seamless Transition in the US?" Working Paper 2022/129, International Monetary Fund, Washington, DC. https://www.imf.org/en/Publications/WP/Issues/2022/07/01/From-Polluting-to-Green-Jobs-A-Seamless-Transition-in-the-U-S-520244. Accessed 25 August 2022.

Berger, P. 1976. "Pontchartrain and the Grain Trade During the Famine of 1693." *The Journal of Modern History* 48(S4): 37–86.

Berkessel, J. B., Gebauer, J. E., Joshanloo, M., Bleidorn, W., Rentfrow, P. J., Potter, J., and Gosling, S. D. 2021. "National Religiosity Eases the Psychological Burden of Poverty." *Proceedings of the National Academy of Sciences* 118(39): 1–6.

Berman, E. P. 2022. "Thinking Like an Economist." In *Thinking Like an Economist.* Princeton, NJ: Princeton University Press.

Bermes, A. 2021. "Information Overload and Fake News Sharing: A Transactional Stress Perspective Exploring the Mitigating Role of Consumers' Resilience During Covid-19." *Journal of Retailing and Consumer Services* 61: 1–10.

Bernstein, A. S., Ando, A. W., Loch-Temzelides, T., Vale, M. M., Li, B. V., Li, H., Busch, J., and others. 2022. "The Costs and Benefits of Primary Prevention of Zoonotic Pandemics." *Science Advances* 8(5): eabl4183.

Berry, H. L., Bowen, K., and Kjellstrom, T. 2010. "Climate Change and Mental Health: A Causal Pathways Framework." *International Journal of Public Health* 55(2): 123–132.

Berry, H. L., Waite, T. D., Dear, K. B., Capon, A. G., and Murray, V. 2018. "The Case for Systems Thinking About Climate Change and Mental Health." *Nature Climate Change* 8(4): 282–290.

Besley, T. J., and Persson, T. 2020. "Escaping the Climate Trap? Values, Technologies, and Politics." Unpublished paper.

Besley, T. J., and Persson, T. 2021. "Science as Civil Society: Implications for a Green Transition." CEPR Discussion Paper DP16840, Centre for Economic Policy Research, London.

Besley, T. J., and Persson, T. 2022. "The Political Economics of Green Transitions." CEPR Discussion Paper DP17242, Centre for Economic Policy Research, London.

Bhugra, D., and Becker, M. A. 2005. "Migration, Cultural Bereavement and Cultural Identity." *World Psychiatry* 4(1): 18–24.

Bianchi, F., Bianchi, G., and Song, D. 2021. "The Long-Term Impact of the Covid-19 Unemployment Shock on Life Expectancy and Mortality Rates." NBER Working Paper 28304, National Bureau of Economic Research, Cambridge, MA.

Biasi, B., Dahl, M. S., and Moser, P. 2021. "Career Effects of Mental Health." NBER Working Paper 29031, National Bureau of Economic Research, Cambridge, MA.

Bilgrami, A. 2020. *Nature and Value.* New York: Columbia University Press.

BIS (Bank for International Settlements). 2021. *Climate-Related Financial Risks—Measurement Methodologies.* Basel, Switzerland.

Black, R., Busby, J., Dabelko, G. D., de Coning, C., Maalim, H., McAllister, C., Ndiloseh, M., and others. 2022. *Environment of Peace: Security in a New Era of Risk.* Stockholm, Stockholm International Peace Research Institute.

Blanchette, I., and Richards, A. 2010. "The Influence of Affect on Higher Level Cognition: A Review of Research on Interpretation, Judgement, Decision Making and Reasoning." *Cognition and Emotion* 24(4): 561–595.

Block, M., Á González , Reyes Morales, H., Cahuana Hurtado, L., Balandrán, A., and Méndez, E. 2020. "Mexico: Health System Review." *Health Systems in Transition* 22(2): 1–222.

Blofield, M., Giambruno, C., and Pribble, J. 2021. "Breadth and Sufficiency of Cash Transfer Responses in Ten Latin American Countries During the First 12 Months of the Covid-19 Pandemic." Commitment to Equity Working Paper 114, Tulane University, Department of Economics, New Orleans, LA.

Blumer, H. 1951. "Collective Behavior." *New Outline of the Principles of Sociology*: 166–222.

Blumer, H. 1995. "Social Movements." In Lyman, S.M., (ed.), *Social Movements: Main Trends of the Modern World.* London: Palgrave Macmillan.

Blyth, M. 2013. *Austerity: The History of a Dangerous Idea.* Oxford, UK: Oxford University Press.

Boelen, P. A., de Keijser, J., and Smid, G. 2015. "Cognitive–Behavioral Variables Mediate the Impact of Violent Loss on Post-Loss Psychopathology." *Psychological Trauma: Theory, Research, Practice, and Policy* 7(4): 382–390.

Boese, V. A., Alizada, N., Lundstedt, M., Morrison, K., Natsika, N., Sato, Y., Tai, H., and Lindberg, S. I. 2022. *Democracy Report 2022: Autocratization Changing Nature?* Gothenburg, Sweden: Varieties of Democracy Institute at the University of Gothenburg.

Bollen, J., Ten Thij, M., Breithaupt, F., Barron, A. T., Rutter, L. A., Lorenzo-Luaces, L., and Scheffer, M. 2021. "Historical Language Records Reveal a Surge of Cognitive Distortions in Recent Decades." *Proceedings of the National Academy of Sciences* 118(30): e2102061118.

Bolt, J., and van Zanden, J. 2020. "Maddison Style Estimates of the Evolution of the World Economy: A New 2020 Update." Maddison-Project Working Paper WP-15, The Maddison Project, Groningen, The Netherlands.

Bolton, P., Adrian, T., and Kleinnijenhuis, A. 2022. "The Great Carbon Arbitrage." IMF Working Paper 2022/102, International Monetary Fund, Washington, DC.

Bolton, P., Despress, M., da Silva, L., Samama, F., and Svartzman, R. 2020. *The Green Swan—Central Banking and Financial Stability in the Age of Climate Change.* Basel, Switzerland, Bank for International Settlements.

Bonn, G. 2015. "Primary Process Emotion, Identity, and Culture: Cultural Identification's Roots in Basic Motivation." *Frontiers in Psychology* 6: 218.

Bonomi, G., Gennaioli, N., and Tabellini, G. 2021. "Identity, Beliefs, and Political Conflict." *The Quarterly Journal of Economics* 136(4): 2371–2411.

Bordalo, P., Gennaioli, N., and Shleifer, A. 2012. "Salience Theory of Choice under Risk." *The Quarterly Journal of Economics* 127(3): 1243–1285.

Bordalo, P., Gennaioli, N., and Shleifer, A. 2021. "Salience." NBER Working Paper 29274, National Bureau of Economic Research, Cambridge, MA.

Bosi, L., Giugni, M., and Uba, K. 2016. "The Consequences of Social Movements: Tacking Stock and Looking Forward." In Bosi, L., Giugni, M., and Uba, K., (eds.), *The Consequences of Social Movements.* Cambridge, UK: Cambridge University Press.

Bosqui, T. J., Marshoud, B., and Shannon, C. 2017. "Attachment Insecurity, Posttraumatic Stress, and Hostility in Adolescents Exposed to Armed Conflict." *Peace and Conflict: Journal of Peace Psychology* 23(4): 372–382.

Bostrom, N. 2002. "Existential Risks: Analyzing Human Extinction Scenarios and Related Hazards." *Journal of Evolution and Technology* 9(1): 1–31.

Bostrom, N. 2013. "Existential Risk Prevention as Global Priority." *Global Policy* 4(1): 15–31.

Boulton, C. A., Lenton, T. M., and Boers, N. 2022. "Pronounced Loss of Amazon Rainforest Resilience since the Early 2000s." *Nature Climate Change* 12(3): 271–278.

Bowen, T., Del Ninno, C., Andrews, C., Coll-Black, S., Johnson, K., Kawasoe, Y., Kryeziu, A., and others. 2020. *Adaptive Social Protection: Building Resilience to Shocks.* Washington, DC: World Bank.

Bowles, S., and Carlin, W. 2021. "Shrinking Capitalism: Components of a New Political Economy Paradigm." *Oxford Review of Economic Policy* 37(4): 794–810.

Bown, C. P. B., Thomas J. 2021. "How Covid-19 Vaccine Supply Chains Emerged in the Midst of a Pandemic." PIIE Working Paper 21–12, Peterson Institute for International Economics, Washington, DC.

Boxell, L., Gentzkow, M., and Shapiro, J. M. 2020. "Cross-Country Trends in Affective Polarization." NBER Working Paper 26669, National Bureau of Economic Research, Cambridge, MA.

Box-Steffensmeier, J. M., Burgess, J., Corbetta, M., Crawford, K., Duflo, E., Fogarty, L., Gopnik, A., and others. 2022. "The Future of Human Behaviour Research." *Nature Human Behaviour* 6(1): 15–24.

Boyd, D., and Keene, S. 2021. "Human Rights-Based Approaches to Conserving Biodiversity: Equitable, Effective and Imperative." Policy Brief 1. Office of the United Nations High Commissioner for Refugees, Geneva. https://www.ohchr.org/Documents/Issues/Environment/SREnvironment/policy-briefing-1.pdf.

Boyd, R., Richerson, P. J., and Henrich, J. 2011. "The Cultural Niche: Why Social Learning Is Essential for Human Adaptation." *Proceedings of the National Academy of Sciences* 108(Supplement 2): 10918–10925.

Boyle, M. H., Georgiades, K., Duncan, L., Wang, L., Comeau, J., and 2014 Ontario Child Health Study Team. 2019. "Poverty, Neighbourhood Antisocial Behaviour, and Children's Mental Health Problems: Findings from the 2014 Ontario Child Health Study." *The Canadian Journal of Psychiatry* 64(4): 285–293.

Bozdag, E. 2013. "Bias in Algorithmic Filtering and Personalization." *Ethics and Information Technology* 15: 209–227.

BP. 2020. *Energy Outlook: 2020 Edition.* London.

Bradtmöller, M., Grimm, S., and Riel-Salvatore, J. 2017. "Resilience Theory in Archaeological Practice—an Annotated Review." *Quaternary International* 446: 3–16.

Brady, W. J., Wills, J. A., Jost, J. T., Tucker, J. A., and Van Bavel, J. J. 2017. "Emotion Shapes the Diffusion of Moralized Content in Social Networks." *Proceedings of the National Academy of Sciences* 114(28): 7313–7318.

Brannen, S., Haig, C., and Schmidt, K. 2020. "The Age of Mass Protests: Understanding an Escalating Global Trend." Center for Strategic and International Studies, Washington, DC.

Brännlund, A., Strandh, M., and Nilsson, K. 2017. "Mental-Health and Educational Achievement: The Link between Poor Mental-Health and Upper Secondary School Completion and Grades." *Journal of Mental Health* 26(4): 318–325.

Bratman, G. N., Anderson, C. B., Berman, M. G., Cochran, B., De Vries, S., Flanders, J., Folke, C., and others. 2019. "Nature and Mental Health: An Ecosystem Service Perspective." *Science Advances* 5(7).

Brenisen, W. 2020. "Loss of Agency: How Domestic Violence Impacts Mental Health." Women's Advocates, Saint Paul, MN. https://www.wadvocates.org/2020/05/26/loss-of-agency-how-domestic-violence-impacts-mental-health/. Accessed 30 Aug 2021.

Brennan, G., and Sayre-McCord, G. 2018. "On 'Cooperation'." *Analyse & Kritik* 40(1): 107–130.

Breukers, S., and Wolsink, M. 2007. "Wind Power Implementation in Changing Institutional Landscapes: An International Comparison." *Energy Policy* 35(5): 2737–2750.

Brierley, C., Manning, K., and Maslin, M. 2018. "Pastoralism May Have Delayed the End of the Green Sahara." *Nature Communications* 9(1): 1–9.

Bringezu, S., Ramaswami, A., Schandl, H., O'Brien, M., Pelton, R., Acquatella, J., Ayuk, E., and others. 2017. "Assessing Global Resource Use: A System Approach to Resource Efficiency and Pollution Reduction." United Nations Environment Programme, International Resource Panel, Nairobi.

Brook, T. 2010. *The Troubled Empire: China in the Yuan and Ming Dynasties.* Cambridge, MA: Harvard University Press.

Brooke, J. 2015. *Climate Change and the Course of Global History: A Rough Journey.* Cambridge, UK: Cambridge University Press.

Brown, R. P., and Gerbarg, P. L. 2005. "Sudarshan Kriya Yogic Breathing in the Treatment of Stress, Anxiety, and Depression: Part I—Neurophysiologic Model." *Journal of Alternative & Complementary Medicine* 11(1): 189–201.

Bruine de Bruin, W., Saw, H.-W., and Goldman, D. P. 2020. "Political Polarization in US Residents' Covid-19 Risk Perceptions, Policy Preferences, and Protective Behaviors." *Journal of Risk and Uncertainty* 61(2): 177–194.

Bruneau, E., Hameiri, B., Moore-Berg, S. L., and Kteily, N. 2021. "Intergroup Contact Reduces Dehumanization and Meta-Dehumanization: Cross-Sectional, Longitudinal, and Quasi-Experimental Evidence from 16 Samples in Five Countries." *Personality and Social Psychology Bulletin* 47(6): 906–920.

Bryan, K., Lemus, J., and Marshall, G. 2020. "Crises and the Direction of Innovation." https://ssrn.com/abstract=3587973.

Brynjolfsson, E. 2022. "The Turing Trap: The Promise & Peril of Human-Like Artificial Intelligence." *Daedalus* (Spring 2022).

Brynjolfsson, E., and McAfee, A. 2015. "Moore's Law and the Second Half of the Chessboard." In *The Second Machine Age: Work, Progress, and Prosperity in a Time of Brilliant Technologies.* New York: W. W. Norton & Company.

Bubonya, M., Cobb-Clark, D. A., and Wooden, M. 2017. "Mental Health and Productivity at Work: Does What You Do Matter?" *Labour Economics* 46: 150–165.

Buchanan, A. 2020. *Our Moral Fate: Evolution and the Escape from Tribalism.* Cambridge, MA: MIT Press.

Buchanan, A., and Powell, R. 2018. *The Evolution of Moral Progress: A Biocultural Theory.* Oxford, UK: Oxford University Press.

Buckley, B. M., Anchukaitis, K. J., Penny, D., Fletcher, R., Cook, E. R., Sano, M., Nam L. C., and others. 2010. "Climate as a Contributing Factor in the Demise of Angkor, Cambodia." *Proceedings of the National Academy of Sciences* 107(15): 6748–6752.

Buell, B., Cherif, R., Chen, C., Seo, H.-J., Tang, J., and Wendt, N. 2021. "Impact of Covid-19: Nowcasting and Big Data to Track Economic Activity in Sub-Saharan Africa." Working Paper 2021/124. International Monetary Fund, Washington, DC.

Buggle, J. C., and Durante, R. 2021. "Climate Risk, Cooperation and the Co-Evolution of Culture and Institutions." *The Economic Journal* 131(637): 1947–1987.

Burke, M., Hsiang, S. M., and Miguel, E. 2015. "Climate and Conflict." *Annual Review of Economics* 7(1): 577–617.

Burnet, J. E. 2021. "Transitional Justice as Interruption: Adaptive Peacebuilding and Resilience in Rwanda." In Clark, J. N., and Ungar, M., (eds.), *Resilience, Adaptive Peacebuilding and Transitional Justice: How Societies Recover after Collective Violence.* Cambridge, UK: Cambridge University Press.

Bursztyn, L., and Yang, D. 2021. "Misperceptions About Others." University of Chicago, Becker Friedman Institute for Economics.

Bursztyn, L., González, A. L., and Yanagizawa-Drott, D. 2018. "Misperceived Social Norms: Female Labor Force Participation in Saudi Arabia." NBER Working Paper 24736, National Bureau of Economic Research, Cambridge, MA.

Business of Apps. 2022. "Dating App Revenue and Usage Statistics 2022." https://www.businessofapps.com/data/dating-app-market/. Accessed 8 August 2022.

Butler, L. D., Waelde, L. C., Hastings, T. A., Chen, X. H., Symons, B., Marshall, J., Kaufman, J., and others. 2008. "Meditation with Yoga, Group Therapy with Hypnosis, and Psychoeducation for Long-Term Depressed Mood: A Randomized Pilot Trial." *Journal of Clinical Psychology* 64(7): 806–820.

Buyalskaya, A., Gallo, M., and Camerer, C. F. 2021. "The Golden Age of Social Science." *Proceedings of the National Academy of Sciences* 118(5): e2002923118.

Cai, Y. 2020. "The Role of Uncertainty in Controlling Climate Change." *arXiv preprint arXiv:2003.01615*.

Callander, E. J., and Schofield, D. J. 2018. "Psychological Distress Increases the Risk of Falling into Poverty Amongst Older Australians: The Overlooked Costs-of-Illness." *BioMedCentral Psychology* 6(1): 1–9.

Callaway, F., Jain, Y. R., Opheusden, B. v., Das, P., Iwama, G., Gul, S., Krueger, P. M., and others. 2022. "Leveraging Artificial Intelligence to Improve People's Planning Strategies." *Proceedings of the National Academy of Sciences* 119(12).

Calo, R., Coward, C., Spiro, E., Starbird, K., and West, J. 2021. "How Do You Solve a Problem Like Misinformation?" *Science Advances* 7(50).

Campbell, B. 2016. *The Great Transition: Climate, Disease and Society in the Late-Medieval World*. Cambridge, UK: Cambridge University Press.

Campbell, B. 2017. "Global Climates, the 1257 Mega-Eruptions of Samalas Volcano, Indonesia, and the English Food Crisis of 1258." *Transactions of the Royal Historical Society* 27: 87–121.

Campiglio, E., Dafermos, Y., Monnin, P., Ryan-Collins, J., Schotten, G., and Tanaka, M. 2018. "Climate Change Challenges for Central Banks and Financial Regulators." *Nature Climate Change* 8(6): 462–468.

CARE (Cooperative for Cooperative for Assistance and Relief Everywhere). 2019. "Strengthening Resilience and Promoting Inclusive Governance Program (STRENPO)." Geneva. https://careclimatechange.org/wp-content/uploads/2019/03/Leaflet-STRENPO.pdf.

CARE (Cooperative for Cooperative for Assistance and Relief Everywhere). 2020. "She Told Us So. Rapid Gender Analysis: Filling the Data Gap to Build Back Equal." https://www.care.org/wp-content/uploads/2020/09/RGA_SheToldUsSo_9.18.20.pdf.

Carlson, C. J., Albery, G. F., Merow, C., Trisos, C. H., Zipfel, C. M., Eskew, E. A., Olival, K. J., and others. 2022. "Climate Change Increases Cross-Species Viral Transmission Risk." *Nature* 607: 555–562.

Carothers, T., and O'Donohue, A., (eds.). 2019. *Democracies Divided, the Global Challenge of Political Polarization*. Washington, DC: Brookings Institution Press.

Carter, B., Roelen, K., Enfield, S., and Avis, W. 2019. "Social Protection: Topic Guide." K4D Emerging Issues Report, Institute of Development Studies, Brighton, UK.

Carter, K. N., Kruse, K., Blakely, T., and Collings, S. 2011. "The Association of Food Security with Psychological Distress in New Zealand and Any Gender Differences." *Social Science & Medicine* 72(9): 1463–1471.

Carver, C. S., Scheier, M. F., and Segerstrom, S. C. 2010. "Optimism." *Clinical Psychology Review* 30(7): 879–889.

Case, A., and Deaton, A. 2015. "Rising Morbidity and Mortality in Midlife among White Non-Hispanic Americans in the 21st Century." *Proceedings of the National Academy of Sciences* 112(49): 15078–15083.

Case, A., and Deaton, A. 2020. *Deaths of Despair and the Future of Capitalism*. Princeton, NJ: Princeton University Press.

Castegnetti, G., Zurita, M., and Martino, B. D. 2021. "How Usefulness Shapes Neural Representations During Goal-Directed Behavior." *Science Advances* 7(15): eabd5363.

Center on the Developing Child. 2013. "Early Childhood Mental Health. Inbrief." https://www.developingchild.harvard.edu. Accessed 29 January 2021.

Center on the Developing Child. 2021. "Brain Architecture." https://developingchild.harvard.edu/science/key-concepts/brain-architecture/. Accessed 29 January 2021.

Cerra, V., Eichengreen, B., El-Ganainy, A., and Schindle, M. 2021. *How to Achieve Inclusive Growth*. Oxford, UK: Oxford University Press.

Chancel, L., Piketty, T., Saez, E., and Zucman, G. 2022. *World Inequality Report 2022*. Paris: World Inequality Lab, Paris School of Economics.

Chandan, J. S., Thomas, T., Bradbury-Jones, C., Russell, R., Bandyopadhyay, S., Nirantharakumar, K., and Taylor, J. 2020. "Female Survivors of Intimate Partner Violence and Risk of Depression, Anxiety and Serious Mental Illness." *The British Journal of Psychiatry* 217(4): 562–567.

Chen, Y., and Zhong, S. 2021. "Uncertainty Motivates Morality: Evidence and Theory." https://ssrn.com/abstract=3737959.

Cheng, J. T., Tracy, J. L., Foulsham, T., Kingstone, A., and Henrich, J. 2013. "Two Ways to the Top: Evidence That Dominance and Prestige Are Distinct yet Viable Avenues to Social Rank and Influence." *Journal of Personality and Social Psychology* 104(1): 103–125.

Chittka, L., Skorupski, P., and Raine, N. 2009. "Speed–Accuracy Tradeoffs in Animal Decision Making." *Trends in Ecology & Evolution* 24(7): 400–407.

Choi, V. K., Shrestha, S., Pan, X., and Gelfand, M. J. 2022. "When Danger Strikes: A Linguistic Tool for Tracking America's Collective Response to Threats." *Proceedings of the National Academy of Sciences* 119(4): e2113891119.

Christensen, J., and Moynihan, D. P. 2020. "Motivated Reasoning and Policy Information: Politicians Are More Resistant to Debiasing Interventions Than the General Public." *Behavioural Public Policy*: 1–22.

Christian, C., Hensel, L., and Roth, C. 2019. "Income Shocks and Suicides: Causal Evidence from Indonesia." *Review of Economics and Statistics* 101(5): 905–920.

Christiansen, J. 2009. "Four Stages of Social Movements." EBSCO Research Starters 1248.

Chung, M. G., and Liu, J. 2022. "International Food Trade Benefits Biodiversity and Food Security in Low-Income Countries." *Nature Food* 3(5): 349–355.

Ciancaglini, V., Gibson, C., Sancho, D., McCarthy, O., Eira, M., Amann, P., and Klayn, A. 2020. "Malicious Uses and Abuses of Artificial Intelligence." Trend Micro Research, European Union Agency for Law Enforcement Cooperation, The Hague, The Netherlands.

Cianconi, P., Betrò, S., and Janiri, L. 2020. "The Impact of Climate Change on Mental Health: A Systematic Descriptive Review." *Frontiers in Psychiatry* 11: 74–90.

Cicchiello, A. F., Kazemikhasragh, A., Monferrá, S., and Girón, A. 2021. "Financial Inclusion and Development in the Least Developed Countries in Asia and Africa." *Journal of Innovation and Entrepreneurship* 10(1): 1–13.

Cimino, A. N., Yi, G., Patch, M., Alter, Y., Campbell, J. C., Gundersen, K. K., Tang, J. T., Tsuyuki, K., and Stockman, J. K. 2019. "The Effect of Intimate Partner Violence and Probable Traumatic Brain Injury on Mental Health Outcomes for Black Women." *Journal of Aggression, Maltreatment & Trauma* 28(6): 714–731.

Circle Economy. 2020. *The Circularity Gap Report*. Amsterdam.

Clark, R., Anderson, N. B., Clark, V. R., and Williams, D. R. 1999. "Racism as a Stressor for African Americans: A Biopsychosocial Model." *American Psychologist* 54(10): 805–816.

Clark, W. C., and Harley, A. G. 2020. "Sustainability Science: Toward a Synthesis." *Annual Review of Environment and Resources* 45(1): 331–386.

Claussen, M., Dallmeyer, A., and Bader, J. 2017. "Theory and Modeling of the African Humid Period and the Green Sahara." *Oxford Research Encyclopedia of Climate Science*.

Clayton, S. 2020. "Climate Anxiety: Psychological Responses to Climate Change." *Journal of Anxiety Disorders* 74: 102263.

Clouston, S., Rubin, M., Phelan, J., and Link, B. 2016. "A Social History of Disease: Contextualizing the Rise and Fall of Social Inequalities in Cause-Specific Mortality." *Demography* 53(5): 1631–1656.

Cockrill, K., and Biggs, A. 2018. "Can Stories Reduce Abortion Stigma? Findings from a Longitudinal Cohort Study." *Culture, Health & Sexuality* 20(3): 335–350.

Coeckelbergh, M. 2011. "Human Development or Human Enhancement? A Methodological Reflection on Capabilities and the Evaluation of Information Technologies." *Ethics and Information Technology* 13(2): 81–92.

Cohen, D., Shin, F., and Liu, X. 2019. "Meanings and Functions of Money in Different Cultural Milieus." *Annual Review of Psychology* 70(1): 475–497.

Cohen, J., Ericson, K. M., Laibson, D., and White, J. M. 2020. "Measuring Time Preferences." *Journal of Economic Literature* 58(2): 299–347.

Colander, D., and Roland, K. 2014. *Complexity and the Art of Public Policy: Solving Society's Problems from the Bottom Up*. Princeton, NJ: Princeton University Press.

Cole, M. A., Ozgen, C., and Strobl, E. 2020. "Air Pollution Exposure and Covid-19 in Dutch Municipalities." *Environmental and Resource Economics* 76(4): 581–610.

Collier, P., Coyle, D., Mayer, C., and Wolf, M. 2021. "Capitalism: What Has Gone Wrong, What Needs to Change, and How It Can Be Fixed." *Oxford Review of Economic Policy* 37(4): 637–649.

Collins, A., Florin, M.-V., and Sachs, R. 2021. "Risk Governance and the Low-Carbon Transition." École Polytechnique Fédérale de Lausanne, International Risk Governance Center, Lausanne, Switzerland.

Collins, D., Morduch, J., Rutherford, S., and Ruthven, O. 2009. *Portfolios of the Poor.* Princeton, NJ: Princeton University Press.

Collins, L. T., and Curiel, D. 2021. "Synthetic Biology Approaches for Engineering Next-Generation Adenoviral Gene Therapies." *ACS Nano* 5(9): 13970–13979.

Comim, F. 2011. "Developing Children's Capabilities: The Role of Emotions and Parenting Style." In Biggeri, M., Ballet, J., and Comim, F., (eds.), *Children and the Capability Approach.* London: Palgrave Macmillan.

Computational Story Lab. n.d. "Average Happiness for Twitter, Hedonometer." https://hedonometer.org/timeseries/en_all/?from=2020-01-01&to=2020-12-31. Accessed 4 May 2022.

Connolly, E. J., and Jackson, D. B. 2019. "Adolescent Gang Membership and Adverse Behavioral, Mental Health, and Physical Health Outcomes in Young Adulthood: A within-Family Analysis." *Criminal Justice and Behavior* 46(11): 1566–1586.

Conradie, I., and Robeyns, I. 2013. "Aspirations and Human Development Interventions." *Journal of Human Development and Capabilities* 14(4): 559–580.

Contraloría General de la República de Costa Rica. 2020. "Informe De Auditoría Operativa Sobre La Eficacia Y Eficiencia Del Bono Proteger Implementado Por El Ministerio De Trabajo Y Seguridad Social Y El Instituto Mixto De Ayuda Social Ante La Emergencia Sanitaria Provocada Por La Enfermedad Covid-19." Área de Fiscalización de Servicios Sociales, San José.

Cook, E. R., Woodhouse, C. A., Eakin, C. M., Meko, D. M., and Stahle, D. W. 2004. "Long-Term Aridity Changes in the Western United States." *Science* 306(5698): 1015–1018.

Cooney, P., and Shaefer, H. L. 2021. "Material Hardship and Mental Health Following the Covid-19 Relief Bill and American Rescue Plan Act. Poverty Solutions." University of Michigan, Ann Arbor, MI. http://sites.fordschool.umich.edu/poverty2021/files/2021/05/PovertySolutions-Hardship-After-COVID-19-Relief-Bill-PolicyBrief-r1.pdf.

Coote, A., and Percy, A. 2020. *The Case for Universal Basic Services.* Hoboken, NJ: John Wiley & Sons.

Cosmides, L., and Tooby, J. 2013. "Evolutionary Psychology: New Perspectives on Cognition and Motivation." *Annual Review of Psychology* 64(1): 201–229.

Cosmides, L., Barrett, H. C., and Tooby, J. 2010. "Adaptive Specializations, Social Exchange, and the Evolution of Human Intelligence." *Proceedings of the National Academy of Sciences* 107(supplement 2): 9007–9014.

Costa, D. 2021. "Health Shocks of the Father and Longevity of the Children's Children." NBER Working Paper 29553, National Bureau of Economic Research, Cambridge, MA.

Costello, E. J., Compton, S. N., Keeler, G., and Angold, A. 2003. "Relationships between Poverty and Psychopathology: A Natural Experiment." *JAMA* 290(15): 2023–2029.

Coyle, D. 2021. *Cogs and Monsters: What Economics Is, and What It Should Be.* Princeton, NJ: Princeton University Press.

Crabtree, A. 2012. "Climate Change and Mental Health Following Flood Disasters in Developing Countries, a Review of the Epidemiological Literature: What Do We Know, What Is Being Recommended." *Australasian Journal of Disaster and Trauma Studies* 1: 21–30.

Crabtree, A. 2022a. "The Anthropocene, Nature-Based Security and Mental Health." Background paper for Human Development Report 2021/2022, UNDP–HDRO, New York.

Crabtree, A. 2022b. "Looking Forward: Eco-Emotions, Planetary Pressures and Nature-Based Human Development." Background paper for Human Development Report 2021/2022, UNDP–HDRO, New York.

Crona, B., Folke, C., and Galaz, V. 2021. "The Anthropocene Reality of Financial Risk." *One Earth* 4(5): 618–628.

Crutchfield, L. R. 2018. *How Change Happens: Why Some Social Movements Succeed While Others Don't.* Hoboken, NJ: John Wiley & Sons.

Crutzen, P. J., and Stoermer, E. F. 2000. "The Anthropocene." *Global Change Newsletter* 41: 17–18.

Cruz, M. S., Silva, E. S., Jakaite, Z., Krenzinger, M., Valiati, L., Gonçalves, D., Ribeiro, E., Heritage, P., and Priebe, S. 2021. "Experience of Neighbourhood Violence and Mental Distress in Brazilian Favelas: A Cross-Sectional Household Survey." *The Lancet Regional Health-Americas* 4: 1–8.

Cuartas, J., and Leventhal, T. 2020. "Exposure to Community Violence and Children's Mental Health: A Quasi-Experimental Examination." *Social Science & Medicine* 246: 2–41.

Cui, J., Chang, H., Burr, G. S., Zhao, X., and Jiang, B. 2019. "Climatic Change and the Rise of the Manchu from Northeast China During AD 1600–1650." *Climatic Change* 156(3): 405–423.

Cukier, K., Mayer-Schönberger, V., and de Véricourt, F. 2022. *Framers: Human Advantage in an Age of Technology and Turmoil.* London: Penguin.

Cunsolo, A., and Ellis, N. R. 2018. "Ecological Grief as a Mental Health Response to Climate Change-Related Loss." *Nature Climate Change* 8(4): 275–281.

Cunsolo, A., Harper, S. L., Ford, J. D., Edge, V. L., Landman, K., Houle, K., Blake, S., and Wolfrey, C. 2013. "Climate Change and Mental Health: An Exploratory Case Study from Rigolet, Nunatsiavut, Canada." *Climatic Change* 121(2): 255–270.

CUNY Advanced Science Research Center. 2021. "Green and Gray Infrastructure-Dependent Pathways for Human Development: Contemporary State and Analytics, Project Report." Background paper for Human Development Report 2021/2022, UNDP–HDRO, New York.

Curtis, D. R., and Dijkman, J. 2019. "The Escape from Famine in the Northern Netherlands: A Reconsideration Using the 1690s Harvest Failures and a Broader Northwest European Perspective." *The Seventeenth Century* 34(2): 229–258.

Curtis, P. G., Slay, C. M., Harris, N. L., Tyukavina, A., and Hansen, M. C. 2018. "Classifying Drivers of Global Forest Loss." *Science* 361(6407): 1108–1111.

Cutler, D., Deaton, A., and Lleras-Muney, A. 2006. "The Determinants of Mortality." *Journal of Economic Perspectives* 20(3): 97–120.

Cyranoski, D., and Ledford, H. 2018. "Genome-Edited Baby Claim Provokes International Outcry." *Nature* 563(7731): 607–609.

Czeisler, M. É., Lane, R. I., Petrosky, E., Wiley, J. F., Christensen, A., Njai, R., Weaver, M. D., and others. 2020. "Mental Health, Substance Use, and Suicidal Ideation During the Covid-19 Pandemic—United States, June 24–30, 2020." *Morbidity and Mortality Weekly Report* 69(32): 1049.

D'Acunto, F., Hoang, D., Paloviita, M., and Weber, M. 2021. "Human Frictions in the Transmission of Economic Policies." NBER Working Paper 29279, National Bureau of Economic Research, Cambridge, MA.

Dallman, M. F. 2010. "Stress-Induced Obesity and the Emotional Nervous System." *Trends in Endocrinology & Metabolism* 21(3): 159–165.

Dami, B., James, A., Zubairu, D., Karick, H., and Dakwak, S. 2018. "Combat Exposure and PTSD among Military Combatants in North East Nigeria." *Journal of Psychology & Clinical Psychiatry* 9(4): 400–404.

Danese, A., and Lewis, S. J. 2017. "Psychoneuroimmunology of Early-Life Stress: The Hidden Wounds of Childhood Trauma?" *Neuropsychopharmacology* 42(1): 99–114.

Danese, A., Dove, R., Belsky, D., Henchy, J., Williams, B., Ambler, A., and Arseneault, L. 2014. "Leptin Deficiency in Maltreated Children." *Translational Psychiatry* 4(9): e446.

Dannenberg, A., and Barrett, S. 2018. "Cooperating to Avoid Catastrophe." *Nature Human Behaviour* 2(7): 435–437.

Darbyshire, E., and Weir, D. 2021. "How Does War Contribute to Climate Change?" Conflict and Environment Observatory Blog, 14 June. https://ceobs.org/how-does-war-contribute-to-climate-change/. Accessed 25 August 2022.

Darwall, S. 2009. *The Second-Person Standpoint.* Cambridge, MA: Harvard University Press.

Dasgupta, P. 2021. *The Economics of Biodiversity: The Dasgupta Review.* London: HM Treasury.

Dasgupta, P., and Maskin, E. 2005. "Uncertainty and Hyperbolic Discounting." *American Economic Review* 95(4): 1290–1299.

Daugherty, J. C., Verdejo-Román, J., Pérez-García, M., and Hidalgo-Ruzzante, N. 2020. "Structural Brain Alterations in Female Survivors of Intimate Partner Violence." *Journal of Interpersonal Violence* 37(7–8): 1–34.

Dávideková, M. 2016. "Digitalization of Society: Smartphone—a Threat?" Paper presented at the International Research Conference on Management Challenges in the 21st Century, 12 April, Bratislava. http://www.cutn.sk/Library/proceedings/mch_2016/editovane_prispevky/30_Davidekova.pdf.

Davies, M., Béné, C., Arnall, A., Tanner, T., Newsham, A., and Coirolo, C. 2013. "Promoting Resilient Livelihoods through Adaptive Social Protection: Lessons from 124 Programmes in South Asia." *Development Policy Review* 31(1): 27–58.

Davies, S., Pettersson, T., and Öberg, M. 2022. "Organized violence 1989-2021 and drone warfare." *Journal of Peace Research* 59(4).

Davis, M. 2002. *Late Victorian Holocausts: El Niño Famines and the Making of the Third World.* New York: Verso Books.

Davydov, D. M., Stewart, R., Ritchie, K., and Chaudieu, I. 2010. "Resilience and Mental Health." *Clinical Psychology Review* 30(5): 479–495.

Dawes, R. M., and Thaler, R. H. 1988. "Anomalies: Cooperation." *Journal of Economic Perspectives* 2(3): 187–197.

de Ágreda, Á. G. 2020. "Ethics of Autonomous Weapons Systems and Its Applicability to Any Ai Systems." *Telecommunications Policy* 44(6): 101953.

de Bruijn, E.-J., and Antonides, G. 2021. "Poverty and Economic Decision Making: A Review of Scarcity Theory." *Theory and Decision* 92: 1–33.

De Coning, C. 2018. "Adaptive Peacebuilding." *International Affairs* 94(2): 301–317.

De Coning, C. 2020a. "Adaptive Peace Operations: Navigating the Complexity of Influencing Societal Change without Causing Harm." *International Peacekeeping* 27(5): 836–858.

De Coning, C. 2020b. "The Six Principles of Adaptive Peacebuilding." *Conflict Trends* 2020(1): 3–10.

De Moor, A. 2013. "Creativity Meets Rationale: Collaboration Patterns for Social Innovation." *Creativity and Rationale*: 1–29.

de Raús Maúre, E., Terauchi, G., Ishizaka, J., Clinton, N., and DeWitt, M. 2021. "Globally Consistent Assessment of Coastal Eutrophication." *Nature Communications* 12(1): 1–9.

de Souza, J. G., Robinson, M., Maezumi, S. Y., Capriles, J., Hoggarth, J. A., Lombardo, U., Novello, V. F., and others. 2019. "Climate Change and Cultural Resilience in Late Pre-Columbian Amazonia." *Nature Ecology & Evolution* 3(7): 1007–1017.

Dean, J. A. 2022. "A Golden Decade of Deep Learning: Computing Systems & Applications." *Daedalus* (Spring 2022).

Dean, M., and Ortoleva, P. 2019. "The Empirical Relationship between Nonstandard Economic Behaviors." *Proceedings of the National Academy of Sciences* 116(33): 16262–16267.

Deaton, A. 2003. "Health, Inequality, and Economic Development." *Journal of Economic Literature* 41(1): 113–158.

Deaton, A. 2013a. *The Great Escape: Health, Wealth, and the Origins of Inequality.* Princeton, NJ: Princeton University Press.

Deaton, A. 2013b. "What Does the Empirical Evidence Tell Us About the Injustice of Health Inequalities." In Eyal, N., Hurst, S. A., Norheim, O. F., and D. Wikler, (eds.), *Inequalities in Health: Concepts Measures, and Ethics.* Oxford, UK: Oxford University Press.

Deb, J. 2020. "Cooperation and Community Responsibility." *Journal of Political Economy* 128(5): 1976–2009.

Decker, M. 2009. *Tilling the Hateful Earth: Agricultural Production and Trade in the Late Antique East.* Oxford, UK: Oxford University Press.

DeFries, R. 2020. *What Would Nature Do? A Guide for Our Uncertain Times.* New York: Columbia University Press.

DeFronzo, J., and Gill, J. 2020. *Social Problems and Social Movements.* London: Rowman & Littlefield Publishers.

Degrave, J., Felici, F., Buchli, J., Neunert, M., Tracey, B., Carpanese, F., Ewalds, T., and others. 2022. "Magnetic Control of Tokamak Plasmas through Deep Reinforcement Learning." *Nature* 602(7897): 414–419.

Degroot, D. 2018. *The Frigid Golden Age: Climate Change, the Little Ice Age, and the Dutch Republic, 1560–1720.* Cambridge, UK: Cambridge University Press.

Degroot, D. 2019. "Little Ice Age Lessons." https://aeon.co/essays/the-little-ice-age-is-a-history-of-resilience-and-surprises. Accessed 20 March 2022.

Degroot, D., Anchukaitis, K., Bauch, M., Burnham, J., Carnegy, F., Cui, J., de Luna, K., and others. 2021. "Towards a Rigorous Understanding of Societal Responses to Climate Change." *Nature* 591(7851): 539–550.

Dein, S. 2020. "Religious Healing and Mental Health." *Mental Health, Religion & Culture* 23(8): 657–665.

Delgado, C. 2022. "War in the Breadbasket: The Ripple Effects on Food Insecurity and Conflict Risk Beyond Ukraine." WritePeace Blog, 1 April. https://www.sipri.org/commentary/blog/2022/war-breadbasket-ripple-effects-food-insecurity-and-conflict-risk-beyond-ukraine. Accessed 28 April 2022.

Demeke, H. B., Merali, S., Marks, S., Pao, L. Z., Romero, L., Sandhu, P., Clark, H., and others. 2021. "Trends in Use of Telehealth among Health Centers During the Covid-19 Pandemic -- United States, June 26 - November 6, 2020." *Morbidity and Mortality Weekly Report* 70(7): 240–244.

Demeritt, A., and Hoff, K. 2018. "The Making of Behavioral Development Economics." *History of Political Economy* 50(S1): 303–322.

Demirgüç-Kunt, A., Klapper, L., Singer, D., and Ansar, S. 2022. *The Global Findex Database 2021.* Washington, DC: World Bank.

Denning, P. J., and Yaholkovsky, P. 2008. "Getting to 'We'." *Communications of the ACM* 51(4): 19–24.

De-Shalit, A. 1995. *Why Posterity Matters.* Abingdon, UK: Routledge.

Desiderio, M. V. 2016. "Integrating Refugees into Host Country Labor Markets: Challenges and Policy Options." Migration Policy Institute, Washington, DC.

Deuze, M. 2006. "Participation, Remediation, Bricolage: Considering Principal Components of a Digital Culture." *The Information Society* 22(2): 63–75.

Devroey, J., P., 2003. *Économie Rurale Et Société Dans L›europe Franque (Vie-Ixe Siècles).* Paris: Belin.

Di Domenico, G., Sit, J., Ishizaka, A., and Nunan, D. 2021. "Fake News, Social Media and Marketing: A Systematic Review." *Journal of Business Research* 124: 329–341.

Diamond, J. 2005. *Collapse: How Societies Choose to Fail or Succeed.* New York: Penguin.

Diamond, L. 2015. "Facing up to the Democratic Recession." *Journal of Democracy* 26(1): 141–155.

Díaz, S., Settele, J., Brondízio, E. S., Ngo, H. T., Agard, J., Arneth, A., Balvanera, P., and others. 2019. "Pervasive Human-Driven Decline of Life on Earth Points to the Need for Transformative Change." *Science* 366(6471): eaax3100.

Díaz-Bonilla, E., Piñeiro, V., De Salvo, C. P., and Laborde Debucquet, D. 2021. "Haiti: The Impact of Covid-19 and Preliminary Policy Implications: Interim Report." LAC Working Paper 18. International Food Policy Research Institute, Washington, DC.

Dickerson-Amaya, N., and Coston, B. M. 2019. "Invisibility Is Not Invincibility: The Impact of Intimate Partner Violence on Gay, Bisexual, and Straight Men's Mental Health." *American Journal of Men's Health* 13(3): 1–12.

Dierkhising, C. B., Sánchez, J. A., and Gutierrez, L. 2019. "'It Changed My Life': Traumatic Loss, Behavioral Health, and Turning Points among Gang-Involved and Justice-Involved Youth." *Journal of Interpersonal Violence* 36(17): 8027–8049.

DiMaggio, P. 1997. "Culture and Cognition." *Annual Review of Sociology* 23(1): 263–287.

DiMaggio, P., and Hargittai, E. 2001. "From the 'Digital Divide' to 'Digital Inequality': Studying Internet Use as Penetration Increases." Working Paper 15, Princeton University, Woodrow Wilson School, Center for Arts and Cultural Policy Studies, Princeton, NJ. https://digitalinclusion.typepad.com/digital_inclusion/documentos/digitalinequality.pdf.

Diorio, J., and Meaney, M. J. 2007. "Maternal Programming of Defensive Responses through Sustained Effects on Gene Expression." *Journal of Psychiatry and Neuroscience* 32(4): 275–284.

Dodds, P. S., Clark, E. M., Desu, S., Frank, M. R., Reagan, A. J., Williams, J. R., Mitchell, L., and others. 2015. "Human Language Reveals a Universal Positivity Bias." *Proceedings of the National Academy of Sciences* 112(8): 2389–2394.

Doel, R. E. 2003. "Constituting the Postwar Earth Sciences: The Military's Influence on the Environmental Sciences in the USA after 1945." *Social Studies of Science* 33(5): 635–666.

Dolgin, E. 2021a. "How Covid Unlocked the Power of RNA Vaccines." *Nature* 589(7841): 189–192.

Dolgin, E. 2021b. "The Tangled History of mRNA Vaccines." *Nature* 597(7876): 318–324.

Doll, C. H., Muller, J.-P., and Elvidge, C. D. 2000. "Night-Time Imagery as a Tool for Global Mapping of Socioeconomic Parameters and Greenhouse Gas Emissions." *AMBIO: A Journal of the Human Environment* 29(3): 157–162.

Domingos, E. F., Grujić, J., Burguillo, J. C., Kirchsteiger, G., Santos, F. C., and Lenaerts, T. 2020. "Timing Uncertainty in Collective Risk Dilemmas Encourages Group Reciprocation and Polarization." *iScience* 23(12): 101752.

Dorison, C. A., Minson, J. A., and Rogers, T. 2019. "Selective Exposure Partly Relies on Faulty Affective Forecasts." *Cognition* 188: 98–107.

Dorison, C. A., Wang, K., Rees, V. W., Kawachi, I., Ericson, K. M., and Lerner, J. S. 2020. "Sadness, but Not All Negative Emotions, Heightens Addictive Substance Use." *Proceedings of the National Academy of Sciences* 117(2): 943–949.

Dosio, A., Mentaschi, L., Fischer, E. M., and Wyser, K. 2018. "Extreme Heat Waves under 1.5 C and 2 C Global Warming." *Environmental Research Letters* 13(5): 054006.

Drèze, J., and Sen, A. 1989. *Hunger and Public Action.* Oxford, UK: Oxford University Press.

Druckman, J. N. 2017. "The Crisis of Politicization within and Beyond Science." *Nature Human Behaviour* 1(9): 615–617.

Druckman, J. N., and McDermott, R. 2008. "Emotion and the Framing of Risky Choice." *Political Behavior* 30(3): 297–321.

Dryhurst, S., Schneider, C. R., Kerr, J., Freeman, A. L., Recchia, G., Van Der Bles, A. M., Spiegelhalter, D., and Van Der Linden, S. 2020. "Risk Perceptions of Covid-19 around the World." *Journal of Risk Research* 23(7–8): 994–1006.

Dukes, D., Abrams, K., Adolphs, R., Ahmed, M. E., Beatty, A., Berridge, K. C., Broomhall, S., and others. 2021. "The Rise of Affectivism." *Nature Human Behaviour* 5(7): 816–820.

Dunbar, R. I. M. 1992. "Neocortex Size as a Constraint on Group Size in Primates." *Journal of Human Evolution* 22(6): 469–493.

Dunn, B. D., Dalgleish, T., and Lawrence, A. D. 2006. "The Somatic Marker Hypothesis: A Critical Evaluation." *Neuroscience & Biobehavioral Reviews* 30(2): 239–271.

Durand, M., Fitoussi, J.-P., and Stiglitz, J. E. 2018. *For Good Measure: Advancing Research on Well-Being Metrics Beyond GDP.* Paris: Organisation for Economic Co-operation and Development.

Durante, F., Fiske, S. T., Gelfand, M. J., Crippa, F., Suttora, C., Stillwell, A., Asbrock, F., and others. 2017. "Ambivalent Stereotypes Link to Peace, Conflict, and Inequality across 38 Nations." *Proceedings of the National Academy of Sciences* 114(4): 669–674.

Ebi, K. L., Woodruff, R., von Hildebrand, A., and Corvalan, C. 2007. "Climate Change-Related Health Impacts in the Hindu Kush–Himalayas." *EcoHealth* 4(3): 264–270.

EcoPeace Middle East. n.d. "EcoPeace Middle East." https://ecopeaceme.org. Accessed 29 Oct 2021.

Edwards, P. N. 2012. "Entangled Histories: Climate Science and Nuclear Weapons Research." *Bulletin of the Atomic Scientists* 68(4): 28–40.

Edwards, S. 2021. "Macroprudential Policies and the Covid-19 Pandemic: Risks and Challenges for Emerging Markets." NBER Working Paper 29441, National Bureau of Economic Research, Cambridge, MA.

Eeckhout, J. 2021. *The Profit Paradox: How Thriving Firms Threaten the Future of Work.* Princeton, NJ: Princeton University Press.

EIU (Economist Intelligence Unit). 2021. *Democracy Index 2020: In Sickness and in Health?* London.

Eklund, A., Nichols, T. E., and Knutsson, H. 2016. "Cluster Failure: Why fMRI Inferences for Spatial Extent Have Inflated False-Positive Rates." *Proceedings of the National Academy of Sciences* 113(28): 7900–7905.

Elhacham, E., Ben-Uri, L., Grozovski, J., Bar-On, Y. M., and Milo, R. 2020. "Global Human-Made Mass Exceeds All Living Biomass." *Nature* 588(7838): 442–444.

Ellis, E. 2022. "Anthropocene Opportunities: Guiding the Evolution of Social-Ecological Development." Background paper for Human Development Report 2021/2022, UNDP–HDRO, New York.

Ellis, E. C. 2019. "Sharing the Land between Nature and People." *Science* 364(6447): 1226–1228.

Ellis, E. C. 2021. "Land Use and Ecological Change: A 12,000-Year History." *Annual Review of Environment and Resources* 46(1): 1–33.

Ellis, E. C., Gauthier, N., Goldewijk, K. K., Bird, R. B., Boivin, N., Díaz, S., Fuller, D. Q., and others. 2021. "People Have Shaped Most of Terrestrial Nature for at Least 12,000 Years." *Proceedings of the National Academy of Sciences* 118(17): e2023483118.

Elster, J. 1998. "Emotions and Economic Theory." *Journal of Economic Literature* 36(1): 47–74.

Elster, J. 2015. *Explaining Social Behavior: More Nuts and Bolts for the Social Sciences.* New York: Cambridge University Press.

Elster, J. 2021a. "Enthusiasm and Anger in History." *Inquiry* 64(3): 249–307.

Elster, J. 2021b. *France before 1789. The Unraveling of an Absolutist Regime* Princeton, NJ: Princeton University Press.

Enders, A. M., and Armaly, M. T. 2018. "The Differential Effects of Actual and Perceived Polarization." *Political Behavior* 41: 815–839.

Engebretsen, R., and Anderson, C. 2020. "The Impact of Coronavirus (Covid-19) and the Global Oil Price Shock on the Fiscal Position of Oil-Exporting Developing Countries." Organisation for Economic Co-operation and Development, Paris.

Enke, B. 2019. "Kinship, Cooperation, and the Evolution of Moral Systems." *The Quarterly Journal of Economics* 134(2): 953–1019.

Enke, B., and Graeber, T. 2019. "Cognitive Uncertainty." NBER Working Paper 26518, National Bureau of Economic Research, Cambridge, MA.

Enke, B., and Graeber, T. 2021. "Cognitive Uncertainty in Intertemporal Choice." NBER Working Paper 29577, National Bureau of Economic Research, Cambridge, MA.

Enke, B., Rodriguez-Padilla, R., and Zimmermann, F. 2021. "Moral Universalism: Measurement and Economic Relevance." *Management Science* 68(5): 3590–3603.

Eom, K., Kim, H. S., Sherman, D. K., and Ishii, K. 2016. "Cultural Variability in the Link between Environmental Concern and Support for Environmental Action." *Psychological Science* 27(10): 1331–1339.

Epeli Hao'ofa. 2008. *We Are the Ocean: Selected Works.* Honolulu, HI: University of Hawaii Press.

Epstein, S., R., 2006. *Freedom and Growth: The Rise of States and Markets in Europe, 1300–1750.* Abingdon, UK: Routledge.

Erev, I., Wallsten, T. S., and Budescu, D. V. 1994. "Simultaneous Over- and Underconfidence: The Role of Error in Judgment Processes." *Psychological Review* 101(3): 519–527.

Erickson, P., Asselt, H. v., Koplow, D., Lazarus, M., Newell, P., Oreskes, N., and Supran, G. 2020. "Why Fossil Fuel Producer Subsidies Matter." *Nature* 578(7793): E1–E4.

Eriksen, S., Schipper, E. L. F., Scoville-Simonds, M., Vincent, K., Adam, H. N., Brooks, N., Harding, B., and others. 2021. "Adaptation Interventions and Their Effect on Vulnerability in Developing Countries: Help, Hindrance or Irrelevance?" *World Development* 141: 105383.

Erikson, E. 1993. *Childhood and Society.* New York and London: WW Norton & Company.

Erlanger, S., and Sengupta, S. 2021. "Europe Unveils Plan to Shift from Fossil Fuels, Setting up Potential Trade Spats." *New York Times,* 14 July.

Etheridge, B., and Spantig, L. 2020. "The Gender Gap in Mental Well-Being During the Covid-19 Outbreak: Evidence from the UK." ISER Working Paper 2020–08, University of Essex, Institute for Social and Economic Research, Colchester, UK. https://lisaspantig.com/wp-content/uploads/UK_gendergap_covidecon.pdf.

European Comission. 2021. "Proposal for a Regulation of the European Parliament and of the Council on Ensuring a Level Playing Field for Sustainable Air Transport." 2021/0205(COD). European Comission, Brussels. https://eur-lex.europa.eu/legal-content/EN/TXT/HTML/?uri=CELEX:52021PC0561&from=EN.

European Comission. 2022. "Digital Services Act: Commission Welcomes Political Agreement on Rules Ensuring a Safe and Accountable Online Environment." https://ec.europa.eu/commission/presscorner/detail/en/ip_22_2545. Accessed 25 August 2022.

European Parliament, European Council, European Economic and Social Committee, European Committee of the Regions. 2018. "Action Plan against Disinformation." https://ec.europa.eu/info/sites/default/files/eu-communication-disinformation-euco-05122018_en.pdf.

Evans, D. 2011. "The Internet of Things: How the Next Evolution of the Internet Is Changing Everything." White Paper, CISCO, San Jose, CA.

Evans, G. W., and Kim, P. 2012. "Childhood Poverty and Young Adults' Allostatic Load: The Mediating Role of Childhood Cumulative Risk Exposure." *Psychological Science* 23(9): 979–983.

Evans, G. W., and Wachs, T. D. 2010. *Chaos and Its Influence on Children's Development. An Ecological Perspective.* Washington: DC: American Psychological Association.

Evans, G. W., Li, D., and Whipple, S. S. 2013. "Cumulative Risk and Child Development." *Psychological Bulletin* 139(6): 1342–1396.

Evans, J. A. 2008. "Electronic Publication and the Narrowing of Science and Scholarship." *Science* 321: 395–399.

Evans, J. 2021. "Setting Ethical Limits on Human Gene Editing after the Fall of the Somatic/Germline Barrier." *Proceedings of the National Academy of Sciences* 118(22): e2004837117.

Fajardo-Gonzalez, J., and Sandoval, C. E. 2021. "Income Support Programs and Covid-19 in Developing Countries." Development Futures Series Working Paper, United Nations Development Programme, Global Policy Network, New York.

Falk, A., Becker, A., Dohmen, T., Enke, B., Huffman, D., and Sunde, U. 2018. "Global Evidence on Economic Preferences." *The Quarterly Journal of Economics* 133(4): 1645–1692.

Fan, R., Varol, O., Varamesh, A., Barron, A., van de Leemput, I. A., Scheffer, M., and Bollen, J. 2019. "The Minute-Scale Dynamics of Online Emotions Reveal the Effects of Affect Labeling." *Nature Human Behaviour* 3(1): 92–100.

Fang, P., Kennedy, A., and Resnick, D. 2020. "Scaling up and Sustaining Social Protection under Covid-19." COVID-19 Policy Response Portal Project Note 3, International Food Policy Research Institute, Washington, DC.

FAO (Food and Agriculture Organization of the United Nations). 2017. FAOSTAT. https://www.fao.org/faostat/en/#home. Accessed 21 July 2022.

FAO (United Nations Food and Agriculture Organization). 2021. "Haiti: Response Overview." Office of Emergencies and Resilience, Rome. https://www.fao.org/publications/card/en/c/CB5697EN/.

FAO (Food and Agriculture Organization of the United Nations) and UNEP (United Nations Environment Programme). 2020. *The State of the World's Forests 2020: Forests, Biodiversity and People.* Rome.

FAO (Food and Agriculture Organization of the United Nations), IFAD (International Fund for Agricultural Development), UNICEF (United Nations Children's Fund), WFP (World Food Programme) and WHO (World Health Organization). 2021. *The State of Food Security and Nutrition in the World 2021: Transforming Food Systems for Affordable Healthy Diets.* Rome.

Farhi, E., and Gabaix, X. 2020. "Optimal Taxation with Behavioral Agents." *American Economic Review* 110(1): 298–336.

Farrell, H., and Schneier, B. 2019. "Democracy's Dilemma." Boston Review. https://bostonreview.net/forum/forum-henry-farrell-bruce-schneier-democracys-dilemma/. Accessed 25 August 2022.

FeldmanHall, O., and Chang, L. J. 2018. "Social Learning: Emotions Aid in Optimizing Goal-Directed Social Behavior." In Morris, R., Bornstein, A., and Shenhav, A., (eds), *Goal-Directed Decision Making.* Cambridge, MA: Academic Press.

FeldmanHall, O., and Shenhav, A. 2019. "Resolving Uncertainty in a Social World." *Nature Human Behaviour* 3: 426–435.

Fernbach, P. M., and Van Boven, L. 2022. "False Polarization: Cognitive Mechanisms and Potential Solutions." *Current Opinion in Psychology* 43: 1–6.

Ferree, M. M. 1992. "The Political Context of Rationality: Rational Choice Theory and Resource Mobilization." In Morris A. D., and McClurg Mueller, C., (eds.), *Frontiers in Social Movement Theory.* New Haven, CT: Yale University Press.

Ferreira, F. H. G. 2021. "Inequality in the Time of Covid-19." *Finance & Development,* June 2021.

Ferreira, J., Lennox, G. D., Gardner, T. A., Thomson, J. R., Berenguer, E., Lees, A. C., Mac Nally, R., and others. 2018. "Carbon-Focused Conservation May Fail to Protect the Most Biodiverse Tropical Forests." *Nature Climate Change* 8(8): 744–749.

Fetzer, T., Hensel, L., Hermle, J., and Roth, C. 2021. "Coronavirus Perceptions and Economic Anxiety." *Review of Economics and Statistics* 103(5): 968–978.

Fetzer, T. R., Witte, M., Hensel, L., Jachimowicz, J., Haushofer, J., Ivchenko, A., Caria, S., and others. 2020. "Global Behaviors and Perceptions at the Onset of the Covid-19 Pandemic." NBER Working Paper 27082, National Bureau of Economic Research, Cambridge, MA.

FEWS NET (Famine Early Warning Systems Network). 2021a. "Haiti. Food Security Outlook: February to September 2021." Washington, DC. https://fews.net/central-america-and-caribbean/haiti. Accessed 25 August 2022.

FEWS NET (Famine Early Warning Systems Network). 2021b. "Haiti. Food Security Outlook: June 2021-January 2022." Washington, DC. https://fews.net/central-america-and-caribbean/haiti. Accessed 25 August 2022.

First Post. 2020. "Mental Health in a Time of National Turmoil: Amid CAA Protests, Building Resilience Is Key to Healing from Trauma." https://www.firstpost.com/india/mental-health-in-a-time-of-national-turmoil-amid-caa-protests-building-resilience-is-key-to-healing-from-trauma-7861341.html. Accessed 27 September 2021.

Fischhoff, B., and Bruine De Bruin, W. 1999. "Fifty–Fifty=50%?" *Journal of Behavioral Decision Making* 12(2): 149–163.

Fishback, P. V. 2022. "Safety Nets and Social Welfare Expenditures in World Economic History." NBER Working Paper 30067, National Bureau of Economic Research, Cambridge, MA.

Fishkin, J., Siu, A., Diamond, L., and Bradburn, N. 2021. "Is Deliberation an Antidote to Extreme Partisan Polarization? Reflections on 'America in One Room'." *American Political Science Review* 115(4): 1464–1481.

Flam, H. 1990. "Emotional 'Man': I. The Emotional 'Man' and the Problem of Collective Action." *International Sociology* 5(1): 39–56.

Fleurbaey, M. 2018. *A Manifesto for Social Progress: Ideas for a Better Society.* Cambridge, UK: Cambridge University Press.

Fligstein, N., and McAdam, D. 2012. *A Theory of Fields.* Oxford, UK: Oxford University Press.

Florini, A. 2013. *The Coming Democracy: New Rules for Running a New World.* Washington, DC: Island Press.

Florini, A., LaForge, G., and Sharma, S. 2022. "Governance for Systemic and Transformational Change: Redesigning Governance for the Anthropocene." Background paper for Human Development Report 2021/2022, UNDP–HDRO, New York.

Foa, R. S., Klassen, A., Slade, M., Rand, A., and Collins, R. 2020. *The Global Satisfaction with Democracy Report 2020.* Cambridge, UK: University of Cambridge, Bennett Institute for Public Policy.

Fokum, V. Y., Fonjong, L. N., and Adams, M. J. 2020. "Increasing Women's Representation in the Cameroon Parliament: Do Numbers Really Matter?" *Women's Studies International Forum* 80: 102369.

Folke, C., Polasky, S., Rockström, J., Galaz, V., Westley, F., Lamont, M., Scheffer, M., and others. 2021. "Our Future in the Anthropocene Biosphere." *Ambio* 50(4): 834–869.

Forester, S., Kelly-Thompson, K., Lusvardi, A., and Weldon, L. S. 2022. "New Dimensions of Global Feminist Influence: Tracking Feminist Mobilization Worldwide, 1975–2015." *International Studies Quarterly* 66(1) sqab093. https://doi.org/10.1093/isq/sqab093.

Fouquet, R. 2016. "Historical Energy Transitions: Speed, Prices and System Transformation." *Energy Research & Social Science* 22: 7–12.

Fowler, P. J., Tompsett, C. J., Braciszewski, J. M., Jacques-Tiura, A. J., and Baltes, B. B. 2009. "Community Violence: A Meta-Analysis on the Effect of Exposure and Mental Health Outcomes of Children and Adolescents." *Development and Psychopathology* 21(1): 227–259.

Frank, M. R., Autor, D., Bessen, J. E., Brynjolfsson, E., Cebrian, M., Deming, D. J., Feldman, M., and others. 2019. "Toward Understanding the Impact of Artificial

Intelligence on Labor." *Proceedings of the National Academy of Sciences* 116(14): 6531–6539.

Frank, R. H. 1988. *Passions within Reason: The Strategic Role of the Emotions.* New York: WW Norton & Co.

Frank, R. H. 2020. *Under the Influence: Putting Peer Pressure to Work.* Princeton NJ: Princeton University Press.

Frankel, T., Mucha, L., and Sadof, K. 2018. "The Hidden Costs of Cobalt Mining." *The Washington Post,* 28 February.

Fransen, J., Peralta, D. O., Vanelli, F., Edelenbos, J., and Olvera, B. C. 2021. "The Emergence of Urban Community Resilience Initiatives During the Covid-19 Pandemic: An International Exploratory Study." *The European Journal of Development Research*: 1–23.

Frazão, S. L., Silva, M. S., Norton, P., and Magalhães, T. 2014. "Domestic Violence against Elderly with Disability." *Journal of Forensic and Legal Medicine* 28: 19–24.

Frederick, S. 2005. "Cognitive Reflection and Decision Making." *Journal of Economic Perspectives* 19(4): 25–42.

Freed, D., Palmer, J., Minchala, D. E., Levy, K., Ristenpart, T., and Dell, N. 2017. "Digital Technologies and Intimate Partner Violence: A Qualitative Analysis with Multiple Stakeholders." *Proceedings of the Association for Computing Maschines on Human-Computer Interaction* 1(CSCW): 1–22.

Freedom House. 2021. "Freedom in the World 2021: Haiti." Washington, DC. https://freedomhouse.org/country/haiti/freedom-world/2021. Accessed 25 August 2022.

Freyd, J. J. 1994. "Betrayal Trauma: Traumatic Amnesia as an Adaptive Response to Childhood Abuse." *Ethics & Behavior* 4(4): 307–329.

Freyd, J. J., DePrince, A. P., and Gleaves, D. H. 2007. "The State of Betrayal Trauma Theory: Reply to Mcnally —Conceptual Issues, and Future Directions." *Memory* 15(3): 295–311.

Fruttero, A., Muller, N., and Calvo-González, Ó. 2021. "The Power and Roots of Aspirations: A Survey of the Empirical Evidence." Policy Research Working Paper 9729, World Bank, Washington, DC.

Frye, M. 2019. "The Myth of Agency and the Misattribution of Blame in Collective Imaginaries of the Future." *The British Journal of Sociology* 70(3): 721–730.

Fuentes-Nieva, R. 2022. "The Rise and Fall of Liberal Democracy (and the Spiders of Inequality)." Background paper for Human Development Report 2021/2022, UNDP–HDRO, New York.

Fujita, Y., and Sabogal, A. 2021. "Perspective of Localization of Aid During Covid-19: Reflecting on the Tensions between the Top-Down and Bottom-up Responses to the Health Emergency in Haiti." ISS Working Paper Series/General Series 673, Erasmus University Rotterdam, International Institute of Social Studies, The Hague, The Netherlands.

Fuller, R., Landrigan, P. J., Balakrishnan, K., Bathan, G., Bose-O'Reilly, S., Brauer, M., Caravanos, J., and others. 2022. "Pollution and Health: A Progress Update." *The Lancet Planetary Health.*

Funda Wande. 2021. "Funda Wande Appoints Nangamso Mtsatse as New CEO." 6 July.

Funke, M., Schularick, M., and Trebesch, C. 2016. "Going to Extremes: Politics after Financial Crises, 1870–2014." *European Economic Review* 88: 227–260.

Funtowicz, S., and Ravetz, J. 1993. "Science for the Post-Normal Age." *Futures* 25(7): 739–755.

Furman, J., and Seamans, R. 2018. "AI and the Economy." NBER Working Paper 24689, National Bureau of Economic Research, Cambridge, MA.

Gabriel, M., Curtiss, J., Hofmann, S. G., and Khalsa, S. B. S. 2018. "Kundalini Yoga for Generalized Anxiety Disorder: An Exploration of Treatment Efficacy and Possible Mechanisms." *International Journal of Yoga Therapy* 28(1): 97–105.

Gal, D., and Rucker, D. D. 2018. "The Loss of Loss Aversion: Will It Loom Larger Than Its Gain?" *Journal of Consumer Psychology* 28(3): 497–516.

Galam, S. 2004. "Contrarian Deterministic Effects on Opinion Dynamics: 'The Hung Elections Scenario'." *Physica A: Statistical Mechanics and its Applications* 333: 453–460.

Galesic, M., Barkoczi, D., and Katsikopoulos, K. 2018. "Smaller Crowds Outperform Larger Crowds and Individuals in Realistic Task Conditions." *Decision* 5(1): 1–15.

Gallagher, K., and Franco Maldonado, C. 2020. "The Role of IMF in the Fight against Covid-19: The IMF Covid-19 Recovery Index." *Covid Economics* 42: 112–142.

Gallotti, R., Valle, F., Castaldo, N., Sacco, P., and Domenico, M. D. 2020. "Assessing the Risks of 'Infodemics' in Response to Covid-19 Epidemics." *Nature Human Behaviour* 4: 1285–1293.

The Gallup Organization. 2022. *Gallup Global Emotions 2022.* Washington, DC.

Gambhir, A., Green, F., and Pearson, P. J. 2018. "Towards a Just and Equitable Low-Carbon Energy Transition." Grantham Institute Briefing Paper 26. Imperial College London, London.

Gandhi, R., Sharma, A., Mahoney, W., Sousan, W., Zhu, Q., and Laplante, P. 2011. "Dimensions of Cyber-Attacks: Cultural, Social, Economic, and Political." *IEEE Technology and Society Magazine* 30(1): 28–38.

Gao, J., Zheng, P., Jia, Y., Chen, H., Mao, Y., Chen, S., Wang, Y., and others. 2020. "Mental Health Problems and Social Media Exposure During Covid-19 Outbreak." *PLOS ONE* 15(4).

Gardiner, S. E. Forthcoming. *The Oxford Handbook of Intergenerational Ethics.* Oxford, UK: Oxford University Press.

Garfield, Z. H., Syme, K. L., and Hagen, E. H. 2020. "Universal and Variable Leadership Dimensions across Human Societies." *Evolution and Human Behavior* 41(5): 397–414.

Garfield, Z. H., von Rueden, C., and Hagen, E. H. 2019. "The Evolutionary Anthropology of Political Leadership." *The Leadership Quarterly* 30(1): 59–80.

Garretson, J., and Suhay, E. 2016. "Scientific Communication About Biological Influences on Homosexuality and the Politics of Gay Rights." *Political Research Quarterly* 69(1): 17–29.

Garrett, S. B. 2016. "Foundations of the Cultural Repertoire: Education and Social Network Effects among Expectant Mothers." *Poetics* 55: 19–35.

Gates, S., Hegre, H., Nygård, H. M., and Strand, H. 2012. "Development Consequences of Armed Conflict." *World Development* 40(9): 1713–1722.

Gaupp, F., Hall, J., Hochrainer-Stigler, S., and Dadson, S. 2020. "Changing Risks of Simultaneous Global Breadbasket Failure." *Nature Climate Change* 10(1): 54–57.

Geertz, C. 1973. *The Interpretation of Cultures.* New York: Basic Books.

Gelfand, M. J. 2019. "Explaining the Puzzle of Human Diversity." *Science* 366(6466): 686–687.

Gelfand, M. J. 2021. "Cultural Evolutionary Mismatches in Response to Collective Threat." *Current Directions in Psychological Science* 30(5): 401–409.

Gelfand, M. J., and Jackson, J. C. 2016. "From One Mind to Many: The Emerging Science of Cultural Norms." *Current Opinion in Psychology* 8: 175–181.

Gelfand, M. J., Nishii, L. H., and Raver, J. L. 2006. "On the Nature and Importance of Cultural Tightness-Looseness." *Journal of Applied Psychology* 91(6): 1225–1244.

Gelfand, M. J., Raver, J. L., Nishii, L., Leslie, L. M., Lun, J., Lim, B. C., Duan, L., and others. 2011. "Differences between Tight and Loose Cultures: A 33-Nation Study." *Science* 332(6033): 1100–1104.

Genicot, G., and Ray, D. 2017. "Aspirations and Inequality." *Econometrica* 85(2): 489–519.

Genicot, G., and Ray, D. 2020. "Aspirations and Economic Behavior." *Annual Review of Economics* 12(1): 715–746.

Gentilini, U. 2021. "A Game Changer for Social Protection? Six Reflections on Covid-19 and the Future of Cash Transfers." Let's Talk Development [blog], 11 January. https://blogs.worldbank.org/developmenttalk/game-changer-social-protection-six-reflections-covid-19-and-future-cash-transfers. Accessed 5 October 2021.

Gentilini, U., Almenfi, M., Blomquist, J., Dale, P., Giuffra, L. D. I. F., Desai, V., Fontenez, M. B., and others. 2021. "Social Protection and Jobs Responses to Covid-19: A Real-Time Review of Country Measures." World Bank, Washington, DC.

Gentle, P., and Maraseni, T. N. 2012. "Climate Change, Poverty and Livelihoods: Adaptation Practices by Rural Mountain Communities in Nepal." *Environmental Science & Policy* 21: 24–34.

Genz, S. 2022. "The Nuanced Relationship between Cutting-Edge Technologies and Jobs: Evidence from Germany." Policy Brief, Brookings Institution, Center on Regulation and Markets, Washington, DC.

Georgieva, K. 2020. "The Financial Sector in the 2020s: Building a More Inclusive System in the New Decade."

Speech at the Pearson Institute for International Economics, 17 January, Washington, DC. https://www.imf.org/en/News/Articles/2020/01/17/sp01172019-the-financial-sector-in-the-2020s. Accessed 31 March 2022.

Georgieva, K., Gopinath, G., and Pazarbasioglu, C. 2022. "Why We Must Resist Geoeconomic Fragmentation—and How." IMFBlog, 22 May. https://blogs.imf.org/2022/05/22/why-we-must-resist-geoeconomic-fragmentation-and-how/. Accessed 1 June 2022.

Geraci, A., Nardotto, M., Reggiani, T., and Sabatini, F. 2018. "Broadband Internet and Social Capital." IZA Discussion Paper 11855, Institute of Labor Economics, Bonn, Germany. https://ftp.iza.org/dp11855.pdf.

Gethin, A., Martínez-Toledano, C., and Piketty, T. 2021. Political Cleavages and Social Inequalities. Cambridge, MA: Harvard University Press.

Gezie, L. D., Yalew, A. W., Gete, Y. K., Azale, T., Brand, T., and Zeeb, H. 2018. "Socio-Economic, Trafficking Exposures and Mental Health Symptoms of Human Trafficking Returnees in Ethiopia: Using a Generalized Structural Equation Modelling." International Journal of Mental Health Systems 12(1): 1–13.

Gibney, E. 2022. "Nuclear-Fusion Reactor Smashes Energy Record." Nature 602: 371.

Gidron, N., Adams, J., and Horne, W. 2020. American Affective Polarization in Comparative Perspective. Cambridge, UK: Cambridge University Press.

Gigerenzer, G., and Gaissmaier, W. 2011. "Heuristic Decision Making." Annual Review of Psychology 62(1): 451–482.

Gill, I., and Saavedra, J. 2022. "We Are Losing a Generation: The Devastating Impacts of Covid-19." Voice [blog], 1 February. https://blogs.worldbank.org/voices/we-are-losing-generation-devastating-impacts-covid-19. Accessed 6 May 2022.

Gill, J., and DeFronzo, J. 2009. "A Comparative Framework for the Analysis of International Student Movements." Social Movement Studies 8(3): 203–224.

Gill, R. B. 2000. The Great Maya Droughts: Water, Life, and Death. Albuquerque, NM: University of New Mexico Press.

Giuliano, P., and Nunn, N. 2020. "Understanding Cultural Persistence and Change." The Review of Economic Studies 88(4): 1541–1581.

Glied, S., and Lleras-Muney, A. 2008. "Technological Innovation and Inequality in Health." Demography 45(3): 741–761.

Goffman, E. 1963. Stigma: Notes on the Management of Spoiled Identity. New York: Simon and Schuster.

Goldfarb, E. S., and Lieberman, L. D. 2021. "Three Decades of Research: The Case for Comprehensive Sex Education." Journal of Adolescent Health 68(1): 13–27.

Goldman-Mellor, S., Margerison-Zilko, C., Allen, K., and Cerda, M. 2016. "Perceived and Objectively-Measured Neighborhood Violence and Adolescent Psychological Distress." Journal of Urban Health 93(5): 758–769.

Golembe, J., Leyendecker, B., Maalej, N., Gundlach, A., and Busch, J. 2020. "Experiences of Minority Stress and Mental Health Burdens of Newly Arrived LGBTQ* Refugees in Germany." Sexuality Research and Social Policy: 1–11.

Golub, B., and Jackson, M. O. 2012. "How Homophily Affects the Speed of Learning and Best-Response Dynamics." The Quarterly Journal of Economics 127(3): 1287–1338.

Goodwin, J., and Jasper, J. M. 2006. "Emotions and Social Movements." In Stets, J. E., and Turner, J. H., (eds.), Handbook of the Sociology of Emotions. Boston, MA: Springer.

Goodwin, J., Jasper, J., and Polletta, F. 2000. "The Return of the Repressed: The Fall and Rise of Emotions in Social Movement Theory." Mobilization: An International Quarterly 5(1): 65–83.

Gordon, A. M., and Mendes, W. B. 2021. "A Large-Scale Study of Stress, Emotions, and Blood Pressure in Daily Life Using a Digital Platform." Proceedings of the National Academy of Sciences 118(31): e2105573118.

Goubert, P. 1982. Beauvais Et Le Beauvaisis De 1600 À 1730: Contribution À L'histoire Sociale De La France Du Xviie Siècle. Paris: Éditions de l'École des hautes études en sciences sociales, Ed Sorbonne.

Gough, I. 2019. "Universal Basic Services: A Theoretical and Moral Framework." The Political Quarterly 90(3): 534–542.

Gough, I. 2021. "Move the Debate from Universal Basic Income to Universal Basic Services." United Nations Educational Scientific and Cultural Organization, Inclusive Policy Lab.

Gould, C. C. 2018. "Solidarity and the Problem of Structural Injustice in Healthcare." Bioethics 32(9): 541–552.

Graham, M. H., and Svolik, M. W. 2020. "Democracy in America? Partisanship, Polarization, and the Robustness of Support for Democracy in the United States." American Political Science Review 114(2): 392–409.

Graham-Rowe, D. 2011. "Agriculture: Beyond Food Versus Fuel." Nature 474(7352): S6–S8.

Granovetter, M. 1985. "Economic Action and Social Structure: The Problem of Embeddedness." American Journal of Sociology 91(3): 481–510.

Granovetter, M. 2005. "The Impact of Social Structure on Economic Outcomes." Journal of Economic Perspectives 19(1): 33–50.

Green, D. P., Wilke, A. M., and Cooper, J. 2020. "Countering Violence against Women by Encouraging Disclosure: A Mass Media Experiment in Rural Uganda." Comparative Political Studies 53(14): 2283–2320.

Greenaway, K. H., Frye, M., and Cruwys, T. 2015. "When Aspirations Exceed Expectations: Quixotic Hope Increases Depression among Students." PLOS ONE 10(9): e0135477.

Greene, C. A., Chan, G., McCarthy, K. J., Wakschlag, L. S., and Briggs-Gowan, M. J. 2018. "Psychological and Physical Intimate Partner Violence and Young Children's Mental Health: The Role of Maternal Posttraumatic Stress Symptoms and Parenting Behaviors." Child Abuse & Neglect 77: 168–179.

Greer, B., Robotham, D., Simblett, S., Curtis, H., Griffiths, H., and Wykes, T. 2019. "Digital Exclusion among Mental Health Service Users: Qualitative Investigation." Journal of Medical Internet Research 21(1): 1–10.

Greif, A., and Mokyr, J. 2017. "Cognitive Rules, Institutions, and Economic Growth: Douglass North and Beyond." Journal of Institutional Economics 13(1): 25–52.

Grix, M., and McKibbin, P. 2015. Needs and Well-Being. London: Routledge.

Grix, M., and Watene, K. 2022. "Communities and Climate Change: Why Practices and Practitioners Matter." Ethics and International Affairs 36(2): 215–230.

Gronholm, P. C., Henderson, C., Deb, T., and Thornicroft, G. 2017. "Interventions to Reduce Discrimination and Stigma: The State of the Art." Social Psychiatry and Psychiatric Epidemiology 52(3): 249–258.

Gros, D., Lane, P. R., Langfield, S., Matikainen, S., Pagano, M., Schoenmaker, D., and Suarez, J. 2016. "Too Late, Too Sudden: Transition to a Low-Carbon Economy and Systemic Risk." Report of the Advisory Scientific Committee 6, European Systemic Risk Board, Frankfurt, Germany.

Gross, J., and Böhm, R. 2020. "Voluntary Restrictions on Self-Reliance Increase Cooperation and Mitigate Wealth Inequality." Proceedings of the National Academy of Sciences 117(46): 29202–29211.

Gross, J., and Dreu, C. K. W. D. 2019. "Individual Solutions to Shared Problems Create a Modern Tragedy of the Commons." Science Advances 5(4): eaau7296.

Gross, J., Veistola, S., De Dreu, C. K. W., and Van Dijk, E. 2020. "Self-Reliance Crowds out Group Cooperation and Increases Wealth Inequality." Nature Communications 11(1): 5161.

Grupe, D. W., and Nitschke, J. B. 2013. "Uncertainty and Anticipation in Anxiety: An Integrated Neurobiological and Psychological Perspective." Nature Reviews Neuroscience 14(7): 488–501.

Grusky, D. B., Hall, P. A., and Markus, H. R. 2019. "The Rise of Opportunity Markets: How Did It Happen & What Can We Do?" Daedalus 148(3): 19–45.

Guillet, S., Corona, C., Stoffel, M., Khodri, M., Lavigne, F., Ortega, P., Eckert, N., and others. 2017. "Climate Response to the Samalas Volcanic Eruption in 1257 Revealed by Proxy Records." Nature Geoscience 10(2): 123–128.

Guo, Y., Gasparrini, A., Armstrong, B. G., Tawatsupa, B., Tobias, A., Lavigne, E., Coelho, M. d. S. Z. S., and others. 2016. "Temperature Variability and Mortality: A Multi-Country Study." Environmental Health Perspectives 124(10): 1554–1559.

Guriev, S., Melnikov, N., and Zhuravskaya, E. 2019. "3G Internet and Confidence in Government." CEPR Discussion Paper 14022, Center for Economic and Policy Research, Washington, DC.

Gutiérrez, K. D., and Rogoff, B. 2003. "Cultural Ways of Learning: Individual Traits or Repertoires of Practice." Educational Researcher 32(5): 19–25.

Haberl, H., Fischer-Kowalski, M., Krausmann, F., Martinez-Alier, J., and Winiwarter, V. 2011. "A Socio-Metabolic Transition Towards Sustainability? Challenges for Another Great Transformation." *Sustainable Development* 19(1): 1–14.

Hacker, J. 2018a. "Economic Insecurity." In Stiglitz, J., Fitoussi, J. and Durand, M., (eds.), *For Good Measure: Advancing Research on Well-Being Metrics Beyond GDP.* Paris: Organisation for Economic Co-operation and Development.

Hacker, J. 2018b. *The Great Risk Shift: The New Economic Insecurity and the Decline of the American Dream. Second Edition.* Oxford, UK: Oxford University Press.

Hacker, J. 2018c. "The Great Risk Shift." In Grusky, D., and Hill, J., (eds.), *Inequality in the 21st Century.* Abingdon, UK: Routledge.

Hackett, R. A., and Steptoe, A. 2017. "Type 2 Diabetes Mellitus and Psychological Stress—a Modifiable Risk Factor." *Nature Reviews Endocrinology* 13(9): 547–560.

Haelermans, C., Korthals, R., Jacobs, M., de Leeuw, S., Vermeulen, S., van Vugt, L., Aarts, B., and others. 2022. "Sharp Increase in Inequality in Education in Times of the Covid-19 Pandemic." *PLOS ONE* 17(2): e0261114.

Haenfler, R., Johnson, B., and Jones, E. 2012. "Lifestyle Movements: Exploring the Intersection of Lifestyle and Social Movements." *Social Movement Studies* 11(1): 1–20.

Haenssgen, M. J., and Ariana, P. 2018. "The Place of Technology in the Capability Approach." *Oxford Development Studies* 46(1): 98–112.

Haerpfer, C., Inglehart, R., Moreno, A., Welzel, C., Kizilova, K., Diez-Medrano J., Lagos, M., and others, (eds.). 2022. "World Values Survey: Round Seven – Country-Pooled Datafile." Madrid, Spain, and Vienna, Austria: JD Systems Institute & World Values Survey Association Secretariat.

Haider, L. J., Schlüter, M., Folke, C., and Reyers, B. 2021. "Rethinking Resilience and Development: A Co-evolutionary Perspective." *Ambio* 50: 1304–1312.

Hale, T., Angrist, N., Goldszmidt, R., Kira, B., Petherick, A., Phillips, T., Webster, S., and others. 2021. "A Global Panel Database of Pandemic Policies (Oxford Covid-19 Government Response Tracker)." *Nature Human Behaviour* 5(4): 529–538.

Hall, J. D., and Madsen, J. M. 2022. "Can Behavioral Interventions Be Too Salient? Evidence from Traffic Safety Messages." *Science* 376(6591): eabm3427.

Hall, P. 1997. "The Role of Interests, Institutions and Ideas in the Comparative Political Economy of Industrialized Countries." In Lichbach, M. I., and Zuckerman, A. S., (eds.)." *Comparative Politics: Rationality, Culture and Structure.* Cambridge, UK: Cambridge University Press.

Hammad, M, Bacil, F., and Soares, F. V. 2021. *Next Practices — Innovations in the COVID-19 Social Protection Responses and Beyond.* Research Report 60. New York and Brasília: United Nations Development Programme and International Policy Centre for Inclusive Growth.

Hammarberg, K., Tran, T., Kirkman, M., and Fisher, J. 2020. "Sex and Age Differences in Clinically Significant Symptoms of Depression and Anxiety among People in Australia in the First Month of Covid-19 Restrictions: A National Survey." *The BMJ* 10(11): e042696.

Hanna, R., and Olken, B. A. 2018. "Universal Basic Incomes Versus Targeted Transfers: Anti-Poverty Programs in Developing Countries." *Journal of Economic Perspectives* 32(4): 201–26.

Harmer, B., Lee, S., TvH, D., and Saadabadi, A. 2022. *Suicidal Ideation.* Treasure Island, FL: StatPearls Publishing. https://pubmed.ncbi.nlm.nih.gov/33351435/. Accessed 2 June 2022.

Harper, G., Sommerville, R., Kendrick, E., Driscoll, L., Slater, P., Stolkin, R., Walton, A., and others. 2019. "Recycling Lithium-Ion Batteries from Electric Vehicles." *Nature* 575(7781): 75–86.

Harvard Medical School. 2020. "Understanding the Stress Response." *Harvard Health Publishing*, 6 July. https://www.health.harvard.edu/staying-healthy/understanding-the-stress-response. Accessed 25 August 2022.

Hataway, J. 2017. "More Than 8.3 Billion Tons of Plastics Made: Most Has Now Been Discarded." *Science-Daily*, 19 July.

Hauser, O. P., and Norton, M. I. 2017. "(Mis) Perceptions of Inequality." *Current Opinion in Psychology* 18: 21–25.

Hauser, O. P., Rand, D. G., Peysakhovich, A., and Nowak, M. A. 2014. "Cooperating with the Future." *Nature* 511(7508): 220–223.

Hausfather, Z., and Forster, P. 2021. "Analysis: Do COP26 Promises Keep Global Warming Below 2C?" *Carbon Brief*, 10 November. https://www.carbonbrief.org/analysis-do-cop26-promises-keep-global-warming-below-2c/. Accessed 25 August 2022.

Hausfather, Z., Marvel, K., Schimdt, G. A., Nielsen-Gamon, J. W., and Zelinka, M. 2022. "Climate Simulations: Recognize the 'Hot Model' Problem." *Nature* 605: 26–29.

Hayes, K., Blashki, G., Wiseman, J., Burke, S., and Reifels, L. 2018. "Climate Change and Mental Health: Risks, Impacts and Priority Actions." *International Journal of Mental Health Systems* 12(1): 1–12.

Head, A., Manguin, M., Tran, N., and Blumenstock, J. E. 2017. "Can Human Development Be Measured with Satellite Imagery?" ICTD '17: Proceedings of the Ninth International Conference on Information and Communication Technologies and Development 8: 1–11.

Headey, D., and Fan, S. 2010. "Reflections on the Global Food Crisis: How Did It Happen? How Has It Hurt? And How Can We Prevent the Next One?" Research Monograph 165, International Food Policy Research Institute, Washington, DC.

Heard-Garris, N. J., Cale, M., Camaj, L., Hamati, M. C., and Dominguez, T. P. 2018. "Transmitting Trauma: A Systematic Review of Vicarious Racism and Child Health." *Social Science & Medicine* 199: 230–240.

Heckman, J. J. 2019. "Cognitive Skills Aree Not Enough." https://heckmanequation.org/resource/cognitive-skills-are-not-enough/. Accessed 3 October 2019.

Heckman, J. J., and Rubinstein, Y. 2001. "The Importance of Noncognitive Skills: Lessons from the GED Testing Program." *American Economic Review* 91(2): 145–149.

Hedin, M., Hahs, A. K., Mata, L., and Lee, K. 2022. "Connecting Biodiversity with Mental Health and Wellbeing—A Review of Methods and Disciplinary Perspectives." *Frontiers in Ecology and Evolution*: 10: 865727.

Heffernan, O. 2019. "Seabed Mining Is Coming--Bringing Mineral Riches and Fears of Epic Extinctions." *Nature* 571(7766): 465–469.

Helbing, D. 2013. "Globally Networked Risks and How to Respond." *Nature* 497(7447): 51–59.

Heller, L., and LaPierre, A. 2012. *Healing Developmental Trauma: How Early Trauma Affects Self-Regulation, Self-Image, and the Capacity for Relationship.* Berkeley, CA: North Atlantic Books.

Helliwell, J. F., Layard, R., Sachs, J. D., De Neve, J.-E., Aknin, L. B., and Wang, S. 2022. *World Happiness Report 2022.* New York: Sustainable Development Solutions Network.

Helmholtz Centre for Ocean Research Kiel. 2021. "DISCOL – a DIS-Turbance and re-COL-onization Experiment." https://www.discol.de/. Accessed 1 October 2021.

Henderson, D. 2020. "Are Epistemic Norms Fundamentally Social Norms?" *Episteme* 17(3): 281–300.

Henrich, J. 2018. *The Secret of Our Success: How Culture Is Driving Human Evolution, Domesticating Our Species, and Making Us Smarter.* Princeton, NJ: Princeton University Press.

Henrich, J. 2020. *The WEIRDEST People in the World: How the West Became Psychologically Peculiar and Particularly Prosperous.* New York: Farrar, Strauss, and Giroux.

Henrich, J., and Gil-White, F. J. 2001. "The Evolution of Prestige: Freely Conferred Deference as a Mechanism for Enhancing the Benefits of Cultural Transmission." *Evolution and Human Behavior* 22(3): 165–196.

Henrich, J., and Muthukrishna, M. 2021. "The Origins and Psychology of Human Cooperation." *Annual Review of Psychology* 72(1): 207–240.

Henrich, J., Bauer, M., Cassar, A., Chytilová, J., and Purzycki, B. G. 2019. "War Increases Religiosity." *Nature Human Behaviour* 3(2): 129–135.

Henrich, J., Blasi, D. E., Curtin, C. M., Davis, H. E., Hong, Z., Kelly, D., and Kroupin, I. 2022. "A Cultural Species and Its Cognitive Phenotypes: Implications for Philosophy." *Review of Philosophy and Psychology.*

Henrich, J., Boyd, R., Derex, M., Kline, M. A., Mesoudi, A., Muthukrishna, M., Powell, A. T., and others. 2016. "Understanding Cumulative Cultural Evolution." *Proceedings of the National Academy of Sciences* 113(44): E6724–E6725.

Henrich, J., Heine, S. J., and Norenzayan, A. 2010a. "Beyond WEIRD: Towards a Broad-Based Behavioral

Science." *Behavioral and Brain Sciences* 33(2–3): 111–135.

Henrich, J., Heine, S. J., and Norenzayan, A. 2010b. "Most People Are Not WEIRD." *Nature* 466(7302): 29.

Herman, J. L. 1992. *Trauma and Recovery: The Aftermath of Violence--from Domestic Abuse to Political Terror.* New York: Basic Books.

Hertel, T. 2009. "Analyzing the Global Poverty Impacts of Biofuel Mandates." GTAP Resource 2999, Global Trade Analysis Project, West Lafayette, IN.

Hertwig, R. 2017. "When to Consider Boosting: Some Rules for Policy-Makers." *Behavioural Public Policy* 1(2): 143–161.

Hewlett, S. A., Marshall, M., and Sherbin, L. 2013. "How Diversity Can Drive Innovation." *Harvard Business Review* 91(12): 30.

Heymann, J., Raub, A., Waisath, W., McCormack, M., Weistroffer, R., Moreno, G., Wong, E., and Earle, A. 2020. "Protecting Health During Covid-19 and Beyond: A Global Examination of Paid Sick Leave Design in 193 Countries." *Global Public Health* 15(7): 925–934.

High Ambition Coalition for Nature and People. 2022. "HAC for Nature and People." https://www.hac fornatureandpeople.org/. Accessed 13 April 2022.

Hilbert, M. 2022. "Digital Technology and Social Change: The Digital Transformation of Society from a Historical Perspective." *Dialogues in Clinical Neuroscience.*

Hill, K. 2020. "Another Arrest, and Jail Time, Due to a Bad Facial Recognition Match." *The New York Times,* 29 December.

Hillis, S., Mercy, J., Amobi, A., and Kress, H. 2016. "Global Prevalence of Past-Year Violence against Children: A Systematic Review and Minimum Estimates." *Pediatrics* 137(3): e20154079.

Hinrichs, K. 2021. "Recent Pension Reforms in Europe: More Challenges, New Directions. An Overview." *Social Policy & Administration* 55(3): 409–422.

Hirai, T., Comim, F., and Ikemoto, Y. 2016. "Happiness and Human Development: A Capability Perspective." *Journal of International Development* 28(7): 1155–1169.

Hjelm, L., Handa, S., de Hoop, J., Palermo, T., Zambia, C., and Teams, M. E. 2017. "Poverty and Perceived Stress: Evidence from Two Unconditional Cash Transfer Programs in Zambia." *Social Science & Medicine* 177: 110–117.

HM Treasury. 2021. "Nature Is a Blind Spot in Economics That We Ignore at Our Peril, Says Dasgupta Review." London.

Hobolt, S. B., Leeper, T. J., and Tilley, J. 2021. "Divided by the Vote: Affective Polarization in the Wake of the Brexit Referendum." *British Journal of Political Science* 51(4): 1476–1493.

Hodder, C. 2021. "Climate Change and Security in the United Nations Assistance Mission in Somalia." Climate-Fragility Policy Brief, Climate Security Expert Network, Adelphi Research, Berlin.

Hoey, J., and Schröder, T. 2022. "Disruption of Social Orders in Societal Transitions as Affective Control of Uncertainty." *American Behavioral Scientist.*

Hoff, K., and Stiglitz, J. E. 2016. "Striving for Balance in Economics: Towards a Theory of the Social Determination of Behavior." *Journal of Economic Behavior & Organization* 126: 25–57.

Hoff, K., and Walsh, J. S. 2019. "The Third Function of Law Is to Transform Cultural Categories." Policy Research Working Paper 8954, World Bank, Washington, DC.

Hogg, M. A. 2007. "Uncertainty–Identity Theory." *Advances in Experimental Social Psychology* 39: 69–126.

Hogg, M. A. 2021. "Self-Uncertainty and Group Identification: Consequences for Social Identity, Group Behavior, Intergroup Relations, and Society." In Gawronski, B., (ed.), *Advances in Experimental Social Psychology,* Vol. 64. Amsterdam: Elsevier.

Holst, C., Sukums, F., Radovanovic, D., Ngowi, B., Noll, J., and Winkler, A. S. 2020. "Sub-Saharan Africa —the New Breeding Ground for Global Digital Health." *The Lancet Digital Health* 2(4): 160–162.

Hooli, L. J. 2016. "Resilience of the Poorest: Coping Strategies and Indigenous Knowledge of Living with the Floods in Northern Namibia." *Regional Environmental Change* 16(3): 695–707.

Hoppen, T. H., and Morina, N. 2019. "The Prevalence of PTSD and Major Depression in the Global Population of Adult War Survivors: A Meta-Analytically Informed Estimate in Absolute Numbers." *European Journal of Psychotraumatology* 10(1): 2–13.

Horn, J. 2020. "Decolonising Emotional Well-Being and Mental Health in Development: African Feminist Innovations." *Gender & Development* 28(1): 85–98.

Hornor, G. 2005. "Domestic Violence and Children." *Journal of Pediatric Health Care* 19(4): 206–212.

Hosonuma, N., Herold, M., De Sy, V., De Fries, R. S., Brockhaus, M., Verchot, L., Angelsen, A., and Romijn, E. 2012. "An Assessment of Deforestation and Forest Degradation Drivers in Developing Countries." *Environmental Research Letters* 7(4): 044009.

Hotaling, J. M., Jarvstad, A., Donkin, C., and Newell, B. R. 2019. "How to Change the Weight of Rare Events in Decisions from Experience." *Psychological Science* 30(12): 1767–1779.

Hromatko, I., Tonković, M., and Vranic, A. 2021. "Trust in Science, Perceived Vulnerability to Disease, and Adherence to Pharmacological and Non-Pharmacological Covid-19 Recommendations." *Frontiers in Psychology* 12: 1425.

Hsiang, S. M., Burke, M., and Miguel, E. 2013. "Quantifying the Influence of Climate on Human Conflict." *Science* 341(6151): 1235367.

Hsieh, N., and Ruther, M. 2016. "Sexual Minority Health and Health Risk Factors: Intersection Effects of Gender, Race, and Sexual Identity." *American Journal of Preventive Medicine* 50(6): 746–755.

Huambachano, M. 2018. "Enacting Food Sovereignty in Aotearoa New Zealand and Peru: Revitalizing Indigenous Knowledge, Food Practices and Ecological Philosophies." *Agroecology and Sustainable Food Systems* 42(9): 1003–1028.

Huambachano, M. 2020. "Indigenous Good Living Philosophies and Regenerative Food Systems in Aotearoa New Zealand and Peru." In Duncan, J., Carolan, M. S., and Wiskerke, J. S., (eds.), *Routledge Handbook of Sustainable and Regenerative Food Systems.* London: Routledge.

Huettel, S. A., and Kranton, R. E. 2012. "Identity Economics and the Brain: Uncovering the Mechanisms of Social Conflict." *Philosophical Transactions of the Royal Society B: Biological Sciences* 367(1589): 680–691.

Hughes, K., Bellis, M. A., Hardcastle, K. A., Sethi, D., Butchart, A., Mikton, C., Jones, L., and Dunne, M. P. 2017. "The Effect of Multiple Adverse Childhood Experiences on Health: A Systematic Review and Meta-Analysis." *The Lancet Public Health* 2(8): 356–366.

Hughes, T. P., Anderson, K. D., Connolly, S. R., Heron, S. F., Kerry, J. T., Lough, J. M., Baird, A. H. and others. 2018. "Spatial and Temporal Patterns of Mass Bleaching of Corals in the Anthropocene." *Science* 359(6371): 80–83.

Hulme, M. 2020. "One Earth, Many Futures, No Destination." *One Earth* 2(4): 309–311.

Human Rights Campaign. 2018. *LGBTQ Youth Report 2018.* Washington, DC. https://assets2.hrc.org/files/assets/resources/2018-YouthReport-NoVid.pdf.

Human Rights Watch. 2017. "Qatar: New Law Gives Domestic Workers Labor Rights, Needs Enforcement Mechanisms." 24 August. https://www.hrw.org/news/2017/08/24/qatar-new-law-gives-domestic-workers-labor-rights. Accessed 25 August 2022.

Human Rights Watch. 2020a. "Syria: Protesters Describe Beatings, Arrests." https://www.hrw.org/news/2020/06/28/syria-protesters-describe-beatings-arrests. Accessed 27 September 2021.

Human Rights Watch. 2020b. "Transgender, Third Gender, No Gender: Part I." 8 September. https://www.hrw.org/news/2020/09/08/transgender-third-gender-no-gender-part-i. Accessed 25 August 2022.

Human Rights Watch. 2021. "'People Can't Be Fit into Boxes': Thailand's Need for Legal Gender Recognition." 15 December. https://www.hrw.org/report/2021/12/15/people-cant-be-fit-boxes/thailands-need-legal-gender-recognition. Accessed 25 August 2022.

Humanitarian Pratice Network. 2017. "Sexual Violence and the Boko Haram Crisis in North-East Nigeria." https://odihpn.org/publication/sexual-violence-and-the-boko-haram-crisis-in-north-east-nigeria/. Accessed 16 March 2021.

Hund, K., La Porta, D., Fabregas, T., Laing, T., and Dexhage, J. 2020. *Minerals for Climate Action: The Mineral Intensity of the Clean Energy Transition.* Washington, DC: World Bank.

Huntingford, C., Fisher, R. A., Mercado, L., Booth, B. B., Sitch, S., Harris, P. P., Cox, P. M., and others. 2008. "Towards Quantifying Uncertainty in Predictions of Amazon 'Dieback'." *Philosophical Transactions of the Royal Society B: Biological Sciences* 363(1498): 1857–1864.

Huppert, E., Cowell, J. M., Cheng, Y., Contreras-Ibáñez, C., Gomez-Sicard, N., Gonzalez-Gadea, M. L., Huepe, D., and others. 2019. "The Development of Children's Preferences for Equality and Equity across 13 Individualistic and Collectivist Cultures." *Developmental Science* 22(2): e12729.

Hussam, R. N., Kelley, E. M., Lane, G. V., and Zahra, F. T. 2021. "The Psychosocial Value of Employment." NBER Working Paper 28924, National Bureau of Economic Research, Cambridge, MA.

Huszár, F., Ktena, S. I., O'Brien, C., Belli, L., Schlaikjer, A., and Hardt, M. 2021. "Algorithmic Amplification of Politics on Twitter." *Proceedings of the National Academy of Sciences* 119(1): e2025334119.

Hyde, S. D. 2020. "Democracy's Backsliding in the International Environment." *Science* 369(6508): 1192–1196.

Hynes, W., Trump, B., Love, P., and Linkov, I. 2020. "Bouncing Forward: A Resilience Approach to Dealing with Covid-19 and Future Systemic Shocks." *Environment Systems and Decisions* 40(2): 174–184.

Hynie, M., Umubyeyi, B., Gasanganwa, M. C., Bohr, Y., McGrath, S., Umuziga, P., and Mukarusanga, B. 2015. "Community Resilience and Community Interventions for Post-Natal Depression: Reflecting on Maternal Mental Health in Rwanda." In Khanlou, N., and Pilkington, F. B., (eds.), *Women's Mental Health*. New York: Springer.

IAEA (International Atomic Energy Agency). 2018. *Status and Trends in Spent Fuel and Radioactive Waste Management*. Vienna.

ICAO (International Council on Civil Aviation). 2019. "CORSIA Eligble Fuels." CORSIA at a Glance Series, International Civil Aviation Organization, Montreal, Canada. https://www.icao.int/environmental-protection/CORSIA/Documents/CORSIA%20Leaflets/CorsiaLeaflet-EN-9-WEB.pdf.

ICRC (International Committee of the Red Cross). 2020. "South Sudan: Depression, Anxiety Common as Huge Gaps Remain in Mental Health Care." https://www.icrc.org/en/document/mental-health-south-sudan. Accessed 18 March 2021.

IEA (International Energy Agency). 2014. *Africa Energy Outlook: A Focus on Energy Prospects in Sub-Saharan Africa*. World Energy Outlook Special Report. Paris. https://www.icafrica.org/en/knowledge-hub/article/africa-energy-outlook-a-focus-on-energy-prospects-in-sub-saharan-africa-263. Accessed 25 August 2022.

IEA (International Energy Agency). 2019. *Africa Energy Outlook 2019*. World Energy Outlook Special Report. Paris. https://www.iea.org/reports/africa-energy-outlook-2019. Accessed 25 August 2022.

IEA (International Energy Agency). 2020a. "ETP Clean Energy Technology Guide." https://www.iea.org/articles/etp-clean-energy-technology-guide. Accessed 25 August 2022.

IEA (International Energy Agency). 2020b. *Energy Technology Perspectives 2020: Special Report on Clean Energy Innovation. Accelerating Technology Progress for a Sustainable Future*. Paris.

IEA (International Energy Agency). 2020c. *World Energy Outlook 2020*. Paris.

IEA (International Energy Agency). 2021a. *Net Zero by 2050: A Roadmap for the Global Energy Sector*. Paris.

IEA (International Energy Agency). 2021b. "The Role of Critical Minerals in Clean Energy Transitions." In *World Energy Outlook Special Report*. Paris.

IEA (International Energy Agency). 2021c. "World Energy Balances: Overview." Paris.

IEA (International Energy Agency). 2021d. *Global Energy Review 2021*. Paris.

IEA (International Energy Agency). 2022. IEA Fossil Fuel Subsidies Database. https://www.iea.org/data-and-statistics/data-product/fossil-fuel-subsidies-database#subsidies-database. Accessed 21 July 2022.

IEP (Institute for Economics & Peace). 2020. *Positive Peace Report 2020: Analysing the Factors That Sustain Peace*. Sydney, Australia.

IEP (Institute for Economics & Peace). 2021. *Ecological Threat Report 2021: Understanding Ecological Threats, Resilience and Peace*. Sydney, Australia.

Iglesias-Rios, L., Harlow, S. D., Burgard, S. A., Kiss, L., and Zimmerman, C. 2018. "Mental Health, Violence and Psychological Coercion among Female and Male Trafficking Survivors in the Greater Mekong Sub-Region: A Cross-Sectional Study." *BioMed Central Psychology* 6(1): 1–15.

Ignatow, G. 2021. "Cognitive Sociology after Relational Biology 1." Sociological Forum, Wiley Online Library. https://onlinelibrary.wiley.com/doi/abs/10.1111/socf.12764. Accessed 24 March 2022.

Igreja, V., Kleijn, W., and Richters, A. 2006. "When the War Was over, Little Changed: Women's Posttraumatic Suffering after the War in Mozambique." *The Journal of Nervous and Mental Disease* 194(7): 502–509.

IHME (Institute for Health Metrics and Evaluation). 2021. "Global Health Data Exchange." http://ghdx.healthdata.org/gbd-results-tool. Accessed 6 July 2021.

ILO (International Labor Organization). 2018a. "Social Protection for Older Persons: Policy Trends and Statistics 2017–19." Social Protection Policy Paper 17. Geneva.

ILO (International Labor Organization). 2018b. *World Employment and Social Outlook 2018: Greening with Jobs*. Geneva.

ILO (International Labor Organization). 2020a. "Extending Social Protection to Informal Workers in the Covid-19 Crisis: Country Responses and Policy Considerations." Social Protection Spotlight, Geneva.

ILO (International Labour Organization). 2020b. *Youth and Covid-19: Impacts on Jobs, Education, Rights and Mental Wellbeing*. Geneva. https://www.ilo.org/wcmsp5/groups/public/---ed_emp/documents/publication/wcms_753026.pdf.

ILO (International Labour Organization). 2021a. "Labour Force Participation Rate by Sex and Age (%) - Annual." https://www.ilo.org/shinyapps/bulkexplorer0/?lang=en&segment=indicator&id=EAP_DWAP_SEX_AGE_RT_A. Accessed 13 September 2021.

ILO (International Labour Organization). 2021b. *The Role of Digital Labour Platforms in Transforming the World of Work*. https://www.ilo.org/global/research/global-reports/weso/2021/WCMS_771749/lang--en/index.htm. Accessed 30 June 2021.

ILO (International Labour Organization). 2021c. *World Social Protection Report 2020–22: Social Protection at the Crossroads — in Pursuit of a Better Future*. Geneva.

IMF (International Monetary Fund). 2017. "State-Contingent Debt Instruments for Sovereigns." Policy paper, Washington, DC.

IMF (International Monetary Fund). 2021a. "Fiscal Monitor April 2021." Washington, DC.

IMF (International Monetary Fund). 2021b. "Fiscal Monitor October 2021: Strengthening the Credibility of Public Finances." Washington, DC.

IMF (International Monetary Fund). 2021c. World Economic Outlook Database. http://www.imf.org/en/Publications/WEO/weo-database/2021/October. Accessed 21 April 2022.

IMF (International Monetary Fund). 2022. World Economic Outlook Database. https://www.imf.org/en/Publications/WEO/weo-database/2022/April. Accessed 21 April 2022.

Immordino-Yang, M. H., Christodoulou, J. A., and Singh, V. 2012. "Rest Is Not Idleness: Implications of the Brain's Default Mode for Human Development and Education." *Perspectives on Psychological Science* 7(4): 352–364.

Imperial College London. 2020a. "Covid-19: Insights on Face Mask Use: Global Review." Institute for Global Health Innovation, London.

Imperial College London. 2020b. "Covid-19: Physical Distancing, Perceptions of Vulnerability and Severity." Institute for Global Health Innovation, London.

Imperva. 2016. "Bot Traffic Report 2016." https://www.imperva.com/blog/bot-traffic-report-2016/. Accessed 25 August 2022.

The Independent Panel for Pandemic Preparedness and Response. 2021. *Covid-19: Make It the Last Pandemic*. Geneva: World Health Organization.

International IDEA (Institute for Democracy and Electoral Assistance). 2021. *The Global State of Democracy 2021: Building Resilience in a Pandemic Era*. Stockholm.

International Rivers Network. 2011. "The Myitsone Dam on the Irrawaddy River: A Briefing." https://archive.internationalrivers.org/resources/the-myitsone-dam-on-the-irrawaddy-river-a-briefing-3931. Accessed 25 August 2022.

IPBES (Intergovernmental Science-Policy Platform on Biodiversity and Ecosystem Services). 2019a. *Global Assessment Report on Biodiversity and Ecosystem Services of the Intergovernmental Science-Policy Platform on Biodiversity and Ecosystem Services*. Bonn, Germany. https://doi.org/10.5281/zenodo.3831673.

IPBES (Intergovernmental Science-Policy Platform on Biodiversity and Ecosystem Services). 2019b. *Summary for Policymakers of the Global Assessment Report on Biodiversity and Ecosystem Services of the*

Intergovernmental Science-Policy Platform on Biodiversity and Ecosystem Services. Bonn, Germany.

IPCC (Intergovernmental Panel on Climate Change). 2019. *Global Warming of 1.5°C: An IPCC Special Report on the Impacts of Global Warming of 1.5°C above Pre-Industrial Levels and Related Global Greenhouse Gas Emission Pathways, in the Context of Strengthening the Global Response to the Threat of Climate Change, Sustainable Development, and Efforts to Eradicate Poverty.* Geneva.

IPCC (Intergovernmental Panel on Climate Change). 2021. *Climate Change 2021: The Physical Science Basis: Summary for Policymakers.* Geneva.

IPCC (Intergovernmental Panel on Climate Change). 2022a. "Annex I: Glossary." In Masson-Delmotte, V., Zhai, P., Pörtner, H.-O., Roberts, D., Skea, J., Shukla, P. R., Pirani, A., and others, (eds.), *Global Warming of 1.5°C: IPCC Special Report on Impacts of Global Warming of 1.5°C above Pre-Industrial Levels in Context of Strengthening Response to Climate Change, Sustainable Development, and Efforts to Eradicate Poverty.* Cambridge, UK: Cambridge University Press.

IPCC (Intergovernmental Panel on Climate Change). 2022b. "Summary for Policymakers" In *Climate Change 2022: Impacts, Adaptation, and Vulnerability.* Geneva: Contribution of Working Group II to the Sixth Assessment Report of the Intergovernmental Panel on Climate Change. Geneva.

Ipsos and Bill & Melinda Gates Foundation. 2018. "Goalkeepers Global Youth Outlook Poll." Washington DC. https://www.ipsos.com/en-us/news-polls/Gates-goalkeepers-youth-optimism. Accessed 25 August 2022.

IRENA (International Renewable Energy Agency) 2020. *Renewable Power Generation Costs in 2019.* Abu Dhabi.

IRENA (International Renewable Energy Agency). 2021. *World Energy Transitions Outlook: 1.5° C Pathway.* Abu Dhabi.

IRENA (International Renewable Energy Agency) and International Labor Organization (ILO). 2021. *Renewable Energy and Jobs – Annual Review 2021.* Abu Dhabi and Geneva.

ISSA (International Social Security Association). 2021. "Beyond Covid-19: Towards Inclusive and Resilient Social Protection Systems." https://ww1.issa.int/analysis/beyond-covid-19-towards-inclusive-and-resilient-social-protection-systems. Accessed 25 August 2022.

ITU (International Telecommunication Union). 2021. "How Covid-19 Accelerated Digital Healthcare." https://www.itu.int/en/myitu/News/2021/04/07/07/25/COVID-accelerating-digital-healthcare. Accessed 27 September 2021.

Ivany, A. S., Bullock, L., Schminkey, D., Wells, K., Sharps, P., and Kools, S. 2018. "Living in Fear and Prioritizing Safety: Exploring Women's Lives after Traumatic Brain Injury from Intimate Partner Violence." *Qualitative Health Research* 28(11): 1708–1718.

Iyengar, S., Sood, G., and Lelkes, Y. 2012. "Affect, Not Ideology: A Social Identity Perspective on Polarization." *Public Opinion Quarterly* 76(3): 405–431.

Izdebski, A., Mordechai, L., and White, S. 2018. "The Social Burden of Resilience: A Historical Perspective." *Human Ecology* 46(3): 291–303.

Izdebski, A., Pickett, J., Roberts, N., and Waliszewski, T. 2016. "The Environmental, Archaeological and Historical Evidence for Regional Climatic Changes and Their Societal Impacts in the Eastern Mediterranean in Late Antiquity." *Quaternary Science Reviews* 136: 189–208.

Izuan, A. Z., Azhar, S. S., Tan, M. K. S., and Syed-Sharizman, S. A. R. 2018. "Neighbourhood Influences and Its Association with the Mental Health of Adolescents in Kuala Lumpur, Malaysia." *Asian Journal of Psychiatry* 38: 35–41.

Jabko, N. 2013. "The Political Appeal of Austerity." *Comparative European Politics* 11(6): 705–712.

Jackson, J. C., Gelfand, M., and Ember, C. R. 2020. "A Global Analysis of Cultural Tightness in Non-Industrial Societies." *Proceedings of the Royal Society B: Biological Sciences* 287(1930): 20201036.

Jackson, M. 2020. *Where to Next? Decolonisation and the Stories of the Land.* Wellington: Bridgett Williams Books.

Jacob, J., and Akpan, I. 2015. "Silencing Boko Haram: Mobile Phone Blackout and Counterinsurgency in Nigeria's Northeast Region." *Stability: International Journal of Security and Development* 4(1).

Jaeger, C. B., Brosnan, S. F., Levin, D. T., and Jones, O. D. 2020. "Predicting Variation in Endowment Effect Magnitudes." *Evolution and Human Behavior* 41(3): 253–259.

Jafino, B. A., Walsh, B., Rozenberg, J., and Hallegatte, S. 2020. "Revised Estimates of the Impact of Climate Change on Extreme Poverty by 2030." Policy Research Working Paper 9417, World Bank, Washington, DC.

Jaidka, K., Giorgi, S., Schwartz, H. A., Kern, M. L., Ungar, L. H., and Eichstaedt, J. C. 2020. "Estimating Geographic Subjective Well-Being from Twitter: A Comparison of Dictionary and Data-Driven Language Methods." *Proceedings of the National Academy of Sciences* 117(19): 10165–10171.

Jain, S., Venkataraman, A., Wechsler, M., and Peppas, N. 2021. "Messenger RNA-Based Vaccines: Past, Present, and Future Directions in the Context of the Covid-19 Pandemic." *Advanced Drug Delivery Reviews* 179(114000).

James, P., and Van Seters, P. 2014. *Globalization and Politics. Volume II. Global Social Movements and Global Civil Society.* Washington, DC: Sage.

Jaramillo, C. F. 2022. "Education Is One of the Most Powerful Tools against Racism in Latin America." Latin America and the Caribbean [blog], 23 March. https://blogs.worldbank.org/latinamerica/education-one-most-powerful-tools-against-racism-latin-america. Accessed 24 June 2022.

Jarvstad, A. 2021. "Beyond Nudging: Generalisable and Transferable Learning in Human Decision-Making." PsyArXiv. March 4. https://doi.org/10.31234/osf.io/9q6xk.

Jasanoff, S., and Hurlbut, B. 2018. "A Global Observatory for Gene Editing." *Nature* 555: 435–437.

Jasper, J. M. 2011. "Emotions and Social Movements: Twenty Years of Theory and Research." *Annual Review of Sociology* 37: 285–303.

Jasper, J. M. 2021. "Fear of the Angry Mob." *Dynamics of Asymmetric Conflict* 14(2): 121–137.

Jenkins, J. C., Wallace, M., and Fullerton, A. S. 2008. "A Social Movement Society?: A Cross-National Analysis of Protest Potential." *International Journal of Sociology* 38(3): 12–35.

Jenner, L. C., Rotchell, J. M., Bennett, R. T., Cowen, M., Tentzeris, V., and Sadofsky, L. R. 2022. "Detection of Microplastics in Human Lung Tissue Using μFTIR Spectroscopy." *Science of the Total Environment* 831: 154907.

Jeswani, H. K., Chilvers, A., and Azapagic, A. 2020. "Environmental Sustainability of Biofuels: A Review." *Proceedings of the Royal Society A* 476(2243): 20200351.

Jetten, J., Haslam, C., Haslam, S. A., and Branscombe, N. R. 2009. "The Social Cure." *Scientific American Mind* 20(5): 26–33.

Jimenez, D., Harper, C., and George, R. 2021. "Mobilising for Change: How Women's Social Movements Are Transforming Gender Norms." ALIGN Report, Overseas Development Institute, London.

Johnston, D. W., Shields, M. A., and Suziedelyte, A. 2020. "Macroeconomic Shocks, Job Security, and Health: Evidence from the Mining Industry." *American Journal of Health Economics* 6(3): 348–371.

Johnston, H., Larana, E., and Gusfield, J. R. 1994. "Identities, Grievances, and New Social Movements." In Laraña, E., Johnston, H., and Gusfield, J. R., (eds.), *New Social Movements: From Ideology to Identity.* Philadelphia, PA: Temple University Press.

Jonas, E., McGregor, I., Klackl, J., Agroskin, D., Fritsche, I., Holbrook, C., Nash, K., and others. 2014. "Threat and Defense: From Anxiety to Approach." In Olson, J. M., and Zanna, M. P., (eds.), *Advances in Experimental Social Psychology*, Vol. 49. Amsterdam: Elsevier.

Jones, L., Hughes, M., and Unterstaller, U. 2001. "Post-Traumatic Stress Disorder (PTSD) in Victims of Domestic Violence: A Review of the Research." *Trauma, Violence, & Abuse* 2(2): 99–119.

Jonsson, K. R., Vartanova, I., and Södergren, M. 2018. "Ethnic Variations in Mental Health among 10–15-Year-Olds Living in England and Wales: The Impact of Neighbourhood Characteristics and Parental Behaviour." *Health & Place* 51: 189–199.

Jordà, Ò., Knoll, K., Kuvshinov, D., Schularick, M., and Taylor, A. M. 2019. "The Rate of Return on Everything, 1870–2015." *The Quarterly Journal of Economics* 134(3): 1225–1298.

Joshi, G., and Yenneti, K. 2020. "Community Solar Energy Initiatives in India: A Pathway for Addressing Energy Poverty and Sustainability?" *Energy and Buildings* 210: 109736.

June, C., O'Connor, R., Kawalekar, O., Ghassemi, S., and Milone, M. C. 2018. "Car T Cell Immunotherapy for Human Cancer." *Science* 359(6382): 1361–1365.

Juris, J. S. 2004. "Networked Social Movements: Global Movements for Global Justice." In Castells, M., (ed.), *The Network Society: A Cross-Cultural Perspective*. Cheltenham, UK: Edward Elgar.

Kadir, A., Shenoda, S., Pitterman, S., and Goldhagen, J. 2018. "The Effects of Armed Conflict on Children." *Pediatrics* 142(6).

Kahan, D. M. 2013. "Ideology, Motivated Reasoning, and Cognitive Reflection: An Experimental Study." *Judgment and Decision Making* 8: 407–424.

Kahan, D. M., Landrum, A., Carpenter, K., Helft, L., and Hall Jamieson, K. 2017a. "Science Curiosity and Political Information Processing." *Political Psychology* 38(S1): 179–199.

Kahan, D. M., Peters, E., Dawson, E. C., and Slovic, P. 2017b. "Motivated Numeracy and Enlightened Self-Government." *Behavioural Public Policy* 1(1): 54–86.

Kahn, L. B. 2010. "The Long-Term Labor Market Consequences of Graduating from College in a Bad Economy." *Labour Economics* 17(2): 303–316.

Kahneman, D. 2003. "Maps of Bounded Rationality: Psychology for Behavioral Economics." *American Economic Review* 93(5): 1449–1475.

Kahneman, D. 2011. *Thinking, Fast and Slow*. New York: Farrar, Strauss and Giroux.

Kahneman, D., and Tversky, A. 1979. "Prospect Theory: An Analysis of Decision under Risk." *Econometrica* 47(2): 263–291.

Kahneman, D., and Tversky, A. 2013. "Prospect Theory: An Analysis of Decision under Risk." *Handbook of the Fundamentals of Financial Decision Making: Part I*. Singapore: World Scientific.

Kakkar, H., and Sivanathan, N. 2017. "When the Appeal of a Dominant Leader Is Greater Than a Prestige Leader." *Proceedings of the National Academy of Sciences* 114(26): 6734–6739.

Kao, A., and Couzin, I. 2014. "Decision Accuracy in Complex Environments Is Often Maximized by Small Group Sizes." *Proceedings of the Royal Society B: Biological Sciences* 281(20133305).

Kapur, V., and Boulton, A. 2021. "Covid-19 Accelerates the Adoption of Telemedicine in Asia-Pacific Countries." Bain & Company. https://www.bain.com/insights/covid-19-accelerates-the-adoption-of-telemedicine-in-asia-pacific-countries/. Accessed 27 September 2021.

Kasman, M., Heuberger, B., and Hammond, R. A. 2018. "A Review of Large Scale Youth Financial Literacy Education Policies and Programs." The Brookings Institution, Washington, DC.

Katz, L., Chen, Y. Y., Gonzalez, R., Peterson, T. C., Zhao, H., and Baltz, R. H. 2018. "Synthetic Biology Advances and Applications in the Biotechnology Industry: A Perspective." *Journal of Industrial Microbiology and Biotechnology*, 45(7): 449–461.

Kaur, S., Mullainathan, S., Oh, S., and Schilbach, F. 2021. "Do Financial Concerns Make Workers Less Productive?" NBER Working Paper 28338, National Bureau of Economic Research, Cambridge, MA.

Kawakatsu, M., Lelkes, Y., Levin, S. A., and Tarnita, C. E. 2021. "Interindividual Cooperation Mediated by Partisanship Complicates Madison's Cure for 'Mischiefs of Faction'." *Proceedings of the National Academy of Sciences* 118(50): e2102148118.

Kay, J., and King, M. 2020. *Radical Uncertainty: Decision-Making Beyond the Numbers*. New York: WW Norton & Company.

Kazan, H. 2020. Cyber Bullying and Violence Literacy in the Context of Digitalization." In *Handbook of Research on Multidisciplinary Approaches to Literacy in the Digital Age*. Hershey, PA: IGI Global. https://www.igi-global.com/chapter/cyber-bullying-and-violence-literacy-in-the-context-of-digitalization/240423. Accessed 6 October 2021.

Kearns, A., and Whitley, E. 2019. "Associations of Internet Access with Social Integration, Wellbeing and Physical Activity among Adults in Deprived Communities: Evidence from a Household Survey." *BioMed Central Public Health* 19(1): 1–15.

Keenan, R. J., Reams, G. A., Achard, F., de Freitas, J. V., Grainger, A., and Lindquist, E. 2015. "Dynamics of Global Forest Area: Results from the FAO Global Forest Resources Assessment 2015." *Forest Ecology and Management* 352: 9–20.

Kelbessa, W. 2022. "Environmental Ethics and Policy." Reimagining the Human-Environment Relationship paper series, United Nations University–United Nations Environment Programme. New York.

Keller, F. B., Schoch, D., Stier, S., and Yang, J. 2021. "Political Astroturfing on Twitter: How to Coordinate a Disinformation Campaign." *Political Communication* 37(2): 256–280.

Keynes, J. M. 1909. "A Treatise on Probability." *Diamond* 3(2): 12.

Keys, P. W., Galaz, V., Dyer, M., Matthews, N., Folke, C., Nyström, M., and Cornell, S. E. 2019. "Anthropocene Risk." *Nature Sustainability* 2(8): 667–673.

Khadgi, A. 2021. "A Group of Activists Strives to End Forced Imposition of the Third Gender Label." *The Katmandu Post*, 22 October.

Khamis, S. 2019. "Arab Women's Feminism(S), Resistance(S), and Activism(S) within and Beyond the "Arab Spring": Potentials, Limitations, and Future Prospects." In Oren, T., and Press, A. L., (eds.), *The Routledge Handbook of Contemporary Feminism*. London: Routledge.

Khan, L. M. 2017. "The Ideological Roots of America's Market Power Problem." *The Yale Law Journal Forum* 127: 960–979.

Khan, M., Ilcisin, M., and Saxton, K. 2017. "Multifactorial Discrimination as a Fundamental Cause of Mental Health Inequities." *International Journal for Equity in Health* 16(1): 1–12.

Khandii, O. 2019. "Social Threats in the Digitalization of Economy and Society." SHS Web of Conferences 67, 06023. https://www.shs-conferences.org/articles/shsconf/abs/2019/08/shsconf_NTI-UkrSURT2019_06023/shsconf_NTI-UkrSURT2019_06023.html. Accessed 6 October 2021.

Khaw, M. W., Glimcher, P. W., and Louie, K. 2017. "Normalized Value Coding Explains Dynamic Adaptation in the Human Valuation Process." *Proceedings of the National Academy of Sciences* 114(48): 12696–12701.

Khaw, M. W., Li, Z., and Woodford, M. 2021. "Cognitive Imprecision and Small-Stakes Risk Aversion." *The Review of Economic Studies* 88(4): 1979–2013.

Khushf, G. 2006. "An Ethic for Enhancing Human Performance through Integrative Technologies." In Bainbridge, W., and Roco, M., (eds.), *Managing Nano-Bio-Info-Cogno Innovations: Converging Technologies in Society*. Dordrecht, The Netherlands: Springer.

Kimbrough, K. 2021. "These Are the Sectors Where Green Jobs Are Growing in Demand." http's://www.weforum.org/agenda/2021/09/sectors-where-green-jobs-are-growing-in-demand/. Accessed 24 August 2022.

Kimmerer, R. W. 2013. *Braiding Sweetgrass: Indigenous Wisdom, Scientific Knowledge and the Teachings of Plants*. Minneapolis, MN: Milkweed Editions.

King, D. L., Delfabbro, P. H., Kaptsis, D., and Zwaans, T. 2014. "Adolescent Simulated Gambling Via Digital and Social Media: An Emerging Problem." *Computers in Human Behavior* 31: 305–313.

Kingdon, J. W. 1984. *Agendas, Alternatives, and Public Policies*. Boston, MA: Little, Brown.

Kinzig, A. P., and Socolow, R. H. 1994. "Human Impacts on the Nitrogen Cycle." *Physics Today* 47(11).

Kirby, J. 2022. "Why Grain Can't Get out of Ukraine." *Vox*, 20 June.

Klein, K. M., and Kruglanski, A. W. 2013. "Commitment and Extremism: A Goal Systemic Analysis." *Journal of Social Issues* 69(3): 419–435.

Klugman, J., Hanmer, L., Twigg, S., Hasan, T., McCleary-Sills, J., and Santamaria, J. 2014. *Voice and Agency: Empowering Women and Girls for Shared Prosperity*. Washington, DC: World Bank.

Knabe, A., and Rätzel, S. 2011. "Scarring or Scaring? The Psychological Impact of Past Unemployment and Future Unemployment Risk." *Economica* 78(310): 283–293.

Knight, F. H. 1921. *Risk, Uncertainty and Profit*. Boston, MA: Houghton Mifflin.

Knobloch-Westerwick, S., Mothes, C., Johnson, B. K., Westerwick, A., and Donsbach, W. 2015. "Political Online Information Searching in Germany and the United States: Confirmation Bias, Source Credibility, and Attitude Impacts." *Journal of Communication* 65(3): 489–511.

Knol, E., and Ijssennagger, N. 2017. "Origin of the Dutch Coastal Landscape: Long-Term Landscape Evolution of the Netherlands During the Holocene." In Hines, J., and Ijssennagger, N., (eds.), *Frisians and Their North Sea Neighbours: From the Fifth Century to the Viking Age*. Woodbridge, UK: Boydell.

Knowledge Portal on Innovation and Access to Medicines. 2021. "Covid-19 Vaccine R&D Investments." https://www.knowledgeportalia.org/covid19-r-d-funding. Accessed 5 October 2021.

Kohrt, B. A., Asher, L., Bhardwaj, A., Fazel, M., Jordans, M. J., Mutamba, B. B., Nadkarni, A., and others. 2018. "The Role of Communities in Mental Health Care in Low- and Middle-Income Countries: A Meta-Review of Components and Competencies." *International Journal of Environmental Research and Public Health* 15(6): 1279–1299.

Koonin, L. M., Hoots, B., Tsang, C. A., Leroy, Z., Farris, K., Jolly, B., Antall, P., and others. 2020. "Trends in the Use of Telehealth During the Emergence of the Covid-19 Pandemic—United States, January–March 2020." *Morbidity and Mortality Weekly Report* 69(43): 1595–1599.

Kopasker, D., Montagna, C., and Bender, K. A. 2018. "Economic Insecurity: A Socioeconomic Determinant of Mental Health." *Social Science & Medicine-Population Health* 6: 184–194.

Korinek, A., and Stiglitz, J. E. 2021. "Covid-19 Driven Advances in Automation and Artificial Intelligence Risk Exacerbating Economic Inequality." *The BMJ* 372: n367.

Kőszegi, B., and Rabin, M. 2006. "A Model of Reference-Dependent Preferences." *The Quarterly Journal of Economics* 121(4): 1133–1165.

Kőszegi, B., and Rabin, M. 2007. "Reference-Dependent Risk Attitudes." *American Economic Review* 97(4): 1047–1073.

Kotz, M., Wenz, L., and Levermann, A. 2021. "Footprint of Greenhouse Forcing in Daily Temperature Variability." *Proceedings of the National Academy of Sciences* 118(32): e2103294118.

Kotz, M., Wenz, L., Stechemesser, A., Kalkuhl, M., and Levermann, A. 2021. "Day-to-Day Temperature Variability Reduces Economic Growth." *Nature Climate Change* 11(4): 319–325.

Kovacevic, A., and Nikolic, D. 2015. "Cyber Attacks on Critical Infrastructure: Review and Challenges." In Portela, I. M., and Cruz-Cunha, M. M., (eds.), *Handbook of Research on Digital Crime, Cyberspace Security, and Information Assurance.* Hershey, PA: IGI Global.

Kozlowski, J., Veldkamp, L., and Venkateswaran, V. 2020. "Scarring Body and Mind: The Long-Term Belief-Scarring Effects of Covid-19." NBER Working Paper 27439, National Bureau of Economic Research, Cambridge, MA.

Kpobi, L., and Swartz, L. 2019. "Indigenous and Faith Healing for Mental Health in Ghana: An Examination of the Literature on Reported Beliefs, Practices and Use of Alternative Mental Health Care in Ghana." *African Journal of Primary Health Care & Family Medicine* 11(1): 1–5.

Krampe, F. 2021. "Why United Nations Peace Operations Cannot Ignore Climate Change." Stockholm International Peace Research Institute, Stockholm. https://www.sipri.org/commentary/topical-backgrounder/2021/why-united-nations-peace-operations-cannot-ignore-climate-change. Accessed 25 August 2022.

Kranton, R., Pease, M., Sanders, S., and Huettel, S. 2020. "Deconstructing Bias in Social Preferences Reveals Groupy and Not-Groupy Behavior." *Proceedings of the National Academy of Sciences* 117(35): 21185–21193.

Krausmann, F., Fischer-Kowalski, M., Schandl, H., and Eisenmenger, N. 2008. "The Global Sociometabolic Transition: Past and Present Metabolic Profiles and Their Future Trajectories." *Journal of Industrial Ecology* 12(5–6): 637–656.

Kremer, M., Rao, G., and Schilbach, F. 2019. "Behavioral Development Economics." In Bernheim, B. D., Dellavigna, S., and Laibson, D., (eds.), *Handbook of Behavioral Economics: Applications and Foundations 1.* Amsterdam: North-Holland.

Kreps, S. 2020. "The Role of Technology in Online Misinformation." The Brookings Institution, Washington, DC.

Kreps, S. E., and Kriner, D. L. 2020. "Model Uncertainty, Political Contestation, and Public Trust in Science: Evidence from the Covid-19 Pandemic." *Science Advances* 6(43): eabd4563.

Kristensen, H., and Korda, M. 2021. "World Nuclear Forces." In *SIPRI Yearbook 2021: Armaments, Disarmament and International Security.* Oxford, UK: Oxford University Press.

Kruglanski, A. W. 1989. "The Psychology of Being 'Right': The Problem of Accuracy in Social Perception and Cognition." *Psychological Bulletin* 106(3): 395–409.

Kruglanski, A. W., Gelfand, M. J., Bélanger, J. J., Sheveland, A., Hetiarachchi, M., and Gunaratna, R. 2014. "The Psychology of Radicalization and Deradicalization: How Significance Quest Impacts Violent Extremism." *Political Psychology* 35: 69–93.

Kruglanski, A. W., Molinario, E., Jasko, K., Webber, D., Leander, N. P., and Pierro, A. 2022. "Significance-Quest Theory." *Perspectives on Psychological Science*: 17(4): 1050–1071.

Krugman, P. 2022. "Food, Fertilizer and the Future." *New York Times,* 26 April.

Kteily, N., Hodson, G., and Bruneau, E. 2016. "They See Us as Less Than Human: Metadehumanization Predicts Intergroup Conflict Via Reciprocal Dehumanization." *Journal of Personality and Social Psychology* 110(3): 343–370.

Kumar, S., Jeyaseelan, L., Suresh, S., and Ahuja, R. C. 2005. "Domestic Violence and Its Mental Health Correlates in Indian Women." *The British Journal of Psychiatry* 187(1): 62–67.

Kupers, R., and Wilkinson, A. 2014. *The Essence of Scenarios.* Amsterdam: Amsterdam University Press.

Kupferschmidt, K. 2020. "'A Completely New Culture of Doing Research.' Coronavirus Outbreak Changes How Scientists Communicate." ScienceInsider, 26 February. https://www.science.org/content/article/completely-new-culture-doing-research-coronavirus-outbreak-changes-how-scientists. Accessed 1 June 2022.

Kwon, J. Y., Wormley, A. S., and Varnum, M. E. W. 2021. "Changing Cultures, Changing Brains: A Framework for Integrating Cultural Neuroscience and Cultural Change Research." *Biological Psychology* 162: 108087.

La Ferrara, E. 2019. "Presidential Address: Aspirations, Social Norms, and Development." *Journal of the European Economic Association* 17(6): 1687–1722.

Lachvier, M. 1991. *Les Années De Misère: La Famine Au Temps Du Grand Roi, 1680–1720* Paris: Fayard.

Lade, S. J., Haider, L. J., Engström, G., and Schlüter, M. 2017. "Resilience Offers Escape from Trapped Thinking on Poverty Alleviation." *Science Advances* 3(5): e1603043.

Lafta, R. K., Aziz, Z. S., and AlObaidi, A. 2014. "Post-traumatic Stress Disorder (PTSD) among Male Adolescents in Baghdad." *Journal of Psychological Abnormalities* 3(3): 1–5.

Laibson, D. 1997. "Golden Eggs and Hyperbolic Discounting." *The Quarterly Journal of Economics* 112(2): 443–477.

Lambe, F., Ran, Y., Jürisoo, M., Holmlid, S., Muhozà, C., Johnson, O., and Osborne, M. 2020. "Embracing Complexity: A Transdisciplinary Conceptual Framework for Understanding Behavior Change in the Context of Development-Focused Interventions." *World Development* 126: 104703.

Lambin, E. F., Gibbs, H. K., Heilmayr, R., Carlson, K. M., Fleck, L. C., Garrett, R. D., le Polain de Waroux, Y., and others. 2018. "The Role of Supply-Chain Initiatives in Reducing Deforestation." *Nature Climate Change* 8(2): 109–116.

Lamont, M. 2000. *The Dignity of Working Men: Morality and the Boundaries of Race, Class, and Immigration.* Cambridge, MA: Harvard University Press.

Lamont, M. 2018. "Addressing Recognition Gaps: Destigmatization and the Reduction of Inequality." *American Sociological Review* 83(3): 419–444.

Lamont, M. 2019. "From 'Having' to 'Being': Self-Worth and the Current Crisis of American Society." *The British Journal of Sociology* 70(3): 660–707.

Lamont, M. Forthcoming. *Who Matters: How to Redefine Worth in Our Divided World.* New York: Simon and Schuster.

Lamont, M., Adler, L., Park, B. Y., and Xiang, X. 2017. "Bridging Cultural Sociology and Cognitive Psychology in Three Contemporary Research Programmes." *Nature Human Behaviour* 1(12): 866–872.

The Lancet Global Health. 2020. "Editorial: Mental Health Matters." *The Lancet Global Health* 8(11): E1352.

Landrigan, P. J., Fuller, R., Acosta, N. J., Adeyi, O., Arnold, R., Baldé, A. B., Bertollini, R., and others. 2018. "The Lancet Commission on Pollution and Health." *The Lancet* 391(10119): 462–512.

Lanphier, E., Urnov, F., Haecker, S. E., Werner, M., and Smolenski, J. 2015. "Don't Edit the Human Germ Line." *Nature* 519(7544): 410–411.

Lavigne, F., Degeai, J.-P., Komorowski, J.-C., Guillet, S., Robert, V., Lahitte, P., Oppenheimer, C., and others. 2013. "Source of the Great Ad 1257 Mystery Eruption Unveiled, Samalas Volcano, Rinjani Volcanic Complex, Indonesia." *Proceedings of the National Academy of Sciences* 110(42): 16742–16747.

Lazard, O. 2021. "The Power of Soil: How Our Precarious Climate Shaped the Arab Spring." *Middle East Eye,* 1 January.

Lazard, O., and Youngs, R., (eds.). 2021. *The EU and Climate Security: Toward Ecological Diplomacy.* Carnegie Europe, Open Society European Policy Institute, Brussels.

Lazer, L. 2021. "A Just Transition to a Zero-Carbon World Is Possible. Here's How." Insights, World Resources Institute, Washington, DC. https://www.wri.org/insights/just-transition-zero-carbon-world-possible-heres-how. Accessed 25 August 2022.

Leach, M., Reyers, B., Bai, X., Brondizio, E. S., Cook, C., Díaz, S., Espindola, G., and others. 2018. "Equity and Sustainability in the Anthropocene: A Social–Ecological Systems Perspective on Their Intertwined Futures." *Global Sustainability* 1(e13): 1–13.

Lear, J. 2006. *Radical Hope: Ethics in the Face of Cultural Devastation.* Cambridge, MA: Harvard University Press.

Lebling, K., Ge, M., Levin, K., Waite, R., Friedrich, J., Elliott, C., Chan, C., and others. 2020. *State of Climate Action: Assessing Progress toward 2030 and 2050.* Washington, DC: World Resource Institute.

Lèbre, É., Stringer, M., Svobodova, K., Owen, J. R., Kemp, D., Côte, C., Arratia-Solar, A., and Valenta, R. K. 2020. "The Social and Environmental Complexities of Extracting Energy Transition Metals." *Nature Communications* 11(1): 1–8.

LeDoux, J. E., and Brown, R. 2017. "A Higher-Order Theory of Emotional Consciousness." *Proceedings of the National Academy of Sciences* 114(10): E2016–E2025.

Lee, H., Ahn, H., Choi, S., and Choi, W. 2014. "The SAMS: Smartphone Addiction Management System and Verification." *Journal of Medical Systems* 38(1): 1–10.

Lee, H., and Waite, L. J. 2018. "Cognition in Context: The Role of Objective and Subjective Measures of Neighborhood and Household in Cognitive Functioning in Later Life." *The Gerontologist* 58(1): 159–169.

Lee, S. 2020. "Environment and Wellbeing." *New Left Review* 123.

Lee, S. H., Ripke, S., Neale, B. M., Faraone, S. V., Purcell, S. M., Perlis, R. H., Mowry, B. J., and others. 2013. "Genetic Relationship between Five Psychiatric Disorders Estimated from Genome-Wide Snps." *Nature Genetics* 45(9): 984–995.

Lees, J. 2022. "Political Violence and Inaccurate Metaperceptions." *Proceedings of the National Academy of Sciences* 119(19): e2204045119.

Lees, J., and Cikara, M. 2021. "Understanding and Combating Misperceived Polarization." *Philosophical Transactions of the Royal Society B: Biological Sciences* 376(1822).

Lehman, C., Loberg, S., Wilson, M., and Gorham, E. 2021. "Ecology of the Anthropocene Signals Hope for Consciously Managing the Planetary Ecosystem." *Proceedings of the National Academy of Sciences* 118(28).

Lengfelder, C. 2021. "Displaced, Traumatised and Human Development Deprived: The Psychology of Impaired Capabilities." Working Paper. https://www.researchgate.net/profile/Christina-Lengfelder-3/publication/354006655_ Displaced_traumatised_and_human_development_deprived_The_psychology_of_impaired_capabilities/links/611e7be1169a1a01031200c4/Displaced-traumatised-and-human-development-deprived-The-psychology-of-impaired-capabilities.pdf.

Lenton, T. M. 2019. "Biodiversity and Global Change: From Creator to Victim." In Dasgupta, P., Raven, P. H. and Mcivor, A. L., (eds.), *Biological Extinction: New Perspectives.* Cambridge, UK: Cambridge University Press.

Lenton, T. M., Pichler, P.-P., and Weisz, H. 2016. "Revolutions in Energy Input and Material Cycling in Earth History and Human History." *Earth System Dynamics* 7(2): 353–370.

Lenton, T. M., Rockström, J., Gaffney, O., Rahmstorf, S., Richardson, K., Steffen, W., and Schellnhuber, H. J. 2019. "Climate Tipping Points—Too Risky to Bet Against." *Nature* 575: 592–595.

Leonard, A., Ahsan, A., Charbonnier, F., and Hirmer, S. 2022. "The Resource Curse in Renewable Energy: A Framework for Risk Assessment." *Energy Strategy Reviews* 41: 100841.

Lerner, J. S., and Keltner, D. 2001. "Fear, Anger, and Risk." *Journal of Personality and Social Psychology* 81(1): 146.

Lerner, J. S., Li, Y., Valdesolo, P., and Kassam, K. S. 2015. "Emotion and Decision Making." *Annual Review of Psychology* 66(1): 799–823.

Lerner, J. S., Small, D. A., and Loewenstein, G. 2004. "Heart Strings and Purse Strings: Carryover Effects of Emotions on Economic Decisions." *Psychological Science* 15(5): 337–341.

Leslie, J. 1996. *The End of the World: The Science and Ethics of Human Extinction.* Abingdon, UK: Routledge.

Levin, A. T., Owusu-Boaitey, N., Pugh, S., Fosdick, B. K., Zwi, A. B., Malani, A., Soman, S., and others. 2022. "Assessing the Burden of Covid-19 in Developing Countries: Systematic Review, Meta-Analysis and Public Policy Implications." *BMJ Global Health* 7(5): e008477.

Levine, P. A. 2008. *Healing Trauma: A Pioneering Program for Restoring the Wisdom of the Body.* Louisville, KY: Sounds True.

Levine, P. A. 2010. *In an Unspoken Voice: How the Body Releases Trauma and Restores Goodness.* Berkeley, CA: North Atlantic Books.

Levine, P. A., and Frederick, A. 1997. *Waking the Tiger: Healing Trauma: The Innate Capacity to Transform Overwhelming Experiences.* Berkeley, CA: North Atlantic Books.

Levine, R. 2019. "Closing the Gap between Social Movements and Policy Change." Hewlett Foundation. https://hewlett.org/closing-the-gap-between-social-movements-and-policy-change/. Accessed 25 August 2022.

Levitsky, S., and Ziblatt, D. 2018. *How Democracies Die.* New York: Broadway Books.

Levy, J. S. 1997. "Prospect Theory, Rational Choice, and International Relations." *International Studies Quarterly* 41(1): 87–112.

Levy, N. 2021. "Echoes of Covid Misinformation." *Philosophical Psychology*: 1–18.

Levy, N. 2022. *Bad Beliefs: Why They Happen to Good People.* Oxford, UK: Oxford University Press.

Levy, N., and Savulescu, J. 2021. "After the Pandemic: New Responsibilities." *Public Health Ethics* 14(2): 120–133.

Levy, R. e. 2021. "Social Media, News Consumption, and Polarization: Evidence from a Field Experiment." *American Economic Review* 111(3): 831–870.

Lewandowsky, S., Ballard, T., and Pancost, R. D. 2015. "Uncertainty as Knowledge." *Philosophical Transactions of the Royal Society A: Mathematical, Physical and Engineering Sciences* 373(2055): 20140462.

Lichtenberg, P. A., Stickney, L., and Paulson, D. 2013. "Is Psychological Vulnerability Related to the Experience of Fraud in Older Adults?" *Clinical Gerontologist* 36(2): 132–146.

Lichtenberg, P. A., Sugarman, M. A., Paulson, D., Ficker, L. J., and Rahman-Filipiak, A. 2016. "Psychological and Functional Vulnerability Predicts Fraud Cases in Older Adults: Results of a Longitudinal Study." *Clinical Gerontologist* 39(1): 48–63.

Lieberman, B., and Gordon, E. 2018. *Climate Change in Human History: Prehistory to the Present.* London: Bloomsbury.

Lieu, J., Hanger-Kopp, S., van Vliet, O., and Sorman, A. H. 2020. "Assessing Risks of Low-Carbon Transition Pathways." *Environmental Innovation and Societal Transitions* 35: 261–270.

Lindbeck, A., Nyberg, S., and Weibull, J. 1999. "Social Norms and Economic Incentives in the Welfare State." *Quarterly Journal of Economics* 114(1): 1–35.

Lindh, A., and McCall, L. 2020. "Class Position and Political Opinion in Rich Democracies." *Annual Review of Sociology* 46: 419–441.

Loewenstein, G. 2000. "Emotions in Economic Theory and Economic Behavior." *American Economic Review* 90(2): 426–432.

Loibl, C., Drost, M. A., Huisman, M., Suanet, B., de Bruin, W. B., McNair, S., and Summers, B. 2021. "Worry About Debt Is Related to Social Loneliness in Older Adults in the Netherlands." *Ageing & Society*: 1–23.

Long, K. N. G., Kim, E. S., Chen, Y., Wilson, M. F., Worthington Jr., E. L., and VanderWeele, T. J. 2020. "The Role of Hope in Subsequent Health and Well-Being for Older Adults: An Outcome-Wide Longitudinal Approach." *Global Epidemiology* 2: 100018.

Lopes da Silva, D., Tian, N., and Marksteiner, A. 2021. "Trends in World Military Expenditure." Stockholm International Peace Research Institute, Stockholm. https://sipri.org/sites/default/files/2021-04/fs_2104_milex_0.pdf.

Lorenzo, V. d., Prather, K. L., Chen, G.-Q., O'Day, E., Kameke, C. v., Oyarzún, D. A., Hosta-Rigau, L., and others. 2018. "The Power of Synthetic Biology for Bioproduction, Remediation and Pollution Control." *EMBO Reports* 19(4): e45658.

Lough, B. J., Carroll, M., Bannister, T., and Borromeo, K. 2018. *State of the World's Volunteerism Report 2018:*

The Thread That Binds: Volunteerism and Community Resilience. Bonn, Germany: United Nations Volunteers programme.

Lövbrand, E., Beck, S., Chilvers, J., Forsyth, T., Hedrén, J., Hulme, M., Lidskog, R., and Vasileiadou, E. 2015. "Who Speaks for the Future of Earth? How Critical Social Science Can Extend the Conversation on the Anthropocene." *Global Environmental Change* 32: 211–218.

Lovejoy, T. E. H., Lee. 2019. *Biodiversity and Climate Change: Transforming the Biosphere*. New Haven, CT: Yale University Press.

Lowes, S., Nunn, N., Robinson, J. A., and Weigel, J. L. 2017. "The Evolution of Culture and Institutions: Evidence from the Kuba Kingdom." *Econometrica* 85(4): 1065–1091.

Lu, J. G., Jin, P., and English, A. S. 2021. "Collectivism Predicts Mask Use During Covid-19." *Proceedings of the National Academy of Sciences* 118(23): e2021793118.

Lübke, C. 2021. "Socioeconomic Roots of Climate Change Denial and Uncertainty among the European Population." *European Sociological Review* 38(1): 153–168.

Lund, C., Breen, A., Flisher, A. J., Kakuma, R., Corrigall, J., Joska, J. A., Swartz, L., and Patel, V. 2010. "Poverty and Common Mental Disorders in Low and Middle Income Countries: A Systematic Review." *Social Science & Medicine* 71(3): 517–528.

Lundberg, J., Kristenson, M., and Starrin, B. 2009. "Status Incongruence Revisited: Associations with Shame and Mental Wellbeing." *Sociology of Health & Illness* 31(4): 478–493.

Lustig, N., Martinez Pabon, V., Neidhöfer, G., and Tommasi, M. 2019. "Short and Long-Run Distributional Impacts of Covid-19 in Latin America." Commitment to Equity Working Paper 96, Tulane University, Department of Economics, New Orleans, LA.

Lybbert, T. J., and Wydick, B. 2018. "Poverty, Aspirations, and the Economics of Hope." *Economic Development and Cultural Change* 66(4): 709–753.

Lynch, A., Broomhall, S., and Davidson, J. 2019. *A Cultural History of the Emotions*. New York: Bloomsbury Academic.

Lyver, P., Timoti, P., Jones, C., Richardson, S., Tahi, B., and Greenhalgh, S. 2017. "An Indigenous Community-Based Monitoring System for Assessing Forest Health in New Zealand." *Biodiversity and Conservation* 26(13): 3183–3212.

Mace, G. M., Reyers, B., Alkemade, R., Biggs, R., Chapin, F. S., Cornell, S. E., Díaz, S., and others. 2014. "Approaches to Defining a Planetary Boundary for Biodiversity." *Global Environmental Change* 28: 289–297.

Mach, K. J., and Field, C. B. 2017. "Toward the Next Generation of Assessment." *Annual Review of Environment and Resources* 42: 569–597.

Mach, K. J., and Kraan, C. M. 2021. "Science–Policy Dimensions of Research on Climate Change and Conflict." *Journal of Peace Research* 58(1): 168–176.

Macy, M. W., Ma, M., Tabin, D. R., Gao, J., and Szymansk, B. K. 2021. "Polarization and Tipping Points."

Proceedings of the National Academy of Sciences 118(50): e2102144118.

Maffi, L. 2005. "Linguistic, Cultural, and Biological Diversity." *Annual Review of Anthropology* 34(1): 599–617.

Maguen, S., Metzler, T. J., Litz, B. T., Seal, K. H., Knight, S. J., and Marmar, C. R. 2009. "The Impact of Killing in War on Mental Health Symptoms and Related Functioning." *Journal of Traumatic Stress* 22(5): 435–443.

Maguire, G. 2020. "Human Erosion: Indigenous Peoples and Well-Being in the Anthropocene." *Irish Studies in International Affairs* 31: 113–130.

Makridis, C., and Rothwell, J. T. 2020. "The Real Cost of Political Polarization: Evidence from the Covid-19 Pandemic." https://ssrn.com/abstract=3638373.

Malhi, Y. 2017. "The Concept of the Anthropocene." *Annual Review of Environment and Resources* 42(1): 77–104.

Malone, T., Rus, D., and Laubacher, R. 2020. "Artificial Intelligence and the Future of Work." Research Brief 17, Massachusetts Institute of Technology, Work of the Future, Cambridge, MA.

Månberger, A., and Stenqvist, B. 2018. "Global Metal Flows in the Renewable Energy Transition: Exploring the Effects of Substitutes, Technological Mix and Development." *Energy Policy* 119: 226–241.

Maner, J. K., and Case, C. R. 2016. "Dominance and Prestige: Dual Strategies for Navigating Social Hierarchies." In Olson, J. M., and Zanna, M. P., (eds.), *Advances in Experimental Social Psychology*, Vol. 54. Amsterdam: Elsevier.

Mani, A., Mullainathan, S., Shafir, E., and Zhao, J. 2013. "Poverty Impedes Cognitive Function." *Science* 341(6149): 976–980.

Manning, J. G., Ludlow, F., Stine, A. R., Boos, W. R., Sigl, M., and Marlon, J. R. 2017. "Volcanic Suppression of Nile Summer Flooding Triggers Revolt and Constrains Interstate Conflict in Ancient Egypt." *Nature Communications* 8(1): 900.

Mansbridge, J., and Flaster, K. 2007. "The Cultural Politics of Everyday Discourse: The Case of 'Male Chauvinist'." *Critical Sociology* 33(4): 627–660.

Marani, M., Katul, G. G., Pan, W. K., and Parolari, A. J. 2021. "Intensity and Frequency of Extreme Novel Epidemics." *Proceedings of the National Academy of Sciences* 118(35): e2105482118.

Marcus, R. 2018. "Education and Gender Norm Change." ALIGN Report, Overseas Development Institute, London. https://www.alignplatform.org/sites/default/files/2018-12/align_education_thematic_guide_-_formatted_v4.pdf.

Markus, H. R. 2016. "What Moves People to Action? Culture and Motivation." *Current Opinion in Psychology* 8: 161–166.

Markus, H. R., and Kitayama, S. 1991. "Culture and the Self: Implications for Cognition, Emotion, and Motivation." *Psychological Review* 98(2): 224.

Marmot, M. 2005. "Social Determinants of Health Inequalities." *The Lancet* 365(9464): 1099–1104.

Marra, F., Armon, M., Adam, O., Zoccatelli, D., Gazal, O., Garfinkel, C. I., Rostkier-Edelstein, D., and others. 2021. "Toward Narrowing Uncertainty in Future Projections of Local Extreme Precipitation." *Geophysical Research Letters* 48(5): e2020GL091823.

Marselle, M. R., Martens, D., Dallimer, M., and Irvine, K. N. 2019. "Review of the Mental Health and Well-Being Benefits of Biodiversity." In Marselle, M., Stadler, J., Korn, H., Irvine, K., and Bonn, A., (eds.), *Biodiversity and Health in the Face of Climate Change*. Cham, Switzerland: Springer.

Marshman, J., Blay-Palmer, A., and Landman, K. 2019. "Anthropocene Crisis: Climate Change, Pollinators, and Food Security." *Environments* 6(2): 22.

Martin-Carrasco, M., Evans-Lacko, S., Dom, G., Christodoulou, N. G., Samochowiec, J., González-Fraile, E., Bienkowski, P., and others. 2016. "EPA Guidance on Mental Health and Economic Crises in Europe." *European Archives of Psychiatry and Clinical Neuroscience* 266(2): 89–124.

Martinez A., C. 2022. "What Makes Hate a Unique Emotion – and Why That Matters." *Psyche*. https://psyche.co/ideas/what-makes-hate-a-unique-emotion-and-why-that-matters. Accessed 25 August 2022.

Martínez Franzoni, J., and Sánchez-Ancochea, D. 2016. *The Quest for Universal Social Policy in the South: Actors, Ideas and Architectures*. Cambridge, UK: Cambridge University Press.

Martínez Franzoni, J., and Sánchez-Ancochea, D. 2022a. "A Lost Opportunity to Build Social Protection for All? Scenarios Following Emergency Cash Transfers in Central America." United Nations Research Institute for Social Development, Geneva.

Martínez Franzoni, J., and Sánchez-Ancochea, D. 2022b. "The Pandemic as an Opportunity? A Call for a Contextual Approach." Background paper for Human Development Report 2021/2022, UNDP–HDRO, New York.

Martínez, I. F., and Atuesta, L. H. 2018. "Mourning Our Dead: The Impact of Mexico's War on Drugs on Citizens' Depressive Symptoms." *International Journal of Drug Policy* 60: 65–73.

Martino, B. D., Camerer, C. F., and Adolphs, R. 2010. "Amygdala Damage Eliminates Monetary Loss Aversion." *Proceedings of the National Academy of Sciences* 107(8): 3788–3792.

Martins, M. d. J. D., and Baumard, N. 2020. "The Rise of Prosociality in Fiction Preceded Democratic Revolutions in Early Modern Europe." *Proceedings of the National Academy of Sciences* 117(46): 28684–28691.

Masco, J. 2010. "Bad Weather: On Planetary Crisis." *Social Studies of Science* 40(1): 7–40.

Mas-Colell, A., Whinston, M. D., and Green, J. R. 1995. *Microeconomic Theory*. Oxford, UK: Oxford University Press.

MaterialFlows. 2022. http://www.materialflows.net/. Accessed 13 June 2022.

Mather, A. S. 1992. "The Forest Transition." *Area* 24: 367–379.

Mathieu, E., Ritchie, H., Ortiz-Ospina, E., Roser, M., Hasell, J., Appel, C., Giattino, C., and Rodés-Guirao,

L. 2021. "A Global Database of Covid-19 Vaccinations." *Nature Human Behavior* 5: 947–953.

Mattingly, H. H., and Emonet, T. 2022. "Collective Behavior and Nongenetic Inheritance Allow Bacterial Populations to Adapt to Changing Environments." *Proceedings of the National Academy of Sciences* 119(26): e2117377119.

Maurer, M., and Holbach, T. 2016. "Taking Online Search Queries as an Indicator of the Public Agenda: The Role of Public Uncertainty." *Journalism & Mass Communication Quarterly* 93(3): 572–586.

Mauss, A. L. 1975. *Social Problems as Social Movements.* Philadelphia, PA: Lippincott.

McCarthy, N. 2021. "Which Companies Received the Most Covid-19 Vaccine R&D Funding?" [Infographic]. *Forbes,* 6 May.

McClanahan, K. J., Maner, J. K., and Cheng, J. T. 2021. "Two Ways to Stay at the Top: Prestige and Dominance Are Both Viable Strategies for Gaining and Maintaining Social Rank over Time." *Personality and Social Psychology Bulletin.*

McCool, W. C., Codding, B. F., Vernon, K. B., Wilson, K. M., Yaworsky, P. M., Marwan, N., and Kennett, D. J. 2022. "Climate Change Induced Population Pressure Drives High Rates of Lethal Violence in the Prehispanic Central Andes." *Proceedings of the National Academy of Sciences* 119(17): e2117556119.

McCoy, D. C., Roy, A. L., and Raver, C. C. 2016. "Neighborhood Crime as a Predictor of Individual Differences in Emotional Processing and Regulation." *Developmental Science* 19(1): 164–174.

McCoy, J., Rahman, T., and Somer, M. 2018. "Polarization and the Global Crisis of Democracy: Common Patterns, Dynamics, and Pernicious Consequences for Democratic Polities." *American Behavioral Scientist* 62(1): 16–42.

McCrea, R., Walton, A., and Leonard, R. 2014. "A Conceptual Framework for Investigating Community Well-being and Resilience." *Rural Society* 23(3): 270–282.

McEwen, C. A., and McEwen, B. S. 2017. "Social Structure, Adversity, Toxic Stress, and Intergenerational Poverty: An Early Childhood Model." *Annual Review of Sociology* 43: 445–472.

McGregor, D. 2009. "Honouring Our Relations: An Anishnaabe Perspective." In Agyeman, J., Cole, P., Haluza-DeLay, R., and O'Riley, P., (eds.), *Speaking for Ourselves: Environmental Justice in Canada.* Vancouver, Canada: University of British Columbia Press.

McGuire, J., Kaiser, C., and Bach-Mortensen, A. M. 2022. "A Systematic Review and Meta-Analysis of the Impact of Cash Transfers on Subjective Well-Being and Mental Health in Low-and Middle-Income Countries." *Nature Human Behaviour:* 1–12.

McKenzie, D., Mohpal, A., and Yang, D. 2021. "Aspirations and Financial Decisions: Experimental Evidence from the Philippines." Policy Research Working Paper 9586, World Bank, Washington, DC. https://documents1.worldbank.org/curated/en/475171615987748251/pdf/Aspirations-and-Financial-Decisions-Experimental-Evidence-from-the-Philippines.pdf.

McLaughlin, K. A., Green, J. G., Alegría, M., Costello, E. J., Gruber, M. J., Sampson, N. A., and Kessler, R. C. 2012. "Food Insecurity and Mental Disorders in a National Sample of US Adolescents." *Journal of the American Academy of Child & Adolescent Psychiatry* 51(12): 1293–1303.

McMillen, C. 2006. *Pandemics: A Very Short Introduction.* Oxford, UK: Oxford University Press.

McNally, R. J. 2007. "Betrayal Trauma Theory: A Critical Appraisal." *Memory* 15(3): 280–294.

Meckling, J., and Allan, B. B. 2020. "The Evolution of Ideas in Global Climate Policy." *Nature Climate Change* 10(5): 434–438.

Mehra, S., Stopnitzky, Y., and Alloush, M. 2018. "Economic Shocks and Personality Traits of the Ultra-Poor." http://www.yanivstopnitzky.com/wp-content/uploads/2019/03/Personality.pdf.

Mehravar, M., Shirazi, A., Nazari, M., and Banan, M. 2019. "Mosaicism in CRISPR/Cas9-Mediated Genome Editing." *Developmental Biology* 445(2): 156–162.

Meier, A. N. 2022. "Emotions and Risk Attitudes." *American Economic Journal: Applied Economics* 14(3): 527–558.

Meinshausen, M., Lewis, J., McGlade, C., Gütschow, J., Nicholls, Z., Burdon, R., Cozzi, L., and Hackmann, B. 2022. "Realization of Paris Agreement Pledges May Limit Warming Just Below 2 °C." *Nature* 604(7905): 304–309.

Meng, F., and Ellis, T. 2020. "The Second Decade of Synthetic Biology: 2010–2020." *Nature Communications* 11.

Menker, S. 2022. "Putin's War Has Started a Global Food Crisis." *The New York Times,* April 5.

Mental Health Foundation. 2021. "Digital Mental Health." https://www.mentalhealth.org.uk/a-to-z/d/digital-mental-health. Accessed 28 May 2021.

Mernyk, J. S., Pink, S. L., Druckman, J. N., and Willer, R. 2022. "Correcting Inaccurate Metaperceptions Reduces Americans' Support for Partisan Violence." *Proceedings of the National Academy of Sciences* 119(16): e2116851119.

Mesoudi, A. 2016. "Cultural Evolution: A Review of Theory, Findings and Controversies." *Evolutionary Biology* 43(4): 481–497.

Mesoudi, A. 2021. "Cultural Selection and Biased Transformation: Two Dynamics of Cultural Evolution." *Philosophical Transactions of the Royal Society B: Biological Sciences* 376(1828): 20200053.

Messing, S., and Weisel, R. 2017. *Partisan Conflict and Congressional Outreach.* Washington, DC: Pew Research Center.

Meta. 2022. "Transparency Center: False News." https://transparency.fb.com/de-de/policies/community-standards/false-news/. Accessed 26 August 2022.

Meyfroidt, P., and Lambin, E. F. 2011. "Global Forest Transition: Prospects for an End to Deforestation." *Annual Review of Environment and Resources* 36: 343–371.

Meyfroidt, P., Roy Chowdhury, R., de Bremond, A., Ellis, E. C., Erb, K. H., Filatova, T., Garrett, R. D., and others. 2018. "Middle-Range Theories of Land System Change." *Global Environmental Change* 53: 52–67.

MHIN (Mental Health Innovation Network). 2022. "BasicNeeds Mental Health and Development Model." https://www.mhinnovation.net/innovations/basicneeds-mental-health-and-development-model. Accessed 8 April 2022.

Middleton, J., Cunsolo, A., Jones-Bitton, A., Wright, C. J., and Harper, S. L. 2020. "Indigenous Mental Health in a Changing Climate: A Systematic Scoping Review of the Global Literature." *Environmental Research Letters* 15(5).

Midgley, C., Thai, S., Lockwood, P., Kovacheff, C., and Page-Gould, E. 2021. "When Every Day Is a High School Reunion: Social Media Comparisons and Self-Esteem." *Journal of Personality and Social Psychology* 121(2): 285–307.

Miles-Novelo, A., and Anderson, C. A. 2019. "Climate Change and Psychology: Effects of Rapid Global Warming on Violence and Aggression." *Current Climate Change Reports* 5(1): 36–46.

Mintrom, M. 1997. "Policy Entrepreneurs and the Diffusion of Innovation." *American Journal of Political Science* 41(3): 738–770.

Miodunka, P. 2020. "A City Is Not an Island: Early Modern Krakow and Natural Resources." In Izdebski, A., and Szmytka, R., (eds.), *Kraków. An Ecobiography.* Pittsburgh, PA: Pittsburgh University Press.

Miranda, K. L. d., and Snower, D. J. 2022. "The Societal Responses to Covid-19: Evidence from the G7 Countries." *Proceedings of the National Academy of Sciences* 119(25): e2117155119.

Mirchandani, M. 2018. "Digital Hatred, Real Violence: Majoritarian Radicalisation and Social Media in India." ORF Occasional Paper 167, Observer Research Foundation, New Delhi.

Mitchell, A., Gottfried, J., Barthel, M., and Shearer, E. 2016. *The Modern News Consumer: News Attitudes and Practices in the Digital Era.* Washington, DC: Pew Research Center.

Mitchell, A., Gottfried, J., and Matsa, K. E. 2015. "Millennials and Political News: The Local TV for the Next Generation." Pew Research Center, Washington, DC.

Mitchell, T. 2005. "The Work of Economics: How a Discipline Makes Its World." *European Journal of Sociology / Archives Européennes de Sociologie / Europäisches Archiv für Soziologie* 46(2): 297–320.

Mobjörk, M., Krampe, F., and Tarif, K. 2021. "Pathways of Climate Insecurity: Guidance for Policymakers." Stockholm International Peace Research Institute, Stockholm. https://www.sipri.org/publications/2020/sipri-policy-briefs/pathways-climate-insecurity-guidance-policymakers. Accessed 25 August 2022.

Moehler, M. 2019. "Diversity, Stability, and Social Contract Theory." *Philosophical Studies* 176(12): 3285–3301.

Moghadam, V. M. 2022. "Institutional Changes and Women's Citizenship in the Maghreb: Toward a New Gender Regime?" In Hirschmann, N. J. and Thomas, D.

A., (eds.), *Citizenship on the Edge: Sex/Gender/Race*. Philadelphia, PA: University of Pennsylvania Press.

Mohan, N. 2021. "Perspective: Tackling Misinformation on YouTube." YouTube Official Blog, 25 August. https://blog.youtube/inside-youtube/tackling-misinfo/. Accessed 25 August 2022.

Mokyr, J. 2013. "Cultural Entrepreneurs and the Origins of Modern Economic Growth." *Scandinavian Economic History Review* 61(1): 1–33.

Mokyr, J. 2016. *A Culture of Growth*. Princeton, NJ: Princeton University Press.

Molina, G. G., and Ortiz-Juarez, E. 2020. "Temporary Basic Income: Protecting Poor and Vulnerable People in Developing Countries." Transitions Series Working Paper, United Nations Development Programme, Global Policy Network, New York.

Moody-Adams, M. M. 1999. "The Idea of Moral Progress." *Metaphilosophy* 30(3): 168–185.

Moore, F. C., Lacasse, K., Mach, K. J., Shin, Y. A., Gross, L. J., and Beckage, B. 2022. "Determinants of Emissions Pathways in the Coupled Climate–Social System." *Nature* 603(7899): 103–111.

Moore, M.-L., Olsson, P., Nilsson, W., Rose, L., and Westley, F. R. 2018. "Navigating Emergence and System Reflexivity as Key Transformative Capacities." *Ecology and Society* 23(2): 38.

Moore, M.-L., Tjornbo, O., Enfors, E., Knapp, C., Hodbod, J., Baggio, J. A., Norström, A., and others. 2014. "Studying the Complexity of Change: Toward an Analytical Framework for Understanding Deliberate Social-Ecological Transformations." *Ecology and Society* 19(4): 54.

Moore-Berg, S. L., Parelman, J. M., Lelkes, Y., and Falk, E. B. 2020. "Neural Polarization and Routes to Depolarization." *Proceedings of the National Academy of Sciences* 117(46): 28552–28554.

Morris, G., Berk, M., Maes, M., Carvalho, A. F., and Puri, B. K. 2019. "Socioeconomic Deprivation, Adverse Childhood Experiences and Medical Disorders in Adulthood: Mechanisms and Associations." *Molecular Neurobiology* 56(8): 5866–5890.

Morris, M. W., Chiu, C.-y., and Liu, Z. 2015. "Polycultural Psychology." *Annual Review of Psychology* 66(1): 631–659.

Morse, I. 2021. "A Dead Battery Dilemma." *Science* 372(6544): 780–783.

Moulding, N., Franzway, S., Wendt, S., Zufferey, C., and Chung, D. 2021. "Rethinking Women's Mental Health after Intimate Partner Violence." *Violence Against Women* 27(8): 1064–1090.

Mousavi, S., and Gigerenzer, G. 2017. "Heuristics Are Tools for Uncertainty." *Homo Oeconomicus* 34(4): 361–379.

Mukhopadhyay, T., Rivera-Vazquez, C., and Tapia, H. 2019. "Gender Inequality and Multidimensional Social Norms." Working Paper, UNDP–HDRO, New York.

Muldoon, R., Lisciandra, C., Colyvan, M., Martini, C., Sillari, G., and Sprenger, J. 2014. "Disagreement

Behind the Veil of Ignorance." *Philosophical Studies* 170(3): 377–394.

Mulgan, T. 2018. "Answering to Future People: Responsibility for Climate Change in a Breaking World." *Journal of Applied Philosophy* 35(3): 532–548.

Mulgan, T. Forthcoming. "From Brad to Worse: Rule-Consequentialism and Undesirable Futures." *Ratio*.

Mulgan, T., Enright, S., Grix, M., Jayasuriya, U., Ka 'ili, T. O., Lear, A. M., Māhina, A. N. M., and others. 2021. "Charting Just Futures for Aotearoa New Zealand: Philosophy for and Beyond the Covid-19 Pandemic." *Journal of the Royal Society of New Zealand* 51: S167–S178.

Müller, J. W. e. 2002. *Memory and Power in Post-War Europe: Studies in the Presence of the Past*. Cambridge, UK: Cambridge University Press.

Müller, J.-W. 2021. *Democracy Rules*. New York: Farrar, Straus and Giroux.

Mumey, A., Sardana, S., Richardson-Vejlgaard, R., and Akinsulure-Smith, A. M. 2020. "Mental Health Needs of Sex Trafficking Survivors in New York City: Reflections on Exploitation, Coping, and Recovery." *Psychological Trauma: Theory, Research, Practice, and Policy* 13(2): 185–192.

Mutahi, P., and Kimari, B. 2017. "The Impact of Social Media and Digital Technology on Electoral Violence in Kenya." IDS Working Paper 493, Institute of Development Studies, Brighton, UK.

Muthukrishna, M., and Henrich, J. 2016. "Innovation in the Collective Brain." *Philosophical Transactions of the Royal Society B: Biological Sciences* 371(1690): 20150192.

Muthukrishna, M., Bell, A. V., Henrich, J., Curtin, C. M., Gedranovich, A., McInerney, J., and Thue, B. 2020. "Beyond Western, Educated, Industrial, Rich, and Democratic (WEIRD) Psychology: Measuring and Mapping Scales of Cultural and Psychological Distance." *Psychological Science* 31(6): 678–701.

Muthukrishna, M., Henrich, J., and Slingerland, E. 2021. "Psychology as a Historical Science." *Annual Review of Psychology* 72(1): 717–749.

Mutu, M., and McCully, M. 2003. *Te Whanau Moana I Nga Kaupapa Me Nga Tikanga: Customs and Protocols [the Customs and Protocols of Te Whanau Moana]*. Auckland: Reed.

Na, J., Grossmann, I., Varnum, M. E. W., Kitayama, S., Gonzalez, R., and Nisbett, R. E. 2010. "Cultural Differences Are Not Always Reducible to Individual Differences." *Proceedings of the National Academy of Sciences* 107(14): 6192–6197.

Narayanan, V., Barash, V., Kelly, J., Kollanyi, B., Neudert, L.-M., and Howard, P. 2018. "Polarization, Partisanship and Junk News Consumption over Social Media in the US." COMPROP Data Memo 2018.1, University of Oxford, Oxford Internet Institute, Program on Democracy and Technology, Oxford, UK.

National Academies of Sciences, Engineering, and Medicine. 2017. *Communities in Action: Pathways to Health Equity*. Washington, DC: The National Academies Press. https://www.nap.edu/download/24624. Accessed 8 February 2021.

National Academy of Engineering and National Research Council. 2013. *Positioning Synthetic Biology to Meet the Challenges of the 21st Century: Summary Report of a Six Academies Symposium Series*. Washington, DC: The National Academies Press.

National Geographic. 2022. "Dead Zone." Resource Library. https://education.nationalgeographic.org/resource/dead-zone. Accessed 18 July 2022.

National Scientific Council on the Developing Child. 2020. "Connecting the Brain to the Rest of the Body: Early Childhood Development and Lifelong Health Are Deeply Intertwined." Working Paper 15, Harvard University, Center on the Developing Child, Cambridge, MA. https://www.developingchild.harvard.edu. Accessed 29 January 2021.

Navarro-Mantas, L., de Lemus, S., and Megías, J. L. 2021. "Mental Health Consequences of Intimate Partner Violence against Women in El Salvador." *Violence Against Women* 27(15–16): 2927–2944.

Nel, E., and Binns, T. 2000. "Rural Self-Reliance Strategies in South Africa: Community Initiatives and External Support in the Former Black Homelands." *Journal of Rural Studies* 16(3): 367–377.

Neophytou, E., Manwell, L. A., and Eikelboom, R. 2021. "Effects of Excessive Screen Time on Neurodevelopment, Learning, Memory, Mental Health, and Neurodegeneration: A Scoping Review." *International Journal of Mental Health and Addiction* 19(3): 724–744.

Newman, N., Fletcher, R., Robertson, C. T., Eddy, K., and Kleis Nielsen, R. 2022. *Digital News Report 2022*. Oxford, UK: University of Oxford, Reuters Institute for the Study of Journalism.

Newson, J., Pastukh, V., Sukhoi, O., Taylor, J., and Thiagarajan, T. 2021. *Mental State of the World 2020*. Sapiens Labs. https://sapienlabs.org/wp-content/uploads/2021/03/Mental-State-of-the-World-Report-2020-1.pdf.

NGFS (Network for Greening the Financial System). 2019. "A Call for Action: Climate Change as a Source of Financial Risk." London.

NGFS (Network for Greening the Financial System). 2021. "Network for Greening the Financial System." https://www.ngfs.net/en. Accessed 1 October 2021.

Nguyen, T., Hui, P.-M., Harper, M., Terveen, L., and Konstan, J. A. 2014. "Exploring the Filter Bubble: The Effect of Using Recommender Systems on Content Diversity." Paper presented at the 23rd International Conference on the World Wide Web, 7 April, Seoul.

Ni, M. Y., Yao, X. I., Leung, K. S., Yau, C., Leung, C. M., Lun, P., Flores, F. P., and others. 2020. "Depression and Post-Traumatic Stress During Major Social Unrest in Hong Kong: A 10-Year Prospective Cohort Study." *The Lancet* 395(10220): 273–284.

Nichols, M. 2018. "U.N. Chief Warns Leaders of 'Increasingly Chaotic' World Order." Reuters, 25 September. https://www.reuters.com/article/us-un-assembly-guterres-idUSKCN1M51SZ. Accessed 4 May 2022.

Nightingale, A. J., Eriksen, S., Taylor, M., Forsyth, T., Pelling, M., Newsham, A., Boyd, E., and others. 2020. "Beyond Technical Fixes: Climate Solutions and the Great Derangement." *Climate and Development* 12(4): 343–352.

Nisbett, R., and Norenzayan, A. 2002. "Culture and Cognition." In Thompson-Schill, S. L., (ed.), *Stevens' Handbook of Experimental Psychology Vol. 3.* Hoboken, NJ: John Wiley & Sons, Inc.

Njwambe, A., Cocks, M., and Vetter, S. 2019. "Ekhayeni: Rural–Urban Migration, Belonging and Landscapes of Home in South Africa." *Journal of Southern African Studies* 45(2): 413–431.

Norris, P., and Inglehart, R. 2016. "Trump, Brexit, and the Rise of Populism: Economic Have-Nots and Cultural Backlash." *Harvard JFK School of Government Faculty Working Papers Series:* 1–52.

North, D. C. 1990. *Institutions, Institutional Change and Economic Performance.* Cambridge, UK: Cambridge University Press.

North, D. C. 1991. "Institutions." *Journal of Economic Perspectives* 5(1): 97–112.

Nowotny, H. 2015. *The Cunning of Uncertainty.* Hoboken, NJ: John Wiley & Sons.

Nowotny, H. 2021. *In AI We Trust: Power, Illusion and Control of Predictive Algorithms.* Hoboken, NJ: John Wiley & Sons.

Nunn, N. 2021. "History as Evolution." In Bisin, A., and Federico, G., (eds.), *The Handbook of Historical Economics.* London: Elsevier.

Nunn, N. 2022. "On the Dynamics of Human Behavior: The Past, Present, and Future of Culture, Conflict, and Cooperation." NBER Working Paper 29804, National Bureau of Economic Research, Cambridge, MA.

Nussbaum, M. C. 1995. "Emotions and Women's Capabilities." In Nussbaum, M. C., and Glover, J., (eds.), *Women, Culture and Development: A Study of Human Capabilities.* Oxford, UK: UNU-Wider Studies in Development Economics, Oxford University Press.

Nussbaum, M. C. 2003a. "Capabilities as Fundamental Entitlements: Sen and Social Justice." *Feminist Economics* 9(2–3): 33–59.

Nussbaum, M. C. 2003b. *Upheavals of Thought: The Intelligence of Emotions.* Cambridge, UK: Cambridge University Press.

Nussbaum, M. C. 2015. "Philosophy and Economics in the Capabilities Approach: An Essential Dialogue." *Journal of Human Development and Capabilities* 16(1): 1–14.

Nydegger, L. A., Quinn, K., Walsh, J. L., Pacella-La-Barbara, M. L., and Dickson-Gomez, J. 2019. "Polytraumatization, Mental Health, and Delinquency among Adolescent Gang Members." *Journal of Traumatic Stress* 32(6): 890–898.

O'Callaghan, B., and Murdock, E. 2021. "Are We Building Back Better? Evidence from 2020 and Pathways for Inclusive Green Recovery Spending." United Nations Environment Programme, Nairobi. https://www.unep.org/resources/publication/are-we-building-back-better-evidence-2020-and-pathways-inclusive-green. Accessed 25 August 2022.

O'Donnell, M., Dev, A. S., Antonoplis, S., Baum, S. M., Benedetti, A. H., Brown, N. D., Carrillo, B., and others. 2021. "Empirical Audit and Review and an Assessment of Evidentiary Value in Research on the Psychological Consequences of Scarcity." *Proceedings of the National Academy of Sciences* 118(44).

O'Donoghue, T., and Rabin, M. 1999. "Doing It Now or Later." *American Economic Review* 89(1): 103–124.

O'Madagain, C., and Tomasello, M. 2022. "Shared Intentionality, Reason-Giving and the Evolution of Human Culture." *Philosophical Transactions of the Royal Society B: Biological Sciences* 377(1843): 20200320.

O'Neil, C. 2016. *Weapons of Math Destruction: How Big Data Increases Inequality and Threatens Democracy.* New York: Crown.

O'Rand, A. M., and Hamil-Luker, J. 2005. "Processes of Cumulative Adversity: Childhood Disadvantage and Increased Risk of Heart Attack across the Life Course." *The Journals of Gerontology Series B: Psychological Sciences and Social Sciences* 60(2): 117–S124.

Occhipinti, J.-A., Skinner, A., Doraiswamy, P. M., Fox, C., Herrman, H., Saxena, S., London, E., and others. 2021. "Mental Health: Build Predictive Models to Steer Policy." *Nature* 597: 633–636. https://www.nature.com/articles/d41586-021-02581-9. Accessed 20 October 2021.

Ochab, E. 2020. "Are These Tech Companies Complicit in Human Rights Abuses of Child Cobalt Miners in Congo?" *Forbes,* 13 Jan.

OECD (Organisation for Economic Co-operation and Development). 2019a. *Global Material Resources Outlook to 2060.* Paris.

OECD (Organisation for Economic Co-operation and Development). 2019b. *OECD Employment Outlook 2019: The Future of Work.* Paris.

OECD (Organisation for Economic Co-operation and Development). 2020a. *Management and Disposal of High-Level Radioactive Waste: Global Progress and Solutions.* Paris.

OECD (Organisation for Economic Cooperation and Development). 2020b. "Paid Sick Leave to Protect Income, Health and Jobs through the Covid-19 Crisis." Paris.

Oehlschlaeger, M. A., Wang, H., and Sexton, M. N. 2013. "Prospects for Biofuels: A Review." *Journal of Thermal Science and Engineering Applications* 5(2): 021006.

OHCHR (Office of the United Nations High Commissioner for Human Rights). 2019. *Born Free and Equal: Sexual Orientation and Gender Identity in International Human Rights Law.* 2nd Edition. Geneva.

OHCHR (Office of the United Nations High Commissioner for Human Rights) and Equitas – International Centre for Human Rights Education. 2022. *Bridging Our Diversities: A Compendium of Good Practices in Human Rights Education.* Geneva and Montréal, Canada.

OHCHR (Office of the United Nations High Commissioner for Human Rights) and Heinrich Böll Foundation. 2018. *The Other Infrastructure Gap: Sustainability, Human Rights and Environmental Perspectives.* Geneva and Berlin.

Oinonen, M., Alenius, T., Arppe, L., Bocherens, H., Etu-Sihvola, H., Helama, S., Huhtamaa, H., and others. 2020. "Buried in Water, Burdened by Nature—Resilience Carried the Iron Age People through Fimbulvinter." *PLOS ONE* 15(4): e0231787.

Okeja, U. B., and Watene, K. 2020. "Reimagining Justice: Options in African Philosophy." *Ethical Perspectives* 27(1).

Okonjo-Iweala, N., Shanmugaratnam, T., and Summers, L. H. 2021. "Rethinking Multilateralism for a Pandemic Era." *Finance & Development,* December: 4–9.

Olsson, P., Moore, M.-L., Westley, F. R., and McCarthy, D. D. P. 2017. "The Concept of the Anthropocene as a Game-Changer: A New Context for Social Innovation and Transformations to Sustainability." *Ecology and Society* 22(2): 31.

Oosterlaken, I. 2009. "Design for Development: A Capability Approach." *Design Issues* 25(4): 91–102.

Oosterlaken, I., and Hoven, J., (eds.). 2012. *The Capability Approach, Technology and Design.* Dodrecht, The Netherlands: Springer.

OpenAI and Pilipiszyn, A. 2022. "GPT-3 Powers the Next Generation of Apps." https://openai.com/blog/gpt-3-apps/. Accessed 10 June 2022.

The Open-ended Working Group on the Post-2020 Global Biodiversity Framework. 2022. "Preparation of the Post-2020 Global Biodiversity Framework—Draft Recommendation Submitted by the Co-Chairs." Geneva. https://www.cbd.int/doc/c/c949/b2cc/a311c0c411d3a81134e2c7f3/wg2020-03-l-02-en.pdf.

Ord, T. 2020. *The Precipice: Existential Risk and the Future of Humanity.* Abingdon, UK: Bloomsbury.

Oreopoulos, P., von Wachter, T., and Heisz, A. 2012. "The Short- and Long-Term Career Effects of Graduating in a Recession." *American Economic Journal: Applied Economics* 4(1): 1–29.

Oreskes, N. 2019. *Why Trust Science.* Princeton, NJ: Princeton University Press.

Oreskes, N., and Conway, E. M. 2011. *Merchants of Doubt: How a Handful of Scientists Obscured the Truth on Issues from Tobacco Smoke to Global Warming.* New York: Bloomsbury Press.

Orhan, Y. E. 2022. "The Relationship between Affective Polarization and Democratic Backsliding: Comparative Evidence." *Democratization* 29(4): 714–735.

Osman, M. B., Tierney, J. E., Zhu, J., Tardif, R., Hakim, G. J., King, J., and Poulsen, C. J. 2021. "Globally Resolved Surface Temperatures since the Last Glacial Maximum." *Nature* 599(7884): 239–244.

Osman, S., and Wood, J. 2018. "Gang Membership, Mental Illness, and Negative Emotionality: A Systematic Review of the Literature." *International Journal of Forensic Mental Health* 17(3): 223–246.

Osman-Elasha, B. n.d. "Women…In the Shadow of Climate Change." UN Chronicle. https://www.un.org/en/chronicle/article/womenin-shadow-climate-change. Accessed 8 May 2022.

Østby, G., Aas Rustad, S., and Arasmith, A. 2021. "Children Affected by Armed Conflict 1990 - 2020." Conflict Trends 4, Peace Research Institute Oslo, Oslo.

Österblom, H., and Paasche, Ø. 2021. "Earth Altruism." *One Earth* 4(10): 1386–1397.

Ottisova, L., Smith, P., Shetty, H., Stahl, D., Downs, J., and Oram, S. 2018. "Psychological Consequences of Child Trafficking: An Historical Cohort Study of Trafficked Children in Contact with Secondary Mental Health Services." *PLOS ONE* 13(3): 1–14.

Our World in Data. 2022. "Coronavirus (Covid-19) Vaccinations." https://ourworldindata.org/covid-vaccinations. Accessed 21 June 2022.

Oyer, P. 2006. "Initial Labor Market Conditions and Long-Term Outcomes for Economists." *Journal of Economic Perspectives* 20(3): 143–160.

Pachter, L. M., and Coll, C. G. 2009. "Racism and Child Health: A Review of the Literature and Future Directions." *Journal of Developmental and Behavioral Pediatrics* 30(3): 255–263.

Padhy, S. K., Sarkar, S., Panigrahi, M., and Paul, S. 2015. "Mental Health Effects of Climate Change." *Indian Journal of Occupational and Environmental Medicine* 19(1): 3–7.

PAHO (Pan American Health Organization). 2019. "Mental Health Problems Are the Leading Cause of Disability Worldwide, Say Experts at PAHO Directing Council Side Event." https://www3.paho.org/hq/index.php?option=com_content&view=article&id=15481:mental-health-problems-are-the-leading-cause-of-disability-worldwide-say-experts-at-paho-directing-council-side-event&Itemid=72565&lang=en. Accessed 25 June 2022.

Palinkas, L. A., and Wong, M. 2020. "Global Climate Change and Mental Health." *Current Opinion in Psychology* 32: 12–16.

Palozzi, G., Schettini, I., and Chirico, A. 2020. "Enhancing the Sustainable Goal of Access to Healthcare: Findings from a Literature Review on Telemedicine Employment in Rural Areas." *Sustainability* 12(8): 3318.

Pancost, R. D. 2017. "Climate Change Narratives." *Nature Geoscience* 10(7): 466–468.

Papachristou, E., Flouri, E., Kokosi, T., and Francesconi, M. 2019. "Main and Interactive Effects of Inflammation and Perceived Neighbourhood Cohesion on Psychological Distress: Results from a Population-Based Study in the UK." *Quality of Life Research* 28(8): 2147–2157.

Pardi, N., Hogan, M., Porter, F., and Weissman, D. 2018. "mRNA Vaccines — a New Era in Vaccinology." *Nature Reviews Drug Discovery* 17: 261–279.

Parfit, D. 1984. *Reasons and Persons*. Oxford, UK: Oxford University Press.

Parker, G. 2013. *Global Crisis: War, Climatic Change, and Catastrophe in the Seventeenth Century*. New Haven, CT: Yale University Press.

Parlement Français. 1840. "Rapport par M. Le Baron Ch. Dupin." Chambre des Pairs, Paris.

Patterson, O. 2014. "Making Sense of Culture." *Annual Review of Sociology* 40(1): 1–30.

Pavel, C. C., Lacal-Arántegui, R., Marmier, A., Schüler, D., Tzimas, E., Buchert, M., Jenseit, W., and Blagoeva, D. 2017. "Substitution Strategies for Reducing the Use of Rare Earths in Wind Turbines." *Resources Policy* 52: 349–357.

Payne, B., and Bellamy, R. 2014. "Novel Respiratory Viruses: What Should the Clinician Be Alert For?" *Clinical Medicine* 14(6): s12–s16.

Payne, J. L., and Wagner, A. 2019. "The Causes of Evolvability and Their Evolution." *Nature Reviews Genetics* 20(1): 24–38.

Pereira, H. M., Navarro, L. M., and Martins, I. S. 2012. "Global Biodiversity Change: The Bad, the Good, and the Unknown." *Annual Review of Environment and Resources* 37: 25–50.

Pereira, L., Frantzeskaki, N., Hebinck, A., Charli-Joseph, L., Drimie, S., Dyer, M., Eakin, H., and others. 2020. "Transformative Spaces in the Making: Key Lessons from Nine Cases in the Global South." *Sustainability Science* 15(1): 161–178.

Perlman, A. 2016. "The Precarity and Politics of Media Advocacy Work." In Curtin, M., and Sanson, K., (eds.), *Precarious Creativity: Global Media, Local Labor*. Oakland, CA: University of California Press.

Perrings, C., Hechter, M., and Mamada, R. 2021. "National Polarization and International Agreements." *Proceedings of the National Academy of Sciences* 118(50): e2102145118.

Persson, P., and Rossin-Slater, M. 2018. "Family Ruptures, Stress, and the Mental Health of the Next Generation." *American Economic Review* 108(4–5): 1214–1252.

Persson, T., and Tabellini, G. 2020. "Culture, Institutions and Policy." https://ssrn.com/abstract=3680457.

Pessoa, L. 2019. "Embracing Integration and Complexity: Placing Emotion within a Science of Brain and Behaviour." *Cognition and Emotion* 33(1): 55–60.

Peszko, G., Van Der Mensbrugghe, D., Golub, A., Ward, J., Marijs, C., Schopp, A., Rogers, J., and Midgley, A. 2020. *Diversification and Cooperation in a Decarbonizing World: Climate Strategies for Fossil Fuel-Dependent Countries*. Washington, DC: World Bank.

Petrarca, C. S., Giebler, H., and Weßels, B. 2022. "Support for Insider Parties: The Role of Political Trust in a Longitudinal-Comparative Perspective." *Party Politics* 28(2): 329–341.

Petrović, A., Manley, D., and van Ham, M. 2020. "Freedom from the Tyranny of Neighbourhood: Rethinking Sociospatial Context Effects." *Progress in Human Geography* 44(6): 1103–1123.

Pettersson, T., and Öberg, M. 2020. "Organized Violence, 1989–2019." *Journal of Peace Research* 57(4): 597–613.

Pettersson, T., Davies, S., Deniz, A., Engström, G., Hawach, N., Högbladh, S., Sollenberg, M., and Öberg, M. 2021. "Organized Violence 1989–2020, with a Special Emphasis on Syria." *Journal of Peace Research* 58(4): 809–825.

Pew Research Center. 2021. *Economic Attitudes Improve in Many Nations Even as Pandemic Endures—But Majorities Say Next Generation Will Be Worse Off Financially*. Washington, DC.

Phelan, J., and Link, B. 2005. "Controlling Disease and Creating Disparities: A Fundamental Cause Perspective." *The Journals of Gerontology Series B: Psychological Sciences and Social Sciences* 60(Special Issue 2): S27–S33.

Phillips, F., Chang, J., and Su, Y.-S. 2019. "When Do Efficiency and Flexibility Determine a Firm's Performance? A Simulation Study." *Journal of Innovation & Knowledge* 4(2): 88–96.

Pierson, P. 1994. *Dismantling the Welfare State*. Cambridge, UK: Cambridge University Press.

Pigliucci, M. 2008. "Is Evolvability Evolvable?" *Nature Reviews Genetics* 9(1): 75–82.

Piketty, T. 2020. *Capital and Ideology*. Cambridge, MA: Harvard University Press.

Pimm, S. 2022. "We Can Have Biodiversity and Eat Too." *Nature Food* 3(5): 310–311.

Pinker, S. 2010. "The Cognitive Niche: Coevolution of Intelligence, Sociality, and Language." *Proceedings of the National Academy of Sciences* 107(Supplement 2): 8993–8999.

Pinto Benítez, M. C., Blanco Escobar, J. A., Cortéz Arévalo, G. A., Marroquín Jiménez, W. A., and Romero Martínez, L. H. 2014. "Evaluación Del Sistema Integrado De Escuela Inclusiva De Tiempo Pleno Implementado Por El Ministerio De Educación De El Salvador." Universidad Tecnológica de El Salvador, San Salvador.

Pinto, P., Hammond, D., Killelea, S., and Etchell, A. 2022. "The Paradox of Progress with Polarisation." Background paper for Human Development Report 2021/2022, UNDP–HDRO, New York.

Plank, G., Marcus, R., and Jones, N. 2018. "Social Protection and Gender Norm Change." ALIGN Report, Overseas Development Institute, London.

Pleeging, E., Burger, M., and van Exel, J. 2021. "Hope Mediates the Relation between Income and Subjective Well-Being." *Journal of Happiness Studies* 22(5): 2075–2102.

Pleyers, G. 2020. "The Pandemic Is a Battlefield. Social Movements in the Covid-19 Lockdown." *Journal of Civil Society* 16(4): 295–312.

Polak, S., and Trottier, D., (eds.). 2020. *Violence and Trolling on Social Media: History, Affect, and Effects of Online Vitriol*. Amsterdam: Amsterdam University Press B.V.

Polasky, S., Crépin, A.-S., Biggs, R., Carpenter, S. R., Folke, C., Peterson, G., Scheffer, M., and others. 2020. "Corridors of Clarity: Four Principles to Overcome Uncertainty Paralysis in the Anthropocene." *BioScience* 70(12): 1139–1144.

Polletta, F., and Jasper, J. M. 2001. "Collective Identity and Social Movements." *Annual Review of Sociology* 27: 283–305.

Pomeroy, R. 2022. "How the Ukraine War Is Driving up Food and Energy Prices for the World." World Economic Forum Podcast, 25 March. https://www.weforum.

org/agenda/2022/03/ukraine-energy-and-food-radio-davos/. Accessed 6 May 2022.

Pomey, M.-P., Morgan, S., Church, J., Forest, P.-G., Lavis, J. N., McIntosh, T., Smith, N., and others. 2010. "Do Provincial Drug Benefit Initiatives Create an Effective Policy Lab? The Evidence from Canada." *Journal of Health Politics, Policy and Law* 35(5): 705–742.

Pörtner, H. O., Scholes, R. J., Agard, J., Archer, E., Arneth, A., Bai, X., Barnes, D., and others. 2021. "IPBES-IPCC Co-Sponsored Workshop Report on Biodiversity and Climate Change." Intergovernmental Science-Policy Platform on Biodiversity and Ecosystem Services, Bonn, Germany, and Intergovernmental Panel on Climate Change, Geneva. https://ipbes.net/sites/default/files/2021-06/20210609_workshop_report_embargo_3pm_CEST_10_june_0.pdf.

Postmus, J. L., Hoge, G. L., Breckenridge, J., Sharp-Jeffs, N., and Chung, D. 2020. "Economic Abuse as an Invisible Form of Domestic Violence: A Multicountry Review." *Trauma, Violence, & Abuse* 21(2): 261–283.

Potts, L. C., and Henderson, C. 2021. "Evaluation of Anti-Stigma Social Marketing Campaigns in Ghana and Kenya: Time to Change Global." *BMC Public Health* 21: 886.

Power, K. 2020. "The Covid-19 Pandemic Has Increased the Care Burden of Women and Families." *Sustainability: Science, Practice and Policy* 16(1): 67–73.

Prabhune, M. 2022. "Diseases CRISPR Could Cure: Latest Updates on Research Studies and Human Trials." *Synthego*, 23 March.

Prange de Oliveira, S. 2021. "Brazil: Policy Effort on Violence against Women and Children/Domestic Violence before and since Covid-19." GIGA Working Paper 1. German Institute for Global and Area Studies, Hamburg, Germany.

Preston, C. 2018. *The Synthetic Age: Outdesigning Evolution, Resurrecting Species, and Reengineering Our World.* Cambridge, MA: MIT Press.

Pribble, J. 2013. *Welfare and Party Politics in Latin America.* Cambridge, UK: Cambridge University Press.

Pritchard, E., and Choonara, I. 2017. "Armed Conflict and Child Mental Health." *BioMedical Journal Paediatrics Open* 1(1): 1–2.

Proto, E., and Quintana-Domeque, C. 2021. "Covid-19 and Mental Health Deterioration by Ethnicity and Gender in the UK." *PLOS ONE* 16(1): 1–16.

Przeworski, A. 1991. *Democracy and the Market: Political and Economic Reforms in Eastern Europe and Latin America.* Cambridge, UK: Cambridge University Press.

Purplesec. 2021. "2020 Cyber Security Statistics." https://purplesec.us/resources/cyber-security-statistics/. Accessed 5 March 2021.

Purves, K. L., Coleman, J. R., Meier, S. M., Rayner, C., Davis, K. A., Cheesman, R., Bækvad-Hansen, M., and others. 2020. "A Major Role for Common Genetic Variation in Anxiety Disorders." *Molecular Psychiatry* 25(12): 3292–3303.

Qi, B., Wang, X., and Sutton, P. 2021. "Can Nighttime Satellite Imagery Inform Our Understanding of Education Inequality?" *Remote Sensing* 13(5): 843.

Quayle, A. F., and Sonn, C. C. 2019. "Amplifying the Voices of Indigenous Elders through Community Arts and Narrative Inquiry: Stories of Oppression, Psychosocial Suffering, and Survival." *American Journal of Community Psychology* 64(1–2): 46–58.

Quéré, C. L., and Mayot, N. 2022. "Climate Change and Biospheric Output." *Science* 375(6585): 1091–1092.

Rabin, M. 1998. "Psychology and Economics." *Journal of Economic Literature* 36(1): 11–46.

Rabin, M., and Thaler, R. H. 2001. "Anomalies: Risk Aversion." *Journal of Economic Perspectives* 15(1): 219–232.

Race, N. S. 2019. "Sustainable Space Mining." *Nature Astronomy* 3: 465.

Rajan, R. 2021. "Communities, the State, and Markets: The Case for Inclusive Localism." *Oxford Review of Economic Policy* 37(4): 811–823.

Ramankutty, N., Mehrabi, Z., Waha, K., Jarvis, L., Kremen, C., Herrero, M., and Rieseberg, L. H. 2018. "Trends in Global Agricultural Land Use: Implications for Environmental Health and Food Security." *Annual Review of Plant Biology* 69(1): 789–815.

Rao, G. 2019. "Familiarity Does Not Breed Contempt: Generosity, Discrimination, and Diversity in Delhi Schools." *American Economic Review* 109(3): 774–809.

Rathje, S., Van Bavel, J. J., and van der Linden, S. 2021. "Out-Group Animosity Drives Engagement on Social Media." *Proceedings of the National Academy of Sciences* 118(26).

Ravallion, M. 2017. "Interventions against Poverty in Poor Places." WIDER Annual Lecture, World Institute of Development Economics, Helsinki.

Rawls, J. 1971. *A Theory of Justice.* Oxford, UK: Oxford University Press.

Raymond, C., Horton, R. M., Zscheischler, J., Martius, O., AghaKouchak, A., Balch, J., Bowen, S. G., and others. 2020. "Understanding and Managing Connected Extreme Events." *Nature Climate Change* 10(7): 611–621.

Raymond, C., Suarez-Gutierrez, L., Kornhuber, K., Pascolini-Campbell, M., Sillmann, J., and Waliser, D. E. 2022. "Increasing Spatiotemporal Proximity of Heat and Precipitation Extremes in a Warming World Quantified by a Large Model Ensemble." *Environmental Research Letters* 17(3): 035005.

Raymond, L., Kelly, D., and Hennes, E. P. 2021. "Norm-Based Governance for Severe Collective Action Problems: Lessons from Climate Change and Covid-19." *Perspectives on Politics*: 1–14.

Raymond, L., Weldon, S. L., Kelly, D., Arriaga, X. B., and Clark, A. M. 2014. "Making Change: Norm-Based Strategies for Institutional Change to Address Intractable Problems." *Political Research Quarterly* 67(1): 197–211.

Razavi, S. 2006. "Islamic Politics, Human Rights and Women's Claims for Equality in Iran." *Third World Quarterly* 27(7): 1223–1237.

Razavi, S., Behrendt, C., Bierbaum, M., Orton, I., and Tessier, L. 2020. "Reinvigorating the Social Contract and Strengthening Social Cohesion: Social Protection Responses to Covid-19." *International Social Security Review* 73(3): 55–80.

Redford, K., Adams, W., Carlson, R., Mace, G., and Ceccarelli, B. 2014. "Synthetic Biology and the Conservation of Biodiversity." *Oryx* 48(3): 330–336.

Rehbein, J. A., Watson, J. E., Lane, J. L., Sonter, L. J., Venter, O., Atkinson, S. C., and Allan, J. R. 2020. "Renewable Energy Development Threatens Many Globally Important Biodiversity Areas." *Global Change Biology* 26(5): 3040–3051.

Reinhart, C., and Graf von Luckner, C. 2022. "The Return of Global Inflation." Voices from the Third World [blog], 14 February. https://blogs.worldbank.org/voices/return-global-inflation. Accessed 24 August 2022.

Repucci, S., and Slipowitz, A. 2022. *Freedom in the World 2022: The Global Expansion of Authoritarian Rule.* Washington, DC: Freedom House. https://freedomhouse.org/sites/default/files/2022-02/FIW_2022_PDF_Booklet_Digital_Final_Web.pdf.

Reyers, B. 2017. "Resilience Thinking: Science for Uncertain Futures." *Re.Think*, 26 January. https://rethink.earth/resilience-thinking-science-for-uncertain-futures/. Accessed 25 August 2022.

Reyers, B., Moore, M.-L., Haider, L. J., and Schlüter, M. 2022. "The Contributions of Resilience to Reshaping Sustainable Development." *Nature Sustainability*: 1–8.

Ricciardi, W., Pita Barros, P., Bourek, A., Brouwer, W., Kelsey, T., and Lehtonen, L. 2019. "How to Govern the Digital Transformation of Health Services." *European Journal of Public Health* 29(3): 7–12.

Richerson, P. J., Gavrilets, S., and de Waal, F. B. M. 2021. "Modern Theories of Human Evolution Foreshadowed by Darwin'sDescent of Man." *Science* 372(6544): eaba3776.

Richerson, P., Baldini, R., Bell, A. V., Demps, K., Frost, K., Hillis, V., Mathew, S., and others. 2016. "Cultural Group Selection Plays an Essential Role in Explaining Human Cooperation: A Sketch of the Evidence." *Behavioral and Brain Sciences* 39: e30.

Ridley, M. W., Rao, G., Schilbach, F., and Patel, V. H. 2020. "Poverty, Depression, and Anxiety: Causal Evidence and Mechanisms." *Science* 370(6522): 282–284.

Riede, F. 2008. "The Laacher See-Eruption (12,920 BP) and Material Culture Change at the End of the Allerød in Northern Europe." *Journal of Archaeological Science* 35(3): 591–599.

Rights and Resources Initiative. 2020. "Rights-Based Conservation: The Path to Preserving Earth's Biological and Cultural Diversity?" Technical Report, Rights and Resources Initiative, Washington, DC.

Riley, A., Varner, A., Ventevogel, P., Taimur Hasan, M., and Welton-Mitchell, C. 2017. "Daily Stressors, Trauma Exposure, and Mental Health among Stateless Rohingya Refugees in Bangladesh." *Transcultural Psychiatry* 54(3): 304–331.

Ritchie, J. 2021. "Movement from the Margins to Global Recognition: Climate Change Activism by Young People and in Particular Indigenous Youth." *International Studies in Sociology of Education* 30(1–2): 53–72.

Roberts, G. L., Lawrence, J. M., Williams, G. M., and Raphael, B. 1998. "The Impact of Domestic Violence on Women's Mental Health." *Australian and New Zealand Journal of Public Health* 22(7): 796–801.

Robeyns, I. 2017. *Wellbeing, Freedom and Social Justice: The Capability Approach Re-Examined.* Cambridge, UK: Open Book Publishers.

Robeyns, I. 2019. "What, If Anything, Is Wrong with Extreme Wealth?" *Journal of Human Development and Capabilities* 20(3): 251–266.

Robinson, L., Schulz, J., Blank, G., Ragnedda, M., Ono, H., Hogan, B., Mesch, G. S., and others. 2020a. "Digital Inequalities 2.0: Legacy Inequalities in the Information Age." *First Monday* 25(7).

Robinson, L., Schulz, J., Dunn, H. S., Casilli, A. A., Tubaro, P., Carvath, R., Chen, W., and others. 2020b. "Digital Inequalities 3.0: Emergent Inequalities in the Information Age." *First Monday* 25(7): ff10.5210/fm.v25i7.10842. https://dspace.uni.lodz.pl/bitstream/handle/11089/32152/Digital%20inequalities%2020.pdf?sequence=2&isAllowed=y.

Robinson, L., Wiborg, Ø., and Schulz, J. 2018. "Interlocking Inequalities: Digital Stratification Meets Academic Stratification." *The American Behavioral Scientist* 62(9): 1251–1272.

Rocha, J. C., Peterson, G. D., and Biggs, R. 2015. "Regime Shifts in the Anthropocene: Drivers, Risks, and Resilience." *PLOS ONE* 10(8): e0134639.

Rodenburg, R., Benjamin, A., de Roos, C., Meijer, A. M., and Stams, G. J. 2009. "Efficacy of EMDR in Children: A Meta-Analysis." *Clinical Psychology Review* 29(7): 599–606.

Rogers, C., and Oldroyd, G. 2014. "Synthetic Biology Approaches to Engineering the Nitrogen Symbiosis in Cereals." *Journal of Experimental Botany* 65(8): 1939–1946.

Rohde, N., Tang, K. K., Osberg, L., and Rao, D. P. 2017. "Is It Vulnerability or Economic Insecurity That Matters for Health?" *Journal of Economic Behavior & Organization* 134: 307–319.

Rohr, J. R., Barrett, C. B., Civitello, D. J., Craft, M. E., Delius, B., DeLeo, G. A., Hudson, P. J., and others. 2019. "Emerging Human Infectious Diseases and the Links to Global Food Production." *Nature Sustainability* 2(6): 445–456.

Roll, M. 2021. "Institutional Change through Development Assistance: The Comparative Advantages of Political and Adaptive Approaches." Discussion Paper 28/2021, German Institute of Development and Sustainability, Bonn, Germany.

Ronay, R., Maddux, W. W., and von Hippel, W. 2020. "Inequality Rules: Resource Distribution and the Evolution of Dominance- and Prestige-Based Leadership." *The Leadership Quarterly* 31(2): 101246.

Roos, P., Gelfand, M., Nau, D., and Lun, J. 2015. "Societal Threat and Cultural Variation in the Strength of Social Norms: An Evolutionary Basis." *Organizational Behavior and Human Decision Processes* 129: 14–23.

Roser, M. 2020. "Why Did Renewables Become So Cheap So Fast?" https://ourworldindata.org/cheap-renewables-growth. Accessed 9 May 2022.

Roser, M. 2021. "Child Mortality: An Everyday Tragedy of Enormous Scale That We Can Make Progress against - We Live in a World in Which 10 Children Die Every Minute." Our World in Data. https://ourworldindata.org/child-mortality-big-problem-in-brief. Accessed 7 June 2022.

Rotondi, V., Kashyap, R., Pesando, L. M., Spinelli, S., and Billari, F. C. 2020. "Leveraging Mobile Phones to Attain Sustainable Development." *Proceedings of the National Academy of Sciences* 117(24): 13413–13420.

Rovera, D. 2014. "Rovera, Escape from Hell: Torture and Sexual Slavery in Islamic State Captivity in Iraq." Amnesty International. https://www.amnesty.org/en/documents/mde14/021/2014/en/. Accessed 7 October 2021.

The Royal Society. 2019. "Sustainable Synthetic Carbon Based Fuels for Transport." Policy Briefing. London.

Ruckert, A., Huynh, C., and Labonté, R. 2018. "Reducing Health Inequities: Is Universal Basic Income the Way Forward?" *Journal of Public Health* 40(1): 3–7.

Rudel, T. K., Meyfroidt, P., Chazdon, R., Bongers, F., Sloan, S., Grau, H. R., Van Holt, T., and Schneider, L. 2020. "Whither the Forest Transition? Climate Change, Policy Responses, and Redistributed Forests in the Twenty-First Century." *Ambio* 49(1): 74–84.

Ruggeri, K., Većkalov, B., Bojanić, L., Andersen, T., Ashcroft-Jones, S., Nélida Ayacaxli, Barea-Arroyo, P., and others. 2021. "The General Fault in Our Fault Lines." *Nature Human Behaviour* 5: 1369–1380.

Ruhm, C. J. 2018. "Deaths of Despair or Drug Problems?" NBER Working Paper 24188, National Bureau of Economic Research, Cambridge, MA.

Ruiz, C., Hernández-Fernaud, E., Rolo-González, G., and Hernández, B. 2019. "Neighborhoods' Evaluation: Influence on Well-Being Variables." *Frontiers in Psychology* 10: 1736.

Rulli, M., Bellomi, D., Cazzoli, A., De Carolis, G., and D'Odorico, P. 2016. "The Water-Land-Food Nexus of First-Generation Biofuels." *Scientific Reports* 6(22521): 1–10.

Russell, S. 2022. "If We Succeed." *Dædalus* 151(2): 43–57.

Rwanda Ministry of Health. 2018. "Fourth Health Sector Strategic Plan July 2018-June 2024." Rwanda Ministry of Health, Kigali. https://www.childrenandaids.org/sites/default/files/2018-05/Rwanda_Nat%20Health%20Sector%20Plan_2018-2024.pdf.

Ryfe, D. M. 2005. "Does Deliberative Democracy Work?" *Annual Review of Political Science* 8: 49–71.

Saavedra, J. 2021. "A Silent and Unequal Education Crisis: And the Seeds for Its Solution." Education for Global Development [blog], 5 January. https://blogs.worldbank.org/education/silent-and-unequal-education-crisis-and-seeds-its-solution. Accessed 24 August 2022.

Sabin-Miller, D., and Abrams, D. M. 2020. "When Pull Turns to Shove: A Continuous-Time Model for Opinion Dynamics." *Physical Review Research* 2(043001).

Saeed, S. A., Antonacci, D. J., and Bloch, R. M. 2010. "Exercise, Yoga, and Meditation for Depressive and Anxiety Disorders." *American Family Physician* 81(8): 981–986.

Sagan, C. 1983. "Nuclear War and Climatic Catastrophe: Some Policy Implications." *Foreign Affairs* 62(2): 257–292.

Sagan, C. 1994. *Pale Blue Dot: A Vision of the Human Future in Space.* New York: Random House.

Sahay, A. 2021. "The Silenced Women: What Works in Encouraging Women to Report Cases of Gender-Based Violence?" Let's Talk Development [blog], 26 March. https://blogs.worldbank.org/developmenttalk/silenced-women-what-works-encouraging-women-report-cases-gender-based-violence. Accessed 26 March 2021.

Salvatore, M. A., and Grundy, E. 2021. "Area Deprivation, Perceived Neighbourhood Cohesion and Mental Health at Older Ages: A Cross Lagged Analysis of UK Longitudinal Data." *Health & Place* 67: 102470.

Samji, S., and Kapoor, M. 2022. "Funda Wande through the Lens of PDIA: Showcasing a Flexible and Iterative Learning Approach to Improving Educational Outcomes." RISE Insight 2022/036. https://doi.org/10.35489/BSG-RISE-RI_2022/036.

Sampi, J., and Jooste, C. 2020. "Nowcasting Economic Activity in Times of Covid-19: An Approximation from the Google Community Mobility Report." Policy Research Working Paper, 9247, World Bank, Washington, DC.

Samuelson, W., and Zeckhauser, R. 1988. "Status Quo Bias in Decision Making." *Journal of Risk and Uncertainty* 1(1): 7–59.

Sanchez, M., Lamont, M., and Zilberstein, S. 2022. "How American College Students Understand Social Resilience and Navigate Towards the Future During Covid and the Movement for Racial Justice." *Social Science & Medicine* 301: 114890.

Sandel, M. J. 2020. *The Tyranny of Merit: What's Become of the Common Good?* London: Penguin.

Sanderson, E. W., Walston, J., and Robinson, J. G. 2018. "From Bottleneck to Breakthrough: Urbanization and the Future of Biodiversity Conservation." *Bioscience* 68(6): 412–426.

Santos, F. C., and Pacheco, J. M. 2011. "Risk of Collective Failure Provides an Escape from the Tragedy of the Commons." *Proceedings of the National Academy of Sciences* 108(26): 10421–10425.

Santos, F. C., Santos, M. D., and Pacheco, J. M. 2008. "Social Diversity Promotes the Emergence of Cooperation in Public Goods Games." *Nature* 454(7201): 213–216.

Santos, H. C., Varnum, M. E. W., and Grossmann, I. 2017. "Global Increases in Individualism." *Psychological Science* 28(9): 1228–1239.

Sarhadi, A., Ausín, M. C., Wiper, M. P., Touma, D., and Diffenbaugh, N. S. 2018. "Multidimensional Risk in a Nonstationary Climate: Joint Probability of Increasingly Severe Warm and Dry Conditions." *Science Advances* 4(11): eaau3487.

Sarku, R. 2022. "Deciding Just Transformations under Uncertainty for Digital Farming in Africa for Tomorrow, Today." Background paper for Human Development Report 2021/2022, UNDP–HDRO, New York.

Satake, K. 2014. "Advances in Earthquake and Tsunami Sciences and Disaster Risk Reduction since the 2004 Indian Ocean Tsunami." *Geoscience Letters* 1: 15.

Satariano, B. 2019. "Diverse Socioeconomic Processes Influencing Health and Wellbeing across Generations in Deprived Neighbourhoods in Malta." *Social Science & Medicine* 232: 453–459.

Save the Children. 2021. "The Number of Children Living in Deadliest War Zones Rises Nearly 20% to Highest in over a Decade." https://www.savethechildren.net/news/number-children-living-deadliest-war-zones-rises-nearly-20-highest-over-decade-%E2%80%93-save-children. Accessed 21 June 2022.

Saxena, S. 2018. "Excess Mortality among People with Mental Disorders: A Public Health Priority." *The Lancet Public Health* 3(6): e264–e265.

Schäfer, A., and Schwander, H. 2019. "'Don't Play If You Can't Win': Does Economic Inequality Undermine Political Equality?" *European Political Science Review* 11(3): 395–413.

Schaffner, B. F., and Luks, S. 2018. "Misinformation or Expressive Responding? What an Inauguration Crowd Can Tell Us About the Source of Political Misinformation in Surveys." *Public Opinion Quarterly* 82(1): 135–147.

Scheffer, M., van de Leemput, I., Weinans, E., and Bollen, J. 2021. "The Rise and Fall of Rationality in Language." *Proceedings of the National Academy of Sciences* 118(51): e2107848118.

Scheffer, M., van de Leemput, I., Weinans, E., and Bollen, J. 2022. "Reply to Sun: Making Sense of Language Change." *Proceedings of the National Academy of Sciences* 119(26): e2206616119.

Scheffler, S. 2013. *Death and the Afterlife.* Oxford, UK: Oxford University Press.

Schell, J. 1982. *The Fate of the Earth.* New York: Knopf.

Scheufele, D. A., Krause, N., Freiling, I., and Brossard, D. 2021. "What We Know About Effective Public Engagement on CRISPR and Beyond." *Proceedings of the National Academy of Sciences* 118(22): e2004835117.

Schilbach, F., Schofield, H., and Mullainathan, S. 2016. "The Psychological Lives of the Poor." *American Economic Review* 106(5): 435–440.

Schill, C., Anderies, J. M., Lindahl, T., Folke, C., Polasky, S., Cárdenas, J. C., Crépin, A.-S., and others. 2019. "A More Dynamic Understanding of Human Behaviour for the Anthropocene." *Nature Sustainability* 2(12): 1075–1082.

Schilling, J., Locham, R., and Scheffran, J. 2018. "A Local to Global Perspective on Oil and Wind Exploitation, Resource Governance and Conflict in Northern Kenya." *Conflict, Security & Development* 18(6): 571–600.

Schimmelpfennig, R., Razek, L., Schnell, E., and Muthukrishna, M. 2022. "Paradox of Diversity in the Collective Brain." *Philosophical Transactions of the Royal Society B: Biological Sciences* 377(1843): 20200316.

Schipper, E. L. F., Eriksen, S. E., Fernandez Carril, L. R., Glavovic, B. C., and Shawoo, Z. 2021. "Turbulent Transformation: Abrupt Societal Disruption and Climate Resilient Development." *Climate and Development* 13(6): 467–474.

Schlesinger, W., and Bernhardt, E. 2013. *Biogeochemistry: An Analysis of Global Change.* Waltham, MA: Elsevier, Academic Press.

Schlosser, J. A. 2013. "'Hope, Danger's Comforter': Thucydides, Hope, Politics." *The Journal of Politics* 75(1): 169–182.

Schmelz, K., and Bowles, S. 2022. "Opposition to Voluntary and Mandated Covid-19 Vaccination as a Dynamic Process: Evidence and Policy Implications of Changing Beliefs." *Proceedings of the National Academy of Sciences* 119(13): e2118721119.

Schmidt, C. 2010. "Synthetic Biology: Environmental Health Implications of a New Field." *Environmental Health Perspectives* 118(3): 118–123.

Schmidt, O., Hawkes, A., Gambhir, A., and Staffell, I. 2017. "The Future Cost of Electrical Energy Storage Based on Experience Rates." *Nature Energy* 2: 17110.

Schofield, H., and Venkataramani, A. S. 2021. "Poverty-Related Bandwidth Constraints Reduce the Value of Consumption." *Proceedings of the National Academy of Sciences* 118(35): e2102794118.

Schui, F. 2014. *Austerity: The Great Failure.* New Haven, CT: Yale University Press.

Schwandt, H., and Von Wachter, T. 2019. "Unlucky Cohorts: Estimating the Long-Term Effects of Entering the Labor Market in a Recession in Large Cross-Sectional Data Sets." *Journal of Labor Economics* 37(1): 161–198.

Schwandt, H., and Von Wachter, T. 2020. "Socioeconomic Decline and Death: Midlife Impacts of Graduating in a Recession." NBER Working Paper 26638, National Bureau of Economic Research, Cambridge, MA.

Schwandt, H., Currie, J., Bär, M., Banks, J., Bertoli, P., Bütikofer, A., Cattan, S., and others. 2021. "Inequality in Mortality between Black and White Americans by Age, Place, and Cause and in Comparison to Europe, 1990 to 2018." *Proceedings of the National Academy of Sciences* 118(40): e2104684118.

Schwarzmueller, F., and Kastner, T. 2022. "Agricultural Trade and Its Impacts on Cropland Use and the Global Loss of Species Habitat." *Sustainability Science.*

Science and Security Board. 2021. "2021 Doomsday Clock Statement: It Is 100 Seconds to Midnight." Bulletin of the Atomic Scientists. https://thebulletin.org/doomsday-clock/. Accessed 25 August 2022.

Scott, R. 2008. *Institutions and Organizations*, 3rd Edition. London: Sage Publications.

Scoville, C., McCumber, A., Amironesei, R., and Jeon, J. 2022. "Mask Refusal Backlash: The Politicization of Face Masks in the American Public Sphere During the Early Stages of the Covid-19 Pandemic." *Socius* 8: 23780231221093158.

Searcey, D., Lipton, E., and Gilbertson, A. 2021. "Hunt for the 'Blood Diamond of Batteries' Impedes Green Energy Push." *New York Times,* 29 November.

Sears, N. A. 2020. "Existential Security: Towards a Security Framework for the Survival of Humanity." *Global Policy* 11(2): 255–266.

Sears, N. A. 2021. "International Politics in the Age of Existential Threats." *Journal of Global Security Studies* 6(3): ogaa027.

Seedat, S., and Rondon, M. 2021. "Women's Wellbeing and the Burden of Unpaid Work." *The BMJ* 374: n1972.

Selee, A., and Bolter, J. 2022. "Colombia's Open-Door Policy: An Innovative Approach to Displacement?" *International Migration* 60(1): 113–131.

Selfa, T., Lindberg, S., and Bain, C. 2021. "Governing Gene Editing in Agriculture and Food in the United States: Tensions, Contestations, and Realignments." *Elementa: Science of Anthropocene* 9(1): 00153.

Sellare, J., Börner, J., Brugger, F., Garrett, R., Günther, I., Meemken, E.-M., Pelli, E. M., and others. 2022. "Six Research Priorities to Support Corporate Due-Diligence Policies." *Nature* 606: 861–863.

Sen, A. 1973. "Behaviour and the Concept of Preference." *Economica* 40(159): 241–259.

Sen, A. 1977. "Rational Fools: A Critique of the Behavioral Foundations of Economic Theory." *Philosophy & Public Affairs* 6(4): 317–344.

Sen, A. 1979. "Equality of What?" *The Tanner Lecture on Human Values* 1.

Sen, A. 1985. "Well-Being, Agency and Freedom: The Dewey Lectures 1984." *The Journal of Philosophy* 82(4): 169–221.

Sen, A. 1989. "Development as Capability Expansion." *Journal of Development Planning* 19: 41–58.

Sen, A. 1993. "Internal Consistency of Choice." *Econometrica* 61(3): 495–521.

Sen, A. 1997a. "Human Capital and Human Capability." In Fukuda-Parr, S., and Shiva Kumar, A. K., (eds.), *Readings in Human Development.* Oxford, UK: Oxford University Press.

Sen, A. 1997b. "Maximization and the Act of Choice." *Econometrica* 65(4): 745–779.

Sen, A. 1999. *Development as Freedom.* New York: Knopf.

Sen, A. 2002. *Rationality and Freedom.* Cambridge, MA: Harvard University Press.

Sen, A. 2005. "Human Rights and Capabilities." *Journal of Human Development* 6(2): 151–166.

Sen, A. 2008. "The Idea of Justice." *Journal of Human Development* 9(3): 331–342.

Sen, A. 2009a. "The Fog of Identity." *Politics, Philosophy & Economics* 8(3): 285–288.

Sen, A. 2009b. *The Idea of Justice.* Cambridge, MA: Harvard University Press.

Senate of the Republic of Chile. 2020. "Agenda De Género Covid-19: Plantean Prioridades a La Ministra De La Mujer Y Equidad De Género." Santiago.

Sepulveda, N. A., Jenkins, J. D., Edington, A., Mallapragada, D. S., and Lester, R. K. 2021. "The Design Space for Long-Duration Energy Storage in Decarbonized Power Systems." *Nature Energy* 6(5): 506–516.

Shah, A. K., Zhao, J., Mullainathan, S., and Shafir, E. 2018. "Money in the Mental Lives of the Poor." *Social Cognition* 36(1): 4–19.

Shapiro, F. 1996. "Eye Movement Desensitization and Reprocessing (EMDR): Evaluation of Controlled PTSD Research." *Journal of Behavior Therapy and Experimental Psychiatry* 27(3): 209–218.

Sharot, T., and Sunstein, C. R. 2020. "How People Decide What They Want to Know." *Nature Human Behaviour* 4(1): 14–19.

She is a Revolution. 2020. "The Remarkable Contributions of Girls and Women During the Covid-19 Pandemic." Iraqi Civil Society Solidarity Initiative, 25 March. https://www.iraqicivilsociety.org/archives/11408. Accessed 25 August 2022.

Shearer, J. C., Abelson, J., Kouyaté, B., Lavis, J. N., and Walt, G. 2016. "Why Do Policies Change? Institutions, Interests, Ideas and Networks in Three Cases of Policy Reform." *Health Policy and Planning* 31(9): 1200–1211.

Sheingate, A. D. 2003. "Political Entrepreneurship, Institutional Change, and American Political Development." *Studies in American Political Development* 17(2): 185–203.

Shen, C., Sambamoorthi, U., and Rust, G. 2008. "Co-Occurring Mental Illness and Health Care Utilization and Expenditures in Adults with Obesity and Chronic Physical Illness." *Disease Management* 11(3): 153–160.

Shen, S., and Kusunoki, Y. 2019. "Intimate Partner Violence and Psychological Distress among Emerging Adult Women: A Bidirectional Relationship." *Journal of Women's Health* 28(8): 1060–1067.

Sherman, L., Proctor, J., Druckenmiller, H., Tapia, H., and Hsiang, S. 2022. "Estimating the United Nations Human Development Index at High-Resolution Using Satellite Imagery." Unpublished working paper.

Shi, L., Romić, I., Ma, Y., Wang, Z., Podobnik, B., Stanley, H. E., Holme, P., and Jusup, M. 2020. "Freedom of Choice Adds Value to Public Goods." *Proceedings of the National Academy of Sciences* 117(30): 17516–17521.

Shigeoka, H. 2019. "Long-Term Consequences of Growing up in a Recession on Risk Preferences." NBER Working Paper 26352, National Bureau of Economic Research, Cambridge, MA.

Shiller, R. J. 2017. "Narrative Economics." *American Economic Review* 107(4): 967–1004.

Shiller, R. J. 2019. "Narrative Economics." Cowles Foundation Discussion Paper 2069, Yale University, Cowles Foundation for Research in Economics, New Haven, CT.

Shultz, J. M., Rechkemmer, A., Rai, A., and McManus, K. T. 2019. "Public Health and Mental Health Implications of Environmentally Induced Forced Migration." *Disaster Medicine and Public Health Preparedness* 13(2): 116–122.

Silagadze, N., Christensen, H. S., Sirén, R., and Grönlund, K. 2022. "Perceptions of Inequality and Political Participation: The Moderating Role of Ideology." *Political Studies Review*: 14789299221082037.

Silva, E. P., Ludermir, A. B., Lima, M. C., Eickmann, S. H., and Emond, A. 2019. "Mental Health of Children Exposed to Intimate Partner Violence against Their Mother: A Longitudinal Study from Brazil." *Child Abuse & Neglect* 92: 1–11.

Silver, S. M., Rogers, S., and Russell, M. 2008. "Eye Movement Desensitization and Reprocessing (EMDR) in the Treatment of War Veterans." *Journal of Clinical Psychology* 64(8): 947–957.

Simon, H. A. 1955. "A Behavioral Model of Rational Choice." *The Quarterly Journal of Economics* 69(1): 99–118.

Singh, A. K., and Singh, P. K. 2019. "Digital Addiction: A Conceptual Overview." *Library Philosophy and Practice.*

Singh, N. N., Lancioni, G. E., Winton, A. S., Adkins, A. D., Wahler, R. G., Sabaawi, M., and Singh, J. 2007. "Individuals with Mental Illness Can Control Their Aggressive Behavior through Mindfulness Training." *Behavior Modification* 31(3): 313–328.

Singhal, S. 2019. "Early Life Shocks and Mental Health: The Long-Term Effect of War in Vietnam." *Journal of Development Economics* 141: 102244.

SIPRI (Stockholm International Peace Research Institute). 2021. *Anthropocene (in)Securities: Reflections on Collective Survival 50 Years after the Stockholm Conference.* Oxford, UK: Oxford University Press.

Skinner, H., Biscope, S., and Poland, B. 2003. "Quality of Internet Access: Barrier Behind Internet Use Statistics." *Social Science & Medicine* 57(5): 875–880.

Smil, V. 2022. *How the World Really Works: The Science Behind How We Got Here and Where We're Going.* London: Viking.

Smirl, J. D., Jones, K. E., Copeland, P., Khatra, O., Taylor, E. H., and Van Donkelaar, P. 2019. "Characterizing Symptoms of Traumatic Brain Injury in Survivors of Intimate Partner Violence." *Brain Injury* 33(12): 1529–1538.

Smith, C., and Brower, D. 2022. "Petrol Prices in US Hit $5 a Gallon as Inflation Picks Up." *Financial Times,* 11 June.

Smith, E., Ali, D., Wilkerson, B., Dawson, W. D., Sobowale, K., Reynolds, C., Berk, M., and others. 2021. "A Brain Capital Grand Strategy: Toward Economic Reimagination." *Molecular Psychiatry* 26(1): 3–22.

Smith, J. C. 1975. "Meditation as Psychotherapy: A Review of the Literature." *Psychological Bulletin* 82(4): 558–564.

Smith, S. G., Zhang, X., Basile, K. C., Merrick, M. T., Wang, J., Kresnow, M.-j., and Chen, J. 2018. *The National Intimate Partner and Sexual Violence Survey: 2015 Data Brief–Updated Release.* Atlanta, GA: Centers for Disease Control and Prevention, National Center for Injury Prevention and Control.

Smith, S. L., Kayiteshonga, Y., Misago, C. N., Iyamuremye, J. D., Dusabeyezu, J. d. A., Mohand, A. A., Osrow, R. A., and others. 2017. "Integrating Mental Health Care into Primary Care: The Case of One Rural District in Rwanda." *Intervention* 15(2): 136–150.

Smits, J., and Permanyer, I. 2019. "The Subnational Human Development Database." *Scientific Data* 6: 190038.

Snow, D. A., and Benford, R. D. 1988. "Ideology, Frame Resonance, and Participant Mobilization." *International Social Movement Research* 1(1): 197–217.

Snow, D. A., Soule, S. A., Kriesi, H., and McCammon, H. J., (eds.). 2018. *The Wiley Blackwell Companion to Social Movements.* Malden, MA: Blackwell Publishing Ltd.

Snower, D. 2020. "The Socio-Economics of Pandemics Policy." IZA Policy Paper 162, Institute of Labor Economics, Bonn, Germany.

Snyder-Beattie, A. E., Ord, T., and Bonsall, M. B. 2019. "An Upper Bound for the Background Rate of Human Extinction." *Scientific Reports* 9(1): 1–9.

Soens, T. 2018. "Resilient Societies, Vulnerable People: Coping with North Sea Floods before 1800." *Past & Present* 241(1): 143–177.

Soens, T. 2020. *Resilience in Historical Disaster Studies: Pitfalls and Opportunities.* New York: Springer VS.

Soga, M., Evans, M. J., Tsuchiya, K., and Fukano, Y. 2021. "A Room with a Green View: The Importance of Nearby Nature for Mental Health During the Covid-19 Pandemic." *Ecological Applications* 31(2): e2248.

Somer, M. 2005. "Failures of the Discourse of Ethnicity: Turkey, Kurds, and the Emerging Iraq." *Security Dialogue* 36: 109–128.

Somer, M., and McCoy, J. 2018. "Déjà Vu? Polarization and Endangered Democracies in the 21st Century." *American Behavioral Scientist* 62(1): 3–15.

Sonter, L. J., Dade, M. C., Watson, J. E., and Valenta, R. K. 2020. "Renewable Energy Production Will Exacerbate Mining Threats to Biodiversity." *Nature Communications* 11(1): 1–6.

Sovacool, B. K. 2016. "How Long Will It Take? Conceptualizing the Temporal Dynamics of Energy Transitions." *Energy Research & Social Science* 13: 202–215.

Sovacool, B. K., Ali, S. H., Bazilian, M., Radley, B., Nemery, B., Okatz, J., and Mulvaney, D. 2020. "Sustainable Minerals and Metals for a Low-Carbon Future." *Science* 367(6473): 30–33.

Speer, P. W., Christens, B. D., and Peterson, N. A. 2021. "Participation in Community Organizing: Cross-Sectional and Longitudinal Analyses of Impacts on Sociopolitical Development." *Journal of Community Psychology* 49(8): 3194–3214.

Statista. 2022. "Number of Smartphone Subscriptions Worldwide from 2016 to 2027." https://www.statista.

com/statistics/330695/number-of-smartphone-users -worldwide/. Accessed 13 July 2022.

Steenbergen, M., and Colombo, C. 2018. "Heuristics in Political Behavior." In Mintz, A., and Terris, L., (eds.), *The Oxford Handbook of Behavioral Political Science.* Oxford, UK: Oxford Handbooks Online.

Steffen, W., Grinevald, J., Crutzen, P., and McNeill, J. 2011. "The Anthropocene: Conceptual and Historical Perspectives." *Philosophical Transactions of the Royal Society A: Mathematical, Physical and Engineering Sciences* 369(1938): 842–867.

Steffen, W., Richardson, K., Rockström, J., Cornell, S. E., Fetzer, I., Bennett, E. M., Biggs, R., and others. 2015. "Planetary Boundaries: Guiding Human Development on a Changing Planet." *Science* 347(6223).

Steinberger, J. 2018. "Climate Breakdown, Capitalism and Democracy." *Medium,* 13 October. https://jksteinberger.medium.com/climate-breakdown -capitalism-and-democracy-e11b16c7d9ef. Accessed 25 August 2022.

Sterelny, K. 2017. "Cultural Evolution in California and Paris." *Studies in History and Philosophy of Science Part C: Studies in History and Philosophy of Biological and Biomedical Sciences* 62: 42–50.

Stevens, F., Nurse, J. R., and Arief, B. 2020. "Cyber Stalking, Cyber Harassment, and Adult Mental Health: A Systematic Review." *Cyberpsychology, Behavior, and Social Networking* 24(6): 367–376.

Stevenson, S., Coats, S., Touma, D., Cole, J., Lehner, F., Fasullo, J., and Otto-Bliesner, B. 2022. "Twenty-First Century Hydroclimate: A Continually Changing Baseline, with More Frequent Extremes." *Proceedings of the National Academy of Sciences* 119(12): e2108124119.

Stewart, A. J., McCarty, N., and Bryson, J. J. 2020. "Polarization under Rising Inequality and Economic Decline." *Science Advances* 6(50).

Stewart, A. J., Plotkin, J. B., and McCarty, N. 2021. "Inequality, Identity, and Partisanship: How Redistribution Can Stem the Tide of Mass Polarization." *Proceedings of the National Academy of Sciences* 118(50): e2102140118.

Stewart, A., Mosleh, M., Diakonova, M., Arechar, A., Rand, D., and Plotkin, J. 2019. "Information Gerrymandering and Undemocratic Decisions." *Nature* 573(117–121).

Stiglitz, J. E., and Guzman, M. M. 2021. "Economic Fluctuations and Pseudo-Wealth." *Industrial and Corporate Change* 30(2): 297–315.

Stiglitz, J. E., Fitoussi, J.-P., and Durand, M. 2018. *Beyond GDP: Measuring What Counts for Economic and Social Performance.* Paris: Organisation for Economic Co-operation and Development.

Stojanovski, K., Zhou, S., King, E., Gjorgjiovska, J., and Mihajlov, A. 2018. "An Application of the Minority Stress Model in a Non-Western Context: Discrimination and Mental Health among Sexual and Gender Minorities in Macedonia." *Sexuality Research and Social Policy* 15(3): 367–376.

Stone, D. 2011. *Policy Paradox. The Art of Political Decision Making.* New York: W.W. Norton & Company.

Stone, D. F. 2020. "Just a Big Misunderstanding? Bias and Bayesian Affective Polarization." *International Economic Review* 61(1): 189–217.

Stoyanovich, J., Bavel, J. J. V., and West, T. V. 2020. "The Imperative of Interpretable Machines." *Nature Machine Intelligence* 2: 197–199.

Straiton, M. L., Aambø, A. K., and Johansen, R. 2019. "Perceived Discrimination, Health and Mental Health among Immigrants in Norway: The Role of Moderating Factors." *BMC Public Health* 19(1): 1–13.

Strassburg, B. B. N., Iribarrem, A., Beyer, H. L., Cordeiro, C. L., Crouzeilles, R., Jakovac, C. C., Braga Junqueira, A., and others. 2020. "Global Priority Areas for Ecosystem Restoration." *Nature* 586(7831): 724–729.

Strømme, A., Sapiezynska, E., Fylkesnes, G. K., Salarkia, K., and Edwards, J. 2020. *Stop the War on Children 2020: Gender Matters.* London: Save the Children International.

Studley, M. 2021. "Onshoring through Automation; Perpetuating Inequality?" *Frontiers in Robotics and AI* 8: 185.

Suárez-Álvarez, A., and López-Menéndez, A. 2022. "Is Covid-19 Vaccine Inequality Undermining the Recovery from the Covid-19 Pandemic?" *Journal of Global Health* 12: 05020.

Sun, K. 2022. "Colloquialization as a Key Factor in Historical Changes of Rational and Emotional Words." *Proceedings of the National Academy of Sciences* 119(26): e2205563119.

Sunstein, C. R. 1999. *The Law of Group Polarization.* Chicago, IL: University of Chicago Law School.

Supran, G., and Oreskes, N. 2021. "Rhetoric and Frame Analysis of ExxonMobil's Climate Change Communications." *One Earth* 4(5): 696–719.

Swidler, A. 1986. "Culture in Action: Symbols and Strategies." *American Sociological Review* 51(2): 273–286.

Swidler, A. 2013. *Talk of Love: How Culture Matters.* Chicago, IL: University of Chicago Press.

Swinkels, M. 2020. "How Ideas Matter in Public Policy: A Review of Concepts, Mechanisms, and Methods." *International Review of Public Policy* 2(3): 281–316.

Szaflarski, M., and Bauldry, S. 2019. "The Effects of Perceived Discrimination on Immigrant and Refugee Physical and Mental Health." In Frank, R., (ed.), *Immigration and Health.* Advances in Medical Sociology Vol. 19. Bingley, UK: Emerald Publishing Limited.

Szekely, A., Lipari, F., Antonioni, A., Paolucci, M., Sánchez, A., Tummolini, L., and Andrighetto, G. 2021. "Evidence from a Long-Term Experiment That Collective Risks Change Social Norms and Promote Cooperation." *Nature Communications* 12(1): 1–7.

Táíwò, O. O. 2022. *Reconsidering Reparations.* Oxford, UK: Oxford University Press.

Tamarit, A., de la Barrera, U., Mónaco, E., Schoeps, K., and Castilla, I. M. 2020. "Psychological Impact of Covid-19 Pandemic in Spanish Adolescents: Risk and Protective Factors of Emotional Symptoms." *Revista de Psicología Clínica con Niños y Adolescentes* 7(3): 73–80.

Tang, S., Xiang, M., Cheung, T., and Xiang, Y.-T. 2021. "Mental Health and Its Correlates among Children and Adolescents During Covid-19 School Closure: The Importance of Parent-Child Discussion." *Journal of Affective Disorders* 279: 353–360.

Tankari, M. 2018. "Rainfall Variability and Farm Households Food Insecurity in Burkina Faso: The Nonfarm Enterprises as Coping Strategy." *Food Security*: 1–12.

Tanovic, E., Gee, D. G., and Joormann, J. 2018. "Intolerance of Uncertainty: Neural and Psychophysiological Correlates of the Perception of Uncertainty as Threatening." *Clinical Psychology Review* 60: 87–99.

Tappin, B. M., Pennycook, G., and Rand, D. G. 2020. "Rethinking the Link between Cognitive Sophistication and Politically Motivated Reasoning." *Journal of Experimental Psychology: General.* 150(6): 1095–1114.

Tasnim, S., Hossain, M. M., and Mazumder, H. 2020. "Impact of Rumors and Misinformation on Covid-19 in Social Media." *Journal of Preventive Medicine and Public Health* 53(3): 171–174.

Tauli-Corpuz, V., Alcorn, J., and Molnar, A. 2018. "Cornered by Protected Areas: Replacing 'Fortress' Conservation with Rights-Based Approaches Helps Bring Justice for Indigenous Peoples and Local Communities, Reduces Conflict, and Enables Cost-Effective Conservation and Climate Action." Rights and Resources Initiative, Washington, DC.

Tay, A., Riley, A., Islam, R., Welton-Mitchell, C., Duchesne, B., Waters, V., Varner, A., and others. 2019. "The Culture, Mental Health and Psychosocial Wellbeing of Rohingya Refugees: A Systematic Review." *Epidemiology and Psychiatric Sciences* 28(5): 489–494.

Taylor, P., and Keeter, S. 2010. "Millennials: Confident. Connected. Open to Change." Pew Research Center, Washington, DC.

Taylor, S. 2020. "Anxiety Disorders, Climate Change, and the Challenges Ahead: Introduction to the Special Issue." *Journal of Anxiety Disorders* 76: 102313.

Tetlock, P. E., and Gardner, D. 2015. *Superforecasting: The Art and Science of Prediction.* New York: Crown.

Thaler, M. 2020. "The Fake News Effect: Experimentally Identifying Motivated Reasoning Using Trust in News." *arXiv preprint arXiv:2012.01663.*

Thaler, R. 1980. "Toward a Positive Theory of Consumer Choice." *Journal of Economic Behavior & Organization* 1(1): 39–60.

Thaler, R. H. 2018. "From Cashews to Nudges: The Evolution of Behavioral Economics." *American Economic Review* 108(6): 1265–1287.

Thaler, R. H., and Sunstein, C. R. 2003. "Libertarian Paternalism." *American Economic Review* 93(2): 175–179.

Thiery, W., Lange, S., Rogelj, J., Schleussner, C.-F., Gudmundsson, L., Seneviratne, S. I., Andrijevic, M., and others. 2021. "Intergenerational Inequities in Exposure to Climate Extremes." *Science* 374(6564): 158–160.

Thompson, K. L., Hill, C., Ojeda, J., Ban, N. C., and Picard, C. R. 2020. "Indigenous Food Harvesting as Social–Ecological Monitoring: A Case Study with the Gitga'at First Nation." *People and Nature* 2(4): 1085–1099.

Thompson, R. 2011. "Radicalization and the Use of Social Media." *Journal of Strategic Security* 4(4): 167–190.

Thompson, T. 2021. "Young People's Climate Anxiety Revealed in Landmark Survey." *Nature* 597(7878): 605. https://www.nature.com/articles/d41586-021-02582-8. Accessed 20 October 2021.

Thrasher, J., and Vallier, K. 2015. "The Fragility of Consensus: Public Reason, Diversity and Stability." *European Journal of Philosophy* 23(4): 933–954.

Tierney, J. E., Poulsen, C. J., Montañez, I. P., Bhattacharya, T., Feng, R., Ford, H. L., Hönisch, B., and others. 2020. "Past Climates Inform Our Future." *Science* 370(6517).

Tigchelaar, M., Battisti, D. S., Naylor, R. L., and Ray, D. K. 2018. "Future Warming Increases Probability of Globally Synchronized Maize Production Shocks." *Proceedings of the National Academy of Sciences* 115(26): 6644–6649.

Tillmann, S., Tobin, D., Avison, W., and Gilliland, J. 2018. "Mental Health Benefits of Interactions with Nature in Children and Teenagers: A Systematic Review." *Journal of Epidemiol Community Health* 72(10): 958–966.

Tilly, C. 1977. *From Mobilization to Revolution.* Reading, MA: Addison-Wesley.

Timmermann, A., and Friedrich, T. 2016. "Late Pleistocene Climate Drivers of Early Human Migration." *Nature* 538(7623): 92–95.

Timperley, J. 2021. "The Fight to End Fossil-Fuel Subsidies." *Nature*: 403–405.

Toff, B., and Nielsen, R. K. 2018. "'I Just Google It': Folk Theories of Distributed Discovery." *Journal of Communication* 68(3): 636–657.

Tokita, C. K., Guess, A. M., and Tarnita, C. E. 2021. "Polarized Information Ecosystems Can Reorganize Social Networks Via Information Cascades." *Proceedings of the National Academy of Sciences* 118(50): e2102147118.

Tom, S. M., Fox, C. R., Trepel, C., and Poldrack, R. A. 2007. "The Neural Basis of Loss Aversion in Decision-Making under Risk." *Science* 315(5811): 515–518.

Tomasello, M. 2016. "The Ontogeny of Cultural Learning." *Current Opinion in Psychology* 8: 1–4.

Tomasello, M. 2018. "How Children Come to Understand False Beliefs: A Shared Intentionality Account." *Proceedings of the National Academy of Sciences* 115(34): 8491–8498.

Tomasello, M. 2020. "The Ontogenetic Foundations of Epistemic Norms." *Episteme* 17(3): 301–315.

Toor, J., Echeverria-Londono, S., Li, X., Abbas, K., Carter, E. D., Clapham, H. E., Clark, A., and others. 2021. "Lives Saved with Vaccination for 10 Pathogens across 112 Countries in a Pre-Covid-19 World." *Elife* 10.

The Trevor Project. 2021. "National Survey on LGBTQ Youth Mental Health." https://www.thetrevorproject.org/survey-2021/. Accessed 9 July 2021.

Troller-Renfree, S. V., Costanzo, M. A., Duncan, G. J., Magnuson, K., Gennetian, L. A., Yoshikawa, H., Halpern-Meekin, S., and others. 2022. "The Impact of a Poverty Reduction Intervention on Infant Brain Activity." *Proceedings of the National Academy of Sciences* 119(5): e2115649119.

Trosset, J.-Y., and Carbonell, P. 2015. "Synthetic Biology for Pharmaceutical Drug Discovery." *Drug Development, Design and Therapy* 9: 6285–6302.

Trudell, J. P., Burnet, M. L., Ziegler, B. R., and Luginaah, I. 2021. "The Impact of Food Insecurity on Mental Health in Africa: A Systematic Review." *Social Science & Medicine* 278: 113953.

Tucker, J. A., Guess, A., Barberá, P., Vaccari, C., Siegel, A., Sanovich, S., Stukal, D., and Nyhan, B. 2018. "Social Media, Political Polarization, and Political Disinformation: A Review of the Scientific Literature." https://ssrn.com/abstract=3144139.

Tunyasuvunakool, K., Adler, J., Wu, Z., Green, T., Zielinski, M., Žídek, A., Bridgland, A., and others. 2021. "Highly Accurate Protein Structure Prediction for the Human Proteome." *Nature* 596(7873): 590–596.

Tvauri, A. 2014. "The Impact of the Climate Catastrophe of 536–537 AD in Estonia and Neighbouring Areas." *Estonian Journal of Archaeology* 18(1): 30.

Tversky, A., and Kahneman, D. 1974. "Judgment under Uncertainty: Heuristics and Biases." *Science* 185(4157): 1124–1131.

Tversky, A., and Kahneman, D. 1991. "Loss Aversion in Riskless Choice: A Reference-Dependent Model." *The Quarterly Journal of Economics* 106(4): 1039–1061.

Tversky, A., and Kahneman, D. 1992. "Advances in Prospect Theory: Cumulative Representation of Uncertainty." *Journal of Risk and Uncertainty* 5(4): 297–323.

Tyng, C. M., Amin, H. U., Saad, M. N., and Malik, A. S. 2017. "The Influences of Emotion on Learning and Memory." *Frontiers in Psychology* 8: 1454.

UN (United Nations). 1972. *Report of the United Nations Conference on the Human Environment, Stockholm 5–16 June 1972.* New York.

UN (United Nations). 2013. "Quality Education Can Help Prevent Racism and Xenophobia – UN Expert." UN News, 14 June. https://news.un.org/en/story/2013/06/442302-quality-education-can-help-prevent-racism-and-xenophobia-un-expert. Accessed 24 June 2022.

UN (United Nations). 2020a. "E-Government Survey 2020." New York.

UN (United Nations). 2020b. "Peacebuilding and Sustaining Peace." Report of the Secretary-General, A/74/976-S/2020/773, New York.

UN (United Nations). 2020c. *Report of the Secretary General: Roadmap for Digital Cooperation.* Nairobi.

UN (United Nations). 2021a. "The Impact of Digital Technologies." https://www.un.org/en/un75/impact-digital-technologies. Accessed 27 May 2021.

UN (United Nations). 2021b. "What Is Domestic Abuse?" https://www.un.org/en/coronavirus/what-is-domestic-abuse. Accessed 28 Aug 2021.

UN (United Nations). 2021c. *Our Common Agenda: Report of the Secretary-General.* New York. https://www.un.org/en/content/common-agenda-report/assets/pdf/Common_Agenda_Report_English.pdf.

UN (United Nations). 2021d. "Secretary-General's Statement on the IPCC Working Group 1 Report on the Physical Science Basis of the Sixth Assessment." 9 August. https://www.un.org/sg/en/content/secretary-generals-statement-the-ipcc-working-group-1-report-the-physical-science-basis-of-the-sixth-assessment. Accessed 24 August 2022.

UN (United Nations). 2022a. "Secretary General's Remarks to the General Assembly on His Priorities for 2022." https://www.un.org/sg/en/content/sg/statement/2022-01-21/secretary-generals-remarks-the-general-assembly-his-priorities-for-2022-bilingual-delivered-scroll-down-for-all-english-and-all-french. Accessed 1 April 2022.

UN (United Nations). 2022b. "Social Media Poses 'Existential Threat' to Traditional, Trustworthy News: UNESCO." 10 March. https://news.un.org/en/story/2022/03/1113702. Accessed 25 August 2022.

UN (United Nations). 2022c. "Secretary-General's Remarks at the Launch of the Second Brief by the Global Crisis Response Group." 8 June. https://www.un.org/sg/en/content/sg/speeches/2022-06-08/secretary-generals-remarks-the-launch-of-the-second-brief-the-global-crisis-response-group. Accessed 24 August 2022.

UN (United Nations). 2022d. "Secretary-General's Remarks to the Global Food Security Call to Action Ministerial [as Delivered]." 18 May. https://www.un.org/sg/en/content/sg/statement/2022-05-18/secretary-generals-remarks-the-global-food-security-call-action-ministerial-delivered. Accessed 24 August 2022.

UN Global Crisis Response Group on Food, Energy and Finance. 2022. "Global Impact of the War in Ukraine: Billions of People Face the Greatest Cost-of-Living Crisis in a Generation." Brief 2, New York.

UN OCHA (United Nations Office for the Coordination of Humanitarian Affairs). 2020. "Haiti: Tropical Storm Laura Situation Report 4." Port-au-Prince. https://reliefweb.int/sites/reliefweb.int/files/resources/tropical_storm_laura_sitrep4_-_ocha_haiti_-_eng_-_final.pdf.

UN Women (United Nations Entity for Gender Equality and the Empowerment of Women). 2021a. *Measuring the Shadow Pandemic: Violence against Women During Covid-19.* New York.

UN Women (United Nations Entity for Gender Equality and the Empowerment of Women). 2021b. "Surveys Show That Covid-19 Has Gendered Effects in Asia and the Pacific." https://data.unwomen.org/resources/surveys-show-covid-19-has-gendered-effects-asia-and-pacific. Accessed 1 October 2021.

UN Women (United Nations Entity for Gender Equality and the Empowerment of Women) and UNDP (United Nations Development Programme). 2022. *Government Responses to Covid-19: Lessons on Gender Equality for a World in Turmoil.* New York.

UN Women (United Nations Entity for Gender Equality and the Empowerment of Women), ILO (International Labor Organization), IOM (International Organization for Migration) and AiW (Arab Institute for Women) 2021. "Migrant Workers' Rights and Women's

Rights: Women Migrant Domestic Workers in Lebanon: A Gender Perspective." New York.

UNDESA (United Nations Department of Economic and Social Affairs). 2022a. *World Economic Situation and Prospects 2022.* New York. https://www.un.org/development/desa/dpad/publication/world-economic-situation-and-prospects-2022/. Accessed 4 May 2022.

UNDESA (United Nations Department of Economic and Social Affairs). 2022b. *World Population Prospects: The 2022 Revision.* New York. https://population.un.org/wpp/. Accessed 11 July 2022.

UNDP (United Nations Development Programme). 1990. *Human Development Report 1990: Concept and Measurement of Human Development.* New York.

UNDP (United Nations Development Programme). 2001. *Human Development Report 2001: Making New Technologies Work for Human Development.* New York.

UNDP (United Nations Development Programme). 2015. *Human Development Report 2015: Work for Human Development.* New York.

UNDP (United Nations Development Programme). 2019. *Human Development Report 2019: Beyond Income, Beyond Averages, Beyond Today: Inequalities in Human Development in the 21st Century.* New York.

UNDP (United Nations Development Programme). 2020a. *Human Development Report 2020: The Next Frontier: Human Development and the Anthropocene.* New York.

UNDP (United Nations Development Programme). 2020b. *Tackling Social Norms, a Game Changer for Gender Inequalities.* Human Development Perspectives. New York.

UNDP (United Nations Development Programme). 2021a. *Climate Finance for Sustaining Peace: Making Climate Finance Work for Conflict-Affected and Fragile Contexts.* New York.

UNDP (United Nations Development Programme). 2021b. *Trapped: High Inequality and Low Growth in Latin America and the Caribbean, Regional Human Development Report 2021.* New York.

UNDP (United Nations Development Programme). 2022a. "Integrating Mental Health and Psychosocial Support into Peacebuilding." Guidance Note. New York.

UNDP (United Nations Development Programme). 2022b. *New Threats to Human Security in the Anthropocene: Demanding Greater Solidarity.* New York.

UNDP (United Nations Development Programme). 2022c. *Arab Human Development Report 2022 Expanding Opportunities for an Inclusive and Resilient Recovery in the Post-Covid Era.* New York.

UNDP (United Nations Development Programme) and OPHI (Oxford Poverty and Human Development Initiative). 2020. *2020 Global Multidimensional Poverty Index: Charting Pathways out of Multidimensional Poverty: Achieving the SDGs.* New York.

UNEP (United Nations Environment Programme). 2021. *Emissions Gap Report 2021: The Heat Is on – a World of Climate Promises Not yet Delivered.* Nairobi.

UNESCO (United Nations Educational, Scientific and Cultural Organization). 2017. "Preventing Violent Extremism." https://en.unesco.org/preventingviolentextremism. Accessed 25 August 2022.

UNESCO (United Nations Educational, Scientific and Cultural Organization). 2018. "International Technical Guidance on Sexuality Education: An Evidence-Informed Approach." Paris.

UNESCO (United Nations Educational, Scientific and Cultural Organization). 2021. "Políticas De Educación Inclusiva." Estudios sobre políticas educativas en América Latina. Santiago.

UNESCO (United Nations Educational, Scientific and Cultural Organization) Institute for Statistics. 2022. UIS Developer Portal, Bulk Data Download Service. https://apiportal.uis.unesco.org/bdds. Accessed 28 April 2022.

UNFPA (United Nations Population Fund). 2021. "The State of World Population 2021." [Data file.] https://www.unfpa.org/modules/custom/unfpa_global_sowp_portal/data-file/SWOP-Data-2021.xlsx. Accessed 13 September 2021.

Ungar, M., and Theron, L. 2020. "Resilience and Mental Health: How Multisystemic Processes Contribute to Positive Outcomes." *The Lancet Psychiatry* 7(5): 441–448.

UNHCR (United Nations High Commissioner for Refugees). 2021. *Global Trends: Forced Displacement in 2020.* Copenhagen.

UNHCR (United Nations High Commissioner for Refugees). 2022a. "Figures at a Glance." https://www.unhcr.org/en-us/figures-at-a-glance.html. Accessed 16 June 2022.

UNHCR (United Nations High Commissioner for Refugees). 2022b. "Ukraine Emergency." https://www.unhcr.org/en-us/ukraine-emergency.html. Accessed 25 July 2022.

UNHCR (United Nations High Commissioner for Refugees). 2022c. "UNHCR: Ukraine, Other Conflicts Push Forcibly Displaced Total over 100 Million for the First Time." Press Release, 23 May. https://www.unhcr.org/news/press/2022/5/628a389e4/unhcr-ukraine-other-conflicts-push-forcibly-displaced-total-100-million.html. Accessed 25 July 2022.

UNICEF (United Nations Children's Fund). 2020a. "Averting a Lost Covid Generation: A Six Point Plan to Respond, Recover and Reimagine a Post-Pandemic World for Every Child." New York.

UNICEF (United Nations Children's Fund). 2020b. "The Impact of Covid-19 on the Mental Health of Adolescents and Youth." https://www.unicef.org/lac/en/impact-covid-19-mental-health-adolescents-and-youth. Accessed 19 February 2021.

UNICEF (United Nations Children's Fund). 2021a. "The Changing Childhood Project." New York.

UNICEF (United Nations Children's Fund). 2021b. "Gender Transformative Education: Reimagining Education for a More Just and Inclusive World." New York.

UNICEF (United Nations Children's Fund). 2021c. *The State of the World's Children 2021: On My Mind:*

Promoting, Protecting and Caring for Children's Mental Health. New York. https://www.unicef.org/reports/state-worlds-children-2021. Accessed 21 October 2021.

UNICEF (United Nations Children's Fund). 2022. "Nearly 37 Million Children Displaced Worldwide – Highest Number Ever Recorded." https://www.unicef.org/press-releases/nearly-37-million-children-displaced-worldwide-highest-number-ever-recorded. Accessed 21 June 2022.

United Nations Security Council. 1992. "The Responsibility of the Security Council in the Maintenance of International Peace and Security." UN Security Council, New York.

United Nations Security Council. 2021. "Risk of Instability, Tension Growing, Amid Glaring Inequalities in Global Covid-19 Recovery, Top United Nations Officials Warn Security Council." SC/14422, New York. https://www.un.org/press/en/2021/sc14422.doc.htm. Accessed 25 August 2022.

UNODA (United Nations Office for Disarmament). 2018. *Securing Our Common Future: An Agenda for Disarmament.* New York.

UNODC (United Nations Office on Drugs and Crime). 2021. "Human Trafficking." https://www.unodc.org/unodc/en/human-trafficking/human-trafficking.html. Accessed 24 September 2021.

UNSD (United Nations Statistics Division). 2022. National Accounts Main Aggregates Database. http://unstats.un.org/unsd/snaama. Accessed 27 April 2022.

Upper, C. 2017. "Macroprudential Frameworks, Implementation and Relationship with Other Policies-Overview." BIS Paper 94, Bank for International Settlements, Basel, Switzerland.

Urbisz Golkowska, K. 2014. "Arab Women in the Gulf and the Narrative of Change: The Case of Qatar." *International Studies* 16(1): 51–64.

USAID (United Sates Agency for International Development). 2020. "Climate Risks to Resilience Food Security in Bureau for Humanitarian Assistance Geographies Haiti." Climate Risk Profile. Washington, DC.

Vamos, E. P., Mucsi, I., Keszei, A., Kopp, M. S., and Novak, M. 2009. "Comorbid Depression Is Associated with Increased Healthcare Utilization and Lost Productivity in Persons with Diabetes: A Large Nationally Representative Hungarian Population Survey." *Psychosomatic Medicine* 71(5): 501–507.

van Baar, J. M., Halpern, D. J., and FeldmanHall, O. 2021. "Intolerance of Uncertainty Modulates Brain-to-Brain Synchrony During Politically Polarized Perception." *Proceedings of the National Academy of Sciences* 118(20): e2022491118.

Van Bavel, B., Curtis, D., Dijkman, J., Hannaford, M., De Keyzer, M., Van Onacker, E., and Soens, T. 2020. *Disasters and History: The Vulnerability and Resilience of Past Societies.* Cambridge, UK: Cambridge University Press.

Van Bavel, J. J., Cichocka, A., Capraro, V., Sjåstad, H., Nezlek, J. B., Pavlović, T., Alfano, M., and others. 2022. "National Identity Predicts Public Health Support During a Global Pandemic." *Nature Communications* 13(1): 517.

van den Berg, D. P., de Bont, P. A., van der Vleugel, B. M., de Roos, C., de Jongh, A., Van Minnen, A., and van der Gaag, M. 2015. "Prolonged Exposure Vs Eye Movement Desensitization and Reprocessing Vs Waiting List for Posttraumatic Stress Disorder in Patients with a Psychotic Disorder: A Randomized Clinical Trial." *JAMA Psychiatry* 72(3): 259–267.

Van der Kolk, B. A. 2015. *The Body Keeps the Score: Brain, Mind, and Body in the Healing of Trauma.* New York: Penguin Books.

Van der Kolk, B. A., and Fisler, R. 1995. "Dissociation and the Fragmentary Nature of Traumatic Memories: Overview and Exploratory Study." *Journal of Traumatic Stress* 8(4): 505–525.

Van der Kolk, B. A., Roth, S., Pelcovitz, D., Sunday, S., and Spinazzola, J. 2005. "Disorders of Extreme Stress: The Empirical Foundation of a Complex Adaptation to Trauma." *Journal of Traumatic Stress: Official Publication of The International Society for Traumatic Stress Studies* 18(5): 389–399.

van der Kolk, B. A., Spinazzola, J., Blaustein, M. E., Hopper, J. W., Hopper, E. K., Korn, D. L., and Simpson, W. B. 2007. "A Randomized Clinical Trial of Eye Movement Desensitization and Reprocessing (EMDR), Fluoxetine, and Pill Placebo in the Treatment of Posttraumatic Stress Disorder: Treatment Effects and Long-Term Maintenance." *Journal of Clinical Psychiatry* 68(1): 37–46.

van der Lugt, M. 2022. "Look on the Dark Side." https://aeon.co/essays/in-these-dark-times-the-virtue-we-need-is-hopeful-pessimism. Accessed 18 July 2022.

van Munster, R., and Sylvest, C. 2021. "Nuclear Weapons, Extinction, and the Anthropocene: Reappraising Jonathan Schell." *Review of International Studies* 47(3): 294–310.

van Panhuis, W. G., Grefenstette, J., Jung, S. Y., Chok, N. S., Cross, A., Eng, H., Lee, B. Y., and others. 2013. "Contagious Diseases in the United States from 1888 to the Present." *New England Journal of Medicine* 369(22): 2152–2158.

van Prooijen, J.-W. 2021. "The Psychology of Political Polarization: An Introduction." In *The Psychology of Political Polarization.* New York: Routledge.

van Prooijen, J.-W., and Krouwel, A. P. 2019. "Psychological Features of Extreme Political Ideologies." *Current Directions in Psychological Science* 28(2): 159–163.

Vanderschraaf, P. 2019. *Strategic Justice: Convention and Problems of Balancing Divergent Interests.* Oxford, UK: Oxford University Press.

Varma, P., Junge, M., Meaklim, H., and Jackson, M. L. 2021. "Younger People Are More Vulnerable to Stress, Anxiety and Depression During Covid-19 Pandemic: A Global Cross-Sectional Survey." *Progress in Neuro-Psychopharmacology and Biological Psychiatry* 109.

Varnum, M. E. W., and Grossmann, I. 2021. "The Psychology of Cultural Change: Introduction to the Special Issue." *American Psychologist* 76(6): 833–837.

Vasconcelos, V. V., Constantino, S. M., Dannenberg, A., Lumkowsky, M., Weber, E., and Levin, S. 2021.

"Segregation and Clustering of Preferences Erode Socially Beneficial Coordination." *Proceedings of the National Academy of Sciences* 118(50): e2102153118.

Veidis, E. M., LaBeaud, A. D., Phillips, A. A., and Barry, M. 2022. "Tackling the Ubiquity of Plastic Waste for Human and Planetary Health." *The American Journal of Tropical Medicine and Hygiene* 106(1): 12–14.

Verdade, L. M., Piña, C. I., and Rosalino, L. M. 2015. "Biofuels and Biodiversity: Challenges and Opportunities." *Environmental Development* 15: 64–78.

Vickers, C., and Ziebarth, N. 2019. "Lessons for Today from Past Periods of Rapid Technological Change." Background paper for *World Economic and Social Survey 2018.* United Nations Department of Economic and Social Affairs, New York.

Vignoles, V. L., Owe, E., Becker, M., Smith, P. B., Easterbrook, M. J., Brown, R., González, R., and others. 2016. "Beyond the 'East–West' Dichotomy: Global Variation in Cultural Models of Selfhood." *Journal of Experimental Psychology: General* 145(8): 966–1000.

Vinichenko, V., Cherp, A., and Jewell, J. 2021. "Historical Precedents and Feasibility of Rapid Coal and Gas Decline Required for the 1.5° C Target." *One Earth* 4(10): 1477–1490.

Viscusi, W. K. 1985. "A Bayesian Perspective on Biases in Risk Perception." *Economics Letters* 17(1): 59–62.

Viscusi, W. K. 1989. "Prospective Reference Theory: Toward an Explanation of the Paradoxes." *Journal of Risk and Uncertainty* 2(3): 235–263.

von Grebmer, K., Bernstein, J., Wiemers, M., Schiffer, T., Hanano, A., Towey, O., Ní Chéilleachair, R., and others. 2021. *Global Hunger Index 2021: Hunger and Food Systems in Conflict Settings.* Bonn, Germany, and Dublin: Welthungerhilfe.

von Hippel, W., and Fox, N. 2021. "The Evolution of Extremism." In Kruglanski, A. W., Kopetz, C., and Szumowska, E., (eds.), *The Psychology of Extremism: A Motivational Perspective.* New York: Routledge.

Voosen, P. 2022a. "Bogs, Lakebeds, and Sea Floors Compete to Become Anthropocene's 'Golden Spike'." *Science* 376(6593): 562–563.

Voosen, P. 2022b. "Use of 'Too Hot' Climate Models Exagerates Impacts of Global Warming." *Science,* 4 May.

Vörösmárty, C., Green, P., Walsh, K., Corsi, F., and Cak, A. 2020. "CUNY UNDP Sustainable Solutions for Human Development." City University of New York, The Graduate Center, Advanced Science Resource Center. Background paper for Human Development Report 2021/2022, UNDP–HDRO, New York.

Vos, P. 2015. *Origin of the Dutch Coastal Landscape: Long-Term Landscape Evolution of the Netherlands During the Holocene.* Kooiweg, The Netherlands: Barkhuis.

Vosoughi, S., Roy, D., and Aral, S. 2018. "The Spread of True and False News Online." *Science* 359(6380): 1146–1151.

Vu, T. V. 2022. "Linking LGBT Inclusion and National Innovative Capacity." *Social Indicators Research* 159(1): 191–214.

Wade, M., Prime, H., Johnson, D., May, S. S., Jenkins, J. M., and Browne, D. T. 2021. "The Disparate Impact of Covid-19 on the Mental Health of Female and Male Caregivers." *Social Science & Medicine* 275: 113801.

Wagner-Pacifici, R. 2017. *What Is an Event?* Chicago, IL: University of Chicago Press.

Walicki, N., Ioannides, M. J., and Tilt, B. 2017. "Dams and Displacement - an Introduction." Case Study Series - Dam Displacement, Internal Displacement Monitoring Centre, Geneva.

Walker, A., Lyall, K., Silva, D., Craigie, G., Mayshak, R., Costa, B., Hyder, S., and Bentley, A. 2020. "Male Victims of Female-Perpetrated Intimate Partner Violence, Help-Seeking, and Reporting Behaviors: A Qualitative Study." *Psychology of Men & Masculinities* 21(2): 213–223.

Waltz, E. 2022. "GABA-Enriched Tomato Is First CRISPR-Edited Food to Enter Market." *Nature Biotechnology* 40(1): 9–11.

Waltz, E., and Nature Biotechnology. 2021. "CRISPR-Edited Tomatoes Are Supposed to Help You Chill Out." *Scientific American,* 24 December.

Wang, M., Rieger, M. O., and Hens, T. 2016. "How Time Preferences Differ: Evidence from 53 Countries." *Journal of Economic Psychology* 52: 115–135.

Wang, P., D'Cruze, H., and Wood, D. 2019. "Economic Costs and Impacts of Business Data Breaches." *Issues in Information Systems* 20(2): 162–171.

Wassénius, E., and Crona, B. I. 2022. "Adapting Risk Assessments for a Complex Future." *One Earth* 5(1): 35–43.

Waszak, P. M., Kasprzycka-Waszak, W., and Kubanek, A. 2018. "The Spread of Medical Fake News in Social Media–the Pilot Quantitative Study." *Health Policy and Technology* 7(2): 115–118.

Watene, K. 2022. "Indigenous Philosophy and Intergenerational Justice." Reimagining the Human-Environment Relationship paper series, United Nations University–United Nations Environment Programme. New York.

Watene, K. Forthcoming. "Kaitiakitanga: Māori Philosophy and Intergenerational Justice." In Gardiner, S. E., (ed.), *The Oxford Handbook of Intergenerational Ethics.* Oxford, UK: Oxford University Press.

Watene, K., and Palmer, E. 2020. *Reconciliation, Transitional and Indigenous Justice.* New York: Routledge.

Wathelet, M., Duhem, S., Vaiva, G., Baubet, T., Habran, E., Veerapa, E., Debien, C., and others. 2020. "Factors Associated with Mental Health Disorders among University Students in France Confined During the Covid-19 Pandemic." *Journal of the American Medical Association Network Open* 3(10): 1–13.

Watson, B., and Osberg, L. 2017. "Healing and/or Breaking? The Mental Health Implications of Repeated Economic Insecurity." *Social Science & Medicine* 188: 119–127.

Watson, O. J., Barnsley, G., Toor, J., Hogan, A. B., Winskill, P., and Ghani, A. C. 2022. "Global Impact of the First Year of Covid-19 Vaccination: A Mathematical Modelling Study." *The Lancet Infectious Diseases.*

Way, R., Ives, M., Mealy, P., and Farmer, J. D. 2021. "Empirically Grounded Technology Forecasts and the Energy Transition." INET Oxford Working Paper 2021–01, University of Oxford, Institute for New Economic Thinking at the Oxford Martin School, Oxford, UK.

WCED (World Commission on Environment and Development). 1987. *Our Common Future*. New York: Oxford University Press.

Webb, A., and Coates, D. 2012. "Biofuels and Biodiversity." CBD Technical Series 65, Secretariat of the Convention on Biological Diversity, Montreal.

Webber, D., Babush, M., Schori-Eyal, N., Vazeou-Nieuwenhuis, A., Hettiarachchi, M., Bélanger, J. J., Moyano, M., and others. 2018. "The Road to Extremism: Field and Experimental Evidence That Significance Loss-Induced Need for Closure Fosters Radicalization." *Journal of Personality and Social Psychology* 114(2): 270–285.

Webber, D., Kruglanski, A., Molinario, E., and Jasko, K. 2020. "Ideologies That Justify Political Violence." *Current Opinion in Behavioral Sciences* 34: 107–111.

WEF (World Economic Forum). 2020a. *The Future of Jobs Report 2020*. Geneva.

WEF (World Economic Forum). 2020b. "Uncertainty and Instability: The World in Two Words, Says UN Secretary-General." News Release, 24 January. https://www.weforum.org/press/2020/01/uncertainty-and-instability-the-world-in-two-words-says-un-secretary-general. Accessed 18 July 2022.

WEF (World Economic Forum). 2022. *Global Gender Gap Report 2022: Insight Report*. Geneva.

Wehi, P. M., Scott, N. J., Beckwith, J., Rodgers, R. P., Gillies, T., Van Uitregt, V., and Watene, K. 2021a. "A Short Scan of Māori Journeys to Antarctica." *Journal of the Royal Society of New Zealand*: 1–12.

Wehi, P. M., van Uitregt, V., Scott, N. J., Gillies, T., Beckwith, J., Rodgers, R. P., and Watene, K. 2021b. "Transforming Antarctic Management and Policy with an Indigenous Māori Lens." *Nature Ecology & Evolution* 5(8): 1055–1059.

Weisburd, D., Cave, B., Nelson, M., White, C., Haviland, A., Ready, J., Lawton, B., and Sikkema, K. 2018. "Mean Streets and Mental Health: Depression and Post-Traumatic Stress Disorder at Crime Hot Spots." *American Journal of Community Psychology* 61(3–4): 285–295.

Weiss, B. 2022. "Why the Past 10 Years of American Life Have Been Uniquely Stupid." *The Atlantic*, 11 April.

Weiss, H. 2017. *Megadrought, Collapse, and Causality*. Oxford, UK: Oxford University Press.

Weldon, L., Forester, S., Kaitlin, K.-T., and Amber, L. 2018. "Handmaidens or Heroes? Feminist Mobilization as a Force for Economic Justice." Working Paper 2, Simon Fraser University, Feminist Mobilization and Empowerment Project, Burnaby, Canada.

Weobong, B., Weiss, H. A., McDaid, D., Singla, D. R., Hollon, S. D., Nadkarni, A., Park, A.-L., and others. 2017. "Sustained Effectiveness and Cost-Effectiveness of the Healthy Activity Programme, a Brief Psychological Treatment for Depression Delivered by Lay Counsellors in Primary Care: 12-Month Follow-up of a Randomised Controlled Trial." *PLOS Medicine* 14(9): 1–13.

Whaling, K. M., and Sharkey, J. 2020. "Differences in Prevalence Rates of Hopelessness and Suicidal Ideation among Adolescents by Gang Membership and Latinx Identity." *Child and Adolescent Social Work Journal* 37(5): 557–569.

Wheeler, B. W., Lovell, R., Higgins, S. L., White, M. P., Alcock, I., Osborne, N. J., Husk, K., and others. 2015. "Beyond Greenspace: An Ecological Study of Population General Health and Indicators of Natural Environment Type and Quality." *International Journal of Health Geographics* 14(1): 1–17.

The White House. 2022. "Executive Order on Climate-Related Financial Risk." https://www.whitehouse.gov/briefing-room/presidential-actions/2021/05/20/executive-order-on-climate-related-financial-risk/. Accessed 10 May 2022.

Whitten-Woodring, J., Kleinberg, M. S., Thawnghmung, A., and Thitsar, M. T. 2020. "Poison If You Don't Know How to Use It: Facebook, Democracy, and Human Rights in Myanmar." *The International Journal of Press/Politics* 25(3): 407–425.

WHO (World Health Organization). 2012. "Understanding and Addressing Violence against Women: Intimate Partner Violence." https://apps.who.int/iris/handle/10665/77432. Accessed 21 September 2021.

WHO (World Health Organization). 2016. "Global Health Observatory (Gho) Data: Telehealth." https://www.who.int/data/gho. Accessed 5 June 2021.

WHO (World Health Organization). 2017. "Mental Health of Older Adults." https://www.who.int/news-room/fact-sheets/detail/mental-health-of-older-adults. Accessed 10 March 2021.

WHO (World Health Organization). 2018. "Addictive Behaviours: Gaming Disorder." https://www.who.int/news-room/q-a-detail/addictive-behaviours-gaming-disorder. Accessed 26 2021.

WHO (World Health Organization). 2021a. "Definition and Typology of Violence. Violence Prevention Alliance." https://www.who.int/groups/violence-prevention-alliance/approach. Accessed 29 April 2022.

WHO (World Health Organization). 2021b. "Dementia." https://www.who.int/news-room/fact-sheets/detail/dementia. Accessed 7 April 2022.

WHO (World Health Organization). 2021c. "Depression." https://www.who.int/news-room/fact-sheets/detail/depression. Accessed 10 March 2021.

WHO (World Health Organization). 2021d. "Fact Sheet Suicide." https://www.who.int/news-room/fact-sheets/detail/suicide. Accessed 25 June 2021.

WHO (World Health Organization). 2021e. "The Global Health Observatory." https://www.who.int/data/gho/. Accessed 23 September 2021.

WHO (World Health Organization). 2021f. "Mental Health." https://www.who.int/health-topics/mental-health#tab=tab_1. Accessed 10 March 2021.

WHO (World Health Organization). 2021g. "Climate Change and Health." https://www.who.int/news-room/fact-sheets/detail/climate-change-and-health. Accessed 4 May 2022.

WHO (World Health Organization). 2022a. "Mental Health and Covid-19: Early Evidence of the Pandemic's Impact." Scientific Brief. https://www.who.int/publications/i/item/WHO-2019-nCoV-Sci_Brief-Mental_health-2022.1. Accessed 3 March 2022.

WHO (World Health Organization). 2022b. "Mental Health: Strengthening Our Response." https://www.who.int/news-room/fact-sheets/detail/mental-health-strengthening-our-response. Accessed 26 July 2022.

WHO (World Health Organization). 2022c. *World Mental Health Report: Transforming Mental Health for All*. Geneva. https://www.who.int/publications/i/item/9789240049338. Accessed 22 June 2022.

Whyte, K. P. 2013. "Justice Forward: Tribes, Climate Adaptation and Responsibility." In Koppel Maldonado, J., Colombi, B. and Pandya, R., (eds.), *Climate Change and Indigenous Peoples in the United States*. New York: Springer.

Whyte, K. P. 2017. "Our Ancestors' Dystopia Now: Indigenous Conservation and the Anthropocene." In Heise, U., Christensen, J., and Niemann, M., (eds.), *The Routledge Companion to the Environmental Humanities*. Abingdon, UK: Routledge.

Wilkinson, R., and Pickett, K. 2009. *The Spirit Level: Why Greater Equality Makes Societies Stronger*. New York: Bloomsbury Publishing USA.

Williams, D. R., and Sternthal, M. 2010. "Understanding Racial-Ethnic Disparities in Health: Sociological Contributions." *Journal of Health and Social Behavior* 51(1_suppl): S15–S27.

Willis, M. M., and Schor, J. B. 2012. "Does Changing a Light Bulb Lead to Changing the World? Political Action and the Conscious Consumer." *The Annals of the American Academy of Political and Social Science* 644(1): 160–190.

Wilson, A. E., Parker, V. A., and Feinberg, M. 2020. "Polarization in the Contemporary Political and Media Landscape." *Current Opinion in Behavioral Sciences* 34: 223–228.

Wing, O. E., Lehman, W., Bates, P. D., Sampson, C. C., Quinn, N., Smith, A. M., Neal, J. C., and others. 2022. "Inequitable Patterns of US Flood Risk in the Anthropocene." *Nature Climate Change* 12(2): 156–162.

Winthrop, R. 2020. "Learning to Live Together: How Education Can Help Fight Systemic Racism." Education Plus Development [blog], 5 June. https://www.brookings.edu/blog/education-plus-development/2020/06/05/learning-to-live-together-how-education-can-help-fight-systemic-racism/. Accessed 24 June 2022.

Witkower, Z., Tracy, J. L., Cheng, J. T., and Henrich, J. 2020. "Two Signals of Social Rank: Prestige and Dominance Are Associated with Distinct Nonverbal Displays." *Journal of Personality and Social Psychology* 118(1): 89–120.

Witze, A. 2020. "How a Small Nuclear War Would Transform the Entire Planet." *Nature* 579(7797): 485–488.

Wojcieszak, M., and Garrett, R. K. 2018. "Social Identity, Selective Exposure, and Affective Polarization: How Priming National Identity Shapes Attitudes toward Immigrants Via News Selection." *Human Communication Research* 44(3): 247–273.

Wojcieszak, M., and Warner, B. R. 2020. "Can Inter-party Contact Reduce Affective Polarization? A Systematic Test of Different Forms of Intergroup Contact." *Political Communication* 37(6): 789–811.

Wolff, S., Schrammeijer, E. A., Schulp, C. J. E., and Verburg, P. H. 2018. "Meeting Global Land Restoration and Protection Targets: What Would the World Look Like in 2050?" *Global Environmental Change* 52: 259–272.

Working Group on the 'Anthropocene' (Subcommission on Quaternary Stratigraphy). 2019. "Results of Binding Vote by AWG, Released 21st May 2019." http://quaternary.stratigraphy.org/working-groups/anthropocene/. Accessed 3 May 2022.

World Bank. 2015. *World Development Report 2015: Mind, Society, and Behavior.* Washington, DC.

World Bank. 2017a. "Pastoralism & Stability in the Sahel and Horn of Africa (Passha)—P153713." Washington, DC. https://projects.worldbank.org/en/projects-operations/project-detail/P153713. Accessed 25 August 2022.

World Bank. 2017b. *World Development Report 2017: Governance and the Law.* Washington, DC.

World Bank. 2020a. *Poverty and Shared Prosperity 2020: Reversals of Fortune.* Washington, DC.

World Bank. 2020b. *State and Trends of Carbon Pricing 2020.* Washington, DC.

World Bank. 2022a. "Regional Pastoral Livelihoods Resilience Project—P129408." Washington, DC.

World Bank. 2022b. "Regional Sahel Pastoralism Support Project - P147674." Washington, DC. https://projects.worldbank.org/en/projects-operations/project-detail/P147674. Accessed 25 August 2022.

World Bank. 2022c. World Development Indicators Database. Washington, DC.

Wörmann, X., Wilmes, S., Seifert, D., and Anders, S. 2021. "Males as Victims of Intimate Partner Violence—Results from a Clinical-Forensic Medical Examination Centre." *International Journal of Legal Medicine*: 1–9.

Worster, D. 1985. *Nature's Economy: A History of Ecological Ideas.* Cambridge, UK: Cambridge University Press.

Wozniak, A. 2010. "Are College Graduates More Responsive to Distant Labor Market Opportunities?" *Journal of Human Resources* 45(4): 944–970.

Wuepper, D., and Lybbert, T. J. 2017. "Perceived Self-Efficacy, Poverty, and Economic Development." *Annual Review of Resource Economics* 9: 383–404.

Wurtzel, E., Vickers, C., Hanson, A. D., Millar, H., Cooper, M., Voss-Fels, K., Nikel, P., and Erb, T. 2019. "Revolutionizing Agriculture with Synthetic Biology." *Nature Plants* 5(5): 1207–1210.

Wurzel, S., and Hsu, S. 2022. "Progress toward Fusion Energy Breakeven and Gain as Measured against the Lawson Criterion." *Physics of Plasmas* 29(062103).

WWF (World Wildlife Foundation). 2020. *Living Planet Report 2020: Bending the Curve of Biodiversity Loss.* Gland, Switzerland: WWF.

WWF (World Wildlife Foundation) Australia. 2021. "The Lifecycle of Plastics." https://www.wwf.org.au/news/blogs/the-lifecycle-of-plastics. Accessed 10 May 2022.

Xiang, Y., Graeber, T., Enke, B., and Gershman, S. J. 2021. "Confidence and Central Tendency in Perceptual Judgment." *Attention, Perception, & Psychophysics* 83(7): 3024–3034.

Xu, C., Kohler, T. A., Lenton, T. M., Svenning, J.-C., and Scheffer, M. 2020. "Future of the Human Climate Niche." *Proceedings of the National Academy of Sciences* 117(21): 11350–11355.

Xue, B., and McMunn, A. 2021. "Gender Differences in Unpaid Care Work and Psychological Distress in the UK Covid-19 Lockdown." *PLOS ONE* 16(3).

Yan, B., Zhang, X., Wu, L., Zhu, H., and Chen, B. 2020. "Why Do Countries Respond Differently to Covid-19? A Comparative Study of Sweden, China, France, and Japan." *The American Review of Public Administration* 50(6–7): 762–769.

Yang, S., Keller, F. B., and Zheng, L. 2016. *Social Network Analysis: Methods and Examples.* Washington, DC: Sage Publications.

Yang, W., Roig, M., Jimenez, M., Perry, J., and Shepherd, A. 2016. *Report on the World Social Situation: Leaving No One Behind: The Imperative of Inclusive Development.* New York: United Nations Department of Economic and Social Affairs.

Yekefallah, M., Imani, S., Borji, M., Sadighpour, M., Gheitarani, B., Kheradmand, M., and Ghahari, S. 2018. "Comparison of Depression and General Health among Victims of Domestic Violence among the Elderly and Their Peers in Savojbolagh-Iran." *Community Health* 5(2): 132–140.

Yiğit-Gençten, V. 2022. "Nature-Based Learning Settings and the Transition to Formal Schooling." *Handbook of Research on Innovative Approaches to Early Childhood Development and School Readiness.* Hershey, PA: IGI Global.

Youngs, R. 2020. "Introduction." In *Global Civil Society in the Shadow of Coronavirus.* Washington, DC: Carnegie Endowment for International Peace.

Youssef, N. A., Lockwood, L., Su, S., Hao, G., and Rutten, B. P. 2018. "The Effects of Trauma, with or without PTSD, on the Transgenerational DNA Methylation Alterations in Human Offsprings." *Brain Sciences* 8(5): 83–99.

Yu, H., Xue, L., and Barrangou, R. 2021. "Toward Inclusive Global Governance of Human Genome Editing." *Proceedings of the National Academy of Sciences* 118(47): e2118540118.

Zalasiewicz, J., Waters, C. N., Summerhayes, C. P., Wolfe, A. P., Barnosky, A. D., Cearreta, A., Crutzen, P., and others. 2017. "The Working Group on the Anthropocene: Summary of Evidence and Interim Recommendations." *Anthropocene* 19: 55–60.

Zald, M. N., Morrill, C., and Rao, H. 2005. "The Impact of Social Movements on Organizations." In Davis, G. F., McAdam, D., Scott, W.R., and Zald, M. N., (eds.), *Social Movements and Organization Theory* Cambridge, UK: Cambridge University Press.

Zappia, N., A., 2014. *Traders and Raiders: The Indigenous World of the Colorado Basin, 1540–1859.* Chapel Hill, NC: UNC Press Books.

Zaremba, H. 2022. "John Kerry: Green Transition Will Be Bigger Than the Industrial Revolution." *Oilprice.com.* https://oilprice.com/Energy/Energy-General/John-Kerry-Green-Transition-Will-Be-Bigger-Than-The-Industrial-Revolution.html. Accessed 24 August 2022.

Zeifman, I. 2017. "Bot Traffic Report 2016." https://www.imperva.com/blog/bot-traffic-report-2016/. Accessed 8 June 2022.

Zelizer, V. A. 1989. "The Social Meaning of Money: 'Special Monies'." *American Journal of Sociology* 95(2): 342–377.

Zelizer, V. A. 2017. *The Social Meaning of Money: Pin Money, Paychecks, Poor Relief, and Other Currencies.* Princeton, NJ: Princeton University Press.

Zhang, L., Zhou, S., and Kwan, M.-P. 2019. "A Comparative Analysis of the Impacts of Objective Versus Subjective Neighborhood Environment on Physical, Mental, and Social Health." *Health & Place* 59: 102170.

Ziegler, M., and Trancik, J. 2021. "Re-Examining Rates of Lithium-Ion Battery Technology Improvement and Cost Decline." *Energy & Environmental Science* 4.

Zilberstein, S., Lamont, M., and Sanchez, M. 2021. "Enabling Hope in a Better Future: Braiding Cultural Repertoires When Facing Uncertainty." Paper presented at the 33rd Annual Meeting of the Society for the Advancement of Socio-Economics, 5 July.

Zoellick, R. 2008. "World Bank Chief: Biofuels Boosting Food Prices." Radio Broadcast, 11 April, National Public Radio. https://www.npr.org/templates/story/story.php?storyId=89545855&t=1643790563262&t=1643790801947. Accessed 25 August 2022.

Zraly, M., and Nyirazinyoye, L. 2010. "Don't Let the Suffering Make You Fade Away: An Ethnographic Study of Resilience among Survivors of Genocide-Rape in Southern Rwanda." *Social Science & Medicine* 70(10): 1656–1664.

Zscheischler, J., Martius, O., Westra, S., Bevacqua, E., Raymond, C., Horton, R. M., van den Hurk, B., and others. 2020. "A Typology of Compound Weather and Climate Events." *Nature Reviews Earth & Environment* 1(7): 333–347.

Zuboff, S. 2019. *The Age of Surveillance Capitalism: The Fight for a Human Future at the New Frontier of Power.* New York: PublicAffairs.

Zurbrügg, C., Drescher, S., Patel, A., and Sharatchandra, H. 2004. "Decentralised Composting of Urban Waste—an Overview of Community and Private Initiatives in Indian Cities." *Waste Management* 24(7): 655–662.

Zurbrügg, F. 2022. "Macroprudential Policy Beyond the Pandemic: Taking Stock and Looking Ahead." Bank for International Settlements, International Center for Monetary and Banking Studies, Basel, Switzerland.

Statistical annex

Statistical annex

Readers guide

The statistical tables in this annex provide an overview of key aspects of human development. The seven tables contain the family of composite human development indices and their components estimated by the Human Development Report Office (HDRO). The sixth table, on multidimensional poverty, is produced in partnership with the Oxford Poverty and Human Development Initiative.

Tables 1–7 are included in the 2021/2022 Human Development Report. The five human development dashboards previously included as part of the Report are now published online. The full set of seven statistical tables and five dashboards is available for download at https://hdr.undp.org/human-development-report-2021-22. Unless otherwise noted, tables use data available to the HDRO as of 30 April 2022. All indices and indicators, along with technical notes on the calculation of composite indices and additional source information, are available at https://hdr.undp.org/data-center.

Countries and territories are ranked by 2021 Human Development Index (HDI) value. Robustness and reliability analysis has shown that for most countries differences in HDI are not statistically significant at the fourth decimal place. For this reason countries with the same HDI value at three decimal places are listed with tied ranks.

Sources and definitions

Unless otherwise noted, the HDRO uses data from international data agencies with the mandate, resources and expertise to collect national data on specific indicators.

Definitions of indicators and sources for original data components are given at the end of each table, with full source details in *Statistical references*.

Methodology updates

The 2021/2022 Report retains all the composite indices from the family of human development indices—the HDI, the Inequality-adjusted Human Development Index (IHDI), the Gender Development Index (GDI), the Gender Inequality Index (GII), the Multidimensional Poverty Index (MPI) and the Planetary pressures-adjusted Human Development Index (PHDI). The methodology used to compute the indices is the same as the one used in the 2020 Human Development Report. For details, see *Technical notes 1–6* at http://hdr.undp.org/sites/default/files/hdr2022_technical_notes.pdf.

Comparisons over time and across editions

Because national and international agencies continually improve their data series, the data—including the HDI values and ranks—presented in this report are not comparable to those published in earlier editions. For HDI comparability across years and countries, see table 2, which presents trends using consistent data, or https://hdr.undp.org/data-center, which presents interpolated consistent data.

Discrepancies between national and international estimates

National and international data can differ because international agencies harmonize national data using a consistent methodology and occasionally produce estimates of missing data to allow comparability across countries. In other cases international agencies might not have access to the most recent national data. When HDRO becomes aware of discrepancies, it brings them to the attention of national and international data authorities.

Country groupings and aggregates

The tables present weighted aggregates for several country groupings. In general, an aggregate is shown only when data are available for at least half the countries and represent at least two-thirds of the population in that grouping. Aggregates for each grouping cover only the countries for which data are available.

Human development classification

HDI classifications are based on HDI fixed cutoff points, which are derived from the quartiles of distributions of the component indicators. The cutoff points are HDI of less than 0.550 for low human development, 0.550–0.699 for medium human development, 0.700–0.799 for high human development and 0.800 or greater for very high human development.

Regional groupings

Regional groupings are based on United Nations Development Programme regional classifications. Least Developed Countries and Small Island Developing States are defined according to UN classifications (see https://www.un.org/ohrlls/).

Developing countries

The aggregates for developing countries are based on information from all developing countries that are included in a regional grouping.

Organisation for Economic Co-operation and Development

Of the 38 Organisation for Economic Co-operation and Development members, 33 are considered developed countries and 5 (Costa Rica, Chile, Colombia, Mexico and Türkiye) are considered developing countries. Aggregates refer to all countries from the group for which data are available.

Country notes

Data for China do not include Hong Kong Special Administrative Region of China, Macao Special Administrative Region of China or Taiwan Province of China.

As of 2 May 2016, Czechia is the short name to be used for the Czech Republic.

As of 1 June 2018, the Kingdom of Eswatini is the name of the country formerly known as Swaziland.

As of 14 February 2019, the Republic of North Macedonia (short form: North Macedonia) is the name of the country formerly known as the former Yugoslav Republic of Macedonia.

As of 1 June 2022, Türkiye is the name of the country formerly known as Turkey.

Symbols

A dash between two years, as in 2010–2021, indicates that the data are from the most recent year available during the period specified. Growth rates are usually average annual rates of growth between the first and last years of the period shown.

The following symbols are used in the tables:

..	Not available
0 or 0.0	Nil or negligible
—.	Not applicable

Statistical acknowledgements

The Report's composite indices and other statistical resources draw on a wide variety of the most respected international data providers in their specialized fields. HDRO is particularly grateful to Eurostat; the Global Carbon Project; ICF Macro; the International Labour Organization; the International Monetary Fund; the Inter-Parliamentary Union; the Luxembourg Income Study; the United Nations Maternal Mortality Estimation Inter-Agency Group; the Organisation for Economic Co-operation and

Development; the Socio-Economic Database for Latin America and the Caribbean; the United Nations Children's Fund; the United Nations Department of Economic and Social Affairs; the United Nations Educational, Scientific and Cultural Organization Institute for Statistics; the United Nations Environment Programme; the United Nations Statistics Division; the World Bank; and the World Inequality Database. The international education database maintained by Robert Barro (Harvard University) and Jong-Wha Lee (Korea University) was another invaluable source for the calculation of the Report's indices.

Statistical tables

The seven tables relate to the six composite human development indices and their components. Since the 2010 Human Development Report, four composite human development indices—the HDI, the IHDI, the GII and the MPI for developing countries—have been calculated. The 2014 Report introduced the GDI, which compares the HDI calculated separately for women and men. The 2020 Report introduced the PHDI, which adjusts the HDI for excessive human pressure on the planet.

For indicators that are global Sustainable Development Goals indicators or can be used in monitoring progress towards specific goals, the table headers include the relevant goals and targets.

Table 1, Human Development Index and its components, ranks countries by 2021 HDI value and details the values of the three HDI components: longevity, education (with two indicators) and income per capita. The table also presents the difference in rankings by HDI value and gross national income per capita, as well as the rank on the 2020 HDI, calculated using the most recently revised historical data available in 2022.

Table 2, Human Development Index trends, 1990–2021, provides a time series of HDI values allowing 2021 HDI values to be compared with those for previous years. The table uses the most recently revised historical data available in 2022 and the same methodology applied to compute 2021 HDI values. The table also includes the change in HDI rank over the last six years and the average annual HDI growth rate across four time intervals: 1990–2000, 2000–2010, 2010–2021 and 1990–2021.

Table 3, Inequality-adjusted Human Development Index, contains two related measures of inequality—the IHDI and the overall loss in HDI due to inequality. The IHDI looks beyond the average achievements of a country in longevity, education and income to show how these achievements are distributed among its residents. The IHDI value can be interpreted as the level of human development when inequality is accounted for. The relative difference between IHDI and HDI values is the loss due to inequality in distribution of the HDI within the country. The table presents the coefficient of human inequality, which is the unweighted average of inequalities in the three dimensions. In addition, the table shows each country's difference in rank on the HDI and the IHDI. A negative value means that taking inequality into account lowers a country's rank on the HDI. The table also presents the income shares of the poorest 40 percent, the richest 10 percent and the richest 1 percent of the population, as well as the Gini coefficient.

Table 4, Gender Development Index, measures disparities on the HDI by gender. The table contains HDI values estimated separately for women and men, the ratio of which is the GDI value. The closer the ratio is to 1, the smaller the gap between women and men. Values for the three HDI components—longevity, education (with two indicators) and income per capita—are also presented by gender. The table includes five country groupings by absolute deviation from gender parity in HDI values.

Table 5, Gender Inequality Index, presents a composite measure of gender inequality using three dimensions: reproductive health, empowerment and the labour market. The reproductive health indicators are maternal mortality ratio and adolescent birth rate. The empowerment indicators are the percentage of parliamentary seats held by women and the percentage of population with at least some secondary education by gender. The labour market indicator is participation in the labour force by gender. A low GII value indicates low inequality between women and men, and vice-versa.

Table 6, Multidimensional Poverty Index, captures the multiple deprivations that people in developing countries face in their health, education and standard of living. The MPI shows both the incidence of nonincome multidimensional poverty (a headcount of those in multidimensional poverty) and its intensity (the average deprivation score experienced by multidimensionally poor people). Based on deprivation score thresholds, people are classified as multidimensionally poor, in severe multidimensional poverty or vulnerable to multidimensional poverty. The table includes the contribution of deprivation in

each dimension to overall multidimensional poverty. It also presents measures of income poverty—population living below the national poverty line and population living on less than $1.90 in purchasing power parity terms per day.

Table 7, Planetary pressures-adjusted Human Development Index, adjusts the HDI for planetary pressures in the Anthropocene to reflect a concern for intergenerational inequality, similar to the Inequality-adjusted HDI adjustment, which is motivated by a concern for intragenerational inequality. The PHDI value can be interpreted as the level of human development adjusted by carbon dioxide emissions per person (production-based) and material footprint per person to account for excessive human pressure on the planet. The table presents the relative difference between PHDI and HDI values as well as each country's difference in rank on the HDI and the PHDI. A negative value means that taking planetary pressures into account lowers a country's rank on the HDI.

Human development composite indices

TABLE 1

Human Development Index and its components

		Human Development Index (HDI)	SDG 3 Life expectancy at birth	SDG 4.3 Expected years of schooling	SDG 4.4 Mean years of schooling	SDG 8.5 Gross national income (GNI) per capita	GNI per capita rank minus HDI rank	HDI rank
		Value	(years)	(years)	(years)	(2017 PPP $)		
HDI RANK		2021	2021	2021[a]	2021[a]	2021	2021[b]	2020
Very high human development								
1	Switzerland	0.962	84.0	16.5	13.9	66,933	5	3
2	Norway	0.961	83.2	18.2[c]	13.0	64,660	6	1
3	Iceland	0.959	82.7	19.2[c]	13.8	55,782	11	2
4	Hong Kong, China (SAR)	0.952	85.5[d]	17.3	12.2	62,607	6	4
5	Australia	0.951	84.5	21.1[c]	12.7	49,238	18	5
6	Denmark	0.948	81.4	18.7[c]	13.0	60,365	6	5
7	Sweden	0.947	83.0	19.4[c]	12.6	54,489	9	9
8	Ireland	0.945	82.0	18.9[c]	11.6[e]	76,169[f]	-3	8
9	Germany	0.942	80.6	17.0	14.1[e]	54,534	6	7
10	Netherlands	0.941	81.7	18.7[c,e]	12.6	55,979	3	10
11	Finland	0.940	82.0	19.1[c]	12.9	49,452	11	12
12	Singapore	0.939	82.8	16.5	11.9	90,919[f]	-10	10
13	Belgium	0.937	81.9	19.6[c]	12.4	52,293	7	16
13	New Zealand	0.937	82.5	20.3[c]	12.9	44,057	16	13
15	Canada	0.936	82.7	16.4	13.8[e]	46,808	9	15
16	Liechtenstein	0.935	83.3	15.2	12.5[g]	146,830[t,h]	-15	14
17	Luxembourg	0.930	82.6	14.4	13.0[i]	84,649[f]	-13	17
18	United Kingdom	0.929	80.7	17.3	13.4	45,225	9	17
19	Japan	0.925	84.8	15.2[e]	13.4	42,274	12	19
19	Korea (Republic of)	0.925	83.7	16.5	12.5[e]	44,501	9	20
21	United States	0.921	77.2	16.3	13.7	64,765	-14	21
22	Israel	0.919	82.3	16.1	13.3[e]	41,524	10	22
23	Malta	0.918	83.8	16.8	12.2	38,884	12	26
23	Slovenia	0.918	80.7	17.7	12.8	39,746	10	23
25	Austria	0.916	81.6	16.0	12.3	53,619	-8	23
26	United Arab Emirates	0.911	78.7	15.7	12.7	62,574	-15	25
27	Spain	0.905	83.0	17.9	10.6	38,354	10	27
28	France	0.903	82.5	15.8	11.6	45,937	-2	28
29	Cyprus	0.896	81.2	15.6	12.4	38,188	9	29
30	Italy	0.895	82.9	16.2	10.7	42,840	0	32
31	Estonia	0.890	77.1	15.9	13.5	38,048	8	30
32	Czechia	0.889	77.7	16.2	12.9	38,745	4	30
33	Greece	0.887	80.1	20.0[c]	11.4	29,002	17	33
34	Poland	0.876	76.5	16.0	13.2	33,034	8	36
35	Bahrain	0.875	78.8	16.3	11.0	39,497	-1	35
35	Lithuania	0.875	73.7	16.3	13.5	37,931	5	34
35	Saudi Arabia	0.875	76.9	16.1	11.3	46,112	-10	38
38	Portugal	0.866	81.0	16.9	9.6	33,155	3	39
39	Latvia	0.863	73.6	16.2	13.3	32,803	4	37
40	Andorra	0.858	80.4	13.3[i]	10.6[e]	51,167[k]	-19	45
40	Croatia	0.858	77.6	15.1	12.2[e]	30,132	8	41
42	Chile	0.855	78.9	16.7	10.9[e]	24,563	14	43
42	Qatar	0.855	79.3	12.6	10.0[e]	87,134[f]	-39	42
44	San Marino	0.853	80.9	12.3	10.8	52,654	-25	46
45	Slovakia	0.848	74.9	14.5	12.9	30,690	1	40
46	Hungary	0.846	74.5	15.0[e]	12.2	32,789	-2	44
47	Argentina	0.842	75.4	17.9	11.1[e]	20,925	17	47
48	Türkiye	0.838	76.0	18.3[c]	8.6	31,033	-3	48
49	Montenegro	0.832	76.3	15.1	12.2[e]	20,839	16	52
50	Kuwait	0.831	78.7	15.3[e]	7.3[e]	52,920	-32	54
51	Brunei Darussalam	0.829	74.6	14.0	9.2	64,490	-42	49
52	Russian Federation	0.822	69.4	15.8	12.8[i]	27,166	-1	49
53	Romania	0.821	74.2	14.2	11.3	30,027	-4	53
54	Oman	0.816	72.5	14.6	11.7	27,054	-2	51
55	Bahamas	0.812	71.6	12.9[i]	12.6[e]	30,486	-8	58
56	Kazakhstan	0.811	69.4	15.8	12.3[e]	23,943	1	59
57	Trinidad and Tobago	0.810	73.0	14.5[m]	11.6[e]	23,392	1	56
58	Costa Rica	0.809	77.0	16.5	8.8	19,974	8	57
58	Uruguay	0.809	75.4	16.8	9.0	21,269	5	55
60	Belarus	0.808	72.4	15.2	12.1	18,849	8	60
61	Panama	0.805	76.2	13.1[e]	10.5	26,957	-8	67
62	Malaysia	0.803	74.9	13.3	10.6	26,658	-8	61

Continued →

TABLE 1

		Human Development Index (HDI)	SDG 3 Life expectancy at birth	SDG 4.3 Expected years of schooling	SDG 4.4 Mean years of schooling	SDG 8.5 Gross national income (GNI) per capita	GNI per capita rank minus HDI rank	HDI rank
		Value	(years)	(years)	(years)	(2017 PPP $)		
HDI RANK		2021	2021	2021[a]	2021[a]	2021	2021[b]	2020
63	Georgia	0.802	71.7	15.6	12.8	14,664	17	64
63	Mauritius	0.802	73.6	15.2[e]	10.4[e]	22,025	-1	62
63	Serbia	0.802	74.2	14.4	11.4	19,123	4	62
66	Thailand	0.800	78.7	15.9[m]	8.7	17,030	6	64
High human development								
67	Albania	0.796	76.5	14.4	11.3[e]	14,131	17	68
68	Bulgaria	0.795	71.8	13.9	11.4	23,079	-8	64
68	Grenada	0.795	74.9	18.7[c,e]	9.0[i]	13,484	18	70
70	Barbados	0.790	77.6	15.7[e]	9.9[n]	12,306	26	71
71	Antigua and Barbuda	0.788	78.5	14.2[e]	9.3[i]	16,792	2	71
72	Seychelles	0.785	71.3	13.9	10.3	25,831	-17	69
73	Sri Lanka	0.782	76.4	14.1[e]	10.8	12,578	21	75
74	Bosnia and Herzegovina	0.780	75.3	13.8[i]	10.5	15,242	4	73
75	Saint Kitts and Nevis	0.777	71.7	15.4[e]	8.7[i]	23,358	-16	76
76	Iran (Islamic Republic of)	0.774	73.9	14.6	10.6[e]	13,001	15	77
77	Ukraine	0.773	71.6	15.0[e]	11.1[n]	13,256	11	78
78	North Macedonia	0.770	73.8	13.6[e]	10.2	15,918	-3	79
79	China	0.768	78.2	14.2[e]	7.6[n]	17,504	-8	82
80	Dominican Republic	0.767	72.6	14.5[e]	9.3[o]	17,990	-11	82
80	Moldova (Republic of)	0.767	68.8	14.4	11.8	14,875	-1	81
80	Palau	0.767	66.0	15.8[e]	12.5[p]	13,819	5	80
83	Cuba	0.764	73.7	14.4	12.5[e]	7,879[q]	37	73
84	Peru	0.762	72.4	15.4[e]	9.9[e]	12,246	13	85
85	Armenia	0.759	72.0	13.1	11.3	13,158	4	87
86	Mexico	0.758	70.2	14.9	9.2	17,896	-16	88
87	Brazil	0.754	72.8	15.6	8.1[e]	14,370	-5	86
88	Colombia	0.752	72.8	14.4	8.9	14,384	-7	88
89	Saint Vincent and the Grenadines	0.751	69.6	14.7[e]	10.8	11,961	11	82
90	Maldives	0.747	79.9	12.6	7.3	15,448	-14	97
91	Algeria	0.745	76.4	14.6[m]	8.1[e]	10,800	13	96
91	Azerbaijan	0.745	69.4	13.5	10.5	14,257	-8	100
91	Tonga	0.745	71.0	16.0	11.4[n]	6,822	34	90
91	Turkmenistan	0.745	69.3	13.2	11.3	13,021	-1	93
95	Ecuador	0.740	73.7	14.6	8.8	10,312	11	99
96	Mongolia	0.739	71.0	15.0	9.4	10,588	9	90
97	Egypt	0.731	70.2	13.8[e]	9.6[e]	11,732	4	97
97	Tunisia	0.731	73.8	15.4[e]	7.4[e]	10,258	10	94
99	Fiji	0.730	67.1	14.7[e]	10.9[e]	9,980	9	94
99	Suriname	0.730	70.3	13.0[m]	9.8[m]	12,672	-6	92
101	Uzbekistan	0.727	70.9	12.5	11.9	7,917	18	107
102	Dominica	0.720	72.8	13.3[e]	8.1[i]	11,488	0	106
102	Jordan	0.720	74.3	10.6	10.4	9,924	8	104
104	Libya	0.718	71.9	12.9[i]	7.6[r]	15,336	-27	117
105	Paraguay	0.717	70.3	13.0[o]	8.9	12,349	-10	100
106	Palestine, State of	0.715	73.5	13.4	9.9	6,583	21	109
106	Saint Lucia	0.715	71.1	12.9	8.5	12,048	-7	104
108	Guyana	0.714	65.7	12.5[e]	8.6	22,465	-47	107
109	South Africa	0.713	62.3	13.6	11.4	12,948	-17	102
110	Jamaica	0.709	70.5	13.4[m]	9.2[e]	8,834	4	110
111	Samoa	0.707	72.8	12.4	11.4	5,308	24	112
112	Gabon	0.706	65.8	13.0[i]	9.4	13,367	-25	113
112	Lebanon	0.706	75.0	11.3[p]	8.7[i]	9,526	-1	103
114	Indonesia	0.705	67.6	13.7[e]	8.6	11,466	-11	116
115	Viet Nam	0.703	73.6	13.0[s]	8.4	7,867	6	113
Medium human development								
116	Philippines	0.699	69.3	13.1	9.0	8,920	-3	113
117	Botswana	0.693	61.1	12.3[e]	10.3	16,198	-43	110
118	Bolivia (Plurinational State of)	0.692	63.6	14.9	9.8	8,111	0	119
118	Kyrgyzstan	0.692	70.0	13.2	11.4[n]	4,566	26	121
120	Venezuela (Bolivarian Republic of)	0.691	70.6	12.8[p]	11.1[n]	4,811[t]	20	118
121	Iraq	0.686	70.4	12.1[s]	7.9[m]	9,977	-12	122
122	Tajikistan	0.685	71.6	11.7[e]	11.3[n]	4,548	23	126
123	Belize	0.683	70.5	13.0	8.8	6,309	6	120

Continued →

TABLE 1 / HUMAN DEVELOPMENT INDEX AND ITS COMPONENTS

TABLE 1

HDI RANK	Human Development Index (HDI) Value 2021	SDG 3 Life expectancy at birth (years) 2021	SDG 4.3 Expected years of schooling (years) 2021ᵃ	SDG 4.4 Mean years of schooling (years) 2021ᵃ	SDG 8.5 Gross national income (GNI) per capita (2017 PPP $) 2021	GNI per capita rank minus HDI rank 2021ᵇ	HDI rank 2020
123 Morocco	0.683	74.0	14.2	5.9	7,303	1	122
125 El Salvador	0.675	70.7	12.7 ᵒ	7.2	8,296	-8	124
126 Nicaragua	0.667	73.8	12.6 ᵒ	7.1	5,625	6	129
127 Bhutan	0.666	71.8	13.2 ᵉ	5.2 ᵉ	9,438	-15	125
128 Cabo Verde	0.662	74.1	12.6 ᵉ	6.3 ᵖ	6,230	2	127
129 Bangladesh	0.661	72.4	12.4	7.4	5,472	4	128
130 Tuvalu	0.641	64.5	9.4 ᵉ	10.6	6,351	-2	131
131 Marshall Islands	0.639	65.3	10.2	10.9	4,620	12	131
132 India	0.633	67.2	11.9	6.7 ⁿ	6,590	-6	130
133 Ghana	0.632	63.8	12.0	8.3 ⁿ	5,745	-2	135
134 Micronesia (Federated States of)	0.628	70.7	11.5 ʲ	7.8 ˡ	3,696	22	136
135 Guatemala	0.627	69.2	10.6	5.7	8,723	-20	133
136 Kiribati	0.624	67.4	11.8	8.0 ˢ	4,063	14	137
137 Honduras	0.621	70.1	10.1 ᵒ	7.1	5,298	-1	138
138 Sao Tome and Principe	0.618	67.6	13.4	6.2 ᵐ	4,021	13	139
139 Namibia	0.615	59.3	11.9 ᵘ	7.2 ⁿ	8,634	-23	134
140 Lao People's Democratic Republic	0.607	68.1	10.1	5.4	7,700	-18	142
140 Timor-Leste	0.607	67.7	12.6 ᵖ	5.4	4,461	7	140
140 Vanuatu	0.607	70.4	11.5 ᵉ	7.1 ᵛ	3,085	23	142
143 Nepal	0.602	68.4	12.9	5.1 ⁿ	3,877	10	144
144 Eswatini (Kingdom of)	0.597	57.1	13.7 ᵉ	5.6	7,679	-21	141
145 Equatorial Guinea	0.596	60.6	9.7 ˡ	5.9 ʲ	12,074	-47	147
146 Cambodia	0.593	69.6	11.5 ʷ	5.1	4,079	3	148
146 Zimbabwe	0.593	59.3	12.1 ᵉ	8.7 ᵉ	3,810	9	145
148 Angola	0.586	61.6	12.2	5.4	5,466	-14	149
149 Myanmar	0.585	65.7	10.9 ᵉ	6.4	3,851	5	145
150 Syrian Arab Republic	0.577	72.1	9.2	5.1 ˡ	4,192 ˣ	-2	152
151 Cameroon	0.576	60.3	13.1 ᵉ	6.2 ⁿ	3,621	6	150
152 Kenya	0.575	61.4	10.7 ᵘ	6.7	4,474	-6	150
153 Congo	0.571	63.5	12.3 ᵉ	6.2	2,889	11	153
154 Zambia	0.565	61.2	10.9 ʷ	7.2 ⁿ	3,218	7	154
155 Solomon Islands	0.564	70.3	10.3 ᵉ	5.7 ˢ	2,482	13	155
156 Comoros	0.558	63.4	11.9 ᵉ	5.1 ˡ	3,142	6	156
156 Papua New Guinea	0.558	65.4	10.4 ᵘ	4.7	4,009	-4	157
158 Mauritania	0.556	64.4	9.4	4.9 ⁿ	5,075	-20	158
159 Côte d'Ivoire	0.550	58.6	10.7	5.2 ⁿ	5,217	-22	159
Low human development							
160 Tanzania (United Republic of)	0.549	66.2	9.2	6.4 ᵉ	2,664	7	160
161 Pakistan	0.544	66.1	8.7	4.5	4,624	-19	161
162 Togo	0.539	61.6	13.0 ᵉ	5.0 ⁿ	2,167	12	163
163 Haiti	0.535	63.2	9.7 ᵖ	5.6	2,848	2	162
163 Nigeria	0.535	52.7	10.1 ᵘ	7.2 ʷ	4,790	-22	163
165 Rwanda	0.534	66.1	11.2	4.4 ᵉ	2,210	6	165
166 Benin	0.525	59.8	10.8	4.3 ⁿ	3,409	-7	166
166 Uganda	0.525	62.7	10.1 ᵘ	5.7 ⁿ	2,181	6	166
168 Lesotho	0.514	53.1	12.0 ᵉ	6.0 ⁿ	2,700	-2	168
169 Malawi	0.512	62.9	12.7 ᵉ	4.5 ⁿ	1,466	13	169
170 Senegal	0.511	67.1	9.0	2.9 ᵉ	3,344	-10	170
171 Djibouti	0.509	62.3	7.4 ᵉ	4.1 ˡ	5,025	-32	171
172 Sudan	0.508	65.3	7.9 ᵉ	3.8	3,575	-14	171
173 Madagascar	0.501	64.5	10.1 ᵉ	5.1 ᵘ	1,484	8	173
174 Gambia	0.500	62.1	9.4 ᵘ	4.6	2,172	-1	173
175 Ethiopia	0.498	65.0	9.7 ᵉ	3.2	2,361	-5	175
176 Eritrea	0.492	66.5	8.1 ᵉ	4.9 ʸ	1,729 ᶻ	3	176
177 Guinea-Bissau	0.483	59.7	10.6 ᵐ	3.6	1,908	0	177
178 Liberia	0.481	60.7	10.4	5.1	1,289	7	179
179 Congo (Democratic Republic of the)	0.479	59.2	9.8 ᵉ	7.0 ᵐ	1,076	9	180
180 Afghanistan	0.478	62.0	10.3 ᵉ	3.0	1,824	-2	177
181 Sierra Leone	0.477	60.1	9.6 ᵐ	4.6 ⁿ	1,622	-1	181
182 Guinea	0.465	58.9	9.8 ᵉ	2.2 ᵉ	2,481	-13	182
183 Yemen	0.455	63.8	9.1	3.2 ᵛ	1,314	1	183
184 Burkina Faso	0.449	59.3	9.1	2.1 ᵉ	2,118	-8	185
185 Mozambique	0.446	59.3	10.2 ᵉ	3.2 ᵉ	1,198	2	184

Continued →

TABLE 1

HDI RANK	Human Development Index (HDI) Value 2021	SDG 3 Life expectancy at birth (years) 2021	SDG 4.3 Expected years of schooling (years) 2021[a]	SDG 4.4 Mean years of schooling (years) 2021[a]	SDG 8.5 Gross national income (GNI) per capita (2017 PPP $) 2021	GNI per capita rank minus HDI rank 2021[b]	HDI rank 2020
186 Mali	0.428	58.9	7.4[e]	2.3	2,133	-11	186
187 Burundi	0.426	61.7	10.7[e]	3.1[e]	732	4	187
188 Central African Republic	0.404	53.9	8.0[e]	4.3	966	1	188
189 Niger	0.400	61.6	7.0[e]	2.1[n]	1,240	-3	189
190 Chad	0.394	52.5	8.0[e]	2.6[u]	1,364	-7	190
191 South Sudan	0.385	55.0	5.5[e]	5.7	768[aa]	-1	191
Other countries or territories							
Korea (Democratic People's Rep. of)	..	73.3	10.8[p]	..	..	..	..
Monaco	..	85.9	..	..	..	..	..
Nauru	..	63.6	11.7[e]	..	17,730	..	..
Somalia	..	55.3	..	..	1,018	..	..
Human development groups							
Very high human development	0.896	78.5	16.5	12.3	43,752	—	—
High human development	0.754	74.7	14.2	8.3	15,167	—	—
Medium human development	0.636	67.4	11.9	6.9	6,353	—	—
Low human development	0.518	61.3	9.5	4.9	3,009	—	—
Developing countries	0.685	69.9	12.3	7.5	10,704	—	—
Regions							
Arab States	0.708	70.9	12.4	8.0	13,501	—	—
East Asia and the Pacific	0.749	75.6	13.8	7.8	15,580	—	—
Europe and Central Asia	0.796	72.9	15.4	10.6	19,352	—	—
Latin America and the Caribbean	0.754	72.1	14.8	9.0	14,521	—	—
South Asia	0.632	67.9	11.6	6.7	6,481	—	—
Sub-Saharan Africa	0.547	60.1	10.3	6.0	3,699	—	—
Least developed countries	0.540	64.2	10.2	5.2	2,881	—	—
Small island developing states	0.730	70.3	12.4	9.1	16,782	—	—
Organisation for Economic Co-operation and Development	0.899	79.0	16.5	12.3	45,087	—	—
World	**0.732**	**71.4**	**12.8**	**8.6**	**16,752**	**—**	**—**

TABLE 1 / HUMAN DEVELOPMENT INDEX AND ITS COMPONENTS   275

TABLE 1

Notes

a	Data refer to 2021 or the most recent year available.
b	Based on countries for which a Human Development Index value is calculated.
c	In calculating the HDI value, expected years of schooling is capped at 18 years.
d	In calculating the HDI value, life expectancy at birth is capped at 85 years.
e	Updated by HDRO based on data from UNESCO Institute for Statistics (2022).
f	In calculating the HDI value, GNI per capita is capped at $75,000.
g	Updated by HDRO based on data from the Organisation for Economic Cooperation and Development for various years.
h	Estimated using the purchasing power parity (PPP) rate and projected growth rate of Switzerland.
i	Updated by HDRO based on data from OECD (2022) and UNESCO Institute for Statistics (2022).
j	Based on data from the national statistical office.
k	Estimated using the PPP rate of Spain.
l	Based on cross-country regression.
m	Updated by HDRO based on data from UNESCO Institute for Statistics (2022) and United Nations Children's Fund (UNICEF) Multiple Indicator Cluster Surveys for various years.
n	Updated by HDRO based on data from Barro and Lee (2018) and UNESCO Institute for Statistics (2022).
o	Updated by HDRO based on data from CEDLAS and World Bank (2022) and UNESCO Institute for Statistics (2022).
p	Updated by HDRO based on data from the United Nations Educational, Scientific and Cultural Organization Institute for Statistics for various years.
q	HDRO estimate based on cross-country regression and the projected growth rate from UNDESA (2022b).
r	Updated by HDRO using projections from Barro and Lee (2018).
s	Updated by HDRO based on data from UNICEF Multiple Indicator Cluster Surveys for various years.
t	IMF (2021) and UNDESA (2022b).
u	Updated by HDRO based on data from ICF Macro Demographic and Health Surveys for various years and UNESCO Institute for Statistics (2022).
v	Based on projections from Barro and Lee (2018).
w	Updated by HDRO based on data from ICF Macro Demographic and Health Surveys for various years.
x	HDRO estimate based on data from UNDESA (2022b), United Nations Statistics Division (2022) and World Bank (2022).
y	HDRO estimate based on cross-country regression and data from UNESCO Institute for Statistics (2022).
z	HDRO estimate based on data from IMF (2022), United Nations Statistics Division (2022) and World Bank (2022).
aa	HDRO estimate based on data from IMF (2022) and United Nations Statistics Division (2022).

Definitions

Human Development Index (HDI): A composite index measuring average achievement in three basic dimensions of human development—a long and healthy life, knowledge and a decent standard of living. See *Technical note 1* at http://hdr.undp.org/sites/default/files/hdr2022_technical_notes.pdf for details on how the HDI is calculated.

Life expectancy at birth: Number of years a newborn infant could expect to live if prevailing patterns of age-specific mortality rates at the time of birth stay the same throughout the infant's life.

Expected years of schooling: Number of years of schooling that a child of school entrance age can expect to receive if prevailing patterns of age-specific enrolment rates persist throughout the child's life.

Mean years of schooling: Average number of years of education received by people ages 25 and older, converted from education attainment levels using official durations of each level.

Gross national income (GNI) per capita: Aggregate income of an economy generated by its production and its ownership of factors of production, less the incomes paid for the use of factors of production owned by the rest of the world, converted to international dollars using PPP rates, divided by midyear population.

GNI per capita rank minus HDI rank: Difference in ranking by GNI per capita and by HDI value. A negative value means that the country is better ranked by GNI than by HDI value.

HDI rank for 2020: Ranking by HDI value for 2020, calculated using the same most recently revised data available in 2022 that were used to calculate HDI values for 2020.

Main data sources

Columns 1 and 7: HDRO calculations based on data from Barro and Lee (2018), IMF (2022), UNDESA (2022a), UNESCO Institute for Statistics (2022), United Nations Statistics Division (2022) and World Bank (2022).

Column 2: UNDESA 2022a.

Column 3: CEDLAS and World Bank (2022), ICF Macro Demographic and Health Surveys, UNESCO Institute for Statistics (2022) and UNICEF Multiple Indicator Cluster Surveys.

Column 4: Barro and Lee (2018), ICF Macro Demographic and Health Surveys, OECD (2022), UNESCO Institute for Statistics (2022) and UNICEF Multiple Indicator Cluster Surveys.

Column 5: IMF (2022), UNDESA (2022b), United Nations Statistics Division (2022) and World Bank (2022).

Column 6: Calculated based on data in columns 1 and 5.

TABLE 2

Human Development Index trends, 1990–2021

		Human Development Index (HDI)								Change in HDI rank	Average annual HDI growth			
		Value									(%)			
HDI RANK		1990	2000	2010	2015	2018	2019	2020	2021	2015-2021[a]	1990-2000	2000-2010	2010-2021	1990-2021
Very high human development														
1	Switzerland	0.851	0.887	0.942	0.954	0.959	0.962	0.956	0.962	0	0.42	0.60	0.19	0.40
2	Norway	0.838	0.913	0.941	0.953	0.962	0.961	0.959	0.961	0	0.86	0.30	0.19	0.44
3	Iceland	0.811	0.871	0.902	0.945	0.959	0.960	0.957	0.959	0	0.72	0.35	0.56	0.54
4	Hong Kong, China (SAR)	0.788	0.851	0.907	0.935	0.949	0.952	0.949	0.952	3	0.77	0.64	0.44	0.61
5	Australia	0.865	0.896	0.923	0.933	0.941	0.941	0.947	0.951	3	0.35	0.30	0.27	0.31
6	Denmark	0.834	0.889	0.913	0.936	0.942	0.946	0.947	0.948	0	0.64	0.27	0.34	0.41
7	Sweden	0.810	0.904	0.910	0.937	0.942	0.947	0.942	0.947	-2	1.10	0.07	0.36	0.51
8	Ireland	0.737	0.847	0.904	0.925	0.937	0.942	0.943	0.945	6	1.40	0.65	0.40	0.81
9	Germany	0.829	0.889	0.926	0.938	0.945	0.948	0.944	0.942	-5	0.70	0.41	0.16	0.41
10	Netherlands	0.847	0.893	0.917	0.932	0.939	0.943	0.939	0.941	-1	0.53	0.27	0.24	0.34
11	Finland	0.814	0.891	0.911	0.930	0.936	0.939	0.938	0.940	0	0.91	0.22	0.29	0.47
12	Singapore	0.727	0.831	0.910	0.930	0.940	0.943	0.939	0.939	-1	1.35	0.91	0.29	0.83
13	Belgium	0.816	0.887	0.912	0.924	0.933	0.936	0.928	0.937	2	0.84	0.28	0.25	0.45
13	New Zealand	0.806	0.887	0.922	0.931	0.936	0.937	0.936	0.937	-3	0.96	0.39	0.15	0.49
15	Canada	0.860	0.890	0.911	0.926	0.933	0.937	0.931	0.936	-2	0.34	0.23	0.25	0.27
16	Liechtenstein	..	0.873	0.913	0.924	0.928	0.940	0.933	0.935	-1	..	0.45	0.22	..
17	Luxembourg	0.786	0.864	0.912	0.915	0.922	0.927	0.924	0.930	3	0.95	0.54	0.18	0.54
18	United Kingdom	0.804	0.862	0.912	0.924	0.929	0.935	0.924	0.929	-3	0.70	0.57	0.17	0.47
19	Japan	0.845	0.877	0.898	0.918	0.923	0.924	0.923	0.925	0	0.37	0.24	0.27	0.29
19	Korea (Republic of)	0.737	0.825	0.890	0.909	0.919	0.923	0.922	0.925	3	1.13	0.76	0.35	0.74
21	United States	0.872	0.891	0.911	0.920	0.927	0.930	0.920	0.921	-3	0.22	0.22	0.10	0.18
22	Israel	0.787	0.844	0.894	0.909	0.919	0.921	0.917	0.919	0	0.70	0.58	0.25	0.50
23	Malta	0.730	0.779	0.861	0.889	0.910	0.915	0.911	0.918	4	0.65	1.01	0.58	0.74
23	Slovenia	..	0.821	0.890	0.903	0.917	0.921	0.913	0.918	1	..	0.81	0.28	..
25	Austria	0.825	0.871	0.902	0.910	0.917	0.919	0.913	0.916	-4	0.54	0.35	0.14	0.34
26	United Arab Emirates	0.728	0.796	0.835	0.865	0.909	0.920	0.912	0.911	9	0.90	0.48	0.80	0.73
27	Spain	0.757	0.825	0.868	0.889	0.901	0.908	0.899	0.905	0	0.86	0.51	0.38	0.58
28	France	0.791	0.844	0.877	0.892	0.901	0.905	0.898	0.903	-3	0.65	0.38	0.27	0.43
29	Cyprus	0.716	0.797	0.857	0.871	0.892	0.897	0.894	0.896	3	1.08	0.73	0.41	0.73
30	Italy	0.778	0.841	0.882	0.882	0.893	0.897	0.889	0.895	-1	0.78	0.48	0.13	0.45
31	Estonia	0.732	0.787	0.861	0.882	0.891	0.896	0.892	0.890	-2	0.73	0.90	0.30	0.63
32	Czechia	0.742	0.808	0.870	0.891	0.894	0.897	0.892	0.889	-6	0.86	0.74	0.20	0.58
33	Greece	0.759	0.810	0.869	0.880	0.886	0.889	0.886	0.887	-2	0.65	0.71	0.19	0.50
34	Poland	0.716	0.793	0.841	0.868	0.877	0.881	0.876	0.876	-1	1.03	0.59	0.37	0.65
35	Bahrain	0.742	0.798	0.808	0.858	0.879	0.882	0.877	0.875	3	0.73	0.12	0.73	0.53
35	Lithuania	0.734	0.766	0.842	0.862	0.880	0.884	0.879	0.875	1	0.43	0.95	0.35	0.57
35	Saudi Arabia	0.678	0.737	0.816	0.859	0.865	0.873	0.870	0.875	2	0.84	1.02	0.64	0.83
38	Portugal	0.701	0.791	0.829	0.850	0.860	0.867	0.863	0.866	2	1.22	0.47	0.40	0.68
39	Latvia	0.730	0.756	0.824	0.850	0.866	0.871	0.871	0.863	1	0.35	0.87	0.42	0.54
40	Andorra	..	0.818	0.848	0.867	0.872	0.873	0.848	0.858	-6	..	0.36	0.11	..
40	Croatia	..	0.759	0.821	0.843	0.856	0.861	0.855	0.858	5	..	0.79	0.40	..
42	Chile	0.706	0.763	0.813	0.846	0.856	0.861	0.852	0.855	1	0.78	0.64	0.46	0.62
42	Qatar	0.758	0.801	0.834	0.846	0.853	0.859	0.854	0.855	1	0.55	0.40	0.23	0.39
44	San Marino	..	..	..	..	0.860	0.862	0.845	0.853	..	..	..	..	..
45	Slovakia	0.692	0.763	0.840	0.851	0.859	0.862	0.857	0.848	-5	0.98	0.97	0.09	0.66
46	Hungary	0.720	0.773	0.828	0.838	0.849	0.853	0.849	0.846	1	0.71	0.69	0.20	0.52
47	Argentina	0.723	0.779	0.834	0.848	0.850	0.852	0.840	0.842	-4	0.75	0.68	0.09	0.49
48	Türkiye	0.600	0.670	0.749	0.817	0.839	0.842	0.833	0.838	6	1.11	1.12	1.03	1.08
49	Montenegro	..	..	0.808	0.822	0.834	0.837	0.826	0.832	3	..	..	0.27	..
50	Kuwait	0.718	0.787	0.813	0.830	0.836	0.839	0.822	0.831	-1	0.92	0.33	0.20	0.47
51	Brunei Darussalam	0.770	0.808	0.828	0.836	0.830	0.830	0.830	0.829	-3	0.48	0.24	0.01	0.24
52	Russian Federation	0.743	0.732	0.796	0.824	0.841	0.845	0.830	0.822	-2	-0.15	0.84	0.29	0.33
53	Romania	0.703	0.715	0.807	0.813	0.827	0.832	0.824	0.821	3	0.17	1.22	0.16	0.50
54	Oman	..	0.705	0.788	0.823	0.834	0.839	0.827	0.816	-3	..	1.12	0.32	..
55	Bahamas	..	0.799	0.812	0.820	0.827	0.816	0.815	0.812	-2	..	0.16	0.00	..
56	Kazakhstan	0.673	0.680	0.767	0.805	0.814	0.819	0.814	0.811	4	0.10	1.21	0.51	0.60
57	Trinidad and Tobago	0.660	0.712	0.790	0.816	0.815	0.821	0.818	0.810	-2	0.76	1.04	0.23	0.66
58	Costa Rica	0.660	0.710	0.772	0.798	0.811	0.819	0.816	0.809	4	0.73	0.84	0.43	0.66
58	Uruguay	0.701	0.753	0.787	0.811	0.819	0.821	0.821	0.809	0	0.72	0.44	0.25	0.46
60	Belarus	..	0.712	0.790	0.812	0.818	0.817	0.807	0.808	-3	..	1.04	0.21	..
61	Panama	0.669	0.721	0.773	0.800	0.807	0.810	0.801	0.805	0	0.75	0.70	0.37	0.60
62	Malaysia	0.640	0.721	0.769	0.797	0.807	0.810	0.806	0.803	1	1.20	0.65	0.39	0.73

Continued →

TABLE 2 / HUMAN DEVELOPMENT INDEX TRENDS, 1990–2021   277

TABLE 2

		Human Development Index (HDI)								Change in HDI rank	Average annual HDI growth			
		Value									(%)			
HDI RANK		1990	2000	2010	2015	2018	2019	2020	2021	2015-2021[a]	1990-2000	2000-2010	2010-2021	1990-2021
63	Georgia	..	0.702	0.759	0.790	0.804	0.810	0.802	0.802	7	..	0.78	0.50	..
63	Mauritius	0.626	0.681	0.755	0.795	0.811	0.817	0.804	0.802	2	0.85	1.04	0.55	0.80
63	Serbia	..	0.690	0.767	0.794	0.808	0.811	0.804	0.802	4	..	1.06	0.41	..
66	Thailand	0.576	0.653	0.737	0.781	0.795	0.804	0.802	0.800	6	1.26	1.22	0.75	1.07
High human development														
67	Albania	0.647	0.677	0.754	0.795	0.806	0.810	0.794	0.796	-2	0.45	1.08	0.49	0.67
68	Bulgaria	0.684	0.725	0.790	0.809	0.809	0.810	0.802	0.795	-9	0.58	0.86	0.06	0.49
68	Grenada	..	..	0.782	0.790	0.797	0.800	0.792	0.795	2	..	..	0.15	..
70	Barbados	0.725	0.756	0.788	0.791	0.797	0.799	0.788	0.790	-2	0.42	0.42	0.02	0.28
71	Antigua and Barbuda	..	..	0.790	0.791	0.798	0.800	0.788	0.788	-3	..	..	-0.02	..
72	Seychelles	..	0.744	0.776	0.796	0.800	0.802	0.793	0.785	-8	..	0.42	0.10	..
73	Sri Lanka	0.636	0.688	0.737	0.764	0.776	0.778	0.780	0.782	9	0.79	0.69	0.54	0.67
74	Bosnia and Herzegovina	..	0.667	0.725	0.761	0.776	0.783	0.781	0.780	10	..	0.84	0.67	..
75	Saint Kitts and Nevis	..	..	0.759	0.772	0.779	0.783	0.779	0.777	2	..	..	0.21	..
76	Iran (Islamic Republic of)	0.601	0.685	0.745	0.776	0.787	0.783	0.777	0.774	-2	1.32	0.84	0.35	0.82
77	Ukraine	0.729	0.700	0.764	0.774	0.783	0.786	0.775	0.773	-2	-0.41	0.88	0.11	0.19
78	North Macedonia	..	0.675	0.738	0.762	0.779	0.784	0.774	0.770	5	..	0.90	0.39	..
79	China	0.484	0.584	0.691	0.733	0.755	0.762	0.764	0.768	19	1.90	1.70	0.97	1.50
80	Dominican Republic	0.577	0.646	0.708	0.736	0.764	0.771	0.764	0.767	16	1.14	0.92	0.73	0.92
80	Moldova (Republic of)	0.653	0.641	0.730	0.749	0.768	0.774	0.766	0.767	9	-0.19	1.31	0.45	0.52
80	Palau	..	0.739	0.773	0.780	0.778	0.776	0.773	0.767	-7	..	0.45	-0.07	..
83	Cuba	0.680	0.693	0.780	0.773	0.783	0.788	0.781	0.764	-7	0.19	1.19	-0.19	0.38
84	Peru	0.621	0.676	0.725	0.759	0.776	0.780	0.762	0.762	1	0.85	0.70	0.45	0.66
85	Armenia	0.656	0.662	0.746	0.766	0.771	0.778	0.757	0.759	-5	0.09	1.20	0.16	0.47
86	Mexico	0.662	0.709	0.746	0.768	0.777	0.779	0.756	0.758	-8	0.69	0.51	0.15	0.44
87	Brazil	0.610	0.679	0.723	0.753	0.764	0.766	0.758	0.754	1	1.08	0.63	0.38	0.69
88	Colombia	0.610	0.666	0.726	0.754	0.763	0.768	0.756	0.752	-1	0.88	0.87	0.32	0.68
89	Saint Vincent and the Grenadines	..	0.683	0.734	0.759	0.775	0.769	0.764	0.751	-4	..	0.72	0.21	..
90	Maldives	..	0.628	0.688	0.736	0.750	0.755	0.734	0.747	6	..	0.92	0.75	..
91	Algeria	0.591	0.649	0.721	0.740	0.745	0.748	0.736	0.745	2	0.94	1.06	0.30	0.75
91	Azerbaijan	..	0.622	0.727	0.748	0.757	0.761	0.730	0.745	-1	..	1.57	0.22	..
91	Tonga	0.645	0.685	0.713	0.730	0.742	0.744	0.745	0.745	10	0.60	0.40	0.40	0.47
91	Turkmenistan	..	..	0.711	0.740	0.746	0.742	0.741	0.745	2	..	..	0.43	..
95	Ecuador	0.651	0.687	0.736	0.765	0.762	0.760	0.731	0.740	-14	0.54	0.69	0.05	0.41
96	Mongolia	0.579	0.598	0.701	0.732	0.743	0.746	0.745	0.739	4	0.32	1.60	0.48	0.79
97	Egypt	0.572	0.633	0.675	0.706	0.729	0.735	0.734	0.731	13	1.02	0.64	0.73	0.79
97	Tunisia	0.576	0.658	0.720	0.733	0.743	0.745	0.737	0.731	1	1.34	0.90	0.14	0.77
99	Fiji	0.642	0.681	0.714	0.729	0.745	0.746	0.737	0.730	3	0.59	0.47	0.20	0.42
99	Suriname	..	..	0.723	0.744	0.755	0.755	0.743	0.730	-7	..	..	0.09	..
101	Uzbekistan	..	0.607	0.673	0.701	0.720	0.726	0.721	0.727	11	..	1.04	0.70	..
102	Dominica	..	0.695	0.711	0.700	0.726	0.729	0.722	0.720	11	..	0.23	0.11	..
102	Jordan	0.622	0.678	0.725	0.718	0.723	0.727	0.723	0.720	2	0.87	0.67	-0.06	0.47
104	Libya	0.666	0.712	0.739	0.699	0.722	0.722	0.703	0.718	10	0.67	0.37	-0.26	0.24
105	Paraguay	0.595	0.649	0.685	0.723	0.727	0.732	0.730	0.717	-2	0.87	0.54	0.42	0.60
106	Palestine, State of	..	..	0.687	0.710	0.723	0.727	0.716	0.715	2	..	..	0.36	..
106	Saint Lucia	0.690	0.698	0.728	0.737	0.746	0.735	0.723	0.715	-11	0.12	0.42	-0.16	0.11
108	Guyana	0.509	0.577	0.656	0.684	0.701	0.708	0.721	0.714	12	1.26	1.29	0.77	1.10
109	South Africa	0.632	0.633	0.675	0.716	0.726	0.736	0.727	0.713	-4	0.02	0.64	0.50	0.39
110	Jamaica	0.659	0.664	0.704	0.713	0.716	0.719	0.713	0.709	-3	0.08	0.59	0.06	0.24
111	Samoa	..	0.683	0.713	0.716	0.716	0.715	0.712	0.707	-6	..	0.43	-0.08	..
112	Gabon	0.610	0.635	0.664	0.699	0.706	0.709	0.710	0.706	2	0.40	0.45	0.56	0.47
112	Lebanon	..	..	0.770	0.746	0.750	0.745	0.726	0.706	-21	..	..	-0.79	..
114	Indonesia	0.526	0.595	0.664	0.695	0.710	0.716	0.709	0.705	3	1.24	1.10	0.55	0.95
115	Viet Nam	0.482	0.588	0.663	0.684	0.697	0.703	0.710	0.703	5	2.01	1.21	0.53	1.22
Medium human development														
116	Philippines	0.598	0.633	0.674	0.698	0.710	0.718	0.710	0.699	0	0.57	0.63	0.33	0.50
117	Botswana	0.586	0.585	0.660	0.702	0.716	0.717	0.713	0.693	-6	-0.02	1.21	0.44	0.54
118	Bolivia (Plurinational State of)	0.550	0.632	0.662	0.690	0.714	0.717	0.694	0.692	0	1.40	0.46	0.40	0.74
118	Kyrgyzstan	0.638	0.621	0.664	0.690	0.698	0.698	0.689	0.692	0	-0.27	0.67	0.38	0.26
120	Venezuela (Bolivarian Republic of)	0.659	0.684	0.755	0.767	0.738	0.721	0.695	0.691	-41	0.37	0.99	-0.80	0.15
121	Iraq	0.528	0.589	0.640	0.675	0.692	0.696	0.679	0.686	1	1.10	0.83	0.63	0.85
122	Tajikistan	0.628	0.560	0.636	0.657	0.671	0.676	0.664	0.685	3	-1.14	1.28	0.68	0.28
123	Belize	0.593	0.640	0.707	0.708	0.706	0.705	0.690	0.683	-14	0.77	1.00	-0.31	0.46

Continued →

TABLE 2

HDI RANK	Human Development Index (HDI) Value								Change in HDI rank	Average annual HDI growth (%)			
	1990	2000	2010	2015	2018	2019	2020	2021	2015-2021[a]	1990-2000	2000-2010	2010-2021	1990-2021
123 Morocco	0.447	0.521	0.603	0.654	0.676	0.682	0.679	0.683	3	1.54	1.47	1.14	1.38
125 El Salvador	0.525	0.617	0.659	0.668	0.680	0.683	0.672	0.675	-2	1.63	0.66	0.22	0.81
126 Nicaragua	0.490	0.566	0.614	0.647	0.662	0.664	0.654	0.667	1	1.45	0.82	0.76	1.00
127 Bhutan	..	..	0.581	0.627	0.658	0.671	0.668	0.666	6	..	..	1.25	..
128 Cabo Verde	..	0.569	0.644	0.663	0.673	0.676	0.662	0.662	-4	..	1.25	0.25	..
129 Bangladesh	0.397	0.485	0.553	0.602	0.635	0.644	0.655	0.661	11	2.02	1.32	1.64	1.66
130 Tuvalu	0.559	0.597	0.616	0.643	0.642	0.635	0.639	0.641	-2	0.66	0.31	0.36	0.44
131 Marshall Islands	..	..	..	0.638	0.639	0.640	0.639	0.639	-1	..	..	..	..
132 India	0.434	0.491	0.575	0.629	0.645	0.645	0.642	0.633	-1	1.24	1.59	0.88	1.22
133 Ghana	0.460	0.507	0.574	0.607	0.620	0.631	0.632	0.632	5	0.98	1.25	0.88	1.03
134 Micronesia (Federated States of)	..	0.572	0.625	0.626	0.633	0.633	0.629	0.628	0	..	0.89	0.04	..
135 Guatemala	0.484	0.550	0.605	0.639	0.640	0.642	0.635	0.627	-6	1.29	0.96	0.33	0.84
136 Kiribati	..	0.549	0.589	0.622	0.622	0.630	0.623	0.624	-1	..	0.71	0.53	..
137 Honduras	0.516	0.556	0.597	0.613	0.617	0.632	0.621	0.621	0	0.75	0.71	0.36	0.60
138 Sao Tome and Principe	0.485	0.501	0.554	0.596	0.617	0.622	0.619	0.618	4	0.33	1.01	1.00	0.78
139 Namibia	0.579	0.546	0.585	0.628	0.636	0.639	0.633	0.615	-7	-0.59	0.69	0.46	0.19
140 Lao People's Democratic Republic	0.405	0.470	0.551	0.599	0.607	0.610	0.608	0.607	1	1.50	1.60	0.88	1.31
140 Timor-Leste	..	..	0.619	0.614	0.605	0.614	0.614	0.607	-4	..	..	-0.18	..
140 Vanuatu	..	..	0.591	0.595	0.603	0.611	0.608	0.607	3	..	..	0.24	..
143 Nepal	0.399	0.467	0.543	0.579	0.601	0.611	0.604	0.602	4	1.59	1.52	0.94	1.34
144 Eswatini (Kingdom of)	0.545	0.471	0.503	0.575	0.607	0.615	0.610	0.597	4	-1.45	0.66	1.57	0.29
145 Equatorial Guinea	..	0.512	0.579	0.603	0.601	0.605	0.599	0.596	-6	..	1.24	0.26	..
146 Cambodia	0.378	0.425	0.540	0.574	0.591	0.598	0.596	0.593	3	1.18	2.42	0.85	1.46
146 Zimbabwe	0.509	0.452	0.512	0.582	0.602	0.601	0.600	0.593	-1	-1.18	1.25	1.34	0.49
148 Angola	..	0.375	0.510	0.582	0.595	0.595	0.590	0.586	-3	..	3.12	1.27	..
149 Myanmar	0.333	0.410	0.510	0.562	0.590	0.598	0.600	0.585	1	2.10	2.21	1.26	1.83
150 Syrian Arab Republic	0.562	0.587	0.660	0.556	0.580	0.584	0.577	0.577	5	0.44	1.18	-1.21	0.09
151 Cameroon	0.452	0.442	0.513	0.560	0.577	0.583	0.578	0.576	2	-0.22	1.50	1.06	0.79
152 Kenya	0.474	0.481	0.545	0.561	0.577	0.581	0.578	0.575	0	0.15	1.26	0.49	0.63
153 Congo	0.522	0.491	0.561	0.590	0.578	0.570	0.574	0.571	-9	-0.61	1.34	0.16	0.29
154 Zambia	0.412	0.418	0.529	0.562	0.572	0.575	0.570	0.565	-4	0.14	2.38	0.60	1.02
155 Solomon Islands	..	0.486	0.550	0.559	0.566	0.567	0.565	0.564	-1	..	1.24	0.23	..
156 Comoros	..	0.464	0.520	0.544	0.557	0.560	0.562	0.558	0	..	1.15	0.64	..
156 Papua New Guinea	0.370	0.447	0.499	0.541	0.554	0.560	0.560	0.558	2	1.91	1.11	1.02	1.33
158 Mauritania	0.397	0.465	0.510	0.544	0.556	0.563	0.556	0.556	-2	1.59	0.93	0.79	1.09
159 Côte d'Ivoire	0.427	0.457	0.473	0.513	0.542	0.550	0.551	0.550	8	0.68	0.34	1.38	0.82
Low human development													
160 Tanzania (United Republic of)	0.371	0.398	0.493	0.520	0.538	0.548	0.548	0.549	2	0.70	2.16	0.98	1.27
161 Pakistan	0.400	0.441	0.505	0.534	0.545	0.546	0.543	0.544	-2	0.98	1.36	0.68	1.00
162 Togo	0.410	0.446	0.477	0.514	0.528	0.535	0.535	0.539	4	0.85	0.67	1.12	0.89
163 Haiti	0.429	0.470	0.433	0.529	0.541	0.543	0.540	0.535	-3	0.92	-0.82	1.94	0.71
163 Nigeria	..	..	0.482	0.516	0.531	0.538	0.535	0.535	1	..	..	0.95	..
165 Rwanda	0.319	0.340	0.489	0.515	0.528	0.534	0.532	0.534	0	0.64	3.70	0.80	1.68
166 Benin	0.359	0.416	0.492	0.529	0.530	0.530	0.524	0.525	-6	1.48	1.69	0.59	1.23
166 Uganda	0.329	0.394	0.502	0.517	0.522	0.525	0.524	0.525	-3	1.82	2.45	0.41	1.52
168 Lesotho	0.479	0.452	0.467	0.503	0.522	0.524	0.521	0.514	3	-0.58	0.33	0.88	0.23
169 Malawi	0.303	0.374	0.456	0.491	0.510	0.519	0.516	0.512	4	2.13	2.00	1.06	1.71
170 Senegal	0.373	0.388	0.468	0.505	0.512	0.513	0.513	0.511	-1	0.40	1.89	0.80	1.02
171 Djibouti	..	0.361	0.458	0.493	0.506	0.512	0.510	0.509	1	..	2.41	0.96	..
172 Sudan	0.336	0.424	0.486	0.508	0.514	0.514	0.510	0.508	-4	2.35	1.37	0.40	1.34
173 Madagascar	..	0.443	0.492	0.504	0.507	0.510	0.501	0.501	-3	..	1.05	0.16	..
174 Gambia	0.343	0.404	0.460	0.478	0.495	0.503	0.501	0.500	1	1.65	1.31	0.76	1.22
175 Ethiopia	..	0.287	0.412	0.460	0.489	0.498	0.498	0.498	6	..	3.68	1.74	..
176 Eritrea	..	..	0.463	0.483	0.493	0.495	0.494	0.492	-2	..	..	0.55	..
177 Guinea-Bissau	..	..	0.443	0.472	0.482	0.490	0.483	0.483	2	..	..	0.79	..
178 Liberia	..	0.438	0.460	0.473	0.483	0.484	0.480	0.481	0	..	0.49	0.41	..
179 Congo (Democratic Republic of the)	0.386	0.376	0.429	0.463	0.480	0.482	0.479	0.479	1	-0.26	1.33	1.01	0.70
180 Afghanistan	0.273	0.335	0.448	0.478	0.483	0.488	0.483	0.478	-5	2.07	2.95	0.59	1.82
181 Sierra Leone	0.312	0.318	0.427	0.453	0.470	0.480	0.475	0.477	1	0.19	2.99	1.01	1.38
182 Guinea	0.269	0.345	0.415	0.440	0.462	0.467	0.466	0.465	1	2.52	1.86	1.04	1.78
183 Yemen	0.383	0.450	0.510	0.477	0.459	0.461	0.460	0.455	-6	1.63	1.26	-1.03	0.56
184 Burkina Faso	..	0.296	0.372	0.418	0.449	0.452	0.449	0.449	2	..	2.31	1.72	..
185 Mozambique	0.238	0.303	0.402	0.440	0.451	0.456	0.453	0.446	-2	2.44	2.87	0.95	2.05

Continued →

TABLE 2 / HUMAN DEVELOPMENT INDEX TRENDS, 1990–2021

279

TABLE 2

		Human Development Index (HDI)							Change in HDI rank	Average annual HDI growth			
		Value								(%)			
HDI RANK	1990	2000	2010	2015	2018	2019	2020	2021	2015-2021[a]	1990-2000	2000-2010	2010-2021	1990-2021
186 Mali	0.237	0.317	0.404	0.416	0.430	0.433	0.427	0.428	1	2.95	2.45	0.53	1.92
187 Burundi	0.290	0.297	0.405	0.428	0.428	0.431	0.426	0.426	-2	0.24	3.15	0.46	1.25
188 Central African Republic	0.338	0.329	0.372	0.384	0.405	0.411	0.407	0.404	2	-0.27	1.24	0.75	0.58
189 Niger	0.216	0.262	0.338	0.376	0.399	0.406	0.401	0.400	2	1.95	2.58	1.54	2.01
190 Chad	..	0.291	0.362	0.389	0.398	0.403	0.397	0.394	-1	..	2.21	0.77	..
191 South Sudan	..	..	0.430	0.412	0.395	0.393	0.386	0.385	-3	..	..	-1.00	..
Other countries or territories													
Korea (Democratic People's Rep. of)	..	..	..	..	..	..	..	..	..	..	..	..	..
Monaco	..	..	..	..	..	..	..	..	..	..	..	..	..
Nauru	..	..	..	..	..	..	..	..	..	..	..	..	..
Somalia	..	..	..	..	..	..	..	..	..	..	..	..	..
Human development groups													
Very high human development	0.784	0.826	0.868	0.889	0.898	0.902	0.895	0.896	–	0.52	0.50	0.29	0.43
High human development	0.557	0.625	0.700	0.734	0.751	0.756	0.753	0.754	–	1.16	1.14	0.68	0.98
Medium human development	0.453	0.506	0.582	0.627	0.643	0.645	0.642	0.636	–	1.11	1.41	0.81	1.10
Low human development	0.356[b]	0.399	0.477	0.506	0.518	0.522	0.519	0.518	–	1.15	1.80	0.75	1.22
Developing countries	0.513	0.569	0.638	0.673	0.687	0.691	0.687	0.685	–	1.04	1.15	0.65	0.94
Regions													
Arab States	0.555	0.618	0.676	0.697	0.711	0.715	0.708	0.708	–	1.08	0.90	0.42	0.79
East Asia and the Pacific	0.507	0.592	0.684	0.722	0.741	0.748	0.748	0.749	–	1.56	1.45	0.83	1.27
Europe and Central Asia	0.664	0.681	0.746	0.783	0.798	0.802	0.793	0.796	–	0.25	0.92	0.59	0.59
Latin America and the Caribbean	0.633	0.689	0.733	0.758	0.766	0.768	0.755	0.754	–	0.85	0.62	0.26	0.57
South Asia	0.442	0.500	0.576	0.623	0.640	0.641	0.638	0.632	–	1.24	1.43	0.85	1.16
Sub-Saharan Africa	0.407[b]	0.430	0.503	0.534	0.547	0.552	0.549	0.547	–	0.55	1.58	0.77	0.96
Least developed countries	0.357	0.408	0.487	0.520	0.537	0.542	0.542	0.540	–	1.34	1.79	0.94	1.34
Small island developing states	0.601	0.649	0.693	0.723	0.734	0.738	0.732	0.730	–	0.77	0.66	0.47	0.63
Organisation for Economic Co-operation and Development	0.795	0.840	0.875	0.893	0.901	0.905	0.897	0.899	–	0.55	0.41	0.25	0.40
World	**0.601**	**0.645**	**0.697**	**0.724**	**0.736**	**0.739**	**0.735**	**0.732**	**–**	**0.71**	**0.78**	**0.45**	**0.64**

Notes

For HDI values that are comparable across years and countries, use this table or the interpolated data at https://hdr.undp.org/data-center, which present trends using consistent data.

a   A positive value indicates an improvement in rank.

b   Value reported with relaxed aggregation rules. For details on aggregation rules, see *Reader's guide*.

Definitions

Human Development Index (HDI): A composite index measuring average achievement in three basic dimensions of human development—a long and healthy life, knowledge and a decent standard of living. See *Technical note 1* at http://hdr.undp.org/sites/default/files/hdr2022_technical_notes.pdf for details on how the HDI is calculated.

Average annual HDI growth: A smoothed annualized growth of the HDI in a given period, calculated as the annual compound growth rate.

Main data sources

Columns 1–8: HDRO calculations based on data from Barro and Lee (2018), IMF (2022), UNDESA (2022a), UNESCO Institute for Statistics (2022), United Nations Statistics Division (2022) and World Bank (2022).

Column 9: Calculated based on data in columns 4 and 8.

Columns 10–13: Calculated based on data in columns 1, 2, 3 and 8.

TABLE 3

Inequality-adjusted Human Development Index

		Human Development Index (HDI)	Inequality-adjusted HDI (IHDI)			Coefficient of human inequality	Inequality in life expectancy	Inequality-adjusted life expectancy index	Inequality in education[a]	Inequality-adjusted education index	Inequality in income[a]	Inequality-adjusted income index	Income shares held by (%)			Gini coefficient
				Overall loss[b] (%)	Difference from HDI rank[b]								Poorest 40 percent	Richest 10 percent	Richest 1 percent	
		Value	Value				(%)	Value	(%)	Value	(%)	Value				
HDI RANK		2021	2021	2021	2021	2021	2021[c]	2021	2021[d]	2021	2021[d]	2021	2010-2021[e]	2010-2021[e]	2021	2010-2021[e]
Very high human development																
1	Switzerland	0.962	0.894	7.1	-3	6.9	3.1	0.954	2.0	0.902	15.6	0.830	19.9	25.8	11.5	33.1
2	Norway	0.961	0.908	5.5	0	5.4	2.5	0.948	2.3	0.912	11.4	0.866	22.9	22.4	8.9	27.7
3	Iceland	0.959	0.915	4.6	2	4.6	2.0	0.945	2.2	0.938	9.5	0.864	23.9	22.1	8.8	26.1
4	Hong Kong, China (SAR)	0.952	0.828	13.0	-19	12.4	2.1	0.979	9.7	0.802	25.6	0.724	..	..	17.9	..
5	Australia	0.951	0.876	7.9	-6	7.6	2.7	0.966	3.1	0.896	17.1	0.776	19.5	26.6	11.3	34.3
6	Denmark	0.948	0.898	5.3	3	5.2	3.0	0.916	2.5	0.909	10.1	0.870	23.5	23.5	12.9	27.7
7	Sweden	0.947	0.885	6.5	0	6.4	2.6	0.944	3.9	0.885	12.8	0.830	21.9	22.7	10.5	29.3
8	Ireland	0.945	0.886	6.2	2	6.2	2.8	0.927	3.4	0.856	12.3	0.877	21.8	25.1	11.8	30.6
9	Germany	0.942	0.883	6.3	1	6.2	3.4	0.901	2.7	0.917	12.5	0.833	20.8	25.1	12.8	31.7
10	Netherlands	0.941	0.878	6.7	1	6.7	3.3	0.917	4.9	0.875	11.9	0.842	22.3	23.9	6.9	29.2
11	Finland	0.940	0.890	5.3	6	5.2	2.8	0.928	2.4	0.907	10.5	0.839	23.1	23.0	10.9	27.7
12	Singapore	0.939	0.817	13.0	-15	12.4	2.3	0.944	10.0	0.771	25.0	0.750	..	..	14.2	..
13	Belgium	0.937	0.874	6.7	1	6.6	3.6	0.918	5.9	0.859	10.3	0.848	23.2	22.3	8.6	27.2
13	New Zealand	0.937	0.865	7.7	0	7.5	4.2	0.921	1.8	0.914	16.4	0.768	..	..	11.9	..
15	Canada	0.936	0.860	8.1	1	7.9	4.1	0.924	2.5	0.893	17.1	0.770	19.5	25.3	13.9	33.3
16	Liechtenstein	0.935	..	..	..	..	4.7	0.927	..	..	..	..	..	..	..	..
17	Luxembourg	0.930	0.850	8.6	0	8.4	3.9	0.926	4.7	0.794	16.7	0.833	19.1	25.8	10.4	34.2
18	United Kingdom	0.929	0.850	8.5	1	8.2	3.9	0.898	2.8	0.901	18.0	0.758	18.6	26.7	12.7	35.1
19	Japan	0.925	0.850	8.1	2	7.9	2.5	0.972	4.5	0.829	16.7	0.761	20.5	26.4	13.1	32.9
19	Korea (Republic of)	0.925	0.838	9.4	-3	9.3	2.8	0.952	8.8	0.799	16.1	0.773	20.5	24.0	14.7	31.4
21	United States	0.921	0.819	11.1	-5	10.6	5.9	0.828	2.7	0.883	23.2	0.751	15.3	30.8	19.1	41.5
22	Israel	0.919	0.815	11.3	-8	10.9	3.2	0.927	6.3	0.835	23.1	0.700	16.1	27.6	16.6	38.6
23	Malta	0.918	0.849	7.5	2	7.4	3.2	0.950	5.2	0.829	13.9	0.776	21.2	24.8	9.1	31.0
23	Slovenia	0.918	0.878	4.4	13	4.4	2.7	0.908	2.1	0.898	8.3	0.829	24.8	20.7	8.0	24.4
25	Austria	0.916	0.851	7.1	9	6.9	3.3	0.917	2.5	0.832	14.9	0.808	21.2	23.2	10.1	30.2
26	United Arab Emirates	0.911	..	..	..	4.5	0.862	12.6	0.751	..	..	23.0	20.0	15.8	26.0	
27	Spain	0.905	0.788	12.9	-12	12.6	2.9	0.941	15.7	0.717	19.3	0.725	18.5	24.9	12.4	34.3
28	France	0.903	0.825	8.6	2	8.5	3.8	0.925	7.7	0.762	13.9	0.797	20.9	26.7	9.8	32.4
29	Cyprus	0.896	0.819	8.6	2	8.4	2.6	0.917	9.5	0.768	13.0	0.781	21.3	25.5	11.5	31.2
30	Italy	0.895	0.791	11.6	-7	11.2	2.7	0.940	10.1	0.727	20.9	0.724	18.3	25.9	8.7	35.2
31	Estonia	0.890	0.829	6.9	7	6.6	2.9	0.853	2.0	0.876	15.0	0.763	21.0	23.3	11.8	30.8
32	Czechia	0.889	0.850	4.4	14	4.4	3.1	0.860	1.3	0.868	8.8	0.821	24.6	21.5	10.0	25.3
33	Greece	0.887	0.791	10.8	-4	10.7	3.6	0.891	11.7	0.777	16.6	0.714	19.6	24.9	10.8	33.1
34	Poland	0.876	0.816	6.8	4	6.8	3.9	0.834	4.5	0.845	12.1	0.770	21.5	24.0	14.9	30.2
35	Bahrain	0.875	..	..	..	..	4.5	0.863	12.6	0.718	..	..	..	..	25.1	..
35	Lithuania	0.875	0.800	8.6	2	8.3	4.3	0.791	3.6	0.870	17.1	0.744	19.0	27.5	11.0	35.3
35	Saudi Arabia	0.875	..	..	..	..	5.1	0.831	18.1	0.676	..	..	..	..	21.0	..
38	Portugal	0.866	0.773	10.7	-4	10.6	3.2	0.909	13.1	0.685	15.5	0.741	20.4	26.0	9.6	32.8
39	Latvia	0.863	0.792	8.2	2	8.0	4.2	0.790	2.2	0.872	17.5	0.722	19.3	26.6	9.1	34.5
40	Andorra	0.858	..	..	..	..	5.3	0.880	10.0	0.649	..	..	..	..	..	..
40	Croatia	0.858	0.797	7.1	4	7.0	3.8	0.853	4.2	0.791	13.0	0.751	21.7	22.2	10.2	28.9
42	Chile	0.855	0.722	15.6	-8	15.0	4.9	0.862	11.7	0.732	28.3	0.596	15.0	35.8	27.1	44.9
42	Qatar	0.855	..	..	..	..	3.9	0.877	11.2	0.607	..	..	..	..	23.6	..
44	San Marino	0.853	..	..	..	..	2.8	0.910	5.6	0.662	..	..	..	..	..	..
45	Slovakia	0.848	0.803	5.3	8	5.2	4.7	0.805	1.7	0.819	9.1	0.787	24.9	18.8	7.0	23.2
46	Hungary	0.846	0.792	6.4	6	6.4	4.0	0.806	2.9	0.802	12.3	0.767	21.4	23.3	12.3	30.0
47	Argentina	0.842	0.720	14.5	-6	13.8	7.6	0.787	5.8	0.818	28.1	0.580	14.3	30.3	21.7	42.3
48	Türkiye	0.838	0.717	14.4	-7	14.2	5.9	0.811	13.6	0.680	23.1	0.667	15.5	31.6	18.8	41.9
49	Montenegro	0.832	0.756	9.1	2	9.0	2.3	0.847	7.8	0.760	16.9	0.670	16.8	26.0	9.7	36.8
50	Kuwait	0.831	..	..	..	..	5.6	0.853	22.1	0.522	..	..	..	..	19.4	..
51	Brunei Darussalam	0.829	..	..	..	..	7.5	0.778	..	..	..	..	..	..	13.6	..
52	Russian Federation	0.822	0.751	8.6	1	8.4	5.5	0.718	2.0	0.846	17.6	0.697	19.1	29.0	21.0	36.0
53	Romania	0.821	0.733	10.7	1	10.4	4.9	0.793	5.4	0.729	20.9	0.682	17.8	24.5	14.4	34.8
54	Oman	0.816	0.708	13.2	-7	13.0	7.1	0.751	11.9	0.698	20.1	0.676	..	..	19.6	..
55	Bahamas	0.812	..	..	..	..	8.7	0.724	6.9	0.726	..	..	..	..	20.8	..
56	Kazakhstan	0.811	0.755	6.9	5	6.9	7.3	0.704	3.2	0.823	10.3	0.742	23.3	23.4	15.4	27.8
57	Trinidad and Tobago	0.810	..	..	..	..	10.9	0.726	..	..	..	..	..	..	20.8	..

Continued →

TABLE 3

		Human Development Index (HDI)	Inequality-adjusted HDI (IHDI)			Coefficient of human inequality	Inequality in life expectancy	Inequality-adjusted life expectancy index	Inequality in education[a]	Inequality-adjusted education index	Inequality in income[a]	Inequality-adjusted income index	Income shares held by (%)			Gini coefficient
		Value	Value	Overall loss[b] (%)	Difference from HDI rank[b]		(%)	Value	(%)	Value	(%)	Value	Poorest 40 percent	Richest 10 percent	Richest 1 percent	
HDI RANK		2021	2021	2021	2021	2021	2021[c]	2021	2021[d]	2021	2021[d]	2021	2010-2021[e]	2010-2021[e]	2021	2010-2021[e]
58	Costa Rica	0.809	0.664	17.9	-17	17.0	5.9	0.826	11.6	0.666	33.4	0.533	12.1	37.0	19.1	49.3
58	Uruguay	0.809	0.710	12.2	-3	11.8	5.4	0.807	6.5	0.717	23.5	0.619	16.0	29.9	14.7	40.2
60	Belarus	0.808	0.765	5.3	10	5.3	3.3	0.780	2.8	0.803	9.6	0.715	24.8	20.7	9.9	24.4
61	Panama	0.805	0.640	20.5	-19	19.6	10.9	0.771	11.4	0.633	36.6	0.536	11.7	38.0	20.8	49.8
62	Malaysia	0.803	..	..	..	..	6.0	0.794	12.1	0.638	..	..	15.9	31.3	14.9	41.1
63	Georgia	0.802	0.706	12.0	-2	11.4	6.6	0.743	2.8	0.836	24.9	0.566	19.0	26.2	21.1	34.5
63	Mauritius	0.802	0.666	17.0	-11	16.9	10.6	0.736	21.9	0.601	18.2	0.667	18.8	29.9	15.9	36.8
63	Serbia	0.802	0.720	10.2	5	9.9	4.1	0.799	7.2	0.723	18.5	0.647	18.9	26.0	10.9	34.5
66	Thailand	0.800	0.686	14.3	-2	14.2	6.9	0.841	16.8	0.608	18.8	0.630	19.0	27.0	17.8	35.0
High human development																
67	Albania	0.796	0.710	10.8	5	10.8	6.8	0.810	12.3	0.682	13.2	0.649	21.0	23.8	8.9	30.8
68	Bulgaria	0.795	0.701	11.8	2	11.4	5.2	0.756	5.9	0.721	23.0	0.633	16.7	31.4	18.3	40.3
68	Grenada	0.795	..	..	..	9.6	0.764		..	..	..	..	..	..	..	..
70	Barbados	0.790	0.657	16.8	-9	15.7	8.0	0.815	5.5	0.722	33.6	0.483				
71	Antigua and Barbuda	0.788	..	..	..		4.7	0.857	..	..	..	..				
72	Seychelles	0.785	0.661	15.8	-7	15.1	9.4	0.715	6.7	0.681	29.3	0.593	19.6	23.9	20.6	32.1
73	Sri Lanka	0.782	0.676	13.6	-2	13.2	5.2	0.823	12.0	0.663	22.4	0.567	17.9	32.6	20.6	39.3
74	Bosnia and Herzegovina	0.780	0.677	13.2	0	13.0	4.0	0.817	14.8	0.626	20.2	0.606	19.8	25.1	8.9	33.0
75	Saint Kitts and Nevis	0.777	..	..	..		8.0	0.732	..	..	..	..			..	
76	Iran (Islamic Republic of)	0.774	0.686	11.4	5	11.1	8.5	0.758	5.0	0.723	19.7	0.590	16.3	31.7	18.2	40.9
77	Ukraine	0.773	0.726	6.1	18	6.0	5.8	0.748	3.6	0.758	8.5	0.675	24.3	21.8	9.5	25.6
78	North Macedonia	0.770	0.686	10.9	7	10.6	4.4	0.792	8.4	0.659	19.2	0.619	18.5	23.0	6.5	33.0
79	China	0.768	0.651	15.2	-3	14.8	5.3	0.848	11.7	0.573	27.4	0.567	17.4	29.5	14.0	38.2
80	Dominican Republic	0.767	0.618	19.4	-9	19.4	17.6	0.667	15.0	0.605	25.6	0.583	16.9	30.5	20.8	39.6
80	Moldova (Republic of)	0.767	0.711	7.3	16	7.3	8.9	0.685	2.6	0.775	10.4	0.677	24.1	22.0	9.8	26.0
80	Palau	0.767	..	..	..		12.5	0.620	2.2	0.836	..	..				
83	Cuba	0.764	..	..	..		4.6	0.788	9.1	0.743	..	..			16.7	
84	Peru	0.762	0.635	16.7	-3	16.4	8.6	0.736	14.3	0.649	26.3	0.535	14.4	32.9	21.2	43.8
85	Armenia	0.759	0.688	9.4	13	9.1	7.0	0.744	2.9	0.720	17.4	0.609	24.5	21.5	15.4	25.2
86	Mexico	0.758	0.621	18.1	-3	17.6	9.5	0.699	13.5	0.623	29.8	0.550	14.3	35.5	28.4	45.4
87	Brazil	0.754	0.576	23.6	-20	22.3	10.0	0.730	15.7	0.594	41.3	0.440	13.2	39.4	25.7	48.9
88	Colombia	0.752	0.589	21.7	-14	20.6	9.4	0.737	14.6	0.595	37.7	0.468	10.2	42.2	19.9	54.2
89	Saint Vincent and the Grenadines	0.751	..	..	..		9.1	0.694	9.2	0.698	..	..			..	..
90	Maldives	0.747	0.594	20.5	-9	19.8	4.1	0.884	29.3	0.421	25.8	0.565	22.1	23.3	13.3	29.3
91	Algeria	0.745	0.598	19.7	-7	19.1	12.4	0.760	33.3	0.451	11.5	0.626	23.1	22.9	9.9	27.6
91	Azerbaijan	0.745	0.685	8.1	14	7.9	11.3	0.673	3.6	0.700	8.9	0.683			14.3	
91	Tonga	0.745	0.666	10.6	11	10.4	8.7	0.716	4.3	0.790	18.2	0.522	18.2	29.7	..	37.6
91	Turkmenistan	0.745	0.619	16.9	0	16.4	20.0	0.607	2.9	0.720	26.2	0.543			19.9	..
95	Ecuador	0.740	0.604	18.4	0	17.8	8.9	0.752	13.4	0.606	31.1	0.483	13.0	36.0	13.7	47.3
96	Mongolia	0.739	0.644	12.9	10	12.7	9.3	0.711	11.9	0.643	16.9	0.585	20.2	25.7	16.5	32.7
97	Egypt	0.731	0.519	29.0	-21	28.0	10.7	0.690	36.9	0.443	36.5	0.457	21.8	26.9	19.9	31.5
97	Tunisia	0.731	0.588	19.6	-7	19.2	10.0	0.745	30.7	0.469	16.9	0.581	20.1	25.6	10.9	32.8
99	Fiji	0.730	..	..	..		15.2	0.614	2.6	0.753	..	..	21.3	24.2	..	30.7
99	Suriname	0.730	0.532	27.1	-18	25.3	11.0	0.688	18.4	0.562	46.7	0.390			20.8	
101	Uzbekistan	0.727	..	..	..		8.5	0.716	0.6	0.739	..	..			16.9	
102	Dominica	0.720	..	..	..		9.0	0.740	..	..	..	..			..	..
102	Jordan	0.720	0.617	14.3	7	14.2	9.3	0.757	15.4	0.545	17.9	0.570	20.3	27.5	17.5	33.7
104	Libya	0.718	..	..	..		7.8	0.736	..	..	..	..			13.6	..
105	Paraguay	0.717	0.582	18.8	-6	18.3	11.4	0.685	13.2	0.570	30.4	0.506	14.9	33.3	20.8	43.5
106	Palestine, State of	0.715	0.584	18.3	-4	17.6	10.2	0.738	11.0	0.625	31.6	0.432	19.2	25.2	17.9	33.7
106	Saint Lucia	0.715	0.559	21.8	-8	21.3	9.3	0.713	27.3	0.467	27.4	0.525	11.0	38.6	..	51.2
108	Guyana	0.714	0.591	17.2	3	17.1	15.8	0.592	10.4	0.568	25.1	0.613			20.8	
109	South Africa	0.713	0.471	33.9	-22	31.1	18.9	0.529	17.3	0.627	57.0	0.316	7.2	50.5	21.9	63.0
110	Jamaica	0.709	0.591	16.6	5	15.7	8.7	0.709	6.5	0.633	32.0	0.461			20.8	
111	Samoa	0.707	0.613	13.3	13	13.1	10.4	0.727	7.0	0.674	21.9	0.469	17.9	31.3	..	38.7
112	Gabon	0.706	0.554	21.5	-3	21.5	19.7	0.566	23.5	0.517	21.2	0.583	16.8	27.7	11.0	38.0
112	Lebanon	0.706	..	..	..		5.6	0.800	6.2	0.567	..	..	20.6	24.8	21.0	31.8
114	Indonesia	0.705	0.585	17.0	4	16.9	13.2	0.635	17.3	0.552	20.1	0.572	18.1	29.6	18.3	37.3

Continued →

TABLE 3

		Human Development Index (HDI)	Inequality-adjusted HDI (IHDI)			Coefficient of human inequality	Inequality in life expectancy	Inequality-adjusted life expectancy index	Inequality in education[a]	Inequality-adjusted education index	Inequality in income[a]	Inequality-adjusted income index	Income shares held by (%)			Gini coefficient
				Overall loss[b] (%)	Difference from HDI rank[b]								Poorest 40 percent	Richest 10 percent	Richest 1 percent	
		Value	Value				(%)	Value	(%)	Value	(%)	Value				
HDI RANK		2021	2021	2021	2021	2021	2021[c]	2021	2021[d]	2021	2021[d]	2021	2010-2021[e]	2010-2021[e]	2021	2010-2021[e]
115	Viet Nam	0.703	0.602	14.4	14	14.3	13.1	0.717	15.3	0.541	14.6	0.563	18.6	27.5	16.2	35.7
Medium human development																
116	Philippines	0.699	0.574	17.9	2	17.5	14.4	0.649	10.1	0.597	28.1	0.488	16.1	33.5	16.9	42.3
117	Botswana	0.693	..	..	..	..	21.6	0.496	23.3	0.526	..	..	10.9	41.5	22.7	53.3
118	Bolivia (Plurinational State of)	0.692	0.549	20.7	-1	20.5	18.0	0.550	16.5	0.620	26.9	0.486	14.5	32.6	20.8	43.6
118	Kyrgyzstan	0.692	0.627	9.4	23	9.2	10.5	0.688	3.4	0.721	13.8	0.497	22.5	24.0	18.4	29.0
120	Venezuela (Bolivarian Republic of)	0.691	0.592	14.3	14	14.2	12.8	0.678	8.7	0.663	21.0	0.462	..	..	20.8[f]	..
121	Iraq	0.686	0.554	19.2	4	18.8	14.0	0.667	29.7	0.421	12.7	0.607	21.9	23.7	20.7	29.5
122	Tajikistan	0.685	0.599	12.6	19	12.3	16.5	0.663	6.0	0.659	14.5	0.493	19.4	26.4	14.9	34.0
123	Belize	0.683	0.535	21.7	1	20.7	9.2	0.705	14.8	0.559	37.9	0.389	..	..	20.8	..
123	Morocco	0.683	0.504	26.2	-4	25.1	10.9	0.741	41.9	0.343	22.5	0.502	17.4	31.9	15.1	39.5
125	El Salvador	0.675	0.548	18.8	5	18.6	9.5	0.706	23.8	0.450	22.5	0.517	17.1	29.8	14.5	38.8
126	Nicaragua	0.667	0.516	22.6	1	22.1	9.9	0.747	25.8	0.437	30.7	0.422	14.3	37.2	20.8	46.2
127	Bhutan	0.666	0.471	29.3	-6	27.7	14.9	0.678	48.2	0.279	20.0	0.550	17.5	27.9	14.2	37.4
128	Cabo Verde	0.662	..	..	..	..	8.8	0.758	27.4	0.405	..	..	15.4	32.3	13.9	42.4
129	Bangladesh	0.661	0.503	23.9	0	23.1	15.5	0.681	37.3	0.371	16.6	0.504	21.0	26.8	16.3	32.4
130	Tuvalu	0.641	0.541	15.6	8	15.5	14.4	0.587	9.2	0.557	22.9	0.483	17.4	30.8	..	39.1
131	Marshall Islands	0.639	..	..	..	..	17.5	0.575	4.8	0.616	..	..	18.9	27.5	..	35.5
132	India	0.633	0.475	25.0	-2	24.4	16.9	0.604	36.9	0.348	19.4	0.510	19.8	30.1	21.7	35.7
133	Ghana	0.632	0.458	27.5	-6	27.3	22.8	0.520	35.1	0.397	24.1	0.464	14.3	32.2	15.2	43.5
134	Micronesia (Federated States of)	0.628	..	..	..	..	13.9	0.672	..	..	26.4	0.401	16.2	29.7	..	40.1
135	Guatemala	0.627	0.460	26.6	-3	26.1	13.9	0.652	35.0	0.314	29.6	0.475	13.1	38.1	20.8	48.3
136	Kiribati	0.624	0.516	17.3	8	17.2	22.5	0.566	9.6	0.537	19.4	0.451	23.0	22.9	..	27.8
137	Honduras	0.621	0.479	22.9	4	22.2	10.1	0.693	21.6	0.406	34.9	0.390	11.6	34.6	20.8	48.2
138	Sao Tome and Principe	0.618	0.503	18.6	7	18.4	10.4	0.656	18.7	0.470	26.2	0.412	16.8	32.9	9.0	40.7
139	Namibia	0.615	0.402	34.6	-10	32.8	19.9	0.484	25.0	0.428	53.6	0.313	8.6	47.3	21.6	59.1
140	Lao People's Democratic Republic	0.607	0.459	24.4	1	24.2	20.6	0.587	31.3	0.316	20.6	0.521	17.8	31.2	20.1	38.8
140	Timor-Leste	0.607	0.440	27.5	-3	26.2	20.2	0.586	44.9	0.293	13.6	0.496	22.8	24.0	15.7	28.7
140	Vanuatu	0.607	..	..	..	..	14.0	0.667	..	..	19.7	0.416	19.9	24.7	..	32.3
143	Nepal	0.602	0.449	25.4	0	24.3	15.5	0.630	41.1	0.311	16.3	0.462	20.4	26.4	13.9	32.8
144	Eswatini (Kingdom of)	0.597	0.424	29.0	-3	28.6	23.8	0.435	24.1	0.431	37.9	0.407	10.5	42.7	19.3	54.6
145	Equatorial Guinea	0.596	..	..	..	..	30.1	0.437	..	..	..	..	..	..	17.6	..
146	Cambodia	0.593	0.479	19.2	11	19.0	15.4	0.646	27.3	0.355	14.3	0.480	..	..	18.6	..
146	Zimbabwe	0.593	0.458	22.8	4	22.5	24.0	0.459	14.6	0.535	28.8	0.392	15.1	34.8	21.1	50.3
148	Angola	0.586	0.407	30.5 *	-2	30.4	28.2	0.460	34.2	0.341	28.9	0.430	11.5	39.6	26.0	51.3
149	Myanmar	0.585	..	..	..	..	21.2	0.554	26.9	0.377	..	..	21.9	25.5	17.1	30.7
150	Syrian Arab Republic	0.577	..	..	..	..	13.0	0.697	..	..	..	..	..	..	21.2	..
151	Cameroon	0.576	0.393	31.8	-6	31.7	28.5	0.444	31.7	0.389	35.0	0.352	13.0	35.0	15.9	46.6
152	Kenya	0.575	0.426	25.9	3	25.7	21.0	0.503	22.9	0.400	33.1	0.384	16.5	31.6	15.2	40.8
153	Congo	0.571	0.432	24.3	5	24.3	21.0	0.529	20.9	0.433	31.0	0.351	12.4	37.9	20.5	48.9
154	Zambia	0.565	0.390	31.0	-4	30.1	25.1	0.475	20.4	0.432	44.8	0.289	8.9	44.4	23.2	57.1
155	Solomon Islands	0.564	..	..	..	..	12.1	0.681	..	..	..	..	18.4	29.2	..	37.1
156	Comoros	0.558	0.310	44.4	-21	43.1	25.6	0.497	47.6	0.262	56.0	0.229	13.6	33.7	14.2	45.3
156	Papua New Guinea	0.558	0.397	28.9	0	28.5	20.9	0.552	35.7	0.287	28.9	0.396	15.1[g]	31.0[g]	16.7	41.9[g]
158	Mauritania	0.556	0.389	30.0	-2	29.0	25.7	0.507	44.0	0.238	17.3	0.490	19.9	24.9	10.8	32.6
159	Côte d'Ivoire	0.550	0.358	34.9	-8	34.3	30.4	0.414	45.6	0.256	27.0	0.436	18.0	29.0	21.0	37.2
Low human development																
160	Tanzania (United Republic of)	0.549	0.418	23.9	8	23.7	21.7	0.556	27.0	0.342	22.4	0.385	17.4	33.1	18.2	40.5
161	Pakistan	0.544	0.380	30.1	0	29.2	26.9	0.518	43.5	0.221	17.2	0.479	22.7	25.5	16.8	29.6
162	Togo	0.539	0.372	31.0	-1	30.8	27.7	0.463	37.7	0.328	26.9	0.340	15.7	32.9	13.9	42.4
163	Haiti	0.535	0.327	38.9	-12	38.1	26.6	0.488	37.3	0.285	50.4	0.251	15.8	31.2	20.8	41.1
163	Nigeria	0.535	0.341	36.3	-7	36.0	39.6	0.304	40.4	0.310	28.1	0.421	18.7	26.7	11.6	35.1
165	Rwanda	0.534	0.402	24.7	11	24.6	19.4	0.571	27.4	0.334	27.2	0.340	15.8	35.6	19.9	43.7
166	Benin	0.525	0.334	36.4	-7	36.1	32.7	0.413	43.7	0.249	32.0	0.363	18.1	29.9	17.5	37.8
166	Uganda	0.525	0.396	24.6	9	24.4	20.4	0.523	27.9	0.341	24.9	0.350	16.1	34.5	17.1	42.7
168	Lesotho	0.514	0.372	27.6	5	27.4	33.0	0.341	19.6	0.430	29.6	0.351	13.5	32.9	14.5	44.9
169	Malawi	0.512	0.377	26.4	7	26.3	19.7	0.530	28.0	0.361	31.3	0.279	17.9	31.0	28.0	38.5
170	Senegal	0.511	0.354	30.7	2	29.5	18.1	0.593	47.1	0.183	23.4	0.406	18.0	30.5	13.2	38.1

Continued →

TABLE 3 / INEQUALITY-ADJUSTED HUMAN DEVELOPMENT INDEX 283

TABLE 3

	HDI RANK	Human Development Index (HDI) Value 2021	Inequality-adjusted HDI (IHDI) Value 2021	Overall loss[b] (%) 2021	Difference from HDI rank[b] 2021	Coefficient of human inequality 2021	Inequality in life expectancy (%) 2021[c]	Inequality-adjusted life expectancy index Value 2021	Inequality in education[a] (%) 2021[d]	Inequality-adjusted education index Value 2021	Inequality in income[a] (%) 2021[d]	Inequality-adjusted income index Value 2021	Income shares held by (%) Poorest 40 percent 2010-2021[e]	Richest 10 percent 2010-2021[e]	Richest 1 percent 2021	Gini coefficient 2010-2021[e]
171	Djibouti	0.509	..	..	..	..	25.7	0.484	..	..	27.7	0.428	15.8	32.3	15.9	41.6
172	Sudan	0.508	0.336	33.9	-1	33.5	25.0	0.522	42.5	0.200	33.0	0.362	19.9	27.8	15.4	34.2
173	Madagascar	0.501	0.367	26.7	7	26.9	23.7	0.522	29.3	0.320	27.6	0.295	15.7	33.5	15.2	42.6
174	Gambia	0.500	0.348	30.4	4	29.3	23.3	0.496	47.0	0.221	17.5	0.384	19.0	28.7	13.6	35.9
175	Ethiopia	0.498	0.363	27.1	8	26.0	23.1	0.532	42.8	0.214	12.1	0.420	19.4	28.5	13.8	35.0
176	Eritrea	0.492	..	..	..	..	20.3	0.571	..	..	..	..	..	..	13.8	..
177	Guinea-Bissau	0.483	0.306	36.6	-5	36.5	29.5	0.430	42.1	0.240	37.9	0.277	19.4	27.6	17.1	34.8
178	Liberia	0.481	0.330	31.4	2	30.7	30.1	0.438	42.1	0.266	19.7	0.310	18.8	27.1	12.2	35.3
179	Congo (Democratic Republic of the)	0.479	0.341	28.8	7	28.7	31.7	0.412	26.8	0.371	27.6	0.260	15.5	32.0	14.6	42.1
180	Afghanistan	0.478	..	..	..	26.2	0.477	45.4	0.210	..	..	..	..	15.3	..	
181	Sierra Leone	0.477	0.309	35.2	0	34.2	35.1	0.400	47.5	0.220	19.9	0.337	19.6	29.4	15.0	35.7
182	Guinea	0.465	0.299	35.7	-4	34.3	35.1	0.389	50.1	0.172	17.8	0.399	21.6	23.1	12.5	29.6
183	Yemen	0.455	0.307	32.5	1	31.5	26.7	0.493	46.1	0.194	21.8	0.304	18.8	29.4	24.7	36.7
184	Burkina Faso	0.449	0.315	29.8	5	29.3	31.4	0.415	39.2	0.197	17.3	0.381	14.1	37.5	14.6	47.3
185	Mozambique	0.446	0.300	32.7	0	32.4	28.3	0.434	40.5	0.232	28.4	0.269	11.8	45.5	31.1	54.0
186	Mali	0.428	0.291	32.0	-2	31.1	32.8	0.403	43.9	0.159	16.6	0.386	18.7	28.2	9.7	36.1
187	Burundi	0.426	0.302	29.1	3	28.7	25.6	0.477	39.5	0.243	20.9	0.238	17.9	31.0	14.7	38.6
188	Central African Republic	0.404	0.240	40.6	-3	40.1	36.0	0.334	35.2	0.238	49.2	0.174	10.3[h]	46.2[h]	31.0	56.2[h]
189	Niger	0.400	0.292	27.0	2	26.7	28.7	0.456	35.0	0.172	16.4	0.318	19.0	31.1	11.6	37.3
190	Chad	0.394	0.251	36.3	1	36.0	38.6	0.307	42.9	0.176	26.5	0.290	18.2	29.7	15.7	37.5
191	South Sudan	0.385	0.245	36.4	1	36.3	37.0	0.339	39.6	0.208	32.3	0.209	12.5[g]	33.2[g]	15.5	44.1
Other countries or territories																
..	Korea (Democratic People's Rep. of)	..	..	..	..	..	11.0	0.730	..	..	..	..	..	..	14.8	..
..	Monaco	..	..	..	..	..	3.4	0.966	..	..	..	..	..	..	..	..
..	Nauru	..	..	..	..	..	13.5	0.581	..	..	..	..	19.4	27.3	..	34.8
..	Somalia	..	..	..	..	..	38.3	0.335	..	..	24.4	0.265	..	..	12.4	36.8
Human development groups																
	Very high human development	0.896	0.805	10.2	—	9.9	4.7	0.858	6.3	0.814	18.8	0.746	18.4	27.6	15.8	—
	High human development	0.754	0.627	16.8	—	16.5	8.0	0.774	13.9	0.579	27.5	0.550	17.0	31.0	16.8	—
	Medium human development	0.636	0.481	24.4	—	24.0	17.3	0.604	33.6	0.372	21.0	0.496	19.0	30.3	20.3	—
	Low human development	0.518	0.359	30.7	—	30.3	28.9	0.452	38.9	0.260	23.1	0.395	18.6	29.5	15.8	—
Developing countries		0.685	0.538	21.5	—	21.4	14.9	0.653	25.0	0.445	24.2	0.535	18.0	30.4	17.9	—
Regions																
	Arab States	0.708	0.534	24.6	—	24.2	14.1	0.672	33.1	0.408	25.3	0.553	20.8	26.6	17.9	—
	East Asia and the Pacific	0.749	0.630	15.9	—	15.5	7.9	0.788	13.4	0.559	25.4	0.569	17.6	29.5	15.1	—
	Europe and Central Asia	0.796	0.714	10.3	—	10.3	7.3	0.754	7.0	0.726	16.5	0.664	19.7	26.7	15.3	—
	Latin America and the Caribbean	0.754	0.601	20.3	—	19.6	10.1	0.721	14.8	0.605	33.9	0.497	13.6	36.7	23.7	—
	South Asia	0.632	0.476	24.7	—	24.3	17.6	0.606	36.2	0.347	18.9	0.511	20.1	29.3	20.3	—
	Sub-Saharan Africa	0.547	0.383	30.0	—	29.9	28.3	0.442	34.3	0.319	27.1	0.397	16.2	32.6	16.2	—
Least developed countries		0.540	0.390	27.8	—	27.6	24.2	0.516	36.1	0.292	22.5	0.393	17.9	30.9	16.9	—
Small island developing states		0.730	0.557	23.7	—	23.3	15.0	0.658	22.1	0.505	32.9	0.519	..	..	18.3	—
Organisation for Economic Co-operation and Development		0.899	0.800	11.0	—	10.6	4.9	0.863	6.7	0.808	20.4	0.735	17.7	28.8	16.2	—
World		**0.732**	**0.590**	**19.4**	**—**	**19.4**	**13.2**	**0.686**	**21.7**	**0.503**	**23.2**	**0.594**	**18.1**	**29.9**	**17.4**	**—**

SDG 10.1

TABLE 3

Notes

a   See https://hdr.undp.org/inequality-adjusted-human-development-index for the list of surveys used to estimate inequalities.

b   Based on countries for which an Inequality-adjusted Human Development Index value is calculated.

c   Calculated by HDRO based on data from period life tables from UNDESA (2022a).

d   Data refer to 2021 or the most recent year available.

e   Data refer to the most recent year available during the period specified.

f   Refers to 2020.

g   Refers to 2009.

h   Refers to 2008.

Definitions

Human Development Index (HDI): A composite index measuring average achievement in three basic dimensions of human development—a long and healthy life, knowledge and a decent standard of living. See *Technical note 1* at http://hdr.undp.org/sites/default/files/hdr2022_technical_notes.pdf for details on how the HDI is calculated.

Inequality-adjusted HDI (IHDI): HDI value adjusted for inequalities in the three basic dimensions of human development. See *Technical note 2* at http://hdr.undp.org/sites/default/files/hdr2022_technical_notes.pdf for details on how the IHDI is calculated.

Overall loss: Percentage difference between the IHDI value and the HDI value.

Difference from HDI rank: Difference in ranks on the IHDI and the HDI.

Coefficient of human inequality: Average inequality in the three basic dimensions of human development.

Inequality in life expectancy: Inequality in distribution of expected length of life based on data from life tables estimated using the Atkinson inequality index.

Inequality-adjusted life expectancy index: HDI life expectancy index value adjusted for inequality in distribution of expected length of life based on data from life tables listed in Main data sources.

Inequality in education: Inequality in distribution of years of schooling based on data from household surveys estimated using the Atkinson inequality index.

Inequality-adjusted education index: HDI education index value adjusted for inequality in distribution of years of schooling based on data from household surveys listed in Main data sources.

Inequality in income: Inequality in income distribution based on data from household surveys estimated using the Atkinson inequality index.

Inequality-adjusted income index: HDI income index value adjusted for inequality in income distribution based on data from household surveys listed in *Main data sources*.

Income shares: Percentage share of income (or consumption) that accrues to the indicated population subgroups.

Income share held by richest 1%: Share of pretax national income held by the richest 1 percent of the population. Pretax national income is the sum of all pretax personal income flows accruing to the owners of the production factors, labour and capital before the tax/transfer system is taken into account and after the pension system is taken into account.

Gini coefficient: Measure of the deviation of the distribution of income among individuals or households in a country from a perfectly equal distribution. A value of 0 represents absolute equality, a value of 100 absolute inequality.

Main data sources

Column 1: HDRO calculations based on data from Barro and Lee (2018), IMF (2022), UNDESA (2022a), UNESCO Institute for Statistics (2022), United Nations Statistics Division (2022) and World Bank (2022).

Column 2: Calculated as the geometric mean of the values in the inequality-adjusted life expectancy index, inequality-adjusted education index and inequality-adjusted income index using the methodology in *Technical note 2* (available at http://hdr.undp.org/sites/default/files/hdr2022_technical_notes.pdf).

Column 3: Calculated based on data in columns 1 and 2.

Column 4: Calculated based on IHDI values and recalculated HDI ranks for countries for which an IHDI value is calculated.

Column 5: Calculated as the arithmetic mean of the values in inequality in life expectancy, inequality in education and inequality in income using the methodology in *Technical note 2* (available at http://hdr.undp.org/sites/default/files/hdr2022_technical_notes.pdf).

Column 6: Calculated based on complete life tables from UNDESA (2022a).

Column 7: Calculated based on inequality in life expectancy and the HDI life expectancy index.

Columns 8 and 10: Calculated based on data from the Center for Distributive, Labor and Social Studies and the World Bank's Socio-Economic Database for Latin America and the Caribbean; Eurostat's European Union Statistics on Income and Living Conditions; ICF Macro Demographic and Health Surveys; the Luxembourg Income Study database; United Nations Children's Fund Multiple Indicator Cluster Surveys; the United Nations Educational, Scientific and Cultural Organization Institute for Statistics; the World Bank's International Income Distribution Database; and the World Income Inequality Database using the methodology in *Technical note 2* (available at http://hdr.undp.org/sites/default/files/hdr2022_technical_notes.pdf).

Column 9: Calculated based on inequality in education and the HDI education index.

Column 11: Calculated based on inequality in income and the HDI income index.

Columns 12, 13 and 15: World Bank (2022).

Column 14: World Inequality Database (2022).

TABLE 3 / INEQUALITY-ADJUSTED HUMAN DEVELOPMENT INDEX   285

TABLE 4

Gender Development Index

		Gender Development Index		Human Development Index Value		SDG 3 Life expectancy at birth (years)		SDG 4.3 Expected years of schooling (years)		SDG 4.4 Mean years of schooling (years)		SDG 8.5 Estimated gross national income per capita[a] (2017 PPP $)	
		Value	Group[b]	Female	Male	Female	Male	Female	Male	Female	Male	Female	Male
HDI RANK		2021	2021	2021	2021	2021	2021	2021[c]	2021[c]	2021[c]	2021[c]	2021	2021
Very high human development													
1	Switzerland	0.967	2	0.944	0.976	85.9	82.0	16.4	16.6	13.5	14.2	54,597	79,451[d]
2	Norway	0.983	1	0.950	0.966	84.9	81.6	18.9[e]	17.5	13.1	12.9	54,699	74,445
3	Iceland	0.976	1	0.947	0.971	84.2	81.2	20.3[e]	18.1[f]	13.9	13.7	47,136	64,004
4	Hong Kong, China (SAR)	0.976	1	0.941	0.964	88.3[g]	82.7[h]	17.6	17.0	11.8	12.7	51,735	75,307[d]
5	Australia	0.968	2	0.932	0.963	85.8	83.2[h]	21.8[e]	20.3[f]	12.8	12.6	37,486	61,161
6	Denmark	0.980	1	0.937	0.957	83.3	79.5	19.3[e]	18.1[f]	13.2	12.8	49,876	70,961
7	Sweden	0.988	1	0.941	0.952	84.9	81.1	20.5[e]	18.3[f]	12.8	12.4	49,580	59,326
8	Ireland	0.987	1	0.934	0.947	83.8	80.2	19.2[e]	18.6[f]	11.8[i]	11.4[i]	61,104	91,506[d]
9	Germany	0.978	1	0.931	0.952	83.2	78.1	17.0	17.0	13.8[i]	14.3[i]	46,150	63,143
10	Netherlands	0.968	2	0.925	0.956	83.4	80.0	19.0[e,i]	18.4[f,i]	12.4	12.8	46,301	65,778
11	Finland	0.989	1	0.934	0.945	84.7	79.3	19.9[e]	18.3[f]	13.0	12.7	41,698	57,394
12	Singapore	0.992	1	0.935	0.943	84.9	80.6	16.7	16.4	11.6	12.3	75,094[j]	105,348[d]
13	Belgium	0.978	1	0.925	0.946	84.3	79.4	20.7[e]	18.5[f]	12.3	12.4	42,533	62,295
13	New Zealand	0.975	1	0.925	0.948	84.3	80.6	20.8[e]	19.7[f]	12.9	13.0	36,864	51,377
15	Canada	0.988	1	0.929	0.941	84.7	80.6	16.9	15.9	13.9[i]	13.7[i]	38,652	55,065
16	Liechtenstein	..	..	..	..	85.4	81.1	14.2	16.2	..	..	..	..
17	Luxembourg	0.993	1	0.925	0.931	84.8	80.4	14.4	14.4	13.0[k]	13.0[i]	70,117	98,991[d]
18	United Kingdom	0.987	1	0.922	0.934	82.8	78.7	17.8	16.8	13.4	13.4	37,374	53,265
19	Japan	0.970	2	0.908	0.936	87.7[g]	81.8	15.2[i]	15.2[i]	13.3	13.4	30,621	54,597
19	Korea (Republic of)	0.944	3	0.894	0.947	86.8	80.4	16.1	16.9	11.9[i]	13.2[i]	29,300	59,737
21	United States	1.001	1	0.920	0.919	80.2	74.3	16.9	15.6	13.7	13.6	51,539	78,238[d]
22	Israel	0.992	1	0.915	0.922	84.3	80.2	16.7	15.4	13.4[i]	13.3[i]	34,960	48,126
23	Malta	0.980	1	0.907	0.925	86.1	81.4	17.4	16.3	12.0	12.4	30,282	46,821
23	Slovenia	0.999	1	0.915	0.916	83.8	77.6	18.4[e]	16.9	12.8	12.8	33,038	46,386
25	Austria	0.980	1	0.906	0.924	84.1	79.0	16.4	15.6	12.0	12.6	43,414	64,148
26	United Arab Emirates	0.953	2	0.877	0.921	80.9	77.2	16.5	15.2	12.5	12.8	28,921	77,318[d]
27	Spain	0.986	1	0.896	0.909	85.8	80.2	18.4[e]	17.4	10.5	10.7	31,213	45,784
28	France	0.990	1	0.898	0.907	85.5	79.4	16.2	15.5	11.4	11.8	38,403	53,988
29	Cyprus	0.972	2	0.882	0.907	83.2	79.2	15.7	15.6	12.4	12.5	30,617	45,735
30	Italy	0.970	2	0.879	0.906	85.1	80.5	16.6	15.9	10.6	10.9	31,100	55,187
31	Estonia	1.021	1	0.898	0.879	81.2	72.8	16.8	15.1	13.8	13.3	30,995	45,866
32	Czechia	0.989	1	0.884	0.893	80.9	74.7	16.8	15.7	12.7	13.0	30,455	47,289
33	Greece	0.969	2	0.872	0.900	82.9	77.5	20.1[e]	20.0[f]	11.1	11.7	22,890	35,368
34	Poland	1.008	1	0.878	0.872	80.4	72.6	16.8	15.3	13.3	13.0	25,261	41,336
35	Bahrain	0.927	3	0.829	0.894	80.0	77.8	17.0	15.9	10.8	11.2	16,786	53,359
35	Lithuania	1.030	2	0.888	0.862	78.8	68.8	16.7	15.9	13.6	13.4	33,891	42,500
35	Saudi Arabia	0.917	4	0.826	0.901	78.8	75.6	16.2	16.1	10.7	11.7	20,678	64,708
38	Portugal	0.994	1	0.863	0.867	84.1	77.8	17.0	16.7	9.6	9.5	28,713	38,127
39	Latvia	1.025	1	0.873	0.852	77.8	69.2	16.8	15.6	13.6	12.9	27,882	38,506
40	Andorra	..	..	..	..	84.3	77.2	..	..	10.5[i]	10.6[i]	..	..
40	Croatia	0.995	1	0.855	0.859	81.1	74.2	15.9	14.4	11.9[i]	12.5[i]	23,888	36,713
42	Chile	0.967	2	0.838	0.867	81.4	76.5	17.0	16.5	10.8[i]	11.0[i]	17,553	31,677
42	Qatar	1.019	1	0.866	0.850	80.9	78.3	14.5	12.1	11.6[i]	9.6[i]	42,101	104,066[d]
44	San Marino	..	..	..	..	83.5	78.4	11.8	12.8	10.9	10.7	..	..
45	Slovakia	0.999	1	0.847	0.848	78.4	71.5	15.0	14.0	12.9	13.0	24,849	36,813
46	Hungary	0.987	1	0.840	0.851	77.9	71.1	15.3[i]	14.8[i]	12.1	12.4	25,909	40,262
47	Argentina	0.997	1	0.833	0.836	78.6	72.2	19.2[e]	16.6	11.4[i]	10.9[i]	15,581	26,376
48	Türkiye	0.937	3	0.806	0.860	79.1	73.0	17.9	18.8[f]	7.9	9.4	19,079	42,929
49	Montenegro	0.981	1	0.823	0.840	79.8	73.0	15.6	14.6	11.8[i]	12.6[i]	15,935	26,001
50	Kuwait	1.009	1	0.831	0.824	81.5	77.2	17.0[i]	13.9[i]	8.1[i]	6.9[i]	28,086	68,827
51	Brunei Darussalam	0.984	1	0.819	0.833	76.9	72.6	14.4	13.5	9.2[i]	9.2	47,579	80,261[d]
52	Russian Federation	1.016	1	0.828	0.815	74.8	64.2	16.0	15.6	12.8[k]	12.8[k]	21,857	33,288
53	Romania	0.994	1	0.819	0.823	77.9	70.6	14.7	13.8	11.0	11.6	24,554	35,874
54	Oman	0.900	4	0.752	0.835	74.7	71.0	15.0	14.5	12.1	11.4	7,169	39,717
55	Bahamas	..	..	..	..	75.1	68.1	..	..	12.7[i]	12.6[i]	25,897	35,495
56	Kazakhstan	0.998	1	0.809	0.811	73.1	65.5	16.0	15.5	12.4[i]	12.3[i]	18,976	29,305
57	Trinidad and Tobago	0.985	1	0.801	0.814	76.4	69.7	14.8[m]	14.2[m]	11.7[i]	11.5[i]	16,794	30,166
58	Costa Rica	0.996	1	0.806	0.810	79.8	74.4	17.1	16.0	8.9	8.7	16,568	23,376
58	Uruguay	1.022	1	0.812	0.795	79.3	71.7	17.3[n]	15.4[n]	9.3	8.7	17,125	25,680

Continued →

TABLE 4

		Gender Development Index		Human Development Index Value		Life expectancy at birth (years) SDG 3		Expected years of schooling (years) SDG 4.3		Mean years of schooling (years) SDG 4.4		Estimated gross national income per capita[a] (2017 PPP $) SDG 8.5	
		Value	Group[b]	Female	Male	Female	Male	Female	Male	Female	Male	Female	Male
HDI RANK		2021	2021	2021	2021	2021	2021	2021[c]	2021[c]	2021[c]	2021[c]	2021	2021
60	Belarus	1.011	1	0.812	0.803	77.7	67.3	15.3	15.0	12.2	12.1	15,158	23,165
61	Panama	1.017	1	0.812	0.798	79.6	73.0	13.6[i]	12.5[i]	10.8	10.3	23,380	30,531
62	Malaysia	0.982	1	0.794	0.809	77.4	72.7	13.8	12.9	10.6	10.7	20,672	32,380
63	Georgia	1.007	1	0.803	0.798	76.7	66.8	15.9	15.2	12.9	12.8	11,285	18,472
63	Mauritius	0.973	2	0.789	0.811	76.8	70.4	15.9[i]	14.5[i]	10.0[i]	10.9[i]	15,016	29,221
63	Serbia	0.982	1	0.794	0.808	77.2	71.2	15.0	13.9	11.0	11.8	15,306	23,270
66	Thailand	1.012	1	0.805	0.796	83.0	74.5	16.2[m]	15.6[m]	8.6	8.8	15,457	18,694
High human development													
67	Albania	1.007	1	0.799	0.794	79.2	74.1	15.3	13.7	11.7[i]	10.9[i]	11,637	16,630
68	Bulgaria	0.995	1	0.792	0.796	75.5	68.4	14.2	13.6	11.5	11.3	18,109	28,357
68	Grenada	..	..	..	..	77.9	72.2	19.3[e,j]	18.1[i,j]	..	..	..	..
70	Barbados	1.034	2	0.799	0.773	79.4	75.6	17.7[i]	13.8[i]	10.3[o]	9.1[o]	10,235	14,555
71	Antigua and Barbuda	..	..	..	..	80.9	75.8	15.2[i]	13.2[i]	..	..	..	..
72	Seychelles	..	..	..	..	75.7	67.7	15.1	12.9	10.2	10.4	..	..
73	Sri Lanka	0.949	3	0.755	0.795	79.5	73.1	14.5[i]	13.8[i]	10.8	10.8	7,005	18,573
74	Bosnia and Herzegovina	0.940	3	0.754	0.802	77.5	73.1	14.1[p]	13.5[p]	9.8	11.4	10,709	19,917
75	Saint Kitts and Nevis	..	..	..	..	75.3	68.3	16.0[i]	14.9[i]	..	..	..	..
76	Iran (Islamic Republic of)	0.880	5	0.704	0.800	76.8	71.2	14.7	14.5	10.6[i]	10.7[i]	3,767	22,041
77	Ukraine	1.012	1	0.776	0.766	76.7	66.5	15.0[i]	14.9[i]	11.5[o]	10.7[o]	10,370	16,605
78	North Macedonia	0.945	3	0.746	0.789	76.2	71.7	13.9[i]	13.4[i]	9.7	10.8	11,147	20,716
79	China	0.984	1	0.761	0.773	81.2	75.5	14.8[i]	13.7[i]	7.3[o]	7.9[o]	13,980	20,883
80	Dominican Republic	1.014	1	0.772	0.761	76.3	69.3	15.4[i]	13.6[i]	9.6[n]	9.0[n]	13,695	22,248
80	Moldova (Republic of)	1.010	1	0.771	0.763	73.5	64.4	14.8	14.1	11.9	11.8	12,087	17,961
80	Palau	..	..	..	..	70.6	62.4	16.0[i]	15.5[i]	..	..	..	..
83	Cuba	0.961	2	0.745	0.775	76.4	71.2	15.1	13.8	12.6[i]	12.4[i]	5,103	10,693
84	Peru	0.950	2	0.742	0.781	74.7	70.1	15.2[i]	15.5[i]	9.3[i]	10.5[i]	9,813	14,727
85	Armenia	1.001	1	0.757	0.756	77.4	66.6	13.8	12.5	11.3	11.3	8,736	18,558
86	Mexico	0.989	1	0.753	0.761	74.9	66.1	15.2	14.5	9.1	9.4	12,456	23,600
87	Brazil	0.994	1	0.750	0.755	76.0	69.6	16.0	15.2	8.3[i]	7.9[i]	10,903	17,960
88	Colombia	0.984	1	0.744	0.756	76.4	69.4	14.7	14.2	9.0	8.7	10,281	18,599
89	Saint Vincent and the Grenadines	0.970	2	0.739	0.761	72.4	67.4	14.9[i]	14.5[i]	10.9	10.7	8,720	15,075
90	Maldives	0.925	3	0.709	0.766	81.0	79.1	14.2	11.9	7.1	7.5	6,359	22,119
91	Algeria	0.880	5	0.680	0.773	78.0	74.9	15.3[m]	14.0[m]	7.7[i]	8.4[i]	3,550	17,787
91	Azerbaijan	0.974	2	0.734	0.753	73.3	65.6	13.6	13.4	10.2	10.9	10,536	18,076
91	Tonga	0.965	2	0.728	0.754	73.7	68.4	16.3[i]	15.7[i]	11.5[o]	11.2[o]	4,842	8,845
91	Turkmenistan	0.956	2	0.726	0.760	72.7	65.9	13.0	13.4	10.9	11.6	9,227	16,884
95	Ecuador	0.980	1	0.731	0.745	77.5	70.3	14.9	14.3	8.8	8.8	7,451	13,180
96	Mongolia	1.031	2	0.749	0.726	75.7	66.5	15.6	14.4	9.9	8.8	8,541	12,666
97	Egypt	0.882	5	0.666	0.755	72.6	67.9	13.8[i]	13.7[i]	9.8[i]	9.4[i]	3,536	19,741
97	Tunisia	0.931	3	0.697	0.748	77.1	70.7	16.5[i]	14.5[i]	6.9[i]	8.0[i]	4,870	15,778
99	Fiji	0.931	3	0.698	0.750	68.9	65.4	15.0[i]	14.5[i]	11.0[i]	10.8[i]	5,664	14,270
99	Suriname	1.001	1	0.728	0.727	73.6	67.2	14.2[m]	11.9[m]	9.9[m]	9.6[m]	8,866	16,506
101	Uzbekistan	0.944	3	0.703	0.744	73.4	68.3	12.4	12.6	11.7	12.1	5,427	10,403
102	Dominica	..	..	..	..	76.3	69.7	14.6[i]	12.2[i]	..	..	..	..
102	Jordan	0.887	5	0.663	0.748	76.8	72.1	10.8	10.5	10.1	10.8	3,778	15,631
104	Libya	0.975	1	0.708	0.726	74.4	69.6	13.1[q]	12.6[q]	8.5[r]	7.2[r]	9,570	20,960
105	Paraguay	0.990	1	0.713	0.720	73.4	67.4	13.6[n]	12.4[n]	8.9	8.9	9,410	15,265
106	Palestine, State of	0.891	5	0.655	0.735	75.9	71.1	14.3	12.5	9.9	10.0	2,250	10,937
106	Saint Lucia	1.011	1	0.719	0.711	74.7	67.8	13.4	12.4	8.8	8.3	9,991	14,147
108	Guyana	0.978	1	0.704	0.720	69.1	62.5	12.8[i]	12.2[i]	8.7	8.5	14,735	30,534
109	South Africa	0.944	3	0.686	0.727	65.0	59.5	14.0	13.3	9.7	12.2	9,935	16,129
110	Jamaica	0.990	1	0.704	0.711	72.5	68.5	13.7[m]	13.1[m]	9.7[i]	8.5[i]	6,982	10,715
111	Samoa	0.957	2	0.685	0.716	75.5	70.3	13.0	11.9	11.8	11.0	3,223	7,312
112	Gabon	0.908	4	0.667	0.735	68.5	63.5	12.6[q]	13.4[q]	7.8[s]	10.5[s]	9,376	17,212
112	Lebanon	0.882	5	0.650	0.737	77.3	72.8	11.1[t]	11.5[t]	8.5[q]	8.9[q]	3,815	15,586
114	Indonesia	0.941	3	0.681	0.723	69.7	65.5	13.8[i]	13.7[i]	8.2	8.9	7,906	14,976
115	Viet Nam	1.002	1	0.704	0.702	78.2	69.1	13.2[u]	12.7[u]	8.0	8.7	6,932	8,826
Medium human development													
116	Philippines	0.990	1	0.695	0.702	71.5	67.2	13.5	12.8	9.2	8.7	7,487	10,311
117	Botswana	0.981	1	0.686	0.700	63.6	58.7	12.4[i]	12.2[i]	10.3	10.4	13,839	18,618

Continued →

TABLE 4 / GENDER DEVELOPMENT INDEX 287

TABLE 4

		Gender Development Index		Human Development Index		SDG 3 Life expectancy at birth (years)		SDG 4.3 Expected years of schooling (years)		SDG 4.4 Mean years of schooling (years)		SDG 8.5 Estimated gross national income per capita[a] (2017 PPP $)	
		Value	Group[b]	Value Female	Male	Female	Male	Female	Male	Female	Male	Female	Male
HDI RANK		2021	2021	2021	2021	2021	2021	2021[c]	2021[c]	2021[c]	2021[c]	2021	2021
118	Bolivia (Plurinational State of)	0.964	2	0.680	0.705	66.8	60.9	14.9	15.0	9.2	10.5	6,856	9,359
118	Kyrgyzstan	0.966	2	0.675	0.698	74.4	65.8	13.4	13.0	11.6 [o]	11.1 [o]	2,863	6,331
120	Venezuela (Bolivarian Republic of)	0.983	1	0.679	0.691	75.2	66.3	13.8 [t]	11.8 [t]	11.4 [i]	10.8 [i]	2,866	6,796
121	Iraq	0.803	5	0.585	0.728	72.4	68.2	11.5 [u]	12.7 [u]	7.2 [m]	8.4 [m]	2,184	17,748
122	Tajikistan	0.909	4	0.648	0.713	73.7	69.6	11.2 [i]	12.1 [i]	10.9 [o]	11.8 [o]	2,980	6,096
123	Belize	0.975	1	0.672	0.689	74.3	67.1	13.3	12.7	9.0	8.7	4,249	8,345
123	Morocco	0.861	5	0.621	0.722	76.4	71.9	13.9	14.4	5.0	6.9	3,194	11,356
125	El Salvador	0.964	2	0.660	0.685	75.1	66.1	12.7 [n]	12.6 [n]	6.8	7.6	5,824	11,015
126	Nicaragua	0.956	2	0.648	0.678	76.8	70.8	12.7 [i]	12.6 [n]	7.4	6.8	3,646	7,661
127	Bhutan	0.937	3	0.641	0.684	73.8	70.1	13.6 [i]	12.8 [i]	4.5 [i]	5.8 [i]	6,671	11,896
128	Cabo Verde	0.981	1	0.653	0.666	78.5	69.6	12.8 [i]	12.3 [i]	6.0 [t]	6.6 [t]	4,682	7,796
129	Bangladesh	0.898	5	0.617	0.688	74.3	70.6	13.0	11.9	6.8	8.0	2,811	8,176
130	Tuvalu	..	..	..	..	69.1	60.8	9.5 [i]	9.3 [i]	10.4	10.8	..	..
131	Marshall Islands	..	..	..	..	67.2	63.7	10.4	10.1	10.7	11.1	..	..
132	India	0.849	5	0.567	0.668	68.9	65.8	11.9	11.8	6.3 [o]	7.2 [o]	2,277	10,633
133	Ghana	0.946	3	0.614	0.649	66.0	61.6	12.1	12.0	7.8 [o]	9.0 [o]	4,723	6,771
134	Micronesia (Federated States of)	..	..	..	..	74.6	67.1	..	..	..	..	..	..
135	Guatemala	0.917	4	0.596	0.650	72.7	66.0	10.5	10.6	5.2	6.2	4,909	12,614
136	Kiribati	..	..	..	..	69.1	65.5	12.4	11.3	..	..	..	..
137	Honduras	0.960	2	0.607	0.633	72.5	67.9	10.4 [n]	9.9 [n]	6.8	7.4	4,271	6,304
138	Sao Tome and Principe	0.907	4	0.584	0.643	70.4	65.2	13.5	13.3	5.6 [m]	6.8 [m]	2,415	5,635
139	Namibia	1.004	1	0.616	0.613	63.0	55.7	11.9 [v]	11.9 [v]	7.5 [o]	6.9 [o]	7,271	10,094
140	Lao People's Democratic Republic	0.949	3	0.591	0.623	70.1	66.2	9.9	10.3	5.0	5.8	6,757	8,627
140	Timor-Leste	0.917	4	0.580	0.633	69.5	66.1	12.2 [t]	13.0 [t]	4.7	6.2	3,642	5,248
140	Vanuatu	..	..	..	..	72.9	68.4	11.4 [i]	11.7 [i]	..	..	2,354	3,809
143	Nepal	0.942	3	0.584	0.621	70.4	66.6	12.9	12.8	4.2 [o]	6.2 [o]	3,677	4,095
144	Eswatini (Kingdom of)	0.986	1	0.593	0.601	61.2	53.4	13.2 [i]	14.2 [i]	5.7	5.5	6,384	8,993
145	Equatorial Guinea	..	..	..	..	62.7	58.8	..	..	4.2 [p]	7.6 [p]	8,351	15,399
146	Cambodia	0.926	3	0.570	0.615	72.3	66.8	11.0 [w]	11.9 [w]	4.4	5.9	3,464	4,706
146	Zimbabwe	0.961	2	0.580	0.604	62.0	56.2	12.0 [i]	12.3 [i]	8.3 [i]	9.2 [i]	3,286	4,397
148	Angola	0.903	4	0.557	0.617	64.3	59.0	11.5	12.9	4.2	6.9	4,751	6,197
149	Myanmar	0.944	3	0.565	0.599	69.0	62.5	11.1 [i]	10.7 [i]	6.1	6.7	2,619	5,093
150	Syrian Arab Republic	0.825	5	0.503	0.610	75.2	69.1	9.1	9.2	4.6 [q]	5.6 [q]	1,285	7,088
151	Cameroon	0.885	5	0.540	0.610	62.0	58.7	12.4 [i]	13.8 [i]	4.8 [o]	7.5 [o]	2,981	4,264
152	Kenya	0.941	3	0.557	0.592	64.1	58.9	10.3 [i]	11.1 [i]	6.1	7.3	3,873	5,084
153	Congo	0.934	3	0.552	0.590	64.9	62.1	12.2 [i]	12.4 [i]	5.6	6.8	2,532	3,247
154	Zambia	0.965	2	0.554	0.574	63.9	58.5	10.9 [w]	11.0 [w]	7.2 [o]	7.2 [o]	2,615	3,837
155	Solomon Islands	..	..	..	..	72.0	68.9	10.8 [i]	9.9 [i]	..	..	2,173	2,777
156	Comoros	0.891	5	0.522	0.585	65.8	61.2	12.2 [i]	11.7 [i]	4.0 [q]	6.0 [q]	2,014	4,260
156	Papua New Guinea	0.931	3	0.538	0.578	68.4	62.9	9.8 [v]	10.9 [v]	4.1	5.4	3,543	4,445
158	Mauritania	0.890	5	0.518	0.582	66.1	62.7	9.6	9.2	4.6 [o]	5.3 [o]	2,604	7,650
159	Côte d'Ivoire	0.887	5	0.516	0.581	59.9	57.4	10.0	11.3	4.7 [o]	5.7 [o]	3,763	6,643
Low human development													
160	Tanzania (United Republic of)	0.943	3	0.532	0.565	68.3	64.2	9.3	9.1	5.9 [i]	6.9 [i]	2,247	3,092
161	Pakistan	0.810	5	0.471	0.582	68.6	63.8	8.1	9.2	3.9	5.0	1,569	7,620
162	Togo	0.849	5	0.497	0.586	62.4	60.8	12.2 [i]	14.3 [i]	3.4 [o]	6.8 [o]	1,885	2,446
163	Haiti	0.898	5	0.506	0.564	66.1	60.4	9.0 [i]	10.4 [i]	4.6	6.8	2,408	3,295
163	Nigeria	0.863	5	0.495	0.574	53.1	52.3	9.6 [v]	10.8 [v]	6.1 [w]	8.2 [w]	3,759	5,800
165	Rwanda	0.954	2	0.521	0.547	68.2	63.8	11.2	11.2	4.0 [i]	4.9 [i]	1,990	2,440
166	Benin	0.880	5	0.491	0.558	61.4	58.2	9.9	11.6	3.3 [o]	5.4 [o]	2,998	3,819
166	Uganda	0.927	3	0.505	0.545	64.9	60.4	10.2 [v]	10.1 [v]	4.9 [o]	6.7 [o]	1,877	2,492
168	Lesotho	0.985	1	0.511	0.519	55.9	50.4	12.4 [i]	11.7 [i]	6.6 [o]	6.0 [o]	2,107	3,310
169	Malawi	0.968	2	0.502	0.519	66.5	59.5	12.8 [i]	12.5 [i]	4.1 [o]	4.7 [o]	1,232	1,713
170	Senegal	0.874	5	0.475	0.543	69.3	64.8	9.5	8.5	1.6 [i]	4.5 [i]	2,258	4,468
171	Djibouti	..	..	..	..	65.0	59.7	7.5 [i]	7.4 [i]	..	..	2,179	7,911
172	Sudan	0.870	5	0.466	0.535	67.9	62.7	7.7 [i]	8.1 [i]	3.4	4.2	1,833	5,320
173	Madagascar	0.956	2	0.490	0.512	66.9	62.2	10.2 [i]	10.1 [i]	4.9 [v]	5.3 [v]	1,284	1,682
174	Gambia	0.924	4	0.481	0.520	63.5	60.7	10.3 [v]	8.5 [v]	3.8	5.6	1,649	2,701
175	Ethiopia	0.921	4	0.478	0.519	68.3	61.9	9.8 [i]	9.6 [i]	2.2	4.2	1,944	2,774
176	Eritrea	..	..	..	..	68.7	64.3	7.5 [i]	8.6 [i]	..	..	1,387	2,079

Continued →

TABLE 4

	Gender Development Index		Human Development Index Value		SDG 3 Life expectancy at birth (years)		SDG 4.3 Expected years of schooling (years)		SDG 4.4 Mean years of schooling (years)		SDG 8.5 Estimated gross national income per capita[a] (2017 PPP $)	
	Value	Group[b]	Female	Male	Female	Male	Female	Male	Female	Male	Female	Male
HDI RANK	2021	2021	2021	2021	2021	2021	2021[c]	2021[c]	2021[c]	2021[c]	2021	2021
177 Guinea-Bissau	0.867	5	0.448	0.517	61.8	57.4	10.0[i]	11.2[i]	2.4	4.9	1,561	2,264
178 Liberia	0.871	5	0.447	0.513	62.1	59.4	10.1	10.8	3.9	6.3	1,062	1,518
179 Congo (Democratic Republic of the)	0.885	5	0.449	0.507	61.5	57.0	9.6[i]	10.1[i]	5.6[m]	8.5[m]	896	1,259
180 Afghanistan	0.681	5	0.365	0.536	65.3	58.9	7.7[i]	12.7[i]	2.3	3.4	533	3,089
181 Sierra Leone	0.893	5	0.452	0.506	61.4	58.8	9.6[i]	9.9[i]	3.5[o]	5.8[o]	1,453	1,789
182 Guinea	0.850	5	0.426	0.501	60.1	57.6	8.6[i]	11.0[i]	1.3[i]	3.2[i]	2,320	2,645
183 Yemen	0.496	5	0.263	0.529	67.1	60.6	7.7	10.5	2.9[x]	5.1[x]	176	2,428
184 Burkina Faso	0.903	4	0.425	0.471	61.0	57.5	9.1	9.2	1.6[i]	2.7[i]	1,659	2,580
185 Mozambique	0.922	4	0.428	0.464	62.4	56.2	9.8[i]	10.7[i]	2.4[i]	4.1[i]	1,096	1,304
186 Mali	0.887	5	0.399	0.450	60.3	57.6	6.8[i]	7.9[i]	2.4	2.2	1,483	2,770
187 Burundi	0.935	3	0.412	0.441	63.6	59.7	10.9[i]	10.5[i]	2.5[i]	3.9[i]	668	797
188 Central African Republic	0.810	5	0.359	0.443	56.3	51.6	6.7[i]	9.4[i]	3.1	5.6	770	1,162
189 Niger	0.835	5	0.364	0.436	62.8	60.4	6.3[i]	7.6[i]	1.7[o]	2.8[o]	936	1,535
190 Chad	0.770	5	0.339	0.441	54.3	50.8	6.6[i]	9.5[i]	1.5[v]	3.7[v]	965	1,760
191 South Sudan	0.843	5	0.348	0.413	56.5	53.4	4.5[i]	6.6[i]	4.8	6.2	664	873
Other countries or territories												
Korea (Democratic People's Rep. of)	..	..	..	..	75.7	70.8	10.4[t]	11.1[t]	..	..	..	..
Monaco	..	..	..	..	87.7[q]	84.3[h]	..	..	..	..	..	..
Nauru	..	..	..	..	67.3	60.3	13.1[i]	10.4[i]	..	..	..	..
Somalia	..	..	..	..	57.4	53.2	..	..	..	..	545	1,489
Human development groups												
Very high human development	0.986	–	0.889	0.901	81.6	75.6	16.9	16.1	12.2	12.4	33,849	53,887
High human development	0.973	–	0.742	0.763	77.7	71.9	14.6	13.8	8.1	8.5	11,187	19,089
Medium human development	0.880	–	0.586	0.666	69.4	65.6	12.0	11.9	6.5	7.4	2,912	9,668
Low human development	0.864	–	0.477	0.552	63.4	59.3	9.0	9.9	4.1	5.7	1,907	4,107
Developing countries	0.937	–	0.660	0.704	72.3	67.6	12.3	12.3	7.2	7.9	7,097	14,230
Regions												
Arab States	0.871	–	0.645	0.741	73.1	68.9	12.2	12.5	7.6	8.6	4,745	21,667
East Asia and the Pacific	0.978	–	0.740	0.756	78.5	72.9	14.2	13.4	7.6	8.1	12,357	18,711
Europe and Central Asia	0.961	–	0.778	0.810	76.4	69.4	15.3	15.6	10.4	10.8	13,162	25,834
Latin America and the Caribbean	0.986	–	0.747	0.757	75.6	68.8	15.2	14.4	9.0	9.0	10,667	18,486
South Asia	0.852	–	0.568	0.667	69.8	66.1	11.5	11.6	6.3	7.3	2,352	10,426
Sub-Saharan Africa	0.907	–	0.519	0.572	62.1	58.2	10.0	10.6	5.1	6.9	2,970	4,429
Least developed countries	0.894	–	0.508	0.568	66.6	61.9	10.0	10.4	4.5	6.0	1,993	3,777
Small island developing states	0.962	–	0.715	0.743	73.1	67.8	12.5	12.4	8.9	9.4	12,634	20,928
Organisation for Economic Co-operation and Development	0.985	–	0.891	0.905	82.0	76.1	16.8	16.1	12.2	12.4	35,117	55,363
World	**0.958**	**–**	**0.715**	**0.747**	**74.0**	**68.9**	**12.9**	**12.7**	**8.4**	**8.9**	**12,241**	**21,210**

TABLE 4 / GENDER DEVELOPMENT INDEX   289

TABLE 4

Notes

a Because disaggregated income data are not available, data are crudely estimated. See *Definitions* and *Technical note 3* at http://hdr.undp.org/sites/default/files/hdr2022_technical_notes.pdf for details on how the Gender Development Index is calculated.

b Countries are divided into five groups by absolute deviation from gender parity in HDI values.

c Data refer to 2021 or the most recent year available.

d In calculating the male HDI value, estimated gross national income per capita is capped at $75,000.

e In calculating the female HDI value, expected years of schooling is capped at 18 years.

f In calculating the male HDI value, expected years of schooling is capped at 18 years.

g In calculating the female HDI value, life expectancy at birth is capped at 87.5 years.

h In calculating the male HDI value, life expectancy at birth is capped at 82.5 years.

i Updated by HDRO based on data from UNESCO Institute for Statistics (2022).

j In calculating the female HDI value, estimated gross national income per capita is capped at $75,000.

k Updated by HDRO based on data from OECD (2022) and UNESCO Institute for Statistics (2022).

l HDRO estimate based on data from Robert Barro and Jong-Wha Lee, ICF Macro Demographic and Health Surveys, the Organisation for Economic Co-operation and Development, United Nations Children's Fund (UNICEF) Multiple Indicator Cluster Surveys and the United Nations Educational, Scientific and Cultural Organization Institute for Statistics.

m Updated by HDRO based on data from UNESCO Institute for Statistics (2022) and UNICEF Multiple Indicator Cluster Surveys for various years.

n Updated by HDRO based on data from CEDLAS and World Bank (2022) and UNESCO Institute for Statistics (2022).

o Updated by HDRO based on data from Barro and Lee (2018) and UNESCO Institute for Statistics (2022).

p Based on data from the national statistical office.

q Based on cross-country regression.

r Updated by HDRO using projections from Barro and Lee (2018).

s Updated by HDRO based on data from Barro and Lee (2018) and ICF Macro Demographic and Health Surveys for various years.

t Updated by HDRO based on data from the United Nations Educational, Scientific and Cultural Organization Institute for Statistics for various years.

u Updated by HDRO based on data from UNICEF Multiple Indicator Cluster Surveys for various years.

v Updated by HDRO based on data from ICF Macro Demographic and Health Surveys for various years and UNESCO Institute for Statistics (2022).

w Updated by HDRO based on data from ICF Macro Demographic and Health Surveys for various years.

x Based on projections from Barro and Lee (2018).

Definitions

Gender Development Index: Ratio of female to male HDI values. See *Technical note 3* at http://hdr.undp.org/sites/default/files/hdr2022_technical_notes.pdf for details on how the Gender Development Index is calculated.

Gender Development Index groups: Countries are divided into five groups by absolute deviation from gender parity in HDI values. Group 1 comprises countries with high equality in HDI achievements between women and men (absolute deviation of less than 2.5 percent), group 2 comprises countries with medium to high equality in HDI achievements between women and men (absolute deviation of 2.5–5 percent), group 3 comprises countries with medium equality in HDI achievements between women and men (absolute deviation of 5–7.5 percent), group 4 comprises countries with medium to low equality in HDI achievements between women and men (absolute deviation of 7.5–10 percent) and group 5 comprises countries with low equality in HDI achievements between women and men (absolute deviation from gender parity of more than 10 percent).

Human Development Index (HDI): A composite index measuring average achievement in three basic dimensions of human development—a long and healthy life, knowledge and a decent standard of living. See *Technical note 1* at http://hdr.undp.org/sites/default/files/hdr2022_technical_notes.pdf for details on how the HDI is calculated.

Life expectancy at birth: Number of years a newborn infant could expect to live if prevailing patterns of age-specific mortality rates at the time of birth stay the same throughout the infant's life.

Expected years of schooling: Number of years of schooling that a child of school entrance age can expect to receive if prevailing patterns of age-specific enrolment rates persist throughout the child's life.

Mean years of schooling: Average number of years of education received by people ages 25 and older, converted from educational attainment levels using official durations of each level.

Estimated gross national income per capita: Derived from the ratio of female to male wages, female and male shares of economically active population and gross national income (in 2017 purchasing power parity terms). See *Technical note 3* at http://hdr.undp.org/sites/default/files/hdr2022_technical_notes.pdf for details.

Main data sources

Column 1: Calculated based on data in columns 3 and 4.

Column 2: Calculated based on data in column 1.

Columns 3 and 4: HDRO calculations based on data from Barro and Lee (2018), ILO (2022), IMF (2022), UNDESA (2022a), UNESCO Institute for Statistics (2022), United Nations Statistics Division (2022) and World Bank (2022).

Columns 5 and 6: UNDESA (2022a).

Columns 7 and 8: CEDLAS and World Bank (2022), ICF Macro Demographic and Health Surveys, UNESCO Institute for Statistics (2022) and UNICEF Multiple Indicator Cluster Surveys.

Columns 9 and 10: Barro and Lee (2018), ICF Macro Demographic and Health Surveys, OECD (2022), UNESCO Institute for Statistics (2022) and UNICEF Multiple Indicator Cluster Surveys.

Columns 11 and 12: HDRO calculations based on ILO (2022), IMF (2022), UNDESA (2022a), United Nations Statistics Division (2022) and World Bank (2022).

TABLE 5

Gender Inequality Index

		Gender Inequality Index		Maternal mortality ratio	Adolescent birth rate	Share of seats in parliament	Population with at least some secondary education		Labour force participation rate[a]	
				SDG 3.1	SDG 3.7	SDG 5.5	SDG 4.4			
							(% ages 25 and older)		(% ages 15 and older)	
		Value	Rank	(deaths per 100,000 live births)	(births per 1,000 women ages 15–19)	(% held by women)	Female	Male	Female	Male
HDI RANK		2021	2021	2017	2021	2021	2021[b]	2021[b]	2021	2021
Very high human development										
1	Switzerland	0.018	3	5	2.2	39.8	96.9	97.5	61.7	72.7
2	Norway	0.016	2	2	2.3	45.0	99.1	99.3	60.3	72.0
3	Iceland	0.043	8	4	5.4	47.6	99.8	99.7	61.7	70.5
4	Hong Kong, China (SAR)	..	..	..	1.6	..	77.1	83.4	53.5	65.8
5	Australia	0.073	19	6	8.1	37.9	94.6	94.4	61.1	70.5
6	Denmark	0.013	1	4	1.9	39.7	95.1	95.2	57.7	66.7
7	Sweden	0.023	4	4	3.3	47.0	91.8	92.2	61.7	68.0
8	Ireland	0.074	21	5	5.9	27.3	88.1[c]	86.0[c]	56.5	68.6
9	Germany	0.073	19	7	7.5	34.8	96.1[c]	96.5[c]	56.8	66.0
10	Netherlands	0.025	5	5	2.8	39.1	89.8	92.7	62.4	71.3
11	Finland	0.033	6	3	4.2	46.0	99.0	98.5	56.5	64.0
12	Singapore	0.040	7	8	2.6	29.8	80.5	85.9	59.4	76.8
13	Belgium	0.048	10	5	5.3	42.9	87.2	89.7	49.8	58.8
13	New Zealand	0.088	25	9	12.6	49.2	82.0	81.8	65.1	75.3
15	Canada	0.069	17	10	7.0	34.4	100.0[d]	100.0[d]	60.8	69.7
16	Liechtenstein	..	..	..	3.0	28.0	..	..	..	..
17	Luxembourg	0.044	9	5	4.3	35.0	100.0[e]	100.0[e]	58.5	65.5
18	United Kingdom	0.098	27	7	10.5	31.1	99.8	99.8	58.0	67.1
19	Japan	0.083	22	5	2.9	14.2	95.9	92.7	53.3	71.0
19	Korea (Republic of)	0.067	15	11	2.2	19.0	83.1[c]	93.1[c]	53.4	72.4
21	United States	0.179	44	19	16.0	27.0	96.5	96.4	55.2	66.4
22	Israel	0.083	22	3	7.6	28.3	91.6[c]	93.7[c]	58.5	66.1
23	Malta	0.167	42	6	11.5	13.4	82.2	88.1	53.1	71.4
23	Slovenia	0.071	18	7	4.5	21.5	97.6	98.7	53.8	62.2
25	Austria	0.053	12	5	5.5	39.3	100.0[d]	100.0[d]	55.5	66.3
26	United Arab Emirates	0.049	11	3	3.1	50.0	82.0	85.6	46.5	88.0
27	Spain	0.057	14	4	6.3	42.3	78.5	83.2	52.7	62.4
28	France	0.083	22	8	9.5	37.8	83.5	87.9	51.9	59.7
29	Cyprus	0.123	35	6	6.8	14.3	81.1	84.8	56.6	68.8
30	Italy	0.056	13	2	4.0	35.3	78.6	86.1	39.9	57.6
31	Estonia	0.100	28	9	8.8	25.7	97.6	98.1	57.5	70.2
32	Czechia	0.120	34	3	9.7	22.1	99.8	99.8	51.7	68.1
33	Greece	0.119	32	3	8.5	21.7	69.9	77.8	43.3	58.1
34	Poland	0.109	31	2	9.7	27.5	86.5	90.7	49.2	65.5
35	Bahrain	0.181	46	14	8.7	18.8	79.9	83.1	42.4	83.5
35	Lithuania	0.105	30	8	10.4	27.7	95.5	97.9	57.3	67.9
35	Saudi Arabia	0.247	59	17	11.9	19.9	71.3	80.9	30.9	80.1
38	Portugal	0.067	15	8	7.4	40.0	59.7	61.9	54.0	62.2
39	Latvia	0.151	40	19	11.2	29.0	99.7[c]	99.3[c]	54.5	66.8
40	Andorra	..	..	..	5.9	46.4	70.7[c]	72.4[c]	..	..
40	Croatia	0.093	26	8	8.6	31.1	97.0[c]	100.0[c]	45.9	58.8
42	Chile	0.187	47	13	24.1	32.7	80.3[c]	83.5[c]	44.2	65.5
42	Qatar	0.220	54	9	7.1	4.4	79.8[c]	69.6[c]	57.2	95.5
44	San Marino	..	..	..	3.8	33.3	81.8	84.3	..	..
45	Slovakia	0.180	45	5	26.3	22.7	98.9	99.2	54.7	66.4
46	Hungary	0.221	55	12	22.1	13.1	97.6	98.8	52.1	67.2
47	Argentina	0.287	69	39	39.1	44.4	71.0[f]	71.4[f]	50.0	71.6
48	Türkiye	0.272	65	17	16.9	17.3	56.3	75.9	31.8	69.4
49	Montenegro	0.119	32	6	10.4	24.7	92.3[c]	99.2[c]	47.8	62.0
50	Kuwait	0.305	74	12	5.6	1.5	60.9[c]	55.2[c]	47.4	83.8
51	Brunei Darussalam	0.259	61	31	10.0	9.1	70.4	71.2	54.1	72.3
52	Russian Federation	0.203	50	17	15.0	16.5	92.8[e]	95.9[e]	54.5	69.7
53	Romania	0.282	67	19	36.4	18.5	88.8	93.7	42.8	62.3
54	Oman	0.300	72	19	9.9	9.9	96.6	99.9	28.7	85.0
55	Bahamas	0.329	78	70	25.7	20.0	87.0[c]	89.9[c]	65.6	71.5
56	Kazakhstan	0.161	41	10	21.9	24.5	99.8[c]	100.0[c]	63.3	75.5
57	Trinidad and Tobago	0.344	81	67	38.1	32.4	84.8[d]	80.6[d]	46.7	68.0
58	Costa Rica	0.256	60	27	37.1	45.6	56.2	54.5	47.5	71.1
58	Uruguay	0.235	58	17	36.2	26.2	59.6	55.5	54.8	69.3

Continued →

TABLE 5 / GENDER INEQUALITY INDEX 291

TABLE 5

		Gender Inequality Index		Maternal mortality ratio (SDG 3.1)	Adolescent birth rate (SDG 3.7)	Share of seats in parliament (SDG 5.5)	Population with at least some secondary education (SDG 4.4) (% ages 25 and older)		Labour force participation rate[a] (% ages 15 and older)	
		Value	Rank	(deaths per 100,000 live births)	(births per 1,000 women ages 15–19)	(% held by women)	Female	Male	Female	Male
HDI RANK		2021	2021	2017	2021	2021	2021[b]	2021[b]	2021	2021
60	Belarus	0.104	29	2	11.9	34.7	97.5	99.0	57.3	71.4
61	Panama	0.392	96	52	69.9	22.5	70.2	68.7	50.4	72.6
62	Malaysia	0.228	57	29	9.3	14.9	75.0	78.4	51.2	77.6
63	Georgia	0.280	66	25	31.7	19.3	97.1	98.3	51.0	68.0
63	Mauritius	0.347	82	61	24.6	20.0	64.4[c]	70.8[c]	43.4	70.4
63	Serbia	0.131	36	12	14.9	39.2	88.6	95.3	46.6	62.3
66	Thailand	0.333	79	37	32.7	13.9	47.6	51.7	59.0	75.0
High human development										
67	Albania	0.144	39	15	14.5	35.7	95.4[f]	93.0[d]	50.7	66.2
68	Bulgaria	0.210	52	10	38.6	23.8	94.9	96.5	49.1	62.6
68	Grenada	..	..	25	32.7	32.1	..	..	..	..
70	Barbados	0.268	64	27	42.3	29.4	95.4[d]	86.0[d]	56.1	63.7
71	Antigua and Barbuda	..	..	42	33.1	31.4	..	..	..	..
72	Seychelles	..	..	53	53.4	22.9	..	..	..	..
73	Sri Lanka	0.383	92	36	15.7	5.4	84.0	84.2	30.9	68.5
74	Bosnia and Herzegovina	0.136	38	10	9.9	24.6	82.7	94.0	32.3	52.4
75	Saint Kitts and Nevis	..	..	..	38.2	25.0	..	..	..	..
76	Iran (Islamic Republic of)	0.459	115	16	30.2	5.6	71.6[c]	76.0[c]	14.4	68.1
77	Ukraine	0.200	49	19	15.6	20.8	96.2[d]	95.8[f]	48.1	63.6
78	North Macedonia	0.134	37	7	16.4	41.7	61.9	75.1	42.4	63.4
79	China	0.192	48	29	11.0	24.9	78.3[d]	85.4[d]	61.6	74.3
80	Dominican Republic	0.429	106	95	65.6	25.7	77.4[c]	76.9[c]	49.6	75.2
80	Moldova (Republic of)	0.205	51	19	27.8	39.6	96.1	98.0	33.9	43.9
80	Palau	..	..	..	42.5	6.9	96.9	97.3	..	..
83	Cuba	0.303	73	36	48.8	53.4	89.5[c]	91.9[c]	40.3	68.5
84	Peru	0.380	90	88	56.8	40.0	59.3[c]	69.9[c]	66.1	81.9
85	Armenia	0.216	53	26	18.5	33.6	96.0	97.1	42.7	63.0
86	Mexico	0.309	75	33	54.4	49.8	65.1	66.7	43.8	75.4
87	Brazil	0.390	94	60	45.2	14.8	62.4[c]	59.1[c]	49.1	68.2
88	Colombia	0.424	102	83	59.0	19.6	58.9	56.5	52.2	78.0
89	Saint Vincent and the Grenadines	0.390	94	68	47.9	18.2	44.1	39.6	52.9	74.1
90	Maldives	0.348	83	53	7.3	4.6	46.4[d]	41.5[d]	34.3	67.5
91	Algeria	0.499	126	112	11.7	7.5	46.0[c]	56.9[c]	15.7	64.5
91	Azerbaijan	0.294	70	26	40.1	18.2	93.6	97.6	60.4	67.3
91	Tonga	0.631	160	52	19.0	0.0[g]	93.5[d]	93.1[d]	37.3	55.3
91	Turkmenistan	0.177	43	7	21.8	25.0	93.5	92.2	36.5	55.6
95	Ecuador	0.362	85	59	63.2	39.4	53.0	52.0	53.3	76.5
96	Mongolia	0.313	76	45	26.7	17.1	79.3	73.0	51.5	66.6
97	Egypt	0.443	109	37	44.8	22.9	81.6[c]	76.6[c]	15.4	67.1
97	Tunisia	0.259	61	43	6.7	26.3	42.9[c]	51.8[c]	25.5	67.2
99	Fiji	0.318	77	34	26.8	21.6	90.2[d]	87.9[d]	37.7	75.3
99	Suriname	0.427	105	120	56.1	29.4	69.9[h]	70.7[h]	43.4	65.1
101	Uzbekistan	0.227	56	29	15.9	28.7	99.9	100.0	44.9	70.9
102	Dominica	..	..	..	38.5	34.4	..	..	..	..
102	Jordan	0.471	118	46	25.4	11.8	77.4	84.2	13.5	62.3
104	Libya	0.259	61	72	6.9	16.0	70.5[i]	45.1[i]	34.1	61.0
105	Paraguay	0.445	111	84	70.3	16.8	52.5	54.0	59.6	84.2
106	Palestine, State of	..	..	27	43.5	..	67.9	67.6	16.7	66.3
106	Saint Lucia	0.381	91	117	36.9	24.1	49.9	43.8	63.2	73.2
108	Guyana	0.454	114	169	66.6	35.7	69.5	62.2	40.3	64.1
109	South Africa	0.405	97	119	61.2	46.0[j]	68.9	87.7	46.2	59.9
110	Jamaica	0.335	80	80	32.8	31.0	74.3[d]	66.4[d]	56.1	70.0
111	Samoa	0.418	99	43	43.6	7.8	79.1[k]	71.6[k]	30.7	54.2
112	Gabon	0.541	140	252	91.2	18.7	67.2[i]	84.0[i]	39.1	57.0
112	Lebanon	0.432	108	29	20.3	4.7	54.3[k]	55.6[k]	20.8	64.3
114	Indonesia	0.444	110	177	33.9	21.0	51.0	58.2	53.7	81.7
115	Viet Nam	0.296	71	43	34.6	30.3	61.3	69.6	69.6	79.4
Medium human development										
116	Philippines	0.419	101	121	48.2	28.0	73.4	69.1	43.8	68.3
117	Botswana	0.468	117	144	49.3	10.8	91.3	91.8	56.3	65.1
118	Bolivia (Plurinational State of)	0.418	99	155	63.8	48.2	60.1	69.7	68.3	83.8

Continued →

TABLE 5

HDI RANK	Gender Inequality Index		SDG 3.1 Maternal mortality ratio (deaths per 100,000 live births)	SDG 3.7 Adolescent birth rate (births per 1,000 women ages 15-19)	SDG 5.5 Share of seats in parliament (% held by women)	SDG 4.4 Population with at least some secondary education (% ages 25 and older)		Labour force participation rate[a] (% ages 15 and older)	
	Value	Rank				Female	Male	Female	Male
	2021	2021	2017	2021	2021	2021[b]	2021[b]	2021	2021
118 Kyrgyzstan	0.370	87	60	34.7	20.5	100.0 [d]	99.8 [d]	42.1	71.7
120 Venezuela (Bolivarian Republic of)	0.492	123	125	82.7	22.2	79.8 [d]	75.4 [d]	34.3	67.8
121 Iraq	0.558	145	79	62.2	28.9	42.0 [h]	52.9 [h]	11.1	71.8
122 Tajikistan	0.285	68	17	45.4	23.4	93.5 [d]	94.6 [d]	30.2	50.5
123 Belize	0.364	86	36	57.1	19.6	54.5	49.8	46.9	76.8
123 Morocco	0.425	104	70	25.9	20.4	30.9	37.1	22.0	66.0
125 El Salvador	0.376	88	46	55.9	27.4	42.7	51.4	43.6	72.6
126 Nicaragua	0.424	102	98	85.6	50.5	51.2	49.7	46.8	81.3
127 Bhutan	0.415	98	183	19.0	16.7	23.6	32.3	51.6	67.4
128 Cabo Verde	0.349	84	58	55.2	38.9	28.8 [m]	31.2 [m]	46.9	61.7
129 Bangladesh	0.530	131	173	75.5	20.9	50.6	58.5	34.9	78.8
130 Tuvalu	..	..	..	33.1	6.3	60.0	60.7	..	..
131 Marshall Islands	..	..	..	58.0	6.1	91.6	92.5	..	..
132 India	0.490	122	133 [n]	17.2	13.4	41.8 [d]	53.8 [d]	19.2	70.1
133 Ghana	0.529	130	308	64.2	14.5	58.0 [d]	73.2 [d]	64.5	72.2
134 Micronesia (Federated States of)	..	..	88	35.8	7.1	..	..	..	..
135 Guatemala	0.481	121	95	64.1	19.4	29.5	35.8	37.4	80.3
136 Kiribati	..	..	92	40.5	6.7	..	..	..	..
137 Honduras	0.431	107	65	72.0	27.3	35.8	44.8	42.3	78.9
138 Sao Tome and Principe	0.494	124	130	79.4	23.6	39.9 [h]	48.4 [h]	37.1	69.9
139 Namibia	0.445	111	195	64.9	35.6	41.5 [d]	44.1 [d]	54.5	62.2
140 Lao People's Democratic Republic	0.478	120	185	73.2	22.0	37.7	47.7	74.8	78.1
140 Timor-Leste	0.378	89	142	33.9	38.5	33.7	41.8	61.0	72.2
140 Vanuatu	..	..	72	64.1	0.0 [g]	..	..	59.7	78.0
143 Nepal	0.452	113	186	63.8	33.6	28.8 [d]	44.7 [d]	78.7	80.8
144 Eswatini (Kingdom of)	0.540	138	437	69.9	18.4	34.0	36.2	45.6	53.6
145 Equatorial Guinea	..	..	301	139.7	20.3	..	..	49.9	58.5
146 Cambodia	0.461	116	160	45.5	19.8	18.3	31.7	74.0	85.9
146 Zimbabwe	0.532	134	458	94.3	34.6	61.8 [c]	72.4 [c]	79.3	88.9
148 Angola	0.537	136	241	138.4	29.5	28.2	51.5	74.0	79.1
149 Myanmar	0.498	125	250	33.0	15.0	38.5	47.8	41.0	70.0
150 Syrian Arab Republic	0.477	119	31	38.7	11.2	37.1 [o]	43.4 [o]	15.7	70.8
151 Cameroon	0.565	148	529	110.4	31.1	36.8 [d]	55.0 [d]	70.2	80.7
152 Kenya	0.506	128	342	64.2	23.2	31.1 [d]	37.7 [d]	71.0	75.6
153 Congo	0.564	147	378	103.6	13.6	48.0	52.0	65.1	67.6
154 Zambia	0.540	138	213	117.0	15.1	47.1 [d]	56.8 [d]	69.2	77.8
155 Solomon Islands	..	..	104	60.3	8.0	..	..	83.1	87.4
156 Comoros	..	..	273	58.2	16.7	..	..	32.1	54.5
156 Papua New Guinea	0.725	169	145	55.3	0.0 [g]	10.8	15.5	46.3	48.1
158 Mauritania	0.632	161	766	78.0	20.3	14.5 [d]	21.9 [d]	27.4	62.2
159 Côte d'Ivoire	0.613	155	617	105.0	15.6	23.9 [d]	32.2 [d]	45.9	64.9
Low human development									
160 Tanzania (United Republic of)	0.560	146	524	123.7	36.9	13.0 [c]	19.1 [c]	79.5	87.1
161 Pakistan	0.534	135	140	42.3	19.9	22.1	28.7	20.7	78.1
162 Togo	0.580	149	396	77.9	18.7	13.9 [d]	42.3 [d]	55.5	59.4
163 Haiti	0.635	163	480	52.5	2.7 [p]	27.9	41.0	60.7	68.9
163 Nigeria	0.680	168	917	101.7	4.5	40.4 [q]	55.3 [q]	47.9	59.6
165 Rwanda	0.388	93	248	32.4	55.7	11.4 [c]	16.3 [c]	82.5	82.2
166 Benin	0.602	152	397	92.3	8.4	21.1 [d]	34.4 [d]	69.3	72.6
166 Uganda	0.530	131	375	107.9	33.8	29.3	36.3	64.2	71.3
168 Lesotho	0.557	144	544	89.6	22.9	27.2 [f]	24.6 [f]	56.1	71.3
169 Malawi	0.554	142	349	117.9	22.9	21.3 [d]	28.4 [d]	71.6	80.0
170 Senegal	0.530	131	315	66.5	43.0	11.1 [c]	30.9 [c]	33.5	56.7
171 Djibouti	..	..	248	22.7	26.2	..	..	17.2	44.1
172 Sudan	0.553	141	295	79.9	31.0 [f]	16.4	20.1	28.7	67.8
173 Madagascar	0.556	143	335	119.4	17.2	27.3 [s]	29.8 [s]	81.5	87.6
174 Gambia	0.611	153	597	63.2	8.6	29.9	43.2	48.9	66.3
175 Ethiopia	0.520	129	401	69.2	39.5	9.1	20.1	72.3	84.7
176 Eritrea	..	..	480	64.4	22.0 [p]	..	..	70.2	83.6
177 Guinea-Bissau	0.627	159	667	87.5	13.7	9.8	22.8	63.9	78.4

Continued →

TABLE 5 / GENDER INEQUALITY INDEX   293

TABLE 5

HDI RANK	Gender Inequality Index Value 2021	Gender Inequality Index Rank 2021	SDG 3.1 Maternal mortality ratio (deaths per 100,000 live births) 2017	SDG 3.7 Adolescent birth rate (births per 1,000 women ages 15–19) 2021	SDG 5.5 Share of seats in parliament (% held by women) 2021	SDG 4.4 Population with at least some secondary education (% ages 25 and older) Female 2021[b]	SDG 4.4 Population with at least some secondary education (% ages 25 and older) Male 2021[b]	Labour force participation rate[a] (% ages 15 and older) Female 2021	Labour force participation rate[a] (% ages 15 and older) Male 2021
178 Liberia	0.648	164	661	123.4	9.7	20.8	39.2	69.8	79.7
179 Congo (Democratic Republic of the)	0.601	151	473	109.0	14.3	40.3[h]	69.1[h]	61.2	69.1
180 Afghanistan	0.678	167	638	82.6	27.2	6.4	14.9	14.8	66.5
181 Sierra Leone	0.633	162	1,120	100.9	12.3	34.7[d]	51.5[d]	56.1	55.9
182 Guinea	0.621	157	576	114.8	16.7[t]	7.2[c]	19.7[c]	62.1	62.2
183 Yemen	0.820	170	164	54.4	0.3	22.4	37.5	6.0	67.6
184 Burkina Faso	0.621	157	320	110.5	6.3	11.3[c]	17.1[c]	57.2	72.7
185 Mozambique	0.537	136	289	165.8	42.4	10.8[c]	20.2[c]	77.7	78.9
186 Mali	0.613	155	562	150.1	27.3	8.0	15.5	57.7	79.7
187 Burundi	0.505	127	548	53.6	38.9	7.8[c]	13.0[c]	79.0	77.4
188 Central African Republic	0.672	166	829	160.5	12.9	13.9	31.6	63.3	79.5
189 Niger	0.611	153	509	170.5	25.9	9.2[d]	15.2[d]	61.7	84.3
190 Chad	0.652	165	1,140	138.3	32.3	7.7[s]	24.4[s]	46.9	69.9
191 South Sudan	0.587	150	1,150	99.2	32.3	26.5	36.4	70.4	73.6
Other countries or territories									
Korea (Democratic People's Rep. of)	..	..	89	2.3	17.6	..	..	77.2	86.1
Monaco	..	..	..	7.2	33.3			..	..
Nauru	..	..		72.5	10.5	..	..	..	..
Somalia	..	..	829	118.0	24.6	..	..	20.9	47.0
Human development groups									
Very high human development	0.155	–	15	14.1	29.1	87.0	89.4	52.6	68.4
High human development	0.329	–	62	28.0	25.8	72.7	78.0	53.6	73.5
Medium human development	0.494	–	175	38.1	21.8	44.0	54.2	28.8	71.3
Low human development	0.577	–	499	89.5	24.3	22.8	34.1	49.3	73.2
Developing countries	0.487	–	247	46.5	23.9	56.9	64.7	44.4	72.8
Regions									
Arab States	0.536	–	150	45.3	18.3	53.8	60.4	19.3	69.5
East Asia and the Pacific	0.337	–	82	21.6	20.9	71.4	78.2	59.7	75.2
Europe and Central Asia	0.227	–	20	20.1	26.1	83.4	89.7	42.9	67.0
Latin America and the Caribbean	0.381	–	75	53.4	33.2	63.2	63.2	48.6	72.7
South Asia	0.508	–	153	28.9	17.6	42.2	52.8	21.6	71.6
Sub-Saharan Africa	0.569	–	536	100.9	25.7	31.1	44.3	62.1	72.3
Least developed countries	0.562		417	93.7	24.7	27.5	38.7	54.6	75.8
Small island developing states	0.461	–	212	50.9	26.7	62.1	65.7	50.4	68.7
Organisation for Economic Co-operation and Development	0.185	–	18	19.2	32.4	86.7	89.1	51.8	67.8
World	**0.465**	**–**	**225**	**42.5**	**25.9**	**64.2**	**70.3**	**46.2**	**71.7**

TABLE 5

Notes

a   Estimates modelled by the International Labour Organization.

b   Data refer to 2021 or the most recent year available.

c   Updated by HDRO based on data from UNESCO Institute for Statistics (2022).

d   Updated by HDRO based on data from Barro and Lee (2018) and UNESCO Institute for Statistics (2022).

e   Updated by HDRO based on data from OECD (2022) and UNESCO Institute for Statistics (2022).

f   HDRO estimate based on data from Robert Barro and Jong-Wha Lee, ICF Macro Demographic and Health Surveys, the Organisation for Economic Co-operation and Development, United Nations Children's Fund (UNICEF) Multiple Indicator Cluster Surveys and the United Nations Educational, Scientific and Cultural Organization Institute for Statistics.

g   In calculating the Gender Inequality Index, a value of 0.1 percent was used.

h   Updated by HDRO based on data from UNESCO Institute for Statistics (2022) and UNICEF Multiple Indicator Cluster Surveys for various years.

i   Updated by HDRO using projections from Barro and Lee (2018).

j   Excludes the 36 special rotating delegates appointed on an ad hoc basis.

k   Based on cross-country regression.

l   Updated by HDRO based on data from Barro and Lee (2018) and ICF Macro Demographic and Health Surveys for various years.

m   Updated by HDRO based on data from the United Nations Educational, Scientific and Cultural Organization Institute for Statistics for various years.

n   A special update by WHO, UNICEF, UNFPA, World Bank Group and United Nations Population Division (2019), communicated to HDRO on 7 September 2020.

o   Based on projections from Barro and Lee (2018).

p   Refers to 2019.

q   Updated by HDRO based on data from ICF Macro Demographic and Health Surveys for various years.

r   Refers to 2018.

s   Updated by HDRO based on data from ICF Macro Demographic and Health Surveys for various years and UNESCO Institute for Statistics (2022).

t   Refers to 2020.

Definitions

Gender Inequality Index: A composite measure reflecting inequality in achievement between women and men in three dimensions: reproductive health, empowerment and the labour market. See *Technical note 4* at http://hdr.undp.org/sites/default/files/hdr2022_technical_notes.pdf for details on how the Gender Inequality Index is calculated.

Maternal mortality ratio: Number of deaths due to pregnancy-related causes per 100,000 live births.

Adolescent birth rate: Number of births to women ages 15–19 per 1,000 women ages 15–19.

Share of seats in parliament: Proportion of seats held by women in the national parliament expressed as a percentage of total seats. For countries with a bicameral legislative system, the share of seats is calculated based on both houses.

Population with at least some secondary education: Percentage of the population ages 25 and older that has reached (but not necessarily completed) a secondary level of education.

Labour force participation rate: Proportion of the working-age population (ages 15 and older) that engages in the labour market, either by working or actively looking for work, expressed as a percentage of the working-age population.

Main data sources

Column 1: HDRO calculations based on data in columns 3–9.

Column 2: Calculated based on data in column 1.

Column 3: WHO, UNICEF, UNFPA, World Bank Group and United Nations Population Division (2019).

Column 4: UNDESA (2022a).

Column 5: IPU 2022.

Columns 6 and 7: Barro and Lee (2018), ICF Macro Demographic and Health Surveys, OECD (2022), UNESCO Institute for Statistics (2022) and UNICEF Multiple Indicator Cluster Surveys.

Columns 8 and 9: ILO (2022).

TABLE 5 / GENDER INEQUALITY INDEX   295

TABLE 6

Multidimensional Poverty Index: developing countries

Country	Multidimensional Poverty Index[a] Year and survey[b] 2009–2020	Value	Population in multidimensional poverty[a] Headcount (%)	Headcount (thousands) In survey year	Headcount (thousands) 2019	Intensity of deprivation (%)	Inequality among the poor Value	Population in severe multidimensional poverty (%)	Population vulnerable to multidimensional poverty[a] (%)	Contribution of deprivation in dimension to overall multidimensional poverty[a] Health (%)	Education (%)	Standard of living (%)	Population living below income poverty line (%) National poverty line 2009–2019[c]	PPP $1.90 a day 2009–2019[c]
Estimates based on surveys for 2015–2020														
Afghanistan	2015/2016 D	0.272 d	55.9 d	19,783 d	21,269 d	48.6 d	0.020 d	24.9 d	18.1 d	10.0 d	45.0 d	45.0 d	54.5	..
Albania	2017/2018 D	0.003	0.7	20	20	39.1	..e	0.1	5.0	28.3	55.1	16.7	14.3	1.3
Algeria	2018/2019 M	0.005	1.4	594	594	39.2	0.007	0.2	3.6	31.2	49.3	19.5	5.5	0.4
Angola	2015/2016 D	0.282	51.1	14,740	16,264	55.3	0.024	32.5	15.5	21.2	32.1	46.8	32.3	49.9
Armenia	2015/2016 D	0.001 f	0.2 f	6 f	6 f	36.2 f	..e	0.0 f	2.8 f	33.1 f	36.8 f	30.1 f	26.4	1.1
Bangladesh	2019 M	0.104	24.6	40,176	40,176	42.2	0.010	6.5	18.2	17.3	37.6	45.1	24.3	14.3
Belize	2015/2016 M	0.017	4.3	16	17	39.8	0.007	0.6	8.4	39.5	20.9	39.6	..	..
Benin	2017/2018 D	0.368	66.8	7,672	7,883	55.0	0.025	40.9	14.7	20.8	36.3	42.9	38.5	49.6
Bolivia (Plurinational State of)	2016 N	0.038	9.1	1,000	1,043	41.7	0.008	1.9	12.1	18.7	31.5	49.8	37.2	3.2
Botswana	2015/2016 N	0.073 g	17.2 g	372 g	397 g	42.2 g	0.008 g	3.5 g	19.7 g	30.3 g	16.5 g	53.2 g	19.3	14.5
Brazil	2015 Nh	0.016 d,h,i	3.8 d,h,i	7,856 d,h,i	8,108 d,h,i	42.5 d,h,i	0.008 d,h,i	0.9 d,h,i	6.2 d,h,i	49.8 d,h,i	22.9 d,h,i	27.3 d,h,i	..	4.6
Burundi	2016/2017 D	0.409 f	75.1 f	8,131 f	8,659 f	54.4 f	0.022 f	46.1 f	15.8 f	23.8 f	27.2 f	49.0 f	64.9	72.8
Cameroon	2018 D	0.232	43.6	10,992	11,280	53.2	0.026	24.6	17.6	25.2	27.6	47.1	37.5	26.0
Central African Republic	2018/2019 M	0.461	80.4	3,816	3,816	57.4	0.025	55.8	12.9	20.2	27.8	52.0	..	..
Chad	2019 M	0.517	84.2	13,423	13,423	61.4	0.024	64.6	10.7	19.1	36.6	44.3	42.3	38.1
Colombia	2015/2016 D	0.020 d	4.8 d	2,335 d	2,440 d	40.6 d	0.009 d	0.8 d	6.2 d	12.0 d	39.5 d	48.5 d	35.7	4.9
Congo	2014/2015 M	0.112	24.3	1,178	1,306	46.0	0.013	9.4	21.3	23.4	20.2	56.4	40.9	39.6
Congo (Democratic Republic of the)	2017/2018 M	0.331	64.5	54,239	55,996	51.3	0.020	36.8	17.4	23.1	19.9	57.0	63.9	77.2
Costa Rica	2018 M	0.002 i,j	0.5 i,j	27 i,j	27 i,j	37.1 i,j	..e	0.0 i,j	2.4 i,j	40.5 i,j	41.0 i,j	18.5 i,j	21.0	1.0
Côte d'Ivoire	2016 M	0.236	46.1	10,975	11,847	51.2	0.019	24.5	17.6	19.6	40.4	40.0	39.5	29.8
Cuba	2019 M	0.003 i	0.7 i	80 i	80 i	38.1 i	..e	0.1 i	2.7 i	10.1 i	39.8 i	50.1 i	..	..
Ethiopia	2019 D	0.367	68.7	77,039	77,039	53.3	0.022	41.9	18.4	14.0	31.5	54.5	23.5	30.8
Gambia	2018 M	0.204	41.6	948	977	49.0	0.018	18.8	22.9	29.5	34.6	35.9	48.6	10.3
Georgia	2018 M	0.001 i	0.3 i	14 i	14 i	36.6 i	..e	0.0 i	2.1 i	47.1 i	23.8 i	29.1 i	19.5	3.8
Ghana	2017/2018 M	0.111	24.6	7,334	7,494	45.1	0.014	8.4	20.1	23.6	30.5	45.9	23.4	12.7
Guatemala	2014/2015 D	0.134	28.9	4,694	5,078	46.2	0.013	11.2	21.1	26.3	35.0	38.7	59.3	8.8
Guinea	2018 D	0.373	66.2	8,220	8,456	56.4	0.025	43.5	16.4	21.4	38.4	40.3	43.7	36.1
Guinea-Bissau	2018/2019 M	0.341	64.4	1,237	1,237	52.9	0.021	35.9	20.0	19.1	35.0	45.8	69.3	68.4
Guyana	2019/2020 M	0.007	1.7	13	13	38.8	0.006	0.2	6.5	29.2	23.0	47.7	..	..
Haiti	2016/2017 D	0.200	41.3	4,532	4,648	48.4	0.019	18.5	21.8	18.5	24.6	57.0	58.5	24.5
India	2015/2016 D	0.123	27.9	369,643	381,336	43.9	0.014	8.8	19.3	31.9	23.4	44.8	21.9	22.5
Indonesia	2017 D	0.014 d	3.6 d	9,578 d	9,794 d	38.7 d	0.006 d	0.4 d	4.7 d	34.7 d	26.8 d	38.5 d	9.4	2.7
Iraq	2018 M	0.033	8.6	3,319	3,395	37.9	0.005	1.3	5.2	33.1	60.9	6.0	18.9	1.7
Jordan	2017/2018 D	0.002	0.4	43	44	35.4	..e	0.0	0.7	37.5	53.5	9.0	15.7	0.1
Kazakhstan	2015 M	0.002 i,f	0.5 i,f	80 i,f	84 i,f	35.6 i,f	..e	0.0 i,f	1.8 i,f	90.4 i,f	3.1 i,f	6.4 i,f	4.3	0.0
Kiribati	2018/2019 M	0.080	19.8	23	23	40.5	0.006	3.5	30.2	30.3	12.1	57.6	..	..
Kyrgyzstan	2018 M	0.001	0.4	25	25	36.3	..e	0.0	5.2	64.6	17.9	17.5	20.1	0.6
Lao People's Democratic Republic	2017 M	0.108	23.1	1,604	1,654	47.0	0.016	9.6	21.2	21.5	39.7	38.8	18.3	10.0
Lesotho	2018 M	0.084 j	19.6 j	413 j	417 j	43.0 j	0.009 j	5.0 j	28.6 j	21.9 j	18.1 j	60.0 j	49.7	27.2
Liberia	2019/2020 D	0.259	52.3	2,646	2,583	49.6	0.018	24.9	23.3	19.7	28.6	51.7	50.9	44.4
Madagascar	2018 M	0.384	69.1	18,142	18,630	55.6	0.023	45.5	14.3	15.5	33.1	51.5	70.7	78.8
Malawi	2015/2016 D	0.252 f	54.2 f	9,333 f	10,106 f	46.5 f	0.013 f	19.8 f	27.4 f	22.0 f	22.4 f	55.6 f	51.5	69.2
Maldives	2016/2017 D	0.003	0.8	4	4	34.4	..e	0.0	4.8	80.7	15.1	4.2	8.2	0.0
Mali	2018 D	0.376	68.3	13,036	13,433	55.0	0.022	44.7	15.3	19.6	41.2	39.3	42.1	50.3
Mauritania	2015 M	0.261	50.6	2,046	2,288	51.5	0.019	26.3	18.6	20.2	33.1	46.6	31.0	6.0
Mexico	2016 Nk	0.026 i	6.6 i	8,097 i	8,375 i	39.0 i	0.008 i	1.0 i	4.7 i	68.1 i	13.7 i	18.2 i	41.9	1.7
Mongolia	2018 M	0.028 m	7.3 m	230 m	234 m	38.8 m	0.004 m	0.8 m	15.5 m	21.1 m	26.8 m	52.1 m	28.4	0.5
Montenegro	2018 M	0.005	1.2	8	8	39.6	..e	0.1	2.9	58.5	22.3	19.2	24.5	2.5
Morocco	2017/2018 P	0.027 n	6.4 n	2,291 n	2,319 n	42.0 n	0.012 n	1.4 n	10.9 n	24.4 n	46.8 n	28.8 n	4.8	0.9
Myanmar	2015/2016 D	0.176	38.3	20,325	20,708	45.9	0.015	13.8	21.9	18.5	32.3	49.2	24.8	1.4
Nepal	2019 M	0.074	17.5	5,008	5,008	42.5	0.010	4.9	17.8	23.2	33.9	43.0	25.2	15.0
Nigeria	2018 D	0.254	46.4	90,919	93,281	54.8	0.029	26.8	19.2	30.9	28.2	40.9	40.1	39.1
North Macedonia	2018/2019 M	0.001	0.4	8	8	38.2	..e	0.1	2.2	29.6	52.6	17.8	21.6	3.4
Pakistan	2017/2018 D	0.198	38.3	81,352	83,014	51.7	0.023	21.5	12.9	27.6	41.3	31.1	24.3	4.4
Palestine, State of	2019/2020 M	0.002	0.6	29	28	35.0	..e	0.0	1.3	62.9	31.0	6.1	29.2	0.8
Papua New Guinea	2016/2018 D	0.263 d	56.6 d	4,874 d	4,970 d	46.5 d	0.016 d	25.8 d	25.3 d	4.6 d	30.1 d	65.3 d	39.9	38.0
Paraguay	2016 M	0.019	4.5	305	317	41.9	0.013	1.0	7.2	14.3	38.9	46.8	23.5	0.9
Peru	2018 N	0.029	7.4	2,358	2,397	39.6	0.007	1.1	9.6	15.7	31.1	53.2	20.2	2.2

Continued →

TABLE 6

	Multidimensional Poverty Index[a]			Population in multidimensional poverty[a]						Population vulnerable to multidimensional poverty[a]	Contribution of deprivation in dimension to overall multidimensional poverty[a]			Population living below income poverty line (%)	
				Headcount			Intensity of deprivation	Inequality among the poor	Population in severe multidimensional poverty					SDG 1.2 National poverty line	SDG 1.1 PPP $1.90 a day
	Year and survey[b]	Value	(%)	(thousands) In survey year	2019	(%)	Value	(%)	(%)	Health (%)	Education (%)	Standard of living (%)		
Country	2009-2020												2009-2019[c]	2009-2019[c]
Philippines	2017 D	0.024[d]	5.8[d]	6,096[d]	6,266[d]	41.8[d]	0.010[d]	1.3[d]	7.3[d]	20.3[d]	31.0[d]	48.7[d]	16.7	2.7
Rwanda	2014/2015 D	0.259[f]	54.4[f]	6,184[f]	6,869[f]	47.5[f]	0.013[f]	22.2[f]	25.8[f]	13.6[f]	30.5[f]	55.9[f]	38.2	56.5
Sao Tome and Principe	2019 M	0.048	11.7	25	25	40.9	0.007	2.1	17.0	18.7	36.6	44.6	66.7	35.6
Senegal	2019 D	0.263	50.8	8,284	8,284	51.7	0.019	27.7	18.2	20.7	48.4	30.9	46.7	38.5
Serbia	2019 M	0.000[i,o]	0.1[i,o]	10[i,o]	10[i,o]	38.1[i]	..[e]	0.0[i,o]	2.1[i,o]	30.9[i,o]	40.1[i,o]	29.0[i,o]	23.2	5.4
Seychelles	2019 N	0.003[i,p]	0.9[i,p]	1[i,p]	1[i,p]	34.2[i,p]	..[e]	0.0[i,p]	0.4[i,p]	66.8[i,p]	32.1[i,p]	1.1[i,p]	25.3	0.5
Sierra Leone	2019 D	0.293	59.2	4,627	4,627	49.5	0.019	28.0	21.3	23.0	24.1	53.0	56.8	43.0
South Africa	2016 D	0.025	6.3	3,517	3,664	39.8	0.005	0.9	12.2	39.5	13.1	47.4	55.5	18.7
Sri Lanka	2016 N	0.011	2.9	614	623	38.3	0.004	0.3	14.3	32.5	24.4	43.0	4.1	0.9
Suriname	2018 M	0.011	2.9	16	17	39.4	0.007	0.4	4.0	20.4	43.8	35.8	..	..
Tajikistan	2017 D	0.029	7.4	661	694	39.0	0.004	0.7	20.1	47.8	26.5	25.8	26.3	4.1
Tanzania (United Republic of)	2015/2016 D	0.284[f]	57.1[f]	30,274[f]	33,102[f]	49.8[f]	0.016[f]	27.5[f]	23.4[f]	22.5[f]	22.3[f]	55.2[f]	26.4	49.4
Thailand	2019 M	0.002[i]	0.6[i]	402[i]	402[i]	36.7[i]	0.003[i]	0.0[i]	6.1[i]	38.3[i]	45.1[i]	16.7[i]	9.9	0.1
Timor-Leste	2016 D	0.222[f]	48.3[f]	588[f]	624[f]	45.9[f]	0.014[f]	17.4[f]	26.8[f]	29.3[f]	23.1[f]	47.6[f]	41.8	22.0
Togo	2017 M	0.180	37.6	2,896	3,040	47.8	0.016	15.2	23.8	20.9	28.1	50.9	55.1	51.1
Tonga	2019 M	0.003	0.9	1	1	38.1	..[e]	0.0	6.4	38.2	40.7	21.1	22.5	1.0
Tunisia	2018 M	0.003	0.8	92	93	36.5	..[e]	0.1	2.4	24.4	61.6	14.0	15.2	0.2
Turkmenistan	2019 M	0.001[i]	0.2[i]	15[i]	15[i]	34.0[i]	..[e]	0.0[i]	0.3[i]	82.4[i]	15.5[i]	2.1[i]	..	..
Uganda	2016 D	0.281[f]	57.2[f]	22,667[f]	25,308[f]	49.2[f]	0.017[f]	25.7[f]	23.6[f]	24.0[f]	21.6[f]	54.5[f]	21.4	41.3
Zambia	2018 D	0.232	47.9	8,313	8,557	48.4	0.015	21.0	23.9	21.5	25.0	53.5	54.4	58.7
Zimbabwe	2019 M	0.110	25.8	3,779	3,779	42.6	0.009	6.8	26.3	23.6	17.3	59.2	38.3	39.5
Estimates based on surveys for 2009–2014														
Barbados	2012 M	0.009[i]	2.5[i]	7[i]	7[i]	34.2[i]	..[e]	0.0[i]	0.5[i]	96.0[i]	0.7[i]	3.3[i]	..	..
Bhutan	2010 M	0.175[i]	37.3[i]	256[i]	285[i]	46.8[i]	0.016[i]	14.7[i]	17.7[i]	24.2[i]	36.6[i]	39.2[i]	8.2	1.5
Bosnia and Herzegovina	2011/2012 M	0.008[i]	2.2[i]	79[i]	72[i]	37.9[i]	0.002[i]	0.1[i]	4.1[i]	79.7[i]	7.2[i]	13.1[i]	16.9	0.1
Burkina Faso	2010 D	0.523[f]	84.2[f]	13,138[f]	17,109[f]	62.2[f]	0.027[f]	65.3[f]	7.2[f]	20.5[f]	40.4[f]	39.1[f]	41.4	43.8
Cambodia	2014 D	0.170	37.2	5,680	6,131	45.8	0.015	13.2	21.1	21.8	31.7	46.6	17.7	..
China	2014 Nq	0.016[r,s]	3.9[r,s]	54,369[r,s]	55,703[r,s]	41.4[r,s]	0.005[r,s]	0.3[r,s]	17.4[r,s]	35.2[r,s]	39.2[r,s]	25.6[r,s]	0.6	0.5
Comoros	2012 D	0.181	37.3	270	317	48.5	0.020	16.1	22.3	20.8	31.6	47.6	42.4	19.1
Dominican Republic	2014 M	0.015[d]	3.9[d]	394[d]	417[d]	38.9[d]	0.006[d]	0.5[d]	5.2[d]	29.1[d]	35.8[d]	35.0[d]	21.0	0.6
Ecuador	2013/2014 N	0.018[i]	4.6[i]	730[i]	795[i]	39.9[i]	0.007[i]	0.8[i]	7.6[i]	40.4[i]	23.6[i]	35.9[i]	25.0	3.6
Egypt	2014 D	0.020[i,f]	5.2[i,f]	4,737[i,f]	5,259[i,f]	37.6[i,f]	0.004[i,f]	0.6[i,f]	6.1[i,f]	40.0[i,f]	53.1[i,f]	6.9[i,f]	32.5	3.8
El Salvador	2014 M	0.032	7.9	495	507	41.3	0.009	1.7	9.9	15.5	43.4	41.1	22.8	1.3
Eswatini (Kingdom of)	2014 M	0.081	19.2	210	221	42.3	0.009	4.4	20.9	29.3	17.9	52.8	58.9	29.2
Gabon	2012 D	0.070[f]	15.6[f]	273[f]	339[f]	44.7[f]	0.013[f]	5.1[f]	18.4[f]	32.7[f]	21.4[f]	46.0[f]	33.4	3.4
Honduras	2011/2012 D	0.093[t,f]	20.0[t,f]	1,727[t,f]	1,948[t,f]	46.5[t,f]	0.013[t,f]	6.9[t,f]	22.2[t,f]	19.5[t,f]	32.5[t,f]	48.0[t,f]	48.3	14.8
Jamaica	2014 N	0.018[i]	4.7[i]	135[i]	138[i]	38.7[i]	..[e]	0.8[i]	6.4[i]	42.1[i]	17.5[i]	40.4[i]	19.9	..
Kenya	2014 D	0.171[f]	37.5[f]	17,502[f]	19,703[f]	45.6[f]	0.014[f]	12.4[f]	35.8[f]	23.5[f]	15.0[f]	61.5[f]	36.1	37.1
Libya	2014 P	0.007	2.0	127	135	37.1	0.003	0.1	11.4	39.0	48.6	12.4	..	..
Moldova (Republic of)	2012 M	0.004	0.9	38	38	37.4	..[e]	0.1	3.7	9.2	42.4	48.4	7.3	0.0
Mozambique	2011 D	0.417[f]	73.1[f]	17,690[f]	22,209[f]	57.0[f]	0.023[f]	49.9[f]	13.3[f]	18.0[f]	32.1[f]	49.9[f]	46.1	63.7
Namibia	2013 D	0.185[f]	40.9[f]	913[f]	1,020[f]	45.2[f]	0.013[f]	13.1[f]	19.2[f]	31.6[f]	13.9[f]	54.4[f]	17.4	13.8
Nicaragua	2011/2012 D	0.074[f]	16.5[f]	985[f]	1,077[f]	45.3[f]	0.013[f]	5.6[f]	13.4[f]	11.5[f]	36.2[f]	52.3[f]	24.9	3.4
Niger	2012 D	0.601[f]	91.0[f]	16,189[f]	21,206[f]	66.1[f]	0.026[f]	76.3[f]	4.9[f]	21.4[f]	36.7[f]	41.8[f]	40.8	45.4
Saint Lucia	2012 M	0.007[i]	1.9[i]	3[i]	4[i]	37.5[i]	..[e]	0.0[i]	1.6[i]	69.5[i]	7.5[i]	23.0[i]	25.0	4.6
South Sudan	2010 M	0.580	91.9	8,735	10,162	63.2	0.023	74.3	6.3	14.0	39.6	46.5	76.4	76.4
Sudan	2014 M	0.279	52.3	19,873	22,403	53.4	0.023	30.9	17.7	21.1	29.2	49.8	46.5	12.2
Syrian Arab Republic	2009 P	0.029[i]	7.4[i]	1,568[i]	1,262[i]	38.9[i]	0.006[i]	1.2[i]	7.8[i]	40.8[i]	49.0[i]	10.2[i]	..	..
Trinidad and Tobago	2011 M	0.002[i]	0.6[i]	9[i]	9[i]	38.0[i]	..[e]	0.1[i]	3.7[i]	45.5[i]	34.0[i]	20.5[i]	..	..
Ukraine	2012 M	0.001[d,f]	0.2[d,f]	111[d,f]	107[d,f]	34.4[d,f]	..[e]	0.0[d,f]	0.4[d,f]	60.5[d,f]	28.4[d,f]	11.2[d,f]	1.1	0.0
Viet Nam	2013/2014 M	0.019[d]	4.9[d]	4,490[d]	4,722[d]	39.5[d]	0.010[d]	0.7[d]	5.6[d]	15.2[d]	42.6[d]	42.2[d]	6.7	1.8
Yemen	2013 D	0.245[f]	48.5[f]	12,188[f]	14,134[f]	50.6[f]	0.021[f]	24.3[f]	22.3[f]	29.0[f]	30.4[f]	40.6[f]	48.6	18.3
Developing countries	–	0.105	21.7	1,229,179	1,287,528	48.6	0.017	9.5	15.2	25.6	29.7	44.7	20.2	14.8
Regions														
Arab States	–	0.071	14.5	44,861	49,666	48.7	0.018	6.5	8.9	26.3	34.6	39.1	26.1	4.9
East Asia and the Pacific	–	0.023	5.4	108,260	111,232	42.5	0.009	1.0	14.5	27.6	35.5	36.9	4.3	1.2
Europe and Central Asia	–	0.004	1.0	1,074	1,101	38.0	0.004	0.1	3.2	52.8	24.8	22.4	9.8	1.1
Latin America and the Caribbean	–	0.030	6.9	35,814	37,463	42.8	0.011	1.8	7.3	36.3	26.3	37.4	36.9	4.2
South Asia	–	0.131	29.0	516,834	531,715	45.2	0.015	10.2	18.3	29.0	28.6	42.3	22.9	19.2
Sub-Saharan Africa	–	0.286	53.4	522,337	556,351	53.5	0.022	30.8	18.8	21.9	29.5	48.6	41.1	43.7

TABLE 6 / MULTIDIMENSIONAL POVERTY INDEX: DEVELOPING COUNTRIES

TABLE 6

Notes	
a	Cross-country comparisons should take into account the year of survey and the indicator definitions and omissions. When an indicator is missing, weights of available indicators are adjusted to total 100 percent. See Technical note at https://hdr.undp.org/system/files/documents//mpi2021technicalnotespdf.pdf for details.
b	*D* indicates data from Demographic and Health Surveys, *M* indicates data from Multiple Indicator Cluster Surveys, *N* indicates data from national surveys and *P* indicates data from Pan Arab Population and Family Health Surveys (see https://hdr.undp.org/mpi-2021-faqs for the list of national surveys).
c	Data refer to the most recent year available during the period specified.
d	Missing indicator on nutrition.
e	Value is not reported because it is based on a small number of multidimensionally poor people.
f	Revised estimate.
g	Captures only deaths of children under age 5 who died in the last five years and deaths of children ages 12–18 years who died in the last two years.
h	The methodology was adjusted to account for missing indicator on nutrition and incomplete indicator on child mortality (the survey did not collect the date of child deaths).
i	Considers child deaths that occurred at any time because the survey did not collect the date of child deaths.
j	Missing indicator on cooking fuel.
k	Multidimensional Poverty Index estimates are based on the 2016 National Health and Nutrition Survey. Estimates based on the 2015 Multiple Indicator Cluster Survey are 0.010 for Multidimensional Poverty Index value, 2.6 for multidimensional poverty headcount (%), 3,207,000 for multidimensional poverty headcount in year of survey, 3,317,000 for projected multidimensional poverty headcount in 2019, 40.2 for intensity of deprivation (%), 0.4 for population in severe multidimensional poverty (%), 6.1 for population vulnerable to multidimensional poverty (%), 39.9 for contribution of deprivation in health (%), 23.8 for contribution of deprivation in education (%) and 36.3 for contribution of deprivation in standard of living (%).
l	Missing indicator on child mortality.
m	Indicator on sanitation follows the national classification in which pit latrine with slab is considered unimproved.
n	Following the national report, latrines are considered an improved source for the sanitation indicator.
o	Because of the high proportion of children excluded from nutrition indicators due to measurements not being taken, estimates based on the 2019 Serbia Multiple Indicator Cluster Survey should be interpreted with caution. The unweighted sample size used for the multidimensional poverty calculation is 82.8 percent.
p	Missing indicator on school attendance.
q	Based on the version of data accessed on 7 June 2016.
r	Given the information available in the data, child mortality was constructed based on deaths that occurred between surveys—that is, between 2012 and 2014. Child deaths reported by an adult man in the household were taken into account because the date of death was reported.
s	Missing indicator on housing.
t	Missing indicator on electricity.

Definitions

Multidimensional Poverty Index: Proportion of the population that is multidimensionally poor adjusted by the intensity of the deprivations. See Technical note at https://hdr.undp.org/system/files/documents//mpi2021technicalnotespdf.pdf for details on how the Multidimensional Poverty Index is calculated.

Multidimensional poverty headcount: Population with a deprivation score of at least 33 percent. It is expressed as a share of the population in the survey year, the number of multidimensionally poor people in the survey year and the projected number of multidimensionally poor people in 2019.

Intensity of deprivation of multidimensional poverty: Average deprivation score experienced by people in multidimensional poverty.

Inequality among the poor: Variance of individual deprivation scores of poor people. It is calculated by subtracting the deprivation score of each multidimensionally poor person from the intensity, squaring the differences and dividing the sum of the weighted squares by the number of multidimensionally poor people.

Population in severe multidimensional poverty: Percentage of the population in severe multidimensional poverty—that is, those with a deprivation score of 50 percent or more.

Population vulnerable to multidimensional poverty: Percentage of the population at risk of suffering multiple deprivations—that is, those with a deprivation score of 20–33 percent.

Contribution of deprivation in dimension to overall multidimensional poverty: Percentage of the Multidimensional Poverty Index attributed to deprivations in each dimension.

Population living below national poverty line: Percentage of the population living below the national poverty line, which is the poverty line deemed appropriate for a country by its authorities. National estimates are based on population-weighted subgroup estimates from household surveys.

Population living below PPP $1.90 a day: Percentage of the population living below the international poverty line of $1.90 (in purchasing power parity [PPP] terms) a day.

Main data sources

Column 1: Refers to the year and the survey whose data were used to calculate the country's Multidimensional Poverty Index value and its components.

Columns 2–12: HDRO and OPHI calculations based on data on household deprivations in health, education and standard of living from various household surveys listed in column 1 using the methodology described in Technical note (available at https://hdr.undp.org/system/files/documents//mpi2021technicalnotespdf.pdf). Columns 4 and 5 also use population data from UNDESA (2019).

Columns 13 and 14: World Bank (2021).

TABLE 7

Planetary pressures–adjusted Human Development Index

		Human Development Index (HDI)	Planetary pressures-adjusted HDI (PHDI)			Adjustment factor for planetary pressures	SDG 9.4 Carbon dioxide emissions per capita (production)	Carbon dioxide emissions (production) index	SDG 8.4, 12.2 Material footprint per capita	Material footprint index
		Value	Value	Difference from HDI value[a] (%)	Difference from HDI rank[a]	Value	(tonnes)	Value	(tonnes)	Value
HDI RANK		2021	2021	2021	2021	2021	2020	2020	2019	2019
Very high human development										
1	Switzerland	0.962	0.796	17.3	-7	0.828	3.7	0.946	31.1	0.710
2	Norway	0.961	0.734	23.6	-34	0.764	7.6	0.889	38.8	0.639
3	Iceland	0.959	0.633	34.0	-91	0.660	8.6	0.875	59.6	0.445
4	Hong Kong, China (SAR)	0.952	..	..	..	..	4.2	0.939	..	..
5	Australia	0.951	0.637	33.0	-87	0.670	15.4	0.776	46.8	0.564
6	Denmark	0.948	0.803	15.3	0	0.847	4.5	0.934	25.9	0.759
7	Sweden	0.947	0.803	15.2	1	0.848	3.8	0.944	26.7	0.751
8	Ireland	0.945	0.682	27.8	-58	0.722	6.8	0.902	49.3	0.542
9	Germany	0.942	0.804	14.6	4	0.854	7.7	0.888	19.4	0.819
10	Netherlands	0.941	0.745	20.8	-18	0.791	8.1	0.883	32.3	0.700
11	Finland	0.940	0.731	22.2	-28	0.777	7.1	0.897	36.7	0.658
12	Singapore	0.939	0.665	29.2	-61	0.709	7.8	0.887	50.4	0.531
13	Belgium	0.937	0.742	20.8	-17	0.792	7.2	0.895	33.5	0.689
13	New Zealand	0.937	0.756	19.3	-6	0.807	6.9	0.899	30.7	0.714
15	Canada	0.936	0.687	26.6	-46	0.734	14.2	0.793	35.1	0.674
16	Liechtenstein	0.935	..	..	..	..	3.7	0.946	..	..
17	Luxembourg	0.930	0.645	30.6	-73	0.693	13.1	0.810	45.5	0.577
18	United Kingdom	0.929	0.819	11.8	15	0.882	4.9	0.929	17.9	0.834
19	Japan	0.925	0.792	14.4	8	0.856	8.1	0.881	18.2	0.831
19	Korea (Republic of)	0.925	0.752	18.7	-4	0.813	11.7	0.830	22.0	0.795
21	United States	0.921	0.698	24.2	-36	0.758	14.2	0.793	29.7	0.724
22	Israel	0.919	0.744	19.0	-8	0.809	6.5	0.905	30.8	0.714
23	Malta	0.918	0.720	21.6	-22	0.784	3.6	0.947	40.7	0.621
23	Slovenia	0.918	0.769	16.2	8	0.838	6.0	0.912	25.4	0.764
25	Austria	0.916	0.766	16.4	9	0.836	6.7	0.902	24.6	0.771
26	United Arab Emirates	0.911	0.518	43.1	-105	0.569	15.2	0.779	69.0	0.358
27	Spain	0.905	0.819	9.5	24	0.905	4.5	0.935	13.5	0.875
28	France	0.903	0.803	11.1	21	0.890	4.2	0.938	17.1	0.841
29	Cyprus	0.896	0.708	21.0	-22	0.791	5.4	0.922	36.6	0.659
30	Italy	0.895	0.813	9.2	25	0.908	5.0	0.927	11.9	0.890
31	Estonia	0.890	0.684	23.1	-34	0.768	7.9	0.885	37.5	0.651
32	Czechia	0.889	0.748	15.9	6	0.841	8.2	0.880	21.3	0.802
33	Greece	0.887	0.792	10.7	22	0.893	5.0	0.927	15.2	0.859
34	Poland	0.876	0.753	14.0	12	0.859	7.9	0.885	17.9	0.834
35	Bahrain	0.875	0.647	26.1	-51	0.740	20.5	0.701	23.8	0.778
35	Lithuania	0.875	0.679	22.4	-34	0.776	5.1	0.926	40.1	0.626
35	Saudi Arabia	0.875	0.638	27.1	-57	0.729	18.0	0.739	30.0	0.720
38	Portugal	0.866	0.792	8.5	27	0.914	4.0	0.942	12.3	0.886
39	Latvia	0.863	0.716	17.0	-8	0.829	3.6	0.948	31.0	0.711
40	Andorra	0.858	..	..	..	..	6.0	0.912	..	..
40	Croatia	0.858	0.764	11.0	23	0.890	4.1	0.940	17.1	0.841
42	Chile	0.855	0.775	9.4	27	0.906	4.2	0.938	13.5	0.874
42	Qatar	0.855	0.491	42.6	-96	0.574	37.0	0.461	33.7	0.686
44	San Marino	0.853	..	..	..	..	..	..	19.1	0.822
45	Slovakia	0.848	0.738	13.0	8	0.870	5.6	0.918	19.1	0.822
46	Hungary	0.846	0.755	10.8	23	0.893	5.0	0.927	15.3	0.858
47	Argentina	0.842	0.759	9.9	26	0.901	3.5	0.949	15.8	0.853
48	Türkiye	0.838	0.741	11.6	14	0.885	4.7	0.932	17.5	0.837
49	Montenegro	0.832	..	..	..	..	3.7	0.946	..	..
50	Kuwait	0.831	0.452	45.6	-100	0.544	20.8	0.697	65.3	0.392
51	Brunei Darussalam	0.829	0.358	56.8	-109	0.432	23.2	0.662	85.7	0.202
52	Russian Federation	0.822	0.721	12.3	7	0.877	10.8	0.843	9.5	0.912
53	Romania	0.821	0.738	10.1	15	0.898	3.7	0.946	16.0	0.851
54	Oman	0.816	0.710	13.0	1	0.870	12.2	0.823	8.9	0.917
55	Bahamas	0.812	0.634	21.9	-43	0.781	5.9	0.913	37.8	0.648
56	Kazakhstan	0.811	0.590	27.3	-52	0.727	15.5	0.774	34.4	0.680
57	Trinidad and Tobago	0.810	..	..	..	..	25.4	0.631	..	..
58	Costa Rica	0.809	0.746	7.8	26	0.922	1.6	0.977	14.4	0.866
58	Uruguay	0.809	0.733	9.4	15	0.906	1.7	0.976	17.5	0.837

Continued →

TABLE 7

		Human Development Index (HDI)	Planetary pressures-adjusted HDI (PHDI)			Adjustment factor for planetary pressures	SDG 9.4 Carbon dioxide emissions per capita (production)	Carbon dioxide emissions (production) index	SDG 8.4, 12.2 Material footprint per capita	Material footprint index
		Value	Value	Difference from HDI value[a] (%)	Difference from HDI rank[a]	Value	(tonnes)	Value	(tonnes)	Value
HDI RANK		2021	2021	2021	2021	2021	2020	2020	2019	2019
60	Belarus	0.808	0.751	7.1	32	0.930	6.1	0.912	5.6	0.948
61	Panama	0.805	0.740	8.1	24	0.919	2.5	0.964	13.5	0.875
62	Malaysia	0.803	0.681	15.2	-10	0.848	8.4	0.877	19.6	0.818
63	Georgia	0.802	0.749	6.6	34	0.934	2.5	0.964	10.4	0.904
63	Mauritius	0.802	..	..	..	..	3.1	0.954	..	..
63	Serbia	0.802	0.715	10.8	11	0.891	4.9	0.928	15.7	0.854
66	Thailand	0.800	0.735	8.1	24	0.918	3.7	0.946	11.8	0.891
High human development										
67	Albania	0.796	0.739	7.2	28	0.928	1.6	0.977	13.0	0.879
68	Bulgaria	0.795	0.708	10.9	12	0.891	5.4	0.922	15.0	0.860
68	Grenada	0.795	..	..	..	..	2.6	0.962	..	..
70	Barbados	0.790	..	..	..	..	3.8	0.945	..	..
71	Antigua and Barbuda	0.788	..	..	..	..	4.4	0.936	..	..
72	Seychelles	0.785	..	..	..	..	5.0	0.927	..	..
73	Sri Lanka	0.782	0.761	2.7	46	0.973	1.0	0.986	4.4	0.959
74	Bosnia and Herzegovina	0.780	0.691	11.4	6	0.885	6.5	0.905	14.4	0.866
75	Saint Kitts and Nevis	0.777	..	..	..	..	4.0	0.942	..	..
76	Iran (Islamic Republic of)	0.774	0.677	12.5	-4	0.874	8.9	0.871	13.2	0.877
77	Ukraine	0.773	0.703	9.1	11	0.909	4.9	0.929	11.9	0.889
78	North Macedonia	0.770	0.707	8.2	15	0.918	3.4	0.950	12.3	0.886
79	China	0.768	0.648	15.6	-14	0.844	7.4	0.892	22.0	0.796
80	Dominican Republic	0.767	0.719	6.3	24	0.937	2.6	0.963	9.5	0.911
80	Moldova (Republic of)	0.767	0.748	2.5	44	0.975	1.3	0.981	3.4	0.968
80	Palau	0.767	..	..	..	..	12.1	0.824	..	..
83	Cuba	0.764	0.721	5.6	30	0.944	1.8	0.974	9.2	0.914
84	Peru	0.762	0.721	5.4	31	0.946	1.4	0.980	9.4	0.912
85	Armenia	0.759	0.727	4.2	33	0.958	2.0	0.971	6.0	0.945
86	Mexico	0.758	0.704	7.1	21	0.929	2.8	0.960	10.9	0.899
87	Brazil	0.754	0.676	10.3	5	0.896	2.2	0.968	18.9	0.824
88	Colombia	0.752	0.711	5.5	28	0.945	1.8	0.975	9.1	0.915
89	Saint Vincent and the Grenadines	0.751	..	..	..	..	1.9	0.973	..	..
90	Maldives	0.747	..	..	..	..	3.3	0.952	..	..
91	Algeria	0.745	0.687	7.8	16	0.922	3.5	0.949	11.2	0.896
91	Azerbaijan	0.745	0.688	7.7	18	0.924	3.7	0.946	10.6	0.902
91	Tonga	0.745	..	..	..	..	1.4	0.980	..	..
91	Turkmenistan	0.745	0.632	15.2	-20	0.848	12.5	0.818	13.1	0.878
95	Ecuador	0.740	0.704	4.9	27	0.951	1.8	0.974	7.7	0.928
96	Mongolia	0.739	0.557	24.6	-35	0.754	27.0	0.607	10.6	0.901
97	Egypt	0.731	0.692	5.3	25	0.947	2.1	0.970	8.2	0.923
97	Tunisia	0.731	0.687	6.0	21	0.940	2.4	0.965	9.2	0.915
99	Fiji	0.730	..	..	..	..	1.6	0.977	..	..
99	Suriname	0.730	..	..	..	..	3.8	0.945	..	..
101	Uzbekistan	0.727	0.688	5.4	25	0.947	3.4	0.951	6.1	0.943
102	Dominica	0.720	..	..	..	..	1.9	0.972	..	..
102	Jordan	0.720	0.683	5.1	20	0.949	2.5	0.964	7.0	0.935
104	Libya	0.718	0.626	12.8	-12	0.871	7.4	0.893	16.1	0.850
105	Paraguay	0.717	0.648	9.6	5	0.904	1.1	0.985	18.9	0.824
106	Palestine, State of	0.715	..	..	..	..	0.6	0.992	..	..
106	Saint Lucia	0.715	..	..	..	..	2.4	0.965	..	..
108	Guyana	0.714	..	..	..	..	2.8	0.959	..	..
109	South Africa	0.713	0.648	9.1	6	0.909	7.6	0.889	7.6	0.930
110	Jamaica	0.709	0.663	6.5	14	0.935	2.5	0.963	10.0	0.907
111	Samoa	0.707	..	..	..	..	1.2	0.982	..	..
112	Gabon	0.706	0.666	5.7	18	0.943	1.9	0.972	9.2	0.915
112	Lebanon	0.706	0.646	8.5	2	0.915	3.8	0.945	12.4	0.885
114	Indonesia	0.705	0.672	4.7	21	0.953	2.2	0.969	6.8	0.937
115	Viet Nam	0.703	0.662	5.8	17	0.941	2.6	0.962	8.5	0.921
Medium human development										
116	Philippines	0.699	0.664	5.0	20	0.950	1.2	0.982	8.8	0.918
117	Botswana	0.693	0.633	8.7	0	0.914	2.8	0.960	14.2	0.868

Continued →

TABLE 7

		Human Development Index (HDI)	Planetary pressures-adjusted HDI (PHDI)			Adjustment factor for planetary pressures	SDG 9.4 Carbon dioxide emissions per capita (production)	Carbon dioxide emissions (production) index	SDG 8.4, 12.2 Material footprint per capita	Material footprint index
		Value	Value	Difference from HDI value[a] (%)	Difference from HDI rank[a]	Value	(tonnes)	Value	(tonnes)	Value
HDI RANK		2021	2021	2021	2021	2021	2020	2020	2019	2019
118	Bolivia (Plurinational State of)	0.692	0.647	6.5	11	0.934	1.8	0.974	11.3	0.895
118	Kyrgyzstan	0.692	0.658	4.9	18	0.951	1.8	0.974	7.8	0.927
120	Venezuela (Bolivarian Republic of)	0.691	0.645	6.7	9	0.934	3.0	0.957	9.6	0.911
121	Iraq	0.686	0.622	9.3	0	0.907	5.2	0.924	11.9	0.889
122	Tajikistan	0.685	0.662	3.4	24	0.966	1.0	0.986	5.8	0.946
123	Belize	0.683	0.637	6.7	9	0.933	1.5	0.979	12.2	0.886
123	Morocco	0.683	0.652	4.5	22	0.955	1.7	0.975	7.0	0.935
125	El Salvador	0.675	0.652	3.4	24	0.966	0.9	0.986	5.9	0.945
126	Nicaragua	0.667	0.647	3.0	19	0.969	0.8	0.989	5.4	0.950
127	Bhutan	0.666	0.553	17.0	-13	0.831	2.5	0.964	32.4	0.698
128	Cabo Verde	0.662	..	..	..	..	1.0	0.986	..	..
129	Bangladesh	0.661	0.649	1.8	25	0.982	0.6	0.992	2.9	0.973
130	Tuvalu	0.641	..	..	..	..	0.6	0.991	..	..
131	Marshall Islands	0.639	..	..	..	..	2.6	0.963	..	..
132	India	0.633	0.609	3.8	6	0.963	1.8	0.974	5.2	0.951
133	Ghana	0.632	0.618	2.2	8	0.978	0.5	0.993	3.9	0.964
134	Micronesia (Federated States of)	0.628	..	..	..	..	1.3	0.981	..	..
135	Guatemala	0.627	0.601	4.1	7	0.959	1.1	0.985	7.2	0.933
136	Kiribati	0.624	..	..	..	..	0.6	0.992	..	..
137	Honduras	0.621	0.599	3.5	7	0.965	1.0	0.986	6.1	0.944
138	Sao Tome and Principe	0.618	..	..	..	..	0.5	0.993	..	..
139	Namibia	0.615	0.574	6.7	2	0.933	1.5	0.978	11.9	0.889
140	Lao People's Democratic Republic	0.607	0.559	7.9	-3	0.921	4.7	0.932	9.6	0.910
140	Timor-Leste	0.607	..	..	..	..	0.4	0.994	..	..
140	Vanuatu	0.607	..	..	..	..	0.6	0.991	..	..
143	Nepal	0.602	0.584	3.0	7	0.970	0.6	0.992	5.6	0.948
144	Eswatini (Kingdom of)	0.597	..	..	..	..	0.8	0.988	..	..
145	Equatorial Guinea	0.596	0.520	12.8	-14	0.873	7.3	0.894	15.9	0.852
146	Cambodia	0.593	0.573	3.4	5	0.967	0.9	0.987	5.7	0.947
146	Zimbabwe	0.593	0.587	1.0	10	0.989	0.7	0.990	1.2	0.989
148	Angola	0.586	0.577	1.5	10	0.985	0.7	0.990	2.2	0.980
149	Myanmar	0.585	0.577	1.4	11	0.986	0.7	0.990	2.1	0.981
150	Syrian Arab Republic	0.577	0.565	2.1	7	0.978	1.7	0.975	1.9	0.982
151	Cameroon	0.576	0.569	1.2	9	0.988	0.3	0.996	2.1	0.980
152	Kenya	0.575	0.561	2.4	7	0.976	0.3	0.996	4.6	0.957
153	Congo	0.571	0.564	1.2	9	0.987	0.6	0.992	1.9	0.982
154	Zambia	0.565	0.557	1.4	7	0.986	0.4	0.995	2.4	0.978
155	Solomon Islands	0.564	..	..	..	..	0.4	0.994	..	..
156	Comoros	0.558	..	..	..	..	0.3	0.996	..	..
156	Papua New Guinea	0.558	0.541	3.0	4	0.970	0.7	0.989	5.2	0.951
158	Mauritania	0.556	0.533	4.1	3	0.959	0.7	0.989	7.8	0.928
159	Côte d'Ivoire	0.550	0.540	1.8	5	0.982	0.4	0.994	3.3	0.970
Low human development										
160	Tanzania (United Republic of)	0.549	0.544	0.9	8	0.991	0.2	0.997	1.6	0.985
161	Pakistan	0.544	0.531	2.4	5	0.976	1.1	0.985	3.5	0.968
162	Togo	0.539	0.528	2.0	4	0.979	0.3	0.996	4.1	0.961
163	Haiti	0.535	0.528	1.3	5	0.987	0.3	0.996	2.4	0.978
163	Nigeria	0.535	0.524	2.1	3	0.979	0.6	0.991	3.6	0.966
165	Rwanda	0.534	0.529	0.9	8	0.990	0.1	0.999	2.0	0.981
166	Benin	0.525	0.515	1.9	2	0.980	0.6	0.992	3.4	0.968
166	Uganda	0.525	0.520	1.0	5	0.990	0.1	0.998	1.9	0.982
168	Lesotho	0.514	..	..	..	..	1.0	0.985	..	..
169	Malawi	0.512	0.508	0.8	3	0.992	0.1	0.999	1.7	0.984
170	Senegal	0.511	0.499	2.3	3	0.976	0.6	0.991	4.1	0.962
171	Djibouti	0.509	0.470	7.7	-7	0.924	0.4	0.995	15.9	0.852
172	Sudan	0.508	0.480	5.5	-1	0.945	0.4	0.994	11.3	0.895
173	Madagascar	0.501	0.497	0.8	5	0.992	0.1	0.998	1.5	0.986
174	Gambia	0.500	0.490	2.0	3	0.981	0.2	0.997	3.8	0.965
175	Ethiopia	0.498	0.496	0.4	6	0.997	0.1	0.998	0.5	0.996
176	Eritrea	0.492	0.483	1.8	4	0.982	0.2	0.997	3.5	0.968

Continued →

TABLE 7 / PLANETARY PRESSURES-ADJUSTED HUMAN DEVELOPMENT INDEX

TABLE 7

HDI RANK	Human Development Index (HDI) Value 2021	Planetary pressures-adjusted HDI (PHDI) Value 2021	Difference from HDI value[a] (%) 2021	Difference from HDI rank[a] 2021	Adjustment factor for planetary pressures Value 2021	SDG 9.4 Carbon dioxide emissions per capita (production) (tonnes) 2020	Carbon dioxide emissions (production) index Value 2020	SDG 8.4, 12.2 Material footprint per capita (tonnes) 2019	Material footprint index Value 2019
177 Guinea-Bissau	0.483	..	..	..	..	0.1	0.998	..	..
178 Liberia	0.481	0.474	1.5	3	0.986	0.2	0.997	2.7	0.975
179 Congo (Democratic Republic of the)	0.479	0.473	1.3	2	0.987	0.0	1.000	2.8	0.974
180 Afghanistan	0.478	0.474	0.8	5	0.991	0.3	0.995	1.4	0.987
181 Sierra Leone	0.477	0.472	1.0	3	0.989	0.1	0.998	2.1	0.980
182 Guinea	0.465	0.454	2.4	2	0.976	0.3	0.996	4.8	0.956
183 Yemen	0.455	0.448	1.5	1	0.984	0.3	0.995	2.9	0.973
184 Burkina Faso	0.449	0.442	1.6	1	0.985	0.2	0.997	3.0	0.972
185 Mozambique	0.446	0.441	1.1	1	0.988	0.2	0.997	2.2	0.980
186 Mali	0.428	0.418	2.3	0	0.978	0.2	0.998	4.6	0.957
187 Burundi	0.426	0.422	0.9	2	0.992	0.1	0.999	1.7	0.984
188 Central African Republic	0.404	0.401	0.7	1	0.992	0.0	0.999	1.6	0.985
189 Niger	0.400	0.392	2.0	1	0.980	0.1	0.999	4.2	0.961
190 Chad	0.394	0.379	3.8	1	0.961	0.1	0.999	8.3	0.923
191 South Sudan	0.385	0.376	2.3	1	0.977	0.1	0.998	4.8	0.956
Other countries or territories									
.. Korea (Democratic People's Rep. of)	..	..	..	..	0.988	1.1	0.983	0.8	0.993
.. Monaco	..	..	..	..	..	..	..	..	..
.. Nauru	..	..	..	..	..	5.2	0.924	..	..
.. Somalia	..	..	..	..	0.983	0.0	0.999	3.5	0.967
Human development groups									
Very high human development	0.896	0.747	16.6	—	0.833	9.0	0.869	21.6	0.799
High human development	0.754	0.667	11.5	—	0.884	5.4	0.922	16.5	0.846
Medium human development	0.636	0.613	3.6	—	0.964	1.5	0.978	5.3	0.951
Low human development	0.518	0.509	1.7	—	0.982	0.4	0.994	3.1	0.971
Developing countries	0.685	0.636	7.2	—	0.928	3.3	0.952	10.5	0.902
Regions									
Arab States	0.708	0.646	8.8	—	0.912	4.3	0.937	12.3	0.885
East Asia and the Pacific	0.749	0.657	12.3	—	0.877	5.8	0.916	17.4	0.838
Europe and Central Asia	0.796	0.713	10.4	—	0.896	5.2	0.924	14.1	0.869
Latin America and the Caribbean	0.754	0.695	7.8	—	0.921	2.3	0.966	13.3	0.876
South Asia	0.632	0.609	3.6	—	0.963	1.8	0.973	5.1	0.952
Sub-Saharan Africa	0.547	0.536	2.0	—	0.980	0.7	0.989	3.2	0.971
Least developed countries	0.540	0.531	1.7	—	0.983	0.3	0.995	3.1	0.972
Small island developing states	0.730	..	..	—	..	3.0	0.957	..	..
Organisation for Economic Co-operation and Development	0.899	0.755	16.0	—	0.840	8.2	0.881	21.5	0.799
World	**0.732**	**0.667**	**8.9**	**—**	**0.912**	**4.3**	**0.937**	**12.4**	**0.885**

TABLE 7

Notes

a   Based on countries for which a Planetary pressures-adjusted Human Development Index value is calculated.

Definitions

Human Development Index (HDI): A composite index measuring average achievement in three basic dimensions of human development—a long and healthy life, knowledge and a decent standard of living. See *Technical note 1* at http://hdr.undp.org/sites/default/files/hdr2022_technical_notes.pdf for details on how the HDI is calculated.

Planetary pressures-adjusted HDI (PHDI): HDI value adjusted by the level of carbon dioxide emissions and material footprint per capita to account for excessive human pressure on the planet. It should be seen as an incentive for transformation. See *Technical note 6* at http://hdr.undp.org/sites/default/files/hdr2022_technical_notes.pdf for details on how the PHDI is calculated.

Difference from HDI value: Percentage difference between the PHDI value and the HDI value.

Difference from HDI rank: Difference in ranks on the PHDI and the HDI.

Adjustment factor for planetary pressures: Arithmetic average of the carbon dioxide emissions index and the material footprint index. A high value implies less pressure on the planet.

Carbon dioxide emissions per capita (production): Carbon dioxide emissions produced as a consequence of human activities (use of coal, oil and gas for combustion and industrial processes, gas flaring and cement manufacture), divided by midyear population. Values are territorial emissions, meaning that emissions are attributed to the country in which they physically occur.

Carbon dioxide emissions (production) index: Carbon dioxide emissions per capita (production-based) expressed as an index with a minimum value of 0 and a maximum value of 68.72 tonnes per capita. A high value implies less pressure on the planet.

Material footprint per capita: The attribution of global material extraction to domestic final demand of a country, divided by midyear population. Total material footprint is the sum of material footprint for biomass, fossil fuels, metal ores and nonmetal ores, calculated as the raw material equivalent of imports plus domestic extraction minus raw material equivalents of exports. Material footprint per capita describes the average material use for final demand.

Material footprint index: Material footprint per capita expressed as an index with a minimum value of 0 and a maximum value of 107.42 tonnes per capita. A high value implies less pressure on the planet.

Main data sources

Column 1: HDRO calculations based on data from Barro and Lee (2018), IMF (2022), UNDESA (2022a), UNESCO Institute for Statistics (2022), United Nations Statistics Division (2022) and World Bank (2022).

Column 2: Calculated as the product of the HDI and the adjustment factor presented in column 5.

Column 3: Calculated based on data in columns 1 and 2.

Column 4: Calculated based on PHDI values and recalculated HDI ranks for countries for which a PHDI value is calculated.

Column 5: Calculated based on data in columns 7 and 9.

Column 6: Global Carbon Project (2022).

Column 7: Calculated based on data in column 6.

Column 8: United Nations Environment Programme (2022).

Column 9: Calculated based on data in column 8.

Developing regions

Arab States (20 countries or territories)
Algeria, Bahrain, Djibouti, Egypt, Iraq, Jordan, Kuwait, Lebanon, Libya, Morocco, State of Palestine, Oman, Qatar, Saudi Arabia, Somalia, Sudan, Syrian Arab Republic, Tunisia, United Arab Emirates, Yemen

East Asia and the Pacific (26 countries)
Brunei Darussalam, Cambodia, China, Fiji, Indonesia, Kiribati, Democratic People's Republic of Korea, Lao People's Democratic Republic, Malaysia, Marshall Islands, Federated States of Micronesia, Mongolia, Myanmar, Nauru, Palau, Papua New Guinea, Philippines, Samoa, Singapore, Solomon Islands, Thailand, Timor-Leste, Tonga, Tuvalu, Vanuatu, Viet Nam

Europe and Central Asia (17 countries)
Albania, Armenia, Azerbaijan, Belarus, Bosnia and Herzegovina, Georgia, Kazakhstan, Kyrgyzstan, Republic of Moldova, Montenegro, North Macedonia, Serbia, Tajikistan, Türkiye, Turkmenistan, Ukraine, Uzbekistan

Latin America and the Caribbean (33 countries)
Antigua and Barbuda, Argentina, Bahamas, Barbados, Belize, Plurinational State of Bolivia, Brazil, Chile, Colombia, Costa Rica, Cuba, Dominica, Dominican Republic, Ecuador, El Salvador, Grenada, Guatemala, Guyana, Haiti, Honduras, Jamaica, Mexico, Nicaragua, Panama, Paraguay, Peru, Saint Kitts and Nevis, Saint Lucia, Saint Vincent and the Grenadines, Suriname, Trinidad and Tobago, Uruguay, Bolivarian Republic of Venezuela

South Asia (9 countries)
Afghanistan, Bangladesh, Bhutan, India, Islamic Republic of Iran, Maldives, Nepal, Pakistan, Sri Lanka

Sub-Saharan Africa (46 countries)
Angola, Benin, Botswana, Burkina Faso, Burundi, Cameroon, Cabo Verde, Central African Republic, Chad, Comoros, Congo, Democratic Republic of the Congo, Côte d'Ivoire, Equatorial Guinea, Eritrea, Kingdom of Eswatini, Ethiopia, Gabon, Gambia, Ghana, Guinea, Guinea-Bissau, Kenya, Lesotho, Liberia, Madagascar, Malawi, Mali, Mauritania, Mauritius, Mozambique, Namibia, Niger, Nigeria, Rwanda, Sao Tomé and Príncipe, Senegal, Seychelles, Sierra Leone, South Africa, South Sudan, United Republic of Tanzania, Togo, Uganda, Zambia, Zimbabwe

Note: All countries listed in developing regions are included in aggregates for developing countries. Countries included in aggregates for Least Developed Countries and Small Island Developing States follow UN classifications, which are available at https://www.un.org/ohrlls/. Countries included in aggregates for Organisation for Economic Co-operation and Development are listed at http://www.oecd.org/about/membersandpartners/list-oecd-member-countries.htm.

Statistical references

Note: Statistical references relate to statistical material presented in this Statistical Annex and in the full set of statistical tables posted at https://hdr.undp.org/human-development-report-2021-22.

Barro, R. J., and J.-W. Lee. 2018. Dataset of Educational Attainment, June 2018 Revision. http://www.barrolee.com. Accessed 7 April 2022.

CEDLAS (Center for Distributive, Labor and Social Studies) and World Bank. 2022. Socio-Economic Database for Latin America and the Caribbean. https://www.cedlas.econo.unlp.edu.ar/wp/en/estadisticas/sedlac/estadisticas. Accessed 7 April 2022.

Eurostat. 2021. European Union Statistics on Income and Living Conditions. EUSILC UDB 2021 – version of November 2021. Brussels. https://ec.europa.eu/eurostat/web/microdata/european-union-statistics-on-income-and-living-conditions. Accessed 8 February 2022.

Global Carbon Project. 2022. Global Carbon Atlas. https://www.globalcarbonproject.org/. Accessed 23 June 2022.

ICF Macro. Various years. Demographic and Health Surveys. https://dhsprogram.com. Accessed 6 May 2022.

ILO (International Labour Organization). 2022. ILOSTAT database. https://ilostat.ilo.org/data/. Accessed 14 April 2022.

IMF (International Monetary Fund). 2021. World Economic Outlook database. Washington, DC. https://www.imf.org/en/Publications/WEO/weo-database/2021/October. Accessed 21 April 2022.

IMF (International Monetary Fund). 2022. World Economic Outlook database. Washington, DC. http://www.imf.org/en/Publications/WEO/weo-database/2022/April. Accessed 21 April 2022.

IPU (Inter-Parliamentary Union). 2022. Parline database: Monthly ranking of women in national parliaments. https://data.ipu.org/women-ranking. Accessed 14 April 2022.

LIS (Luxembourg Income Study). 2022. Luxembourg Income Study Project. https://www.lisdatacenter.org/data-access. Accessed 31 March 2022.

OECD (Organisation for Economic Co-operation and Development). 2022. *OECD.Stat.* https://stats.oecd.org. Accessed 7 April 2022.

UNDESA (United Nations Department of Economic and Social Affairs). 2019. *World Population Prospects: The 2019 Revision.* Rev 1. New York. https://population.un.org/wpp/. Accessed 8 July 2021.

UNDESA (United Nations Department of Economic and Social Affairs). 2022a. *World Population Prospects: The 2022 Revision.* New York. https://population.un.org/wpp/. Accessed 11 July 2022.

UNDESA (United Nations Department of Economic and Social Affairs). 2022b. *World Economic Situation and Prospects 2022.* https://www.un.org/development/desa/dpad/publication/world-economic-situation-and-prospects-2022/. Accessed 4 May 2022.

UNEP (United Nations Environment Programme). 2022. World Environment Situation Room, Data downloader. https://wesr.unep.org/downloader. Accessed 23 June 2022.

UNESCO (United Nations Educational, Scientific and Cultural Organization) Institute for Statistics. 2022. UIS Developer Portal, Bulk Data Download Service. https://apiportal.uis.unesco.org/bdds. Accessed 28 April 2022.

UNICEF (United Nations Children's Fund). Various years. Multiple Indicator Cluster Surveys. New York. http://mics.unicef.org. Accessed 11 March 2022.

United Nations Statistics Division. 2022. National Accounts Main Aggregates Database. http://unstats.un.org/unsd/snaama. Accessed 27 April 2022.

WHO (World Health Organization), UNICEF (United Nations Children's Fund), UNFPA (United Nations Population Fund), World Bank Group and United Nations Population Division. 2019. *Trends in Maternal Mortality: 2000 to 2017: Estimates by WHO, UNICEF, UNFPA, World Bank Group and the United Nations Population Division.* Geneva: World Health Organization. https://apps.who.int/iris/handle/10665/327595. Accessed 7 February 2022.

World Bank. 2021. World Development Indicators database. Washington, DC. http://data.worldbank.org. Accessed 8 July 2021.

World Bank. 2022. World Development Indicators database. Washington, DC. http://data.worldbank.org. Accessed 28 April 2022.

World Inequality Database. 2022. World Inequality Database. http://wid.world. Accessed 6 July 2022.